New York
New Jersey
Pennsylvania

Red Maples, Delaware Water Gap – Jonathan Wallen

Rhododendron

Jonathan Wallen

About This Guide

The guide is organized by state, each with its own introduction. Within each state, the text is organized into geographical regions: six regions in New York; two regions in New Jersey; and six regions in Pennsylvania. Each Entry Heading is followed by a population figure (where applicable), map reference and tourist information phone number (with Website, when available).

In the text, useful information, such as addresses, recommended visiting times, opening hours, admission charges and telephone numbers, appears in *italics*. Symbols indicate handicapped access &, on-site eating facilities ✗, and on-site parking ▣. The "kids" symbol 🄺🄸🄳 highlights sights of special interest to children. And the "long lines" symbol ⫘ indicates the probability of long waiting lines. Many entries contain digressions, entertaining breaks from sightseeing, that are marked by a purple bar. Those digressions that appear on a map within the guide are indicated by ❶.

Cross-references to destinations described in the text appear in SMALL CAPITALS; consult the **Index** at the back of the guide for the appropriate page number.

White-tailed Doe and Fawn

Contents

Legend

★★★ **Worth the trip**
★★ **Worth a detour**
★ **Interesting**

Sight symbols

Recommended itineraries with departure point

⛪ ⛨	Church, chapel	
○	Town described	
B	Letter locating a sight	
■ ▲	Other points of interest	
⚒ ⌒	Mine – Cave	
𝔜 ⌘	Windmill – Lighthouse	
☆ ♣	Fort – Mission	

■ Building described

▢ Other building

▪ Small building, statue

◎ ♣ Fountain – Ruins

🛈 Visitor information

⬭ ⚓ Ship – Shipwreck

✳ ♨ Panorama – View

Other symbols

🛡	Interstate highway	🛡 US highway	⬭ Other route
	Highway, bridge		Major city thoroughfare
	Toll highway, interchange		City street with median
	Divided highway		One-way street
	Major, minor route		Tunnel – Pedestrian street
18	Distance in miles		Steps – Gate
2149/655	Pass *(elevation in feet/meters)*	🅿 ✉	Parking – Main post office
△ 6288/1917	Mtn. peak *(elevation in feet/meters)*	🚂 🚌	Train station – Bus station
✈ ✛	Airport – Airfield		Cemetery – Swamp
⛴	Ferry: Cars and passengers		International boundary
⛵	Ferry: Passengers only		State boundary
⟨ ← ⟳	Waterfall – Lock – Dam	●	Subway station
🍷	Winery	❶	Digression

Recreation

●–○–○–○–●	Gondola, chairlift		Park, garden – Wooded area
⛴ ◊	Harbor, lake cruise – Marina	🌐	Wildlife reserve
⛷ ⚑	Ski area – Golf Course	🐾	Zoo
⊂⠂⠂⊃	Stadium	– – – – –	Walking path, trail

Abbreviations

NP	National Park	NHS	National Historic Site	SF	State Forest
NWR	National Wildlife Refuge	NHP	National Historical Park	SP	State Park
NRA	National Recreation Area	SHS	State Historic Site	HP	Historic Park
		HS	Historic Site		

Symbols specific to this guide

🚌	Covered bridge	✡	Synagogue

4

Distance Chart

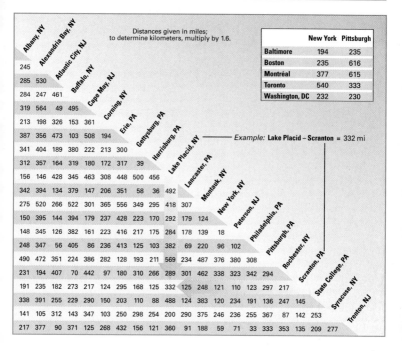

Distances given in miles; to determine kilometers, multiply by 1.6.

	New York	Pittsburgh
Baltimore	194	235
Boston	235	616
Montréal	377	615
Toronto	540	333
Washington, DC	232	230

Example: **Lake Placid – Scranton = 332 mi**

From \ To	Albany, NY	Alexandria Bay, NY	Atlantic City, NJ	Buffalo, NY	Cape May, NJ	Corning, NY	Erie, PA	Gettysburg, PA	Harrisburg, PA	Lake Placid, NY	Lancaster, PA	Montauk, NY	New York, NY	Paterson, NJ	Philadelphia, PA	Pittsburgh, PA	Rochester, NY	Scranton, PA	State College, PA	Syracuse, NY
Alexandria Bay, NY	245																			
Atlantic City, NJ	285	530																		
Buffalo, NY	284	247	461																	
Cape May, NJ	319	564	49	495																
Corning, NY	213	198	326	153	361															
Erie, PA	387	356	473	103	508	194														
Gettysburg, PA	341	404	189	380	222	213	300													
Harrisburg, PA	312	357	164	319	180	172	317	39												
Lake Placid, NY	156	146	428	345	463	308	448	500	456											
Lancaster, PA	342	394	134	379	147	206	351	58	36	492										
Montauk, NY	275	520	266	522	301	365	556	349	295	418	307									
New York, NY	150	395	144	394	179	237	428	223	170	292	179	124								
Paterson, NJ	148	345	126	382	161	223	416	217	175	284	178	139	18							
Philadelphia, PA	248	347	56	405	86	236	413	125	103	382	69	220	96	102						
Pittsburgh, PA	490	472	351	224	386	282	128	193	211	569	234	487	376	380	308					
Rochester, NY	231	194	407	70	442	97	180	310	266	289	301	462	338	323	342	294				
Scranton, PA	191	235	182	273	217	124	295	168	125	332	125	248	121	110	123	297	217			
State College, PA	338	391	255	229	290	150	203	110	88	488	124	383	120	234	191	136	247	145		
Syracuse, NY	141	105	312	143	347	103	250	298	254	200	290	375	246	236	255	367	87	142	253	
Trenton, NJ	217	377	90	371	125	268	432	156	121	360	91	188	59	71	33	333	353	135	209	277

Locator Map

5

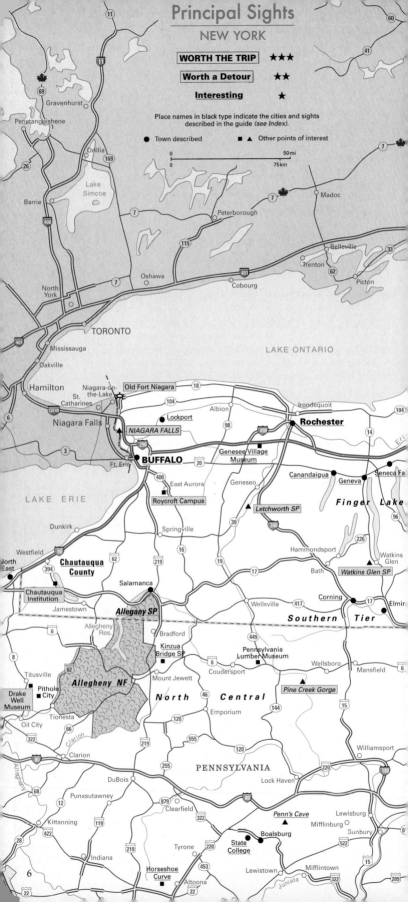

8

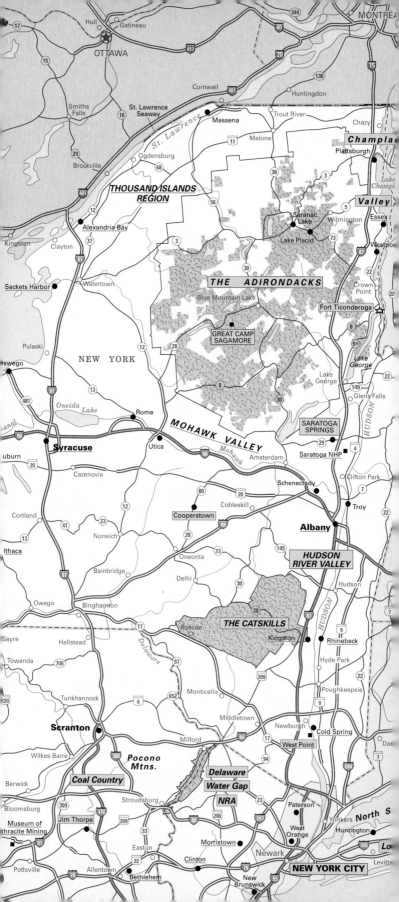

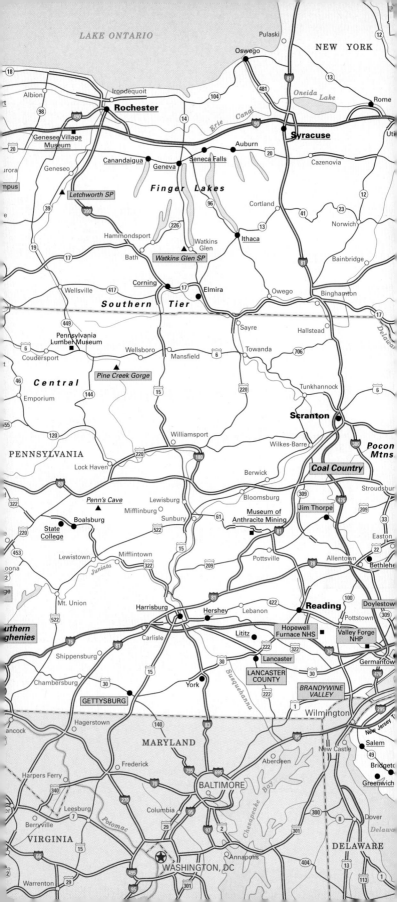

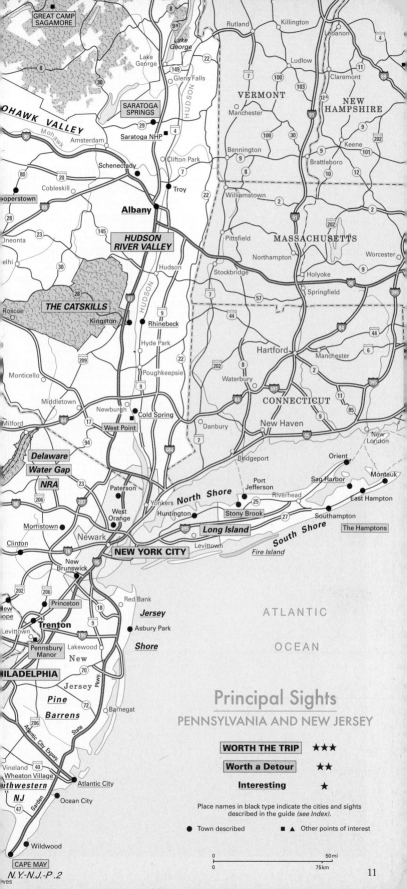

Principal Sights

PENNSYLVANIA AND NEW JERSEY

WORTH THE TRIP	★★★
Worth a Detour	★★
Interesting	★

Place names in black type indicate the cities and sights described in the guide *(see Index)*.

● Town described   ■ ▲ Other points of interest

| 0 | | 50mi |
| 0 | | 75km |

Lower Saranac Lake, Adirondacks – Jonathan Wallen

New York

Introduction to New York

On a visit to the region just after the American Revolution, George Washington quipped that New York had the potential to be "the seat of the Empire." In the two centuries since, the Empire State has made good on that prediction. A world leader in finance and publishing, a driving force in national politics, a pioneer in wilderness preservation, a crucible of social and religious movements, a haven for artists and intellectuals—New York has muscled its way to the top of nearly every field.

Encompassing 47,834sq mi, the state is shaped like a boot, with the toe pointed west and Long Island trailing like a spur from its heel into the Atlantic. New York's roughly 1,100mi periphery is fringed in almost equal parts by water (the Atlantic, Lake Champlain, the St. Lawrence River, the Niagara River, Lake Ontario and Lake Erie) and land (Pennsylvania, New Jersey, Massachusetts, Connecticut and Vermont). It is the only state to touch both the Great Lakes and the Atlantic Ocean.

New York State Facts
Capital: Albany
Land Area: 47,834 square miles
Population: 18,134,226
Nickname: Empire State
Motto: *Excelsior* (Ever Upward)
State Flower: Rose (wild or cultivated)
State Bird: Bluebird

New York ranks only 30th out of the 50 states in size, but it is second in population, having been outstripped by California in 1963. Today some 18 million Americans call themselves New Yorkers, with 7.3 million, or 40 percent of the state, residing in New York City, still the nation's largest metropolis.

Geographical Notes

Geologic Past – A land of true diversity, New York contains eight distinct land regions *(map p 15)*, including two major mountain ranges—the Catskills and the Adirondacks—as well as the smaller Taconic Range. The Catskills and the Taconic Range are part of the northeast Appalachian chain, which formed just after the Paleozoic era (some 400-500 million years ago), when the Eurasian and North American tectonic plates collided, causing the earth's crust to heave upward in a series of parallel folds. In contrast, the Adirondacks—composed of anorthosite, a billion-year-old rock formed beneath the earth's crust—uplifted between 60 million and 20 million years ago. Most of the geographical handiwork, however, was done by glaciers. As recently as 10,000 years ago, a sheet of ice up to 2mi thick spread across almost all of the area that is now New York State. As it retreated, it deepened valleys, rounded off mountaintops, and left a mess of moraine deposits, which dammed up rivers to make lakes, piled up on sedimentary rock to create offshore islands, and formed the foundation of the arable soil in the state's fertile lowlands.

Regional Landscapes – Part of the **Atlantic Coastal Plain**, which stretches from the southern tip of Florida to Massachusetts, Long Island and Staten Island lie just offshore from mainland New York's southeast corner. They are made up of glacial detritus, left in such massive quantities that the islands were able to remain above water as the ocean rose and invaded lower-lying regions. To the north, a finger of land running north-south along New York's eastern border belongs to the **New England Upland**: it includes the western half of the Taconic Range, which has elevations up to 2,000ft; the cliffy banks of the southern Hudson River Valley; and Manhattan Island, the heart of New York City.

Adjacent to the upland is the fertile **Hudson-Mohawk Lowland**, a Y-shaped swath between 10mi and 30mi wide embracing most of the Hudson and Mohawk River Valleys. The west branch of the "Y" ends at the pod-shaped **Tug Hill Plateau**, which rises 1,700ft above the Black River, its eastern boundary. Mostly wilderness, this flat, rocky region lies just north of Syracuse and Utica. The Tug Hill Plateau is but a small extension of the rugged **Appalachian Plateau**, New York's largest land mass, which takes up half the state. In the southeast corner, the CATSKILL MOUNTAINS ascend from approximately 2,000ft to a maximum height of 4,025ft. To the northwest, the FINGER LAKES, a necklace of long, deep, tusk-shaped lakes, were gouged out by glaciers. The rest of the plateau is distinguished by broad uplands at elevations of 800ft to 2,000ft, separated by deep river valleys, such as that on the Genesee River in Letchworth State Park, the deepest canyon east of the Mississippi River.

Abutting the plateau to the north, the **Erie-Ontario Lowland** hugs the southeast shores of these two Great Lakes. It supports swamps, orchards and, on a temperate strip along Lake Erie, vineyards. Tumbling over a dolostone precipice, the NIAGARA FALLS dramatically channel the waters of Lake Erie into Lake Ontario. Roughly 100mi in diameter, the **Adirondack Upland** is New York's second-largest land region. Cradled to the south by the "Y" of the Hudson-Mohawk Lowland and to the north by the **St. Lawrence Lowland**, where many of the state's dairy farms thrive, this circular area contains the mineral-rich ADIRONDACKS—the only Eastern mountains not related to the Appalachians.

Climate – The Empire State is unfortunately known for its long, brutal winters; beautiful, if brief, summers; and practically nonexistent springs. Fall, however, can be as stunning in New York's heavily forested areas as it is in much of New England. Because of their altitude, the central Adirondacks are the coldest part of the state, with an average January temperature of 14°F (–10°C), compared to 30°F (–1°C) on Long Island. In July, temperatures average a pleasant 66°F (19°C) in the central Adirondacks, 74°F (23°C) on Long Island, and around 70°F in many points in between and to the west. Precipitation varies considerably throughout New York, the wettest area being around the Tug Hill Plateau. Because it blocks winter storms coming off Lake Ontario, the plateau also gets saddled with more snow (as much as 225in per year) than any other American region east of the Rockies.

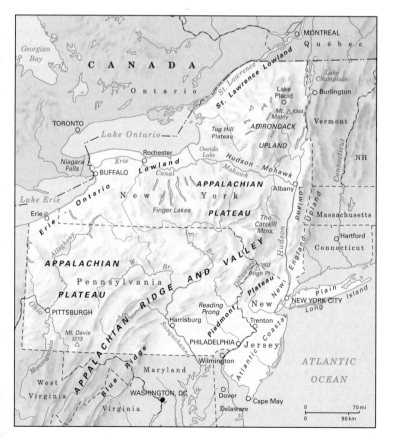

Historical Notes

A Tarnished Chain of Friendship – Before the arrival of European explorers, two of the most powerful Indian groups in North America resided in New York. Until the early 16C, several tribes of Algonquian Indians, including the Lenni Lenape, inhabited the southeastern part of the state. By the mid-17C the mighty Iroquois had conquered most of the Algonquian tribes or pushed them north into Canada. A century later, the Five Nations of the Iroquois—from west to east, the Senecas, Cayugas, Onondagas, Oneidas and Mohawks—were firmly established in vertical bands across the state. Agriculture was the mainstay of their livelihood.

The Indians in New York played a decisive role in shaping the direction of the empire, providing guides for explorers, beaver pelts for the fur trade, and warriors for battle. To their credit, the first European settlers, the Dutch, maintained good relations with the Indians. Laying out the terms for trade in the Hudson River Valley, their treaties called on both groups "to keep the Great Chain of Friendship polished bright." The French and English, however, exacerbated tribal conflicts by engaging opposing groups in their war for control of the Ohio River Valley and the Western frontier. During the French and Indian War *(p 218)*, the Iroquois were generally allied with the English, the displaced Algonquians with the French. All allegiances were fragile, however, because many Indians rejected the whole notion of European occupation. The question was forcefully resolved in 1779, when George Washington sent 3,500 troops to central New York to crush the Iroquois and open the territory for white settlers. In what was known as the Sullivan-Clinton Campaign *(p 138)*, the Indians' crops were torched, cattle killed and homes destroyed. Afterward, white settlement proceeded apace.

Colonial Era – The first European to explore New York was Italian navigator Giovanni da Verrazano, who sailed into New York Bay around 1524. It was not until 1609, however, that Henry Hudson, an Englishman employed by the Dutch East India Company, thoroughly explored the river that bears his name, sailing as far as Albany and claiming New York, New Jersey, Delaware and part of Connecticut for the Dutch; he called the territory New Netherland. Also in 1609, the Frenchman Samuel de Champlain followed Indian guides from Quebec to Lake Champlain, claiming northeastern New York for the French.

While the French remained for the most part in Canada, the Dutch built trading posts along the Hudson. In 1624 they established the first permanent white settlement in New York on the site of present-day Albany. The following year, the Dutch leased Manhattan Island from the Indians for $24 worth of trinkets and started the settlement of New Amsterdam there. In between, a system of **patroonships** *(p 76)* grew up, wherein wealthy businessmen—some not even residing in the country—would be given huge swaths of farmland if they could encourage tenants to cultivate the land. One of the largest, Patroon Van Rensselaer, measured 20sq mi and wasn't broken up until the 1840s.

Although Dutch was spoken in the Hudson River Valley well into the 1820s, the English took over New Amsterdam in 1664 and the rest of New Netherland in 1667. Over the next century, as English colonists poured into southern New York from Massachusetts and Connecticut, the French began to fortify their claims to the Champlain Valley and the mouth of the Niagara River. Beginning in 1690, when Schenectady was raided by the French, a series of skirmishes broke out, culminating in the **French and Indian War** (1754-63). Decisive English victories at FORT TICONDEROGA, FORT NIAGARA and CROWN POINT in 1759 paved the way for the fall of Quebec and Montreal in 1760. Three years later, the Treaty of Paris granted England almost all of France's holdings in North America.

The Empire State – England had little time to savor her prize, however. To pay for the costly war, the Crown tried to raise money by increasing colonists' taxes; instead, it raised the colonists' hackles and sparked a war for independence. Although some 30,000 New Yorkers—the majority of whom were presumed to be Loyalists—left the state during the Revolution, many Patriots remained. On July 9, 1776, the provincial congress met in White Plains and, after overriding vigorous arguments for state sovereignty, approved the Declaration of Independence. A year later, New York claimed one of the most important turning points of the war: British general John Burgoyne's surprise defeat at SARATOGA SPRINGS, after which France announced its pivotal support of the revolutionaries. On ratifying the US Constitution in 1788, New York became the 11th state to enter the Union. In 1789 George Washington was sworn in as the first president of the United States in New York City, the nation's capital from 1785 to 1790.

A wave of land speculation and settlement followed rapidly on the heels of independence. The state saw warfare only once in the 19C—during the unpopular **War of 1812**. Angered at British naval policies, as well as their practice of arming Indians who would raid frontier settlements in the Midwest, Congress declared war on England with the aim to take over Florida from the British-allied Spanish and Canada from the Crown. However, American troops were ill-prepared for the war, the public unenthusiastic and the British blockade of the Eastern Seaboard airtight. Luckily, two naval victories—Oliver Hazard Perry's on Lake Erie in 1813 and Thomas Macdonough's on Lake Champlain in 1814—staved off defeat. The British burned Buffalo to the ground as they retreated from a thwarted land invasion, and a stalemate was formalized in the 1814 Treaty of Ghent. Peace restored, by 1820 New York had a population of almost 1.4 million, more than any other state.

Erie Canal Activities (c.1830), Aquatint by John Hull

The most decisive factor in the state's growth in the early 19C was the opening of the **Erie Canal** *(p 94)* in 1825. Though it was widely ridiculed in its construction phases as "Clinton's Ditch" (after the governor who championed the idea), the 363mi-long canal made New York *the* essential conduit of trade between the Eastern Seaboard and the Great Lakes. The cost of shipping a ton of freight from Buffalo to New York City dropped from $120 to $14 virtually overnight, giving rise to boomtowns like Rochester and Syracuse. Industry and agriculture thrived all over the state, and New York City became the nation's number-one port. The railroad, built between the 1830s and the 1850s by many of the same Irish immigrants who worked on the canal, consolidated the canal's gains. By 1850 New York led the country not just in population, but in manufacturing and commerce as well. Dairying became the most important source of farm income.

Fame and Fortune – As the 19C gave way to the 20C, it was clear that New York really was the Empire State. The nation's first billionaire, John D. Rockefeller, hailed from New York, as did railroad tycoon "Commodore" Cornelius Vanderbilt; bankers J.P. Morgan and Jay Gould were New Yorkers, as were entrepreneurs George Eastman (founder of Eastman Kodak) and Thomas B. Watson (founder of IBM). Industry streaked by agriculture in economic importance, and by 1900 four out of five New Yorkers lived in the 20mi-wide "urban corridor" stretching from the Big Apple north to Albany, then west to Buffalo.

While the Great Depression of the 1930s hit New York hard, the state bounced back in the mid-20C as a center of the nation's defense industry. During World War II, the Korean War and the Vietnam War, cities like Buffalo, New York City, Rochester and Schenectady produced munitions and warships. The post-World War II industrial boom brought economic growth to smaller communities as well, and federal dollars went to finance the construction of hundreds of miles of interstate highways and cultural institutions such as the world-renowned Lincoln Center. The economy slumped once more in the mid-1970s, but unprecedented growth through the 1980s and 90s—especially in the New York Stock Exchange—has brought the state's net worth to giddy new heights.

Social and Religious Ferment – New Yorkers have not always been crass capitalists. In fact, in the early 19C, a wave of general religious fervor swept the state as people embraced Christianity, especially Catholicism. In 1830, Joseph Smith founded his **Mormon Church** near the upstate town of Palmyra, winning thousands of converts—and detractors (he was eventually run out of the state by those who objected to polygamy). The prosperous **Oneida community**—which believed in nonmonogamy, the collective ownership of property, and women's rights—thrived from 1848 to 1879 before transforming itself into a joint-stock company to sell its still-famous silver plate. In 1873 the CHAUTAUQUA INSTITUTION, a summer education/arts colony, blossomed out of a Sunday-school-teacher training camp and spawned a hugely popular national lecture circuit. Patterned after William Morris' famous Arts and Crafts furniture-making workshop in England, Elbert Hubbard's **Roycroft community** *(p 150)*, located on the outskirts of Buffalo in the early 20C, put their faith in the credo "Not how cheap but how good." In August 1969, the youth counterculture reached its peak at the **Woodstock Art and Music Festival**, which drew upward of 450,000 rock-music lovers to a farm in Bethel, New York.

From the far left to the far right, New Yorkers have long made their voices heard in politics. In 1839 tenant farmers in the Hudson River Valley led an **Anti-Rent Movement** that finally put an end to exploitative 17C patroonships and manors. In 1848 Elizabeth Cady Stanton and Lucretia Mott spearheaded the modern-day **Women's Rights Movement** at a convention in SENECA FALLS. New York was long a hotbed of **abolitionism**, with both Harriet Tubman and Frederick Douglass residing in the state. However, in July 1863, nearly 1,000 people, including blacks who were hung by lynch mobs, were killed in **Anti-Draft Riots** in New York City, the most violent riots in American history. (New York would later contribute more troops and supplies to the Union cause than any other state.) A political powerhouse, the state filled the Oval Office during 46 of the 76 years between 1876 and 1952.

Economy

New York's economy has long been one of the strongest in the country due to the state's excellent location, large immigrant labor pool and substantial brain trust in New York City. The opening of the St. Lawrence Seaway in 1959 was a sub-

---

■ Art and Architecture

Given its history of vibrant and contradictory social movements, it's not surprising that New York has long been on the cutting edge of the nation's art scene, finding its clearest expression in its architecture. Louis Sullivan built one of the world's first steel-frame skyscrapers, the Guaranty-Prudential Building, in Buffalo in 1896. The state is also home to some of the nation's Art Deco masterpieces, including Buffalo City Hall, the Chrysler Building and the Empire State Building. Monumental examples of the International style (the Seagram Building by Mies van der Rohe) and Postmodernism (AT&T Headquarters) still stand in New York City. On a smaller scale, **Adirondack architecture**, which combines rustic twig work and indigenous materials with elements of the classic Swiss chalet, is one of New York's few homegrown styles. One of the state's most notorious "firsts" is **Levittown**, a planned community of mass-produced homes on Long Island whose population swelled from 450 in 1946 to 60,000 in the late 1950s, thus ushering in the age of suburbia.

Widely acknowledged as the nation's cultural capital, New York City has nurtured more artists than any other American metropolis: Edgar Allan Poe, Edith Wharton, Henry James, Eugene O'Neill, Dorothy Parker, James Baldwin, Langston Hughes, Jackson Pollock, George Gershwin, Charlie Parker, Theolonious Monk, Woody Allen, Martin Scorsese—the list of artists associated with the Big Apple goes on and on. But other parts of New York State have yielded their share of successes, too. Thomas Cole and Frederic Church, painters of the first distinctly American school of painting, the **Hudson River school** (1825-75), drew their inspiration from the dramatic scenery north of the city. James Fenimore Cooper romanticized New York's frontier era in his best-selling 1826 novel *The Last of the Mohicans*, just as Washington Irving immortalized the Catskills in his popular short stories *Rip Van Winkle* and *The Legend of Sleepy Hollow* (1819-20).

stantial boon for Western New York port cities; nevertheless, in the 1970s many factories closed throughout the state, resulting in the loss of some 600,000 jobs. In the past two decades New York has recovered, thanks to a marked increase in service industries and electronics manufacturing.

Natural Resources – With one of the largest garnet mines in the world located on the outskirts of Glens Falls, New York's **mineral** production is valued at nearly $300 million a year. Niagara Falls are the state's most important source of hydro-electric power. **Lumbering** maintains a toehold in the northeastern corner of the state, providing the wood for Ticonderoga pencils, but other 19C economic staples, such as iron-ore mining, have been largely retired. In fact, protecting or restoring natural resources has become more of an industry than exploiting them. In 1986 New York voters approved a $1.45 billion bond act devoted to cleaning up the state's more than 500 hazardous waste sites.

Service Industries – An umbrella term that includes health care, insurance, law firms, retail, finance, government, transportation and utilities, service industries account for fully 82 percent of New York's gross state product. New York State leads the nation in wholesale and retail trade, and New York City is the financial center of the world, thanks to Wall Street.

Manufacturing – Although manufacturing accounts for only 14 percent of the gross state product, New York is surpassed only by California in this category. The state ranks first in the production of clothing and publications, owing to the plethora of designers and publishers in the Big Apple. New York also boasts a number of regional specialties, such as the imaging-equipment manufacturing industry in Rochester.

Agriculture – While agriculture accounts for only 1 percent of the gross state product, farmland covers one-quarter of the state. The Finger Lakes region is second only to California's Napa Valley in its wine production. Northern New York is one of the nation's leading dairy-farming regions, milk being the state's leading agricultural product. Orchards and vegetable farms are common in the Hudson-Mohawk Lowland and throughout the flatter sections of Western New York.

The State Today

New York prides itself on its diversity. In terms of **population**, it is the quintessential melting pot. Between 1847 and 1860 more than a million Irish immigrants, fleeing the potato famine at home, passed through the port of New York, while others poured in from revolution-torn Europe. In the three-year period of 1852-54, upward of 500,000 Germans alone landed in America. Ellis Island ushered a staggering 12 million immigrants into the New World between 1892 and 1954, and a good number of those ended up staying in New York. Today the state is second only to California in the number of immigrants it welcomes each year. Three out of four mainland Puerto Ricans make New York their home, as do three million Jews—fully half of all Jews in the US. According to the 1990 census, some 30 percent of New Yorkers belong to ethnic minorities.

While New York City draws nearly 30 million visitors a year, and Niagara Falls attracts 20 million, the smart traveler will find countless places well worth exploring in between. Tour the wineries in the Finger Lakes or along Lake Erie. Canoe the mountain lakes of the Adirondacks. Hike up the great Mt. Marcy. Sunbathe in the Hamptons. Attend the August horse races at Saratoga Springs. Ski in Lake Placid. Glimpse what Henry James called "the geography of the ideal" on a tour of the dramatic Hudson River Valley or catch a summer concert or lecture at the Chautauqua Institution. Much more than just its world-famous city and waterfall, the Empire State is, as one 20C writer put it, "a land of wooded slopes and crag and pool, sparkling lakes and noble rivers, of island strands, of gently rolling farms all finely cultivated, and busy towns not too begrimed with soot. It is not a land of staggering wonders but one of varied loveliness."

New York City Area

Now York, known around the world as the "capital" of America, is arguably the most stimulating and sophisticated urban center in the nation. It is also one of the largest. The 320-acre city proper spreads over bits and pieces of mainland, scattered islets, and a chunk of western Long Island occupied by the boroughs of Brooklyn and Queens, which are situated just across the East River from Manhattan. Long Island itself is the biggest land mass adjoining the continental US, covering an estimated 1,723sq mi as it stretches eastward opposite the Connecticut coast almost as far as Rhode Island. It is hard to tell where one town ends and another begins in the densely populated suburbs nearest New York City, but the relatively quiet forked "tail" at the eastern end of the island offers an unforgettably lovely seaside landscape of bluffs, dunes and salt ponds. Potato fields and vineyards perpetuate a 300-year-old agricultural tradition, while fishing ports and rustic villages preserve a strong sense of local history, rich in 19C whaling and maritime lore.

With a population of nearly seven million, Long Island has roughly the same number of residents as New York City, and a constant flow of people between the two keeps them closely linked. Each weekday morning, trains chug into Manhattan's Penn Station bringing hundreds of thousands of Long Island commuters to their jobs in New York; thousands more fight their way through the snarled traffic on the Long Island Expressway, better-known as the "Distressway." Conversely, Long Island is an extremely popular destination for New Yorkers. When the steamy sidewalks of the city empty out on summer weekends, it is often because so many people have fled to the charming villages known collectively as "the Hamptons" on Long Island's South Shore, celebrated for their gorgeous beaches.

Together, the city and "the island," as New Yorkers call it, form a metropolitan area offering every imaginable diversion and recreational pastime that can be found in urban and rural areas alike. Because of the beaches, summer is a great time to visit Long Island, but it is also the busiest season. As a result, many people favor the fall for exploring the greater New York City region. Between early October and mid-November, crowds thin and nature explodes in a blaze of color as Indian Summer arrives. Temperatures are often in the 70s, making it ideal for strolling through Manhattan's Central Park or enjoying a drive out to Long Island to tour a Gilded Age mansion or prowl for antiques. Virtually any activity will offer a welcome taste of one of the East Coast's most diverse and culturally rich destinations.

NEW YORK CITY ★★★

Population 7,380,906
Map p 7
Tourist Information www.nycvisit.com ☎212-484-1222 or 800-692-8474

New York City is a world unto itself by virtue of its dynamic economic activity, its vibrant cultural life and the size and density of its population. This East Coast capital has long been defined by its remarkable diversity, traceable to the successive waves of immigration that arrived through the major port of entry into the New World. The city now claims some 7.3 million residents (twice as many as any other American metropolis). Fine dining and shopping; a dramatic skyline; a rich array of museums, galleries, theaters and nightclubs; and world-class sports events endow "the city that never sleeps" with an irresistible reputation for glamour and excitement that draws some 25 million visitors from around the world annually.

Historical Notes

From Nieuw Amsterdam to New York – Before the arrival of Europeans, the island of Manhattan was inhabited by Algonquian- and Iroquoian-speaking Indians. The Algonquian tribe is credited for naming the island Manhattan, meaning "island of the hills." The first European to land here was Giovanni da Verrazano, an Italian explorer who arrived in 1524 in the service of the French king François I. In 1609 Henry Hudson made his famous journey up the river that now bears his name in his ship, the *Half Moon.* Hudson was on an exploratory voyage for the Dutch East India Company, which founded the colony of New Netherland on the site of present-day New York City in 1614 and established the trading post Nieuw Amsterdam 11 years later.

In 1626 Peter Minuit of the Dutch West India Company leased Manhattan from the Algonquian Indians for 60 guilders, the equivalent of $24. As a repercussion of English and Dutch trading rivalries in Europe, the British, already established in New England to the north, took control of the colony in the late 17C, accepting the surrender of Director-General Peter Stuyvesant in 1664. The city was renamed New York after the Duke of York, brother of the English king Charles II, and in 1667 it came under the English system of municipal government.

New York blossomed as an important trading post in the North American colonies, second only to Boston in the trade of furs and farm products. By 1700 the city claimed some 4,000 residents and spread north beyond the original Dutch palisade fortifications (in the area of present-day Wall Street). The city's increasingly pivotal role as a commercial port placed it in the center of the taxation controversies leading up to the American Revolution—New York was one of the first targets of the British Army. On November 17, 1776, Fort Washington in northern Manhattan fell, and the British occupied all of the area of present-day New York City throughout the War for Independence.

Empire City – In 1784 the city became the capital of New York State and a year later was named US capital under the Articles of Confederation. George Washington, elected first president, took the oath of office at Federal Hall on Wall Street in 1789. Although the federal capital moved to Philadelphia the following year, New York had already established commercial links and financial institutions that would lead the new nation into the Industrial Age. New York was also at the threshold of unprecedented changes in the urban and cultural fabric as it confronted explosive population and physical growth.

By 1820 New York was the most densely inhabited city in the nation with 123,705 residents, and the population skyrocketed in the next decade as immigrants arrived from Germany, Ireland and Scandinavia by the thousands. Following the opening of the Erie Canal in 1825, New York solidified its importance when it became a leading shipbuilding center. The South Street Seaport on the East River was the hub of port activities, handling more trade than all the other US ports combined.

As Manhattan grew in prosperity, it continued to expand steadily to the north, following the 1811 Randel Plan, which platted an even grid of 12 north-south avenues and 155 cross streets north of Houston Street. A devastating fire in 1835 leveled 700 buildings in lower Manhattan, and another in 1845 consumed 300 structures, accelerating the necessary process of building and rebuilding. The improvement of public transportation from horse-drawn omnibuses in the 1830s to street railroads in the 1850s helped speed up the northward march. Inevitably, slums grew along with the city, as "rear buildings" and tenements proliferated in the mid-century and shantytowns filled the vacant lands in upper Manhattan.

Getting There

By Air – John F. Kennedy International Airport: 15mi from midtown; international and domestic flights; ☎718-244-4444. Information centers are located on the baggage-claim level. Metropolitan Transit Authority (MTA) A-train from Howard Beach station to midtown stations *(free shuttle service from airport)*. Taxi service to midtown: 1hr *($30/flat rate)*. **LaGuardia Airport**: 8mi from midtown; domestic flights; ☎718-533-3400. Information center located between concourse C and D on the departure level. The MTA M60 bus departs from each terminal. Taxi service to midtown: 30min *($20 average)*. Rental car agency shuttles are located outside baggage-claim areas at both airports.

By Bus and Train – Bus service to New York City is provided by Greyhound *(☎212-971-6318 or 800-231-2222)* and Peter Pan *(☎212-564-8484 or 800-343-9999)* into the Port Authority Bus Terminal *(42nd St. & Eighth Ave.)*. Amtrak **trains** come into the Pennsylvania Railroad Station *(Seventh Ave. & 32nd St.)*. Regional rail service into Grand Central Railroad Terminal *(42nd St. & Park Ave.)* is available from Metro-North *(☎212-532-4900)*. Long Island Railroad *(☎718-217-5477)* and New Jersey Transit *(☎201-762-5100)* operate out of Pennsylvania Railroad Station.

Getting Around

By Public Transportation – The **Metropolitan Transportation Authority** operates an extensive network of subway, buses and commuter trains throughout the area. The New York City Transit division runs the city bus and subway lines. System fares: $1.50 *(exact fare required for buses; $1 bills not accepted)*. Tokens, accepted by subway or buses, are available at subway stations. The MetroCard automated fare card (available at subway stations and retail outlets) can be used on both systems. System maps and timetables are available *(free)* on buses, at subway stations and visitor information centers. The **Travel Information Center** offers route and fare information for subway and bus lines *(☎718-330-1234)*.

Subway and Buses – Virtually all **subway** lines run 24hrs/day. During off-peak hours (especially after midnight), it is advisable not to ride alone. Platform signs indicate which trains stop at the station (uptown trains are northbound; downtown trains are southbound). New York City Transit **buses** generally operate daily 5:30am–2am. Some routes on major corridors run 24hrs/daily. Pick-up points are indicated by signs (route numbers are clearly marked).

By Car – Given the efficiency of the public transportation system, and the ease with which many sights can be reached on foot, a car is not necessary to visit Manhattan. Keep in mind that streets are usually congested, public parking lots expensive *($6-$12/hr)*, and street parking extremely difficult to find.

By Taxi – All Yellow Medallion *(☎212-692-8294)* cabs are metered and share the same rate schedule (use other cabs at the risk of being overcharged): $2 for the first ⅕ mile, 30¢ each additional ⅕ mile. Taxis are easily hailed from the street in most areas of Manhattan. Taxi stands are located at most hotels, transportation terminals and entertainment centers.

General Information

Visitor Information – To obtain a copy of the *Big Apple Visitor Guide*, which gives information on shopping, accommodations and seasonal events, contact the **New York Convention & Visitors Bureau** *(810 7th Ave., New York NY 10019; www.nycvisit. com* ☎212-397-8222 or 800-692-8474). Stop in at the **Times Square Visitor Center** *(46th St. & Broadway; open year-round daily 8am–8pm)* for citywide information, theater tickets and Metrocards.

Accommodations – *(p 358)* Area visitors' guide including lodging directory is available *(free)* from the New York Convention & Visitors Bureau. Accommodations range from elegant **hotels** located in the vicinity of Fifth, Park and Madison Avenues to lower-priced motels found in the theater district. **Bed-and-breakfast inns** can also be found throughout Manhattan. **Reservation services**: Accommodations Express *(☎609-391-2100 or 800-444-7666)*; Central Reservation Service *(☎407-740-6442 or 800-548-3311)*; Express Hotel Reservations *(☎303-440-8481 or 800-356-1123)*; City Lights Bed & Breakfast *(☎212-737-7049)*; and Urban Ventures, Inc. *(☎212-594-5650)*. **Hostels** provide inexpensive lodging: Chelsea International Youth Hostel *(251 W. 20th St.* ☎212-647-0010); Big Apple Hostel *(119 W. 45th St* ☎212-302-2603); Hosteling International *(891 Amsterdam Ave.* ☎212-932-2300)

Local Press – Daily news: *New York Times* (morning), Sunday arts & leisure and Friday weekend entertainment sections; and *Wall Street Journal* (morning).

Foreign Exchange Offices – *(p 355)* Thomas Cook Currency Services, Inc. *(511 Madison Ave.* ☎212-753-2398 *and 1590 Broadway* ☎212-265-6049*)*; Avis Currency Exchange *(200 Park Ave.* ☎212-661-0826 *and Grand Central Terminal* ☎212-661-7600)*. Currency exchange offices can also be found at Kennedy and LaGuardia airports.

Sports and Leisure

Sightseeing – Tours of Manhattan aboard **double-decker buses** and trolleys are offered year-round; visitors can board (and reboard) at stops located at major attractions. For information, contact New York Apple *(daily 9am–6pm;* ☎201-947-4000 *or 800-876-9868)*; New York Double Decker *(daily 10am–3pm;* ☎212-967-6008)*; or Gray Line *(daily 9am–3pm;* ☎212-397-2600)*. Narrated **neighborhood tours** are provided by Big Onion Tours *(call for schedule & departure points;* ☎212-439-1090)*; Grand Tour of Midtown *(depart from corner of Park Ave. & 42nd St. year-round Fri 12:30pm;* ☎212-818-1777)*; and Harlem Spirituals, Inc. *(p 50)*. The self-guided **walking tours** of the *Heritage Trails New York Guidebook* explore the history and architecture of lower Manhattan *($4; available at kiosk in Federal Hall or from Heritage Trail, 61 Broadway, Suite 2220, New York NY 10006* ☎212-269-1500 *or 888-487-2457)*. Companies offering **boat tours** include NY Waterway *(depart from Pier 78 mid-Mar–Thanksgiving weekend daily;* ☎201-902-8700 *or 800-533-3779)*; and Circle Line *(depart from Pier 83 Mar–Dec daily;* ☎212-563-3200)*.

Entertainment – **Dance & Music Hotline:** ☎768-1818. **The Broadway Line:** ☎563-2929. Consult the arts and entertainment sections of the *New York Times* for schedules of cultural events and addresses of theaters and concert halls. To purchase **tickets**, contact the venue's box office, TKTS *(full and discounted tickets sold;* ☎212-868-1818*)* or Ticketmaster *(*☎212-307-4100*)*. The *Broadway Theater Guide* provides a weekly schedule of Broadway shows *(available free at visitor centers)*.

Venue	Performances	☎
Alice Tully Hall	Music & dance	212-874-6770
Avery Fisher Hall	New York Philharmonic Orchestra	212-874-2424
Carnegie Hall	Music & dance	212-247-7800
Metropolitan Opera House	Metropolitan Opera, American Ballet Theatre	212-362-6000
New York State Theater	New York City Opera, New York City Ballet	212-870-5570 212-496-0600

Spectator Sports – Mets *(*☎718-507-8499*)* and Yankees *(*☎718-293-6000*)* baseball; Giants *(*☎201-935-8222*)* and Jets *(*☎516-560-8200*)* football; Knicks *(*☎465-5867*)* basketball; Islanders *(*☎516-794-9300*)* and Rangers *(*☎465-6741*)* hockey.

Recreation – The city's primary recreation area is **Central Park** *(p 43)*, offering paths for walking, biking and horseback riding *(*☎212-724-5100*)*. The park also features tennis courts, horse-drawn-carriage rides and gondola rides. You can **ice-skate** outdoors at Wollman and Lasker Rinks *(rentals available;* ☎212-396-1010*)* and at The Rink at Rockefeller Plaza *(rentals available;* ☎212-332-7654*)*. **Chelsea Piers** complex *(W. 23rd & Hudson River* ☎212-336-6666*)* incorporates the world's longest indoor running track, a heated outdoor golf driving range, a rock-climbing wall and in-line skating rinks.

Shopping – Numerous fashionable **department stores** and specialty boutiques are located on Fifth Avenue *(between 47th & 57th Sts.)* and Madison Avenue *(between 59th & 79th Sts.)* including Saks Fifth Avenue *(611 Fifth Ave.* ☎212-753-4000)*, Bergdorf Goodman *(754 Fifth Ave.* ☎212-753-7300)* and Tiffany & Co. *(727 Fifth Ave.* ☎212-755-8000)*. Trendy boutiques and **art galleries** abound in SoHo *(p 32)*, TriBeCa *(p 33)*, and Chelsea *(p 42)*. New York City is also home to the nation's fashion industry, centered in the Garment Center on Seventh Avenue, and the **diamond wholesale trade**, concentrated on Diamond and Jewelry Way *(47th St.)*.

Useful Numbers

	☎
Police/Ambulance/Fire	**911**
Dental Referral *(24hrs)*	212-679-3966
Medical Referral	718-238-2100
24hr Pharmacy: Duane Reade *(224 57th St. & Broadway)*	212-541-9708
Main Post Office *(421 Eighth Ave. & W. 33rd St.)*	212-967-8585
Weather (recorded)	212-976-1212

Following the success of America's first World's Fair in 1853, New York established its role as the cultural capital of America through the creation of Central Park (1857), the American Museum of Natural History (1869) and the Metropolitan Museum of Art (1872). As commercial and industrial growth was spurred by large waves of immigration from Europe and the Americas, the population more than doubled every 20 years, exceeding a million persons by 1875.

A City of Immigrants – Between 1880 and 1884 some two million people arrived in New York City. While tenements and sweatshops proliferated, exploiting the new population, Wall Street became the center of banking, finance and insurance in the US. Immigration increased dramatically as the 19C waned, bringing new groups from Southern and Eastern Europe; New York also became home to the largest Jewish community in the world as millions fled Russian persecution.

The ongoing rush of immigration led to the 1892 completion of the Ellis Island facility, where more than 12 million persons were processed by the mid-1920s. Greater New York City was created in 1898, comprising the five boroughs of Manhattan, Brooklyn, the Bronx, Queens and Staten Island. With a population of more than three million, New York was now the world's largest city.

Culture, Crash and the Upward Swing – New architecture and cultural landmarks, as well as economic growth marked the new century. In 1902 one of New York's first skyscrapers, the Flatiron Building, was completed, and two years later the first underground subway opened. In this era, two great Beaux-Arts monuments, the New York Public Library (1911) and Grand Central Terminal (1913), were also completed, along with Cass Gilbert's glorious Gothic Revival Woolworth Building of 1913—which at 792ft stood as the world's tallest building for a generation. By the 1910s, Greenwich Village had become the country's bohemia, attracting avant-garde artists, thespians and writers including Eugene O'Neill, Edna St. Vincent Millay and Theodore Dreiser.

The concentration of African Americans in northern Manhattan's Harlem suburb after the turn of the century created an atmosphere of independence and cultural pride that fostered the 1920s Harlem Renaissance, an internationally recognized flowering of African-American arts and literature that featured writers like Langston Hughes and Zora Neale Hurston and such jazz legends as Duke Ellington and Cab Calloway. The gaiety of the Roaring 20s finally came to an end with the Wall Street stock market crash on Black Thursday, October 24, 1929, signaling the onset of the Great Depression. In the ensuing years, however, New York experienced a period of continued cultural growth, starting with the 1929 founding of the Museum of Modern Art. Construction of Rockefeller Center and the World's Fair during the 1930s buoyed New York as reform mayor Fiorello La Guardia led the city through the trials of the Depression, arresting gangsters like "Lucky" Luciano and supervising huge public works projects.

Standing Tall – Renewed economic growth came in the 1940s, when World War II made New York the busiest port in the world and solidified its international position in industry, commerce and finance. The United Nations (UN) established headquarters in Manhattan in 1945 as the city began building anew, adding more office and apartment towers. The 1950s brought more growth and a new influx of immigrants, with large numbers arriving from Puerto Rico and Asia. During the 1950s and 60s, New York evolved into the cultural capital of the Jet Age, as writers, artists and aesthetes gathered in Greenwich Village's Cedar Tavern, fostering the spontaneity and experimentation of New York school poets like Allen Ginsberg. The period marked a resurgence of African-American literature in New York, with the popularity of poet Amiri Baraka (LeRoi Jones) and author James Baldwin.

In the decade after World War II, a true American avant-garde also flowered, and New York emerged as a cultural mecca and world leader in the production and promotion of modern art. A haven for refugee intelligentsia from Europe, the city also welcomed painters such as Piet Mondrian, Jacques Lipchitz and Fernand Léger. This period of fertile artistic activity culminated in the first radical American artistic movement, Abstract Expressionism, which had its heyday from 1946 to the late 1950s. As the Abstract Expressionists received international recognition, postwar American affluence prompted collecting and gallery activity. New York gradually came to the fore, replacing Paris as the epicenter of the art world, and began fostering a new generation of avant-garde artists like Jackson Pollock, Willem de Kooning, Louise Nevelson and Andy Warhol. Off Broadway theaters enlivened the cultural scene and the city also became a center for film and television.

Racial and labor tensions beset the city in the 1960s. The 1964 Harlem Uprising was the first major manifestation of Northern black unrest in the Civil Rights era, underscored a year later by the assassination of the black leader Malcolm X at the Audubon Ballroom in Harlem. In 1975 an economic downturn forced the city government to default on its debts. These setbacks, however, only stimulated New Yorker pluck, and the city's budget was balanced by 1981. By the late 1980s an upswing in the world economy led to massive expansion on Wall Street and growth throughout the city. Today New York continues to cope with urban challenges on a grand scale as it faces the new century.

MANHATTAN

As the heart of New York's vibrant cultural and commercial activity, Manhattan is the best-known of the five boroughs and is synonymous with the city itself. In addition to an enviable concentration of fine museums, shops and restaurants, the island boasts an unparalleled skyline distinguished by architectural monuments recognized the world over. For all its sophistication, however, Manhattan retains a remarkably diverse physical and social makeup, epitomizing the melting pot that makes New York so interesting to explore. The famous landmarks should not be missed, but a stroll off the beaten path will also reward visitors with a taste of the "real" city, where brownstones and bodegas are as much a part of the urban fabric as skyscrapers and Tiffany's. Some of the most historic sections are found in the area south of 14th Street, known as "Downtown." Manhattan's commercial core is "Midtown," the vicinity between 34th and 59th Streets. "Uptown," or anything above 59th Street, offers a broad cross section of cultural and educational institutions, fashionable residential blocks and well-entrenched neighborhoods.

Statue of Liberty against the Lower Manhattan Skyline

Henryk Kaiser/INDEX STOCK

★★ LOWER MANHATTAN *1½ days. Map p 26.*

New York's financial and government districts dominate most of the area from Chambers Street south to the tip of the island, where the 17C Dutch settlement of Nieuw Amsterdam gave rise to a pattern of winding streets that prevails to this day. Skyscrapers create dramatic canyons of glass and stone, but many 18C and 19C buildings also survive, preserving a human scale even as the surrounding skyline is constantly redefined.

Historical Notes – The small town of Nieuw Amsterdam at the tip of Manhattan was defended to the south by a fort and to the north by a wall of wood planks constructed in 1653 between the Hudson and East Rivers to discourage Indian attacks. Dismantled by the British in 1699, the wall was replaced by a new street. This so-called Wall Street became an administrative and residential thoroughfare, while countinghouses, shops and warehouses flourished at the South Street port on the East River. As shipping and warehousing continued to flourish in down-

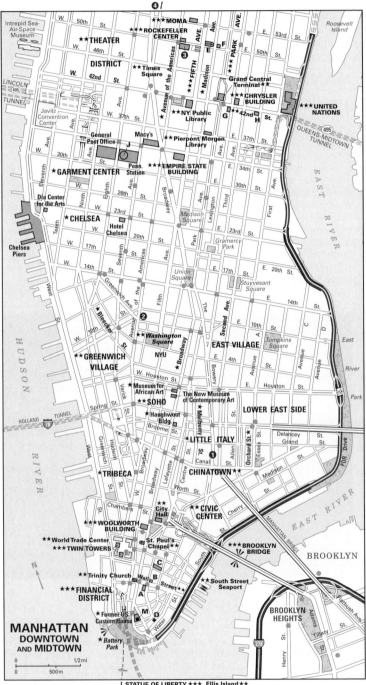

STATUE OF LIBERTY ★★★, Ellis Island ★★

town Manhattan in the 19C, related accounting and banking interests located here as well. Lower Manhattan's history as a gateway for immigrants dates to 1855, when Castle Clinton was converted as a processing center, a prelude to the construction of the Ellis Island station in 1890.

★★ Liberty and Ellis Islands

Kids *Ferry departs from Battery Park South Ferry (Manhattan) or Liberty State Park (p 55) Jun–Sept daily 9:30am–4:30pm every 30min. Rest of the year daily 9:30am–3:30pm every 45min. No service Dec 25. $7 (fare includes round-trip and visits to both the Statue and to Ellis Island).* ✗ ♿ ⅲ *Circle Line* ☎212-269-5755. *Statue of Liberty and Ellis Island Immigration Museum open year-round daily 9:30am–5pm (extended summer hours). Closed Dec 25. Guided and audio tours available.* Located in New York Harbor, Liberty and Ellis Islands symbolize the city's rich immigrant heritage. A dignified, stirring reminder of the ideals upon which the nation was founded, "Miss Liberty" has been welcoming travelers by sea for more than a century. Nearby in the harbor is Ellis Island, where millions passed through the gates to enter the "land of golden opportunity."

★★ Statue of Liberty

★★ **Statue of Liberty** – Located on Liberty Island (known as Bedloe's Island until 1956), this famous monument to hope and opportunity was a gift to America from the people of France. Recently restored, the 225-ton statue, delivered in 220 crates in 1885, is the work of Alsatian sculptor Frédéric-Auguste Bartholdi and the inventive French engineer Alexandre Gustave Eiffel, who created the intricate iron-and-steel frame faced with 300 copper plates. (The right arm, holding the torch, measures 42ft in length and has an 8ft-long index finger.) Noted American architect Richard Morris Hunt designed the base (1886), which contains a second-story exhibit space. An observation deck above offers spectacular **views★★★** of the harbor.

★★ **Ellis Island** – Inaugurated in 1892 on the 27.5-acre site of an abandoned fort, this renowned national monument received more than 12 million immigrants before it slipped into decay and closed in 1954. In the peak years, from 1903 to 1914, an average of 2,000 new arrivals were processed daily, the majority in less than half a day. In 1984 the main structure in the 33-building complex underwent one of the most elaborate renovations of any public building in the US. Restored to reflect its appearance in the early 1920s, it reopened in 1990 as the Ellis Island Immigration Museum. Highlights include the sweeping second-story Registry Room/Great Hall, where thousands of immigrants awaited their fate while queuing inside metal pens. The hall has been left empty, save for a few scattered benches, to serve as a grand, quiet memorial. Another moving exhibit, "Treasures from Home," presents personal belongings donated by immigrants and their families, from a teddy bear to an elaborate wedding gown.

★★ Financial District

This densely built business center covers most of the area below Chambers Street bounded by West Street and Franklin D. Roosevelt Drive. Here, in 1792, 24 brokers met under a buttonwood tree at the intersection of Wall and William Streets to found the forerunner of the New York Stock Exchange. **Wall Street★★**, hub of the district, has since come to symbolize the nation's financial power.

★ **Battery Park** – On the southwestern tip of Manhattan, the maze of stone and steel suddenly gives way to this 21-acre expanse of greenery built on landfill in 1870. Located in the park is the 1811 fortification, **Castle Clinton National Monument** *(open year-round daily 8:30am–5pm; closed Dec 25;* ♿ ☎212-344-7220), which has served as concert hall, aquarium and immigration station before being restored in 1975. The courtyard contains a ticket office for ferries and boat tours to the Statue of Liberty and Ellis Island. Along the bay, a **promenade★★** leads from Castle Clinton east to the Staten Island Ferry Terminal. The meandering walk offers splendid **views★★★** of the harbor, Jersey City, Brooklyn Heights, the Verrazano-Narrows Bridge and Governors Island.

★ **Former US Custom House** – *1 Bowling Green.* Designed in 1907 by Cass Gilbert, this magnificent Beaux-Arts building adorned with sculptures by Daniel Chester French and Augustus Saint-Gaudens was vacated in 1973 when the Customs House moved to the World Trade Center *(p 28).* It is now the splendid setting for the Smithsonian Institution's **National Museum of the American Indian★★ [M]**. Beautifully displayed collections, including masks, weapons and ceremonial garments, represent the history and cultures of indigenous peoples living in North, Central and South America.

★★ **Trinity Church** – *Open year-round Mon–Fri 7am–6pm, Sat & holidays 8am–4pm, Sun 7am–4pm. Guided tours (45min) available, reservations suggested.* ☎212-602-0800. This Gothic Revival edifice, designed by Richard Upjohn, was completed in 1846.

The rose sandstone exterior features a square bell tower with a 280ft spire. Handsome bronze doors (1896, Richard Morris Hunt), inspired by those of the Baptistery in Florence, Italy, lead to the interior. Note the stained-glass windows by Upjohn above the white marble altar (1877). Dotted with old and worn tombstones, the adjacent cemetery offers a pleasant, shady green space among the Financial District's skyscrapers.

★ **New York Stock Exchange [A]** – *8-18 Broad St.* The most recent home for the New York Stock Exchange, founded in 1792, is this 17-story building (1903) distinguished by a majestic facade of Corinthian columns and an elaborate crowning pediment. On an average day, about 410 million shares change hands, valued at more than $16 billion. In the visitor center you will find exhibits that trace the history of the exchange and present the workings of the stock market *(20 Broad St.; open year-round Mon–Fri 9:15am–4pm; closed major holidays; tickets are distributed free outside the building for a same-day visit;* ♿ ☎212-656-5165).

★ **Federal Hall National Memorial [B]** – *26 Wall St. Open year-round Mon–Fri 9am–5pm.* ♿ ☎212-825-6888. This site was first occupied by New York's City Hall (1699), which was remodeled in 1789 to serve as Federal Hall, the first US capitol. It was here in that year that George Washington took his oath of office as the nation's first president. The present building (Town & Davis) dates from 1842 and served as the US Custom House until 1862, when it became the US Subtreasury. An elegant central rotunda with 16 marble Corinthian columns makes this one of the finest Greek Revival interiors in New York.

Federal Reserve Bank of New York [C] – *33 Liberty St. Visit by guided tour (45min) only, year-round Mon–Fri 10:30am & 11:30am, 1:30pm & 2:30pm. Closed major holidays. Advance reservations (minimum 2 weeks) required.* ♿ ☎212-720-6130. Facing the Chase Manhattan Bank, this imposing 14-story Renaissance Revival-style structure, which encompasses an entire block, was completed in 1924. Inside, at a depth of 80ft below the street level, is the Federal Reserve's gold vault. Approximately half the length of a football field, this chamber contains the gold reserves of 80 foreign nations and is thought to house the largest accumulation of the precious metal in the world, with a market value (1993) of more than $107 billion.

★ **Fraunces Tavern [D]** – *54 Pearl St. Open year-round Mon–Fri 10am–4:45pm, weekends noon–4pm. Closed major holidays. $2.50.* ♿ ☎212-425-1778. The original 1719 building on this site was bought in 1763 by Samuel Fraunces, whose tavern here was the scene of George Washington's farewell to his officers in 1783. A speculative reconstruction, the present yellow-brick structure (1904) with its slate roof, portico and balcony, represents a fine example of Georgian Revival architecture. The main floor contains a tavern-style restaurant, while upper-level exhibits trace the early history of New York City. American decorative arts are also displayed in period settings.

★★ **World Trade Center** – Occupying a 16-acre site, this "United Nations of Commerce," devoted to the advancement and expansion of international trade, was completed in 1970 and has since become the central market of world trade. Architects Minoru Yamasaki & Assocs. and Emery Roth & Sons designed the modernistic complex, which comprises seven buildings grouped around a sweeping five-acre plaza. The Center includes a concourse with a Port Authority TransHudson (PATH) railroad terminal, access to the New York subways and eight acres of shops and services.

The main attractions of the World Trade Center are the two 110-story **Twin Towers**★★★, the second-tallest buildings in the nation after the Sears Tower in Chicago, rising to 1,350ft. An innovative structural design, in which the exterior walls bear most of the load, allows a maximum amount of open, column-free floor space. Expansive **views**★★★ of the entire metropolitan area from a downtown vantage point are offered by the glass-enclosed **observation deck** 🄺🄸🄳🅂 of Two WTC *(107th floor; open Jun–Aug daily 9:30am–11:30pm; rest of the year daily 9:30am–9:30pm; $10;* ✖♿ ☎212-323-2340). Weather permitting, it is also possible to take an escalator up to the 110th floor for a stroll on the quarter-mile-high rooftop promenade. On the 107th floor of One WTC, you can enjoy views of the city from Windows of the World restaurant.

★★ **South Street Seaport** – 🄺🄸🄳🅂 *Admission is free to historic district, its shops, restaurants, piers and Fulton Market.* One of New York's leading tourist attractions, the South Street Seaport Historic District encompasses an 11-block area fronting the East River on the edge of the Financial District just south of the Brooklyn Bridge. The area was the hub of New York's worldwide shipping activities during the early 19C, and it contains the largest concentration of early commercial buildings in Manhattan. After a period of neglect, many of the brick and granite countinghouses and warehouses have been rehabilitated for use as specialty shops, offices and housing. Notable among them is **Schermerhorn Row**, a handsome group of 19C Federal-style buildings constructed in 1811-12. Rising from a pier that extends 400ft into the East River, the **Pier 17 Pavilion**★ encompasses more than 100 shops, restaurants and cafes. Another good spot to people-watch is the **Fulton Market Building** (1983), which houses food courts and restaurants. Facing the building across South Street are the stalls of the wholesale **Fulton Fish Market**, in operation for more than a century and a half. (Fish selling begins in the early morning hours and concludes around dawn.)

The **South Street Seaport Museum** maintains several historic buildings, piers, ships, galleries and a printing shop. Stop in at the **visitor center**, located at 12 Fulton Street, to view the permanent exhibit on the history of the seaport. Moored at piers 15 and 16 along South Street is the fleet of **historic ships**★ dating from 1885 to 1935 (*$6 general admission fee covers gallery, historic ships, the museum's special programs, and 50min guided tours, available Dec–Mar daily; purchase tickets at visitor center* ✗ & ☎212-669-9424).

★★ Civic Center

Located at the foot of Brooklyn Bridge, north of the Financial District and west of Chinatown, the Civic Center encompasses Foley Square and City Hall Park. After the completion of City Hall in 1811, several federal, state and municipal buildings were erected in the immediate vicinity. Although the city continued its northward expansion, the area has always remained the heart of government activities in Manhattan.

Foley Square – Standing on the former site of a large body of water known as the Collect Pond, this square is surrounded by monumental structures, including the 1927 **New York State Supreme Court** (*60 Centre St.*), distinguished by a hexagonal plan and an elaborate central rotunda, and the **United States Courthouse** (*40 Centre St.*), completed in 1936 by Cass Gilbert, designer of the Woolworth Building. Located at 1 Centre Street, the colossal, 40-story **Municipal Building**★ culminates in a tower topped by a gilded finial—the heroic 25ft statue *Civic Fame*.

★★ **City Hall** – Surrounded by a pleasant, tree-shaded park, this dignified edifice contains the office of the mayor and the City Council Chamber. The French-inspired Neoclassical structure (1811) designed by Joseph-François Mangin and John McComb, Jr., has been associated with many important events. In 1824 Revolutionary War hero Marquis de Lafayette was officially entertained here during his triumphant return to America. In 1865 Abraham Lincoln's body lay in state inside while 120,000 grief-stricken New Yorkers filed past. The building is considered one of the most beautiful early-19C civic buildings in the US. In the central rotunda, a pair of graceful, cantilevered stairways lead to the second-floor gallery, which is ringed with slender Corinthian columns supporting the coffered dome.

Behind City Hall, the old New York County Courthouse, generally known as the **Tweed Courthouse**, stands as a monument to "Boss" Tweed, who allegedly pocketed some $10 million of the building's $14 million construction cost.

★★★ **Woolworth Building** – *233 Broadway*. This 1913 skyscraper, Cass Gilbert's masterpiece, was the tallest in the world until the Chrysler Building's completion in 1930. Created for F.W. Woolworth (the founder of the ubiquitous five-and-ten-cent store), the Gothic-style building cost more than $13.5 million, which Woolworth paid in cash. Soaring without setbacks to a height of 792ft, the terracotta-clad tower is ornamented with gargoyles, pinnacles, flying buttresses and finials. The three-story **lobby**★★ features a barrel vault covered with Byzantine-style mosaics and frescoed balconies. Note the six whimsical caricatures, among them Woolworth (counting his nickels and dimes) and Gilbert (clutching a model of the building), under the supporting crossbeams on the Barclay Street side.

★★ **St. Paul's Chapel** – *On Broadway, between Fulton and Vesey Sts. Open year-round Mon–Fri 9am–3pm, Sun 7am–3pm. Closed major holidays. Guided tours (40min) available.* & ☎212-602-0800. Belonging to Trinity Church parish, this small chapel (1766) constructed of native Manhattan schist is the oldest extant church in

29

Manhattan and one of the city's finest Georgian-period buildings. The spire and rear portico on Broadway (part of the original plan) were added in 1794. The altar is attributed to Pierre Charles L'Enfant, who later laid out Washington, DC.

★★★ **Brooklyn Bridge** – *The pedestrian walkway can be reached by crossing Park Row from City Hall Park, or from the Brooklyn Bridge–City Hall subway station.* The first bridge to link Manhattan and Brooklyn, this famed structure was one of the great engineering triumphs of the 19C and the world's longest suspension bridge for 20 years. Its history dates back to 1869, when German-born John Augustus Roebling was commissioned to design a bridge linking Manhattan and Brooklyn. Roebling's foot was crushed while he was taking measurements for the piers, gangrene set in and he died three weeks later. His son, Washington Roebling, carried on, adopting new methods in pneumatic construction. Washington himself was stricken with the bends from entering the deep underwater construction chambers, known as caissons. Confined to his sickbed, he nevertheless continued to direct work from a window overlooking the operation. The $25 million project was completed in 1883 and played a significant role in the development and growth of Brooklyn, now the city's most populous borough. With its intricate web of suspension cables and its majestic, pointed arches, the bridge remains an aesthetic and technical masterpiece. For one of the most dramatic walks in New York, stroll across this bridge as the sun sets, when magnificent **views**★★ of the city and harbor filter through the filigree of cables.

★★ CHINATOWN – LITTLE ITALY – LOWER EAST SIDE *½ day. Map p 26.*

Together with the Lower East Side, Chinatown and Little Italy form one of New York City's most distinctive immigrant districts. While each of these three sections of Manhattan was once quite separate, the borders have increasingly blurred over the years. In particular, Chinatown is rapidly encroaching on Little Italy and the Lower East Side, both of which now contain a multitude of Chinese factories and laundries. Throughout the entire area, narrow streets lined with colorful shops, produce stands, cafeterias and restaurants teem with locals and visitors, particularly on weekends.

Chinatown

★★ **Chinatown** – The majority of Manhattan's 110,000 Asians and Asian Americans live in this busy lower Manhattan neighborhood centering around Canal, Mott, Bayard and Pell Streets. A stroll through the area leads past storefronts piled high with displays of herbs and condiments, bean curd, dried fungi and duck eggs. Other shops offer jade and ivory carvings, silks, fans and tea sets. The Chinese culture is kept alive here by a number of Chinese movie theaters, by temples (Buddhist and Eastern Buddhist) and by the local cultural center on Mott Street.

A visit to Chinatown is of course not complete without a meal in a Chinese restaurant. Many regional cuisines are available, including Cantonese, Hunan, Mandarin and Szechuan. The area comes to life with a bang for the Chinese New Year (the first full moon after January 19), celebrated with parades, dancing dragons and fireworks.

The **Museum of Chinese in the Americas** *(70 Mulberry St.; open year-round Tue–Sun 10:30am–5pm; closed major holidays; $3;* ☎*212-619-4785)* is located in a large gallery designed by Chinese-American architect Billie Tsien. The museum focuses on the history and culture of Chinese people in New York.

★ **Little Italy** – Located north of Chinatown between Canal and Houston Streets, Little Italy was first populated by Italian immigrants who arrived at Ellis Island between the 1880s and the 1920s. The friendly atmosphere of neighborhood grocery stores purveying pastas, salamis, olives and cheeses, and the inviting smells drifting from the cafes have turned this area into a popular tourist attraction. The hub of the district is **Mulberry Street**★, also known as the Via San Gennaro after the patron saint of Naples. During the feast of San Gennaro *(mid-September)*, the street becomes a vast alfresco restaurant.

❶ Dim sum

Map p 26. After plunging through bustling Chinatown, take time to sample the district's renowned dim sum eateries. Pick from a variety of delicious appetizers circulating the room, including *bao* (steamed buns), *wonton* (dumplings filled with fish) and *harkow* (steamed shrimp dumplings). Among the best bets: **Triple Eight Palace** *(88 E. Broadway between Division and Market Sts.;* ☎*212-941-8886)*; **Nice Restaurant** *(35 E. Broadway between Catherine and Market Sts.;* ☎*212-406-9510)*, at its liveliest during the lunchtime rush; **H.S.F.** *(46 Bowery at Canal St.;* ☎*212-374-1319)*, where a picture chart helps you identify more than 75 offerings; and **Silver Palace** *(52 Bowery between Canal and Bayard Sts.;* ☎*212-964-1204)*, a longtime favorite for huge wedding banquets.

Lower East Side – Encompassing the area below Houston Street bounded by the Bowery and the East River, the Lower East Side is best known historically as a melting pot for newly arrived immigrants. Once primarily home to Jewish and Ukrainian families, the neighborhood has undergone continual change as successive waves of newcomers have staked their claim to it. Lining the narrow streets, an eclectic ensemble of tenement buildings, bustling open-air markets and shops for discount designer clothing combine to create one of America's landmark ethnic neighborhoods.

The heart of the district is **Orchard Street**★. This busy artery and its surrounding streets are closed to traffic on Sundays, becoming a mecca for bargain-seekers. Enthusiastic merchants and street hawkers vie for their customers' attention with colorful invitations to inspect their merchandise. At no. 90 stands the **Lower East Side Tenement Museum** 🔲 *(open year-round Tue–Fri noon–5pm; 1hr guided tours of the tenement building depart year-round Tue–Fri 1pm–3pm, weekends 11am–4:15pm. $8;* ☎*212-431-0233)*, which features a series of changing exhibits and programs focusing on the history of the area's urban immigrants. The guided tour takes visitors through the partially restored tenement building at 97 Orchard Street, where two cramped apartments give a sense of the deplorable conditions faced by the thousands of families who resided in the area between 1863 and 1935. Other streets worth exploring include the Bowery, once nicknamed "the poor man's Broadway." Although still home to shelters and soup kitchens, the Bowery is also known for stores specializing in lighting fixtures and wholesale restaurant equipment. The congested east-west thoroughfare of Canal Street is noted for its jewelry and diamond merchants. A short detour on Eldridge Street leads to the **Eldridge Street Synagogue**★ *(nos. 12-16)*, the first great house of worship built by Eastern European Jews in America.

★★ SOHO AND THE VILLAGES   *1 day. Map p 26.*

The three contiguous downtown neighborhoods of SoHo, Greenwich Village and the East Village rank among Manhattan's most colorful and trendy. The once largely industrial area of SoHo (an acronym for South of Houston Street) is now an international center for artists and collectors, and the place where the hottest fashions in clothing, collectibles and home furnishings are likely to appear first. Just to the north lies Greenwich Village, long known as New York's bohemia. The East Village, centering around Astor Place and Second Avenue, is a somewhat seedy but lively district that has become a center for dance, theater (Off-Off Broadway), and visual and performance art.

★★ SoHo

The site of the first free black community on the island, this area of lower Manhattan was settled in 1644 by former slaves of the Dutch West India Company who were granted the land for farms. From the 1850s to the 1890s the district was a thriving industrial dry-goods center, with department stores and warehouses located in the area's many cast-iron commercial and warehouse buildings. In the 20C the area languished until SoHo re-emerged as an artistic community in the 1960s, when painters began moving into the old warehouses, or lofts, attracted by low rents and huge, open spaces that could accommodate enormous canvases. As the area became desirable, boutiques and uptown galleries moved in. Lined with T-shirt shops and expensive clothing boutiques alike, West Broadway in particular comes alive on weekends, as it is also home to some of SoHo's best-known galleries, including Mary Boone *(no. 467)*, Leo Castelli and Sonnabend *(no. 420)*, and OK Harris *(no. 383)*.

SoHo is also known for the largest concentration of 19C **cast-iron buildings** in the US. The 26 blocks bounded by Canal, West Houston and Crosby Streets and West Broadway were declared a historic district in 1973.

West Greenwich Village

Lawrence Manning/First Light

★ **Broadway** – Overflowing with traffic, pedestrians and sidewalk vendors, this lively thoroughfare is a street of contrasts, where hardware stores and bargain outlets stand side by side with tony emporiums selling everything from antiques to Armani. At 488-92 Broadway stands the **E.V. Haughwout Building★**, which boasts the oldest complete cast-iron facades in the city, produced by Daniel Badger's ironworks in 1857. Four museums of note are located within walking distance of each other, including the SoHo branch of the Guggenheim Museum *(p 45)* at no. 575 and the Alternative Museum *(no. 594)*, founded in 1975 expressly to offer programs that foster equitable participation by both men and women from all economic, ethnic and social backgrounds.

★ **Museum for African Art** – *593 Broadway. Open year-round Tue–Fri 10:30am–5:30pm, weekends noon–6pm. Closed major holidays. $5.* & ☎*212-966-1313.* This small but active museum with interiors designed by architect Maya Lin (Vietnam War Memorial) is one of only two in the US devoted exclusively to African art. Changing exhibits feature both contemporary and historical works, including painting, sculpture, textiles and masks.

The New Museum of Contemporary Art – *583 Broadway. Open year-round Wed–Sun noon–6pm (Sat 8pm). Closed major holidays. $4.* ⚹ ☎*212-219-1355.* Founded in 1977, the New Museum is an international forum for contemporary artists—many unknown or unrecognized—whose work deals with popular culture, the environment, feminism, the media, politics and health issues such as AIDS.

★ **Greene Street** – One of the richest collections of cast-iron building facades in SoHo is found on this thoroughfare, where the original cobblestones and wide granite sidewalks accentuate the 19C atmosphere. The two stars of the street are the "King" *(no. 72)*, with massive projecting bays, and the "Queen" *(nos. 28-30)*, a six-story Second Empire-style warehouse with an enormous mansard roof; both cast-iron structures date from 1872.

★ **TriBeCa** – This intriguing area gained its acronym (for T̲riangle B̲elow C̲anal Street) in the 1980s from a real estate agent hoping to create an identity as trendy as SoHo's. Roughly bounded by Broadway and Canal, Chambers and West Streets, the wedge-shaped district is notable for its commercial warehouses, art spaces and chic restaurants.

★★ Greenwich Village

Greenwich Village occupies the area bounded by Spring and 14th Streets, between Greenwich Street and Broadway. The heart of this heterogeneous district of winding, tree-shaded lanes is Washington Square and the area just to the west of it. Restaurants and coffeehouses abound, interspersed with craft shops, boutiques, theaters and galleries.

In 1609, when Henry Hudson sailed up the river that was later named for him, the countryside that was to become Greenwich Village was covered with woods and streams. In 1696 a village sprung up, named after the English town of Greenwich. By the early 19C, the area became an elegant residential address, then lost its cachet when industry developed near the waterfront. It was during the early 1900s that "the Village" solidified its reputation as New York's bohemian enclave, becoming a political, artistic and literary center for New York's intelligentsia. Today Greenwich Village still caters to New Yorkers who cherish a diversity of lifestyles and it remains the main stomping ground for the city's gay community.

★★ **Washington Square** – Forming the heart of present-day Greenwich Village, this large plaza stands at the foot of Fifth Avenue, its marble triumphal arch (1892, Stanford White) a fitting gateway to the famous thoroughfare. Following its transformation into a park in 1826, the square spurred the growth of a fashionable enclave of Greek Revival town houses on its north side. Today a large number of the surrounding buildings belong to NYU and the square is the university's unofficial campus—a people-watcher's paradise, alive with impromptu performers and soapbox orators.

New York University – The largest private university in the United States, NYU was founded in 1831 by Albert Gallatin, secretary of the Treasury under Thomas Jefferson. There are now 13 colleges, a staff of 14,500 and more than 45,000 students. Notable NYU buildings in the area include Stanford White's 1893 Judson Memorial Baptist Church *(55 Washington Square South)*, with superb stained-glass windows by John LaFarge; the Elmer Holmes Bobst Library, an imposing red sandstone cube; and the Hagop Kevorkian Center for Near Eastern Studies *(corner of Washington Square South and Sullivan St.)*, a stark granite building whose lovely **entrance hall**★ is a reconstruction of a Syrian courtyard.

★ **Bleecker Street** – This is one of the most active commercial thoroughfares in the Village, along with West Eighth and

➊ **Balducci's**
Map p 26. 424 Ave. of the Americas. ☎*212-673-2600.* Run by the Balducci family since 1916, this old-world former produce stand has long been one of the best-stocked food emporiums in the city. Cramped aisles and displays burst with produce, baked delicacies, prepared gourmet foods, and succulent meats and seafood. Browsers often get treated to generous free samples of focaccia or Italian cookies; the company's own roasted coffee beans make a great gift. The best part is watching locals shop—it's always crowded, but worth it.

Hudson Streets. Part of an old Italian neighborhood, Bleecker is famed for pastry shops and coffeehouses. The four-block stretch between the Avenue of the Americas and LaGuardia Place is an old 1960s stomping ground and still abounds with small cabarets, music clubs and bars.

East Village

Bounded by Houston and 14th Streets east of Broadway, the East Village is a magnet for New York City's youthful counterculture. Eastward toward Second Avenue and Avenue A, secondhand shops, ethnic boutiques, bakeries, restaurants and coffeehouses are an adventure to explore. St. Mark's Place between Second and Third Avenues is packed with shops and stalls where you can buy everything from vintage comic books to leather goods. Popular bars and restaurants proliferate in the **NoHo** (<u>No</u>rth of <u>Ho</u>uston) and **Astor Place** neighborhoods. After the Revolution, the district west of Second Avenue boasted fashionable town houses. Most of the area, however, has a history as a working-class neighborhood, and the blocks farther east were home to Polish, Ukrainian and German immigrants until the early 20C. In the 1950s low rents and an air of romantic seediness attracted such beat-generation writers as Jack Kerouac and William S. Burroughs, followed by the hippies and punks of the 1960s and 70s. The glory days were the 1980s, when rock bands like the B-52's and Talking Heads made their name at the **CBGB Club** *(315 Bowery)*. Tireless denizens of the night also danced the wee hours away at the **Palladium** *(126 E. 14th St.)*, once one of the city's most popular discos.

Second Avenue – The main artery of the East Village is this busy avenue, the spine of the Jewish intellectual community during the first half of the 20C. The Entermedia Theater *(no. 189)*, originally the Yiddish Art Theater, is located here, along with an astounding variety of inexpensive ethnic eateries offering Caribbean, Ukrainian, Russian, Chinese, Yemenite, Italian, Japanese, Tibetan, Mexican and Israeli food. Indian restaurants line both sides of East Sixth Street between Second and First Avenues; the block is now known as "Curry Lane" or **Little India**. Located at the corner of East 10th Street is **St. Mark's-in-the-Bowery Church**, a Georgian-style Episcopal Church built in 1799 on the site of Peter Stuyvesant's 1660 family chapel. It is the second-oldest church in Manhattan after St. Paul's Chapel.

★★★ MIDTOWN *2 days. Maps p 26 and p 47.*

The heart of Manhattan, Midtown is New York City at its most glamorous and exciting. Situated between 34th and 59th Streets, the area is made up of a checkerboard of broad avenues (north-south) crossed by numbered streets (east-west). Among them are some of the city's most famous thoroughfares, defined by a mix of modern skyscrapers, monumental civic buildings, elegant private clubs and hotels, art galleries and designer boutiques. The spine of the district is **Fifth Avenue★★★**, which marks the boundary between the East and West Sides. This former residential street known in the late 19C as "Millionaires' Row" (home to the Goulds, Astors and Vanderbilts) is now bordered by such famous department stores as Bergdorf Goodman, Saks, Lord & Taylor (the city's oldest), and such world-renowned jewelry firms as Cartier and Tiffany & Co. Although the mass-market ventures of Disney, Coca-Cola and Warner Bros. have opened commercial venues here in recent years, attracting camera-toting tourists, the avenue continues to exude a sense of luxury and elegance unequaled in New York.

One block west of Fifth Avenue is the **Avenue of the Americas★**, where an imposing line of

1960s skyscrapers creates a dramatic canyon of glass and steel. **Madison Avenue★**, ranking among New York's most exclusive shopping thoroughfares, is located one block east of Fifth Avenue. Many of the fine brownstones that made Madison a choice residential address in the late 19C remain, now remodeled with stylish storefronts. Another block to the east is **Park Avenue★★★**, home to many midtown banks and high-rise offices that have replaced earlier apartment buildings. Tunneling under this wide boulevard are the railroad tracks running north out of Grand Central Terminal.

Slicing across Manhattan from the East River to the Hudson, **42nd Street★★** is New York's major crosstown street. Following the completion of Grand Central in 1913, a boom in real estate opened up the area to office towers, apartment buildings and hotels. The eastern section of 42nd Street, between the United Nations headquarters and Fifth Avenue, features a lineup of distinguished Art Deco structures, including the Chanin, Chrysler and Daily News Buildings. The main artery spanning the breadth of upper midtown is **57th Street★**, encompassing shops, galleries (a bastion of 20C art) and office towers. Theme clubs, including Planet Hollywood, Hard Rock Cafe, and Jekyll and Hyde, cluster at the street's western end.

★★ **Pierpont Morgan Library** – *29-33 E. 36th St. Open year-round Tue–Fri 10:30am–5pm, Sat 10:30am–6pm, Sun noon–6pm. Closed major holidays. $5. Guided tours (1hr) available. ☎212-685-0610.* This venerable institution houses an outstanding collection assembled by **J. Pierpont Morgan** (1837-1913), whose interest in Western civilizations is represented by rare manuscripts, drawings, prints, paintings and books, including three Gutenberg Bibles (mid-15C). Designed by the firm of McKim, Mead and White, the Italian Renaissance-style main building was completed in 1906, and the equally elegant annex (West Library) was added in 1928. Opulent interiors, including three public rooms and Morgan's former library—with its renowned collection of books and manuscripts—are considered among the most magnificent in New York.

★★★ **Empire State Building** – Kids *350 Fifth Ave. at 34th St. Observatory open year-round daily 9:30am–11:30pm (reduced hours Dec 24–25 & Jan 1). $4.50. ✗ ♿ ☎212-736-3100. Consult visibility chart before buying tickets.* Rising to a height of 1,454ft with a grace, elegance and strength that have made it one of the most breathtaking skyscrapers ever built, this Art Deco masterpiece has remained the most distinctive feature of the Manhattan skyline. Completed in 1931, the needle-nosed tower was the world's tallest for four decades. The top floor was originally intended as a mooring platform for dirigibles, but the project was abandoned after a trial run in 1932 nearly resulted in a catastrophe. The 80mi view from the 86th floor **observatory** is so impressive that two visits are recommended for the full effect: by day, for an overview of the entire region, and again in the evening, to enjoy the spectacle of the city's lights. Another elevator takes visitors to the glass-enclosed circular observatory on the 102nd floor.

Aerial View of Midtown – Henryk Kaiser/INDEX STOCK

★★ **New York Public Library** – *476 Fifth Ave., between W. 40th and 42nd Sts. Open year-round Mon 10am–6pm, Tue–Wed 11am–7:30pm, Thu–Sat 10am–6pm. Closed major holidays. Guided tours (1hr) available Mon–Sat 11am & 2pm.* ♿ ☎212-661-7220. Founded in 1895, the New York Public Library is the second-largest research library in the US, after the Library of Congress, in Washington, DC. Housed in various branches throughout New York City, the collection comprises more than 15 million books and more than 48 million manuscripts and other materials. The stately, marble-faced main building (1911), a Beaux-Arts master-piece by Carrère and Hastings, is a monument to culture and learning and is midtown Manhattan's most striking public edifice. Two famous marble lions (Patience and Fortitude) guard the main entrance. Periodic exhibits are mounted in the lavishly appointed interior. Among the rarities occasionally presented in the **Salomon Room★** are a draft of the Declaration of Independence in Jefferson's own hand and an edition of Galileo's works, which can be read only with a mag-nifying glass.

Located behind the library is **Bryant Park★**, midtown's only large green space. Filled with flower vendors, bookstalls and snack kiosks, it is the scene of summer concerts and art exhibits.

★★★ **Rockefeller Center** – *Between Fifth and Seventh Aves. and 47th and 52nd Sts.* One of the most vital and cohesive urban design complexes in America, Rockefeller Center comprises an imposing group of harmoniously designed skyscrapers dat-ing primarily from the pre-World War II era. Steeped in an air of festivity year-round, this "city within a city" draws some 275,000 office workers and tourists daily.

The complex was the brainchild of oil magnate John Davison Rockefeller (1839-1937) and originally occupied a 12-acre site leased by Rockefeller from Columbia University in 1928. The project's core, including the former RCA Building, was completed in 1940, and seven more buildings were added between 1947 and 1973. The ensemble was designed by a team of seven architects, which included Wallace K. Harrison. Their intent was to provide midtown Manhattan with an urban center that would foster a sense of community. The result is a wonderful combination of buildings, open spaces, restaurants, shops and boutiques today housed in 19 buildings covering about 22 acres.

Centerpiece of Rockefeller Center, the lovely **Channel Gardens★★** incorporate a series of six pools surrounded by flower beds, which are changed regularly dur-ing the temperate months, beginning with Easter lilies on Good Friday. The promenade leads down a gentle slope to a sunken plaza rimmed by the flags of the United Nations' member countries. The west side of the lower plaza is dom-inated by the Center's best-known sculpture, the bronze statue of **Prometheus** (1934, Paul Manship) stealing the sacred fire for humankind. An outdoor cafe in summer, the sunken space serves as a skating rink in winter. Every December, a huge Christmas tree is erected here, and visitors come to admire spectacular lighting displays and to observe the skaters whirling around on the ice below.

★★ **GE (General Electric) Building** – *30 Rockefeller Plaza.* Soaring 850ft above street level, the 70-story GE Building (former RCA Building) is the loftiest and most harmo-nious of the Center's towers. Slight setbacks soften the severity of its lines. A glass and limestone Art Deco panel (1933) enlivens the main entrance. Inside, immense murals by Spanish artist José Maria Sert depict America's develop-ment and man's progress through time. On the 65th floor is the **Rainbow Room★**, the legendary ballroom and restaurant; spectacular views can be enjoyed from all sides. General Electric and the National Broadcasting Company (NBC) are headquartered on other floors.

★ **NBC Studios** – 🧒 *Visit by guided tour only (1hr) Easter Sunday–Labor Day & Thanks-giving Day–Dec daily 9:30am–4:30pm every 15min. Rest of the year Mon–Sat 9:30am–*

③ Rainbow Room
Map p 26. 30 Rockefeller Plaza. ☎212-632-5000. *Jacket and tie required.* It would be difficult to find a place more glamorous, or more *New York*, than the 63rd floor of the GE Building. This is *the* place for a drink with a view (in the Promenade Bar), a swank night of cabaret (Rainbow and Stars), or a pull-out-the-stops romantic evening on the town, including dinner and cheek-to-cheek dancing on the revolving dance floor, with all of glitter-ing Manhattan as a backdrop.

4:30pm every 30min. No tours Jan 1, Easter Sunday, Labor Day, Thanksgiving Day & Dec 25. $10. ☎*212-664-4000.* The tour takes visitors through various NBC studio sets, including that of long-running late-night comedy *Saturday Night Live.* It ends in a simulated mini-studio where visitors appear on camera and learn a meteorologist's tricks for explaining the weather on television.

★★ **Radio City Music Hall** – *1260 Ave. of the Americas. Visit by guided tour (1hr) only, year-round Mon–Sat 10am–5pm, Sun 11am–5pm. Tours depart from main lobby every 30-45min. Prices subject to change.* ☎*212-632-4041.* The Music Hall opened its doors in 1932 under the direction of Samuel "Roxy" Rothafel to present variety shows, and soon it hosted star-studded movie premieres as well. Highlights of the fabulous Art Deco interior include the lobby, with sweeping grand staircase; Ezra Winter's enormous 60ft-by-40ft mural *Fountain of Youth*; and elaborate two-ton chandeliers. The immense proscenium arch (60ft high) is the most striking feature of the 5,882-seat theater.

Today the Music Hall is best known for the musical spectaculars presented live on its Great Stage and for concerts by top performing artists. The world's finest precision dance team, the **Rockettes** have been a star attraction since opening night, December 27, 1932. Major shows are the "Spring Spectacular" *(2 weeks around Easter)* and the "Christmas Spectacular" *(mid-Nov–Jan 5).* Concerts and special events are presented year-round *(for show schedule:* ☎*212-247-4777; for ticket information: Ticketmaster* ☎*212-307-7171).*

★★ **St. Patrick's Cathedral [E]** – *Fifth Ave. between E. 50th and 51st Sts. Open year-round Sun–Fri 7am–6pm, Sat 8am–6pm.* ☎*212-753-2261.* Designed by renowned architect James Renwick (1818-95), New York City's major Roman Catholic cathedral was one of the first examples of Gothic Revival ecclesiastical architecture in the US. When construction of the cathedral began in 1853, churchgoers complained that the building was too far out in the country. However, the city continued its growth northward, and by the time it was consecrated in 1879, St. Patrick's dominated Manhattan's most fashionable residential district.

The elegant granite and marble structure, with its 330ft spires (1888), is reminiscent of the cathedral of Cologne, Germany. Inside, three portals with intricately sculpted bronze doors open into the spacious nave, illuminated by Gothic-style stained-glass windows, most of which were manufactured in France. A series of slender marble pillars supports the cross-ribbed vaults, which rise 110ft above the nave. Note also the elegantly designed baldachin over the high altar (Renwick), and the monumental organ.

★★ **Villard Houses (New York Palace Hotel) [F]** – *451-457 Madison Ave.* This graceful ensemble originated as a U-shape group of six mansions designed in 1882 by McKim, Mead and White for Henry Villard, founder of the Northern Pacific Railroad. The Renaissance Revival composition of rusticated brownstone was intended to appear to passersby as a single mansion. In 1976 the houses were incorporated into the Helmsley Palace Hotel and the luxurious interior detailing, including stained-glass windows by Louis Comfort Tiffany and murals by John Lafarge, were restored. The north wing houses the Urban Center, including the Municipal Art Society, which presents periodic exhibits on design issues; and Urban Center Books, the city's most comprehensive architecture bookstore.

★★ **Museum of Modern Art** – *11 W. 53rd St. Open year-round Sat–Tue 11am–6pm & Thu–Fri noon–8:30pm. Closed Thanksgiving Day, Dec 25. $8.50. Guided tours (1hr) available.* ✗ & ☎*212-708-9750.* One of the world's preeminent cultural institutions, the Museum of Modern Art (MOMA) offers an unparalleled overview of the modern visual arts. The collection encompasses not only painting, drawing and sculpture, but also photography; decorative, graphic and industrial art; architectural plans and models; video; and the most comprehensive film archive in the US. Now much altered, the original 1939 marble-and-glass building by Philip Goodwin and Edward Durell Stone was one of the first examples of the International style in the US. Later modifications were designed by Philip Johnson and Cesar Pelli.

The museum itself dates to 1929, when three private benefactresses—Abby Aldrich Rockefeller, Lillie P. Bliss and Mary Quinn Sullivan—launched a show of Postimpressionists to promote the modern arts in the US. Over the next decade, founding director Alfred H. Barr, Jr. shaped MOMA's philosophy, which emphasizes ideas as much as objects. From an initial 1931 bequest of 235 works—including key paintings by Cézanne, Gauguin, Seurat and Redon—the holdings have grown to encompass more than 100,000 pieces. There are six divisions:

painting and sculpture (all major modern movements from the 1880s to the present); drawings (Dada, Surrealist, school of Paris, Russian avant-garde and American artists); prints and illustrated books (bibliographic arts and print-making, including the graphic arts of Picasso); photography (masters from the 1840s to the present, including Atget, Stieglitz, Cartier-Bresson, Weston and Friedlander); architecture and design (architectural models, posters, decorative arts and transportation); and film and video (silent, experimental, animated, doc-umentary, feature films and stills from around the world). Opening off the ground floor, the Sculpture Garden serves as a gallery for sculptures by Rodin, Moore and Picasso.

★ **Carnegie Hall** – *156 W. 57th St. Visit by guided tour (1hr) only, Jan–Jun & Sept–Dec Mon–Tue, Thu–Fri 11:30am, 2pm & 3pm. $6.* & ☎212-247-7800. Named for its bene-factor, steel magnate and philanthropist Andrew Carnegie *(p 338)*, this majestic concert hall is regarded as one of the world's most prestigious. The Italian Renaissance-style structure opened in 1891 with Russian composer Pëtr Tchaikovsky's American conducting debut and has since hosted luminaries from Gustav Mahler to the Beatles, Winston Churchill and Dr. Martin Luther King, Jr. After narrowly escaping demolition in the 1960s, the building was renovated in 1986. The small **Rose Museum at Carnegie Hall** *(access at no. 154; open year-round Mon–Tue & Thu–Sun 11am–4:30pm; closed major holidays;* & ☎212-903-9629) fea-tures photos, programs and clippings detailing the history of the hall.

★★ **Grand Central Terminal** – *Park Ave. and 42nd St.* Designed by the engineering firm of Reed and Stem and architects Warren & Wetmore, the sumptuous Beaux-Arts building is one of New York's great civic monuments and has remained a beloved symbol of the city since its inception in 1903. The terminal is currently undergoing a $100 million restoration scheduled for completion in fall 1998. Highlight of the design is the cavernous **main concourse★**, measuring 375ft long by 120ft wide, and soaring to a height of 125ft (12 stories). The hall is crowned by a vaulted ceiling decorated with the constellations (pinpointed with electric light) of the winter zodiac. Streams of sunlight from 60ft-tall arched windows flow into the vast and imposing space, where a centrally located brass and onyx clock serves as a traditional rendezvous point. Towering 59 stories over Grand Central is the **MetLife Building** (1963), formerly the Pan Am Building, which was con-ceived by a group of architects that included Walter Gropius of the Bauhaus school. Its nonconforming design raised a storm of protest, which still rumbles occasionally today.

★ **Chanin Building [G]** – *122 E. 42nd St.* A prime example of the Art Deco style, this 56-story building (1929) features a series of setbacks, topped by a buttressed crown, rising from a massive base. Adorning the first four floors, a detailed terra-cotta frieze of floral bas-reliefs reflects typical curvilinear Art Deco elements. Step inside the intricately detailed lobby to view the door frames, convector grilles and mailboxes.

★★★ **Chrysler Building** – *405 Lexington Ave.* Rising to 1,048ft (77 stories), this famous New York landmark is surmounted by a distinctive spire of radiant stainless-steel arches that glimmers in sunlight. Designed by William Van Alen and com-pleted in 1930, it was briefly the tallest building in the world (it was surpassed by the Empire State Building in 1931). It was also one of the first to feature exposed metal as an essential part of its design. The pinnacle resembles a radia-tor cap from a 1930 Chrysler automobile. Abundant automotive decorations adorning the various setbacks under the spire include silver hood ornaments, stylized racing cars and the huge radiator-cap gargoyles at the fourth level, modeled after a 1929 Chrysler. The **lobby★**, a superb example of Art Deco styling, is faced with red African marble. The elevator cabs feature ornate doors and richly paneled interiors.

★ **Daily News Building [H]** – *220 E. 42nd St.* This 1930 building was designed by Howells and Hood for the *Daily News* tabloid. One of the city's first skyscrapers to abandon the Gothic style popular at the time, the Daily News Building fea-tures white-brick piers alternating with patterned red and black brick spandrels in an Art Deco-inspired design, giving the tower a vertical striped look and an illusion of height greater than its actual 37 stories. The lobby is famed for its revolving globe (12ft in diameter) and a clock that gives readings in 17 time zones. The floor is laid out as a giant compass indicating most of the principal cities of the world and their distance, by air, from New York City.

■ Park Avenue Architecture

Since the turn of the century, Park Avenue has offered an illuminating timeline of New York architecture, ranging from Beaux-Arts monuments to groundbreaking experiments in Modernism. All the buildings here date from after 1903, when the railroad tracks running up the center of the thoroughfare, originally called Fourth Avenue, were buried underground as work began on **Grand Central Terminal** *(p 38)*. New engineering techniques allowed vibration-proof construction directly over the train tunnels and resulted in the rapid development of real estate as far north as 50th Street. The newly named and landscaped Park Avenue was quickly lined with uniform rows of clubs, hotels and apartment buildings, and the entire scheme was hailed as a triumph of urban design. In the 1920s and 30s, Art Deco towers appeared, followed by the glass-and-steel high rises, home mainly to banks, that shape the "glass canyon" of Park Avenue's midtown blocks today.

Early Landmarks – The **Helmsley Building★** (1929, Warren & Wetmore) at no. 230 is unquestionably the grande dame of the avenue's Beaux-Arts landmarks, reflecting the academic influence of European Renaissance architecture with its symmetrical design, triumphal arches and sumptuous base sculptures and lobby. This office tower was intended to symbolize the power of the New York Central Railroad Company (originally headquartered inside) and literally straddles Park Avenue like a giant (two portals allow cars to pass through). It is now overshadowed by the colossal **MetLife Building** separating it from Grand Central, but it remains an impressive sight when the gold-leafed pyramidal roof is lit at night.

Another Beaux-Arts building of note is the Italian Renaissance-style **Racquet and Tennis Club** (1919) at no. 30. The elegant McKim, Mead and White design illustrates the firm's custom of modeling club buildings after Italian palazzos. Park Avenue's history as a bastion of New York society is also recalled by the Byzantine-inspired **St. Bartholomew's Church★**, set in a beautiful terraced garden at the corner of East 50th Street. Considered one of architect Bertram G. Goodhue's most successful commissions, this Episcopal church was completed in 1919 and is distinguished by a multicolored dome and salmon-colored brick walls articulated with bands of gray limestone. The triple-arched Romanesque portal was taken from the original St. Bartholomew's Church (Stanford White), which stood on Madison Avenue from 1872 to 1918.

Art Deco Masterworks – In 1916 New York passed the city's first zoning resolution, restricting the floor area of a building to no more than 12 times a site's surface area. The resultant use of setbacks coincided with the Art Deco style to produce elegant, streamlined compositions. A notable example is the **Waldorf-Astoria Hotel★** (1931, Schultze & Weaver), standing on an entire city block at no. 301. Twin chrome-capped towers rise 47 stories from an 18-story granite base into a series of setbacks in limestone and brick. The handsome interior presents a mix of Art Deco ornamentation and Second Empire furnishings. Designed by Cross & Cross to complement St. Bart's, the **General Electric Building★** (formerly RCA Victor Building), towers behind the church at 570 Lexington Avenue as another 1931 Art Deco masterpiece. The GE clock, incorporating lightning bolts and angular figures wearing sun-ray halos, epitomizes the futuristic look of Art Deco ornamentation.

Modern Statements – With the postwar building boom in New York came a wave of glass-curtain-wall buildings, including some of the city's first internationally acclaimed examples of modern architecture. The 21-story, blue-green **Lever House★★** at no. 390 (1952, Skidmore, Owings & Merrill) was pivotal in New York architecture as the first skyscraper to use the vertical slab (turned sideways and rising from a two-story base) to comply with a provision of the 1916 zoning resolution (if a building occupies only 25 percent of the lot, no setbacks are required). At no. 375 the 1958 **Seagram Building★★**, by Philip Johnson and Mies van der Rohe (his only New York City commission), demonstrates an equally compelling approach to commercial design. The harmoniously proportioned headquarters of Joseph E. Seagram & Sons, Inc. towers 38 stories over a granite plaza; given Park Avenue real estate values, the half-acre open space was remarkable for its time. (Step inside the lobby to admire the huge Picasso painting adorning the entrance of the famed restaurant, the Four Seasons.) With their sleek bronze-and-glass facades stripped of ornament and historical references, both buildings are considered jewels of the International style.

Among Park Avenue's own examples are the former **Pepsi-Cola Building** (1960, Skidmore, Owings & Merrill) at no. 500, an 11-story glass rectangle of refined geometry. The green mirrored **Park Avenue Plaza★**, consuming the block between 52nd and 53rd Streets, was designed by the same firm in 1981. With its 30ft, two-story shopping arcade, it remains a monument to the excess of the decade.

★★★ **United Nations** – *First Ave. between E. 42nd and E. 48th Sts. Visit by guided tour (45min) only, Mar–Dec daily 9:15am–4:45pm. Rest of the year Mon–Fri 9:15am–4:45pm. Closed Jan 1, Thanksgiving Day, Dec 25. Children under 5 not admitted on tours. $7.50.* ✗ & ☎212-963-7713. Situated on an 18-acre East River site purchased with $8.5 million donated by John D. Rockefeller, Jr., the United Nations complex comprises four buildings and various gardens. The premise of the 1945 UN Charter is to foster international cooperation regarding economic, social, cultural and humanitarian problems and to forge peaceful solutions to international disputes. There are 185 member states, whose flags front the building, arranged north to south in English alphabetical order (from Afghanistan to Zimbabwe). The buildings were designed in 1946 by a group of international architects, including Le Corbusier (France), Oscar Niemeyer (Brazil) and Sven Markelius (Sweden), under the direction of the American architect Wallace K. Harrison. The Secretariat Building opened in 1950, and two years later the first meetings of the Security Council and the General Assembly were held at the permanent site. Dag Hammarskjöld Memorial Library (Harrison, Abramovitz & Harris) was completed in 1962.

Forming the heart of the United Nations, the low-lying **General Assembly Building**, topped by a lyrically curved roof, contains the vaulted Assembly Hall. Various objects enhance the lobby, including a model of Sputnik I, a Foucault pendulum, a statue of Poseidon and a chunk of moon rock. The space is dominated by a dramatic, 15ft-by-20ft stained-glass window by Marc Chagall.

The five-story **Conference Building,** thus named because of its council and committee meeting rooms, links the Secretariat and the General Assembly buildings. In the front garden is a Japanese peace bell, made of copper coins and metal donated by the children of 60 countries, as well as a sculpture by Henry Moore. Constructed entirely of white Vermont marble and glass-and-aluminum panels, the slab-like **Secretariat Building**★ is striking for its pure, clean lines. The simple grid pattern of the exterior rises 39 floors without a break. Located on the southwest corner of the complex, the **Hammarskjöld Library**, a gift of the Ford Foundation, is dedicated to the memory of the second secretary-general, Dag Hammarskjöld, killed in 1961 in a plane crash during a peacekeeping mission to the Congo. Marble walls enclose 380,000 volumes for the use of UN delegates, Secretariat staff members and scholars.

★★ **THEATER DISTRICT AND CHELSEA**   *2hrs. Maps p 26 and p 47.*

Running the entire length of Manhattan, Broadway, "the longest street in the world," has given its name to the city's famous entertainment and theater district, which extends approximately from 40th to 53rd Streets, between Seventh and Eighth Avenues. Times Square, referred to as the "Crossroads of the World," marks the center of this concentration of world-renowned theaters, cinemas, night spots and bars. Situated to the south, roughly west of the Avenue of the Americas between 14th and 30th Streets, Chelsea is a multifaceted neighborhood that combines refurbished industrial buildings, chic shops and a quiet residential district of historic brownstones. Here, a thriving arts scene and increasingly upscale air contrast with both the glitz of the Times Square area and the grit of the Garment District sandwiched in between.

★★ **Theater District**

At the end of the 19C, the Times Square area was a center for livery stables and harness makers. One of the area's first theaters was opened by Oscar Hammerstein in 1899 at the corner of 42nd Street and Seventh Avenue. Then known as Longacre, the square (actually wedge-shaped) was renamed in 1904 when *The New York Times* moved its headquarters here. In the first decade of the 20C, Times Square abounded with vaudeville houses. As vaudeville waned, live entertainment persisted during the "big band" era of the 1930s and 40s. The legendary Roseland Dance City *(239 W. 52nd St.)* was *the* place for devotees of ballroom dancing, attracting would-be Fred Astaires and Ginger Rogers. In the 1960s the area deteriorated and filled with adult bookstores, X-rated movie theaters, porn shops and other tawdry establishments. Revitalization efforts began in the mid-1970s and have continued into the 1990s, when such big-name commercial enterprises as Disney, MTV, Virgin Megastore and the publishing company Condé Nast agreed to establish a presence here. Much of the pornography has disappeared, and Times Square's resurgence as a mecca of entertainment seems to be sealed.

Today, some 40 theaters cluster between 40th and 57th Streets, and the Avenue of the Americas and Eighth Avenue. Most present musicals, some of which run many years to sold-out houses. Movie theaters dominate the Times Square area, including some "grinds" open around the clock, showing second-run films. Farther north on Broadway, you'll find larger movie houses, originally built to accommodate up to three thousand spectators. Most of these giant pre-World War II houses have been transformed into multiscreen cinemas showing first-run films.

★★ **Times Square** – Located at the intersection of Broadway and Seventh Avenue between 42nd and 43rd Streets, Times Square is best known for its **nighttime illuminations**★★★. It is here that the quick pulse of the city can best be felt, as the milling theater crowds merge with thousands of tourists and theatergoers strolling under the flashing neon signs. Although the first electric advertising sign in the city was erected on Madison Square in 1892, the sign industry soon moved to Times Square, attracted by the huge crowds and large vistas. In 1916 a city zoning bill formally encouraged large electric signs in Times Square, and corporate advertisers still outdo themselves to create eye-catching displays. The square is also often the setting for huge gatherings such as political demonstrations or the annual vigil to celebrate the stroke of midnight on New Year's Eve. One Times Square landmark, the former Times Tower, dominates the southern end of the square; it is now best known for the lighted ball that drops to the accompaniment of a raucous countdown to mark the arrival of the New Year. On the facade, a giant computer-generated display (20ft by 40ft) features a mix of art and advertisements.

Theater District

West 42nd Street – The first target of Times Square's revitalization project, the section of 42nd Street between Broadway and Eighth Avenue is undergoing a dramatic transformation. The long-neglected **New Amsterdam Theater**, commissioned in 1903 by the legendary producers Klaw and Erlanger, and later home to the Ziegfeld Follies, boasts fabulous interiors restored to their Art Nouveau splendor by the Walt Disney Corporation. Across the street stands the **New Victory Theatre** (built in 1900 by Oscar Hammerstein), which reopened as a children's performance venue in 1995, following a much-acclaimed $12 million renovation.

Shubert Alley – Parallel to Broadway, this short private street, reserved for pedestrians, was laid down in 1913, between 44th and 45th Streets. The Shubert brothers built the Booth and Shubert Theaters and were required to leave this passage as a fire exit. At intermission or after a show, many theatergoers drop into Sardi's restaurant, well known for the caricatures of celebrated theatrical personalities lining its walls, and their more or less famous successors who gather in the bar or the restaurant.

★ Chelsea and the Garment Center

Named after the London neighborhood of the same name, Chelsea traces its roots to a country home staked out in 1750 along the Hudson River by Capt. Thomas Clarke. In 1813 the property passed to Clarke's grandson Clement Clarke Moore, a scholar and erudite literary figure who nevertheless remains best remembered for his famous poem "A Visit from St. Nicholas." Moore developed his land as an elegant residential neighborhood with park-like squares and row houses with spacious front yards that still bring distinction to the neighborhood. A historic district, located roughly between 19th and 23rd Streets and Ninth and Tenth Avenues, now preserves one of the largest concentrations of Greek Revival and Italianate row houses in the city; in recent years this beautifully restored area has become an enclave for New York's well-heeled gay community. Chelsea's rejuvenation is also evident along the industrial west side, where many 19C warehouses have been converted to galleries, theaters and performance venues. Overlooking the Hudson River, the reconverted **Chelsea Piers** now house a massive sports and recreational facility. Just to the north of Chelsea is the largely commercial Garment Center, which runs from West 29th to 40th Streets between Broadway and Eighth Avenues. Shops for fabrics and trimmings (mostly wholesale, but some retail) line streets jammed with trucks, while workers crowd the sidewalks wheeling racks of clothing.

④ Carnegie Delicatessen

Map p 47. 854 Seventh Ave. between 54th and 55th Sts. ☎*212-757-2245.* It's hard to tell what this kosher-style deli is more famous for: salty service or mile-high pastrami. At this New York legend, it's best to endure the former for the latter (split a sandwich if you want to save room for the famous cheesecake), and be prepared to share your table—it's all part of the fun here. For film buffs: much of Woody Allen's 1983 film *Broadway Danny Rose* was shot on the premises—there's even a namesake sandwich on the menu.

Dia Center for the Arts – *548 W. 22nd St. Open Sept–Jun Thu–Sun noon–6pm. $4.* ⚧ ♿ ☎*212-989-5912.* Based in SoHo, this center for the arts opened exhibition space in Chelsea in 1987, luring several other galleries from SoHo to the area. Each of four stories of a renovated warehouse is devoted to a large-scale, single-artist project installed for a minimum of a year. The roof features a pavilion made of two-way mirrored glass, along with a coffee bar, video room and great views up and down the Hudson River.

Hotel Chelsea – *222 W. 23rd St., between Seventh and Eighth Aves.* One of the very first cooperative apartment houses in the city, the eclectic Hotel Chelsea (1884) became a residential hotel in 1905. Festooned with cast-iron balconies, it has served as a part- or full-time home to writers and artists from Dylan Thomas and Mark Twain to Jackson Pollock and Andy Warhol, whose cult classic *Chelsea Girls* was filmed here. The somewhat shabby lobby features works by artists past and present.

Madison Square Garden [J] and Pennsylvania Station – *Bounded by Seventh and Eighth Aves. and 31st and 33rd Sts.* On this spot stood the original 1906 Pennsylvania Station designed by McKim, Mead and White. Considered the greatest New York work of this famed architectural firm, the cast-iron and glass structure was torn down in 1964 and replaced by the existing bland design. Enormous controversy over the project precipitated New York City's first landmark legislation, which remains one of the strongest local preservation laws in the country. The railroad-station complex includes the cylindrical **Madison Square Garden Sports Center**, located on the upper five tiers of the nine-story structure. The 20,000-seat "garden" is today home to the New York Knickerbockers basketball team and the New York Rangers hockey team. It is also the site of international horse and dog shows, rock concerts, skating exhibitions, circuses, boxing matches and tennis tournaments.

General Post Office – *At the corner of Eighth Ave. and 33rd St.* Covering two full blocks, this vast granite structure (James A. Farley Building) was designed in 1908 by McKim, Mead and White as a companion to the original Penn Station and features a colonnade of 20 Corinthian columns, each 53ft high. The cornice bears the well-known inscription "Neither snow nor rain nor heat nor gloom of night stays these couriers from the swift completion of their appointed rounds."

Macy's – *Bounded by Broadway, Seventh Ave., 34th and 35th Sts.* Covering an entire city block, the "world's largest store" consists of two parts: the 1901 classically inspired eastern section and the newer western wing, built in the Art Deco style in 1931. In addition to selling almost every imaginable item—from sensible shoes to gourmet chocolates—Macy's sponsors many seasonal events that have become New York institutions, including the annual spring flower show, Fourth of July fireworks and the renowned Thanksgiving Day parade.

★ CENTRAL PARK   *¹/₂ day. Map p 47.*

A sweeping, rectangular greensward located in the geographical center of Manhattan, Central Park covers 843 acres, extending from 59th to 110th Streets between Fifth Avenue and Central Park West. The park opened more than a century ago as the first large-scale public recreation space in America and continues to provide a haven of greenery, light and air to the more than 15 million people who flock here each year.

As early as 1850, editor and poet William Cullen Bryant launched the idea of a park through a press campaign in his newspaper, the *New York Evening Post*, and the design commission was won by landscape architects **Frederick Law Olmsted** (1822-1903) and **Calvert Vaux** (1824-95). Clearing the site (a swamp then inhabited by squatters, pigs and goats) began in 1857 with a labor force of 3,000 and work continued for the next 19 years. Olmsted and Vaux's design skillfully blended natural and man-made elements to create a park inspired by the "picturesque," or Romantic, style highly favored in the mid-19C. Lakes, ponds, hills and dales, rocky crags, trees, bushes and shrubs produce a landscape of great scenic beauty, while open spaces and meadows, bridle paths and carriage drives lend a pastoral charm. Since 1980 renovation of the park has been ongoing. Despite periodic flare-ups in crime, the highly valued green space remains a much-loved and constantly used recreational center for New Yorkers from all walks of life.

Ice-skating in Central Park

Visit – Favorite destinations *(moving roughly south to north)* include the Wollman Memorial Rink, which is used for ice-skating in the winter and in-line skating and roller-skating in summer. Another popular spot is the **Central Park Wildlife Conservation Center**★ 🄺🄸🄳🅂 *(open Apr–Oct Mon–Fri 10am–5pm, weekends & holidays 10:30am–5:30pm; rest of the year daily 10am–4:30pm; $2.50; ✗ ᵫ ☎212-861-6030).* Occupying 5.5 acres, this innovative zoo houses more than 450 animals of 100 species in a newly renovated naturalistic habitat. One of the few formal areas in the park, the nearby **Mall** consists of a straight path lined with handsome elms and two rows of busts depicting famous writers. Lying to the west of the Mall, the Sheep Meadow fills up with summer picnickers who flock into the park after work to enjoy the popular free evening concerts offered by the New York Philharmonic and the City Opera. Considered the centerpiece of the park,

Bethesda Terrace★ resembles a Spanish courtyard with its arcaded bridge adorned with ornate friezes, sweeping stairs and central fountain. Just to the north of this lovely plaza is the **Lake**, with its famous Art Nouveau cast-iron bridge, reproduced innumerable times in engravings and photographs. To the west lie the **Strawberry Fields** and the International Garden of Peace honoring the late Beatle, John Lennon. The three-acre garden, containing 161 species of plants representing the various nations of the world, is steps away from New York's first luxury apartment house, The Dakota, where Lennon lived. He was murdered right outside The Dakota in 1980.

To the north of the lake, the **Ramble** is a heavily wooded hill with hidden paths and a meandering brook. Inside Belvedere Castle is the **Henry Luce Nature Observatory [K]** 🄺🄳🄱 *(open Apr–Oct Tue–Sun 11am–5pm; rest of the year Tue–Sun 11am–4pm; closed Jan 1, Thanksgiving Day, Dec 25; ☎212-772-0210)*. Opened in May 1996, this nature education center hosts hands-on exhibits detailing the city's flora and fauna.

The **Conservatory Garden** at East 103rd Street is the park's only formal garden, featuring a half-acre greensward, crab apple alleys and a wisteria pergola. The south section is known as "The Secret Garden" after Frances Hodgson Burnett's children's classic. The north part, a formal garden in the French style, blooms with two dazzling floral displays each year—20,000 tulips in spring and 5,000 chrysanthemums in fall. At 110th Street is the **Harlem Meer**, stocked with some 50,000 fish, including fathead minnows, largemouth bass, catfish and bluegills. Located at the north end of Harlem Meer, the **Charles A. Dana Discovery Center** 🄺🄳🄱 features nature exhibits and a classroom laboratory.

Museums around Central Park

The buildings bordering the west, south and east sides of Central Park create one of the most striking skylines in Manhattan. Among the landmarks here are some of New York's most famous museums, distinguishing the park along Central Park West and Fifth Avenue on the east. The stretch of Fifth Avenue running from 70th to 103rd Streets boasts so many cultural institutions that it is known as "Museum Mile"; it includes the **National Academy of Design** *(1083 Fifth Ave. ☎212-369-4880)*, the **International Center of Photography★** *(1130 Fifth Ave. ☎212-860-1783)* and **El Museo del Barrio** *(1230 Fifth Ave. ☎212-831-7272)*.

★★ **The New-York Historical Society** – *1hr. 2 W. 77th St. Open year-round Wed–Sun noon–5pm. $5. Guided tours (1hr) available 1pm & 3pm. ☎212-873-3400.* The collections of New York City's oldest museum (founded in 1804) cover three centuries of Americana; a renowned research library is housed on the third floor *(open by appointment only)*. On the brink of financial insolvency, the museum closed its doors to the public in early 1993. It reopened two years later, following a $10 million renovation. Temporary exhibitions related to the history of New York are on display in the main galleries on the first and second floors. Opening

5 Tavern on the Green
Map p 47. West side of Central Park at W. 67th St. ☎*212-873-3200.* The famed tavern is a perfect Sunday brunch spot *(reservations required)*, with stained-glass windows, sand-carved mirrors and glittering crystal chandeliers to brighten even the gloomiest day. Weather permitting, head for the outdoor cafe, lit by thousands of white lights strung through the branches, and enjoy the view of the park. The site of innumerable film and television scenes, this restaurant also serves as the finish line for the New York Marathon.

in 1999, the Henry Luce Center for the Study of American Culture will house the entire museum collection—including a superb assemblage of Hudson River school paintings, Audubon watercolors, Tiffany lamps, silver, furniture and toys.

★★★ **American Museum of Natural History** – 🄺🄳🄱 *1 day. Central Park West, between 77th and 81st Sts. Open year-round Sun–Thu 10am–5:45pm, Fri–Sat 10am–8:45pm. Closed Thanksgiving Day, Dec 25. $8. Guided tours available.* ✕ ♿ ☎*212-769-5100.* Culled on more than 1,000 expeditions since 1869, the holdings of this venerated institution (1874) include more than 30 million artifacts and specimens dealing with all facets of natural history—from mollusks to minerals to gems to dinosaurs.

The museum is arguably best known for the largest collection of fossil vertebrates in the world, and visitors scouting out skeletal remains will not be disappointed. The six **fossil halls**★★ on the top floor, where *Tyrannosaurus rex* towers over tiny *Archaeopteryx lithographica*, represent a visual and intellectual tour de force.

The institution's magnificent displays also include the famed lifelike and life-size dioramas of animals shown in their natural habitats. Of equal interest are the galleries related to the Aztec and Mayan peoples and the Hall of South American Peoples, showcasing Andean and Amazonian treasures. The museum's Asian collection comprises more than 60,000 artifacts, making it one of the largest such assemblages in the Western hemisphere. Don't miss the more than 6,000 specimens of meteorites, rocks, minerals and gems—including the Star of India, the world's largest star sapphire (563 carats).

★★ **The Frick Collection** – *At least 1½hrs. 1 E. 70th St. Open year-round Tue–Sat 10am–6pm, Sun 1pm–6pm. Closed Jan 1, Jul 4, Thanksgiving Day, Dec 24–25. $5. Children under 10 not admitted.* ☎212-288-0700. A Pittsburgh coke and steel industrialist, **Henry Clay Frick** *(p 340)* began collecting works of art on his first trip to Europe, which he took in the company of his friend Andrew Mellon, the primary benefactor of the National Gallery of Art in Washington, DC. First concentrating on 18C English paintings, he later ventured into bronzes, then prints and drawings, enamels, furniture, porcelain and rugs. In 1913 Frick commissioned this 40-room mansion, designed by Carrère and Hastings to display his holdings, including portraits by Hogarth, Romney and Reynolds and a masterpiece by Gainsborough, *The Mall in St. James's Park*. Also of note are the 11 decorative paintings by Jean-Honoré Fragonard (1732-1806) and 16C masterpieces by Bellini and Titian.

★★★ **Metropolitan Museum of Art** – *At least 1 day. Fifth Ave. at E. 82nd St. Open year-round Tue–Sun 9:30am–5:15pm (Fri & Sat 8:45pm). Consult information-desk staff for gallery viewing times. Closed Jan 1, Thanksgiving Day, Dec 25. Suggested contribution $8 (includes same-day admission to the Cloisters, p 51). Guided tours available.* ☎212-535-7710. Founded in 1870, the "Met" has occupied its present location since 1880. A great monument to world culture, the building has continually evolved ever since, incorporating sections designed by Jacob Wrey Mould and Calvert Vaux; Richard Morris Hunt (the limestone Beaux-Arts facade facing Fifth Avenue); McKim, Mead and White (north and south side wings); and Roche, Dinkeloo and Assocs. (several modern wings). The largest museum in the Western hemisphere, the Met today owns nearly three million objects from prehistory to the 20C. Rich collections from four wellsprings of civilization—ancient Egypt (a highlight is the magnificent installation of the Temple of Dendur), ancient Greece, ancient Rome, and the Near East—offer a day's worth of viewing possibilities alone.

The **Medieval collection**★★ comprises more than 4,000 works from the early Christian, Byzantine, Migration, Romanesque and Gothic periods. The galleries of arts from Africa, Oceania and the Americas; Islamic art; arms and armor; and prints and photographs are no less significant.

Among the many privately funded installations that distinguish the museum is the **Robert Lehman Collection**★★, considered one of the finest private art collections in the US. The collection is most famous for its Italian paintings of the 14C and 15C displayed in a series of seven period rooms and galleries ringing a central garden court. Exquisite period rooms, including the newly refurbished Robert Adam rooms in the English galleries, are another highlight, as are the galleries for European sculpture, painting and decorative arts (13C to the present). The superb collection of **Impressionists and Postimpressionists**★★★ is a particular magnet for visitors. Included are works by Cézanne, Manet, Monet, Renoir, Gauguin and Seurat. Equally impressive holdings of painting, sculpture and decorative arts in the **American Wing**★★★ span three centuries and include 25 full-scale room interiors. Sculpture, stained glass and architectural fragments occupy the stunning Charles Engelhard Court on the first floor. Perhaps the most recognizable work, Gilbert Stuart's portrait of George Washington is one of at least 114 that Stuart made of him.

★★ **Solomon R. Guggenheim Museum** – *2hrs. 1071 Fifth Ave. Open year-round Sun–Wed 10am–6pm, Fri–Sat 10am–8pm. Closed Thanksgiving Day, Dec 25. $8. Guided tours available.* ☎212-423-3500. **Solomon R. Guggenheim** (1861-1949) came from a family of German-Swiss immigrants who made a vast fortune mining precious metals in the 19C. In 1937 he and his wife, Irene Rothschild, established the Solomon R. Guggenheim Foundation to encourage art and art education. Six years later renowned architect **Frank Lloyd Wright** *(p 314)* was commissioned to design a permanent home for the foundation's collection, which now comprises more than 6,000 paintings, sculptures and works on paper. Among them are 195 works by Kandinsky—the largest assemblage in the US—and more than 75 pieces by Klee. A selection from the **Thannhauser collection★** is the only permanent display, with works by Pissaro, Renoir, Manet, van Gogh and Picasso. The museum itself is as much a work of art as the sculptures and paintings it contains. Wright considered the idiosyncratic structure, based on a complex trigonometric spiral, his crowning achievement. However, with its interior ramp and sloping walls, it actually proved a difficult place both to view and to display art. As a result, there have been many alterations; most recently, in 1992, the firm of Gwathmey, Siegel & Assocs. added a 10-story annex and restored much of Wright's original design. Few public spaces in New York rival the drama of the refurbished main gallery, encircled by the famous spiraling ramp, more than a quarter-mile long.

★ **Cooper-Hewitt National Design Museum** – *1hr. 2 E. 91st St. Open year-round Tue 10am–9pm, Wed–Sat 10am–5pm, Sun noon–5pm. Closed major holidays. $3.* ⚅ ☎212-860-6868. Devoted to historical and contemporary design, this decorative-arts museum focuses on industrial and interior design, architecture, fashion and advertising. The extensive collection, which encompasses some 250,000 objects spanning more than 3,000 years, is housed in the Beaux-Arts mansion (1898) built by wealthy industrialist Andrew Carnegie. The holdings include delicate textiles dating from the 3C BC; silver, bronze and wrought-iron metalwork; examples of jewelry and goldsmiths' work; wallpaper samples; bandboxes; porcelain, glass and earthenware; and furniture.

★ **The Jewish Museum** – *1hr. 1109 Fifth Ave. Open year-round Mon–Thu 11am–5:45pm (Tue 8pm). Closed Jewish and major holidays. $7.* ✗ ⚅ ☎212-423-3230. This beautifully presented collection of Judaica offers insight into 4,000 years of Jewish history through historical and literary materials, ceremonial objects, Zionist memorabilia and ancient and contemporary art. Its more than 27,000 pieces are housed in a gorgeous 1908 French Gothic-style mansion. The Goodkind Resource Center offers visitors access to television and radio tapes from the National Jewish Archive of Broadcasting.

★★ **Museum of the City of New York** – 🆒 *1½hrs. Fifth Ave. at 103rd St. Open year-round Wed–Sat 10am–5pm, Sun 1pm–5pm. Closed major holidays. $5 contribution requested.* ⚅ ☎212-534-1672. Founded in 1923 as America's first institution dedicated to the history of a city, this museum chronicles the changing face of New York from a modest Dutch trading post to a thriving international metropolis. Housed in a Georgian Revival mansion, the rich collections span three centuries of New York memorabilia, decorative arts, furnishings, silver, prints and paintings. A Toy Gallery features a delightful selection of playthings from the museum's collection of more than 6,000 items, including an exquisite series of **doll houses★**.

★★ UPTOWN   *2 days. Map p 47.*

The northern section of Manhattan above midtown comprises three vibrant and interesting districts: the Upper East Side, the Upper West Side and Harlem. Synonymous with old money and culture, the Upper East Side is known primarily as an enclave of the wealthy and fashionable, although it actually offers a broad cross section of neighborhoods. The colorful Upper West Side, across Central Park, has long attracted artists, actors and musicians, upper- and middle-class Jewish families and many other ethnic groups. Harlem is home to a sizable segment of New York's black and Hispanic communities.

★★ Upper East Side

Covering the area between Central Park and the East River, the Upper East Side stretches roughly from 59th Street to 97th Street. Once dotted with squatters' shanties and a few farms, the area remained rural until the 19C. Attracted by large lots on and near Fifth Avenue, New York's high society began migrating uptown in the 1850s, extending "Millionaires' Row" (Fifth Avenue) ever northward with lavish mansions. Ever since, the posh pockets near Central Park have continued to attract celebrities—Greta Garbo, Andy Warhol, Richard Nixon and Woody Allen among them—as well as old New York families and young Wall Streeters.

★★ **Fifth Avenue** – The section of Fifth Avenue bordering Central Park has long been New York's most prestigious residential area. Luxury apartments abut former mansions, most of which have now become museums, consulates, clubs or cultural institutions. **Grand Army Plaza★★**, a large and flowered square, marks the division between Fifth Avenue's luxury shopping district and its residential area. The **Plaza Hotel★** (1907), designed by Henry J. Hardenbergh in the French Renaissance style, is a New York institution of elegance and standing where coming-out parties and charity balls draw the cream of New York society. The blocks north on Fifth Avenue showcase many fine old residences from the glory days of the 19C, all converted to new uses.

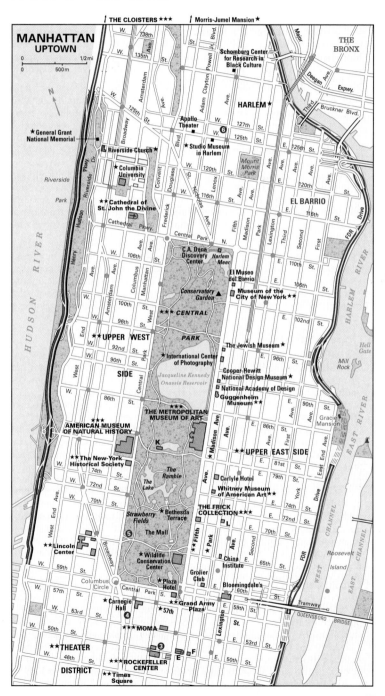

★ **Madison Avenue** – Famed enclave of exclusive stores, galleries and haute couture boutiques, Madison Avenue is a street for moneyed shoppers, where the pedestrians often rival the window displays for looking chic. Most of the small designer boutiques are concentrated south of 79th Street, but the stretch north to 96th Street, with its neighborhood bookstores, shops and trendy bistros, also has great appeal. Several early prestigious apartment buildings and apartment hotels, including the 1929 **Carlyle Hotel** *(35 E. 76th St.)*, also enhance the street's genteel character.

Located at 945 Madison Avenue, the **Whitney Museum of American Art**★★ *(open year-round Wed & Fri–Sun 11am–6pm, Thu 1pm–8pm; closed Jan 1, Jul 4, Thanksgiving Day, Dec 25; $8;* ✗ ⅋ ☎212-570-3676) is dedicated to the advancement of contemporary artists and is known for provocative exhibits. Its outstanding collection of 20C American art is housed in a stark granite building (1966) designed in the Brutalist school of Modernism by Marcel Breuer and Hamilton Smith. More than 10,000 works represent such contemporary painters as Hopper, de Kooning, Kelly, Gorky, Prendergast, Demuth and Motherwell, and sculptors Calder, Nevelson, Noguchi and David Smith.

★ **Park Avenue** – A meticulously landscaped mall and dignified apartment houses define the uptown blocks of Park Avenue, where prosperous New Yorkers erected grand residences in the early 20C. Although primarily residential, the area is also home to many respected organizations, including the **Grolier Club** *(47 E. 60th St.)*, the **China Institute** *(125 E. 65th St.)* and the **Asia Society**★ **[L]** *(725 Park Ave.; open year-round Tue–Wed & Fri–Sat 11am–6pm, Thu 11am–8pm, Sun noon–5pm; closed major holidays; $3;* ⅋ ☎212-288-6400). Housed in a red granite and sandstone building (1981) designed by Edward Larrabee Barnes, the Asia Society was founded by John D. Rockefeller III. Its rooms provide an elegant setting for Indian bronzes, Chinese and Japanese ceramics, exquisite screen paintings and hanging scrolls, wood carvings and manuscripts, and stone sculptures from Southeast Asia.

Lexington Avenue – East of Park Avenue, the atmosphere becomes more casual. With its mix of apartment houses, brownstones, coffee shops and bookstores, Lexington Avenue maintains a neighborhood feel and a pleasant scale unbroken by high-rise buildings. A famous landmark is the Art Deco-style **Bloomingdale's** department store at 59th Street. Here, high fashion applies not only to clothes but to all the merchandise, from designer bonbons to trendy shower curtains.

★★ Upper West Side

This ethnically diverse area reaching northward from Columbus Circle to West 125th Street between the Hudson River and Central Park is home to many of the city's great cultural institutions, including Lincoln Center, Columbia University and the American Museum of Natural History *(p 44)*.

In the late 19C, development reached the rural area of Bloomingdale, then dotted with shantytowns and saloons and populated by stray goats. New York's first luxury apartment house was erected on West 72nd Street and Central Park West in 1884. Even then, the building was considered to be so far out west in the middle of nowhere that it was dubbed the "Dakota." In the 1960s low rents in the old tenement buildings attracted an element of bohemia, while urban renewal projects brought further diversity to the area. Recent gentrification of the older row houses has made the cross streets quite desirable. Tree-lined residential blocks provide a quiet contrast to the bustle of Broadway, the area's commercial spine, which features everything from discount shoe stores to gourmet food shops. As young singles moved to the Upper West Side in the 1970s, Columbus Avenue became almost overnight the site of dozens of specialty shops and sidewalk cafes. In the past few years Amsterdam Avenue has followed suit and is now the setting for several popular bars, coffeehouses and bistros.

★★ **Lincoln Center** – *On Broadway between W. 62nd and 67th Sts. Visit of performance spaces by guided tour (1hr) only, year-round daily 10am–5pm. No tours Jan 1, Thanksgiving Day, Dec 25. Tour includes Metropolitan Opera House, the New York State Theater and Avery Fisher Hall. $8.25. Advance reservations recommended. Tours depart from the concourse level under the Metropolitan Opera House.* ✗ ⅋ 🅿 ☎212-875-5350. Devoted to drama, music and dance, Lincoln Center for the Performing Arts is a 16-acre complex comprising five major theater and concert buildings, a library, a band shell and two outdoor plazas. Construction began in 1959 with Avery Fisher Hall and continued over the next ten years, ending with the Juilliard

Lincoln Center

School. In 1991 the Samuel B. and David Rose Building, a multipurpose structure, was added to the complex, northwest of the Juilliard School. The sleek rectangular buildings of glass and Italian travertine marble can accommodate 13,666 spectators at a time. Distinguished by lobby murals by Marc Chagall, the 1966 **Metropolitan Opera House** forms the centerpiece of the main plaza. Designed by Wallace K. Harrison, the theater hosts both the Metropolitan Opera and the American Ballet Theater. **Avery Fisher Hall**, designed by Max Abramovitz and set to the right of the main plaza, is home to the New York Philharmonic, the country's oldest orchestra, which previously played at Carnegie Hall. To the left of the plaza is the **New York State Theater**, a 1964 Philip Johnson design, which houses the New York City Opera and the New York City Ballet.

Two small stages are also located in the recently renovated Vivian Beaumont Theater and the Mitzi E. Newhouse Theater. The Juilliard Building (1968), contains the Juilliard School (for musicians, actors and dancers) and Alice Tully Hall, used by the Chamber Music Society of Lincoln Center. The New York Film Festival is also held here every fall.

★★ **Cathedral of St. John the Divine** – *On Amsterdam Ave. at W. 112th St. Open year-round daily 7am–6pm. Guided tours (1hr) available Tue–Sat 11am, Sun 1pm ($3).* ☎*212-932-7314.* Seat of the Episcopal Diocese of New York, this is reportedly the largest cathedral in the world built in the Gothic style and can welcome up to 8,000 worshipers at a time. Construction began in 1892 and is still under way. Twenty-five years into the project, the original Romanesque design by Heins and LaFarge was scrapped for a revised plan in the Gothic style by Ralph Adams Cram. The choir and sanctuary were completed in 1916, and the nave was begun in 1925. Another century is needed to finish the towers, central spire, transepts and portal carvings, and limestone interior facing, along with a planned chapter house, sacristy building and Greek amphitheater. The 13-acre site on Amsterdam Avenue between Cathedral Parkway and West 113th Street contains seven ancillary buildings, gardens, a park and a stone-cutting yard, where a crew of apprentice stoneworkers, many of them neighborhood youths, is currently on the job, training under a master mason.

★ **Columbia University** – *W. 114th to 120th Sts., between Amsterdam Ave. and Broadway. Main entrance at W. 116th St. Guided tours (45min) enabling visitors to see the interior of many of the buildings are conducted year-round Mon–Fri 11am & 2pm. Schedule may vary during school vacations & holidays. Reservations required.* ✗ ᏻ ☎*212-854-4902.* The first college in New York (1754) and the fifth-oldest in the nation, Columbia is one of the country's wealthiest and largest private Ivy League universities, with almost 20,000 students, 15 schools, 71 academic departments and some 5,700 faculty. The main campus (1894) in Morningside Heights occupies 36 acres located on the site of the former Bloomingdale Insane Asylum. Designed by Charles McKim, the campus features a formal, axial arrangement typical of the turn-of-the-century Beaux-Arts movement and has been embellished and altered over the years. Among the notable buildings is **Temple Hoyne Buell Hall** (1878), the oldest structure on campus, which serves as a center for the study of American architecture. **St. Paul's Chapel★** (1907), a Northern Italian Renaissance design, features a beautiful vaulted interior with salmon-colored Guastavino tiling and striking cast-iron chandeliers. The elegant Neo-classical **Low Memorial Library★** (1898) with its marble rotunda was the first major structure on the campus, modeled by Charles McKim on the Roman Pantheon. Sculptures by European and American artists also distinguish the campus. Among them are Rodin's famous bronze, *The Thinker*, cast from the 1880 model in 1930, in front of Philosophy Hall; and *Three Way Piece: Points* (1967) by Henry Moore, on the Amsterdam Avenue overpass. Fronting Low Library is the regal *Alma Mater*, designed by Daniel Chester French in 1903. The Neoclassical bronze figure, emblem of the university, survived a bombing during the 1968 student riots.

★ **Riverside Church** – *On Riverside Dr. between W. 120th and 122nd Sts. If west portal is closed, use entrance at 91 Claremont Ave. Open year-round Mon–Fri 8am–10pm, weekends 8am–9pm. Closed (except for services) Dec 25.* ✗ & 🅿 ☎212-870-6700. With its soaring 400ft tower—containing the largest carillon in the world—this streamlined Gothic Revival building is a dominant Upper West Side landmark. Interdenominational and interracial, the church is perhaps best known for its liberal stance on social issues. John D. Rockefeller, Jr. helped fund the present 1927 building of limestone, designed by Allen and Collens and Henry C. Pelton (the south wing was added in 1960). The magnificent west portal faces Riverside Drive and recalls the sculptures at Chartres Cathedral in France. In the narthex are two striking **stained-glass windows★** depicting the life of Christ, made in the 16C for the Cathedral of Bruges in Belgium. Enjoy the stunning 360-degree **panorama★★** from the observation deck *(Sun 12:30pm–4pm; $1)* by taking an elevator to the 20th floor.

★ **General Grant National Memorial** – *On Riverside Dr. at W. 122nd St. Open year-round daily 9am–5pm. Closed major holidays. 30min guided tours available.* ☎212-666-1640. Popularly known as Grant's Tomb, this Neoclassical monument located in Riverside Park is the final resting place of Ulysses Simpson Grant (1822-85) and his wife, Julia Dent Grant (1826-1902). The 1890 white granite mausoleum, crowned by a stepped cone, features a dramatic coffered dome suspended directly over the sunken crypt.

★ **Harlem**

Harlem embraces most of northern Manhattan, above 125th Street and St. Nicholas Avenue on the West Side and above 110th Street on the East Side. This multifaceted "city within a city," with its broad boulevards, brownstones, tenements, bodegas and bargain stores, was world-famous in the 1920s as a center for black arts and culture—an era known as the Harlem Renaissance. Popular nightspots included the original Cotton Club on Lenox Avenue, which drew nightly crowds (some white-only) with jazz greats like Duke Ellington, Count Basie and Cab Calloway. The area also provided a serious cultural forum for emerging writers (Langston Hughes) and artists, and a haven for middle-class black families. By the 1960s Harlem's celebrities were more likely to be civil-rights activists like Malcolm X, who worked with the black Muslim Temple of Islam at 116th Street and Lenox Avenue. In 1965 he was assassinated at the Audubon Ballroom on West 166th Street.

Despite its reputation for poverty and decline, Harlem is actually an interesting destination. Many parts are safe, but it is always wise to exercise caution, especially after dark. **Harlem Spirituals, Inc.** offers various guided tours. Here are some of the more popular ones: visit of Harlem including soul-food lunch *(4hrs 30min; Thu 9am; $37)*; evening visit of Harlem including soul food and jazz *(5hrs; Mon, Thu–Sat 7pm; $75)*; Sunday gospel and visit of Harlem *(5hrs; Sun 9:30am; $57)*; midweek gospel and visit of Harlem *(3hrs 30min; Wed 9am; $35)*. *All tours depart year-round from Ed Sullivan Theater Building, 1697 Broadway. Reservations required* ☎212-391-0900.

Visit – ½ *day.* The main commercial arteries of Harlem are quite lively, particularly Luis Muñoz Marin Street (116th St.) and Martin Luther King Jr. Boulevard (125th St.), where Senegalese vendors offer Kente cloth, wood carvings and jewelry. The legendary **Apollo Theatre** *(253 W. 125th St.;* ☎212-749-5838), famous for its all-black revues of the 1930s, hosts varied shows, including Wednesday's Amateur Night, which still draws would-be stars to the stage. The **Studio Museum in Harlem**★ *(144 W. 125th St.; open year-round Wed–Fri 10am–5pm, weekends 1pm–6pm; closed major holidays; $5; ☎212-864-4500)* offers selections from a permanent collection of 1,400 works by prominent and emerging artists of the African diaspora (African, African-American and Caribbean origins). The **Schomburg Center for Research in Black Culture** *(515 Malcolm X Blvd.)* contains the world's largest archive relating to black heritage, with more than five million books, photographs, manuscripts, films, recordings and works of art *(open year-round Mon–Wed noon–8pm, Thu–Sat 10am–6pm; closed major holidays; ☎212-491-2200)*. The **Morris-Jumel Mansion**★ *(W. 160th St. and Edgecombe Ave.; open year-round Wed–Sun 10am–4pm; closed major holidays; $3; ☎212-923-8008)*, a handsome Georgian mansion, is the only Colonial home to survive in northern Manhattan.

6 Sylvia's

Map p 47. 328 Lenox Ave. between 126th and 127th Sts. ☎*212-996-0660.* The most celebrated soul-food restaurant in Harlem, Sylvia's is also the place for important political and cultural gatherings for the Harlem community. Order the delicious greens, candied yams and Southern fried chicken. For a special treat, come for the Sunday gospel brunch.

Among the most intriguing sites in upper Manhattan is **The Cloisters**★★★, isolated on a hill in Fort Tryon Park. This museum re-creates a fortified monastery, a part of the Old World transplanted to the New. The collections, which include innumerable sculptures, stained-glass windows, tapestries and other objects spanning more than 1,000 years, enjoy an unrivaled reputation among lovers of Medieval art *(open Mar–Oct Tue–Sun 9:30am–5:15pm; rest of the year Tue–Sun 9:30am–4:45pm; closed Jan 1, Thanksgiving Day, Dec 25; $8; & ☎212-923-3700)*.

THE BOROUGHS

Ever since New York City expanded to include Brooklyn, Queens, the Bronx and Staten Island under state charter in 1898, New Yorkers have referred to the districts outside Manhattan as the "outer boroughs." Although an influx of immigrants throughout the city has blurred borders in recent years, these four districts still have a somewhat provincial character that sets them apart, and Manhattanites still regard them with a trace of snobbery. Brooklyn remains best knows for its well-preserved 19C brownstone neighborhoods; Queens for the airports and Shea Stadium; the Bronx for its home team, the Yankees; and Staten Island for the ferry. However, anyone who takes the time to explore these boroughs may also be surprised to discover beautiful parks, historic landmarks, great museums, and some of the best and least expensive ethnic restaurants in the city. New York's excellent public transportation system makes it easy to get around without a car.

THE BRONX *1 day. Map p 52.*

This borough was a part of Westchester County until 1898, when it was incorporated into New York City. By 1949 almost 50 percent of Bronx residents were Jewish. During the 1950s and 60s, blacks and Puerto Ricans relocating from slums in Manhattan moved into the Hunts Point and Morrisania areas of the South Bronx; today Hispanics make up a third of the Bronx's population.

The only New York borough located on the mainland, the Bronx today exemplifies the contradictions of a mature urban environment. Marked by run-down apartment buildings and massive projects, the southern part of the borough is mainly inhabited by low-income groups and is also home to Yankee Stadium. To the north, prosperous sections such as Riverdale are characterized by grand mansions and lush gardens.

★★ **The Bronx Zoo** – 🅺🆒 *Bronx River Pkwy. at Fordham Rd. Open Apr–Oct Mon–Fri 10am–5pm, weekends & holidays 10am–5:30pm. Rest of the year daily 10am–4:30pm. $6.75, $3 off-season (Wed free).* ✗ & 🄿 *($6)* ☎*718-367-1010.* Opened in 1899 by the New York Zoological Society, the 265-acre zoo has grown to encompass the largest urban wildlife park in the US and is ranked among the leading zoos in the country for its exhibit technology and captive management techniques. Over the years it has altered its focus to concentrate on conservation. Today the zoo exhibits 1,824 mammals, 823 birds, and 670 reptiles and amphibians, in addition to a large number of invertebrates, in a series of realistic exhibits that make every effort to replicate the animals' natural habitats.

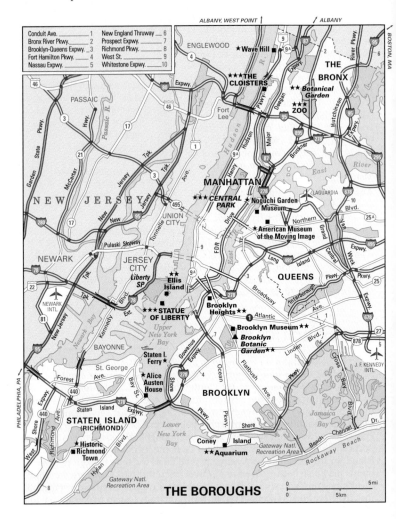

THE BOROUGHS

Highlights include the **Baboon Reserve**★; a popular Gorilla exhibit; **Wild Asia**★★, inhabited by Siberian tigers, red pandas and Asian rhinoceroses; **JungleWorld**★, which re-creates an Asian rain forest; and the **Children's Zoo**★, covering more than three acres of marsh, prairie and woodland, and home to more than 100 animals.

★★ **The New York Botanical Garden** – *200th St. and Southern Blvd. Open Apr–Oct Tue–Sun 10am–6pm. Rest of the year Tue–Sun 10am–4pm. Closed Thanksgiving Day, Dec 25. $3 (additional fees for trolley and some gardens).* ⏴ 🅿 *($4)* ☎*718-817-8700.* Located directly to the north of the zoo, this is one of the largest and oldest gardens (1891) in the country. Numerous walking trails wind through its 250 acres, past thousands of flowering trees, shrubs and plants that reach their peak in spring and early summer. Attractions include the rose garden, rock garden, native plant garden, daylily garden, five demonstration gardens and 40 acres of one of the city's last remaining original forests. The remarkable 1901 **Enid A. Haupt Conservatory**★★ is a Victorian glass confection modeled after the crystal palaces of the 19C; it presents biomes from rain forests to deserts.

★ **Wave Hill** – *625 W. 252nd St. Open mid-May–mid-Oct Tue–Sun 9am–5:30pm (Fri until dusk). Rest of the year Tue–Sun 9am–4:30pm. Closed major holidays. $4.* ✗ & ▯ ☎*718-549-3200.* Opened to the public in 1965, this enchanting 28-acre estate comprises award-winning gardens and greenhouses, rolling meadows and lush woodlands, all overlooking the Hudson River. Built as a country home by William Lewis Morris in 1843, the main mansion was later owned by wealthy publisher William Appleton. Theodore Roosevelt's family occupied it in 1870 and Mark Twain leased the estate in 1901. Some 18 acres of landscaped gardens contain more than 3,000 species of plants and a variety of trees. Of special interest are the greenhouses, the lovely aquatic garden and the fragrant herb garden.

BROOKLYN   *1 day. Map p 52.*

Brooklyn was founded in 1636 by Dutch settlers who called the area *Breuckelen* ("broken land") after a small town near Utrecht. The district, now New York's most populous borough, is situated on the western tip of LONG ISLAND and extends from the East River to Coney Island and from the Narrows to Jamaica Bay. In 1883 the Brooklyn Bridge formed the first direct link with Manhattan, and Brooklyn was integrated into New York City in 1898. Although almost half a million residents now commute to Manhattan, the area has retained a distinctive personality. Among the great variety of neighborhoods is Park Slope, a choice residential neighborhood; Brooklyn Heights, a charming enclave that is still the refuge of a few "old families"; Williamsburg, containing Hasidic Jewish, Hispanic and Italian communities; Brighton Beach, a thriving Russian neighborhood; Flatbush, with fine private homes and lively commercial streets; Bensonhurst, a predominantly Italian section; and Bedford-Stuyvesant, an African-American district.

Park Slope District, Brooklyn Heights

★ **Brooklyn Heights** – In the mid-19C this section of Brooklyn developed into a choice residential area, owing largely to its proximity to Manhattan. Narrow, tree-shaded streets and mews are lined with brownstones and town houses that represent almost every style of 19C American architecture. Willow, Orange, Middagh and Pierrepont Streets are notable for their Federal row houses (including many early-19C wooden examples) and historic buildings in the Greek Revival and picturesque Victorian styles. The **Brooklyn Historical Society** *(128 Pierrepont St.;* ☎*718-624-0890)* features special exhibits, educational programs, concerts and walking tours, and houses the borough's only history museum. Overlooking the harbor, the esplanade offers magnificent **views**★★★ of Manhattan's Financial District. Behind the terrace lies a series of houses with lovely private gardens.

★★ **Brooklyn Museum** – *200 Eastern Pkwy. Open year-round Wed–Sun 10am–5pm. Closed Jan 1, Thanksgiving Day, Dec 25. $4.* ✕ & 🅿 *($6)* ☎718-638-5000. This monumental Beaux-Arts building designed by McKim, Mead and White contains more than 1.5 million artifacts. The outstanding **Egyptian collection**★★ is one of the finest in the world. Galleries are also devoted to the primitive arts, including African works, and art from the Americas ranging from pre-Columbian jewelry and textiles to magnificent totem poles from the Haida Indians on the Northwest Coast. Other exhibits cover Oceanic art; artifacts from China, Korea, Japan and Southeast Asia; paintings, ceramics, carpets and textiles from India, Nepal and Tibet; Islamic calligraphy and carpets; Greek and Roman artifacts; and European painting and sculpture. The Impressionists are well represented with works by Degas, Monet, Morisot, Sisley and Pissarro. The Iris and B. Gerald Cantor **rotunda gallery**★ displays 58 sculptures by Rodin. The museum has also garnered international renown for its fine collection of **American painting**★★, with portraits, genre paintings and landscapes by such important artists as Copley, Eakins, Homer, Cassatt, Chase, Bellows, Bierstadt, Cole and O'Keeffe. Housed in the newly renovated west wing, a gallery of contemporary art showcases 80 works created after World War II by American and European artists.

> **1 Atlantic Avenue**
> *Map p 52.* The main thoroughfare of Brooklyn's Lebanese and Middle Eastern neighborhoods has become one of New York's most popular culinary destinations. Some of the avenue's highlights include **Tripoli** *(no. 156;* ☎*718-596-5800)*, a campy two-level restaurant that serves up hummus, falafel and honeyed desserts. **Almonstaser** *(218 Court St.;* ☎*718-624-1267)* is more intimate and consistent kitchen-wise (the apricot pudding is a must). If you want to take something home with you, visit **Sahadi's Importing Co.** *(no. 187;* ☎*718-624-4550)* for Lebanese pistachios, feta, spices and coffee. To cleanse the palate, stop by **Peter's Ice Cream Shop** *(no. 185;* ☎*718-852-3835)* for a refreshing sorbet; it's also a local favorite for homemade pies.

★★ **Brooklyn Botanic Garden** – *1000 Washington Ave. Open Apr–Sept Tue–Fri 8am–6pm, weekends 10am–6pm. Rest of the year Tue–Fri 8am–4:30pm, weekends 10am–4:30pm. Closed Jan 1, Thanksgiving Day, Dec 25. $3.* ✕ & 🅿 *($6)* ☎718-622-4433. Located to the south of the Brooklyn Museum, this outstanding 52-acre botanical garden contains one of the finest assemblages of roses in the country, along with rows of cherry trees and well-kept gardens. Divided into six areas—including a Tropical Pavilion, Aquatic Exhibit and the country's largest bonsai collection—the **conservatory** displays numerous varieties of flora.

Coney Island – Located to the south of Brooklyn and bordered by the Atlantic Ocean, this beach resort and amusement park attracted over a million people on busy summer Sundays in the early 1900s. Today all but a small section has fallen into disuse. For many, however, a stroll on Coney Island's boardwalk (which runs along a 3.5mi stretch of sandy beach), the hot dog and cotton candy stands, and a handful of attractions still remain a pleasant diversion on a warm summer day. A worthwhile stop is the **Aquarium for Wildlife Conservation**★★ Kids *(W. 8th St and Surf Ave.; open Memorial Day–Labor Day 10am–4:45pm, weekends & holidays 10am–6:45pm; rest of the year daily 10am–4:45pm; $7.75;* ✕ & 🅿 *[$6]* ☎*718-265-3474)*. Don't miss the 90,000-gallon shark tank—holding stingrays and five types of free swimming and bottom-dwelling sharks—and **Discovery Cove**, a 20,000sq ft center featuring 65 exhibits, including a reproduction of a living coral reef and a New England lobster boat.

QUEENS ½ day. Map p 52.

Named after Catherine of Braganza, the wife of Charles II of England, Queens is the largest borough of New York City. Situated on Long Island, east of Brooklyn, it extends from the East River in the north to Jamaica Bay and the Atlantic Ocean in the south. Although known today as New York's air transportation hub, Queens remains a residential area, home to a large number of immigrants hailing primarily from Asia and Latin America. In the 1920s the borough attracted the silent film industry, which operated some 20 studios in Astoria before relocating to sunny Hollywood. On the heels of the 1939 World's Fair, Queens developed a reputation as a haven for sports and recreation. It continues to draw sports fans to the Aqueduct Race Track, Shea Stadium and the USTA National Tennis Center. A cluster of factories in the Long Island City area, where artists have renovated lofts into studio and living spaces, gives way to more residential sections to the southeast, such as Forest Hills and Jamaica.

★ **American Museum of the Moving Image** – Kids *35th Ave. and 36th St. in Astoria. Open year-round Tue–Fri & holidays noon–5pm, weekends 11am–6pm. Closed Thanksgiving Day, Dec 25. $7.* ✗ & ☎718-784-0077. Located on the former site of the Astoria Film Studios (built by Paramount Pictures in the 1920s), this unique museum (1988) is devoted to the history, technology and art of film media, including motion pictures, television and video. Screenings from the film collection are presented on a rotating basis throughout the year.

★ **Isamu Noguchi Garden Museum** – *32-37 Vernon Blvd. Open Apr–Oct Wed–Fri 10am–5pm, weekends 11am–6pm. $4.* ☎718-204-7088. Conflicting and harmonious relationships between nature and the man-made are a recurrent theme in the sculpture of **Isamu Noguchi** (1904-88), the renowned Japanese-American artist whose works include public spaces (Detroit's Hart Plaza), playgrounds (Atlanta's Playscapes), gardens and fountains. Noguchi designed and installed this museum in his former studio quarters in 1985. More than 250 works of art are on display in 12 indoor galleries, while several carved stone pieces adorn the tranquil outdoor sculpture garden, dotted with Japanese black pine trees.

STATEN ISLAND   *½ day. Map p 52.*

The fifth borough of New York City, Staten Island is still a relatively rural area. Dutch merchants passing through here in the early 1600s named the island after the Dutch States General. Most of the island is flat, although it boasts the highest point on the Atlantic coast south of Maine—Todt Hill—rising 410ft above sea level. White sandy beaches run along the southeastern shore; still fairly un-crowded, the best-known are South Beach and the Gateway National Recreation Area. The island grew considerably after integration with the other boroughs in 1898, attracting hardworking immigrants to its farms and factories and hard-playing society folk to its resort hotels. Today Staten Island is primarily a bedroom community, culturally and economically related more closely to New Jersey than to New York.

★ **Staten Island Ferry** – Kids *Departs from Whitehall Terminal in Manhattan to St. George Ferry Terminal on Staten Island year-round daily 24hrs/day every 30min on the half hour. 20min. 50¢, $3/car.* ✗ & 🅿 *($5.50)* ☎718-815-2628. Any visit to New York should include a trip on the Staten Island Ferry. On the windy voyage, the ferry skirts the Statue of Liberty, affording magnificent **views★★★** of Manhattan and the bay.

★ **Alice Austen House** – *2 Hylan Blvd. Visit by guided tour (45min) only, Mar–Dec Thu–Sun noon–5pm. Closed major holidays. $3.* & ☎718-816-4506. A pioneer photographer, **Alice Austen** (1866-1952) captured turn-of-the-century life in New York City, from exclusive society gatherings to poignant scenes of immigrant life. This picturesque gingerbread-trimmed Victorian cottage displays changing exhibits, including prints from her glass-plate negatives.

★ **Historic Richmond Town** – Kids *441 Clarke Ave. Open Jul–Aug Wed–Fri 10am–5pm, weekends 1pm–5pm. Rest of the year Wed–Sun 1pm–5pm. Closed Jan 1, Easter Sunday, Thanksgiving Day, Dec 25. $4.* ✗ 🅿 ☎718-351-1611. This historic village traces the evolution of community life in Richmond Town from the 17C to the 19C through a variety of buildings, furnishings, gardens and implements. The open-air museum comprises 27 structures, including private dwellings, craft shops, a schoolhouse and municipal buildings that have been restored and opened to the public. Staff members dressed in period costumes reenact everyday chores, and artisans occasionally demonstrate crafts.

Excursions

Liberty State Park – *1hr. 9mi north of Staten Island. Take Rte. 440 over the Bayonne Bridge and follow Rte. 169 to Exit 14C. Morris Pesin Dr., Jersey City. Open year-round daily 6am–10pm.* ✗ & 🅿 ☎201-915-3400. This reclamation in progress makes no apologies for its past. Heavily industrialized in the 19C, a center of commuter and commercial rail activity, and finally a waterfront dumping ground, the 1,122 acres that now make up the park have been used hard over the years. Undergrowth scarcely hides the skeletons of cars and the scars of railroad tracks. However, beginning in 1976, this "brownspace" is being transformed to celebrate its past. Here, immigrants fresh from Ellis Island caught trains at the immense CRRNJ Terminal that dispersed them around the country. Today the cavernous terminal *(open seasonally)* has been beautifully restored to its 1889 splendor, when it presided over "the greatest concentration of rail facilities in the New York Harbor area." From here you can see the classic view of the Manhattan skyline. You can catch ferries *(p 27)* from the park to Ellis Island and the Statue of Liberty.

A small interpretive center at the edge of the salt marsh presents exhibits of historical and natural interest, including an investigation of the marshes that line the coast and alternate perpetually between terrestrial and marine habitats with the ebb and flow of the tides. A nature trail (Freedom Way) with interpretive signage provides an opportunity to observe the complex salt marsh and estuary ecosystems that are now beginning to thrive here again. Birds abound; a documented 210 varieties have been spotted in the park.

Liberty Science Center – Kids *2hrs. Liberty State Park, 251 Philip St. Open Apr–Labor Day daily 9:30am–5:30pm. Rest of the year Tue–Sun 9:30am–5:30pm. Closed Thanksgiving Day, Dec 25. $9.50.* ✗ & 🅿 *($5) www.lsc.com* ☎*201-200-1000.* Part fun house and part science museum, this 60,000sq ft behemoth is a bustling, colorful place that rises from the salt marshes in futuristic profile. Inside, visitors encounter an indestructible, kid-friendly kingdom. Two floors and a lower level are organized by theme: Inventions, Health and Environment. Highlights include the Touch Tunnel, where kids line up to navigate in the dark entirely by feel, and the Perception Maze—exploring the wonders of mirrors and refraction—on the Health floor. The quiet Environment floor offers a rock-climbing wall, a honeybee hive and a marvelous creepy-crawly insect zoo. In areas where docents conduct demonstrations, parents and children both get a chance to sit down.

LONG ISLAND ★★

Map p 8
Tourist Information ☎516-951-3440 or 800-441-4601

Claiming some of the finest beaches and best protected harbors on the Atlantic seaboard, Long Island is New York State's oceanside vacationland. While the island is perhaps best known for a fabulous range of recreational opportunities, including swimming, yachting, tennis, golf and horseback riding, it also offers excellent museums, great shopping, and some of the most sophisticated restaurants in the greater metropolitan area.

Measuring 125mi long and 20mi at its widest point, Long Island claims a distinctive fish-shape, with the "mouth" at Jamaica Bay at the west end and the "tailfins" formed by the North and South Forks extending to Orient and Montauk Points to the east. The North Shore borders Long Island Sound and is dominated by dramatic cliffs; on a clear day, you can see Connecticut. Along the South Shore, a string of barrier islands extends from Rockaway Inlet, Queens, to the South Fork, protecting the mainland from the tempestuous Atlantic. Owing to its proximity to the city, the western part of the island has developed into a suburban area while the eastern part has remained more rural.

Historical Notes

First Settlers – Long Island's earliest inhabitants were Native Americans descended from nomadic hunters who walked over from Connecticut 10,000 years ago when the area now covered by Long Island Sound was still marshland. The heritage of the 13 tribes that once lived here is reflected by the Indian names of dozens of towns, such as Massapequa, Montauk and Ronkonkoma. Today two Native American reservations, Poosepatuck and Shinnecock, are located in Suffolk County. In 1524 Italian explorer Giovanni da Verrazano sighted Long Island, and British seafarer Henry Hudson made landfall on its western end in 1609. Early European settlers bartered with local chiefs for permission to establish villages and farms; 12 hatchets, 10 coats and one pair of children's stockings reportedly were part of the price for the Setauket region.

Settlements prospered during the Revolutionary era, when wheat and livestock became the basis of the Long Island economy. After the Battle of Long Island in 1776, British troops occupied the island for seven years. During this period, Long Islanders showed a strong patriotic streak, destroying Tory supply depots, assisting whaleboat raiders from New England and running active spy rings; the most famous spy of the era was Long Island native, Nathan Hale.

Vacationland – By 1900 Long Island had blossomed into a mecca for the new American gentry, who were attracted to a summer colony that not only boasted all the social cachet of such rival watering holes as Newport, Rhode Island, but was also within easy commuting distance by rail to New York City. Between the Civil War and World War II more than 900 estates were built on Long Island. Many were situated on the North Shore, the so-called Gold Coast that inspired the setting for F. Scott Fitzgerald's 1925 novel *The Great Gatsby*. J.P. Morgan, William K. Vanderbilt, William Randolph Hearst, Charles Pratt, Vincent Astor, F.W. Woolworth, Otto Kahn, Marshall Field and Jay Gould were just a few of the dozens of financial and industrial barons who owned houses on the island. Here, the well-heeled residents pursued a frenzy of recreational sports ranging from polo, fox hunting and golf to angling and amateur yachting. Each estate was an ostentatious emblem of Gilded Age excess. Four hundred employees were needed to run the household and grounds of the Pratt family's Glen Cove compound, for example, while Louis Comfort Tiffany's Laurelton Hall boasted 15 greenhouses that supplied weekly thematic floral arrangements for the living quarters.

By World War II, the island had become an important center of aircraft manufacturing and advanced aeronautic engineering. Suburbs burgeoned in the western section of Nassau County in areas contiguous to spurs of the Long Island Railroad, the main commuter artery into New York City. After the war, the population rate skyrocketed and developers invested in thousands of new housing developments, including Levittown (1947-51); here, sales prices for the more than 17,000 homes made of assembly-line parts started at $6,990. During that time, Nassau County alone grew from 672,000 inhabitants in 1950 to more than one million by 1960.

Today Long Island's economy is quite diversified, encompassing light manufacturing, service industries, aerospace industry and agriculture. Suffolk County is the largest producer of agricultural products in the state of New York, and a number of farms are still engaged in truck farming (fruits and vegetables) and dairy and livestock farming. Ducklings and potatoes are noted area products. Enjoying an ever-increasing reputation for fine merlots and chardonnays, Long Island **wineries** cover hundreds of acres on the North and South Forks. Seafood is particularly abundant on the eastern end of the island: oysters, clams, scallops and lobsters have a well-deserved reputation for excellence. This area is also notable for its bountiful local produce. During the summer season, roadside farmstands overflow with fresh vegetables, fruit and bouquets of cut flowers.

NORTH SHORE   *2 days. Map pp 58-59.*

Facing Long Island Sound, the North Shore features rocky necks and beaches, thick woodlands, hilly coves, bays, inlets and steep bluffs; the northern fork extends 25mi to Orient Point. During the 19C, the North Shore became known as the Gold Coast as wealthy landowners from the city began erecting residences here. Today several of these manses are open to the public, offering a glimpse into the lifestyle of the Gilded Age.

The following attractions are presented west to east.

★ **Sands Point Preserve** – *95 Middleneck Rd., Port Washington. Open year-round daily 10am–4:30pm. $1 (May–Oct).* ✗ ♿ 🅿 ☎516-571-7900. This 216-acre park and nature preserve comprises two Gold Coast estates reflecting the grandiose tastes of New York society during the Gilded Age. Six nature trails also permit visitors to explore lawns, meadows, woodlands, gardens, beaches, cliffs and a freshwater pond. Built between 1904 and 1912, the original estate was created by railroad heir Howard Gould (son of Wall Street financier Jay Gould), who commissioned a Tudor-style stone mansion complete with a circular tower and mock fortifications. The property was sold in 1917 to Daniel Guggenheim, a member of the noted family of entrepreneurs and philanthropists who made a fortune mining precious metals in the 19C (David's brother funded the SOLOMON R. GUGGENHEIM MUSEUM in Manhattan). In 1942 Gould's Tudor estate house, which

Guggenheim named Hempstead House, was donated by his widow to the Institute of Aeronautical Sciences and served as a naval training center until 1967. Presently undergoing renovations, it is occasionally open to the public.

Situated across a broad meadow is Castlegould, a turreted limestone "castle" originally planned as stables, carriage houses and servants' quarters. Modeled after Kilkenny Castle in Ireland, this imposing structure now contains an information center and rotating exhibits.

★ **Falaise** – *Visit by guided tour (1hr) only, May–Oct Wed–Sun at noon, 1pm, 2pm & 3pm. $4. Children under 10 not admitted.* ☎516-571-7900. Perched on a cliff (*falaise* in French), this Norman-style manor was erected by **Capt. Harry F. Guggenheim** (son of Daniel), who received 90 acres of the original Gould estate from his father as a gift on the occasion of his second wedding in 1923. A US ambassador to Cuba, Harry Guggenheim pursued an avid interest in aeronautics (his close friend Charles Lindbergh was a frequent guest at Falaise) and also raised racehorses, which he stabled on the property. Upon his death in 1971, Harry deeded his much-loved estate to Nassau County with the stipulation that it remain exactly as it was during his lifetime, down to the clothes hanging in his own closet.

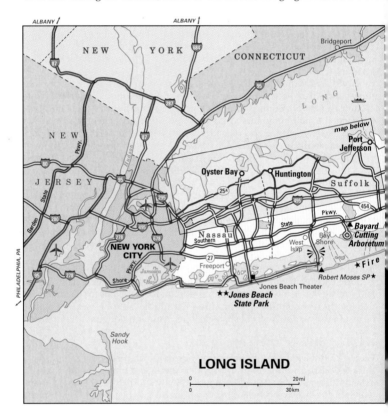

LONG ISLAND

Fronted by a charming walled courtyard filled with potted plants, the two-and-a-half-story house is built of imported Dutch brick and crowned with a steeply pitched slate roof. Inside, surprisingly intimate rooms feature an impressive collection of 16C and 17C French and Spanish artifacts amassed by Capt. Guggenheim and his architect, Frederick Sterner, on several visits to Europe. The interior and a rear terrace and loggia, overlooking the sound, afford excellent views★★ of Hempstead Bay.

Nassau County Museum of Fine Art [M] – *In Roslyn Harbor. Take Rte. 25A east, cross the Roslyn Viaduct and turn left on Museum Dr. Open year-round Tue–Sun 11am–5pm. Closed Dec 25. $4. Guided tours (1hr) available Tue–Thu & Sat 2pm.* ✗ ⅙ ❒ ☎516-484-9337. The museum is headquartered on the grounds of a turn-of-the-century estate built for Lloyd Bryce, the paymaster-general of New York, and acquired in 1919 by Childs Frick, the son of Henry Clay Frick *(p 45)*. Changing art exhibits covering all periods are presented in the elegant Georgian Revival mansion, which has been converted into eight galleries. The attractively landscaped lawns, ponds and gardens, covering 145 acres, offer an ideal outdoor setting for various sculpture shows. Also on the grounds is the Tee Ridder Miniatures Museum, featuring 26 miniature rooms crafted by a Locust Valley artisan.

Oyster Bay – First settled by New Englanders in 1652, this picturesque town with a history of farming and shipping is renowned as a vacation spot and for its sheltered pleasure-craft harbor. Tourists flock to Oyster Bay's historic landmarks, shops and quaint, tree-shaded streets lined with Colonial and Victorian homes. Oyster Bay's most famous resident was Theodore Roosevelt, who spent some 20 years at Sagamore Hill; his grave **[A]** is located in Young's Cemetery.

★ **Planting Fields** – *Planting Fields Rd. Grounds open year-round daily 9am–5pm. Closed Dec 25. $4/car May–Labor Day daily, rest of the year weekends & holidays. Guided tours (1hr) available (*☎*516-922-9511).* & ▯ ☎*516-922-9200.* This 409-acre State Historic Park includes the country home of the late financier William Robertson Coe and its spectacular grounds, designed by noted landscape architects the Olmsted

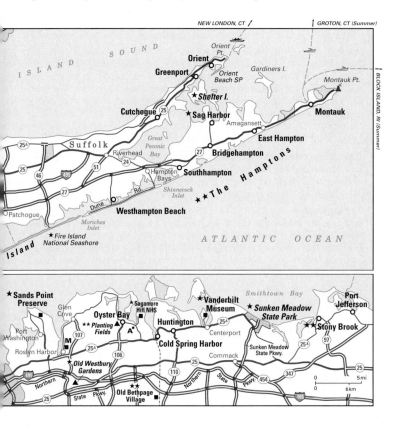

brothers. Situated on the 17C planting fields of the Matinecock Indians, the estate contains 160 acres developed as an arboretum; the remaining land is preserved as a natural habitat. Plant collections include more than 600 rhododendron and azalea species *(in bloom mid-Apr–May)*; the Synoptic Garden, comprising approximately five acres of selected ornamental shrubs for Long Island gardens; the camellia collection, the oldest and largest of its kind under glass *(in bloom Feb–Mar)*; a dwarf conifer garden; a holly collection; a heather garden; and greenhouses filled with orchids, hibiscus, begonias and cacti.

Amid the landscaped gardens and sweeping lawns shaded by beech, elm and linden trees stands **Coe Hall**, a 65-room Tudor Revival mansion, designed by the New York architectural firm of Walker and Gillette *(visit by 30min guided tour Apr–Sept daily noon–3pm; $3.50;* &*).* The epitome of Gold Coast splendor, the massive 1921 residence was inspired by several 16C English estates and incorporates 25 chimneys, 17 fireplaces and 11 bedrooms and baths. Among the highlights of the eccentric interior are a vast paneled "great hall," which served as a library and picture gallery, and a cozy breakfast room detailed with murals of roaming buffalo (Buffalo Bill Cody was one of Coe's good friends).

★ **Sagamore Hill National Historic Site** – *Cove Neck Rd. Visit of mansion by guided tour (30min) only, May–Oct daily 9am–4:30pm. $2.* ▣ ☎516-922-4447. Located east of the village of Oyster Bay, this well-preserved, 23-room Queen Anne-style residence was built by **Theodore Roosevelt** as his permanent home in 1885. Dominated by a broad verandah, the gracious mansion is maintained as it was during Roosevelt's presidency (1901-09), when it served as the Summer White House. Guided tours offer humorous anecdotes on Teddy's life and presidential pursuits. Of special interest is the North Room, furnished with bronzes by Frederic Remington, Japanese artifacts (Roosevelt orchestrated the end of the Russo-Japanese War in 1905) and hunting trophies; note the rhinoceros-foot inkstand. Among the other highlights are Roosevelt's office and study and the original kitchen and baths, which were never modernized despite the fact that Teddy's second wife, Edith Kermit Carow, lived here until her death in 1948. About 90 percent of the furnishings are original to the house.

Also on the park-like grounds is the **Old Orchard Museum**, housed in a brick Georgian Revival residence (1938) built by Theodore Roosevelt, Jr. Exhibits and a biographical film *(20min)* trace President Roosevelt's life at Sagamore Hill.

Raynham Hall – *20 W. Main St. Open Jan–Jun & Sept–Dec Tue–Sun 1pm–5pm (open Mon holidays). Jul–Labor Day Tue–Sun noon–5pm. Closed Jan 1, Thanksgiving Day, Dec 25. $2.* ☎516-922-6808. Surrounded by a white picket fence, this 18C clapboard farmhouse played an important role during the American Revolution. The saltbox structure was the home of Samuel Townsend, whose son, Robert, was General Washington's chief intelligence agent in New York City. The interior, including two handsome front parlors, contains period furniture and memorabilia dating from the 1770s through the 1870s.

Cold Spring Harbor – From 1836 to 1862 the Cold Spring Harbor whaling fleet of nine ships sailed to every navigable ocean in search of whale oil and bone. The commanders of these vessels came from established whaling centers such as New Bedford, Massachusetts, and Sag Harbor *(p 66)*.

★ **Whaling Museum** – *On Main St. (Rte. 25A). Open Jun–Aug daily 11am–5pm. Rest of the year Tue–Sun 11am–5pm. Closed Jan 1, Easter Sunday, Thanksgiving Day, Dec 25. $2.* ♿ ☎516-367-3418. Dedicated to the preservation of the town's history as a whaling port, this museum features several outstanding exhibits, including a fully equipped whaleboat, looking just as it did aboard the whaling brig *Daisy* on her

---

■ The Pine Barrens

Evolving in the dry, sandy outwash plain left after the region's last period of glaciation ended some 8,000 to 10,000 years ago, the pine-barren ecosystem of Long Island constitutes one of only some twenty such rare plant communities in the world. The "barrens" take their name from the relatively poor soil, but are actually lush with hardy, adaptable vegetation: mainly beautiful woodlands of pitch pine, scrub oak and dwarf oak, which filter sunlight to a thriving underlayer of heath. Postwar development has diminished these forests to about 40 percent of the original 250,000-acre tract. The remainder is located primarily in Suffolk County. Some of the best locations to explore these exceptional natural habitats—ideal for bird-watching—are:

Connetquot River State Park, in Oakdale.
Entrance on westbound side of Sunrise Hwy. ☎516-581-2100.

Cranberry Bog County Nature Preserve, in Riverhead.
At Exit 71 off Long Island Expwy., take Rte. 24 to Lake Ave.; travel .9mi south to gate entrance on right side of the road; access by foot only.

David A. Sarnoff State Pine Barrens Preserve, in Riverhead,
adjoining Cranberry Bog Preserve. *Take Exit 71 off Long Island Expwy. and follow Rte. 24 to Lake Ave.; travel .25mi south to gate entrance on left side of the road.*

Quogue Wildlife Refuge, in Quogue.
Old Country Rd., 1.2mi north of Montauk Hwy. ☎516-653-4771.

Sunken Forest/Fire Island National Seashore, in Sailors Haven.
Access by ferry from Sayville. ☎516-597-6183.

1912 voyage out of New Bedford. A diorama of Cold Spring Harbor represents village houses, whaling company buildings and wharves as they appeared in the 1840s, the heyday of Long Island's illustrious whaling industry. Other permanent displays include the skull of an orca (or killer whale); harpoons; navigational instruments; whaling-ship models; prints and maps; and an impressive collection of scrimshaw (carvings on whale jawbones and teeth), the whaler's folk art.

Huntington – Although the earliest residents of this North Shore town founded in 1653 were the Matinecock Indians, its best-known citizen is poet **Walt Whitman**, born here in 1819.

Heckscher Museum of Art – *In Heckscher Park at Prime Ave. and Main St. Open year-round Tue–Fri 10am–5pm, weekends 1pm–5pm. Holiday hours may vary. $2.* ☎516-351-3250. Founded in 1920, the Heckscher Museum presents shows that focus on both historical and contemporary subjects and also feature the work of Long Island artists. In addition to showcasing selections from its 1,200-piece permanent collection of European and American art from the Renaissance to the present, the museum organizes an array of temporary exhibits, lectures, workshops and concerts.

Walt Whitman Birthplace State Historic Site and Interpretive Center – *Off Rte. 110 at 246 Old Walt Whitman Rd. Visit by guided tour (1hr) only, Memorial Day–Labor Day daily 11am–4pm. Rest of the year Wed–Fri 1pm–4pm, weekends 11am–4pm. Closed major holidays. $3.* www.waltwhitman.org ☎516-427-5240. Still standing on its original site, the simple two-story shingled house where poet Walt Whitman was born in 1819 retains several notable features, including much of its original hardware and window glass. An interpretive center opened in 1997 houses a library, multimedia area and exhibits tracing Whitman's life as one of America's most prominent literary figures. Portraits, letters, manuscripts, a first edition of the epic *Leaves of Grass* (1855) and a writing desk used by the author as a young Long Island schoolteacher are on display.

★ **Vanderbilt Museum** – *Little Neck Rd., Centerport. Visit of house by guided tour (1hr) only, year-round daily noon–4pm. Closed Jan 1, Thanksgiving Day, Dec 25. $3. Grounds self-guided $5.* ☎516-854-5579. Overlooking Northport Harbor, this 43-acre estate comprises the Vanderbilt mansion, a marine museum and a planetarium. Known as Eagles Nest, the 24-room, multilevel mansion was built in several stages between 1910 and 1936 in the Spanish Revival style. Design elements include stucco walls, clay-tiled roofs, iron window grilles and a Baroque bell tower. Sprawling down a steep hill overlooking Long Island Sound, the house belonged to William K. Vanderbilt II, an accomplished marine biologist and great-grandson of "Commodore" Cornelius Vanderbilt, who founded the family fortune with the profits from his 19C shipping company. Inside, note the Medieval and Renaissance doors, elaborately carved oak paneling and beautiful tapestries imported from Europe; numerous original family furnishings include the Commodore's desk. Galleries showcase part of Vanderbilt's own extensive marine biology collection gathered during worldwide sea voyages, as well as anthropological specimens collected by his son. Natural history exhibits are on view in the house's lower-level Stoll and Habitat Wings.

Nearby on the grounds is the **Marine Museum**, a two-story Spanish Revival structure constructed by Vanderbilt in 1922 to provide additional exhibit space for his overflowing collection. Displays include tropical shells, embalmed sea snakes and a 2,000-pound stingray caught in the Bahamas in 1916. The **Vanderbilt Planetarium** presents a variety of laser and sky shows throughout the year *(for schedule:* ☎516-854-5544).

★ **Sunken Meadow State Park** – *Open year-round daily 6:30am–sunset.* ($5) ☎516-269-4333. Bordering the Long Island Sound, this 1,266-acre park offers a wide range of recreational facilities, including a golf course (27 holes), driving range, nature trails and bike paths. The main attraction is the pristine white swimming beach bordered by a raised wooden boardwalk *(.75mi long)* offering dramatic views of the rugged North Shore coastline.

★ **Stony Brook** – Founded in the 1930s, this idyllic hamlet occupies a charming rural setting. During the Revolutionary period, the area served as headquarters for George Washington's spy ring. In the early 20C, the town erected a number of reconstructed Colonial and Federal-style buildings. One of the country's first planned business districts, the Stony Brook Village Center (1941) on Main Street houses 35 shops and restaurants in a complex of Colonial Revival structures.

At the center of town *(near the intersection of Rte. 25A & Main St.)*, the nine-acre **Museums at Stony Brook**★★ complex comprises history, art and carriage museums, as well as several historic buildings, including a blacksmith's shop, schoolhouse and barn moved to the site in the 1950s and 60s to ensure their preservation *(museums open Jul–Aug Mon–Sat 10am–5pm, Sun noon–5pm; rest of the year Wed–Sat 10am–5pm, Sun noon–5pm; closed Jan 1, Thanksgiving Day, Dec 24-25, $4; & ▣ ☎516-751-0066).*

Margaret M. Blackwell History Museum – Housed in a renovated 19C lumber mill, the visitor center offers changing exhibits drawn from the museum's collections and those of other institutions. Displays focus on American life from the 18C to the 1900s. There is also a permanent display of antique wildfowl decoys and a gallery of **miniature period rooms** (1in to 1ft scale) depicting interiors from the Colonial period to the 1930s.

★★ **Dorothy and Ward Melville Carriage Museum** – An exceptional collection of some 250 horse-drawn carriages is presented in thematic displays tracing the history of horse-drawn vehicles. Centerpiece of the two-story gallery space is the c.1880 "Grace Darling" omnibus, decorated with carefully conserved landscape paintings. On the upper level, galleries showcase ornate European vehicles from the 18C and 19C, as well as early American gigs, coaches and wagons. The lower level features American coachman-driven carriages; pleasure vehicles; sporting rigs; trade vehicles, including hay, milk, grocery, tea and mail wagons; sleighs, children's vehicles (pulled by goats and dogs); and gaily painted 19C American gypsy wagons. Among the highlights of the horse-drawn fire-fighting equipment also featured is an elegant silver-plated hose carriage made in 1875.

Art Museum – The paintings and drawings of **William Sidney Mount** (1807-68) and other 19C and 20C artists are presented here in changing exhibits. Mount settled at Stony Brook, where he painted anecdotal records of his rural surroundings. Among the best-known works owned by the museum are *Farmer Whetting His Scythe*, *Dancing on the Barn Floor* and *The Banjo Players*.

Port Jefferson – Situated at the head of a beautiful deepwater harbor, Port Jefferson is a busy waterside town filled with antique shops and small boutiques. The village is the Long Island port of call for the Bridgeport and Port Jefferson Steamboat Company, which runs daily auto and passenger ferries between the North Shore and Bridgeport, Connecticut.

Cutchogue – The charm of this unspoiled village is typical of the North Fork's rural towns. Clustered around the historic village green are an 1840 schoolhouse, a carriage house and the early-18C **Wickham Farmhouse** *(open Jul–Aug weekends 1pm–4pm; Jun & Sept by appointment only; $1.50; ▣ ☎516-298-5757).* Opposite the green on East Main Street stands the **Old House**, a post-and-beam building erected around 1649; it represents an excellent example of early English Colonial architecture. Among its notable attributes are the massive clustered brick chimney and beveled oak clapboards.

Greenport – Busiest town on the North Fork, Greenport is a hardworking fishing port where gift shops and tourist emporiums stand side by side with the local hardware store and ship's chandlers. Charter excursions leave from the town docks, and informal seafood houses furnished with picnic tables offer harborside dining—take time to dig into the chowder, fresh clams and lobsters, all local specialties. Located at the Shelter Island ferry dock, the **East End Seaport Maritime Museum** *(end of 3rd St.; open May weekends 10am–4pm; Jun–Labor Day Wed–Sun 10am–6pm; Sept–Oct weekends 10am–4pm; $2; ▣ ☎516-477-2100)* presents exhibits on sea life, shipbuilding and yacht racing. Held in late September, the annual Greenport Maritime Festival centers around a wooden boat regatta, fishing tournament, whaleboat race and clam chowder tasting contest.

Orient – With its tidy shingled houses and shady lanes, this quiet town resembles a bit of New England transplanted. The hamlet was settled in the 17C as the Parish of Oyster Ponds. Today the **Oysterponds Historical Society** *(1555 Village Ln.; open Jun–Sept weekends 1pm–5pm; $3; ▣ ☎516-323-2480)* maintains five 18C and 19C museum buildings, including the c.1750 Webb Tavern, distinguished by an unusual two-story columned porch.

At the tip of the North Fork, the Cross Sound Ferry docks at Orient Point bringing cars and passengers from New London, Connecticut *(departs from Orient Point Jun–Oct daily 7am–9:45pm; Nov–May daily 7am–8:45pm; closed Dec 25; one-way*

1hr 20min; $28, car & driver; reservations suggested; ✗ & Cross Sound Ferry Services
☎*860-443-5281).* A beautiful 2mi drive off Route 25 leads past salt marshes and
osprey nests to **Orient Beach State Park** *(open Jul 4–Labor Day daily 8am–8pm; rest of
the year hours vary; closed Dec 25; $5/car, Memorial Day–Labor Day; ✗ & ▣ ☎516-
323-2440),* where facilities include a bathhouse, refreshment stand and picnic
tables; bike rentals are also available. In summer the park hosts concerts and a
children's theater.

SOUTH SHORE   *2 days. Map pp 58-59.*

Boasting numerous protected harbors and coves, Long Island's scenic southern
coastline is defined by pleasant suburban towns, commercial fishing piers,
marinas and a string of beach resorts ranging from modest blue-collar bungalow
communities to the exclusive "Hamptons" of the South Fork. The south shore's
greatest attractions are its famed beaches: Accessed by causeways or ferries, most
stretch along narrow barrier islands separated from the mainland by a series of
bays. Don't miss the beautiful
coastal drive along Ocean State
Parkway from Jones Beach to
Robert Moses State Park. If
fishing is more to your liking,
chartered deep-sea fishing boats
leave daily from South Shore
communities and Montauk Point.

*The following attractions are pre-
sented west to east.*

★★ **Jones Beach State Park** –
Ocean State Pkwy., Wantaugh. The
world's largest recreational facility when it opened in 1929, this
famed bathing resort is considered one of the most significant
public construction projects of
the 20C. With parking for 23,000
vehicles, the park occupies more
than 6mi of sandy coastline
and features eight beaches, two
Olympic-size swimming pools,

> ### ■ Clamming up
> No visit to Long Island is complete without
> a stop at a dockside clam shack to sam-
> ple the region's famous seafood. Clams
> come in several varieties traditionally pre-
> pared in different ways. **Steamers**, with a
> long neck and thin shell, are served
> steamed with broth and melted butter.
> Hard-shelled **littlenecks** and **cherry-
> stones** are types of tender young
> quahogs (KOE-hogs), typically eaten
> raw, on the half shell, with lemon and a
> dab of cocktail sauce. Mature quahogs,
> which can be fist-sized, are reserved
> for **chowder**. If you know the difference
> between Manhattan (tomato-based) and
> New England (milk-based) chowder, no
> one will peg you for a tourist.

fishing piers and a boat basin, sports fields, picnic areas, refreshment stands,
a modern beachside restaurant and a 1.5mi boardwalk complete with band
shell (music is provided for nightly dancing). Much of the resort, conceived by
the late Long Island parks superintendent Robert Moses, was constructed as
a WPA project. Among the brick-and-sandstone Art Deco landmarks are the
East and West Bathhouses and the 200ft-high central Water Tower (1930), a
modernistic version of the campanile of St. Mark's Church in Venice, Italy. The
popular **Jones Beach Theater** features concerts by pop and rock stars.

Bayard Cutting Arboretum – *Rte. 27A. Open year-round Tue–Sun 10am–sunset.
Closed Jan 1, Martin Luther King, Jr.'s Birthday, Presidents' Day, Dec 25. ✗ & ▣ ($4)*
☎*516-581-1002.* Begun in 1887 in accordance with plans by Frederick Law
Olmsted, the former estate ("Westbrook") of wealthy entrepreneur William
Cutting covers 690 acres of woodlands, meadow, oak-studded lawns and planted
areas. Rhododendrons and azaleas *(in bloom May–Jun)* border the walks and
drives; wildflowers add blazes of color throughout the arboretum. A pinetum
contains one of Long Island's most extensive collections of fir, spruce, pine, hemlock, yew and other specimens. Visitors may also explore the Tudor-style manor
house, detailed with shingled towers, eyebrow windows, hand-carved interior
woodwork and Tiffany windows. Refreshments are served on a porch overlooking the Connetquot River.

★ **Fire Island** – Measuring 32mi long and .5mi to less than 200yds wide, this barrier
island off Great South Bay covers more than 1,400 acres of **National Seashore**★. The
island, which has no roads for automobile traffic, preserves an exquisite but fragile landscape of dunes, scrub pine and wild beach grass. National Seashore
programs at Watch Hill and Sailors Haven feature interpretive walks and special
events. Facilities at both areas include a guarded swimming beach, snack bar and

marina. Ferry service connects Patchogue, Sayville and Bay Shore to the Fire Island communities and the main developed areas of the National Seashore. *Ferry to Watch Hill departs from Patchogue near the train station Memorial Day–Sept Mon–Fri 8am–6pm, weekends 8am–9:15pm. 20min. $5.50. Davis Ferry Co.* ☎516-475-1665. Approached by the Ocean State Parkway or the Robert Moses Causeway from West Islip—which offers spectacular **views**★ of the bay—the western part of

Robert Moses State Park, Fire Island

Fire Island is the site of **Robert Moses State Park**★. Parking facilities and several bathhouses are provided for beachgoers, while dunes and sea grasses offer refuge for myriad waterfowl. At the east end of the island, Smith Point Park *(access by bridge from William Floyd Pkwy.)* is also part of the Fire Island National Seashore. This location has swimming beaches and a boardwalk nature trail. Chartered boat excursions leave from nearby Captree State Park.

Dominating a 35mi stretch of Long Island's South Shore, **The Hamptons**★★ comprise a chain of vacation colonies beginning at Westhampton Beach, which rims Shinnecock Bay, and ending at Amagansett. Long a summer playground for the wealthy, these South Fork villages also attract New York City's young single set and hordes of tourists to their picture-perfect downtowns, cafes, designer boutiques and beautiful beaches. The Hamptons reflect an intriguing mix of the traditional and contemporary. Indeed, the area claims many early historic structures, including 17C farmhouses and nine wooden windmills dating from 1795 to 1820. Near the center of each village, classic shingle-style houses may be glimpsed behind tall boxwood hedges lining shady streets. By contrast, the region's outlying dunes and potato fields have become a noted showcase for experimental beach houses. Because it serves as the South Fork's main artery, Montauk Highway *(Rte. 27)* is frequently congested; expect traffic, particularly on weekends, and leave plenty of time to get to your destination. Biking is a good option and bike rentals are widely available.

Westhampton Beach – Formerly a seafaring community, Westhampton is a lively resort where New Yorkers—among them musicians, writers and artists—spend their weekends or take up summer residence. The annual Westhampton Beach Outdoor Art Show occurs in early August. An attractive beach extends 15mi from Moriches Inlet to Shinnecock Inlet. Take a drive along Dune Road, on the narrow barrier beach, for a prime view of Westhampton's beach houses, including many eccentric modern designs in concrete and glass. *Sections of Dune Rd. are extremely narrow and may be impassable following a storm.*

Southampton – *Self-guided walking-tour maps are available from the Chamber of Commerce (76 Main St.).* This elegant resort began as a small farming community founded in 1640 by settlers from Lynn, Massachusetts. During the mid-18C, when the nearby port of Sag Harbor was a major whaling center, Southampton became home to prosperous ship's captains. The town is now the largest of the Hampton communities and the site of gorgeous estates. A drive down South Main Street, a beautiful tree-shaded boulevard, offers a glimpse of "old" Southampton. Note in particular the **Thomas Halsey House**, a central-chimney shingled saltbox built by a member of one of Southampton's 20 founding families. The earliest section of the house, furnished with 17C and 18C antiques, is believed to date to c.1648. A handsome perennial and boxwood garden embellishes the rear yard. Continue on Gin Street to the west end of Meadow Avenue for a look at dozens of multimillion-dollar residences, complete with dune landscaping and entry gates equipped with elaborate security systems.

Parrish Art Museum – *25 Jobs Ln. Open mid-Jun–mid-Sept Mon–Tue, Thu–Sat 11am–5pm, Sun 1pm–5pm. Rest of the year Mon, Thu–Sat 11am–5pm, Sun 1pm–5pm. Closed first two weeks of Jan. $3.* ♿ 🅿 ☎516-283-2118. Housed in an elegant arcaded brick building designed by society architect Grosvenor Atterbury in 1898, this one-story museum boasts a collection of more than 2,000 19C and 20C American paintings, prints and drawings. Among the highlights are numerous works by William Merrit Chase and Fairfield Porter. Changing exhibits, lectures and concerts are presented regularly. The surrounding gardens, known as the Parrish Arboretum, showcase 250 trees and shrubs, along with sculpture reproductions form the Parrish collection. Note the 18 marble busts of Roman emperors placed in two parallel rows on the east side of the building.

Southampton Historical Museum and Colonial Society – *17 Meeting House Ln. Open mid-Jun–mid-Sept Tue–Sun 11am–5pm. Rest of the year by appointment only. $3.* ☎516-283-2494. Visitors to this collection of historic buildings will find a one-room schoolhouse; carpenter's, blacksmith's and cobbler's shops; and a pre-Revolutionary War barn housing country-store items. Forming the centerpiece of the museum, the Greek Revival Capt. Rogers Homestead was built in 1843 by a prosperous whaling ship captain. The ground floor features changing exhibits and a display of Indian artifacts from the Shinnecock and Montauk tribes.

Bridgehampton – Running through the center of town, the Montauk Highway serves as a main shopping street in this attractive village. Antique shops, cafes and home furnishing stores rank among the finest in the area. The **Bridgehampton Historical Museum**, housed in a two-story farmhouse *(Montauk Hwy. and Crowith Ave.;* ☎516-537-1088), offers changing exhibits on Long Island history and crafts.

East Hampton – This town's quaint charm has long attracted writers and artists; former residents Childe Hassam, Jackson Pollock and Stuart Davis are all buried here. Featuring a central pond flanked by fine old houses, the village green lends East Hampton the appearance of an English country town. Streets bordering the green, lined on both sides by magnificent elm trees, boast several historic structures, including the **Mulford Farmhouse**, a c.1680 saltbox *(5 James Ln.).* **Clinton Academy** *(151 Main St.),* a two-story brick-and-clapboard structure dating to 1784, is used by the East Hampton Historical Society *(☎516-324-6850)* for history exhibits. The Society also maintains the adjacent **East Hampton Townhouse** (1734), possibly the oldest extant schoolhouse on Long Island. Distinguished by a hip-roofed rotunda, the elegant one-story brick **Guild Hall** *(158 Main St.)* was built in 1931 as the East Hampton Cultural Center. It is the setting for a multitude of cultural events often featuring nationally known performers, artists and writers who frequent the Hamptons. At the north end of Main Street sits **Hook Mill**, an 1806 windmill powered by wooden gears; it was built by Nathaniel Dominy, member of a noted Long Island family of craftsmen and furniture makers.

Home Sweet Home Museum –*14 James Ln. Visit by guided tour (20min) only, Mar–Dec Mon–Sat 10am–4pm, Sun noon–4pm. Rest of the year by appointment only. Closed major holidays. $4.* ▯ ☎516-324-0713. Best known as the 1791 birthplace of playwright John Howard Payne (who wrote the 1822 song "Home Sweet Home" for his opera *Clari*), this oak-framed shingled saltbox dates to the 1640s. The house retains its original kitchen lean-to and an impressive collection of pewter, blue Staffordshire and lusterware tea sets. Among the highlights is an elaborately carved blanket chest made by Thomas Mulliner in 1640. Adjacent to the house, the 1804 Pantigo Windmill was moved to the site from the East Hampton Green several decades ago.

★ **Sag Harbor** – Originally known as Sagg Harbor, this charming 17C sea town is one of Long Island's most historic settlements. A protected deepwater harbor made this spot on the north shore of the South Fork an important port for the villages of the Hamptons. The first recorded whaling expedition set out in 1667. Trade with the West Indies was established by 1770, and in 1789 Sagg was named port of entry for the United States by George Washington. (With New York City, it was one of only two such official ports in the country.) By the early 1800s, the town ranked as the fourth-largest whaling port in the world, serving as port of call for some 400 whaling vessels in the peak years of the 1820s to 1850s. In that period, three- to five-year voyages to Alaska, Hawaii and the Orient brought in some $15 million in profits. The last whaler, the *Myra*, left the harbor in 1871. She was condemned, and her cargo, worth $32, sent home on another ship.

Today the well-preserved town is a living museum of Colonial and 19C architecture, including such local types as the one-and-a-half-story fisherman's cottage known as the "half house"; 18C post-and-beam saltboxes; Federal-period merchant houses with elegant entryway fanlights; columned Greek Revival mansions commissioned by wealthy whaling captains; and Victorian cottages adorned with gingerbread trim. A map for a self-guided walking tour of the Sag Harbor National Historic District is available at the Chamber of Commerce, housed in a windmill at the foot of Long Wharf on Bay Street.

Sag Harbor Whaling and Historical Museum – *Main St. Open May–Sept Mon–Sat 10am–5pm, Sun & holidays 1pm–5pm. $3.* ⌖ ▯ ☎516-725-0770. An outstanding example of the Greek Revival style, the former residence of Benjamin Hunting is attributed to Minard Lafever, one of America's most highly regarded 19C builder-architects. Erected in 1845, the two-story clapboard structure features a central temple front with Corinthian columns and a cornice sporting carved blubber spades and harpoons. The house, which also serves as a Masonic temple, contains an eccentric collection of whaling artifacts, toys, tools and Indian arrowheads. Framing the front door are the enormous jawbones of a right whale.

Old Whaler's Church – *Union St.* The First Presbyterian Church of Sag Harbor was completed in 1844 at the height of the town's maritime period. The unusual building is considered one of the country's major monuments in the Egyptian Revival style. Sloping walls recall Egyptian temple pylons, but the design also references the Sag Harbor whaling industry with a cornice cresting trimmed with wooden blubber spades. Once visible from miles away at sea, the original 185ft steeple blew down in a 1938 hurricane.

Custom House – *Main and Garden Sts. Visit by guided tour (1hr 30min) only, May–Oct weekends & holidays 1pm–5pm. $3.* ▯ ☎516-941-9444. US Custom Master Henry Packer Dering collected tariffs on goods from trading vessels in the front room of this 1789 Federal-period house. Furnishings include Dering family pieces.

★ **Shelter Island** – *Ferries from Greenport depart year-round daily 5:40am–11:45pm; ferries from Sag Harbor depart year-round daily 6am–11:45pm; extended summer hours. $1, $6.50/car & driver.* ⌖ ▯ ☎516-749-0399. Nestled between the North and South Forks, peaceful Shelter Island is a short ride by car ferry from Greenport *(8min)* on the North Shore and Sag Harbor *(3min)* to the south *(the cross-island drive from ferry to ferry is 5mi)*. English settlers arrived to this home of the Manhanset Indians in 1652 and the island remained a quiet farming and fishing community. In the 19C, Long Island was a popular site for religious camp meetings, and in 1868 a group of Brooklyn Methodists founded the Shelter Island Grove Camp Meeting Association here. The colorful Victorian cottages of Shelter Island Heights are remnants of this camp community, laid out by Robert Morris Copeland, who also designed the famous Oak Bluffs Campground in Martha's Vineyard, Massachusetts. Whimsical gingerbread trim ornamenting the cottages has inspired the local term, "Shelter Island lace."

Picket fences, boxwood hedges and roadside flower stands (leave your money in a coffee can) seem to outnumber the residents on this lovely island, which is a wonderful spot for biking and hiking.

Mashomack Preserve – *Rte. 114. Open Jan weekends 9am–4pm. Feb–Apr Wed–Mon 9am–4pm. May–Oct Wed–Mon 9am–5pm. Nov–Dec Wed–Mon 9am–4pm. $1.50.* ☎516-749-1001. Edged by 10mi of coastline, this 2,100-acre preserve owned by the Nature Conservancy covers nearly one third of Shelter Island. Passing by wildlife observation stations, four trails lead through woodlands, wetlands, oak and beech forest and grassy meadows. A visitor center offers literature, displays and a small gift shop.

Montauk – Located on the easternmost tip of Long Island and encompassing a 10mi strip of natural woodlands, stark cliffs, dunes and white beaches jutting into the ocean, Montauk is a favorite location for deep-sea fishing and beachside vacations. Begun in 1795, the Montauk Point Lighthouse, rising at the tip of the peninsula, is located in Montauk State Park. Designed by the acclaimed Colonial architect John McComb, Jr. (also responsible for Manhattan's City Hall), the octagonal sandstone tower was originally lit by 13 whale-oil lamps. A lightkeeper's house was added in 1860.

Additional Sights *½ day*

★★ **Old Bethpage Restoration Village** – *Round Swamp Rd. Open Mar–Oct Wed–Sun 10am–5pm. Nov–Dec Wed–Sun 10am–4pm. Closed Thanksgiving Day, Dec 24 & 25. $5. Guided tours available.* ✕ ☎516-572-8400. Nestled in a 200-acre valley, Old Bethpage is an active farm community that re-creates a pre-Civil War American village. More than 25 historic buildings reflecting the history of Long Island's vernacular architecture have been moved to the site of the former Powell farm. Take a leisurely stroll through the village to observe a blacksmith hammering at his anvil, a cobbler making shoes, a tailor, a hatmaker, clerks tending two 19C general stores, and farmers working their fields. Depending on the time of year, sheep shearing, candle making and other seasonal activities may also be viewed.

★ **Old Westbury Gardens** – *Old Westbury Rd. Open late Apr–mid-Dec Wed–Mon 10am–5pm (Nov weekends only 11am–4pm). $6. Guided tours (30min) available.* ✕ ☎516-333-0048. This former Gold Coast estate built in 1906 by financier John S. Phipps and his English bride, Margarita Grace, includes the red-brick mansion they called Westbury House and more than 70 beautifully maintained acres of gardens and park interspersed with woodlands, ponds and meadows. The stately two-and-a-half-story Georgian Revival house has been preserved as it was during the family's residence until the 1950s. The interior showcases antique furnishings, paintings by Thomas Gainsborough and John Singer Sargent, gilded mirrors and objets d'art. Influenced by both English Romantic and French Renaissance landscape design, the grounds envelop formal lawns; rose, boxwood and Japanese gardens; lilac, primrose and bluebell walks; a pinetum; a spectacular collection of rhododendrons *(in bloom mid–late May)*; and a walled garden where perennials bloom from spring to fall.

Hudson River Valley and Catskill Mountains

A scant distance from New York City, the scenery and sites of the Hudson River Valley and the neighboring Catskill Mountains rank easily among the most remarkable in the Northeast. The river and mountains are perhaps best recognized in their shimmering portraits by the Hudson River school of painters who flocked to the region in the mid-19C to capture their incomparable beauty on canvas. In spite of the imprint of 20C life, these luminescent riverine vistas and verdurous forest scenes still capture the power of the place today.

The valley itself is notable for both its natural beauty and its man-made environment. To the river's east, a stunning succession of historic homes represents a veritable living catalog of American history and architecture. Route 9 skirts the riverbank and links most of these sites with quaint towns like Cold Spring and Rhinebeck, where good food and a range of accommodations can be found. West of the river, Route 9W connects a variety of sites—many relating to the Revolutionary War—all basking in the scenic beauty of the Hudson River Valley and Highlands. Seven bridges cross the river at convenient intervals. Just beyond Kingston, the velvety blue-green Catskill Mountains loom on the western horizon with their promise of primeval forests, waterfalls and mountain trails. Scenic Route 28 bisects this 1,500sq mi region, making its way from the heart of the mountains, past the sprawling Ashokan Reservoir and Slide Mountain, the range's high peak at 4,180ft, to the rolling dairy farms of the western Catskills.

> "Whoever has made a voyage up the Hudson must remember the Kaatskill Mountains.... When the weather is fair and settled, they are clothed in blue and purple, and print their bold outlines on the clear evening sky; but sometimes, when the rest of the landscape is cloudless, they will gather a hood of gray vapors about their summits, which, in the last rays of the setting sun, will glow and light up like a crown of glory."
>
> from *Rip Van Winkle* by Washington Irving

Still renowned for its "borscht belt," a region of mountain resorts made popular by Jewish vacationers escaping the heat and congestion of New York City at the turn of the century, the Catskills also present a healthy array of recreational and sightseeing opportunities for both the outdoors enthusiast and the history buff.

Historical Notes – The ridges and hills of the Catskills were formed millions of years ago by the heavy erosion of a high, flat land. Engraved by water and wind, they are not technically mountains, but rather a "dissected plateau." Mountains or not, it is their mystery that has intrigued travelers for centuries. Indeed, tangled forests, shifting light, thundering waterfalls and rocky cloves (clefts in the terrain) imbue the Catskills with a certain magic. Native Americans called them "land in the sky" and trod their paths warily. Henry Hudson claimed the region for Holland on his voyage up the river in 1609. The Dutch, who settled the Hudson Valley, viewed the Catskills (from the Dutch *kaaterskill*, meaning "wildcat creek") superstitiously, peopling them in their folklore with imps and spirits. Washington Irving's famous fictional sleeper, Rip Van Winkle, succumbed to the mountains' spell, napping in their shadows for 20 years.

The Catskills' brooding interior remained largely unexplored until after the War of 1812, when its dense hemlock forests yielded bark to be used in the tanning of leather. Until the 1870s, tanneries thrived in the woods, which thinned considerably as the great hemlocks were felled. Elsewhere in the Catskills, bluestone quarries operating in the late 19C provided New York City with sandstone for its sidewalks until cement became the material of choice. Eventually the romance and beauty of the Catskills began to attract tourists, ushering in an era of elegant vacation resorts as early as the mid-1820s with the opening of the Catskill Mountain House. This legacy lingers, as the region still depends primarily on tourism for its livelihood. It is not, however, unusual to encounter in the rustic outreaches the bleached bones of industry and ingenuity—long-abandoned canals, rusting railroad tracks, overgrown mills—that attest to a flirtation with progress.

■ Meet Me in the Catskills

For more than 70 years, the Catskill Mountains echoed with laughter and applause: large and small resorts alike dispensed a brand of merriment that would forever enliven American entertainment. Modern music and filmmaking, theater and television all inherited the legacy, as hundreds of performers launched their careers from the stages at Grossinger's, the Concord, the Flagler and scores of other resort venues.

Nearly a century before their heyday, Jewish immigrants escaping the pogroms of Europe and the sweatshops on Manhattan's Lower East Side discovered the Catskill Mountains. All met with discrimination, as popular hotels refused them rooms and townsfolk rebuffed them. Soon resourceful Jews opened their own kosher boardinghouses, giving rise to the name "Borscht Belt." Increasingly, visitors expected more than just fresh air and scenery. Boris Thomashevsky produced the first Yiddish plays at his retreat in Hunter, and in 1913, Malke and Slig Grossinger, restaurateurs from New York City, arrived in Ferndale to establish the grande dame of all Catskill resorts. Grossinger's achieved global renown before its decline and sale out of the family in 1985.

In the 1920s, the resorts hit their stride, and a regiment of entertainers traipsed across their stages, including Fanny Brice and Eddie Cantor in the early days, and Sid Caesar and Joan Rivers later on. Among the most famous, Danny Kaye began as a "tummler," or social director, at White Roe Hotel in the 1930s. The Syndicate recognized the Catskill opportunity as well, and the region became a hotbed for illegal gambling, loan sharking and bootlegging. The mountains hummed with activity, legitimate and otherwise, until, by the 1970s, a younger generation had found other places to play, and the era of the grand Catskill resorts faded.

Practical Information

Getting There – Access to **Kingston** and the eastern portions of **Catskills Park** from the north (**Albany,** 56mi) or south (**New York City,** 108mi) via I-87; Route 23 skirts the northeastern border of the park. From the west (**Binghamton,** 69mi) take Route 17 east for access to southwestern Catskills Park, or Route 17 east to Route 30 east for the northwest areas. Route 28 traverses the park east to west from Kingston to Margaretville. International and domestic flights service **Albany International Airport** and **Stewart International Airport** *(Newburgh).* Closest Amtrak train station (☎800-872-7245) is located in Rhinecliff. Adirondack Trailways **bus** service stops at many cities in the region (☎518-465-1491 or 800-858-8555).

Visitor Information – Contact the following agencies for information and brochures on points of interest, seasonal events, recreation and accommodations: **Greene County Promotion Bureau** *(Rte. 23B, Exit 21 Thruway, Catskill NY 12414* ☎518-943-3223 *or* 800-355-2287*);* **Sullivan County Office of Public Information** *(Government Center, Monticello NY 12701* ☎914-794-3000 or 800-882-2287*);* **Ulster County Tourism & Public Information Office** *(244 Fair St., Kingston NY 12401* ☎914-340-3566 or 800-342-5826*).*

Accommodations – *(p 358).* Area visitors' guides including lodging directories are available *(free)* from local tourism agencies *(above).* A wide range of accommodations can be found throughout the area year-round, including **vacation resorts** that offer nightly entertainment and recreational and leisure activities; quaint cabins; historic inns; bed-and-breakfast inns; sporting lodges; hotels and motels. **Campsites** are nestled throughout the region along lakes and waterways. Consult the brochure *Camping in the New York State Forest Preserve (free)* for a list of campgrounds and facilities *(available from the Public Information & Publications Unit, NYS Dept. of Environmental Conservation, 50 Wolf Rd., Room 111, Albany NY 12233; general information* ☎518-457-3521*; campground reservations* ☎800-456-2267*; campground information* ☎518-457-2500*).*

Recreation – The Catskills abound with recreational opportunities throughout the year from public **golf** courses to guided **horseback** trail rides or **bicycle** shops that provide rentals and trail information. Tubing and **rafting** excursions on the Esopus River are also popular activities *(Memorial Day–Labor Day; companies offering rental equipment are located in Phoenicia).* **Fishing** and **hunting** are allowed; contact the New York State Department of Environmental Conservation for details *(Rte. 10, Stamford NY 12167* ☎607-652-7366*).* **Ski** resorts *(p 368),* featuring downhill, cross-country and snowboarding are located primarily in Greene, Ulster and Sullivan counties *(contact Ski the Catskills for more information* ☎800-882-2287*).* **Snowmobile** rentals are available at several ski areas in Greene County.

★ **KINGSTON**   *1 day. Map p 71.*

Wedged between the Hudson River and the Catskills, Kingston is both river town and mountain gateway. Settlement here dates back to a trading post established in 1614, making it among the oldest European communities in the country. It grew to be New York's third-largest city for a time and, briefly in 1777, the first state capital. Eventually its proximity to the river—and by 1829 to the mouth of the Delaware & Hudson Canal—made it both a disembarkation point for Catskill-bound tourists and a major commercial port. Today, after a period of economic decline, Kingston shares the revival mood of fellow river towns, restoring and promoting its sites for a growing number of visitors.

★ **Stockade District** – *Bounded by Clinton Ave. and N. Front, Green and Wall Sts. Self-guided or occasional guided tours begin at the visitor center at 308 Clinton Ave. (open May–Oct daily 11am–5pm;* & ▣ *www.mhrcc.org/kingston/* ☎914-331-7517 or 800-331-1518).* Historic heart of Kingston, this hilltop was originally enclosed by Gov. Peter Stuyvesant to protect Dutch settlers from the native Esopus Indians in 1658. Many of the homes that cluster within the eight-block neighborhood represent variations on the stone house so popular with the first Dutch and northern European settlers in this region. After the British torched the town in 1777, numerous structures were modernized with roof styles from ensuing centuries. A stroll through the quaint district still reveals the essence of the 17C village. Kingston boasts the only intersection left in America with a stone house on each corner *(where Crown St. crosses John St.).* The third incarnation of the **Old Dutch**

Church between Wall and Fair Streets on Main was built of local bluestone in 1852. Like a geode, the church is stern and brooding on the outside but marvelously bright inside, with a beautiful blend of Neoclassical and Colonial elements. Note the Tiffany window above the pulpit, installed in 1891. The worn and fragmented tombstones in the surrounding cemetery reveal a community of French Huguenot and Dutch souls in repose since the 18C.

★ **Senate House State Historic Site** – *296 Fair St. Open mid-Apr–Oct Wed–Sat & holidays 10am–5pm, Sun 1pm–5pm. Rest of the year by appointment only. $3.* 🅿 ☎914-338-2786. Located across the street from the visitor center and occupying the northeast corner of the Stockade District, the Senate House grounds include two buildings of interest. Tours begin from the **museum**, built in 1927, which contains an eclectic variety of materials that relate to the house and to the history of New York State government. The museum also claims the largest collection of works by early American painter **John Vanderlyn** (1775-1852); they are exhibited on a rotating basis on the first floor. Next door, the **Senate House** (*visit by guided tour only*) gained its importance because New York's first state senate convened there in 1777. The senate-appointed Council of Safety fled to nearby Hurley (*p 72*) just one step ahead of the British army, which burned Kingston on October 16, 1777. Begun a century earlier, the house was owned by Abraham Van Gaasbeek, who rented it to the senate as a meeting place. Rooms open to the public include the living room, the parlor and the understated room where the senate met in the midst of revolutionary turmoil, now a shrine to the tenacity of early American democracy.

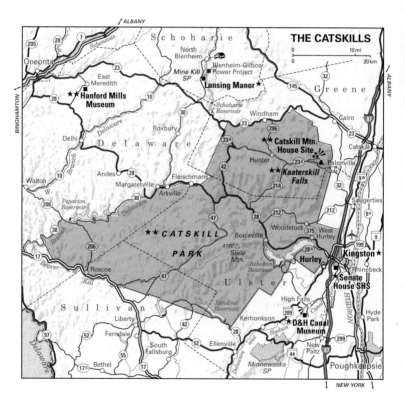

Rondout District – *Along Broadway at Rondout Creek. Visitor center located at 20 Broadway (open May–Oct Mon–Fri 9am–5pm, weekends & holidays 11am–5pm; rest of the year Mon–Fri 9am–5pm; closed major holidays;* & 🅿 *www.mhrcc.org/kingston/* ☎914-331-7517 or 800-331-1518). A short drive across town and down the steep embankment to the river lies the Kingston that was inspired by another revolution, the industrial one. Rondout Creek became the "tidewater terminal" of the Delaware & Hudson Canal (*p 72*). By then the waterfront was bustling, and in 1848 the midstream island was built to store coal for shipment down the Hudson. A row of sturdy Italianate buildings lines the strand, making perfect venues for boutiques, restaurants and bars. Stops of interest in Rondout include the **Trolley Museum** *(89 E. Strand; open May–Oct weekends & holidays noon–5pm; $3;* ♿ 🄿 *www.mhrcc.org/kingston/kgntroll.html* ☎*914-331-3399),* which offers trolley rides to Kingston Point in summer; and the **Maritime Museum** *(1 Rondout Landing; open May–Oct Wed–Mon 11am–5pm; $2;* 🄿 ☎*914-338-0071),* whose collection of vessels includes the 1898 steam tugboat *Mathilda.* Rotating exhibits highlight the various types of craft that plied the Hudson in the 19C and explore the history of industry along the mighty waterway. The 1913 Rondout II Lighthouse, a Hudson sentry at the mouth of the creek, can be toured by taking one of the Maritime Museum's boat rides *(May–Jun weekends 12:30pm–3:30pm; Jul–Aug Wed–Mon 12:30pm–3:30pm; Sept–Oct weekends 12:30pm–3:30pm; $7).*

Excursions

Hurley – *30min. On Rte. 209 just southwest of Kingston.* Famous for being the largest enclave of stone houses in the country, quaint Hurley was established in 1661 and grew to become a renowned producer of pot cheese. Many of its 25 stone houses stand right on Main Street and span the 18C in their construction. Squat and sturdy with steep gables at either end and little *stoeps* at their front doors, these stone houses are of utterly Dutch design. Under the sharply sloping shingle roofs of their ample attics, farm families stored grain and other goods while living on the ground floor. Still privately owned today, the homes are opened once a year in July.

★ **Delaware & Hudson Canal Museum** – *30min. 17mi from Kingston. Take Rte. 209 south and turn left on Rte. 213; follow Rte. 213 east to High Falls for 3mi. Turn right at Clove Valley Trading Post. Museum is on Mohonk Rd. Open May 30–Labor Day Mon & Thu–Sat 11am–5pm, Sun 1pm–5pm. Early May & Oct Sat 11am–5pm, Sun 1pm–5pm. $2.* ♿ 🄿 *www.mhrcc.org/kingston/kqndah.html* ☎*914-687-9311.* The Delaware & Hudson Canal Historical Society operates this small museum, which recounts the history of the D & H Canal, built between 1825 and 1828 to haul anthracite coal from Pennsylvania. Visitors listen to a taped narration as they view dioramas, maps, artifacts and a working model of a gravity railroad *(p 272).* However, the most interesting part of this site is the remnants of the now dried-up canal. Pick up a brochure in the museum and take the self-guided tour through the woods along the five locks that run parallel to Mohonk Road. These were built in 1849 to ease the larger canal boats down a total of 70ft to the aqueduct across Rondout Creek. Though overgrown and crumbling, the wonder of this engineering marvel still lingers. In places, the canal walls remain perfectly plumb, and snubbing posts bear the scars of heavily loaded lines. A small group of buildings at the foot of the canal evokes a sense of the community that existed here. The walking path crosses Route 213 to the site of the Roebling aqueduct abutments and follows Rondout Creek for a **view★** of the upper and lower falls.

★★ **CATSKILL PARK**   *½ day. Map p 71.*

The region's heart beats in Catskill Park, where wilderness and settlement blend to offer hiking, fishing and skiing with plenty of amenities and accommodations. Originally demarcated in 1904, the park today includes more than 700,000 acres. Within its boundaries lies the Catskill Forest Preserve, which began in 1885 when New York State gave over certain of its lands for perpetual protection under the Constitution. Including parcels in four Catskill counties, the preserve now constitutes the largest wilderness area east of the Mississippi. To the northeast, the escarpment rises 3,000ft above the Hudson River Valley, affording spectacular **vistas★** from its precipitous edges. Painter **Thomas Cole**'s effulgent canvases of the surrounding wilderness inspired a generation of artists to render nature at its most sublime.

★★ **Catskill Mountain House Site** – *From Palenville, take Rte. 23A west for 5mi to Haines Falls. Turn right onto Greene County Rte. 18 and follow it to the North-South Lake Public Campground. Look for small brown and yellow signs at the far end of the picnic shelter.* Reached by a short hike, this evocative site captures much of the essence of the Catskills in its scenic beauty, mystery and historic significance. Catskill Mountain House was built in 1823 and operated for nearly 120 years, an archetypal American resort and a favorite destination of the rich and famous. Eventually it fell into ruin and was intentionally burned in 1963. All that remains today is the broad plain on which it stood and the stupendous natural setting that it crowned. **Views★★★** surrounding the site were among the most familiar of the

Stony Clove Creek, Catskill Park

19C, thanks to Thomas Cole and other artists of the Hudson River school and writers like James Fenimore Cooper. Visitors can still scramble up and down the many trails that 19C tourists made the most popular in America, including the 24mi **Escarpment Trail**, portions of which are more than 150 years old.

★★ **Kaaterskill Falls** – *On Rte. 23A, about 3mi west of Palenville. Note: Park in roadside parking area on the south side of Rte. 23A, west of and uphill from the trailhead. Be particularly careful negotiating the way between the parking area and the trail .25mi down the hill. Walking along the highway is tricky as there is no sidewalk and little room between rocks and road.* Beginning at a hairpin turn directly to the left off the road, this 1mi round-trip trail ascends rapidly. Follow the yellow trail markers along boisterous Kaaterskill Creek, past hemlock trees that once dominated the forests. These specimens survived the 19C tanning industry that thrived here by using the tree's bark in the curing process. Rocks and roots akimbo make it a rigorous climb, but the payoff at the end is superb. Looming above, the narrow falls—tallest in the state at 260ft—descend in two cascading tiers. Kaaterskill Falls were once as popular as Niagara, and by 1854 beskirted 19C women clamored up the escarpment on wooden staircases. This is quintessential Catskill terrain, and a few minutes in these woods evokes the awe that made Indians wary and inspired Dutch legends.

★ WESTERN CATSKILLS
½ day. Map p 71.

The counties of Delaware and southern Schoharie roughly define the western perimeter of the Catskill region. Tapering hills roll across their breadth to the Susquehanna River (or, in less scenic terms, to Interstate 88), overlaid by dairy farmland and small towns. In Arkville, the **Delaware and Ulster Rail Ride** runs hour-long train rides in historic "rolling stock" that tour the countryside *(depart May–Jun weekends 11am–3pm; Jul–Aug Wed–Sun 11am–3pm; Sept–Oct weekends 11am–3pm; reservations required; $7;* ✗ **P***)*

Woodstock
Rtes. 212 and 375. Another kind of history pervades Woodstock, and indeed has been the maker of its fortune. Although the hamlet was founded in the 1700s, it acquired its popularity as an artists' colony in 1902 when Ralph Whitehead, a Utopian philosopher, established the Byrdcliffe Arts and Crafts Colony. Woodstock's latest incarnation was heavily influenced by the counterculture invasion of the late 1960s. Since the legendary rock concert (actually held 50mi from here, in Bethel) in 1969, the town has acquired a funky blend of shops, restaurants and people with a delightfully bohemian air. This is the place to stop for a good vegetarian nosh or an afternoon of gallery and boutique hopping.

73

☎*607-652-2821 or 800-225-4132*). This is quiet country, from which philosopher and naturalist **John Burroughs** (1837-1921) drew inspiration for his finely crafted essays on nature. A memorial honors him near his boyhood home in Roxbury.

★ **Lansing Manor** – *South of North Blenheim on Rte. 30. Visit by guided tour (1hr) only, Jun–Oct Wed–Mon 10am–5pm.* ♿ 🅿 ☎*518-527-6121 or 800-724-0309.* As part of the sweeping Blenheim-Gilboa Power Project next door, the New York Power Authority acquired this elegant 1819 manor house, restoring and furnishing it in Federal, Empire and early Victorian styles of the mid-19C. Originally the center of an 842-acre tenant farm owned by Jacob Livingston Sutherland, the house passed through four families, undergoing few changes over the years. The guided tour visits 10 meticulously appointed rooms, lush in color, fabric and furniture. Outbuildings on the property include the dairy barn, which now houses the power plant's visitor center. Despite an odd juxtaposition of historic and modern elements on the landscape, the restoration of Lansing was obviously well endowed by the Power Authority, and the house is nicely maintained.

Blenheim-Gilboa Pumped Storage Power Project Visitors Center – *Next to Lansing Manor, on Rte. 30. Open year-round daily 10am–5pm. Closed Jan 1, Thanksgiving Day, Dec 24–25, Dec 31.* ♿ 🅿 ☎*518-827-6121 or 800-724-0309.* Long on public relations, this center affords visitors a bird's-eye view of the power project and provides historical background on its purpose, siting and construction. Begin downstairs with a 7min introductory video describing the project, which was completed in 1973. Upstairs, the museum offers a look at various ways to make and transmit electricity, along with some history of Schoharie County. The glassed-in viewing area provides a good vista of the plant itself, nestled far below at the edge of the lower reservoir. Only a quarter of it is visible; the rest plunges 10 stories underground. At peak hours of electrical use around the state, water from an upper reservoir falls through conduits to spin turbines and generate electricity. At lulls, the water recycles back again. The Power Authority built nearby **Mine Kill State Park** *(open Jun–Sept daily 8am–8pm; rest of the year daily 8am–4pm; closed Jan 1, Dec 25; $4/car;* ✗ ♿ 🅿 ☎*518-827-6111),* which boasts a lovely waterfall and hiking trails that end at the visitor center. Tours of the plant are available with advance reservations (☎*518-827-6111).*

A short drive down Route 30 intersects Schoharie Creek, which is crossed by the longest single-span **wooden bridge** in the world. Although you cannot drive across it, you can walk its length. The bridge no longer reaches from bank to bank because of a new channel cut by a storm many years ago.

★★ **Hanford Mills Museum** – *On Delaware County Rte. 10 in East Meredith. From Margaretville, continue west on Rte. 28 for 32mi, then turn right onto Rte. 10. Open May–Oct daily 10am–5pm. $4.* ✗ ♿ 🅿 *www.norwich.net/~hanford1* ☎*607-278-5744 or 800-295-4992.* Established as a sawmill in 1846, Hanford Mills grew by accretion over the years into a "rural industrial complex," a segue between traditional rural life and the industrial age. By harnessing the waterpower of nearby Kortright Creek, the complex reached its heyday between 1880 and 1915, operating as a sawmill, gristmill and source of electricity for the town of East Meredith. Begin in the Feed Mill Building, where a comprehensive exhibit offers interesting background and historical context for this fascinating site. Knowledgeable guides (with obvious affection for the site) conduct tours through the working sawmill, where they still cut all manner of wooden products, from broom handles to barrel covers. Beneath the woodworking floor, the behemoth "overshot" waterwheel sets into motion a complicated network of pulleys and power trains to run the saws and woodworking machinery. Everywhere, the pungent smell of sawdust, the rumble of the wheel and pulleys, and the screech of the saws add to the ambience.

HUDSON RIVER VALLEY ★★★

Maps p 75 and p 79
Tourist Information ☎914-294-5151 or 800-232-4782

Between the state capital at Albany and its mouth in the thick of the nation's busiest city, the Hudson River passes through some 145mi of hills, highlands and history. The region's first inhabitants were Algonquian-speaking Indians, whom explorer Henry Hudson encountered when he sailed up the river in 1609. Hudson's glowing reports to his Dutch employers of the fertile bottomlands along the river encouraged Dutch settlement there, mostly in large tenant-farmed estates called patroonships *(p 76)*. Although the English took over the colony in

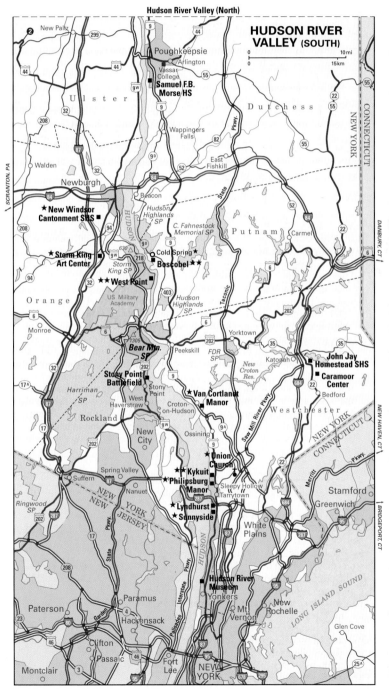

1664, the Hudson River Valley retained much of its Dutch character in the years to come, as the sturdy stone houses that still stand today attest. During the Revolution, the valley took on considerable strategic importance, since the river connected a vast network of waterways that stretched from the Great Lakes north to the St. Lawrence and south to the Atlantic Ocean. Moreover, should it fall to the British, New England would be cut off from the rest of the colonies. Americans spared nothing for the river's defense, which included the establishment of Fortress West Point at its most strategic bend. Although steamships and the Erie Canal increased traffic and commerce along the Hudson in the early 19C, the magnificence of the landscape prevailed. Writers and artists extolled the river's virtues, the wealthy built grand houses along its banks, and ordinary Americans enjoyed its natural charms.

Inexorably, however, road building, quarrying and industry marred the countryside and polluted the water. Tensions over such activity came to a head in the early 1960s as Consolidated Edison planned a power plant at Storm King Mountain. A 17-year battle culminated in a major victory for environmentalists when the plan was abandoned and the Hudson River Valley became a model for the modern environmental movement. Folksinger and activist Pete Seeger has long been a champion of the Hudson River, and vigilant interest in the waterway as an important scenic and natural resource has spawned considerable environmental concern over recent years. Cities like Newburgh, Kingston and Poughkeepsie, having outlived their usefulness as industrious ports, are redefining themselves to attract tourist dollars. Related efforts among 82 riverside communities to create a shoreside greenway reflect a return to a vision of the river as a grand entryway rather than a back door.

■ Lords of the Manor

In 1629, to encourage the settlement of New Netherland with private rather than company money, the Dutch West India Company granted estates, each measuring 16mi along the river, to its shareholders. Called "patroons" (patrons), these landholders agreed to send 50 tenant farmers within four years to cultivate the land. Unique in America, this feudal system worked poorly as the absentee patroons mismanaged their estates and attracted few settlers. Even so, when the English took over in 1664, they converted the patroonships into manors and continued to grant lands up and down the river to wealthy families. As freehold lands grew scarcer, more farmers began to settle as tenants on the manors of such families as the Van Rensselaers, Beekmans and Livingstons, who formed the upper crust of the valley's "nobility." Violent tenant uprisings led to a new state constitution in 1846 outlawing "feudal tenures." Soon, however, new generations of American aristocracy— Vanderbilts, Goulds and Rockefellers among them—would flock to the river's edge to build their mansions amid those of the venerable families of the Hudson Valley. Today a remarkable concentration of historic homes and properties remains the lingering legacy of this centuries-old Dutch settlement pattern.

The following sights along the east and west banks are presented from south to north.

EAST BANK   *4-5 days. Maps p 75 and p 79.*

Hudson River Museum of Westchester – *511 Warburton Ave. in Yonkers. Open year-round Wed–Sun noon–5pm (May–Sept Fri 9pm). Closed major holidays. $3.* ✗ ♿ ▣ ☎*914-963-4550.* Blending an art and history museum, a planetarium and a historic house, this unusual facility offers something for everyone. Glenview, the stone mansion built for local financier John Trevor in 1876, features four Eastlake and Gothic Revival rooms appointed to depict the lifestyle of an upper-middle-class late-Victorian family. Note the lovely ceiling stencils and the occasional Hudson River school painting. A small exhibit uses elements of design and utility from the house to explore late-19C life. The modern wing, added in 1969, displays changing exhibits of art, history and science. Artist Red Grooms created the fanciful bookstore in the new wing in 1979, a decided contrast to the Victorian interiors of Glenview. The **Andrus Planetarium** presents star shows with its Zeiss M1015 projector, capable of projecting 5,000 stars *(Fri 7pm–9pm, weekends 1:30pm–3:30pm; $4 weekends only).*

PRACTICAL INFORMATION

Getting There

By Car – Access to the **East Bank** from New York City via the Henry Hudson Parkway north to Route 9N; from Albany via I-87 to I-90 to Route 9J. To access the **West Bank** from the south, cross the Hudson River via the George Washington Bridge to Palisades Interstate Parkway to Route 9W north; from the north take I-87 south to Route 9W.

By Air – Closest airports are **Stewart International Airport** *(Newburgh)* and **Albany International Airport**; both handle international and domestic flights.

By Bus and Train – Adirondack Trailways (☎518-465-1491 *or* 800-858-8555), Greyhound (☎402-330-2055 *or* 800-847-5263) and New Jersey Transit (☎201-762-5100) provide **bus** service to many cities in the Hudson River Valley. Metro-North *(www.mta.nyc.ny.us* ☎212-532-4900) and Amtrak (☎800-872-7245) **trains** make stops throughout the valley.

General Information

Visitor Information – Contact the following agencies to obtain maps and information on recreation, accommodations and seasonal events: **Historic Hudson Valley** *(150 White Plains Rd., Tarrytown NY 10591* ☎914-631-8200); **Hudson Valley Tourism** *(76 Main St., Cold Spring NY 10516* ☎914-265-3066 *or* 800-232-4782); **Dutchess County Tourism Promotion Agency** *(3 Neptune Rd., Poughkeepsie NY 12601* ☎914-463-4000 *or* 800-445-3131); **Orange County Tourism** *(30 Matthews St., Suite 111, Goshen NY 10924 www.orangetourism.org* ☎914-291-2136); **Ulster County Tourism Information Office** *(PO Box 1800 HGV, Kingston NY 12402* ☎914-340-3566 *or* 800-342-5826).

Accommodations – *(p 358)*. Area visitors' guides including lodging directories are available *(free)* from local tourism agencies *(above)*. Room rates tend to be higher for establishments on the eastern side of the river. Hotels, motels and bed-and-breakfast inns can be found in most cities along the river, especially in New Paltz, Rhinebeck and Poughkeepsie. **B&B reservation service**: American Country Collection *(1353 Union St., Schenectady NY 12308* ☎518-370-4948).

Camping – State parks that allow camping in the Hudson River Valley include Harriman *(Bear Mountain* ☎914-947-2792), Fahnestock *(Carmel* ☎914-225-7207) and Mills-Norrie *(Staatsburg* ☎914-889-4646). Camping is also available at many privately owned campgrounds.

Amenities – Most towns in the Hudson River Valley offer a broad range of shops and restaurants. **"Pick-your-own" farms** selling produce, herbs and plants are located throughout the valley. Contact the agencies listed above or request a copy of the Dutchess County Farm Produce Map *($2; Cornell Cooperative Extension, Attn: Produce Map, PO Box 259, Millbrook NY 12545* ☎914-677-8223).

Sports and Leisure

Cruises – Companies offering cruises on the Hudson River include Great Hudson Sailing Center *(sailboat cruises depart from Haverstraw Apr–Oct; 2hrs;* ☎914-429-1557 *or* 800-237-1557); Hudson Highlands Cruises & Tours *(depart from West Haverstraw & West Point May–Oct; 6hrs 30min & 1hr 30min;* ☎914-446-7171); Hudson River Adventures *(depart from Newburgh Landing, Newburgh May–Oct; 2hrs; ny.frontiernet.net/~hudrivad/* ☎914-782-0685); and Hudson River Cruises *(depart from Roundout Landing, Kingston May–Oct; 2hrs;* ☎914-255-6515 *or* 800-843-7472). **Riverboat** tours are provided by Spirit of St. Joseph *(depart from Riverside Ave., Rensselaer May–Oct; 3hrs;* ☎914-449-2664 *or* 800-828-2364); and Hudson River Boat Co. *(depart from Westerly Rd., Ossining late Mar–Dec; 2-4hrs;* ☎914-762-4564). **Historic** cruises are conducted by NY Waterway *(depart from end of West Main St., Tarrytown mid-Apr–early Nov; 2hrs;* ☎201-902-8700 *or* 800-533-3779).

Recreation – *(p 362)* Many trail systems lace the region, crossing through state and local parks. The **Rails-to-Trails Conservancy** maintains several former railroad tracks throughout the Hudson River Valley that have been converted into paved and dirt paths for bikers and pedestrians *(Rails-to-Trails Conservancy, 1400 16th St. NW, Suite 300, Washington DC 20036* ☎202-797-5400). A portion of the **Appalachian Trail** zigzags through Rockland, Orange, Putnam and Dutchess counties. The lengthy **Heritage**, **Highlands** and **Long Path** trails are all maintained by the New York, New Jersey Trail Conference *(p 365)*. The **Dutchess County Bike Tour** brochure *(free)* is available from the Dutchess County Tourism Promotion Agency *(above)*. Public **horseback riding** stables can be found throughout the valley.

★ **Sunnyside** – *W. Sunnyside Ln., off Rte. 9 in Tarrytown. Visit of house by guided tour (1hr) only, Mar–Oct Wed–Mon 10am–5pm. Nov–Dec Wed–Mon 10am–4pm. Closed Thanksgiving Day, Dec 25. $7. Combination tickets are available for 2 or 3 houses (Sunnyside, Philipsburg and Van Cortlandt).* 🄿 ☎914-591-8763. Focal point of "Sleepy Hollow Country," this quaint hideaway still evokes the storybook setting that its famous owner, **Washington Irving** (1783-1859), cultivated. Irving was among the first writers to employ American themes. His stories about Rip Van Winkle and Ichabod Crane continue to shape our romantic notions of the Hudson River Valley, as does Sunnyside. Its fanciful architecture and verdant surroundings embody the essence of the 19C Romantic landscape, where carefully planned vistas and structures blend into a picturesque and evocative scene. Built by Irving around an existing farmhouse in 1835, this "snuggery" blends English, Dutch, Spanish and Scottish elements, as well as skylights and a system of hot and cold running water he had seen on his world travels. A retreat during his later years, Sunnyside remains warm and welcoming to this day, conjuring up the festive gatherings of family and friends the author so enjoyed. Much evidence of Irving's life remains: the wisteria he planted in 1840 still engulfs the front entryway, and his study seems only just vacated.

★ **Lyndhurst** – *635 S. Broadway, off Rte. 9 in Tarrytown. Visit of house by guided tour (1hr) only, Apr–Oct Tue–Sun 10am–5pm. Rest of the year Sun & holidays 10am–5pm. Closed Thanksgiving Day, Dec 25. $9.* 🍴 ♿ 🄿 ☎914-631-4481. An astonishing Gothic Revival castle in the "pointed style," Lyndhurst was designed in 1838 by Alexander Jackson Davis, the most prolific architect of Gothic country houses in America. The manse represents one of the finest residential examples of this style, associated more often in the US with churches and ivory towers. Sprung from the same Romantic ethos as Sunnyside, Lyndhurst was intended to be picturesque and reminiscent of distant times and places. Davis not only built the home but also designed the interior flourishes and much of its furniture. His pervasive influence gives the home a creative continuity. Railroad tycoon and financier Jay Gould acquired Lyndhurst in 1880, and it came to the National Trust for Historic Preservation upon the death of Gould's youngest daughter in the 1960s. A profusion of peaks, pinnacles, tracery and turrets embellishes the exterior, which was constructed of limestone quarried by inmates at nearby Sing Sing Prison. Inside, dark-wooded Gothic gloom prevails, offset by Tiffany stained-glass windows and fixtures added by Gould. Faux treatments throughout the house, popular during the residency of George Merritt, culminate in the baronial dining room, where trompe l'oeil painting mimics the look of oak, marble and flocked wallpaper to imposing effect. Outside, a stroll or drive around the 67-acre wooded estate affords 360-degree views of the mansion on the bluff and glimpses of the river below. Northeast of the mansion stands the skeleton of the massive 1881 greenhouse, forlornly awaiting the day $3 million can be raised to replace its hand-cut glass panes.

★ **Philipsburg Manor** – *On Rte. 9 in Sleepy Hollow. Visit of house by guided tour (1hr) only, Mar–Oct Wed–Mon 10am–5pm. Nov–Dec Wed–Mon 10am–4pm. Closed Thanksgiving Day, Dec 25. $7. Combination tickets are available for 2 or 3 houses (Sunnyside, Philipsburg and Van Cortlandt).* 🍴 🄿 ☎914-631-3992. Philipsburg Manor conveys a sense of the manor system under which much of the Hudson River Valley was settled. At its zenith, the powerful Philipse family controlled 52,000 acres of land along the Hudson by royal charter. The Philipses erected a stone manor house by the Pocantico River to function largely as a business office and a gristmill to grind the grains that tenant farmers brought in as payment for their rent. Their mill formed the basis of the successful trading network and shipping empire that helped make them the richest family in the colonies. Today, a working mill has been reconstructed on the site (bags of flour are available for sale), and the house has been furnished with the help of a 1750 probate inventory. A barn and tenant farmhouse add to the ambience of the manor.

★★ **Kykuit** – *Tours begin from Philipsburg Manor Visitor Center. Visit by guided tour (2hrs) only, mid-Apr–Oct Wed–Mon 10am–4pm. $18. Reservations required (1 month in advance during summer months).* 🍴 ♿ 🄿 ☎914-631-9491. One of the last grand homes built in the Hudson River Valley, Kykuit (pronounced Kye-cut; the word is Dutch for "lookout"), offers a glimpse into the lives of four generations of Rockefellers. Built between 1906 and 1913 by **John D. Rockefeller, Jr.** for his father, patriarch of Standard Oil, the estate did not begin as the imposing Beaux-Arts edifice that stands today. Conceived in a modest, eclectic style with a steep slate roof and broad encircling porches to please the conservative Baptist sensibilities of its owner, the original home suffered from several shortcomings, leading to a major redesign that included the facade. The new plan better complemented the interior spaces designed by Ogden Codman, Jr., which represent fine examples of the Classical Revival style in the English country home tradition (note especially the decorative plasterwork). Today furnishings and room arrangements date to the residency of New York State governor **Nelson Rockefeller** and his wife, Happy, who succeeded Nelson's parents, Junior and Abby, in 1963. By then the house brimmed with antique furniture, lovely Chinese ceramics of the Han, Tang and Ming dynasties, an assortment of china services and, of course,

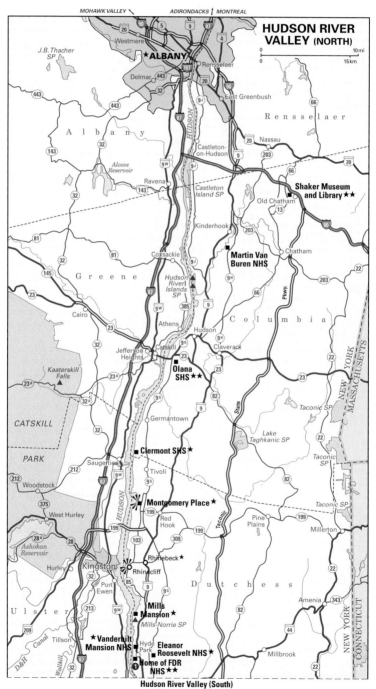

Nelson's burgeoning **modern art collection**★. He acquired his love of contemporary art—particularly sculpture—from his mother, Abby Aldrich Rockefeller, a founder of the Museum of Modern Art in New York. His basement art galleries contain many treasures, including one-of-a-kind tapestries created by Picasso. The **gardens**★ and terraces of Kykuit, designed in the orderly, Beaux-Arts fashion by William Welles Bosworth (who also redesigned the facade), take their inspiration from Italian hilltop gardens. Nelson's careful siting of more than 70 modern sculptures around the grounds only enhances the beauty of the landscaping. Spectacular **views**★ across the Hudson, particularly from the west porch, blend together with gardens and art into breathtaking vistas and painterly tableaux.

★ **Union Church of Pocantico Hills** – *555 Bedford Rd. in Sleepy Hollow. Open Apr–Dec Mon, Wed–Fri 11am–5pm, Sat 10am–5pm, Sun 2pm–5pm. Closed Thanksgiving Day, Dec 25 & during services. $3. Guided tours (45min) available.* & ▣ ☎914-332-6659. Built on Rockefeller land in 1921 to serve the family and other Protestant worshipers, this country stone church harbors sublime surprises, for its stained-glass windows were designed by modern masters Henri Matisse and Marc Chagall. Working from his studio in Nice, France, Matisse completed the church's rose window, dedicated to Abby Aldrich Rockefeller, just days before his death in 1954. Within the framework of an existing window, he arranged his familiar "cutout" forms, organic arabesques infused with pure color, each one a distinct shape. The Chagall windows (nine in all), by contrast, swirl with color, form, texture and light. Figures in Chagall's monumental **Good Samaritan window**★, completed in 1965 to honor John D. Rockefeller, Jr., float in a sea of intense blue. Layering, cutting, chemical engraving and a surface painting-and-etching technique called grisaille create gradations of color and texture that give the illusion of depth and movement. This is the only cycle of windows Chagall executed for an American church.

★ **Van Cortlandt Manor** – *Off Rte. 9 in Croton-on-Hudson. Visit of house by guided tour (1hr) only, Mar–Oct Wed–Mon 10am–5pm. Nov–Dec Wed–Mon 10am–4pm. Closed Thanksgiving Day, Dec 25. $7. Combination tickets are available for 2 or 3 houses (Sunnyside, Philipsburg and Van Cortlandt).* ▣ ☎914-271-8981. Another of the great Hudson Valley manors and home to the Van Cortlandt family for 260 years, the house has been restored to its appearance during the tenure of Pierre Van Cortlandt, patriot and first lieutenant governor of New York State who presided over 86,000 acres. Legend has it that such notable personalities as Benjamin Franklin, the Marquis de Lafayette, the Comte de Rochambeau and John Jay visited the manor.

The house contains original family furnishings, paintings and pewter. Don't miss the large kitchen replete with its original hearth, Dutch oven and cooking utensils. Located on the property, the ferry house, ferry house kitchen, fields and gardens evoke 18C life in the Hudson Valley.

John Jay Homestead State Historic Site – *On Rte. 22 between Katonah and Bedford Village. Visit by guided tour (45min) only, Apr–Oct Wed–Sat 10am–4pm, Sun noon–4pm. Rest of the year by appointment only. $3.* & ▣ ☎914-232-5651. A visit to this home makes a nice excursion into the wilds of Westchester County. Situated on a bluff overlooking the countryside, the modest Federal-style house actually comprises 60 rooms, having grown through successive occupation by four generations of the Jay family. Its first and most famous occupant, **John Jay** (1745-1829), took up permanent residence upon his retirement in 1801. His auspicious career included serving as president of the Continental Congress, as first chief justice under Washington and as governor of New York State. A leading Federalist, Jay believed in the authority of the central government and authored the Federalist Papers to help convince New Yorkers to ratify the Constitution. The land on which the homestead stands had been in the Jay family since 1703, and here Jay the gentleman farmer—a common role assumed by retired gentry of the era—indulged his interest in agriculture and horticulture. A self-guided walking tour of the 64-acre grounds passes outbuildings, orchards and gardens. The home itself is furnished in the Federal style.

Caramoor Center for Music and the Arts – *On Rte. 22 in Katonah. Visit by guided tour (45min) only, May–Oct Wed–Sun 1pm–4pm. Rest of the year by appointment only. $6.* & ▣ *www.caramoor.com* ☎914-232-5035. *Recitals offered in Music Room Apr–Nov Wed at 11am.* Home to metropolitan New York's largest outdoor summer music festival since 1945, this 117-acre wooded compound comprises three performance spaces as well as a fascinating house museum, all representing the legacy of Walter and Lucie Bigelow Rosen. The Rosens built the Mediterranean-style palazzo they called Caramoor between 1930 and 1939, and gave the estate over to music upon the death of their son in World War II. Avid patrons of the arts, they filled their country home with music, a salon of artists and celebrities and a remarkable collection of art and antiques. The eclectic profusion of sculpture, tapestries, stained glass, furniture and pottery that crowds the rooms and corridors of the rectangular stucco villa includes a stunning 40-panel Chinese jade screen of incredible translucency, and a wooden bed carved—in legend at least—for Pope Urban VIII. The Rosens dismantled entire rooms from locations around Europe, reinstalling them at Caramoor. At the heart of the home, the Music Room, a vast space crowned with a 16C coffered ceiling and equipped with a stage at one end, overflows with Renaissance artifacts, many acquired from the fund-raising sales of ill-fated Italian nobles.

Boscobel

★★ **Boscobel** – *On Rte. 9D in Garrison-on-Hudson, 4mi north of junction with Rte. 403. Visit of house by guided tour (1hr) only, Apr–Oct Mon, Wed–Sun 10am–4:15pm. Mar, Nov–Dec Mon, Wed–Sun 9:30am–3:15pm. Closed Thanksgiving Day. $6.* 🅿 ☎914-265-3638. Fastidiously appointed and furnished, this crisply elegant restoration embodies the essence of American Federal architecture, interior design and furniture. Originally built 15mi to the south by States Morris Dyckman in 1804, the house, on the verge of demolition, was purchased in 1955 with the help of philanthropist Lila Acheson Wallace and moved to this lovely Hudson River overlook surrounded by fragrant gardens and orchards. Federal architecture represents one form of the "antique taste" made popular in the 18C by archaeological study of the ancient world. More properly called the Adam style after its leading English proponent, Robert Adam, it presents a light and delicate aspect. Indoors and out, note Boscobel's slight columns, narrow windows and dainty, shallow ornament. In the same spirit, restrained and slender furniture of the period features reeding, inlay, eglomise (reverse painting on glass), veneer and flat carving. Decorative motifs include classical urns and swags, but Americans proudly added eagles and other symbols of the new Republic. Boscobel's magnificent entry hall sets the tone for the rest of the house: its freestanding staircase framed by a lovely archway, the wallpaper a reproduction of an 1804 design, the floor cloth painted in an 18C pattern. Bathed in the unexpectedly bright colors of the era, each room is appointed in detail, many with works by virtuoso furniture maker Duncan Phyfe. While some items are original to the house, most have been carefully selected to suit the period.

Of all the quaint towns that trim the Hudson's eastern edge, none may be so delightfully situated as **Cold Spring**★ *(just north of Boscobel on Rte. 9).* At the heart of the Highlands, it expertly combines the elements that give these towns their charm: antique shops, bed-and-breakfast inns, fine dining, historical interest and lovely vistas of the river. From Cold Spring the view includes the sweep from West Point north to Storm King. The town grew up around the West Point Foundry, created in 1817 to manufacture armaments from the local iron ore. The Chapel of Our Lady, which has overlooked the river since it was built for the ironworkers in the 1830s, is a favorite landmark of the region.

The Samuel F.B. Morse Historic Site (Locust Grove) – *370 South Rd. (Rte. 9) in Poughkeepsie. Visit of home by guided tour (1hr) only Mar–Dec daily 10am–4pm. Closed Thanksgiving Day, Dec 25. $5. 24-hour advance reservations required for spring & winter tours.* P ☎*914-454-4500.* Once owned by Renaissance man **Samuel F.B. Morse** (1791-1872), the house and nature trails at Locust Grove still provide a welcome retreat from the whine of busy Route 9. A painter who invented or an inventor who painted, Morse was a man of diverse accomplishment. A Yale graduate, he studied as a history painter in Europe and returned to the US in 1815 to make a meager living in portraiture. In 1826 he founded the National Academy of Design, and later he held prominent posts at New York University. In a short burst of political activity, he aligned himself with nativists and ran for mayor of New York City in 1836. Telegraphy soon intrigued him, however, and by 1844 he had inaugurated modern, instantaneous communication with the first successful telegraph. Morse owned the Poughkeepsie house from 1847 until his death, shaping it with the help of Alexander Jackson Davis into the picturesque Tuscan villa that stands today. Although the house also contains the extensive collections of subsequent owners, Morse's presence is evident in his landscape design as well as the paintings, family artifacts and telegraph equipment that are on display.

★★ **Home of Franklin D. Roosevelt National Historic Site (Springwood)** – *On Rte. 9 in Hyde Park. Open mid-May–Oct daily 9am–5pm. Rest of the year Thu–Mon 9am–5pm. Closed Jan 1, Thanksgiving Day, Dec 25. $2. Guided tours (45min) available.* P ☎*914-229-2414.* Backdrop for much of Franklin Delano Roosevelt's life, Springwood offers an exceedingly personal glimpse into the "transformation of a charming New York socialite into one of America's great statesmen." Born in the house in 1882, Roosevelt took his bride, Eleanor, to Springwood in 1905 and launched his political career from there, entering New York State government as a senator from Dutchess County in 1910. He enlarged the house over the years, designing the fieldstone wings that flank it today. Stricken with polio in 1921, FDR convalesced at Springwood, and with considerable support from Eleanor, he became governor of New York in 1928. Springwood bustled with political and campaign activity leading up to Roosevelt's first election as president in 1932. During four terms as president, Roosevelt visited Springwood 200 times, conducting political business, entertaining and relaxing. His last visit came two weeks before his death in Warm Springs, Georgia, on April 12, 1945; he is buried beside Eleanor in the rose garden. Today the Roosevelt presence remains palpable: well-used furniture of faded Victorian elegance fills the home; the bed in which FDR was born still occupies his mother's upstairs bedroom; his naval cape hangs in a closet; the chair favored by Roosevelt's beloved Scottie, Fala, still stands by his master's bed. A lover of trees, FDR planted nearly a half-million on the 1,200-acre property between 1911 and 1945. Also on the property is the FDR Library and Museum, designed by President Roosevelt in 1940 to house his papers, mementos and extensive collection of naval history books. A quiet office there served him throughout the war years. Thorough exhibits cover FDR's childhood and family life, his formative

1 Culinary Institute of America

Map p 79. 433 Albany Post Rd., Hyde Park, ☎*914-471-6608. Reservations required.* Under the single roof of a former Jesuit seminary reside the four restaurants of the Culinary Institute. Here, 2,000 chefs-in-training gain practical experience in preparation, cooking and serving under the watchful tutelage of 90 masters. Each of the restaurants offers a different—and excellent—dining experience: the food and atmosphere are outstanding, and the students friendly and earnest. St. Andrew's Cafe serves a range of nutritional and healthy meals; American Bounty features local ingredients; the formal and elegant Escoffier will please the Francophile; and Caterina de Medici serves trattoria fare at two evening seatings.

years, his battle with polio and his political career, and one traces the life and work of Eleanor Roosevelt as she grew from a shy and dependent young wife into a self-confident, influential and determined woman.

★ **Eleanor Roosevelt National Historic Site** – *On Rte. 9G in Hyde Park. Visit by guided tour (45min) only, mid-May–Oct daily 9am–5pm. Nov–Dec & Mar–mid-May weekends 9am–5pm. Closed Jan 1, Thanksgiving Day, Dec 25.* ▯ ☎914-229-9422. Even though **Eleanor Roosevelt** (1884-1962) was both born and married into the Roosevelt clan, a distant cousin of Franklin and niece of President Teddy Roosevelt, she never felt entirely comfortable at Springwood. The ancestral home was truly the domain of Franklin's mother, Sara, so FDR built a stone cottage for Eleanor in 1925 at a favorite family picnic spot on the estate. The timing coincided with Eleanor's transition from domestic to public life, as she stepped up to become politician Franklin's legs and voice during his battle with polio, overcoming in the process her own timidity in public. Named for the stream that flowed close by, Val-Kill remained her retreat until her death in 1962. Here, with friends and political associates Nancy Cook and Marion Dickerman (who lived in the original stone cottage until 1947), she built Val-Kill Industries, employing local workers in making furniture and decorative items for 10 years. When the little factory closed in 1936, Eleanor converted it into a home for herself. After FDR's death in 1945, she took up permanent residence there, continuing her long career as "First Lady of the World." Her unflinching devotion to the cause of human rights culminated in her overseeing the adoption of the UN's Declaration of Human Rights in 1948.

The tour begins in the playhouse with a video about Eleanor's life and proceeds into Val-Kill Cottage, cozily and simply furnished and blanketed with photographs of the people she "collected." Silver candlesticks in the dining room—which was usually crowded with family and friends during her lifetime—seem the only reminder of her connection with Hudson River Valley aristocracy.

★ **Vanderbilt Mansion National Historic Site** – *On Rte. 9 in Hyde Park. Open mid-May–Oct daily 9am–5pm. Rest of the year Thu–Mon 9am–5pm. Closed Jan 1, Thanksgiving Day, Dec 25. $2. Guided tours available.* ▯ ☎914-229-7770. It seems surprising that Franklin Roosevelt was largely responsible for convincing his neighbor, Vanderbilt heir Margaret Van Alen, to deed her uncle's opulent estate to the National Park Service (as he had Springwood), for no two properties could be less alike. Built by Frederick (grandson of "Commodore" Cornelius Vanderbilt) and Louise Vanderbilt in 1898 for fall and spring entertaining, this mansion epitomizes the extravagance of the Gilded Age nouveau riche. Although modest by Vanderbilt standards, the 50-room Beaux-Arts edifice designed by McKim, Mead and White overflows with art and furniture befitting America's self-styled "nobility" and ranging from Renaissance to Rococo in style. The coup de grâce is perhaps Louise's Louis XV bedroom, designed by noted arbiter of Gilded Age style Ogden Codman, who advocated historical veracity in every detail. Of the original 600-acre estate, 211 acres now make up the historic site. Their cultivation reached a peak in the 1820s when landscape architect Andre Parmentier created the park-like setting that exists today. Especially nice are the formal gardens, a short walk south of the mansion.

★ **Mills Mansion** – *Off Rte. 9 on Old Post Rd. in Staatsburgh. Visit by guided tour (45min) only, mid-Apr–Labor Day Wed–Sat 10am–4:30pm, Sun noon–4:30pm. After Labor Day–Oct Wed–Sun noon–4:30pm. In Dec call for hours. Open most Monday holidays. $3.* ▯ ☎914-889-8851. From the outside, this 79-room Beaux-Arts mansion appears somewhat dilapidated; indeed the state is working to remove the ugly gunite sealant sprayed on the exterior in the 1940s to halt its deterioration. Interior spaces, however, belie its weathered facade. Built on land that had been in **Ruth Livingston Mills'** family since 1792, the current mansion engulfs a Greek Revival home constructed in 1832. Improvements were made by Ogden and Ruth Mills, who inherited the property in 1890 and selected architects McKim, Mead and White to transform the home into a "palace royale" for autumn and winter entertaining. They added the two side wings along with decorative embellishments popular at the time. Part English baronial hall (note the heavily wooded entryway), part French palace (the Louis XVI **dining room★** rivals any in the Hudson River Valley for its scale, luster and view), the home boasts 14 bathrooms and other accommodations, indoors and out, for weekend visitors. Indeed, its lavish public and guest areas overwhelm the private family rooms, re-emphasizing the mansion's primary purpose. Mrs. Mills' furnishings remain in situ, and her personal touches demonstrate pride in her Colonial and Revolutionary War heritage as a descendant of the Livingston family. She considered herself heiress, as well, to Mrs. Astor as queen of American society. Outside, the expansive western lawn sweeps down to the Hudson's edge, and trails access Mills-Norrie State Park.

Just north of Staatsburgh, the charming village of **Rhinebeck**★ was named by German settlers in 1713 who pined for their own lovely river. The town grew to service the 19C millionaires who built homes in its environs and installed a railroad station at Rhinecliff for easy access. Rhinebeck is an architectural delight that includes the gingerbread **Delameter House** (1844, Alexander Jackson Davis), which offers lovely accommodations and is operated by the Beekman Arms just down the street. Just outside of Rhinebeck, County Routes 85 and 103 connect some of the region's most beautiful homes and properties—many of them country retreats of the Livingston and Beekman families—dating from the 18C and 19C. Located directly across from Rondout Lighthouse in Kingston, **Rhinecliff** affords panoramic **views**★ of the river.

★ **Montgomery Place** – *Off Rte. 9G on Annandale Rd. in Annandale-on-Hudson. Visit of home by guided tour (1hr) only, Apr–Oct Wed–Mon 10am–5pm. Nov–Dec weekends 10am–4pm. Closed major holidays.* 🄿 *www.hudsonvalley.org* ☎914-758-5461. Much of the early history of the eastern side of the Hudson River Valley entwines with the lives of a handful of families who, by various means, established spreading manors from Albany to New York City. When the first lord of Livingston Manor, Robert, surveyed his lands in 1715, he counted some 160,240 acres. Over the ensuing years, relatives and descendants of his prolific family came to build many of the great houses along this stretch of the Hudson. Janet Livingston Montgomery, of Montgomery Place, was great-grandaunt to Ruth Livingston Mills, of Mills Mansion *(p 83)* to the south, and sister of Chancellor Robert Livingston, Jr., of Clermont *(below)* to the north. Janet Livingston married Gen. Richard Montgomery, who fell two years later at the Battle of Quebec in 1775. She went on, in 1802, to construct a Federal-style home, which she called Chateau Montgomery, farm the land and run a successful seed business. After her death in 1828, the property passed among relatives, remodeled along the way by Alexander Jackson Davis into the current Classical Revival edifice. Historic Hudson Valley acquired the estate in 1986. Much of the success of this restoration revolves around the priceless collection of furnishings, family possessions and even samples of the original wallpapers that stayed with the house. A tremendous archive of family papers—75,000 in all—documents the home and the family. Most of the interiors in the house today are furnished in the pre-Civil War Empire style, a heavy Neoclassicism originating in Napoleonic France. The pleasant stroll from the visitor center through the 434-acre grounds and gardens affords splendid **views** of the Hudson and the Catskills.

> **The Beekman Arms**
>
> *4 Mill St., Rhinebeck,* ☎914-876-7077. "The oldest inn in America" actually comprises a complex of 10 lodgings at the heart of historic Rhinebeck. The Arms itself began as the small stone house of William Traphagen around 1700, growing over the years to accommodate travelers along the old King's Highway (Route 9). George Washington, Benedict Arnold and Aaron Burr visited the inn, and today their presence still lingers around the old stone hearth. The Beekman 1766 Tavern includes two indoor tap and dining areas little changed in 200 years, as well as an airy greenhouse space, where sophisticated repasts are prepared using regional ingredients.

★ **Clermont State Historic Site** – *On Rte. 9G in Germantown. Visit of house by guided tour (45min) only, Apr–Oct Tue–Sun 11am–4pm (Mon holidays 10am–5pm). Nov–Dec weekends 11am–4pm. Grounds open year-round daily 8am–sunset. $3 (grounds free).* ♿ 🄿 ☎518-537-4240. The oldest of the standing Hudson River mansions, Clermont pays tribute to the rich history of one of the valley's most influential families. Constructed in 1730, the simple Georgian home is furnished with the family treasures of seven generations of Livingstons. Robert R. ("Chancellor") Livingston, Jr. may be the most famous of the family. In addition to helping draft the Declaration of Independence, he developed, with Robert Fulton, the first practical steamboat. In 1807, the *Clermont* made its maiden voyage up the Hudson from New York City to Albany in 32 hours, with a stop, of course, at the estate's docks. It was the Chancellor's mother, Margaret Beekman, however, who managed Clermont through the Revolution and rebuilt the mansion after the British burned it in 1777. Today its 485 lush and lovely acres include vestiges of early plantings, but the formal gardens were added in the 20C. Unlike its sister estates, Clermont perches near the edge of the river, its unimpeded view of the Catskills inspiring its French name, "Clear Mountain."

Olana

★★ Olana State Historic Site – *On Rte. 9G in Hudson. Visit of home by guided tour (1hr) only, Apr–Oct Wed–Sun 10am–4pm. Closed major holidays. $3. Reservations suggested. Grounds open year-round daily 8am–sunset.* ⅁ 🅿 ☎*518-828-0135.* Of all the great Hudson River Valley homes, Olana most resembles Sunnyside, at least in spirit. Both picturesque settings took flight from the artistic imaginations of their well-traveled builders. Hudson River school painter **Frederic Edwin Church** (1826-1900) began construction atop this commanding hillside in 1870. With the help of architect Calvert Vaux, Olana took shape over the next several years, a blend of Islamic motifs Church and his wife, Isabel, had admired on a recent tour of the Middle East. Such exoticism evidently appealed to his Romantic inclinations, for he created, decorated and furnished Olana as if it had been one of his great paintings. His love, however, was landscape, and he found the Olana "viewshed" unparalleled. Indeed, the panorama to the southwest extends 60mi down the Hudson and takes in a great sweep of the Catskill Mountains. Church carefully developed the surrounding 250 acres, using the grounds as his canvas to contrive vistas and scenes and make "more and better landscapes" than he could in his studio. Carriage roads that climb the 500ft to the house pass from one scenic vignette to another. Inside the Persian "castle," walls glow with colors that Church mixed himself, a lush palette of ochres, brick reds, purples and moss greens, accented with stencils he applied. Everywhere, Eastern ornamentation adds atmosphere— from cusped Moorish arches to interlocking line designs. Such detailing took four years to complete. Most wonderful are the scores of Church's **paintings** hung in room after room, some rarely seen beyond Olana, and many in frames he designed. A disciple of Thomas Cole, Church executed his best-known works in the 1850s and 60s, devoting much of his later life to his living landscape masterpiece at Olana.

Martin Van Buren National Historic Site – *Rte. 9H (Old Post Rd.), 2mi south of Kinderhook. Visit by guided tour (40min) only, mid-May–Oct daily 9am–4pm. Nov– early Dec Wed–Sun 9am–4pm. $2.* 🅿 *www.nps.gov/mava* ☎*518-758-9689.* **Martin Van Buren** (1782-1862) bought Lindenwald while serving as eighth president of the US in 1839. A native son of Kinderhook, he had gained a reputation in local politics as competent, levelheaded and assertive. An architect of the two-party system, he served as vice president under Andrew Jackson, succeeding him as president. His greatest accomplishment of office was the establishment of an independent treasury, but a bad depression early on undid him when he refused to allow the government to provide public aid. Van Buren ran unsuccessfully for president again in 1840 and 1848, then finally pursued in earnest the life of a gentleman farmer on his 220 acres at Lindenwald. The 18-room home, built in the Federal style in 1797 and remodeled extensively into an Italianate villa in 1850, reveals the aristocratic and masculine tastes of a widower of more than 20 years. Lindenwald is sparsely furnished in the Empire style; note in particular the hand-painted French wallpaper that was removed, restored and rehung in the main hall. Van Buren died in his bedroom here in 1862, undoubtedly saddened by the dissolution of the union he had worked to strengthen.

■ Painters and Poets in an American Paradise

A young painter named Thomas Cole first cast his artist's eye over the Catskills' rocky cloves and the Hudson's towering highlands in 1825. Returning to his studio in New York, he proceeded to paint the craggy, luminescent wilderness he had observed. In so doing, he launched a new style of painting that would come to be called the Hudson River school. Asher B. Durand, John Kensett, Frederic Church and others joined Cole over the years, exulting in the wonder of river wild and forest primeval. Painting the natural chaos of a boulder-strewn mountainside or a tumbling waterfall, they attempted to capture the power of nature's unpredictability. Between 1825 and 1875 they produced hundreds of canvasses of favorite vistas, including Storm King, Kaaterskill Falls and the view from West Point, revealing to the world both the beauty of the American landscape and the talent of American artists.

Similar intent stirred a new literary genre. At its heart, Washington Irving, William Cullen Bryant and James Fenimore Cooper sketched prose and poetic portraits of the region. Inspired by Dutch lore, Revolutionary War history and the evocative scenery of the Catskills and the Hudson, their work constituted an indigenous American literature imbued with the spirit of both landscape and people. These writers shared a friendship with their painting contemporaries, and between them, they cast the spell of beauty and mystery that envelops the region today.

★★ **Shaker Museum and Library** – *Shaker Museum Rd., Old Chatham. Open May–Oct Wed–Mon 10am–5pm. Call for off-season & holidays hours. $6.* ▣ *www.shaker museummoldchat.org* ☎*518-794-9100.* Unlike nearby Mount Lebanon, site of the original Shaker settlement in the US—the Shaker Museum is not a historic village, but rather a collection of representative buildings that house the largest collection of Shaker-made tools, furniture and textiles in existence. After the Victorian excesses of the grand Hudson Valley homes, Shaker simplicity comes as a gift. Brought to America in 1774 from Britain by Mother Ann Lee, Shaker

Shaker Museum

ways sprang from a belief in the imminent second coming of Christ. Celibacy, communal living, temperance and separation but equality between the sexes defined Shaker life. Relying on conversion and adoption to supplement its numbers, the sect—at its peak in 1830—included nearly 6,000 followers living in 20 colonies. Although only a handful of Shakers remains today, the group is among the longest-lived of America's utopian communities. Governed by quietude and simplicity, the Shakers were nonetheless an industrious group who embraced utility, crafting and inventing fine tools and furniture for their own use as well as for sale in "the World." Indeed, the Shaker name has become synonymous with fine workmanship and an elegant plainness of style.

The museum's vast collection comprises more than 18,000 objects, including the largest selection of Shaker **textiles** anywhere. In the orientation gallery, a fine selection of furniture "masterpieces" dating from the early 19C demonstrates well the lean lines and crisp geometry that characterize Shaker chairs, trestle tables, boxes and cupboards. Although largely without ornament, each piece displays an elemental beauty through the use of color and finish. Twenty other galleries throughout the complex feature stoves, kitchenware, tools and machines that reveal the surprising variety and richness of Shaker life. Also on the grounds, the library *(visit by appointment only)* houses more than 19,000 archival documents detailing Shaker life.

★ **Albany** – *Description p 92.*

WEST BANK *2 days. Map p 75.*

Stony Point Battlefield – *Park Rd., off Rte 9W. Open mid-Apr–Oct Wed–Sat 10am–5pm, Sun 1pm–5pm. Closed Memorial Day, Jul 4 & Labor Day. Guided tours available.* ⬤ 🄿 ☎914-786-2521. The British wrested this rocky, strategic promontory from the Americans in 1779, thereby gaining control of the entrance to the Hudson Highlands and safeguarding the Kings Ferry, which connected the east and west banks at this narrow stretch of river. Itching to retrieve it for the colonists, Gen. "Mad" Anthony Wayne mounted a surprise attack on the point in July of that year, fording the marshes below at midnight and overcoming the British in less than an hour. The battle proved to be the last in the north and a tremendous morale-builder for Continental troops. Now a state historic site, this rugged, windswept terrain is studded with interpretive signs that describe the fighting and with picnic spots that afford fine views over the Hudson. In the **museum** *(closes at 4:30pm)*, exhibits and a 12min video detail the battle. The oldest lighthouse *(open weekends 2pm–4:15pm)* on the Hudson River, built in 1826 on the site of the central powder magazine, has been restored to working order with a period Fresnel lens .

Bear Mountain State Park – *On Rte. 9W. Open year-round daily 8am–sunset.* ✗ ⬤ 🄿 *($4)* ☎914-786-2701. Rising 1,305ft from the heart of an enchanted landscape on the west bank of the Hudson, Bear Mountain is surrounded by Dunderberg ("Thunder Hill") just south and Anthony's Nose across the river. Below, at the Hudson's narrowest point, the river twists and turns at its most treacherous; its unpredictable currents, eddies and winds were the bane of early navigators. Here legend holds that the little Dutch Dunderberg Imp conjures up thunder and storms to thwart the sailors who brave this passage. The hazards continue north to Storm King, where the river widens and settles down. This strategic stretch saw considerable activity during the Revolution when forts Clinton and Montgomery occupied the bluffs and Americans stretched a great chain from bank to bank to stop the British navy. Bear Mountain State Park and the adjacent Harriman State Park were established in 1910 through the generosity of Mr. and Mrs. Edward Harriman in the face of quarrying, deforestation and even an effort by the state to relocate Sing Sing prison on the mountain. The lovely lodge, a grand example of the rustic style popular in the Adirondacks, remains today a Bear Mountain landmark. East of the lodge, across Route 9W, are the **Trailside Museums and Wildlife Center** *(open year-round daily 9am–4:30pm; $1;* ⬤*).* The wildlife center offers a refuge for sick and injured animals and its trails include the oldest section (1923) of the Appalachian Trail. Housed in stone buildings constructed in the 1930s, the trailside museums explain local geology, wildlife and history. Also along the way lie the scant remains of the outer redoubt of Ft. Clinton, which fell in pitched battle to the British in 1777. Don't miss the river **overlook** near the historical museum in the shadow of Bear Mountain Bridge.

★★ **West Point** – *On Rte. 218 South. Guided tours (1hr) depart every 30min from the visitor information center Apr–Oct Mon–Sat & holidays 10am–3:30pm, Sun 11am–3:30pm. Rest of the year (weather permitting) at 11:15am & 1:15pm. No tours Jan 1, Thanksgiving Day, Dec 25. $5. 2hr tour ($7) offered Apr–Oct at 11:15am & 1:15pm. West Point Tours, Inc.* ☎914-446-4724. Overlooking the Hudson River, West Point is renowned as the site of the United States Military Academy and the nation's oldest continually occupied military post. Fortress West Point was established in 1778 as a series of fortifications to protect the strategically important Hudson at its most defensible location. After the war, the grounds became a repository for trophies and captured equipment. It was not until 1802 that the US Military Academy, the oldest of the nation's service academies, was established by Congress, and West Point selected as its site. In the academy's first year, five officers trained and instructed the ten students; there are now more than 4,200 men and women cadets. Among its graduates, West Point counts Generals MacArthur (1903), Patton (1909), Eisenhower (1915) and Schwartzkopf (1956). Artist James MacNeill Whistler attended the academy in the 1850s.

Battle Monument, West Point

Visit – *2hrs*. West Point offers layers of history to peel away at leisure, beginning in the **visitor information center**, where films and exhibits introduce its sights and the life of a cadet *(open year-round daily 9am–4:45pm; closed Jan 1, Thanksgiving Day, Dec 25;* ✗ ᪲ 🅿 ☎914-938-2638). The chapels, monuments and museum are open to the public and include the 1910 **Cadet Chapel**, austerely "military Gothic" in style and hung with threadbare battle flags *(open year-round Mon–Sat & holidays 9am–4:15pm, Sun 1pm–4:15pm;* ᪲ 🅿 ☎914-938-4106). The busy and colorful stained-glass windows seem determined to keep light out but are nonetheless impressive in their precise and tiny detail. The Greek Revival Old Cadet Chapel built in 1837 seems sedate by contrast; Doric columns are its most elaborate decoration. Among the bronze plaques memorializing Revolutionary and Mexican War combatants, the treasonous name of Benedict Arnold, the commanding general at West Point who conspired to betray the fortifications in 1780, has been eradicated.

An ascent to **Fort Putnam**★ *(open late May–mid-Nov Mon & Thu 11am–3pm;* 🅿 ☎914-938-3590) is well worthwhile, for this was truly the strategic heart of historic Fortress West Point, with its commanding views 500ft above the river. Within its reconstructed walls, the small McLean Museum offers a concise narrated history of the strategics of the region and fascinating exhibits about the archaeology of the fort. The **Battle Monument** commemorates victims of the Civil War. Farther east, **Trophy Point**★ is laid out in sections relating to America's wars, displaying captured ordnance from each. Among the relics are links from the great chain that spanned the Hudson during the Revolution to impede the progress of British vessels.

The military **museum★★** *(open year-round daily 10:30am–4:15pm; closed Jan 1, Thanksgiving Day, Dec 25; ♿ ☎914-938-3590),* housed in a wing of the former indoor riding ring (Thayer Hall), thoroughly examines the history of warfare, the military, the academy and weapons using dioramas, print materials and hundreds of artifacts, including Napoleon's sword and Goering's jewel-encrusted marshal's baton. Its collection of arms, which traces the development of automatic weapons from the Civil War to the present, began with ordnance captured at the Battle of Saratoga in 1777. Three floors of well-conceived exhibits are densely informative; the interested visitor could spend all day here.

Even though Route 218, the Old Storm King Highway, cuts an ugly scar around the face of Storm King Mountain, it affords magnificent river **views★★** between Cornwall-on-Hudson and West Point.

★ **Storm King Art Center** – *Off Rte. 9W on Old Pleasant Hill Rd. in Mountainville. Sculpture Park open Apr–mid-Nov daily 11am–5:30pm. Indoor exhibits open mid-May–mid-Nov daily 11am–5:30pm. $7. ✗ ♿ 🅿 ☎914-534-3190.* Consider this tranquil 500 acres in the tradition of the 19C Romantic landscape, even though its vistas and picturesque elements are planned around a stunning collection of modern sculpture that includes work by Alexander Calder, Mark di Suvero, Henry Moore, Louise Nevelson, Isamu Noguchi and David Smith.

Begin your visit at the Normandy-style museum building (1935)—once a private residence—to view exhibits of paintings, graphics and smaller sculptures featured in the center's collection. Meadows, hillsides, forests and lawns spread out around the hilltop building, and it is possible to see many of the more than 125 works on the grounds from here. The grove to the west of the building is particularly lovely; smaller works cluster among the greenery, while monumental constructions dominate the fields below. Set off in any direction from here; much of the fun of this site is to encounter these pieces in the context of the landscape, viewing them from all sides and elevations, in different lights and from various angles. Founded in the early 1970s, the art center is a work in progress, changing with the seasons, continued landscaping and new works.

★ **New Windsor Cantonment State Historic Site** – *On Rte. 300 in Vails Gate. Open mid-Apr–Oct Wed–Sat & holidays 10am–5pm, Sun 1pm–5pm. $3 (allows free admission to Washington's Headquarters p 90). 🅿 ☎914-561-1765.* Stroll around the grounds for a while and feel the presence of 7,000 war-weary men hunkered down in 600 huts for the final winter encampment, or "cantonment," of the Revolutionary War in 1782-83. Fortunately, this was not a winter like those at VALLEY FORGE and Morristown, and the climactic battle at Yorktown had been won. But as peace negotiations in Paris dragged on, soldiers chafed to return home and officers wanted long-standing issues of pensions, back pay and land bounties settled before the war's end. Gen. George Washington—headquartered in Newburgh 6mi north—addressed the disgruntled officers in the cantonment's Temple Building. Appealing to their patriotism, he successfully countered a possible rebellion, and a month later the war ended. Begin in the visitor center with a 20min video on the final months of the Revolution. Outside in the "living history" area, buildings and displays reflect routines at the cantonment; one particularly good exhibit describes life for the soldiers here. Don't miss the 18C "Mountainville Hut," which may actually date to the encampment at New Windsor. Camp-life and musket demonstrations round out your visit.

2 Mohonk Mountain House

Map p 75. Lake Mohonk, New Paltz, ☎914-255-1000. Deep in the Shawangunk Mountains at the edge of Lake Mohonk, this magnificent resort (1869) combines the elegance of a Victorian hotel with the stunning beauty of its natural surroundings. Surrounded by 20,100 acres of park and preserve land, as well as meticulously tended lawns and gardens, the Mountain House offers year-round activities from cross-country skiing and hiking to horseback riding and fishing. On the grounds, the 1888 Barn Museum displays historic vehicles and implements and offers blacksmithing demonstrations. Inside the seven-story, 275-room hotel, lush wood-trimmed Victorian interiors, original period furnishings and cozy fireplaces ensconce visitors in an atmosphere of 19C luxury. Day visitors are welcome to enjoy, for a fee, many of the resort's activities.

★ **Washington's Headquarters State Historic Site** – *Corner of Washington and Liberty Sts. in Newburgh. Visit by guided tour (1hr) only, mid-Apr–late Oct Wed–Sat 10am–5pm, Sun 1pm–5pm. Rest of the year by appointment only. Closed major holidays. $3.* ▣ ☎*914-562-1195.* Although "Washington's Headquarters" abound throughout the Northeast, the Hasbrouck House is of particular importance as the one he occupied for the longest period of time during the Revolution. Even with peace imminent, Washington did not trust the British and chose to watch the river from this vantage point 12mi north of West Point. Washington's Headquarters is also the first publicly operated historic site in the country, acquired by the state of New York in 1850. It represents, in a sense, the end of the Revolution as war and the beginning of the Revolution as history. Initial public interest in Hasbrouck House, in fact, inspired the first round of Colonial Revivalism in the years prior to the nation's centennial. Tours begin in the museum building, which presents excellent exhibits on the Continental Army, the defense of the Hudson River and the importance of Hasbrouck House to the collective American memory. The simple Dutch farmhouse-headquarters has been furnished to reflect the activities of Washington and his large retinue of aides and visitors, which included his wife, Martha.

★ **Huguenot Street National Historic Landmark District** – *In New Paltz. Guided tours (1hr 30min & 2hr 30min) of the neighborhood available from the Huguenot Historical Society May–Oct Wed–Sun 9am–4pm. $4 & $7.* ▣ ☎*914-255-1889.* Little changed since the 18C, the charming character of this neighborhood befits its status as the "oldest street in America with its original houses." Twelve Huguenot families—Protestants fleeing religious persecution in Catholic France—began building here in 1692, and Huguenot Street today comprises the historic heart of New Paltz, still home to many descendants of the original pioneers. Six stone houses stand (one remodeled in the Queen Anne style in 1890) along with the reconstructed French Huguenot Church, originally erected in 1717. A host of Huguenots, including the original patentees, lies buried in its mossy churchyard. Navigate your own way around the neighborhood or arrange a tour with the **Huguenot Historical Society** *(6 Broadhead Ave.)*, which also offers excursions to the 1738 Terwilliger House and the 1814 Josiah Hasbrouck House (Locust Lawn) on adjoining lots 4mi south of town.

Central New York

Farm near Cooperstown – © Pete Souza

This triangular territory radiates west from Albany, covering 7,000sq mi between Highways 88 and 90 and anchored by Utica/Rome and Binghamton at its westernmost corners. Seeping into the CATSKILL MOUNTAINS to the south, outlined by the Mohawk Valley along its northern periphery and abutting the FINGER LAKES to the west, Central New York is a bucolic region of family farms and picturesque villages. Indeed, the region abounds in town names ending in "Corners" and "Crossings"—a testament to the area's rural character. Here dairy herds, apple cider, maple sugar and history provide local livelihoods.

For all its modern serenity, however, Central New York served over the years as a stage for dramas of war and nation building. In the 17C, the powerful Mohawk tribe of the Iroquois Confederacy *(p 92)* dominated these strategic lands, declaring war on various neighboring tribes. Their "castles," well-fortified enclaves of longhouses, surmounted the rolling hillsides. As the French and English inserted themselves into the complicated tangle of Indian loyalties and disputes, the landscape echoed with the reverberations of European wars, culminating with the French and Indian War in the 1750s and 60s. Central New York then formed the frontier between French and British claims to North America, but by 1763 the British and Iroquois had driven the French and Hurons out, securing for themselves rich fur-trading networks, fertile farmlands and the best water route west through the Appalachians. Almost a century later, in the 1820s, author James Fenimore Cooper would conjure up the romantic vision of this period, populating his novels with frontiersmen and Indians. Cooper's novel *The Last of the Mohicans* became the most popular book of 1826, and its famous hero, Natty Bumppo—alias Leatherstocking—bequeathed his nickname to the region. Tories, Patriots and Iroquois fought fiercely over Central New York, the northern theater of war during the Revolution. After peace resumed, the floodgates of migration opened as Yankee farmers left the rocky fields of New England in search of better soil, opening an era of rabid speculation and settlement. In an age of Republican zeal, town names and architecture inspired by the classical order proliferated; temple-like Greek Revival homes, manufactories and public buildings cropped up in small towns with names like Rome and Ilion. Improving transportation along the Mohawk River increased the portability of crops produced in the interior, and so thrived both farms and factories throughout the region. Today river industry and valley agriculture still carry on, weathered by the exigencies of depression and recession and greatly diversified. Each year, tourism contributes more to the economy, reviving and renewing interest in sites long forgotten. In addition, more than a dozen state parks offer camping, picnicking, hiking, canoeing and fishing, as well as winter sports.

ALBANY★

Population 103,564
Map p 7
Tourist Information ☎518-434-1217 or 800-732-8259

Albany's low-slung skyline hugs the Hudson River's edge, punctuated by the sleek towers of the Empire State Plaza and the Gothic spires of the D & H Railway Building (now part of the State University of New York). A small city best known as the capital of New York, Albany is the gateway to the Saratoga region north and the Mohawk Valley west. Since the early 19C, Albany has been at the heart of the state's waterway system, which today comprises 524mi of canals along which you can cruise, bike or drive.

Historical Notes – Geography is largely responsible for the region's development. Since Henry Hudson sailed the *Half Moon* this far in 1609, the area has marked the head of tidal navigation on the Hudson River. What began as a Dutch fur-trading post in 1614 grew into both an important outpost—called Beverwyck—of the Dutch West India Company and the seat of the powerful Van Rensselaer patroonship *(p 76)*. When the English took over in 1664, they christened the settlement Albany, and the city was chartered in 1686. The blending of British and Dutch influences that began in this period can be felt in Albany to the present day.

During the American Revolution, the city served as a staging area for American military maneuvers and quickly blossomed. As the gateway to Western New York, the city supplied Yankee pioneers moving to rich forests and farmlands. By 1797 Albany became the state capital. From here, settlers turned west up the Mohawk and, by 1825, along the Erie Canal to the Great Lakes. At this crucial point between the Atlantic and the West, Albany grew into a busy inland seaport surrounded by industries that thrived on the rivers, canals and railroads.

Today government is Albany's biggest business, along with banking and education. Nineteen institutions of higher learning, including the State University of New York and the Rensselaer Polytechnic Institute, make their home here.

■ **The Mighty Iroquois Confederacy**

Long before the arrival of Europeans in the New World, the New York woodlands rustled with life. By at least AD 1300, the restless Iroquois had moved down from the north, pushing the Algonquian tribes south and inhabiting the Mohawk Valley and the Finger Lakes. The five Iroquois tribes—Seneca, Mohawk, Oneida, Cayuga, Onondaga—warred among themselves to the brink of extinction. Finally around 1570 a leader emerged who convinced them to make peace and unite. Called by whites the Iroquois Confederacy or the League of Five Nations, this arrangement allowed each of the tribes autonomy under the aegis of a Great Council. (After the Tuscarora, a southern tribe of Iroquois origin, joined the confederacy in the early 18C, historians referred to the League of Six Nations.) The Onondaga, who lived near the geographic center of the confederacy around present-day Syracuse, became keepers of the council fire where 50 chiefs, or sachems, met each year to settle disputes and make overarching decisions. Under this Great Peace, the Iroquois ceased their infighting, but continued aggressions against neighboring tribes expanded their reach from the Atlantic to the Mississippi, north to Canada and south to Tennessee. After siding with the British during the American Revolution, the league faltered—never to regain its strength—at the hands of the Continental Army, which cut a decimating swath through the Iroquois lands of upstate New York. Its legacy lives on, however. As the first representative democracy in North America, the Iroquois Confederacy served as an inspiration to Benjamin Franklin and James Madison when it came their turn for nation-building in a young America.

SIGHTS *1 day. Map p 99.*

An impression of the city's earliest development lingers in its street grid, though few extant buildings predate the 19C. Start your downtown walk at the **Urban Cultural Park Visitors Center** near the heart of old Beverwyck *(25 Quackenbush Sq.; open year-round daily 10am–4pm; closed Jan 1, Easter Sunday, Thanksgiving Day, Dec 25; ⅄ ⅃ [$3]; www.albany.org ☎518-434-5132)*. The center shows a film on Albany's history and stocks brochures and maps for self-guided walking tours. Note the 1736 **Quackenbush House** *(on the south side of Quackenbush Sq.)*, Albany's oldest Dutch house and one of two still standing with gable fronts.

© Michael Melford

New York State Capitol

★★ **New York State Capitol Building** – *Bounded by State, Swan and Eagle Sts., and Washington Ave. Open year-round Mon–Fri 9am–5pm. Closed major holidays. Guided tours (45min) available; reservations required. ⅄ ⅃ www.ogs.state.ny.us ☎518-474-2418.* Like an elegant chateau set upon a sweeping front lawn, the capitol holds forth with bygone splendor at the northern end of Empire State Plaza *(below)*. Its strata of arched windows and the rough-textured facade contrast dramatically with the sheen of the plaza's smooth exteriors. The legislature declared the $25-million building complete in 1899 after more than 30 years of effort by five architects and hundreds of stone carvers. The first two stories reflect the Italian Renaissance style chosen by architect Thomas Fuller in 1867. **Henry Hobson Richardson** took over in 1876, designing the third and fourth stories with his characteristic Romanesque flair. Skillful stone carvers embellished the granite and sandstone surfaces with a remarkable array of ornamental forms.

Among the interior spaces, the third-floor **Senate Chamber**, restored to Richardson's 1881 design, is most opulent. A rich blend of materials, including carved oak, gold leaf, stained glass, Siena marble and Mexican onyx, creates a stately atmosphere suitable to the work of the 61 senators who sit in session here between January and June. Note the Richardson case clock (the senate's official timepiece) and the huge fireplaces, where members can hobnob in private. Across the courtyard is the **Assembly Chamber** designed by Leopold Eidlitz, the first room to be used in 1879. This space is also ornate; particularly striking are its stained-glass windows. The papier-mâché ceiling here actually helped save the building during a fire in 1911 by retaining water. Showcase of the capitol is Richardson's **Great Western Staircase★** (completed after 13 years, in 1896). Stone carvers transformed its Romanesque grandeur into a veritable sandstone confection that includes more than a thousand tiny, nameless faces, each one unique. On the first floor, the East Lobby houses a thousand battle-worn flags carried by various New York regiments beginning with those who fought in the Civil War.

★ **Empire State Plaza** – *Between Madison Ave. and Swan, State and Eagle Sts. Open year-round daily 6am–11pm. ⅄ ⅃ ($8) ☎518-474-2418.* One's opinion as to the aesthetics of this colossal complex notwithstanding, there is no mistaking its superlative presence at the summit of Albany's capitol hill. In concept and design, Gov. Nelson Rockefeller intended the Empire State Plaza to stand apart from the city, and indeed, the 98-acre site—from the **observation deck** *(open year-round daily 9am– 3:45pm; &)* atop the 42-story Corning Tower to the deepest recesses of the concourses below—constitutes a kind of latter-day acropolis. Built between 1962 and 1978, the plaza's visual kinship with Rockefeller and Lincoln Centers and the UN headquarters in New York City is no accident, since they all shared lead architect Wallace K. Harrison. Of the 11 buildings surrounding the central reflecting pool, the concrete **Performing Arts Center** (fondly called the "Egg") is the most distinctive, its functional appearance contrasting bizarrely with the decorative ornament of the capitol across State Street. The other buildings, tall and squat studies in geometric precision clad in shimmering marbles, house mostly governmental operations. The entire futuristic campus surmounts a five-story concourse where 3.8 million square feet of floor space a quarter-mile long houses restaurants, retail outlets and offices, along with parking. A remarkable feat of engineering, the Empire State Plaza took 16 years and $2 billion to complete. Nelson Rockefeller, who served four terms as New York's governor from 1959 until 1973, actively contributed to the design of the plaza and left his mark as well in the form of a stunning **collection**★ of paintings and sculpture by modern artists ranging from Jackson Pollock to Alexander Calder. Its splashes of color and shape enliven the dreary concourse level as well as the public spaces outside and inside the buildings.

■ **"I got a mule, her name is Sal, fifteen years on the Erie Canal"**

Public skepticism greeted Governor DeWitt Clinton's insistence that a canal between Albany and Buffalo would make the fortune of the Empire State. Fortunately, the state legislature agreed with Clinton, and on July 4, 1817, construction on the 363mi Erie Canal began in Rome. Built in three sections at a cost of $7 million, the full span of "Clinton's Ditch" was completed on October 26, 1825. A remarkable feat in the days before modern construction equipment, the canal was dug by hand and horsepower. It posed new challenges for engineers, including the design of 83 locks to allow boats to climb or descend a 600ft drop in elevation from west to east. Eighteen aqueducts carried boats over rivers, and nearly 300 low bridges crossed the canal over its entire length. Barge-like canal boats pulled by mules that trod a 10ft towpath on either side crowded the waters; in 1833 a boat passed through the Schenectady locks once every seven minutes around the clock. Canal towns boomed as the watery conveyor in their front yards moved settlers west and cargo—from hops to salt to lumber—to eastern markets. Canal culture thrived. Entire families lived and worked aboard their canal boats, and canal-side groceries catered to the needs of passengers and crew. In the winter months when the canal froze over, many canallers tied up in New York City to await the thaw. Ongoing enlargements and improvements, including miles of lateral canals built after 1836, kept the Erie viable, but by 1905 larger boats required a new waterway. Work commenced to shift the canal into the Mohawk River and, finally, in 1918, the wider and deeper New York State Barge Canal opened. The Erie Canal, maker of the Empire State, was then abandoned. Today, under the auspices of the Thruway Authority, the historic New York State Canal System comprises 524mi still in use by recreational and commercial boaters.

New York State Museum – 🧒 *At south end of Empire State Plaza in the Cultural Education Center. Open year-round daily 10am–5pm. Closed Jan 1, Thanksgiving Day, Dec 25. $2.* ⅄ & 🅿 ☎*518-474-5877.* Overlooking the plaza's southern end, this modern museum of history and culture addresses the dichotomy of New York State in two mammoth exhibits covering the urban milieu and the natural environment. **"New York Metropolis"** traces the prodigious growth of that city through various themes, including immigration, transportation and skyscraper construction. A comparable exhibit on the Adirondack wilderness examines the ecology of the region and the impact of human intervention there. Ample in scale, both exhibits feature huge galleries that accommodate life-size dioramas and full-scale artifacts like subway train cars and biplanes. Additional exhibits cover diverse topics, including the state's flora and fauna. Don't miss the handsome gallery on the **"Native Peoples of New York,"** where you can step into a Mohawk Iroquois longhouse for a realistic glimpse of Indian life.

★ **Albany Institute of History and Art** – *125 Washington Ave. Open year-round Wed–Sat noon–5pm. Closed major holidays. $3.* ♿ 🅿 ☎*518-463-4478.* The order of the Institute's title is significant, for here art serves the purposes of history: the museum presents paintings, sculpture and artistically crafted artifacts of daily life for both their beauty and their historical significance. Begin on the second floor, where exhibits devoted to the history and collections of the Institute—which was founded in 1791 as a "Learned Society"—shed light on local themes and highlights the 12 categories—from ceramics to textiles—that the museum now collects. A fine assemblage of early portraits represents the most popular subject of early-American "limners": the human form. With little use for painting other than its utility, these portraitists recorded the faces of the Hudson River Valley, leaving a visual genealogy of its founding families. Works of the Hudson River school are highlighted in an intimate installation in the first-floor Albany Room. Part library and part exhibit, this gallery invites visitors to ponder the Hudson River school ethos through paintings and books, and by leaving their own impressions of the work. The Museum Annex next door houses a gallery for the exhibit, sale and rental of contemporary art, along with a library and reading room.

Historic Cherry Hill – *523 ½ S. Pearl St. Visit by guided tour (45min) only, Feb–Dec Tue–Sat 10am–3pm, Sun 1pm–3pm. Closed major holidays. $3.50.* 🅿 ☎*518-434-4791.* In 1787 Philip and Maria Van Rensselaer erected Cherry Hill, a comfortable Georgian home that was once the center of a 900-acre farm. A member of one of New York's most influential families and a descendant of patroon Kiliaen Van Rensselaer, Philip was himself a successful merchant and a farmer. Occupied by four subsequent generations of the family until 1963, the home today appears much as it did during the tenure of the final owners, brimming with family artifacts and furniture. As such, Cherry Hill represents the evolution of a historic home through stylistic and decorative changes, conversions of the heating and lighting systems, and additions made over time.

★ **Schuyler Mansion State Historic Site** – *32 Catherine St. Visit by guided tour (1hr) only, mid-Apr–Oct Wed–Sat & holidays 10am–5pm, Sun 1pm–5pm. Rest of the year by appointment only. $3.* 🅿 ☎*518-434-0834.* Elegant and sturdy, this brick manse was built by **Philip Schuyler** (1733-1804), American Revolutionary general, between 1761 and 1764, following his 1755 marriage to Catharine Van Rensselaer. His career as military man, businessman, entrepreneur and politician made his home a center of activity. Generous Georgian dimensions define the house: its broad entry hall spans front to back and the characteristic offset staircase ascends to a 20ft-wide gallery designed for elaborate entertaining. A trip to England kept Schuyler from supervising the construction, but he returned with choice wallpapers, fine hardware and other quality accoutrements. As one of four original major generals in the Continental Army, Schuyler conducted military business at home during the war, including detaining British general John Burgoyne and his entourage—with exceeding hospitality—after their defeat at the Battles of Saratoga *(p 121)* in 1777. In 1780 Schuyler's daughter Elizabeth married Alexander Hamilton in the parlor. After Schuyler's death, the house passed out of the family; it was later purchased by the state and opened as a historic site in 1917. A painstaking restoration now under way makes the mansion a stunning work in progress. Based on careful analyses of walls and woodwork, as well as period documentation, curators will return the home to its late-18C appearance, meticulously reproducing the rich paint colors, fashionable furniture and beautiful textured wallpapers Schuyler used. A fine exhibit in the visitor center aligns Philip Schuyler's life with his revolutionary times.

EXCURSIONS *Map p 99*

Watervliet Arsenal Museum [M] – *½hr. 6mi north of Albany in Watervliet on Rte. 32/Broadway. Open year-round Mon–Thu 10am–3pm. Closed major holidays.* ♿ 🅿 *www.wva.army.mil* ☎*518-266-5805.* This "certified Army museum" commemorates the Watervliet Arsenal's history as the country's oldest, continuously active maker of arms and equipment. Now principally a manufacturer of cannon (the "shooter" tube of an artillery weapon, from breech to muzzle), the 140-acre arsenal originated in 1813 to provide military matériel during the War of 1812. Housed in a cavernous 1859 cast-iron storehouse, the museum focuses on arsenal products but also exhibits historic American and European armaments.

Hart-Cluett Mansion – *1hr. 7mi north of Albany in Troy. 59 Second St. Open Feb–Dec 23 Tue–Sat 10am–4pm. Closed major holidays. $2.* & *www.crisny.org/not-for-profit/rchs* ☎518-272-7232. Part of Troy's historic Second Avenue District, the Hart-Cluett mansion was built by an early Troy mayor and later occupied by the Cluett family, who made a fortune manufacturing shirts and collars. Along with the adjacent Carr Building (1837), this 1827 Federal-style town house is home to the Rensselaer County Historical Society. Victorian furnishings throughout its 14 rooms are typically eclectic and can be seen by self-guided tour.

A bustling industrial city, 19C **Troy** attracted merchants who left a legacy of fine town houses and commercial buildings. Troy's neighborhoods retain enough of their Victorian atmosphere to have hosted the filming of Edith Wharton's *The Age of Innocence*. Today you can tour eight historic districts on foot, including the Second Avenue District.

COOPERSTOWN★★

Population 2,033
Map p 7
Tourist Information 607-432-4500 or 800-843-3394

This quintessentially quaint village between the shores of Otsego Lake and the banks of the Susquehanna River has led a charmed life. Never of strategic, commercial or industrial importance, Cooperstown cultivates atmosphere as its primary export. Author James Fenimore Cooper romanticized its already lovely setting in his stories of the New York frontier. His tales still heighten its allure, as does its significance as an ancient Indian rendezvous. Cooper's father established the village in 1786, and the author himself lived here on and off, staging two of his five Leatherstocking tales in its environs. Owing to a devastating fire in 1862, the town's architectural silhouette only dates back to the years after the Civil War, its handsome 19C homes and expansive lawns the very picture of prosperity. Today a crush of summertime visitors comes to see the town's historical heritage as well as more contemporary attractions such as the National Baseball Hall of Fame and Museum. Offerings as diverse as the renowned **Glimmerglass Opera** festival *(July–August)* and the Corvette Hall of Fame and Americana Museum *(south of town on Rte. 28;* ☎607-547-4135) also draw crowds.

SIGHTS   *1 day. Map p 98.*

★★ **National Baseball Hall of Fame and Museum** – **Kids** *25 Main St. Open May–Sept daily 9am–9pm. Rest of the year daily 9am–5pm. Closed Jan 1, Thanksgiving Day, Dec 25. $9.50.* & *www.baseballhalloffame.org* ☎607-547-7200. In 1905 a committee of experts gathered at the behest of sporting goods mogul A.G. Spalding to determine conclusively the origin of baseball. Based largely on the 68-year-old eyewitness recollections of Abner Graves, the commission found that baseball in its modern form was invented in Cooperstown by one Abner Doubleday in 1839. Other evidence, however, suggests that boys in sandlots and empty fields all over the country were playing similar forms of the game by the time Doubleday introduced the diamond-shaped field and the concept of "safe" bases. Real or imagined, Cooperstown makes the perfect birthplace for the national pastime, and here in 1939 a museum was dedicated to the sport. Today, much expanded and augmented by a full-fledged hall of fame, this shrine to baseball and its players covers its subject with encyclopedic thoroughness.

At the heart of the museum's three floors, the reverential **Hall of Fame** honors more than 200 of the greats, inducting new members every year with much ado. Steeped in history, personalities and statistics, bright and imaginative galleries cover every aspect of the sport from the evolution of equipment and uniforms to baseball's great moments. Serious fans will relish the details offered up throughout the museum, especially in the Records Room, where touch screens give instant access to records made and broken. Colorful and clever exhibits include such themes as baseball music, the story of women's participation and the Negro Leagues. The entire second floor explores the history of baseball, and here relics abound, foremost among them a well-worn, hand-sewn ball that may have belonged to Abner Doubleday. In the Grandstand Theatre, a stirring **multimedia presentation** pays tribute to the game and contains remarkable historic footage of professional and amateur play; the theater itself has been ingeniously imbued

Baseball Hall of Fame

with ballpark ambience. If you still haven't gotten your fill, visit the library, where an exhibit explores baseball reporting since the 1850s, and where clips from baseball movies play continuously.

★★ **The Farmers' Museum** – [Kids] *1mi north of Cooperstown on Lake Rd. Open Jun–Labor Day daily 9am–5pm. Feb–May & Sept–Dec call for hours. $9.* ✗ & ☐ *www.nysha.org* ☎*607-547-1400.* In the tradition of the great open-air living-history museums, this tidy collection of historic buildings from around the state re-creates a typical New York "village crossroads" and explores many aspects of 19C country life. Once owned and worked by James Fenimore Cooper and a succession of other gentlemen farmers, this land most recently supported a dairy farm. The handsome Colonial Revival barn that today houses the main exhibit galleries was completed as a modern dairy barn in 1918. Since the museum was established here in 1943 under the aegis of the New York State Historical Association, various buildings have been added, including a schoolhouse, doctor's office, church, farmhouse and general store. Dedicated to both the content and the process of rural culture, the Farmers' Museum conveys a sense of daily farm life through its extensive collections of household implements, agricultural tools and other artifacts, and its demonstrations of crafts and trades.

Begin in the main barn, which houses decorative and folk arts and crafts, and an incredible inventory of **tools**★ related to the building trades, metalworking, leatherworking and housekeeping. Demonstrations given here range from broom making to wallpaper printing. From the barn, stroll around the village peopled with blacksmiths, spinners and weavers, printers and other interpreters who will gladly discuss the rhythms and routines of rural life. Many of the buildings, including the 1795 Bump Tavern, include period room settings. One curious bit of arcana is the Cardiff Giant, a 10ft stone hoax perpetrated on upstate residents in 1869 by an enterprising entrepreneur. George Hull had the petrified "prehistoric" human form carved, buried and "discovered," then charged admission to eager viewers. The Cardiff Giant (so-called for its "unearthing" in Cardiff, New York) today reclines peacefully in a tent that simulates the 19C version.

★ **Fenimore House Museum** – *On Lake Rd. across from Farmers' Museum. Open Jul–Labor Day daily 9am–6pm. Apr–Jun & Sept–Dec call for hours. $9.* ✗ & ☐ *www. nysha.org* ☎*607-547-1400.* Graciously situated on the shores of Otsego Lake, the Fenimore House Museum occupies the site of the farmhouse owned by James Fenimore Cooper between 1810 and 1828. The Georgian Revival mansion was built in 1932 by local philanthropist Edward S. Clark. Administered by the New York State Historical Association, today it houses an elegant, if eclectic, assemblage of American and Native American art and folk art. Its stunning centerpiece is the new American Indian wing, home of the **Eugene and Clare Thaw Collection**★★. Dealers of fine arts, the Thaws developed a taste for Indian crafts and acquired more than 600 superlative examples of beadwork, basketry, textiles, masks and costume items from tribes around North America. The thematic organization of the exhibits—by culture group in one gallery and by cosmology in the other—treats the artifacts, as well as the beliefs and lifeways they represent, with dignity and respect. In addition, exquisite lighting shows off the collection to best advantage.

Works by the Hudson River school, folk portraits and genre paintings, along with Cooper family memorabilia, are also on display. A small gallery of bronze life masks by 19C sculptor John Browere includes the venerable visages of John Adams, Dolley Madison and others whose collective gaze makes a lasting impression.

MOHAWK VALLEY ★

Map pp 98-99
Tourist Information ☎315-866-1500

Flowing nearly 150mi across the center of New York from Rome to Albany, the Mohawk River is the Hudson's largest tributary. Already well-traveled by Indians and fur traders, the valley was the easiest way west across the Appalachians for many early settlers. Even before the canal system, it was possible—though arduous—to travel by water from the Atlantic Ocean, up the Hudson and Mohawk rivers, across a short portage and on to the Great Lakes. Dutch, Palatinate Germans and Scotch-Irish made up the first contingent of pioneers to settle along the riverbanks, building reputations as expert farmers. Place names today—Amsterdam, Palatine, Scotia—still reflect their influence. During the Revolution, the river played a key role in a British plan to slice the colonies in two and commandeer these rich farmlands, which by then fed Continental troops. Failing that, Loyalists and their Iroquois allies laid waste the countryside in raids against Patriot farmers throughout the Mohawk and Schoharie Valleys, staging one particularly brutal massacre in Cherry Valley in 1778. As many as 300,000 Yankee immigrants from New England all but displaced the first settlers by 1810. In the 1820s the Erie Canal (p 94) from Albany to Buffalo only made the journey easier, bypassing rapids, spring floods and oxbows, and expediting the transport of people and huge quantities of goods. Mills and factories—guns in Ilion, textiles in Utica, leather goods in Gloversville—hummed throughout the valley. By 1918 the Erie had been replaced by the New York State Barge Canal, which accommodated larger and deeper vessels and still serves as an important artery. Today, however, the New York State Thruway carries most traffic up and down this well-trodden corridor, paralleling the river and connecting towns, historic forts and homes, and family farms.

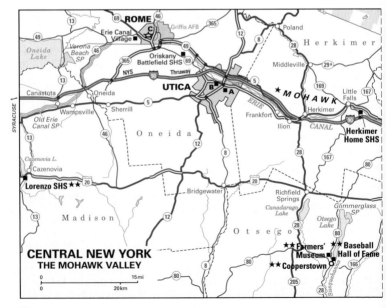

SIGHTS *2 days. Map pp 98–99.*

Busy I-90 *(toll road)* and quiet Route 5 offer easy access to the following sights, presented from east to west along the Mohawk River.

Schenectady – Founded by Dutch settlers on land purchased from the Mohawk Indians in 1661, Schenectady grew through thick and thin to become "the city that lights and hauls the world." At first a river town that thrived on boatbuilding, the city suffered a devastating fire in 1819 and its fate took another downturn when the Erie Canal shifted its port of entry for westbound goods to Troy and Albany. As the railroads converged in Schenectady after 1831, the city took up locomotive manufacture and began to prosper anew. **Thomas Edison** *(p 184)* opened a machine shop to manufacture electrical equipment along the banks of the Mohawk in 1886, and the young General Electric Co. made Schenectady its headquarters six years later. The town became a mecca for researchers, scientists and technicians, among them Charles Steinmetz, the great electrical engineer who pioneered the study of alternating current and served in later life as a professor at Union College.

★ **Stockade District** – *Bounded by the Mohawk River, Washington Ave. and Ferry and State Sts.* Dutch cottages crowd Italianate town houses in this lovely residential district at the heart of old Schenectady. At the edge of Dutch settlement, the outpost was burned by the French and Indians in 1690, but rebuilt and refortified, it continued to grow. The waterfront bustled with commercial activity, and fur traders and merchants built their homes along the nearby blocks.

Begin a walking tour at the **Schenectady Historical Society** *(32 Washington Ave.; visit by 1hr guided tour only year-round Mon–Sat 1pm–5pm; closed major holidays; $2; & ▣ ☎518-374-0263)*, a relative newcomer built in 1895. Appointed with 19C period furnishings, the home contains artifacts dating back to Dutch settlement as well as a collection of 18C paintings. From here, continue to the district's earliest building at 14 North Church Street: once the home of Hendrick Brouwer, it may date back to as early as 1692 and encompass an even older building. At the intersection of Front, Ferry and Green Streets stood the first British fort, constructed in 1705 in the strategically important Mohawk Valley.

Union College – *Enter off Union St. through Payne Gate. Guided tours depart from the admissions office year-round Mon–Fri 10am–4pm. www.union.edu ☎518-388-6112.* Even though the glittering Gothic Victorian dome of the landmark **Nott Memorial** dominates the campus' skyline, Union College presents, on the whole, the profile of an early-19C institution. The original college, chartered in 1795, moved from the Stockade District in 1814 into the first buildings constructed according to a design by Joseph Jacques Ramée, which included the South and North Colleges. Ramée's work represented the first unified campus plan ever conceived

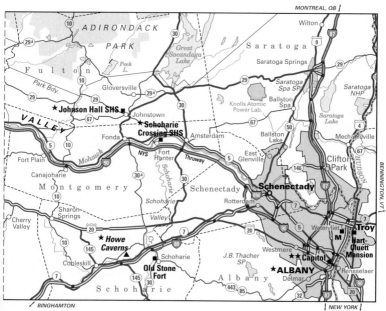

for an American college, predating Thomas Jefferson's University of Virginia by several years. Over time, much of his original plan for the central campus was executed, most recently the Humanities and Social Science buildings completed on the east side of the main quadrangle only 30 years ago. Even the picturesque Nott Memorial (named for Eliphalet Nott, the college president who moved Union to its present site), though not consistent with Ramée's Neoclassical vision, occupies a place he reserved for a central "round building." Designed by Edward Tuckerman Potter, a student of Richard Upjohn, the 16-sided cylindrical edifice features a dazzling 100ft dome illuminated by 709 tiny windows arranged like a constellation. No stroll through campus should bypass the eight acres of **Jackson's Garden**, a peaceful green space designed in 1830 to contrast with the symmetrical formality of the campus proper.

★ **Schoharie Crossing State Historic Site** – *129 Schoharie St. in Fort Hunter. Buildings open mid-May–Oct Wed–Sat 10am–5pm, Sun 1pm–5pm. Grounds open year-round daily dawn–dusk (weather permitting).* ♿ 🅿 ☎*518-829-7516.* There is much to see at this site, which stretches out along 3mi of canal towpath between Schoharie Creek and Yankee Hill Lock. Hikes or bike rides between the site's various features take in wildlife and canal history aplenty. Or, you can drive along Queen Anne's Road for a look at both ends. In any case, begin at the visitor center on Schoharie Street. Here, remnants of the original Erie Canal (this portion completed in 1821) and the enlarged canal (1841) furrow the landscape, and the truncated ruin of the 624ft **aqueduct**, built in 1842 to ease the treacherous crossing of the creek, looms above the water. Follow the towpath east on foot or drive to Yankee Hill Lock, the site of a double lock and restored canal grocery. The serenity here is misleading: during the heyday of canal travel, such a locale—the heart of canalside culture—bustled with activity as men and women hurried to stock up on provisions and exchange news while their vessels locked through.

★ **Johnson Hall State Historic Site** – *Hall Ave. in Johnstown. Open mid-May–Oct Wed–Sat & holidays 10am–5pm, Sun 1pm–5pm. $3.* 🅿 ☎*518-762-8712.* Few white men had more pre-Revolutionary influence in the Mohawk Valley than **Sir William Johnson** (1715-74). He arrived in the region as a young man in 1738 to oversee his uncle's lands. By the time he built Johnson Hall in 1763, he had earned a baronetcy for his faithful service to the Crown, defeated the French at the Battle of Lake George in 1755, and been appointed superintendent of Indian Affairs. His huge estate exceeded any other in size, as did his fortune. Johnson Hall stood at the center of the baronet's empire, which included 700,000 acres, the town of Johnstown and an active trading post. At five windows wide, the Hall, a sturdy Georgian country manse, boasts ample dimensions and massive thresholds. As in many Georgian homes of this period, a broad central hall connects the front and back doors; two bedrooms and two parlors open onto it from either side. Such construction promoted a cross-breeze in summer, but made for a cold

---

■ **The Unsinkable Molly Brant**

Sir William Johnson's rapport with the Mohawk people distinguished his career. He learned their language and treated them as equals. They made him a war chief, calling him *Warraghiyagey* ("He Who Does Much"). Such mutual regard helped to strengthen the bond between Iroquois and British that would weaken the French presence in the Mohawk Valley in the 1750s and 60s and threaten the success of the American Revolution a decade later. Johnson also had the good fortune to ally himself with Molly Brant, sister of Mohawk leader Joseph Brant, who exerted a strong influence among her people. Molly believed that an Iroquois alliance with the British would protect Indian lands from American encroachment, and she and her brother worked hard to convince the Mohawks, Senecas and Cayugas to enter the Revolution on the British side. The formidable Molly personified the powerful role of Iroquois women; a contemporary remarked that "one word from her goes farther with them [the Iroquois] than a thousand from any white man without exception." Johnson's house and grounds at Johnstown clamored with hundreds of Iroquois, who came and went freely, made all the more welcome by Molly, who ran the household and bore Johnson nine children. She outlived William and the Revolution, seeking refuge with the British and acting as a valuable liaison between them and their Indian allies. In exchange, the British established her in Kingston, Ontario, after the war. She died in 1796.

passageway in the winter. Though no original furniture remains, the home is authentically appointed based on a 1774 inventory. Its elegant furnishings and Native American decorative items bespeak Johnson's blended life as baronet and frontiersman. Note the handsome **balustrade**—its mahogany a sign of wealth—vandalized by Continental troops who came to arrest Johnson's son during the Revolution. John Johnson inherited the home following his father's death in 1774, but, a Loyalist, he fled to Canada to assemble troops against the revolutionaries. A compact exhibit in one of two stone houses that flank the Hall gives a good sense of William Johnson's life and times.

Herkimer Home State Historic Site – *Rte. 169 at Thruway Exit 29A in Little Falls. Visit by guided tour (1hr) only, mid-May–Oct Wed–Sat 10am–5pm, Sun & holidays 1pm–5pm. Rest of the year by appointment only. Closed Memorial Day & Labor Day. $3.* ☎315-823-0398. Patriot general Nicholas Herkimer probably planned his substantial Georgian residence to compete with that of William Johnson, his Loyalist neighbor to the east. Its gambrel roof and brick construction, however, reveal a different heritage: Herkimer descended from Palatinate German refugees whose flight from war and persecution in their Rhineland homes had led them to the Mohawk Valley. Nicholas made a success of farming and trading, becoming an important local figure. As he led the militia to aid the besieged Ft. Stanwix in August 1777, British troops ambushed and mortally wounded him at the fierce Battle of Oriskany (*p 104*). He died in his home 10 days later and is buried on the grounds. The house passed out of the family in 1814, and soon thereafter the Erie Canal cut its swath through the back of the property. The Herkimer home served some checkered years as a canal tavern, falling into disrepair until acquired by the state in 1913. Today costumed interpreters demonstrate facets of Colonial farm life and conduct tours through the home's Georgian-style interior. The kitchen garden endures in the 18C style, and the 19C barn has been converted into an interpretive center where a visit to the home begins.

In historical parlance, a "fort" might be any place of safety. Therefore, many private homes, churches and other buildings in the Mohawk Valley were called forts to imply a local refuge from danger.

EXCURSIONS   *Map p 99*

Old Stone Fort Museum Complex – *1hr. N. Main St. in Schoharie. Open May–Jun Tue–Sat & holidays 10am–5pm, Sun noon–5pm. Jul–Aug Mon–Sat & holidays 10am–5pm, Sun noon–5pm. Sept–Oct Tue–Sat & holidays 10am–5pm, Sun noon–5pm. $5.* 🅿 ☎518-295-7192. Built as a church in 1772, this stalwart structure served to protect the local population who gathered within its walls at signs of approaching danger. Rich farmland had earned this region the epithet "breadbasket of the American Revolution," which made it an important target for Col. John Johnson, Iroquois chief Joseph Brant and other British Loyalists who systematically raided the settlements here. Despite their devastating sweep through the countryside in 1780, the Old Stone Fort remained impenetrable, bearing today the mark of only a single cannonball. Note the names of those who helped to build the church engraved on its exterior—and the obliteration of the names of those who sided with the British. A museum since 1889, the Old Stone Fort exhibits in its musty spaces a collection of relics—from fossils to the oldest fire engine in the US—along with military paraphernalia from each of America's wars. Materials pertaining to local Revolutionary War history are most interesting and include a letter written by Joseph Brant, who was educated at the forerunner to Dartmouth College. Across the street, an assemblage of unrelated buildings moved from various sites includes an early-18C Dutch barn and a schoolhouse.

★ **Howe Caverns** – 🄺🄸🄳🅂 *1½hrs. Off Rte. 7 in Howes Cave. Visit by guided tour (1hr 30min) only, year-round daily 9am–6pm. Closed Jan 1, Thanksgiving Day, Dec 25. $12.* ✗ 🅿 *www.howecaverns.com* ☎518-296-8900. *The caverns maintain a temperature of approximately 50°F year-round, so bring a sweater or jacket.* This classic American "tourist attraction" has a long and venerable history, having been explored and exploited by local dairy farmer Lester Howe in 1842. Howe's cows seemed to enjoy congregating around a cool rocky opening in the earth on hot days, and the intrepid Lester determined to discover what lay beyond. Realizing the magnitude of his find, he began to escort tourists into his caverns—a treacherous expedition that cost 50 cents a head and involved eight hours of climbing, slipping and slogging. Not surprisingly, Howe's enterprise failed. It was not until the 1920s that another entrepreneur engineered an elevator, walkways, bridges and an electrical lighting system to make the caverns accessible. Carved out over millennia by a subterranean river, the caverns and their fabulous **limestone formations** are fun for young spelunkers; the youthful guides are friendly and well practiced in the scripted spiel that narrates each tour. From the lodge above ground, note the sweeping vista of the Schoharie Valley.

UTICA and ROME
Map p 7
Tourist Information ☎315-724-7221 or 800-426-3132

Offspring of the Industrial Revolution and bustling rest stops on the journey west by water, rail and turnpike, both villages boomed as the 19C dawned and the great migration from New England funneled through their city limits. Today fairly quiet towns, Utica and Rome mark the western end of the pleasant Mohawk Valley.

UTICA *½ day. Map p 98.*

Utica grew as a small trading post surrounding a British fort erected in 1758. Waves of settlers swelled the population after the Revolution and the town truly blossomed following the 1825 opening of the Erie Canal. Earning a reputation for manufacturing steam engines, pottery and plows, Utica also prospered in the textile industry when the first woolen mill opened in 1847. Some thirty years later, F.W. Woolworth introduced his first five-and-dime store here.

Munson-Williams-Proctor Institute [A] – *310 Genesee St. Open year-round Tue–Sat 10am–5pm, Sun 1pm–5pm. Closed Jan 1, Thanksgiving Day, Dec 25.* ♿ 🅿 *www.mwpi. edu* ☎315-797-0000. Utica's cultural heart, and a healthy one at that, this compact institution encompasses a museum of fine and decorative art, performing-arts facilities and film series; a 19C Italianate house museum; and a school of art that annually serves more than 2,000 students. A legacy of the city's early prosperity, the institute was founded in 1919 with an endowment from the Proctor family, whose pioneer forebears had established woolen and textile mills in town. Their ancestral home, **Fountain Elms** (named for the lovely trees that were once the glory of the Mohawk Valley), has been restored to its 1850s appearance and made a showcase for the high Victorian furnishings of the museum's decorative-arts collection. Philip Johnson's 1960 International-style building houses an impressive collection of painting and sculpture, including, in the handsome second-floor American gallery, Thomas Cole's massive four-canvas allegory *The Voyage of Life.* The museum's several other permanent galleries feature works by artists such as William Glackens, Georgia O'Keeffe, Jackson Pollock, Piet Mondrian, Paul Klee and Pablo Picasso. Paintings from the museum's 20,000-piece collection are also exhibited on a temporary basis.

Matt Brewing Company [B] – *811 Edward St. Visit by guided tour (1hr) only, Jun–Aug Mon–Sat 10am–4pm, Sun noon–4pm. Rest of the year Mon–Fri noon–3pm, Sat 11am–3pm. Closed major holidays. $3.* ♿ *www.saranac.com* ☎315-732-0022. Sixty minutes after the repeal of Prohibition in 1933, the Matt Brewing Co. became the first brewery to retrieve its license. Putting ginger ale and root beer on the back burner, the Matt family revitalized the brewing tradition begun by F.X. Matt in 1888. In spite of a healthy reputation built on its Utica Club label, the brewery faltered in the 1980s, depending largely on contract brewing. Matt's retooled to take advantage of the microbrew trend, introducing its Saranac line of specialty beers, now distributed in 20 states. The Matt Brewery ranks today as 12th-largest in the US and second-oldest among its family-owned competitors. Fun and friendly tours begin in the visitor center, which is housed in the original bottle works. The seven-story brew house was added after World War II; its gleaming copper kettles, huge aging vats and pungent aroma epitomize the brewery tour experience. Particularly fascinating is the amazing mechanized choreography of the bottling plant. You'll also appreciate the beer (or root beer) tasting at tour's end, held in the Victorian atmosphere of the 1888 tavern.

ROME *2hrs. Map p 98.*

At Rome, the Mohawk River turns north and peters out. Until the early 19C, travelers going west from here carried their canoes or bateaux to Wood Creek to continue on to the Great Lakes and Canada. The British built Ft. Stanwix in 1758 to protect the portage during the French and Indian War. After the Revolution, Rome grew up around the fort, which, reconstructed, still dominates the city's downtown. Construction on the Erie Canal began in Rome in 1817; this middle section of the canal was completed by 1819. The **Erie Canal Village** 🎠 *(Route 49W in Rome; open Memorial Day–Labor Day daily 9:30am–6pm; $6;* 🅿 ☎*315-337-3999)* —a reconstructed 1840s canal town—and a 36mi National Recreational Trail along the abandoned canal between Rome and Syracuse preserve a fragment of canal culture and the imprint of the old Erie Canal. Rome today manufactures metal goods and wire and cable.

Fort Stanwix

★ **Fort Stanwix National Monument [C]** – *At the intersection of Rtes. 365, 49, 46 and 69. Open Apr–Dec daily 9am–5pm. Closed Thanksgiving Day & Dec 25. $2.* ♿ ☎*315-336-2090.* At the head of the Mohawk Valley, 30mi beyond the northwesternmost corner of settlement, the British built Ft. Stanwix in 1758. Guarding the back door of the colonies, as well as the mile-long portage between the Mohawk River and Wood Creek, the wood and sod fort of Stanwix loomed large on the frontier. Garrisoned to stem the tide of French encroachment during the French and Indian War, the fort was phased out by the British at war's end. It was here that, in 1768, British representatives and Indians signed the Boundary Line Treaty, which extended south to Tennessee; colonists settled east of the line, Indians to the west. The Americans rebuilt the dilapidated fort in 1776 and renamed it Ft. Schuyler. It's most famous history dates back to the Revolution when the fort came under siege by the British attempting to execute their three-legged strategy to cut off New England from the southern colonies by converging on Albany from the west along the Mohawk, from the south up the Hudson and from the north down Lake Champlain Valley. Largely due to British disdain for the colonial "rabble," the siege failed (as did the entire campaign), leaving the Mohawk Valley unconquered. With a frustrated vengeance, the British and their Iroquois allies turned to raiding valley settlements until Washington sent troops to destroy the Indian villages and debilitate the Iroquois. At Ft. Stanwix in 1784, Americans and Indians signed their peace treaty, forcing the broken Iroquois Confederacy to cede its lands to the US. The fort became a storehouse for military supplies and slipped gradually into disuse. During reconstruction to its impressive 1777

103

appearance, archaeologists unearthed 400,000 18C-20C artifacts on the site. A small fraction of the findings—tools, coins, garment accessories and so on—are exhibited in the **museum**★ behind the visitor center.

A short way down Route 69, the **Oriskany Battlefield State Historic Site** *(open mid-May–mid-Oct Wed–Sat 10am–5pm, Mon holidays & Sun 1pm–5pm;* ▣ ☎315-768-7224)* commemorates one of the bloodiest battles of the Revolution. On their way to aid the besieged Ft. Stanwix, 800 troops led by Brig. Gen. Nicholas Herkimer fell victim to a wilderness ambush by John Johnson and Indian leader Joseph Brant. Herkimer himself was mortally wounded and his militia decimated, but they had provided enough of a distraction to allow soldiers from Ft. Stanwix to sneak out and silently seize British arms and supplies. Weakened by the Oriskany battle and the loss of equipment, betrayed by his disillusioned Indian allies and apprehensive of rumors of approaching American reinforcements, British colonel Barry St. Leger gave up his siege on Ft. Stanwix and returned to Oswego. The obelisk monument was erected at Oriskany in 1884.

EXCURSIONS

★★ **Lorenzo State Historic Site** – *2hrs. From Rome, take Rte. 13 to Cazenovia. Lorenzo is located past town, just south of Rte. 20. Visit by guided tour (45min) only, mid-May–mid-Oct Wed–Sat & holidays 10am–5pm, Sun 1pm–5pm. Rest of the year by appointment only. $3.* ♿ ▣ ☎315-655-3200. A lovely **drive**★ down Route 13 follows the course of Chittenango Creek and, passing its namesake falls, arrives in the attractive lakeside town of Cazenovia. Shortly beyond and overlooking Cazenovia Lake stands the mansion Lorenzo. Town and home are both products of the 18C land speculation that settled much of upstate New York. In this case, a Dutch land company purchased more than three million wilderness acres in 1792, then laid out the town of Cazenovia (Theophile Cazenove represented the Dutch banks that financed the operation), surveyed lots and set about attracting buyers. Field agent John Lincklaen, who had discovered and promoted the site, acquired ten percent of the land for himself, including the knoll on which he would ultimately construct his Federal manse, Lorenzo. Lincklaen and his family moved into the home in 1808. The house remained in the family until the 1960s, a happy circumstance that ensured its seamless survival with furnishings and architectural integrity intact. New York State acquired the property in 1968 and has undertaken a fastidious restoration of its 25 rooms to their early-20C appearance. Vibrant reproduction turn-of-the-century wall, window and floor coverings set off the home's stunning collection of furniture and decorative arts, which spans the 19C. Architecturally, Lorenzo retains its Federal essence: its rectilinear plan, the fan- and sidelights that surround the front door and the quiet, balustraded roof line (the pediments were added in 1815). Particularly handsome are the interior moldings and fireplace mantels, their delicate, bas-relief swags restored and renewed. Outbuildings on the estate were erected after 1890; today the carriage barn houses an informative exhibit, which makes good use of artifacts and documents to place Lorenzo and the Lincklaen family in their historic context.

North Country

Below the Thousand Islands International Bridge – Jonathan Wallen

If New York State is shaped like a hiking boot with the toe pointing west, then North Country occupies the part extending from the top of the foot to the ankle, a roughly trapezoidal chunk of land in the northeast part of the state bounded by Canada and the St. Lawrence River to the north, Lake Champlain (and Vermont) to the east, Lake Ontario to the west, and the Mohawk River to the south. One of the best-protected wilderness areas in the nation, Adirondack Park comprises some six million acres of public and private land, forming the stunning centerpiece of North Country. It is girdled by other resort areas, including Saratoga Springs, famous for its 19C thoroughbred racetrack and Victorian architecture; the Champlain Valley, rich with 18C military history; and the Thousand Islands region, a resort mecca.

Thought to be the first European explorer of North Country, Samuel de Champlain was led by Native Americans from Quebec down Lake Champlain in 1609. At the time, North Country was mainly occupied by tribes affiliated with the Alqonquian family and the Iroquois Confederacy. Beginning in the mid-17C, many Indians became involved in the fur trade. Allied with both French and English trading partners, they also became embroiled in the French and Indian War, which resulted in British dominion over most of North America. While the waterways surrounding North Country—Lake Champlain, the St. Lawrence River, the Hudson River and Lake Ontario—were wrangled over during this war and the Revolutionary War that followed quickly on its heels, the interior remained largely unexplored until the mid-19C. As access to mountainous areas improved, lumbering and mining grew more widespread, as did tourism. After a protracted struggle, the latter won out, resulting in the creation and expansion of the Adirondack Forest Preserve. Dairy farms and fruit orchards thrived on the surrounding lowlands.

Today North Country remains largely open space—from the rolling farmland on the periphery to the densely forested mountains in its heart. Some of the back roads here are among the most scenic in the state. Most of the towns in Adirondack Park (with the exception of touristy Lake Placid and Lake George) exude a sort of no-frills charm, their diners, mom-and-pop grocery stores, and rustic lodges catering as much to locals as to the visitors who come to hike, canoe, fish, ski and snowmobile. Towns in the Champlain Valley (Ticonderoga, Crown Point, Plattsburgh) tend to be markedly less prosperous than their preppy Vermont neighbors (Burlington, Middlebury). The Thousand Islands (actually more than 1,700 islands) along the western edge of North Country attract a wealthy summertime crowd, while Saratoga Springs serves as a culturally rich gateway to the Adirondacks for visitors arriving from the Eastern Seaboard.

THE ADIRONDACKS ★★★

Maps p 7 and p 107
Tourist Information ☎518-846-8016

Sprawling across the northeast lobe of New York State, Adirondack Park comprises some six million acres (9,400sq mi) of public and private land, or one-fifth of the state's total area. Roughly the size of New Hampshire, it is bigger than Yellowstone, Grand Canyon and Yosemite national parks combined. More than 4,000 lakes, ponds, swamps and bogs are sprinkled throughout the verdant park, as are 2,000 peaks in the five overlapping ranges that make up the Adirondacks. Some 31,500mi of rivers, brooks and streams support dozens of species of fish, and more than a billion second- and third-growth trees shelter animals including beavers, black bears, white-tailed deer, foxes, coyotes and otters. With many of its most scenic spots not accessible by car, the park is a nature-lover's dream.

Historical Notes

"Dismal Wilderness" – Geologically the Adirondacks are young: They began to rise between ten million and twenty million years ago, when the magma under the earth's crust reached infernal temperatures, pushing the land above it upward. The mountains rose some 10,000ft, though due to erosion, today the highest peak, Mt. Marcy, measures only 5,344ft. Mile-high glaciers during the Wisconsin glaciation, which ended less than 10,000 years ago, did the decorating by smoothing down jagged peaks, gouging out riverbeds, damming up streams and creating kettle ponds.

The Iroquois Confederacy controlled the Adirondacks prior to the 1600s, venturing into the mountains to hunt, and farming the surrounding lowlands. In the 17C and early 18C, both the French and the Dutch and English engaged Indians to gather pelts in exchange for cloth, guns and rum. Perhaps due to their remoteness, the Adirondacks saw little or no warfare during the French and Indian War. Indeed, they remained largely unexplored "dismal wilderness" well into the 1770s. Land speculators nevertheless bought millions of acres on the cheap from Native Americans, believing that the land's value would increase when it was cleared and cultivated. After many attempts at farming failed—the soil was too thin and rocky, the growing season too short—logging and mining took hold. By 1850 New York was the biggest logging state in the Union.

Even as the wilderness was being devoured by industry, there was a growing interest in preserving it. In 1837 the state ordered the first geological survey of the mountains. By the mid-1800s artists and intellectuals including Ralph Waldo Emerson, Winslow Homer and Thomas Cole were trekking up to the Adirondacks for inspiration. Next came the so-called robber barons, whose "great camps" *(p 113)* allowed them to enjoy both the splendor of nature and the sumptuous pleasures of civilization. In the 1890s it was believed that simply breathing the air around Saranac Lake would cure tuberculosis.

The "Blue Line" – Meanwhile the state of New York began accumulating land in the Adirondacks and CATSKILL MOUNTAINS in order to protect the watershed which was believed to be threatened by logging. In 1885 the state lands were legally deemed a forest preserve, but the protected areas were few and fa between. In 1892 a blue line was drawn on an official map around some 2.8 million acres of wilderness, with the hope that over time the state would consolidate its holdings inside the boundary. Two years later, legislators amended the state constitution to ensure that all forest preserve lands would be "forever wild"— that is, not leased, logged or developed. Today no other land in the nation is as well protected by law, though it is still threatened by civilization. While the state of New York has increased its holdings from one-fifth to nearly one-half of the land inside the "blue line" during the past century, 57 percent still remains in private hands. Conflicts among developers, environmentalists, loggers, miners, hunters, anglers and state bureaucrats over what constitutes wilderness and what private owners have a right to do with their land have been constant and, on several occasions, violent.

Despite this ongoing tension, Adirondack Park has retained a mellow, backwoods feel you won't find in the more traveled forests of neighboring New England. Although homes are being built at the alarming rate of 1,000 a year, the mountain towns have not yet succumbed to unsightly sprawl. And while some 10 million visitors come here every year to hike, ski and fish, the 130,000 year-round residents—as well as the high taxes and development restrictions—keep most of the Adirondacks from becoming an overcommercialized theme park. Indeed, Adirondack Park has been called an "accidental wilderness" because it has, miraculously, escaped the forces that have turned much of the country into farms, cities and ever-expanding suburbs. Its pristine trails, untainted lakes and rivers, historic "great camps" and celebratory museums offer a persuasive argument for continued preservation.

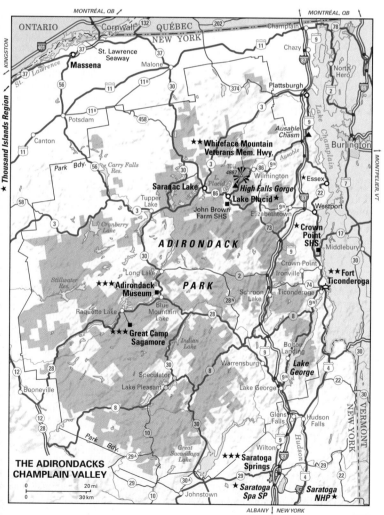

★ LAKE PLACID

Self-proclaimed "birthplace of winter sports in America," Lake Placid put itself on the map by hosting the 1932 and 1980 Winter Olympics. Today the village draws athletes year-round with its state-of-the-art ice rinks, ski jumps and training facilities. Its proximity to scores of trailheads makes it a popular stepping-off point for hikes into the High Peaks.

Historical Notes – Situated not on Lake Placid but on Mirror Lake, Lake Placid Village began developing as a resort community in the 1850s. Small hotels catered to the general public, while the shores of Lake Placid sprouted dozens of private "camps" and exclusive clubs. In the winter of 1904-05, Melvil Dewey (inventor of the Dewey Decimal library cataloging system) kept his influential Lake Placid Club open for organized winter sports for the first time. In 1918 the first sanctioned skating competition took place here, and in 1928 Melvil's son Godfrey was appointed the Olympic ski coach. Almost single-handedly, Godfrey persuaded the Olympic committee to hold the 1932 Winter Games in Lake Placid, whose residents numbered only 2,930. Fifty-eight years later, the still-tiny town (pop. 2,731) hosted the Winter Games again.

Today the village of Lake Placid bustles with tourist activity, both during the winter ski season and the summer hiking season. Skirting the western edge of Mirror Lake, Main Street is lined with upscale restaurants and boutiques, sports outfitters, bookstores, bike and ski rental shops, and outlet stores. In the temperate months, wood-hulled boats carry visitors on the crystal-clear waters of Lake Placid itself, the shores of which are still privately owned. During the tour, guides

PRACTICAL INFORMATION .... Area Code: 518

Getting There

By Car – I-87 runs north to south along the eastern Adirondacks, offering access from **Plattsburgh** or **Saratoga Springs**. Route 30 winds north to south through the center of the park providing access from **Malone** or **Amsterdam**. Routes 3 and 28 cross the park from east to west.

By Air – Closest airports are **Albany International Airport**, international and domestic flights; and **Adirondack Regional Airport** *(Saranac Lake)*, limited domestic flights.

By Bus and Train – Adirondack Trailways *(☎465-1491 or 800-858-8555)* and Greyhound *(☎793-5052 or 800-231-2222)* provide **bus** service to many cities in and around the Adirondacks. Amtrak **trains** come into Westport *(☎800-872-7245)*.

General Information

Visitor Information – Contact the following agencies to obtain maps and information on recreation, accommodations and seasonal events: **Adirondack Regional Tourism Council** *(PO Box 51, West Chazy NY 12992-0051 www.adirondacks.org ☎846-8016)*; **Lake Placid/Essex County Visitors Bureau** *(Olympic Center, Lake Placid NY 12946 www.lakeplacid.com ☎523-2999 or 800-275-2243)*; **Hamilton County Deptartment of Tourism** *(White Birch Ln., Indian Lake NY 12842-0771 www.blacdisc. com/tour/tour1. html ☎648-5239)*; **Franklin County Tourism** *(63 W. Main St., Malone NY 12953 www.adirondacklakes.org ☎483-2900)*; **Adirondack North Country Association** *(183 Broadway, Saranac Lake NY 12983-1328 ☎891-6200)*. Adirondack Park operates **Visitor Interpretive Centers** *(open year-round daily 9am–5pm; closed Thanksgiving Day, Dec 25)* in the villages of Newcomb *(Rte. 28N, 14mi east of Long Lake; ☎582-2000)* and Paul Smiths *(Rte. 30, 12mi north of Saranac Lake; ☎327-3000)*.

Accommodations – *(p 358)* Area visitors' guides including lodging directories are available *(free)* from local tourism agencies *(above)*. Hotels, motels, bed-and-breakfast inns and cabins can be found in most cities throughout the area, especially in Lake Placid, Saranac Lake and Wilmington.

Camping – Campsites are spread throughout the region, scattered over islands and along lakes and waterways. Consult *Camping in the New York State Forest Preserve (free)* for a comprehensive listing of campgrounds and facilities *(available from Public Information & Publications Unit, NYS Dept. of Environmental Conservation, 50 Wolf Rd., Room 111, Albany NY 12233; general information ☎457-3521; campground reservations ☎800-456-2267; campground information ☎457-2500)*.

regale visitors with stories and myths about this historic lake *(late Jun–Labor Day daily 10:30am–4pm; 1hr cruises depart from Lake Placid Marina mid-May–late Oct; call for off-season hours; $6; ☎518-523-9704).*

Sights *1½ days. Map p 107.*

Olympic Center – *216 Main St. Guided tours (45min) offered seasonally and by appointment.* ☎*518-523-1655 or 800-462-6236.* This hulking modern structure looms over the village of Lake Placid like a giant spaceship. Hosting four ice rinks, dating from 1931 to 1980, it is reputedly the largest facility of its kind in the world. Some 28mi of underground pipes carry coolant to the outdoor speed-skating oval, where Eric Heiden won his record five gold medals at the 1980 Games. The indoor rinks are now used 20 to 22 hours a day in the summer for hockey, figure skating and short-track speed skating; competitions take place year-round. Watching the skaters twirl around on the ice in the middle of the summer makes for a chilly treat.

Museum – *Open Memorial Day–late Oct daily 10am–5pm. Apr–May weekends 10am–4pm. $3.* ♿ *www.orda.org* ☎*518-523-1655 or 800-462-6236.* Tucked on the ground floor of the Olympic Center, the small museum was opened in 1994 to celebrate Lake Placid's winter-sports heritage. An introductory video *(5min)* provides a patriotic account of the 1932 and 1980 games. Photographs of athletes in action flank the walls, and footage of the 1980 "Miracle on Ice" hockey game—in which the US unexpectedly upset the Soviets—plays continuously. Exhibits include medals; uniforms; antique and modern sporting equipment, including the skates

---

Area Code: 518 .... **PRACTICAL INFORMATION**

Sports and Leisure

Sightseeing – Visitors can tour the Adirondacks by rail or car. The **Adirondack Scenic Railroad** offers excursions between Utica and Old Forge in northern Herkimer County *(May–Nov; 1hr 30min one-way;* ☎*315-369-6290).* The publication *Byways ($3)* lists 11 **scenic driving tours**, organized by themes such as the Colonial, Olympic and Revolutionary trails *(available from the Adirondack North Country Assn., p 108).*

Canoeing and Kayaking – Many areas in the Adirondack Forest Preserve are limited to nonmotorized craft and may be miles removed from paved roads. For a reasonable fee, professional outfitters will rent gear, shuttle your car and provide navigational instruction. Routes such as the **Adirondack Canoe Route** *(140mi)* from Old Forge to the Saranac Lakes and the **St. Regis Canoe Area** *(57mi)* near Saranac Lake are composed of interconnecting waterways, following strings of lakes, ponds and rivers. Offering some of the best freshwater **fishing** in the eastern US, the waterways of the Adirondacks are home to many species of game fish. Specialized guides take clients to productive fishing waters year-round. Contact tourism agencies for a list of licensed guides. *Adirondack Waterways* published by the Adirondack Regional Tourism Council *(p 108)* provides information on lakes and rivers, campsites, outfitters and guides.

Hiking – *p 110.*

Mountain Biking – Bicycles and all motorized vehicles are prohibited from areas designated as wilderness or primitive in the Adirondack Forest Preserve. Bicycles are permitted on all other roads and trails, except where posted. Trail information is available from the Tourism Information Center *(Main St., PO Box 68, Old Forge, NY 13420,* ☎*315-369-6983);* the Lake Placid/Essex County Visitors Bureau *(p 108);* and the Adirondack North Country Assn.

Winter Sports – With their rugged terrain and annual snowfall of over 150 inches, the Adirondacks offer ample opportunities for winter recreation. **Downhill skiing** is available in Franklin County at Mt. Pisgah, Big Tupper and Titus Mountain; in Hamilton County at Oak Mountain; in Essex County at Whiteface Mountain; and in Herkimer County at McCauley Mountain. Many of these resorts also offer **snowboarding**. Well-groomed **cross-country-skiing** trails can be found at Malone, Tupper Lake, Saranac Lake (Franklin County) and in the Lake Placid area. Stores in Lake Placid offer rentals and trail information for **snowshoeing** and **snowmobiling**; guide service is also available.

that local hero John Shea wore to win his two gold medals in speed skating in 1932; and the "lucky" red dress that figure skater Linda Fratianne wore to capture the silver in 1980.

Ski jumps – *2mi south of downtown on Rte. 73. Open mid-May–late Oct daily 9am–4pm. Late Mar–mid-May Wed–Sun 9am–4pm. $3, chairlift/elevator $7.* ▯ ☎518-523-2202. The village of Lake Placid built these state-of-the-art jumps for the 1980 Games, in the same place the original 1921 jump once stood. Concrete was poured into molds continuously for 15 days to create the 120-meter jump; the 90-meter jump took nine days. The two gray towers are visible from miles around. A chairlift brings visitors to the top of the slope, and a 26-story elevator continues up to the 120-meter SkyDeck and vertiginous takeoff platform. In the summer the 90-meter ramp and slope are covered with plastic "grass" and ceramic tiles that simulate snow, making it one of the best off-season Nordic practice jumps in the world *(call ahead for practice times)*.

Less than a mile from the ski-jump site is the **John Brown Farm State Historic Site** *(.75mi down John Brown Rd. off Rte. 73; open late May–late Oct Wed–Sat & holidays 10am–5pm, Sun 1pm–5pm;* ▯ ☎518-523-3900), where the famous anti-slavery activist built his farmhouse in 1855 and elected to be buried in 1859. Two of his sons were also interred here in 1885 and 1899. Today the modest house and peaceful graveyard are open to the public, and display panels tell the story of the historic raid that Brown led on the US Arsenal in Harper's Ferry, Virginia. After his hanging in 1859, Brown came to be considered one of the anti-slavery movement's foremost martyrs.

Excursions

Saranac Lake – *1hr. 9mi west of Lake Placid on Rte. 86.* Called "the little Switzerland in the Adirondacks" by Robert Louis Stevenson, Saranac Lake began its heyday as a health resort in the 1880s, after Dr. Edward Livingston Trudeau

---

■ Hiking in the Adirondacks

To hiking enthusiasts, visiting the Adirondacks without venturing forth into her pristine wilderness would be like visiting Versailles and not seeing the palace. Two thousand miles of trails, many developed from old logging and fire roads, plunge into the deep forest, tracing cool mountain streams, skirting lakes, marshes and bogs, and offering heavenly views.

Nearly half of the total trail mileage in the park is concentrated in the eastern High Peaks region, situated southeast of Lake Placid. Here hikers will find the Adirondacks' most vigorous and popular trails, those that scale the heights of Mt. Marcy (the highest point in New York State at 5,344ft), Algonquin Mountain (5,114ft), Mt. Haystack (4,964ft), and other massive peaks in the MacIntyre Range. Heavily trafficked in July and August, many of these routes originate at the famed Adirondak Loj *(☎518-523-3441)*. Besides providing lodging, lakeside campsites and home-cooked meals, the all-season lodge is an invaluable clearinghouse for information on equipment, weather conditions and trails throughout the park.

Indeed, some of the lesser-known trails are the most rewarding. In the High Peaks, the secluded trail up Giant Mountain (4,627ft) offers stunning vistas without the parade of foot traffic found on Mt. Marcy, and a local hiking expert has called the trail up Jenkins Mountain "the best-designed trail in the park" due to its varied vegetation and gentle switchbacks. Outside the High Peaks region, the Pharaoh Lake Wilderness Area (east of Schroon Lake), the Five Ponds Wilderness Area (near Cranberry Lake), and the Siamese Ponds Wilderness Area have been touted as hidden treasures.

To get the most out of a hike in the Adirondacks, planning ahead is key. Be sure to match the difficulty of the trail to your ability level; some trails are extremely steep, especially near the summits. Always sign in at trail registers, and bring a detailed trail map with you. For your own safety and to prevent erosion, stay on marked trails. Wear sturdy boots and clothing made of wool instead of cotton, even in warm weather, and bring plenty of water, food, sunscreen, a compass and a flashlight. For full trail descriptions and information, consult the *ADK Guides to Adirondack Trails* series or the *Discover the Adirondacks* series, available at local outfitters and through the Adirondack Mountain Club *(814 Goggins Rd., Lake George NY 12845;* ☎518-668-4447), or drop in at the Adirondak Loj, where hiking afficionados will help you pick the trail that's best for you.

---

popularized the notion that "taking the air" here could cure tuberculosis. The picturesque mountain town maintains a sizable year-round population and exudes a friendly, laid-back ethos in its natural-foods store, restaurants, bars and shops.

★ **Robert Louis Stevenson Cottage** – *11 Stevenson Ln. From the town hall follow Main St. east approx. .25mi to its terminus at Triangle Park and Pine St. Turn left on Stevenson Ln. off Pine St. Open Jul–mid-Sept Tue–Sun & holidays 9:30am–4:30pm. Rest of the year by appointment only. $2.* ▣ ☎*518-891-1462.* Scottish-born Robert Louis Stevenson (1850-94), author of the popular 1883 novel *Treasure Island,* spent the winter of 1887-88 in the back half of this modest farmhouse, hoping to recover from tuberculosis as a patient of Dr. Trudeau's. Of the harsh weather he wrote, it is "a bleak blackguard beggarly climate, of which I can say no good except it suits me well, by whom all right it ought to kill." One of five museums commemorating places in which the peripatetic writer once lived, the house contains the largest collection of Stevenson's personal effects in the US, including photographs, first editions, scrapbooks, correspondence and an accomplished series of 18 woodcuts that Stevenson carved in Switzerland. Note in particular the cigarette burns that Stevenson left on the wooden mantelpiece and the dandyish black velvet cap and jacket he wore while he wrote.

★★ **Whiteface Mountain Veterans Memorial Highway** – *2hrs. From Lake Placid, take Rte. 86 to Rte. 431 in downtown Wilmington. Continue 3mi to toll booth. Open mid-May–late Jun daily 9am–4pm. Late Jun–Labor Day daily 9am–6pm. Sept–mid-Oct daily 9am–4pm. $8/car & driver, $4/passenger ($25 max.).* ✕ ▣ ☎*518-946-2223. Highway may be closed at any time due to inclement weather; call ahead.* A notable exception to the 1894 "forever wild" clause, this two-lane road was built in 1927 as a memorial to the veterans of World War I. It provides the only automobile access to a summit in the High Peaks. Starting in the forest, the highway climbs 5mi through a series of switchbacks toward the scrubby peak, offering ever-expanding vistas from roadside turnouts; informative panels describe features of the landscape and the geology of the area. On top, a rocky, .2mi trail ascends steeply from Whiteface Castle (1936) to the wind-whipped summit (4,867ft), the fifth-highest in New York State *(an elevator is accessible from the parking lot).* The 360-degree view★★★ extends 110mi on a clear day from nearby Lake Placid across the tree-covered mountains to Lake Champlain.

High Falls Gorge – *1hr. From Lake Placid, take Rte. 86. east for 8mi. Open Memorial Day–Jun daily 9am–4:15pm. Jul–Aug daily 8:30am–4:45pm. Sept–mid-Oct daily 9am–4:15pm. $5.50.* ✕ ᴴ ▣ *www.lake-placid.ny.us/highfallsgorge* ☎*518-946-2278.* The Ausable River drops 275ft in the 700ft-long series of four **falls**★ at High Falls Gorge. Following a woodplank path along the lip of the gorge, visitors can learn about the geology of the area—which includes 35ft-deep glacial "potholes," a mature climax forest and some of the oldest rock deposits in the world. Some 40mi farther east, the river descends into the long and narrow **Ausable Chasm** *(open Memorial Day–Jun daily 9:30am–4pm; Jul–Labor Day daily 9:30am–5pm; Sept–mid-Oct daily 9:30am–4pm; $19;* ⚠ ᴴ ▣ ☎*518-334-7454).* Paths carved into the rock and a series of bridges afford close-up views of the tumbling waters. The adventurous can float down the last 2mi of the chasm aboard inflatable rafts.

James Randklev/Tony Stone Images

Ausable River, Adirondacks

★★★ ADIRONDACK MUSEUM

At the intersection of Rte. 30 and Rte. 28 in the hamlet of Blue Mountain Lake.

Commanding a picturesque **view**★ of Blue Mountain Lake, this 32-acre compound of historic buildings, galleries and exhibit halls has been rightly called "the Smithsonian of the Adirondacks." Indeed, nowhere else in the park can you get such a complete view of the region's history—from its geology, flora and fauna, to its vernacular art and architecture, to its unique, present-day status as a public-private entity.

The museum was first opened in 1957 on the site of the popular 19C Blue Mountain House resort. Although the main hotel structure was torn down to make way for new exhibit space, an 1876 log house from the resort remains on-site, and a handful of other notable buildings—including a 1907 schoolhouse, an early-20C trolley-*cum*-diner and several whimsical cottages—have been imported from other parts of Adirondack Park. Newer structures contain exhibits on such topics as transportation, logging, mining and the environment, and display selections from the museum's 61,000-piece collection of Adirondack images, including works by Hudson River school founders Thomas Cole and Asher B. Durand; painters A.F. Tait, Winslow Homer and Frederic Remington; and the celebrated Glens Falls-based historian and photographer Seneca Ray Stoddard.

Visit   ½ *day. Map p 107.*

Open Memorial Day–mid-Oct daily 9:30am–5:30pm. $10. ✗ ♿ ▣ *www.adkmuseum.org*
☎*518-352-7311.* If time allows, begin your visit by watching the 35min film *The Adirondacks: The Life and Times of an American Wilderness,* a meticulously researched and thought-provoking overview of the history of the park. Continue your tour of the complex by following the map handed out at the entrance. Standout exhibits include:

★ **Adirondack architecture** – Reputedly the finest surviving example of rustic twig work built on an architectural scale, **Sunset Cottage**★ is completely covered with split spruce branches set in sunbursts and diamond patterns. Nearby, **Gustav Wiegand's Studio**, built on-site, contains a simple twig-work bed. **Bull Cottage**★, a whimsical structure atop Merwin Hill, features many pieces of bark furniture by Ernest Stowe. Widely acknowledged to be the master of the form, Stowe left Saranac Lake for Florida in 1911 and never came back.

★★ **Boats and Boating in the Adirondacks** – One of the museum's most acclaimed exhibits, this is the largest collection of freshwater boats in the country. Dating from c.1425 through the 1960s, the boats range from simple dugout canoes—the Adirondacks' earliest form of transportation—to gleaming wood-and-brass powerboats. Note especially the large room devoted to **guideboats**★★. Developed in the Adirondacks around 1849, these handsome double-ended rowboats were

Adirondack Guideboat

built sturdy enough to hold a guide, his client and their gear, yet light enough (50-75 pounds) so that the guide could carry the boat on his shoulders over the 1-2mi spits of land—or "carries"—sometimes found between lakes. Made with pine or cedar planking supported by spruce-root ribs, guideboats have become a symbol of the Adirondack wilderness, and their construction remains a time-honored art.

★ **Road and Rail Transportation Building** – Some 45,000sq ft of exhibition space is devoted to the single greatest impediment to the region's development in the 19C: transportation. Fifty horse-drawn sleighs, buggies and wagons, as well as exhibits on blacksmithing and wagon making, illustrate over-ground conveyance up to the railroad era. An exquisitely restored, fully furnished private **Pullman railroad car**★★ (1890)—complete with mahogany paneling, built-in liquor cabinets and a marble bath—shows the kind of wealth the robber barons brought with them to their Adirondack great camps.

Outside stands the 1900 **steam engine** and a passenger car of the Marion River Carry Railroad, the shortest standard-gauge railroad in the world (it ran a whopping three-quarters of a mile), financed by great-camp developer William West Durant.

★★ **GREAT CAMP SAGAMORE**   *4mi south of the town of Raquette Lake, off Rte. 28.*

Enjoyed by the Vanderbilt family for more than 50 years, this prototypical "great camp"—the only one regularly open to the public—was actually a 1,500-acre, self-contained village in its heyday. A wilderness playground, it encompassed dozens of outbuildings, an outdoor bowling alley, more than 20 fireplaces and sleeping quarters for 100 guests. Today the 19-acre complex, a National Historic Site, is expertly interpreted by the Sagamore Institute, a nonprofit educational organization.

Historical Notes – For **William West Durant**, son of railroad tycoon Dr. Thomas C. Durant, Sagamore and the two prior great camps he designed (Pine Knot and Uncas) were more business ventures than art projects. Called back from Europe in 1873 to develop his father's substantial land holdings in the Adirondacks (some 500,000 acres), Durant set about constructing charming "rustic" villages for the nouveau riche of the day. Pairing the twig ornamentation, notched logs and natural bark textures of Adirondack architecture with the gables, bay windows, massive fieldstone chimneys and large roof overhangs of Swiss chalets, Durant is credited with inventing a wholly new aesthetic. His first camp, Pine Knot, completed in the late 1880s, set off a flurry of great-camp construction by such families as the Guggenheims and the Whitneys, just as the developer had hoped. However, Durant was plagued by money problems. Sued by his sister for squandering the family fortune, he was forced to surrender his second great camp, Uncas (1895), to financier J.P. Morgan to pay off a loan. Sagamore, completed in 1897, was also sold at a loss, to Alfred G. Vanderbilt in 1901. In the ensuing half-century, as Vanderbilt—and later, his second wife, Margaret Emerson— continuously expanded and improved the luxuriously appointed camp, Durant made his living surveying the land he once owned. Willed to Syracuse University in the 1950s, the camp was bought by the Sagamore Institute in the 1970s and has been undergoing renovation ever since.

Visit *2hrs. Map p 107.*

Visit by guided tour (2hrs) only, Jul 4–mid-Oct daily 10am & 1:30pm. $7. ✕ 🅿 www. sagamore.org ☎315-354-5311. Guided tours begin with a slide presentation *(20min)* setting out the history of Adirondack Park and the peculiar Gilded Age philosophy that led to the rise of the great camps. For robber barons, as for the artists and intellectuals who preceded them, the Adirondacks represented an antidote to urban malaise. Yet even as the Vanderbilts and their ilk trekked more than 30 hours from Manhattan to Sagamore, they refused to leave behind the comforts of Park Avenue and Newport, virtually blocking out nature with a battalion of servants, sumptuous living quarters and an array of games imported from New York City. Moreover, the money used to build the great camps was often acquired by rapaciously consuming the very wilderness this "haute rustic" elite so admired. Guides explore these and other provocative themes during the tour of the complex.

Upper camp – This compound of simple board-and-batten structures includes a carriage barn (c.1898); a giant woodshed (c.1898); a schoolhouse (c.1911) used for children of workers at Sagamore and in neighboring camps; and a chalet (1915), which still houses Sagamore's staff. During their tenure here, the Vanderbilt family kept 40 to 200 servants employed year-round. Most of the original ironwork chandeliers, hinges and fixtures you'll see in the lower camp were made by highly skilled craftsmen in the blacksmith's shop (1897).

Lower camp – Splayed out on a peninsula jutting into scenic Raquette Lake, the buildings here give visitors a good sense of what made up a great camp. Boasting cedar-bark siding and a yellow birch twig-work railing on the outside, and a two-ton fieldstone mantel and dark wood paneling within, the **Wigwam★** was formerly used as a men's lodge. Word has it that the walls were once hung with paintings by Renoir and Remington. The three-and-a-half-story **main lodge★★** typifies Durant's Swiss-chalet-meets-Adirondack-rustic aesthetic. While the spruce logs on the outside are decorative rather than structural, the roof overhang successfully protects the foundation from rain and snow. Note the sporty red window trim, a classic Durant touch. The interior is flanked with knotty white pine paneling and contains the original table and iron chandelier, made onsite. Expanded twice during the Vanderbilt era, the paneled, bay-windowed **dining room** features lake views from three sides and more intricate ironwork. Fiercely competitive, Margaret Emerson reigned over the **playhouse**—once jam-packed with stuffed game, a Ping-Pong table, a billiard table, a roulette wheel and other diversions—and the famous outdoor **bowling alley★** (1913), so sturdily constructed that it functions to this day.

CHAMPLAIN VALLEY★★

Map pp 7-8
Tourist Information ☎518-563-1000

Skirting the eastern edge of Adirondack Park, this fertile valley lies between two mountain ranges—the Adirondack foothills to the west and Vermont's Green Mountains to the east—and centers on 125mi-long Lake Champlain, "the sixth Great Lake." Millions of years after the surrounding mountains rose out of the ocean floor, retreating glaciers melted to form the lake and create the moraines, kettle ponds, cirques and erratic boulders that pock the area. The Iroquois Confederacy ruled the valley well into the 17C, long after French explorer Samuel de Champlain "discovered" the lake in 1609. During the mid-18C French and Indian War, both British and French forts and settlements grew up along Champlain's shores. After considerable back-and-forth, Britain won control of the valley, but the victory was short-lived; Americans snatched back the forts during the Revolutionary War and trounced the Brits again at the Battle of Plattsburgh, fought on Lake Champlain on September 11, 1814.

In the early 19C the valley's pines were clear-cut, not only to fuel the burgeoning demand for timber, but to stoke the numerous charcoal furnaces in which iron was made from ore. Mining and logging dominated the valley's economy until the mid-19C, when farmers began growing crops on the deforested land. While small settlements thrived here and there, in the early 20C the valley fell into a slump from which it has not yet fully recovered. Logging in the park has become increasingly controversial; small family farms are having a hard time competing with agribusiness; a large military base in Plattsburgh closed in the early 1990s. In recent years tourism has taken up some of the slack. Two historic forts—one rebuilt, one in intriguing ruins—bring the area's 18C history alive, and several small towns retain a quaint 19C feel. Vacation homes, summer camps and resorts dot the shores of the beautiful lake, and, of course, the celebrated mountains both to the east and to the west extend a tantalizing range of outdoor recreation options.

SIGHTS *2 days. Map p 107.*

Most museums are open only May through October. For information on sights and accommodations, contact the Champlain Valley Heritage Network, Rte. 1, Box 220, Crown Point, NY 12928; ☎518-597-4646.

★★ **Fort Ticonderoga** – 🖼 *On Rte. 74, 1mi east of village of Ticonderoga. Open early May–late Oct daily 9am–5pm (Jul–Aug 6pm). $8. ✗ ♿ 🅿 www.neinfo.net ☎518-585-2821.* More than 100,000 visitors throng "Fort Ti" each year, making it the most popular tourist attraction in the Champlain Valley. From its commanding perch, the enormous reconstructed fort offers bird's-eye views of Lake Champlain and a glimpse of 18C military life.

The French built the star-shaped, log-and-stone fort in the fall of 1755 to defend the southeast border of their fur-trade empire. In the years that followed, the British attacked the mighty fortification (which the French called Carillon) repeatedly, finally capturing it for King George in 1759—but not before the French blew their majestic creation to bits. Rebuilding the fort and renaming it Ticonderoga (a Mohawk word for "place between the waters," referring to lakes George and Champlain), the Redcoats held it until May 1775, when Ethan Allen and his Green Mountain Boys, along with Benedict Arnold, heroically raided it "in the name of the Great Jehovah and the Continental Congress." The supplies captured here were used the following spring by George Washington to drive the British out of Boston, but in July 1777 it was the Americans who were driven out of Ticonderoga. Simply by hacking a path to the top of nearby Mt. Defiance and placing cannons there, British Gen. John Burgoyne and his troops forced the Revolutionaries to surrender.

In the early 19C, wealthy merchant William Ferris Pell purchased the fort and the 600-acre peninsula surrounding it to protect the ruins. Reconstruction began in 1908 based on archaeological research, historical descriptions and maps. Incorporating the old fort's ruins, the colossal limestone replica appears as formidable today as the original likely did in the 18C. High, sloping walls rise up from a deep ditch, and diamond-shaped bastions bristle with cannons pointed in every direction. Within the central parade ground, costumed guides roam around, coalescing now and then to relate the fort's history, perform musket and cannon demonstrations, or march with the drum-and-fife corps. Visitors are invited to explore the cavernous powder magazine, the cool, dark bakehouse and casemates, and a selection of the fort's 26,000 **artifacts★** (only a small fraction of which were excavated on-site, mostly related to 18C and early-19C military history.

Penfield Homestead Historical Museum – *From Rte. 9N, turn left on Rte. 74 and continue to County Rte. 2. Turn right and proceed for 3mi to Ironville Rd. Open mid-May–Jun Wed–Sun 10am–4pm. Jul–Aug daily 10am–4pm. Sept–mid-Oct Wed–Sun 10am–4pm.* 🅿 ☎*518-597-3804.* Situated in historic Ironville, an intriguing little hamlet that is now part of Crown Point, this 1828 homestead was built for Allen Penfield, part-owner of the local ironworks. Though his was only one of more than 200 ironworks in the Adirondack region in the 1800s, Penfield's operation had two claims to fame: it contributed material for such grand 19C projects as the Brooklyn Bridge and the famous Civil War ship *Monitor*, and it saw the first industrial use of electricity. Penfield's Federal-style dwelling contains heirlooms, an exhibit on the local iron industry, and glass cases packed with trinkets and photographs. Ironville, today consisting of eight Federal and Greek Revival structures set in a clearing in the woods, was placed on the National Register of Historic Places in 1974.

Indian Kettles

On Rte. 9; 5mi south of Ticonderoga; 2mi north of Hague. ☎518-543-6576. Don't let the moose head in the timbered dining room scare you away. For a casual lunch or dinner with a phenomenal view of Lake George and the surrounding mountains, this venerable 51-year-old institution can't be beat. Weather permitting, the expansive back deck, high above the lake, is dotted with umbrella tables from which you can ogle formidable Roger's Rock as well as the glacial "kettles" in which Native Americans once stored and cooked food. (Hence the name Indian Kettles.) The fare is standard (burgers and fries for lunch; seafood and steak for dinner), the service is friendly, and the setting is extraordinary. See for yourself.

★ Crown Point State Historic Site – *Return to Rte. 9N. The fort is 4mi east of the junction of Rtes. 9N and 22, at the foot of Lake Champlain Bridge. The path is not paved; wear good shoes. Open year-round Mon–Tue 9am–4:30pm, Wed–Sun 9am–6pm (hours may be extended during the summer). $4/car.* ☎518-597-3666. The fascinating, eerie ruins on this scenic peninsula are all that's left of Ft. St. Frédéric, completed in 1737 by the French, and of "His Majesty's Fort of Crown Point," built by the British in 1759. Altered mainly by the elements—but impeccably interpreted by the New York State Park Service—the ruins provide a perfect complement to fully reconstructed Ft. Ticonderoga *(p 114)* 15mi to the south. Though a relatively small stronghold, Ft. St. Frédéric established French control over the Champlain Valley for more than 20 years. The garrison withstood four attacks by the British between 1755 and 1758 before falling in 1759. The British decided to build a brand-new fort just southwest of the French site. One of the most ambitious military engineering projects they undertook in the colonies yielded the gigantic, star-shaped complex of redoubts and blockhouses. Raided in 1775 by American colonists, it was retaken by Gen. John Burgoyne's army in 1776 and remained under British control for the rest of the Revolutionary War.

Today a one-story visitor center (*open mid-May–mid-Oct Wed–Sat 10am–5pm, Sun 1pm–5pm; closed Memorial Day, Jul 4, Labor Day*) provides a historical overview of the site with an entertaining slide show (*10min*), neatly curated exhibits and hundreds of artifacts (hinges, bolts, pottery shards, powder horns and guns) excavated from the grounds and the bottom of Lake Champlain. A walking tour studded with interpretive signs leads visitors around the provocative ruins, which range from the pile of rubble marking the place where the four-story, eight-sided citadel of Ft. St. Frédéric once stood to the elegant Georgian-style barracks of Crown Point, now roofless and floored with grass. The dirt trail along the top of the scarp around the British fort provides magnificent **views**★★ of the ruins, the lake and the nearby bridge to Vermont.

Just across Bridge Road from the ruins stands the **Champlain Memorial and Lighthouse** (*open mid-Apr–mid-Oct daily 10am–6pm, weather permitting; $3/car*), completed in 1912 following the tercentennial celebration of Samuel de Champlain's discovery of the lake. The unique design by architects Dillon, McClellan and Beadle features a cylindrical granite tower encircled by eight Doric columns and a stepped copper roof; decorations include a bronze statue of Champlain with his explorer cohorts resting in a niche above the protruding prow of a canoe. Climb the 62-step spiral staircase to the parapet for great panoramic **views**★★.

Traveling north from Crown Point toward Plattsburgh, consider taking scenic Route 22 all the way to Exit 33 off the Northway (I-87). The road snakes along Lake Champlain from Crown Point to **Westport**, an affluent town with a yacht club, a sloping village green flanked by 19C B&Bs and mansions, a couple of gourmet restaurants and shops. North of Westport the road darts inland—notice the New England-style fieldstone walls separating the farms and estates—until it reaches **Essex**★. Founded in 1765, this charming former port town has been called "the jewel of Lake Champlain's western shore" for its meticulously preserved and greatly varied 18C and 19C architecture and its historic downtown shopping district, now tastefully lined with craft shops, antique stores, boutiques, B&Bs and an 1815 dock house converted to a popular lakeside restaurant (*a ferry to Vermont leaves from the adjacent pier;* ☎*802-864-9804*). After Essex, Route 22 cuts back into the thickly forested Adirondack foothills. Rejoin I-87 and continue north to **Plattsburgh**. Although the closing of a large Air Force base prompted a major economic downturn here, a number of industries—including bottling, railroads and education—keep this struggling city alive.

★ **Kent-Delord House Museum** – *17 Cumberland Ave., Plattsburgh. Open Mar–Dec Tue–Sat noon–4pm. $3.* ♿ ☎*518-561-1035.* Six first-floor rooms may be seen at this handsome lakeside dwelling, which was briefly commandeered by the British during the War of 1812, just prior to their defeat at the Battle of Plattsburgh. One of the oldest residences in the area, the Federal-style house (1797) was occupied by the Delord family from 1810 to 1913. Today the vastness of the family's collection of furniture, art and collectibles allows the museum to depict a different era every two years: 1810-30, 1830-60, and 1860-1913. Among the items consistently on view are an extensive collection of blue and white Canton porcelain dating from the 1700s; paintings by Abraham Tuthill, Henry Inman and others; a 1735 tall-case clock (the oldest piece of furniture in the house); and a wooden mess chest left behind by the British during their occupation.

Across the street there is a small waterfront park with a 1909 monument to French explorer Samuel de Champlain.

SUNY-Plattsburgh Art Museum – *101 Broad St., Plattsburgh. Open year-round daily noon–4pm (Thu 8pm). Closed major holidays.* ✗♿🅿 ☎*518-564-2474.* Founded in 1989, this "museum without walls" is spread over various buildings and plazas of Brutalist-style State University of New York (SUNY) Plattsburgh campus. It comprises outdoor sculptures, a fledgling permanent collection, temporary installations, student art, and—the museum's greatest strength—significant holdings of work by 20C artists Rockwell Kent and Nina Winkel.

Tucked in a corner of the Feinberg Library, the **Rockwell Kent Gallery** *(2nd floor)* contains the most complete collection of the versatile artist's work in the US. The museum's small permanent collection is also located here. An attractive two-story glass atrium located on the second floor of the John P. Myers Fine Arts Building, the **Nina Winkel Sculpture Court**★ houses more than 40 sculptures by this celebrated artist. Set off by greenery and fountains, the mostly representational sculptures, made over the course of 50 years, are at turns dramatic and playful, many depicting the cycle of life and death.

★ **Alice T. Miner Museum** – *On Rte. 9, Chazy, 12mi north of Plattsburgh. Open Feb–Dec 22 Tue–Sat 10am–4pm. Closed major holidays. $3.* 🅟 ☎518-846-7336. "Eclectic" does not come close to describing this far-flung accretion of knick-knacks, art and collectibles, which range from historically significant artifacts to rather unusual mummified objects. The museum's founder, Alice T. Miner, the wife of wealthy railroad inventor and noted philanthropist William H. Miner, was a leading light in the Colonial Revival movement. At that time, Colonial Revival was loosely interpreted as anything old or interesting. Largely unchanged since Alice's death in 1950, this one-of-a-kind museum is set up to resemble a house, though the Miners never lived in it (they occupied a sprawling, 18,000-acre experimental farm nearby). A kitchen with a beamed ceiling and an open hearth, a children's room and a weaving room all recall a bygone era, as do the plentiful portraits of George Washington and Abraham Lincoln—Colonial Revival favorites. Other items in the collection include miniature furniture; massive holdings of china, porcelain and pressed glass; needlework samplers; Revolutionary War weapons; Lincoln's inkwell; ruins from Pompeii; and a piece of George Washington's first coffin. Fascinating stories accompany some of the more offbeat items.

SARATOGA SPRINGS ★★★

Population 25,118
Map p 7
Tourist Information ☎518-584-3255 or 800-526-8970

Renowned for its rejuvenating mineral waters, thoroughbred racetrack and luxury hotels, Saratoga Springs was considered the premier summer getaway for the 19C social elite. While today many of the mammoth resorts have given way to quaint B&Bs and hotels, an air of summery aristocracy lingers in block after block of resplendent Victorian homes and in a downtown shopping district lined with antique stores, artsy coffeeshops and outdoor restaurants. The town's tourist season reaches its festive peak during August, when the historic track opens for thoroughbred racing six days a week. During the rest of the year, a handful of unique museums and historic sites, a great state park, and a genial collegiate atmosphere provide a window to life in Saratoga Springs, past and present.

Historical Notes

As early as the 14C, Mohawk Indians came to the area around what is now Saratoga Springs on their annual hunting expeditions because they found an unusually large aggregation of game here. The discovery that the animals were drawn to the high salt content of the naturally carbonated springs—which originate between layers of limestone 100ft to 1,000ft below the earth's surface and bubble up through the Saratoga Fault—led to the belief that the springs possessed various curative powers. Beginning in the mid-1700s, Indian guides led wealthy Europeans to the springs. After British Indian agent Sir William Johnson, Gen. Philip Schuyler, George Washington and Alexander Hamilton attested to some magic in the area—owing perhaps to the decisive Revolutionary War victories at the Battles of Saratoga *(p 121)* in 1777—tourists flooded in, with hucksters not far behind.

Though it could never be proven that the springs themselves provided relief for "the overweight, the languid, and those suffering from indigestion, gout and gravel," Saratoga Springs' fresh air and pleasant social diversions offered a genuine tonic to both the healthy and the infirm. Between 1865 and 1890 the population grew from 7,000 to 12,000 as grand hotels sprung up along Broadway, rambling Victorian summer cottages took over the surrounding neighborhoods and the Canfield Casino and historic Saratoga Racetrack gobbled up the wealthy tourists' money. Saratoga Springs began to take on its present character in the early 20C. After the casino closed in 1907, the excesses of the superwealthy were less in evidence, but fun-loving New York dandies continued to make the trek up for the fashionable racing season. The town also gained favor among artists and intellectuals, due to the combined presence of Skidmore College, the exclusive artists' retreat Yaddo, and the summer residencies of the New York City Ballet and the Philadelphia Orchestra. Today the sidewalk cafes, gourmet shops, bookstores, restaurants, bars and galleries on and around historic Broadway reflect a mix of urban and resort-town sensibilities.

SIGHTS 1 day. Map below.

With 900 of the town's buildings on the National Register of Historic Places, even a quiet stroll through downtown Saratoga Springs can be enlightening. A good place to start is the **Urban Cultural Park Visitor Center** (*297 Broadway; open Apr–Nov daily 9am–4pm; rest of the year Mon–Fri 9am–4pm; closed Easter Sunday, Thanksgiving Day & Fri after, & Dec 25; & www.albany.net/~cultural ☎518-587-3241*), which contains a wealth of brochures on historic sites, accommodations and special events, as well as self-guided walking-tour maps. Hundreds of Victorian summer "cottages" testify to the residential building boom that transformed the sleepy hamlet into the nation's premier resort town between 1865 and 1900. Queen Anne was perhaps the most popular style, but Greek Revival, Gothic, Italianate, Second

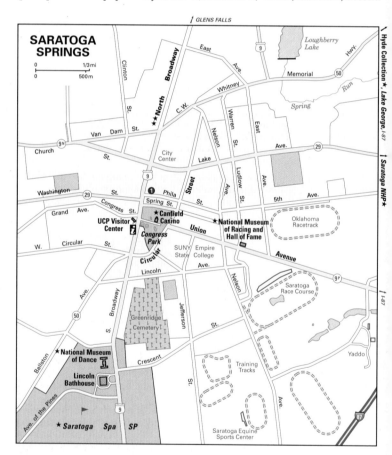

Empire and Bungalow structures were also common, and there are many cases where elements of several styles have been combined for original, whimsical effects. The most ritzy and least trafficked of Saratoga's grand thoroughfares is **North Broadway★★** between downtown and the Skidmore campus. The whole East Side is also ripe for exploration. While the larger structures, many now renovated as B&Bs and offices, are congregated along **Union Avenue** and **Circular Street**, the quiet back streets contain hundreds of hidden gems.

Saratoga Race Course

★ **National Museum of Racing and Hall of Fame** – *191 Union Ave. Open late Jul–Labor Day daily 9am–5pm. Rest of the year Mon–Sat 10am–4:30pm, Sun noon–4:30pm. Closed Jan 1, Easter Sunday, Thanksgiving Day, Dec 25. $5.* 🅿 ☎*518-584-0400.* Everything you wanted to know about thoroughbred racing and more has been wedged into this one-story brick museum located across the street from the Saratoga Racetrack. Encircling a central courtyard, exhibit rooms bursting with portraits, trophies and equestrian paraphernalia tell the story of the elite sport from when it arrived in the New World in the 17C to the present era, with one room focusing on the track at Saratoga—the nation's oldest. Colorful jockey's silks; a 19C "take-down purse" that first-place riders used to snatch at the finish line (hence today's term "purse" for winnings); and a full-size thoroughbred skeleton rank among the highlights of the museum's enormous collection. Interactive exhibits and an 18min wide-screen film provide still more details on how winning horses were bred, how much they cost, who owned them, trained them and raced them, as well as how to place a bet.

Congress Park – *Broadway between Spring and Circular Sts.* Bordering the southern edge of downtown, verdant Congress Park originated in the early 1800s as a small private garden where visitors could stroll after imbibing the waters from the Congress and Columbian springs. Expanded and enhanced three times over

---

■ **Racing Season**

In Saratoga there are essentially two seasons: the six-week racing season beginning the third week of July and the rest of the year. Live entertainment is offered at venues throughout the city every night during those precious six weeks, and on the first and last weekends of the season, Hats Off to Saratoga, a festive fair, fills the streets with vendors and music. A couple of chic restaurants (Siro's and The Lodge) open their doors only during the racing season. The seat of the action, of course, centers around the celebrated 1864 racetrack, where some of the finest thoroughbreds in the world run neck-in-neck in up to ten races a day, six days a week *(the track is closed Tuesday)*. The prestigious Travers Stakes takes place in late August. On regular race days, a modest fee ($2) buys admission to the grounds, where you can spread a blanket on the grass and feel the thunder of the horses' hooves as they come out of a turn; grandstand seats ($4) offer a bird's-eye view of the action. Continuing the track's dandy tradition are the $50-minimum betting windows, the box seats handed down from generation to generation, and the dress code enforced at two of the track's four restaurants. Another tradition, the **early-morning breakfast**★★ at the beautiful, often mist-shrouded track, can be enjoyed by anyone. Whether you sip your coffee in the stands or enjoy a trackside meal at the historic clubhouse, the main attraction is watching the horses exercise as an expert delivers an informative commentary. It's a great way to get the inside scoop on the winners.

the century, mostly notably by Frederick Law Olmsted in the 1870s, the park now comprises two square blocks of rolling hills, walking paths, fountains, duck ponds, Italian gardens and statuary; the two historic springs are sheltered by attractive pavilions.

Centerpiece of the park, the imposing **Canfield Casino★**, a luxuriously appointed Italianate structure, is now home to the **Historical Society of Saratoga Springs** *(open Jun–Sept Mon–Sat & holidays 10am–4pm, Sun 1pm–4pm; rest of the year Wed–Sat & holidays 10am–4pm, Sun 1pm–4pm; $3;* ☎*518-584-6920)*. Built in 1870 by John Morrissey, a legendary prize fighter, banker and Tammany Hall politician, the casino was purchased and substantially refurbished by New York City gambler Richard Canfield in 1894. Though gambling was technically illegal, Canfield's casino enjoyed a reputation as one of the Empire State's flashiest gaming parlors until 1907. Today the Historical Society uses a handful of the casino's smaller rooms to fill out various aspects of Saratoga Springs' past; its comprehensive exhibit on the history of the town *(2nd floor)* is by far the region's best. To get a sense of the casino's true grandeur, however, ask to see the palatial colonnaded dining hall (which is capped with a marvelous barrel-vaulted ceiling honeycombed with colored-glass windows) and the plush gaming parlor, which boasts massive chandeliers, floor-to-ceiling windows, domed skylights and rich mahogany woodwork.

★ **Saratoga Spa State Park** – *1mi south of downtown; main entrance on Rte. 9. Open year-round daily 8am–dusk. $4/car.* ✗ ▯ ☎*518-584-2535.* Two golf courses, clay and hardtop tennis courts, two swimming-pool complexes, a historic hotel, a huge performing-arts amphitheater and numerous picnicking areas take up much of this 2,200-acre site, though a quiet walking/running path does meander along Geyser Brook beneath a canopy of hemlocks. The park was created by the state legislature in 1909 to protect Saratoga's springs from the carbonated-beverage industry, which had drilled more than 200 wells in the area in order to extract the waters' naturally occurring carbon dioxide gas. In 1927 New York governor Franklin D. Roosevelt appointed a commission to develop a spa at Saratoga. Completed in 1935, the complex of classically inspired buildings on the park grounds is now a National Historic Landmark. Fizzy mineral baths and an array of massages and herbal wraps are still offered at the 1920 **Lincoln Bathhouse** *(for reservations, call* ☎*518-583-2880).*

★ **National Museum of Dance** – *99 South Broadway. Open year-round Tue–Sun 10am–5pm. Closed major holidays. $3.50.* ♿ ▯ *www.spac.org* ☎*518-584-2225.* Established in 1986, this exquisite museum, located within the state park in the former Washington Bath Pavilion, a 1909 Arts and Crafts structure, has expertly found its footing among the region's finest arts institutions. The only museum in the country devoted solely to dance, it pays tribute to ballet, modern, jazz and tap legends with a style and simplicity these dancers and choreographers would admire. Twenty-four great dancers, choreographers, and dance promoters—including George Balanchine, Isadora Duncan, Bill "Bojangles" Robinson, Martha Graham, Alvin Ailey and Fred Astaire—are honored individually in the Hall of Fame with large, expressive photographs, well-written biographical sketches and, when possible, performance videos. State-of-the-art practice studios are located behind the museum; visitors are invited to watch rehearsals of visiting dance troupes.

★ **Saratoga National Historical Park** – *Entrance is on Rte. 4, 10mi east of downtown. Visitor center is 2.5mi from the*

① Lyrical Ballad Bookstore

Map p 118. 7 Phila St., Saratoga Springs. ☎*518-584-8779.* Don't judge this book by its cover. Behind the humble storefront shaded by the striped awning lies a labyrinth of passageways and back rooms lined floor-to-ceiling with more than 75,000 used books. Founded in 1971, Lyrical Ballad has earned a reputation as one of the finest rare and antiquarian booksellers in the area. Dealers from around the world stop in regularly to look in the vault, which contains an exceptional array of first editions, leather-bound sets, and rare books on (you guessed it) thoroughbred racing. For the amateur bibliophile, great sections on film, drama, literary criticism, philosophy, and visual art offer hours of browsing pleasure.

entrance. *Visitor center open year-round daily 9am–5pm. Closed Jan 1, Thanksgiving Day, Dec 25. Tour road open to vehicles Apr–Nov. $4/car.* ♿ 🅿 ☎518-664-9821. History changed its course at the Battles of Saratoga in 1777. In the summer of that year Gen. John Burgoyne and his British comrades had planned a massive, three-pronged attack to gain control of the Hudson River from the American patriots. Traveling south from Canada, Burgoyne captured mighty Ft. Ticonderoga *(p 114)* on July 6 after a four-day siege, but here, during two battles, he and his troops were routed. A fast ship brought the news to Europe, and on December 6, King Louis XVI announced France's decisive support of the American Revolution.

Today a modern visitor center affords a panoramic view of the 2,800-acre battle site. Audiovisual exhibits, Revolutionary War artifacts, and a 21min film provide detailed accounts of the battles, many from an 18C perspective. A 10mi **tour road★** features turnouts to 10 significant sites; to get the full story of the battles, rent the audiotape *(1hr 30min)* to accompany you on your drive or take a horse-drawn carriage tour with a Park Service-trained guide. To simply enjoy the natural beauty of the site, consider bicycling the tour road or hiking the wooded, 4.2mi Wilkinson Trail.

A related site is the handsome, Federal **Philip Schuyler House** *(7mi north of battle-field on Rte. 4; visit by 25min guided tour Jun–Labor Day Fri–Sun 10am–4pm;* 🅿 *)*, built in November 1777 after General Burgoyne burned the much larger original structure during his retreat from the Americans. Restored to its 1787-1804 appearance, the airy summer home filled with period furnishings is interpreted by informative costumed guides. A wealthy landowner, politician and general, Schuyler *(p 95)* hosted George Washington, Thomas Jefferson and the Marquis de Lafayette here. Alexander Hamilton, who married one of Schuyler's daughters, had his own room in the attic.

EXCURSIONS

★ **Hyde Collection** – *1hr. 25mi north of Saratoga Springs via I-87. Take Exit 18 to Glen Falls and follow signs to downtown. 161 Warren St., Glens Falls. Open May–Oct Tue–Sun 10am–5pm. Rest of the year Wed–Sun noon–5pm. Closed major holidays.* ♿ 🅿 ☎518-792-1761. Combining the intimacy of a historic house with the spectacular holdings of a world-class museum, the Hyde Collection is a diamond in a somewhat rough part of Glens Falls, a former milltown. Louis Fiske Hyde (1866-1934) and Charlotte Pruyn Hyde (1867-1963) financed their formidable art collection with money from Charlotte's father's successful paper company. Starting with European old masters, they gradually acquired an important selection of 18C Italian Renaissance and French antiques, as well as works by Impressionists, Cubists and 19C American artists. Works by a shocking number of great artists—Botticelli, da Vinci, El Greco, Rubens, Rembrandt, Cézanne, Renoir, Whistler, van Gogh and Picasso, among many others—cover the walls of the Hydes' stately Italian Renaissance villa (1912), whose exquisitely furnished rooms are arranged around a two-story skylit courtyard studded with sculpture and tropical plants. An Education Wing (1989) includes three gallery spaces featuring temporary exhibits, an auditorium, an art studio and a museum shop.

Lake George – *2hrs. 29mi north of Saratoga Springs via I-87 & Rte. 9.* A slim finger of blue measuring 32mi long and up to 3mi wide, Lake George parallels the southeast edge of Adirondack Park and boasts some 179 islands and 159mi of mostly private shoreline. The lake was discovered and dubbed Lac du St. Sacrement by Isaac Jogues, a French Jesuit priest, in 1646, but Adirondack explorer Sir William Johnson renamed it in the mid-18C in honor of King George II of England. The lake played a pivotal role in both the French and Indian War and the American Revolution.

At the southernmost tip of the lake, the village of Lake George hosts a carnival-esque profusion of motels, sports bars and shops hawking T-shirts, ice cream, fudge and souvenirs. Just south of town, rock-lined **Prospect Mountain Veterans Memorial Highway** wends its way to the 2,030ft summit, offering up to 100mi views of Lake George from an expansive mountaintop parking lot. Another way to see the lake is by boat. Two companies located on Beach Road offer narrated cruises: **Shoreline** *(departs from Shoreline Marina May–Oct daily; round-trip 1-2hrs; commentary; $8;* ✗ ♿ 🅿 ☎518-668-4644) and the **Lake George Steamboat Co.** *(departs from Steel Pier May–Oct daily; round-trip 1hr-4hrs 30min; commentary; reservations required; $7.75-$29.95;* ✗ ♿ 🅿 *[$5]* ☎518-668-2015 or 800-553-2628).

Fort William Henry – *Pedestrian entrance on Beach Rd. Open May–Jun daily 10am–5pm. Jul–Aug daily 9am–10pm. Sept–Oct daily 10am–5pm. $8.50.* ✗ & 🄿 *www.fortwilliam henry.com* ☎518-668-5471. The log-and-earth fort that the British erected in 1775 on this site overlooking Lake George was never intended to withstand a full-scale attack by the French, but it did just that during a five-day siege in March 1757.

Four months later, however, the French and their Indian allies tried again, and this time British troops—vastly outnumbered, short on supplies and munitions, and fighting off a smallpox epidemic—agreed to an honorable surrender. Disgruntled with their role as hired guns for the French, though, the Indians swept in and massacred hundreds of men, women and children. Afterward the French burned the fort, but the British returned to the site a year later to embark on their first unsuccessful attack on Ft. Ticonderoga *(p 114)*, a massive bastion anchoring the northern tip of the lake. Located next to the sprawling motor lodge that bears its name, the reconstructed fort was built on the 18C foundations according to original British plans. While not everything here is historically accurate, costumed guides relate grisly details about 18C military life and perform cannon- and musket-firing demonstrations.

★ **Marcella Sembrich Memorial Studio** – *1hr. 9mi north of Lake George on Rte. 9N. 4800 Lakeshore Dr., Bolton Landing. Open Jun–Sept daily 10am–5:30pm. $2.* & 🄿 *www.lgdigitalads.com/sembrich* ☎516-644-9839. Stuffed full of fascinating musical mementos, art and antiques, this pink stucco teaching studio (1924) located on a scenic wooded peninsula overlooking Lake George preserves the memory of one of the greatest opera singers of the fin-de-siècle era. A coloratura soprano, Polish-born **Marcella Sembrich** (1858-1935) dominated opera stages in the US and Europe from 1879 until 1909. After retiring from performance, she became a celebrated teacher, founding the illustrious voice programs at Juilliard and the Curtis School of Music. Tributes from such musical greats as Liszt, Rachmaninoff, Puccini and Enrico Caruso (her longtime singing partner) bedeck the interior, along with a 1905 Steinway baby grand piano, dozens of trophies and gilded laurels, glittering costumes and scores of librettos and photographs. A scenic loop trail *(.25mi)* offers **views**★★ of Lake George and cuts back through the woods to the house.

> **The Grist Mill**
> *River St., Warrensburg.*
> ☎518-623-3949.
> This picturesque 1824 mill on the Schroon River once produced some 15 tons of grain a day; today the mill's owners pay homage to that heritage with an award-winning gourmet restaurant and an array of historic exhibits. The spacious main dining room boasts a sloping timbered ceiling, candlelit tables, and river views. The healthful, inventive cuisine, which can be sampled here year-round, incorporates seasonal vegetables, succulent meats and fish, and natural grains, reflecting the restaurant's milling past. Tastefully tucked here and there on both the upper and lower levels are photographs, paintings, and a documentary video on milling and logging in the region, as well as the miller's office and artifacts including the original mill stone and swing hoist and a reconstructed water wheel.

THOUSAND ISLANDS REGION★

Map p 7
Tourist Information ☎315-482-2520

Flowing northeast over the shoulder of New York State, the St. Lawrence River forms the backbone of this scenic region and the Thousand Islands area beats at its heart. As it leaves Lake Ontario, the river filters past the islands (which actually number more than 1,700) and then on for 700mi to the sea through a corridor of great beauty, historical interest and sporting opportunities. The river blurs the border between the US and Canada, which divides Lake Ontario and winds through the Thousand Islands, leaving two-thirds of them in Canada.

Historical Notes

When Jacques Cartier first paddled North America's longest east-west river in 1535, he hoped it would lead to China, or at least to a land as rich as the Spaniards had found in Mexico. The French, however, would have to settle for the bounty of the fur trade. Allying themselves with the indigenous Algonquian peoples, the French dominated the region until the end of the French and Indian War in 1763. As Americans, British and Indians vied for control of western lands after the Revolution, the waterways of the St. Lawrence and Great Lakes played a key role, and during the War of 1812 conflict raged in the North Country. Today historical markers along the 454mi **Seaway Trail** *(p 364)* that skirts the water's edge from Lake Erie to Massena, identify 42 important sites connected with the war. At the same time, trade with Canada was paramount to life in the region and continued at the hands of smugglers who operated under cover of the Thousand Islands throughout the war.

After 1825 the Erie Canal deflected trade and travelers away from the lake routes, and towns along the waterway staggered until the 1870s when, largely due to publicity surrounding visits by former president Ulysses S. Grant, the Thousand Islands blossomed as a vacation destination among the wealthy. Fishing parties became all the rage, nimble St. Lawrence skiffs and tasty shore dinners *(p 128)* their legacy. Besides tourism, North Country communities lived on lumbering, boatbuilding, paper milling and dairy farming. The idea for a US-Canadian seaway to enable deep-draft navigation between Lake Superior and the Atlantic

---

Practical Information .... Area Code: 315

Getting There – I-81 provides access to the entire Thousand Islands area from **Syracuse** to **Alexandria Bay**. Routes 12 and 27 follow the St. Lawrence Seaway from **Clayton** to **Massena**. **Syracuse-Hancock International Airport** handles international and domestic flights; limited domestic flights service **Massena International Airport** and **Watertown Municipal Airport**. Closest Amtrak **train** station (☎*800-872-7245)* is located in Syracuse. Greyhound **bus** service (☎*402-330-2055 or 800-231-2222)* runs to Oswego.

Visitor Information – Contact the following agencies for information and brochures on points of interest, seasonal events, recreation and accommodations: **Thousand Islands International Council Visitors Center** *(43373 Collins Landing, Alexandria Bay NY 13607 www.1000islands.com* ☎*482-2520 or 800-847-5263)*; **County of Oswego Department of Promotion and Tourism** *(46 E. Bridge St., Oswego NY 13126* ☎*349-8322)*; **Sackets Harbor Chamber of Commerce** *(PO Box 17, Sackets Harbor NY 13685* ☎*646-1700)*; **Alexandria Bay Chamber of Commerce** *(PO Box 365, Alexandria Bay NY 13607* ☎*482-9531 or 800-541-2100)*. The Fish•N•Fun hotline provides fishing reports and information about upcoming events: ☎800-248-4386.

Accommodations – *(p 358)* Area visitors' guides including lodging directories and campgrounds are available *(free)* from local tourism agencies *(above)*. Hotels, motels, bed-and-breakfast inns and cabins can be found in Sackets Harbor, Cape Vincent, Alexandria Bay and Clayton. Campsites (some accessible only by boat) are scattered throughout the area. For a list of **campground** facilities in state parks, contact the Thousand Islands State Park Region *(PO Box 247, Alexandria Bay NY 13607* ☎*482-2593)*.

Recreation – The Thousand Islands region offers an abundance of water sports. **Fishing** is one of the most popular activities year-round. The waters along the islands have yielded world-record-setting catches. Bait shops and marinas are located in most area towns. Contact the Department of Environmental Conservation for regional fishing information *(317 Washington St., Watertown NY 13601* ☎*785-2262)*. Guides and charter services provide gear and tackle, and take clients to good fishing waters. For a list of licensed guides, contact the Fishing Guides Assn. *(54 Anthony St., Alexandria Bay NY 13607)* or the agencies listed above. Salmon River & Eastern Lake Ontario **Fishing Reports**: www. salmon-river.com/welcome.htm. Companies offering **cruises** include Uncle Sam *(p 126)*; and Antique Boat Museum *(depart from 750 Mary St., Clayton Jun–Aug; 1hr;* ☎*686-4104)*.

surfaced in 1892, but politics on the American side delayed its construction. In 1959 the **St. Lawrence Seaway** opened: It deepened the river, calmed its rapids, bypassed its waterfalls and created a $470 million, 2,342mi trade route connecting the Great Lakes to the world. While outdoor recreation continues to lure vacationers, port towns along the river, battered by the economic cycles of recent years, are reclaiming their waterfronts and dusting off their history in an effort to attract more tourism.

OSWEGO *2hrs*

Like many frontier settlements, Oswego began as a fortification in 1722 built by the British to counter the French at Ft. Niagara *(p 158)*. The town, laid out in 1797, grew up around the mouth of the Oswego River and became an American naval base during the War of 1812. After the war, Oswego made its name as a major freshwater port strategically located at the nexus of the Erie Canal and Great Lakes trade routes. Salt, lumber and textiles came and went from Oswego in abundance. The lucrative lake trade suffered with the advent of the railroads, but the St. Lawrence Seaway reinvigorated the entrepôt of Oswego. Modern nuclear-power plants at Nine Mile Point make different use of Lake Ontario's aqueous resources and contribute to the economic health of the city.

Fort Ontario State Historic Site – *One E. Fourth St. Open May–Oct Wed–Sat & holidays 10am–5pm, Sun 1pm–5pm. $3.* ⊞ ☎*315-343-4711.* Although this impressive five-bastioned fort has been restored to its 1867-72 appearance, its antecedents date to 1755, when this commanding bluff above Lake Ontario and the mouth of the Oswego River seemed the perfect place for the British to defend their territorial claims. Use of the fort ebbed and flowed until after the Civil War, when a company of the Veteran Reserve Corps was garrisoned there. Like other convalescing Civil War veterans, these soldiers remained in the East on active duty so that the able-bodied could go West. Thorough exhibits in the enlisted men's barracks describe the fort's history and the quiet daily life of Company F. Across the parade ground, the officers' quarters housed two wounded Civil War commanders and their families between 1868 and 1869. In 1903 the fort overflowed its walls to house a battalion, and by 1941 it had been expanded to include 125 buildings. Three years later, the fort became the only refugee camp in the country for victims of the Holocaust. Climb the ramparts for a sweeping view of the lake and Oswego harbor.

Richardson-Bates House Museum – *135 E. Third St. Visit by guided tour (1hr) only, Apr–late Dec Tue–Fri 10am–5pm, weekends 1pm–5pm. Early Jan–Mar Tue–Fri 10am–5pm. Closed major holidays. $2.* ☎*315-343-1342.* An oddly frivolous edifice for the hardworking port city of Oswego, this Victorian-era Tuscan villa was begun in 1867 by Mayor Maxwell Richardson. A well-traveled lifelong bachelor with flamboyant taste, Richardson reveled in the revival styles popular at the time, blending Egyptian and French Renaissance motifs in furnishing and decorating his home, which is dominated by doorways and window frames of amazing proportion. He added a second wing in the 1880s, sparing no expense on wood carved by hand and other decorative detailing. The Oswego County Historical Society maintains the house and has undertaken an extravagant and careful restoration of the first floor. An extensive collection of local archives and artifacts occupies the second floor, where several rooms have been converted into exhibit galleries.

★ SACKETS HARBOR *½ day*

A more perfect natural harbor than this would be hard to find on Lake Ontario, and indeed, its proximity to Canada, large size, deep water, protected anchorage and rich timberlands gave Sackets Harbor promising potential as a port of trade. The first land speculators arrived here in 1801, and settlers developed a thriving potash (a by-product of felled timber) trade with Canada. Soon, however, this ideal harbor would become the nerve center of American naval activity on the Great Lakes. As anti-British sentiment flourished in the years before the War of 1812, the watery frontier between the US and British North America (Canada) grew increasingly important. Both sides knew that control of the lakes meant control of the West. The American navy arrived in Sackets Harbor in 1808 to enforce the failing US trade embargo that was a response to the British seizure of American sailors on the high seas. As tensions mounted, American leaders began to think that capturing Canada might persuade Britain to respect US commercial maritime rights. During the ensuing war, Sackets Harbor became the nation's largest shipbuilding facility and base of operations for the northern theater of action, and therefore a primary target for two British attacks. After the war, the military maintained a presence here through World War II.

Meanwhile, although its commercial importance diminished as lake trade faltered, Sackets Harbor became a favorite retreat for tourists who came to enjoy the area's natural beauty and to gawk at the largest ship of its day, the unfinished 212ft frigate *New Orleans*, begun in 1814 and dry-docked there until its dismantling in 1884. Sites in and around this lovely village relate to the many phases of its history.

Downtown – This compact area merits exploring just for the architecture of shops, churches and homes—many of them newly refurbished. Designs span the tastes of a century, ranging from Federal to Bungalow styles. Of particular note are the **Union Hotel** on Main and Ray Streets, erected between 1817 and 1818; the **Pickering Cottage and House** (1809 and 1817) at the edge of the battlefield on Main Street; and the stately, Adamesque **Elisha Camp House** (c.1816) at 310 General Smith Drive. The **Augustus Sacket House** on Main Street houses the Sackets Harbor Heritage Area Visitors Center *(open Jun–Sept Mon–Sat & holidays 10am–5pm, Sun noon–4pm; rest of the year by appointment only;* ♿ 🅿 ☎315-646-2321*)*. Village founder Augustus Sacket built the elegant little Palladian-style house in 1802, and it served as a hospital and officers' quarters during the war. The center offers exhibits on the growth of Sackets Harbor, as well as an excellent 15min video.

★ **Sackets Harbor Battlefield State Historic Site** – *Along the lakefront at end of Main St. Buildings open Memorial Day–Labor Day Wed–Sat & holidays 10am–5pm, Sun 1pm–5pm. Sept Sat 10am–5pm, Sun 1pm–5pm. Grounds open year-round. $1.* 🅿 ☎*315-646-3634.* At the heart of Sackets Harbor history, of course, is this 34-acre battlefield. Futilely bombarded by the British a month after the war's start, the harbor was secured with various fortifications and barracks built along the waterfront and encircling the town. The bloody second battle took place here in May of 1813 as the British attempted to destroy the *General Pike*, a major warship under construction at the yard. Although the Americans held the attackers off throughout the four-hour battle, the Brits unnecessarily set fire to the ship.

Adjacent to the battlefield, the structures occupying the navy yard restoration date from the 1840s and include the **Commandant's House**, which can be visited by guided tour, and the **stable** 🄺, which houses an exhibit on life aboard the 20-gun brig *Jefferson* that is particularly fun for children. One of 11 warships built at this shipyard, the vessel was left to rot and sink off the dock after the war and has been the subject of extensive underwater archaeology.

Madison Barracks, located off Old Military Road, is today a ghostly collection of buildings currently being transformed by adaptive re-use. Begun in 1815, this installation once housed Ulysses S. Grant and served the US Army until its closing after World War II. Pike Road encircles the parade and polo grounds, winding past **Old Stone Row** (1816-19), a stone water tower built in 1892 and brick officers' homes that date to the mid-1890s. On the lake side stand the Romanesque Revival **mess hall** (1895), with its distinctive octagonal tower, the gray limestone hospital (1838) and the early-20C headquarters building. Toward the end of the loop, the overgrown remains of Ft. Pike, an 1812 fortification, are barely visible. The fort was named for Gen. Zebulon Pike, discoverer of the eponymous Colorado mountain peak, who died at York (present-day Toronto) in 1813. South of Madison Barracks, the Military Cemetery lies along Dodge Avenue. Here repose the remains of General Pike and other American service personnel who have died since the War of 1812.

Excursion

Paddock Mansion – *30min. 7mi from Sackets Harbor in Watertown. 228 Washington St. Open May–Nov Tue–Fri 10am–5pm, Sat noon–5pm. Rest of the year Tue–Fri 10am–5pm. Closed major holidays. $2.* ♿ 🅿 ☎*315-782-3491.* Jefferson County Historical Society makes its home in this 1876 Victorian mansion trimmed in the Swiss chalet style. The downstairs parlors have been restored and furnished to their high Victorian appearance, down to the gewgaws and knickknacks so beloved by 19C decorators. Local history exhibits include a display of turbines that harnessed the furious Black River, which drops more than 200ft in Watertown. The barn houses a 1910 Babcock automobile and carriages manufactured in town, and the home's backyard blooms with Victorian plantings.

Across the street, the gleaming Beaux-Arts library was built in 1904 in memory of native son and New York governor Roswell P. Flower. Though small, the lobby rotunda features the classic elements of the Beaux-Arts style so popular for such buildings around the turn of the century.

★ ALEXANDRIA BAY   *1 day*

The quintessential Thousand Islands hamlet, Alex Bay offers riverside atmosphere and easy access to the waterway. Built on an awkward jigsaw-puzzle promontory, the town exists more in the water than out of it. In the 19C, it made a convenient supply and fueling stop for passing ships and later grew into a center of sport fishing and tourism. As wealthy vacationers built homes on nearby islands, the town became the mainland anchor of a scattered community of riverine hideaways. Since the **Cornwall Brothers Store** was established in the 1820s, the waterfront has served as a supply and retail center. Today the store houses exhibits of local history and crafts, while boutiques, restaurants and T-shirt shops inhabit the surrounding web of waterfront streets.

Thousand Islands Skydeck – *Between spans of the Thousand Islands International Bridge, Hill Island, Ontario, Canada. Open mid-Apr–mid-Jun daily 8:30am–6:30pm. Mid-Jun–Aug daily 8:30am–8:30pm. Sept–Oct daily 8:30am–6:30pm. $6.95.* ✗ ⅙ ▯ ☎*613-659-2335.* A brief foray into Canada will yield a most spectacular **view**★★ of the surrounding countryside. From this 425ft aerie on a clear summer day you can see many of the region's sites and geographic features, all set against a variegated background of greenery and sparkling blue waters. The sweeping perspective helps orient the visitor to the islands, coastline and river towns that define this complicated landscape. Thousand Islands International Bridge, opened in 1938, consists of five spans that stretch over a total of 8.5mi to connect the islands between the US and Canada.

★ Uncle Sam Boat Tours – *Depart from end of James St. at the river May–Oct daily 9am–7pm. Round-trip 2hrs 15min. Commentary. $13.* ✗ ⅙ ▯ ☎*315-482-2611 or 800-253-9229.* The character (and name) of the Thousand Islands derives from the unruly archipelago that clutters the upper reaches of the St. Lawrence River between Cape Vincent and Morristown. There is no better way to explore this domain of millionaires, rumrunners, smugglers and river rats than to voyage among the islands themselves, from the smallest, Tom Thumb, to 8,000-acre Wellesley. Boats of varying sizes offer several tour options depending on your time frame and interest. Islands and stories abound to fill several hours, and the narrated tour entertains with both facts and fables about the waters between Alexandria Bay and Canada. Tours pass through Millionaires' Colony, where privately owned islands sport grand houses with names like Casablanca and Seven Gables. Many of them once were owned by the rich industrialists of the 19C and early 20C, and they are still maintained in elegant fashion as summer "cottages."

Boldt Castle – *Open mid-May–mid-Oct daily 10am–6:30pm. $3.75.* ⅙ *www.boldtcastle. com* ☎*315-482-2501 or 800-847-5263.* Passengers may disembark and spend an hour or a day on Heart Island, home to the grandest, and most peculiar, of the island mansions. Begun in 1900 by George Boldt for his beloved wife, Louise, construction ceased in 1904 when she died. Boldt acquired Hart Island (named for its former owner) in 1895, changed the island's name, reshaped it to resemble a heart and set about planning for a magnificent Medieval-style residence. Since 1977, under the auspices of the Thousand Islands Bridge Authority, the shell of that residence and other buildings on the island have been undergoing extensive stabilization and restoration.

Today it bustles with reconstruction work, and several first-floor rooms have been completed. Visitors are welcome to roam through the 120 empty spaces, where several generations of graffiti cover the walls. A video and exhibit on the first floor recount the Boldts' story and something of the history of the Thousand Islands. Across the channel stand the **yacht house★** and captain's quarters *(accessible via shuttle boat)*, which are, in sharp contrast to the castle, elegantly restored. The eclectic Shingle-style structure could accommodate the family's many boats in slips 128ft long. Huge doors and towering ceilings admitted tall-masted vessels, with room for racing launches and a houseboat. A display of antique skiffs, sailing canoes and, especially, numbered race boats, now occupies the space.

Excursions

★ **Antique Boat Museum** – *2hrs. 11mi west of Alexandria Bay. 750 Mary St. in Clayton. Open mid-May–mid-Oct daily 9am–4pm. $6.* ♿ 🅿 ☎*315-686-4104.* The nautical heritage of the St. Lawrence River, and particularly the Thousand Islands region, has been long and lively. From the earliest Native American canoes to today's huge cargo-carrying "lakers" and "salties," vessels of every description have plied these waters. Perhaps most distinctive, however, are the various species of gleaming wooden craft that inhabit this museum. Whether powered by sail, oar, steam or fuel, the 150 or so freshwater boats on exhibit all share an elegance of craftsmanship, line and material that conjures up a bygone day of transportation and sport on the river. Small craft are housed in the Pauline Morgan Dodge and Adelaide Gaffney buildings and include numerous examples of the indigenous St. Lawrence skiff. A blend of rowboat, canoe and sailing dinghy, the skiff was developed as a workboat to transport fishing parties in the 1860s as the sport grew popular. Other buildings feature stately steam launches, powerful runabouts and sprightly race boats, both outboard and inboard. Powerboat racing became a fashionable pastime among the islands' wealthy residents before 1910, keeping local boatbuilders busy designing faster and sleeker competitors. The 48ft *Pardon Me*, built in 1948 as the world's largest runabout with an 1,800-horsepower engine, epitomizes the quest. At the museum's docks, it is a pleasure to see several boats from the collection afloat, where they look most at home. The museum also offers demonstrations and classes on boatbuilding and restoration, as well as exhibits that explore life and history along the river.

★ **Frederic Remington Art Museum** – *1hr. 36mi east of Alexandria Bay. 303 Washington St., Ogdensburg. Open May–Oct Mon–Sat & holidays 9am–5pm, Sun 1pm–5pm. Rest of the year Wed–Sat 11am–5pm, Sun 1pm–5pm. Closed Jan 1, Easter Sunday, Thanksgiving Day, Dec 25. $4.* ♿ *www.northnet.org/broncho* ☎*315-393-2425.* While the connection that western artist **Frederic Remington** (1861-1909) had to North Country may be little known, it was here that he spent a portion of his childhood and summers throughout his life. After his death his widow occupied this 1810 home for several years, and the museum grew from her inspiration. Recent renovation has linked the historic house with a later home next door, adding 6,000sq ft to the gallery, curatorial and public space. The museum has amassed the largest single collection of Remington's works in the world, including 70 oils and hundreds of watercolors and pen-and-ink drawings, as well as 16 sculptures, which are displayed in two major galleries in permanent and rotating installations. Several smaller exhibits use personal possessions and artifacts to explore the now-forsaken wax method of bronze casting that Remington employed, along with the stages of his life and the workings of his artistic process. In addition, the museum presents traveling exhibitions that deal with the artist's times and context.

Courtesy Frederic Remington Art Museum

End of the Day (1904) by Frederic Remington

Also of note in Ogdensburg is the 1810 **Customs House** *(127 Water St.)*, the oldest government-owned building in the US. The Georgian-style brick edifice began life as a store and warehouse owned by merchant David Parish, who also built the home now occupied by the Remington Museum.

MASSENA *2hrs*

Originally a lumber town, Massena is located on the Grasse and Raquette rivers, which also made it ideal for wool and grain mills. The therapeutic sulfur content of the Raquette attracted spa-goers until the end of the 19C. In 1898 Alcoa Aluminum established a facility here, as did General Motors later; both remain major employers in the area. During the building of the Robert Moses-Robert H. Saunders Power Dam in the 1950s, Massena bustled with the influx of thousands of workers who crowded the boarding houses and taverns during the four years of construction.

Eisenhower Lock – *Rte. 131.* Along the 2,342mi of the St. Lawrence Seaway, 15 locks lift and lower freighters between the Atlantic at sea level and the 600ft elevation of Duluth, Minnesota, on Lake Superior. The Eisenhower Lock does its part by raising or lowering vessels 42ft, and the visitor center and observation deck *(open May–Oct daily 9am–5pm;* ▯ ☎*315-764-3200)* here provide an opportunity to see the "locking through" process in action and learn about the history and mechanics of the seaway. A video monitor in the center lists the day's transits, and you can call ahead *(☎315-764-3200)* to plan your visit around a ship's arrival. The observation deck also provides stunning **views**★ up and down the St. Lawrence Seaway.

Robert Moses-Robert H. Saunders Power Dam – *In Robert Moses State Park, Rte. 131. Open Jan–May Mon–Fri 9am–4:30pm. Memorial Day–Labor Day daily 9:30am–6pm. Sept–mid-Oct daily 9am–4:30pm. Rest of the year Mon–Fri 9am–4:30pm.* △ 占 ▯ *www.stl.nypa.gov* ☎*315-764-0226.* The St. Lawrence-FDR Power Project, a massive four-year construction effort begun in 1954, relocated seven communities and produced three dams including this one to harness the St. Lawrence and generate electricity for the US and Canada. The river's descent to the sea (225ft between Lake Ontario and Montreal) makes it an ideal source for hydropower, which requires a steady and forceful flow of water. Taming the wild rapids along this stretch of the river, the project created Lake St. Lawrence, directing the flow of the river over the Moses-Saunders Power Dam, where it falls 80ft to spin giant turbines and create electricity. Begin your visit on the fifth-floor observation deck for a view of the dam, half in the US and half in Canada, and the surrounding countryside. On this floor, hands-on exhibits exploring electricity and hydropower will intrigue children, and a 12min video *(shown every 30min)* on the fourth floor relates the fascinating story of the dam's construction using lively oral-history recollections of the men who worked on it. Films of the dam in the process of being built capture the sheer immensity of the endeavor: Coffer dams constructed around the site rerouted the river so that the dam could be built on the dry riverbed. Two vibrant murals commissioned from Thomas Hart Benton for the dam's opening hang on the third floor, where visitors can also observe activity in the control room.

■ **Shore Dinner: An American Favorite**

Like clambakes and fish boils, the shore dinner occupies a special place in the pantheon of regional American seafood feasts. Although variations on this favorite can be found in waterside dining establishments coast to coast, authentic shore dinners originated among the Thousand Islands. As the region grew popular in the 19C, eager anglers clamored to sport-fish the St. Lawrence's abundant waters, giving rise to a fraternity of fishing guides who knew the waterway intimately and offered their skills and skiffs for hire. No such river trip would be complete without an island picnic built around the day's catch fried in fatback and served with salt potatoes, corn, strong coffee and delicious French toast with maple syrup. Legend has it that Thousand Island dressing—a blend of mayonnaise, chili sauce, chopped eggs, relish and parsley—originated as a shore-dinner condiment. While powerboats have replaced the little skiffs, modern guides still prepare shore dinners for their fishing parties, searing their freshly caught muskie, perch, walleye and pike over an open fire at one of many shady luncheon sites throughout the islands.

Finger Lakes

Watkins Glen State Park near Ithaca – © Dick Dietrich

At the heart of upstate New York hang the 11 Finger Lakes, suspended like slender pendants from an invisible chain. Each one a jewel in its own right, together these narrow lakes form the framework for landscape, leisure and life in this region. At largest estimates, the Finger Lakes region covers 9,000 acres from Lake Ontario south to Pennsylvania, east to SYRACUSE and west to ROCHESTER, encompassing 14 counties. Among the lakes, Cayuga is the longest at 40mi, and Seneca the deepest, reaching down more than 600ft in places. Tiny Canadice Lake, 3mi long, is highest in elevation at 1,099ft above sea level. Each lake hosts quaint communities at its north and south ends where commerce and culture thrive.

The peaceful, gently undulating landscape around the lakes belies a dramatic past under tons of grinding glacier. Two glacial advances during the last Ice Age carved the lakes from streambeds and bulldozed the surrounding terrain. Other stunning features of the area—precipitous glens and gorges and their boisterous waterfalls—are products of ongoing postglacial water erosion. Today farms and fruit trees thrive between the lakes, cradled in the fertile valleys and temperate microclimates around their shores. Perfect for viticulture, these conditions make the Finger Lakes the second-largest winemaking region in the US after California's Napa Valley.

Human habitation began with the Algonquian Indians, whom the Iroquois displaced around AD 1300. Organized into the League of Nations by Hiawatha around 1600, the six tribes formed North America's first democracy, which is said to have inspired Benjamin Franklin *(p 230)* some 150 years later. During the Revolution, when much of the Iroquois Confederacy supported the British, the Continental Army mounted a fierce campaign against the Indians, driving west those who were not killed. Land speculators, war veterans and tax-weary New Englanders and Pennsylvanians settled the region thereafter, and by 1825 the Erie Canal *(p 94)* cut its swath north of the lakes, bringing more settlers and industry. Steamboats once plied the lakes, hauling the local bounty of industry and agriculture to canal and, later, railroad. This is the birthplace, as well, of several religious movements, notably Mormonism. Directed by a vision to Hill Cumorah near Palmyra in 1827, **Joseph Smith** reputedly found inscribed tablets and based his new religion on them. In 1848 the women's movement was born in Seneca Falls with the first convention for women's rights.

This confluence of history, waterways and winemaking attracts millions of visitors to the Finger Lakes region each year.

ITHACA ★

Population 28,507
Map p 132
Tourist Information ☎607-272-1313 or 800-284-8422

Nestled at the southern tip of Cayuga Lake, among state parks, waterfalls and gorges, Ithaca captures much of the essence of the Finger Lakes in its blend of commerce, culture and beauty. Founded strategically at the head of the lake in 1788, the settlement grew to become the seat of Tompkins County and an entrepôt for gypsum and other goods bound to and from the Erie Canal. Since 1868 Cornell University has crowned the heights above the city. Today, in an easy amalgam of town and gown, the city bustles with a mixture of students, vacationers and residents.

★★ CORNELL UNIVERSITY *3hrs*

It is easy to see why Ezra Cornell envisioned a university on his farmland high above Lake Cayuga. Surrounded by uplifting natural beauty, yet close to a bustling commercial center, such an institution would offer students the best of all worlds. Cornell was chartered in 1865 as New York's land-grant university to provide an education in both the liberal and practical arts. **Ezra Cornell** (1807-74) had made his fortune in the telegraph business (he strung the line that carried Morse's first transmission). He donated 300 acres and a generous endowment to the college, and his vision of a university where "any person can find instruction

Cornell University Campus

in any study" materialized in 1868. Cornell's love of mechanics and agriculture was tempered by co-founder and first president, Andrew Dickson White, who insisted on the benefits of an education in the humanities as well. The university prides itself on its milestones in practical education: it awarded the first degree in veterinary medicine, established schools of hotel administration and labor relations and sponsored the first university press in the nation. Today the 745-acre campus offers 1,800 courses and educates 19,500 students in more than 100 fields. Of the 11 colleges and schools located here, many are organized around quadrangles, lending a feeling of intimacy to this sprawling institution.

Campus – *A good way to visit the campus and its environs is to use the Founders Loop trail on the Cornell Plantations Path (below). Park at Plantations headquarters and begin your walking tour from there. Campus maps are available at booths at campus entrances. Guided campus tours (1hr 15min) depart from the Information & Referral Center in Day Hall year-round Mon–Fri 9am–3pm, Sat 9am–1pm, Sun 1pm. Closed Thanksgiving Day, Dec 25–Jan 1.* & ▣ *($6) www.cornell.edu* ☎607-254-4636. A visit to the campus offers spectacular scenery and interesting history bound together by miles of walking trails. **Founders Loop** circles through the oldest parts of campus, past such classic structures as the Gothic-style Willard Straight Hall (1925) and McGraw Tower (1891), whose carillon takes 21 days to repeat a tune. Climb the 161 steps up the tower and take in the breathtaking **view**★ of Ithaca and Lake Cayuga beyond. Ezra Cornell rests in **Sage Chapel**, dedicated in 1872 and replete with a Tiffany window in its north wall. The path skirts the brink of Libe Slope, a 45-degree incline guaranteed to strengthen the legs of the students who climb it daily. In the Arts Quad the loop passes "Old Stone Row," the oldest buildings on campus and, in marvelous juxtaposition, the contemporary **Herbert F. Johnson Museum of Art** *(open year-round Tue–Sun 10am–5pm; closed major holidays;* & *www.museum.cornell.edu* ☎607-255-6464*)*. Designed by I.M. Pei in 1973, the museum houses a diverse collection particularly strong in Asian and American works. Two libraries of note along this path are Olin, the largest of 17 at Cornell, and the underground Carl Kroch Library, which contains rare books, Asian materials and a witchcraft collection.

★ **Cornell Plantations** – *One Plantation Rd. Open year-round daily sunrise–sunset.* ▣ ☎607-255-3020. *Maps are available at the Garden Gift Shop.* A living laboratory of local and non-native flora alike, Cornell Plantations manages 200 acres on campus and 2,700 adjacent acres, including an arboretum and gardens. The complex evolved from the university's first arboretum, built in 1875, and from early movements for gorge preservation in the area. The **Plantations Path**, seven miles laid out in 1994, cuts a lovely swath among campus quads and bowers alike and offers a good way to see both the natural and the man-made environment here. For a view of waterfalls and gorge ecology, try the Cascadilla Gorge Path *(closed in winter)* that ascends about 400ft and connects Ithaca with the campus. Stonework erected by the Civilian Conservation Corps still marks the way. Note as well nature's stonework, called architectural jointing: rock planes cleft with astonishingly precise angularity caused by compression and pressure. Other loops along the Plantations Path network wind eastward into the campus, around Beebe Lake, into the Mundy Wildflower Garden, through the arboretum and along lovely Fall Creek.

Sapsucker Woods Bird Sanctuary – *159 Sapsucker Woods Rd. Open year-round Mon–Thu 8am–5pm, Fri 8am–4pm, Sat 10am–4pm. Closed major holidays.* & ▣ ☎607-254-2473. Airport noise and a highway's whine compete with but lose to this peaceful 200-acre sanctuary. A quiet indoor observatory overlooks a 10-acre pond and feeding garden frequented by a wide variety of birds. Walls display a selection of bird prints by Louis Agassiz Fuertes, who worked around the turn of the century and is considered by many second only to John James Audubon for his artistry. Outside, 4mi of trails wind through wetland and forest. Besides being a popular destination for bird lovers, the sanctuary is also a research center run by the Cornell Laboratory of Ornithology. It maintains the largest collection of recorded natural sounds in the world, including some of endangered or extinct creatures.

EXCURSIONS

★ **Taughannock Falls State Park** – *2hrs. 10mi north of Ithaca on Rte. 89 in Trumansburg. Open year-round daily sunrise–sunset. $5/car (free in winter).* △ & ▣ ☎607-387-6739. This 783-acre state park has something for everyone, including a nice beach on Lake Cayuga, woodsy hiking trails, picnic grounds and of course the breathtaking falls. Visitors can drive to overlook the falls or take one of three foot trails. The shortest *(.75mi one way)* ends at the base of the falls, which plunge over a rock lip 215ft up—45ft higher than the falls at Niagara. Steep gorge walls rise 400ft through layers of shale from a softly undulating limestone floor. Like others in the Finger Lakes, this gorge began to form after the glaciers retreated, eroded by the relentless scouring of the soft rock by Taughannock Creek. As the gorge receded upstream, the rock became harder to erode, stranding the stream high above the gorge floor. From there it tumbles over the caprock with power enough to carve the 30ft plunge pool below.

If you drive south from the falls on Route 89, note the lovely view of Cornell University across Lake Cayuga.

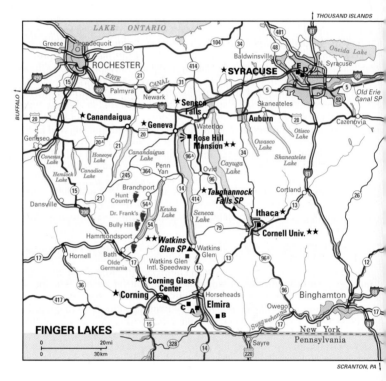

★★ **Watkins Glen State Park** – *(p 129). 2hrs. 23mi southwest of Ithaca on Rte. 14 (Franklin St.) in Watkins Glen. Open year-round daily 8am–dusk. $5/car.* ⚠ 🅿 ☎607-535-4511. At the tip of Lake Seneca, 1.5mi-long Watkins is perhaps the most spectacular glen in the Finger Lakes. The gorge was formed as the rushing waters of glacial runoff cut easily through soft sedimentary rock beginning some 12,000 years ago. Today Glen Creek still dances down the canyon through 19 waterfalls, into crystal-clear plunge pools and over well-worn rock formations. Venturing into this slash in the earth—halfway between sunlight and shadow, warm and cool—both excites and exhilarates. Walkers along the gorge trail are liable to get wet as they skirt various falls. Elsewhere the flow ebbs to a trickle: moving water barely glazes the streambed and proceeds sedately downward over rocks that descend with stairstep precision. Past all of this the 1.5mi hike into the narrow gorge ascends 832 steps and 700ft in elevation; climb Jacob's Ladder (a steep staircase) at the end and return along one of the upper trails. (From here, don't be surprised if the thunder of race cars at Watkins Glen International Speedway replaces the tumult of the waterfalls.) The steps and bridges of the path were originally opened to the public by an enterprising newspaperman in 1863. He called it a "book of nature," and indeed, its wonder lies not only in its breathtaking beauty but in the glimpse it offers into water erosion, gorge building, geology and microclimates. Take in the view from the 85ft suspension bridge that crosses the gorge and connects the Indian and South Rim Trails.

A succession of charming, historic, lake-end towns anchors the northern section of the Finger Lakes. Settled largely by New Englanders after the Revolution in an era of widespread land speculation, they are in plan and early architecture reminiscent of towns in Connecticut and Massachusetts. Their fortunes made by the surrounding lakes and rivers, which supplied power, transportation and beauty, these towns remain a blend of tourism and industry. For today's visitor, each of them offers a wealth of sites to explore.

★ CANANDAIGUA *2hrs*

The Seneca Indians believed that they originated along the shores of Lake Canandaigua, and the word means "the chosen place." Canandaigua became the focus of white settlement in western New York in 1792 as the center of land sales for developers from Massachusetts. Its public square still reflects its New England heritage. In 1794 the Iroquois and the US signed the Treaty of Canandaigua here. Susan B. Anthony (*p 162*) was tried here in 1873 for attempting to register to vote. Found guilty, she refused to pay the $100 fine.

★ **Sonnenberg Gardens and Mansion** – *151 Charlotte St. Open mid-May–mid-Oct daily 9:30am–5:30pm. $7.50.* ✗ ◨ ☎716-394-2128. Set on 50 beautifully landscaped acres, this Queen Anne-style mansion, embellished with Tudor, Romanesque and Chateauesque touches, was begun in 1885 as the summer home of Frederick Ferris and Mary Clark Thompson. The Thompsons had acquired the estate in 1863 and began planting extensive gardens, nine of which still surround the manse. He made his money as a founder of what is today the First National Bank of New York, and she was a world traveler and collector who loved birds. (Part of her aviary, which once housed more than 400 varieties of birds, remains on the property.) The gardens, each of a different design, reflect the Victorian fascination with landscape planning. They are lovingly tended and in various states of restoration. The serene Japanese Garden includes a furnished teahouse, and the Moonlight Garden shimmers with evening-bloom-

> ### Finger Lakes Facts
> ■ **Longest:** Cayuga, 40mi
> ■ **Deepest:** Seneca, 600⁺ft
> ■ **Shortest:** Canadice, 3mi
> ■ **Highest:** Canadice, 1,099ft above sea level
> ■ **Lowest:** Cayuga, 384ft above sea level
> ■ **Steepest shoreline:** Seneca
> ■ **Widest:** Cayuga, 3.5mi
> ■ **Most wineries:** Seneca
> ■ **Clearest:** Skaneateles
>
> The Indians described the Finger Lakes in highly practical terms by identifying their prominent characteristics. White settlers adapted and formalized these names:
>
> *Canandaigua*: the chosen spot, or a place selected for settlement
> *Keuka*: canoe landing
> *Seneca*: a place of stone
> *Cayuga*: lake at the mucky land (low-lying Cayuga has a marshy shoreline)
> *Owasco*: outlet and crossing place
> *Skaneateles*: long lake
> *Canadice*: also means long lake
> *Otisco*: water-dried (perhaps because the lake had shrunk)
> *Conesus*: berry place
> *Honeoye*: finger lying (from the story of an Indian who had amputated his snake-bitten finger)

ing white flowers. Well-weathered stone cherubs, winged creatures, satyrs and sprites populate the grounds. Inside the house, a docent conducts informal tours. Photos on exhibit shed interesting light on how the home once looked.

★ **Granger Homestead and Carriage Museum** – *295 N. Main St. Visit by guided tour (1hr 30min) only, Jun–Aug Tue–Sun 1pm–5pm. Mid-late May & Sept–mid-Oct Tue–Fri 1pm–5pm. $4.* ◨ ☎716-394-1472. Occupying a pleasant, grassy 12-acre site are four buildings paying homage to Canandaigua history. Built in 1816, the Federal-style **mansion** was commissioned by former state politician and postmaster general Gideon Granger (1767-1822) to serve as a base from which he could administer his western land tracts. Over the years, the homestead has been extensively renovated and enlarged, even housing a girls' school from 1876 to 1906. Today the beautifully restored rooms—furnished with period pieces and sporting ornate mantelpieces and moldings—reflect the tastes and aspirations of early- to mid-19C society. Evoking a different period is a re-creation of a dormitory room on the second floor.

Housed in two barns behind the mansion, the **carriage museum** showcases more than 50 horse-drawn vehicles from the Western New York area; most have been lovingly restored. Highlights include an 1864 crane-neck fire engine, "Old Betsy"; an 1875 hearse; and a 1900 three-seater Surrey complete with fringe on top. The fourth building sited on the grounds is the Walter Hubbell Law Office (1820).

★ GENEVA   *2hrs. Map p 132.*

While a Seneca village had long existed here, the British realized Geneva's strategic location and built a stockade on the site in 1756, making it the oldest non-native settlement in western New York. Geneva came into full flower in 1794 as the vision of developer Charles Williamson, who laid out South Main Street and the town center at Pulteney Park. He succeeded in attracting wealthy Southerners and New Englanders who built many of the Federal homes that still encircle the park. As the town prospered, South Main continued as a popular neighborhood and is today lined with homes in an array of 18C and 19C styles. Located in the Prouty-Chew House at 543 S. Main Street is the **Geneva Historical Society**, featuring 19C furnishings, decorative arts, toys and a fine collection of period costumes *(open Jul–Aug Tue–Fri 9:30am–4:30pm, weekends 1:30pm–4:30pm; rest of the year Tue–Fri 9:30am–4:30pm, Sat 1:30pm–4:30pm; closed daily noon–1:30pm & major holidays;* ☎315-789-5151*)*. Geneva College, now Hobart, has the distinction of having granted the first medical degree to a woman, Elizabeth Blackwell, in 1849.

★★ **Rose Hill Mansion** – *3mi east of Geneva on Rte. 96A. Visit by guided tour (1hr) only, May–Oct Mon–Sat 10am–4pm, Sun 1pm–5pm. $3.* 🅿 ☎315-789-3848. A charming Greek Revival mansion dating back to 1839, Rose Hill has been meticulously restored and furnished to reflect the period. Its temple-like exterior beautifully imitates Classical style and symmetry, from the well-proportioned Ionic colonnade to the Greek fretwork on the front door panel. Rose Hill passed through a procession of owners; it is named for Virginian Robert Rose, who built and lived in what is now the visitor center in 1802. Banker and wool merchant William Strong built the standing mansion. Gentleman farmer Robert Swan, who owned the property between 1850 and 1890, made it a model working farm. More owners and years of decay ensued. Finally, in the mid-1960s, a Swan descendant bought the property for $15,000 and made the restoration possible. Rose Hill is listed on the National Register of Historic Places as a remarkable example of American Greek Revival architecture.

Tours begin with a 7min video, and the house is well served by enthusiastic and knowledgeable guides. Note the sprawling **view** of Lake Seneca from the front porch. Inside, plasterwork, wall colors and floor coverings blend into an authentic backdrop for period furnishings. (All of the pieces are antiques, some original to the house.) Although the balance and classicism of the Empire style predominate, this is a home on the verge of the lush Victorian era. Compare the ornate furnishings of the gold bedroom (crafted by inmates at Auburn prison in the 1850s) with the mahogany Empire sleigh bed in the blue bedroom. Note the Duncan Phyfe sofa with its original upholstery in the family parlor. In the dining room, the reproduction French Empire wallpaper conveys a marvelous illusion of dimension and texture.

★ SENECA FALLS   *2hrs*

A 30ft waterfall in the Seneca River made this an excellent site to locate gristmills and industry: 19C textile mills and ironworks thrived on the power and transportation the river offered. A link to the Erie Canal was dug in 1827, and in 1915 the falls were obliterated by the merger of that waterway and the river. Today the Seneca & Cayuga Canal joins the lakes of the same names to the New York State Barge Canal. Against this industrial backdrop the **women's rights movement** was born. Inspired largely by the growing abolitionist movement, a cadre of women in Seneca Falls determined to extend the spirit of reform to the plight of American women, whose legal rights were extremely limited. Using the powerful language of the Declaration of Independence, they drafted a manifesto of women's rights called the Declaration of Sentiments, and in 1848 held the first Women's Rights Convention in the Wesleyan Methodist Chapel on Seneca Falls' main street.

★ **Women's Rights National Historical Park Visitor Center** – *136 Fall St. Open year-round daily 9am–5pm. Closed Jan 1, Thanksgiving Day, Dec 25. $2.* ⅃ ▣ *www.nps.gov/wor* ☎*315-568-2991.* This fascinating landmark comprises several diverse locations important to the history of the women's rights movement. At its heart, and the best place to begin a tour, is the **visitor center**. A thoughtful exhibit explores themes of womanhood using passages from the Declaration of Sentiments along with a timeline of women's history. The exhibit also addresses contemporary issues: interactive computer games and videotaped "debates" encourage visitors to draw their own conclusions on issues and case law surrounding the draft, sexual harassment, women's studies, equal education and divorce. In Declaration Park next door, the remains of **Wesleyan Chapel**, where the 1848 convention took place, have been enshrined like an ancient temple. Other sites in the park include homes connected to the movement's progenitors: the Elizabeth Cady Stanton House *(32 Washington St.)*; the home of Mary Ann and Thomas M'Clintock, where the declaration was drafted; and the home of Quaker abolitionist Jane Hunt. The latter two are both in neighboring Waterloo. For a litany of noted American women and their accomplishments, visit the National Women's Hall of Fame at 76 Fall Street. Although not part of the park, the gallery honors women from all walks of life, adding new inductees each year.

Seneca Falls Historical Society – *55 Cayuga St. Visit by guided tour (45min) only, Jul–Aug Mon–Fri 9am–5pm, weekends 1pm–4pm. Rest of the year Mon–Fri 9am–5pm. Closed major holidays. $3.* ▣ ☎*315-568-8412.* Remodeled in 1880 around a small Italianate home, this sprawling Queen Anne mansion was occupied by one family up through 1961. It now houses the Historical Society, founded in 1896. Lavishly furnished Victorian period rooms fea-

Susan B. Anthony (left) and Elizabeth Cady Stanton

ture lovely Arts and Crafts detail (note in particular the stained- and painted-glass windows). Exhibits focus on local history, firefighting and circus toys. The society's collection of glass-plate negatives documenting the women's rights movement is unique in the country. Other rooms present rotating exhibits related to life and industry in the city.

AUBURN *2hrs*

Straddling the Owasco River just north of the eponymous lake, Auburn was once the site of a major Cayuga settlement. White occupation began with a series of mills along the river after the Revolution, and industry flourished. Today plastics and auto parts have replaced grist and woolens, but manufacturing continues unabated. Constructed in 1816, the Auburn Correctional Facility is the oldest of New York's prisons. South of the city stands the modest home *(180 South St.; ☎315-252-2081)* of **Harriet Tubman**. Escaping from slavery in 1849, this amazing woman delivered 300 people from bondage on 19 excursions into the South and was later employed by the Union Army to guide troops around the Southern landscape she knew so well. A friend of William Seward *(p 136)*, she settled in Auburn after the war.

★ **The Seward House** – *33 South St. Visit by guided tour (1hr 30min) only, Apr–Dec Tue–Sat 1pm–4pm. Closed major holidays. $3.25.* ▣ ☎*315-252-1283.* Although this home is a fine example of Federal architecture, the most important story here is that of the man who occupied it for 48 years. **William Henry Seward** (1801-72) may be best remembered as President Lincoln's secretary of State, but his long and distinguished career extended from the New York State governor's office to the US Senate as well. His home reflects a rich and full life and conveys something of Seward's gregarious nature. And because five generations of the family lived here over the years, the house is remarkably appointed with personal posses-sions, from costume items and china to artwork and furniture. Each piece has a story: a youthful Brigham Young carved the parlor mantel; many of the 10,000 books in the collection contain flowers from Civil War battlefields pressed by Seward's daughter; friends commissioned the massive Thomas Cole painting in the impressive parlor in 1839; a small Federal-style desk served a delegate to the first Constitutional Congress. A remarkable portrait gallery on the second-floor landing depicts the many dignitaries Seward met during his wide-ranging career. Seward himself died in the house in 1872, and the last of his line died here in 1957. Originally built in 1816, the home was later "Victorianized" by the family and is furnished accordingly. A wonderfully thorough tour includes several rooms of artifacts relating to the attempt on Seward's life in 1865, to the Alaska Purchase ("Seward's folly") and to the Civil War.

Willard Memorial Chapel – *17 Nelson St. Open year-round Tue–Fri 10am– 4pm. Closed major holidays. $2.* ☎315-252-0339. Originally built as part of the Auburn Theological Seminary between 1892 and 1894, this is the only complete

---

■ **Winemaking in the Finger Lakes**

Winemaking in the Finger Lakes region celebrates a long and interesting history. Best known in the early years for sparkling and sweet wines squeezed from native Catawba and Concord grapes, the local cultivation of European grapes—or vinifera—has caused considerable excitement over the last four decades. Today nearly 50 wineries of various sizes cluster around Lakes Seneca, Cayuga, Keuka and Canandaigua at the heart of Finger Lakes wine country, providing the visitor with ample opportunity to tour and taste against a backdrop of spectacular coun-tryside.

A Little History – The first large-scale viticulture began in the region at the south-ern tip of Keuka Lake when a cooperative venture of local grape growers formed the Pleasant Valley Wine Company in 1860. (California's Napa Valley had another year to wait before its first winery was established.) By 1867 their sparkling wine had taken Europe by storm as the "greatest champagne of the Western world." The Great Western label shortly became a favorite wine of the Finger Lakes, and other vintners rushed to set up shop. By 1900 more than 20,000 acres of vines trimmed the shorelines of the lakes, divided among 50 vineyards and dominated by the great names of Taylor and Widmer, Pleasant Valley and Urbana. The double blow of Prohibition and Depression decimated New York's winemakers. Smaller winer-ies failed, leaving the larger ones to produce sacramental wines and fruit juices (labeled with strict instructions not to add yeast and ferment lest alcohol result). Taylor and Widmer wineries survived and went on to build huge operations that pur-chased local grapes and imported California wines to blend and soften the Finger Lakes vintages. For a time, it seemed as though the character of Finger Lakes wines would be lost. In 1976 the state opened up the field by passing the Farm Winery Law, encouraging small growers to return to winemaking and allowing them to sell directly to consumers. Boutique and family wineries sprang up around the lakes, experimenting with native, hybrid and vinifera grapes to create a huge and increasingly sophisticated body of local wines. Today, reminiscent of the grand grape-growing valleys of California, Finger Lakes "wine trails," winery tours, tast-ings and special events are attracting a growing audience.

Treading the Trails – Often located at the end of dirt roads or atop rolling hills, Finger Lakes wineries afford magnificent vistas well off the beaten path. Add the lush vineyard landscape and a tasting or tour here and there, and the result is a delightful day of exploring wines and countryside. At a leisurely pace, three or four stops in a day will satisfy. Some wineries feature restaurants or shops where cheese, crackers and, of course, wine can be purchased for a picnic lunch. Each of the major Finger Lakes has its own "wine trail," or recommended route connect-ing the local wineries. Follow one of these *(brochures available at visitor centers and information kiosks in towns)* or try this sample winery tour around Lake Keuka, where Finger Lakes winemaking began.

and unaltered chapel interior by artist **Louis Comfort Tiffany** (1848-1933) known to exist. It is indeed a lovely space that includes a rare figurative stained-glass window by Tiffany depicting Christ and the apostle Peter. Other elements add up to a catalog of Tiffany's decorative techniques: note the mosaic floor, opalescent windows, "Mooresque" leaded-glass chandeliers, oak wainscoting, carved oak trim and gold stenciling. Designed by Rochester architect A.J. Warner, the building's Romanesque Revival exterior in gray limestone and red portage stone is equally distinctive.

SOUTHERN TIER

Map pp 6-7
Tourist Information ☎607-734-5137 (Elmira) or 607-936-4686 (Corning)

In the southern reaches (sometimes called the "Southern Tier") of the Finger Lakes lie the neighboring towns of Corning and Elmira, connected by the Chemung River and Route 17. Iroquois villages once dotted this landscape, but Revolutionary War campaigns drove them from the region. Elmira, named in 1825, grew rapidly as a 19C river town manufacturing and transporting a plethora of goods from flour to skin lotion. By 1890 the city boasted 539 manufactories in 80 industries, and the architecture of the historic Near Westside reflects the good fortune of 19C Elmira.

Selected Wineries

Olde Germania *(8299 Pleasant Valley Rd., Hammondsport; ☎607-569-2218)* – This small newcomer is beautifully sited, overlooking the valley in a complex of historic buildings constructed between 1880 and 1903 by Germania Wine Cellars, and once housing Taylor's sherry-making process. The pride of this winery is its cream sherry, which contains elements of 62 historic vintages.

Bully Hill *(8843 Greyton H. Taylor Memorial Dr., Hammondsport; ☎607-868-3610)* – Bully Hill affords a spectacular view of Lake Keuka and the surrounding hills. Owned by the grandson of Walter Taylor, founder of Taylor Wine Company in the 19C, the eccentric character of Bully Hill is largely a product of young Walter's dispute with the Taylor Co. over the use of the name. Engaging and enthusiastic employees offer tours, and the tastings are lively and fun. The complex includes an informal museum, acres of vineyards, a shop and a restaurant. The most popular of Bully Hill's 60 wines is Love My Goat, a red varietal.

Dr. Frank's Vinifera Wine Cellar *(Middle Rd., Hammondsport; ☎607-868-4884)* – Dr. Konstantin Frank made his name by cultivating European vinifera varieties in New York. Still a family operation, this well-established winery offers little to see but a good tasting experience. Its flagship is a lovely 1995 Johannesburg Riesling, and it is the only US winery to use the rkatsiteli grape originally grown on Mt. Ararat (in Turkey) to make a robust "workingman's" red.

Hunt Country Vineyards *(4021 Italy Hill Rd., Branchport; ☎315-595-2812)* – This small vineyard operates in a farmlike setting, offering informal tastings and tours for the asking. Its signature wine is Foxy Lady, a semisweet blush.

Vineyards along Seneca Lake – © Cosmo Condina/Tony Stone Images

Corning, incorporated in 1851, made its living off the river as well, beginning as a lumbering center. In 1868, however, the Brooklyn Flint Glass Company came to town, clinching the town's reputation as the "Crystal City."

Today both cities thrive on tourism. As the summer home of Mark Twain for nearly two decades, Elmira offers Twain lovers several sites of interest. In Corning, the Glass Center attracts nearly a half-million visitors each year and is the third-largest tourist stop in the state.

ELMIRA   *2hrs. Map p 132.*

Mark Twain Exhibit and Study [A] – *On Elmira College campus off Park Pl. Open mid-Jun–Labor Day Mon–Sat 9am–5pm, Sun noon–5pm. Rest of the year by appointment only. & ☎607-735-1941.* Mark Twain (Samuel Clemens, 1835-1910) may owe as much to the Chemung River as to the Mississippi, for it was overlooking its valley that he wrote most of his tales. Beginning in the early 1870s, Twain spent 20 productive summers at Quarry Farm, the home of his in-laws, bringing Tom Sawyer Huckleberry Finn and other characters to life. Just outside Elmira, the farm today houses a center of Twain scholarship. For the casual visitor, however, a three-room exhibit about Twain and his years in Elmira can be found in Hamilton Hall on the Elmira College campus. Across the street, the little octagonal study where Twain did his writing occupies a grassy knoll. The cozy lair had been built for him by his sister-in-law in 1874 and was moved from Quarry Farm to the college in 1952

Take a moment to enjoy the surrounding historic buildings of Elmira College founded in 1855 as the first women's college in the US to grant degrees equal to those given men. **Woodlawn Cemetery** *(at the end of Walnut St.)*, where Twain is buried, boasts a park-like Victorian setting. In a shady grove, surrounded by his children and wife's family, the author shares a tall monument with the son-in-law who had requested to be buried at Twain's feet.

Sullivan's Monument Park and Newtown Battlefield Reservation [B] – *455 Oneida Rd. Open May–Oct daily 10am–sunset. △ ✗ & ☎607-737-2907.* A drive to this site winds deep into the New York woods, terminating at the summit of a hill with a wonderful view of the Newtown Battlefield and the Chemung River Valley. An interpretive label at the overlook describes the Revolutionary Sullivan-Clinton campaign—largely an effort to punish the Iroquois who had sided with the British in violent attacks against upstate settlers. The Battle of Newtown on August 29, 1779, was a decisive one. Instructed by Washington to "lay waste all the settlements around," generals John Sullivan and James Clinton did just that burning crops and destroying Indian villages throughout the Finger Lakes Monuments above the overlook honor fallen Continental soldiers, British and Iroquois alike. Battle reenactments and encampments are presented seasonally and the 330-acre park also offers hiking, camping and picnicking.

National Soaring Museum [C] – *51 Soaring Hill Dr. in Harris Hill (take Exit 51 from Rte. 17). Open year-round daily 10am–5pm. Closed Jan 1, Thanksgiving Day, Dec 25 $4. ✗ & www.soaringmuseum.org ☎607-734-3128.* This museum shares a high plateau above an expansive and busy public park with an airstrip devoted to motorless flight. At 1,700ft, Harris Hill offers a panoramic vista of the surrounding countryside and provides an ideal place to watch the sailplanes silently come and go. Here in 1930 the first national soaring and gliding contest was held, and it has been a mecca for the sport ever since. Technically, soaring refers to the ascent of heavier-than-air craft on up-currents and thermals, while gliding describes their gradual descent. Sailplanes are generally more efficient gliders with an ability to remain airborne longer.

The museum itself, founded in 1969, is housed in a hangar-like building and contains exhibits about the physics of motorless flight, soaring technique, instrumentation, history, communications and, of course, craft. Selected originals and full-scale replica planes from the museum's collection of 68 hang from the ceiling. Other highlights include historic films depicting soaring in the 1920s and 30s and 120 scale models representing the most popular sailplanes and gliders since the 1880s.

★ CORNING   *½ day. Map p 132.*

★★ **Corning Glass Center** – *151 Centerway. Open Jul–Aug daily 9am–8pm. Rest of the year daily 9am–5pm. Closed Jan 1, Thanksgiving Day, Dec 25. $7. ✗ & www.corning glasscenter.com ☎607-974-8271. The center is currently undergoing an elaborate renovation to add new orientation and innovation centers; enlarge the museum; and renovate* *the auditorium, retail areas and the Hot Glass Show. Completion is scheduled for the year 2001.* Opened in 1951 by Corning Inc., this huge complex is divided into a museum of glass, a hall of science and industry *(closed for renovations until mid-1999)*, and the Hot Glass Show. Shops offer glass items in every price range. The current building, itself a monumental work of glass, was designed by Gunnar Birkerts and opened in 1980. Its unusual periscopic construction allows visitors to see out without admitting an excess of damaging sunlight.

★★ **Corning Museum of Glass** – This bustling and beautiful place presents a wealth of exquisite glassware crafted over 3,500 years. Housed in a huge serpentine space, the galleries are arranged chronologically in bays that each explore different glassmaking cultures, techniques and eras. Most impressive about this assemblage of glass delicacies is its seemingly infinite range of form and function, color and style. Glass afficianados will revel in the study collections arranged within the exhibit bays, which present an amazing array of pieces. Visitors overwhelmed by this massing of objects and centuries will enjoy the collection highlights quietly sequestered in the connecting hallway: note the diminutive and rare glass bust of Pharaoh Amenhotep (made originally of blue glass but turned tan from years of burial), Roman glassware

Corning Museum of Glass

© Scott Barrow

resplendent in dappled colors, and elaborately detailed 18C Chinese vases. Also of interest is a startled glass salamander peering from a 19C French paperweight with remarkable verisimilitude. Extraordinary works, beginning with those of Tiffany, Lalique, Carder and Galle, span the 20C and attest to the adaptability and timeless appeal of glass.

★ **The Rockwell Museum** – *111 Cedar St. Open year-round Mon–Sat 9am–5pm, Sun noon–5pm. Closed Jan 1, Thanksgiving Day, Dec 24–25. $5. & www.stny.lrun.com/ rockwellmuseum* ☎607-937-5386. At the heart of this idiosyncratic museum is the largest collection of American western art on the East Coast. It includes Remingtons, Russells, Bierstadts and Morans amassed by Robert F. Rockwell, Jr., Corning department store scion. Rockwell also collected antique toys and the stunning art-glass creations of Frederick Carder (1863-1963), co-founder of Steuben Glass Works. The gallery devoted to his work (more than 2,000 pieces) shimmers with the indescribable surfaces and colors he pioneered.

Market Street

A successful cooperative effort in the aftermath of a devastating 1972 hurricane made four blocks of this town's main street a viable and useful shopping district; an arts, crafts, entertainment and dining corridor; and a tourist attraction. Cute and crafty galleries exist side-by-side with traditional barber shops. Glass and jewelry artisans share the blocks with insurance agents and drugstores. Both locals and tourists gather here. Architecturally, Market Street represents a blend of eras, dating from the 1880s. Each storefront has been restored to its original appearance; be sure to note the terra-cotta touches that ornament many of the facades. Walking-tour maps are available.

Benjamin Patterson Inn Museum – *59 W. Pulteney St. Open Apr–Nov Mon–Fri 10am–4pm. $3.* ⚹ 🅿 ☎*607-937-5281.* Built as an inn to attract land investors to the region in 1796, this structure has undergone many changes over the years. Restored by the historical society to its original appearance and furnished with period pieces, the building offers a glimpse into life on the New York frontier. Several other buildings have been moved to this property as well to create a collection of local history; a log cabin, a 19C barn and an 1878 one-room schoolhouse share the site.

SYRACUSE ★

Population 155,865
Map p 132
Tourist Information ☎315-470-1800 or 800-234-4797

At the intersection of two major expressways, New York's fifth-largest city occupies the northeast corner of the Finger Lakes region. Its central location and excellent transportation systems have served the city well since its earliest settlement and still make possible a diversified manufacturing economy; commodities from chinaware to jet engines originate in Syracuse. Overlooking the downtown area from its handsome hilltop campus, Syracuse University educates nearly 14,000 students each year and is one of the city's ten top employers. To the northwest, Onondaga Lake and its shoreside park provide the city with a lovely backyard for outdoor recreation.

Historical Notes

White Gold – Long before Routes 81 and 90 intersected at Syracuse, the area had been a crossroads at the geographic center of the Iroquois Confederacy. Here the Onondaga Indians settled on the shores of the eponymous lake and became keepers of the council fire. To white settlers, the lake yielded up the salt deposits that were vestiges of the ancient sea that once covered the region. By 1794 large-scale efforts to coax salt from briny springs around the lake began in earnest. The industry would make the city's early fortunes. Although it remained viable until 1926, salt production peaked in 1862 when the harvest yielded nine million bushels. With the completion of the Erie Canal in 1825, Syracuse boomed as products, people and ideas floated past on the "horse ocean." From an enclave of 600 in 1820, the city grew to accommodate more than 11,000 people by 1840. Many were European immigrants who came to work the salt manufactories or build the canals.

When railroad transportation began to replace canals in the mid-19C, Syracuse remained a hub of mercantile activity. With its ready labor force and central location, the city's manufacturing base expanded to include an array of industries to succeed the slackening salt trade. Syracuse boomed after the Civil War, expanding horizontally and, with the advent of the passenger elevator in the 1890s, vertically. Into this bustling industrial milieu, Syracusan **Gustav Stickley** (1858-1942) and a cadre of local artists and architects introduced the Arts and Crafts movement to the US, advocating a return to simplicity and handcrafting in the domestic arts. Stickley's Mission-style furniture and his seminal publication *The Craftsman* had a far-reaching effect on Americans growing weary of the fussiness of Victoriana and the general decline in quality that characterized machine-made goods. His house still stands at 438 Columbus Avenue.

Renewal and Preservation – Comfortably supported by its broad base of manufacturing and transportation, Syracuse thrived until the years of the Great Depression and the world wars. Its subsequent fortunes echo those of other American cities abandoned by residents seeking a better life in the suburbs. In an effort to reverse the trend, urban renewal changed the texture of Syracuse's historic downtown, but preservation efforts begun in the late 1960s have halted the wholesale demolition of many of its notable structures. One such success story is that of the **Landmark Theatre Building** (1928) at 362 Salina Street, a moving-picture palace in the grand tradition. Entered on the National Register of Historic Places in 1977, the theater's restored lobby glitters with fairy-tale Mesopotamian extravagance. Its 2,900-seat auditorium hosts a variety of stage performances.

Surrounded by New York's fertile farmland, Syracuse is the home of the state fair, attended by well over 800,000 people during its 12-day run in late summer. Music lovers flock to the city from around Central New York throughout the concert season to hear the Syracuse Symphony Orchestra and the city's opera (the third-largest in the state). In June, venues around downtown host the Northeast's largest "free jazz" festival, a weeklong showcase for jazz musicians of all stripes. For specialty shopping or a casual night out, the historic Armory Square neighborhood offers a growing variety of bistros, boutiques and nightclubs.

SIGHTS *1 day. Map below.*

Elaborate 19C bank buildings built on a foundation of salt and canal fortunes punctuate a downtown landscape where modern edifices pale in comparison to the eclectic blend of historic styles, including Romanesque Revival (City Hall, 1892), Second Empire (Gridley Building, 1867), Gothic Revival (Fleet Bank, 1875) and Art Deco (Niagara Mohawk Building, 1932). The most interesting sites are organized around squares, circles, parks and plazas. **Hanover** and **Clinton Squares** border the footprint of the Erie Canal, while **Armory Square** grew up around railroad terminals. In the vicinity of Columbus Circle congregate historic buildings of religious and civic importance dating from 1871. Walking-tour maps of each neighborhood are available from the Urban Cultural Park Visitor Center at the Erie Canal Museum.

★ **Erie Canal Museum** – *318 Erie Blvd. E. at Montgomery St. Open year-round daily 10am–5pm. Closed major holidays.* & 🖻 *www.syracuse.com/eriecanal* ☎315-471-0593. When the canal was filled in through Syracuse in the 1920s, the 1850 Greek Revival **Weighlock Building**—designed to weigh canal boats for toll-taking purposes—was the only surviving structure of its kind not destroyed. Today it houses the Urban Cultural Park Visitor Center, stocked with brochures and maps on Syracuse; and the Erie Canal Museum, which presents an overview of the city's history and explores the canal's contributions to culture, science and other fields. Loafers, for instance, were first made in Syracuse in 1937, and typewriters were once a staple manufacture. Upstairs are period settings of various local businesses, including a stone cutter, a china studio and a general store. The highlight of a visit here, however, is the 65ft canal boat replica "docked" outside in the weighlock. A stroll through the boat evokes a feel for traveling on it, and exhibits in its cabins offer a capsule history of the canal's influence on the city. North across the street, notice the old tow path and the site of the confluence of the Erie and Oswego Canals, where streets of the same names now meet. At the museum's entrance, a colorful two-story mural depicts a bustling canal warehouse.

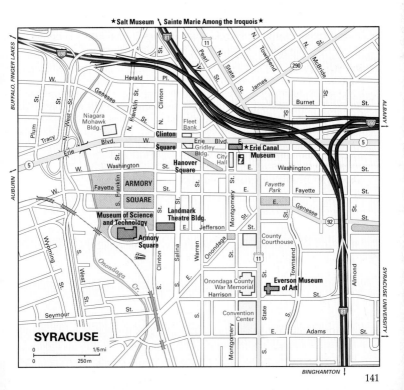

Everson Museum of Art – *401 Harrison St. Open year-round Tue–Fri & Sun noon–5pm (7:30pm 1st Thu of the month), Sat 10am–5pm. Closed major holidays. $2.* ℵ ⅋ *www.everson.org* ☎*315-474-6064.* I.M. Pei's first museum commission (1968), this cantilevered concrete edifice presents a stern profile to the street. Among the exterior sculptures, however, five fanciful monumental vases suggest the wealth of ceramics inside. Indeed, the lower level houses the Center for the Study of Ceramics, a 2,500-piece study collection including examples of the earthenware of ancient cultures to Meissen porcelain to American art pottery, all arranged chronologically. In addition to ceramics, the Everson's collections include portraits, sculpture, video art and photography, all displayed in 10 galleries on three floors. Don't miss the Gustav Stickley furniture exhibit *(main floor)*, which explores the work of this patriarch of the Arts and Crafts movement who lived and worked in a Syracuse suburb in the 1890s.

Museum of Science and Technology – 𝐊𝐢𝐝𝐬 *500 S. Franklin St. Open year-round daily 9:30am–5pm (Fri 9pm). Closed Jan 1, Thanksgiving Day, Dec 25. $9 (exhibits & Omnitheater), $4.50 (exhibits only).* ⅋ *www.sunyocc.edu/community/most* ☎*315-425-9068.* Dominating Armory Square, this three-level venue (known as "MOST") is chock-full of hands-on science exhibits. On the lower level, young scientists can discover the workings of the human body, visit an authentic turn-of-the-century Syracuse apothecary, learn about the biomes of the world and analyze the earth's rock sediments with the MOST drill. To the west, the charming planetarium is especially fun for children. Its upper level is devoted to traveling exhibits. Located on the middle level is the new 220-seat Bristol Omnitheater, where films are projected regularly on the huge 66ft hemispherical screen.

Additional Sights   *Map p 132*

Onondaga Lake pokes into the northwest corner of town, and two sites on its north shore relate to distinct eras in the area's history.

★ **Sainte Marie Among the Iroquois [D]** – 𝐊𝐢𝐝𝐬 *Onondaga Lake Pkwy. (Rte. 370), in Liverpool. Open year-round Tue–Sun 10am–5pm. $3.50.* ⅋ ☎*315-453-6767.* A 7min video and exhibits in the visitor center establish the context for this living-history complex, which represents the first European settlement in the territory of the Iroquois and the only historic French site of that period in the US. Occupied for only 20 months between 1656 and 1658, the mission was established by Jesuits and soldiers in response to an Onondaga invitation. This is a good place to learn about the complicated interrelationships within the Iroquois League, as well as the ramifications of contact with Europeans. Exhibits handle both issues sensitively. Outside, within the stockaded compound, interpreters in period dress demonstrate daily life as it might have been at the mission.

★ **Salt Museum [E]** – 𝐊𝐢𝐝𝐬 *Onondaga Lake Pkwy. (Rte. 370), in Liverpool. Open May–Sept Tue–Sun noon–5pm.* ☎*315-453-6715.* In this interesting museum built on the site of a 19C salt manufactory, exhibits recount the somewhat arcane history of salt harvesting that was an early bastion of Syracuse industry. Unlike rock salt, which is mined, this salt was distilled from local brine springs, first using a boiling method and later a solar evaporation process. Syracuse once provided most of the nation's salt, but by the 1920s salt mining flourished in the West, and the industry here died. Exhibits—including a full-size "boiling block" and "firing pit"—do a good job of describing these salt-gathering techniques, the difficult lives of the salt workers and the culture that surrounded the pursuit of "white gold."

Western New York

Niagara Falls – Jonathan Wallen

A world apart from the Big Apple and its more cosmopolitan eastern neighbors, Western New York is predominantly rural, its gently rolling terrain traversed by scenic back roads and pocked with lakes and towns. Drawing more than 20 million visitors a year, spectacular NIAGARA FALLS far outstrips all other tourist attractions in the area, though the midsize cities of BUFFALO and ROCHESTER draw their share of visitors by offering some of the best music and art in the state outside New York City. Southwestern New York consists mainly of dairy and vegetable farms and second-growth forest. Of special interest here are the CHAUTAUQUA INSTITUTION, a world-renowned summer arts colony, and a chain of picturesque vineyards that thrive in an unusual microclimate along Lake Erie.

Many of Western New York's deep valleys and smoothly sloping hills were created about 10,000 years ago, when a glacier that was 2mi thick in places covered most of the state. As it receded, it rounded off mountains and blocked rivers with sediment. The new paths cut by the rivers sometimes grew into yawning gorges like the ones along the Niagara and Genesee Rivers. The Iroquois tribe inhabited the region long before the first European explorers arrived in the mid-1700s. When the English officially won the French and Indian War in 1763, development took off. By 1788 settlers had bought up large swaths of land in Western New York and began building small farmsteads and flour mills along the Genesee River. The opening of the Erie Canal in 1825 brought about the region's first huge economic and population explosion. The advent of the railroad in the 1850s resulted in a second wave of prosperity. After experiencing a wartime industrial boom in the early to mid-20C, the area has seen its economy shift increasingly toward the service sector.

Today visitors to Western New York will find remnants of nearly every period in American history, from the pioneer-era Genesee Country Village Museum to the quaint Erie Canal boomtown of Lockport, from the idyllic turn-of-the-century Roycroft campus and Chautauqua Institution to the cities of Buffalo and Rochester—both of which boast stunning examples of early-20C architecture and an impressive array of galleries and museums. No less captivating are the timeless treasures of Western New York: the roaring waterfalls of Niagara, miles of country back roads, farmers' markets, vineyards and state parks that offer recreational activities galore.

ALLEGANY STATE PARK ★

Map p 6
Tourist Information ☎716-354-9101

Grassy meadows, rushing streams, placid lakes and dense woodlands studded with mammoth rock outcroppings—Allegany State Park's terrain is as varied as its slate of year-round recreational offerings. Whether you want to camp, hike, bike, swim or fish, you'll find plenty of opportunities to do so here.

VISIT 2½hrs

The only part of New York State not covered by the Wisconsonian glacier, which gouged out the Finger Lakes and the Great Lakes during the last Ice Age 10,000 years ago, Allegany State Park retains its own distinctive geography.

Practical Information .... Area Code: 716

Getting There – Allegany State Park's two principal entrances are on Route 17: **Red House** area (Exit 19) and **Quaker** area (Exit 18). Access from **Buffalo** (64mi) is via Route 219 south to Route 17 west; from **Altoona** (213mi) take I-99 north/220 east to I-80 west to Route 219 north to Route 17 west; from **Pittsburgh** (193mi) take I-79 north to I-90 east to Route 17 east. International and domestic flights service **Buffalo-Niagara Falls International Airport**. Closest Amtrak **train** station (☎800-872-7245) is in Buffalo. Greyhound **bus** service (☎402-330-2055 or 800-231-2222) runs to Salamanca.

Visitor Information – *Allegany State Park is open year-round daily 7am–10pm. $5* ⚠ ⚓ ♿ 🅿 ☎716-354-9121. Contact the following agencies for information and brochures on points of interest, seasonal events, recreation and accommodations: **Allegany State Park** (2373 ASP Rte. 1, Suite 3, Salamanca NY 14779 ☎354-9121); **Cattaraugus County Tourist Bureau** (303 Court St., Little Valley NY 14755 ☎938-9111 or 800-331-0543); **Allegany County Tourism** (County Office Building, Room 208, Belmont NY 14813 ☎268-9229 or 800-836-1869). The park administration office (daily 9am–4:30pm) is located in the Red House area. Park **police**: ☎354-9111.

Accommodations – (p 358) Facilities within the state park include three **campgrounds** with close to 300 campsites and more than 380 **cabins** (almost half are winterized). Reservations are recommended for cabins year-round and for campsites in the summer and over holiday weekends (☎354-9121 or 800-456-2267). Contact one of the tourism agencies listed above for accommodation information in neighboring towns.

Recreation – Allegany State Park offers year-round recreational opportunities. Most facilities and amenities are located around the Red House and Quaker areas. Trail maps and an explanation of trail markers for all routes are available at the administration office (above). Guided nature hikes are offered June through August (free). Daily schedules are posted at campgrounds, rental offices and the administration office. Many of the marked **hiking** and **horseback** trails become **cross-country ski** and **snowmobile** routes in the winter (snowmobilers must have a valid New York State registration and park permit). Cross-country ski rentals are available during the week at the administration office, and at the Warming Hut in the Red House area on weekends. **Bicycle** rentals are available at the Red House Lake boathouse. Both Red House and Quaker lakes offer sandy **beaches** (lifeguards on duty Memorial Day–Labor Day), snackbars and boat rentals. **Fishing** and **hunting** are allowed. The park restaurant (open year-round) is located in the administration building.

Most notably, it contains conglomerate rock formations that date back more than 320 million years. Centuries-old stands of hardwood trees thrived here until the mid-19C, when lumber companies began to ravage the area. Harvesting continued until around 1920, at which time most of the old-growth trees were gone. The New York State legislature founded Allegany State Park in 1921, with a 7,000-acre parcel in the Quaker Run Valley. Science Lake and Red House Lake were created for recreation in 1926 and 1930, respectively. Between 1933 and 1940, the Civilian Conservation Corps built roads, bridges and picnic and camping areas in the park.

Over the years, the park annexed nearby land, growing tenfold to its current size of 65,000 square acres (97sq mi). Today it borders Pennsylvania's 500,000-acre Allegheny National Forest *(p 318)* to the south, the Allegheny Reservoir and river system to the west and north, and Tunuguaat Creek to the east. (The 30,000-acre horseshoe of land surrounding the park in New York State belongs to the Seneca Nation.) The forest has also naturally regenerated. Hardwood trees—sugar maple, hemlock, beech, black cherry and white ash—now cover nearly 95 percent of the parkland. With all the varied tree types, fall foliage is especially beautiful here.

The park contains some 100mi of trails for hiking, biking, horseback riding, cross-country skiing and snowmobiling. Three of the 18 hiking trails are studded with interpretive nature signs, and visitors can arrange guided nature hikes. One site not to miss is **Thunder Rocks★**, an assemblage of enormous quartz boulders that dates back to the Paleozoic era. Some of the smooth, mossy specimens stand nearly 20ft tall.

EXCURSIONS

Located 3mi west of the Red House entrance to Allegany State Park, the small town of **Salamanca** *(Exit 20, off Rte. 17)* harbors several shops and restaurants as well as two small museums offering insight into the region's history and culture. Salamanca is the only city in the country located on an Indian reservation.

Seneca-Iroquois National Museum – *1hr. 814 Broad St. Open Feb–Sept Wed–Sun 9am–5pm. Oct–Dec Wed–Fri 9am–5pm. Closed major holidays. $4.* ♿ 🅿 ☎716-945-1760. This one-story modern museum celebrates the cultural heritage of the Seneca Nation and Iroquois people. Exhibits include a model longhouse: made with slippery-elm walls, this was the most common type of dwelling for Eastern Woodland Indians. Beaded purses and wallets are embellished with designs inspired by nature, and moose-antler and soapstone carvings show how native people used natural materials to create art. Several portraits of Seneca leaders, painted in England in the early 18C, depict the Seneca Nation's initially friendly relationship with some colonists. A large photo essay, devoted to the fight over the 1960s construction of the Kinzua Dam *(p 318)*, which flooded 10,000 acres of Seneca land, illustrates how that relationship has been strained over the years.

Salamanca Rail Museum – *30min. 170 Main St. Open May–Sept Mon–Sat 10am–5pm, Sun noon–5pm. Apr & Oct–Dec Tue–Sat 10am–5pm, Sun noon–5pm. Closed Easter Sunday, Thanksgiving Day, Dec 25. Contribution requested.* ♿ 🅿 ☎716-945-3133. Three major railroads—the Erie, the Baltimore & Ohio and the Pennsylvania Railroad—served Salamanca during the town's turn-of-the-century glory days. Although grass has grown over some of the tracks, this quaint 1912 depot brings the railroad era back to life with old photographs, timetables, models of rolling stock, lanterns, "railroad china" and a fully stocked 1920 ticket office. A 10min video traces the rise and fall of rail travel in the region. Lovingly restored in the 1980s, the depot's dazzling **interior★** features red-oak wainscoting and benches and a two-story skylit ceiling. Outside stand the remnants of a 1918 coaling station, as well as a boxcar, an Erie Railroad camp car and two 1950s cabooses, complete with potbelly stoves and built-in desks and bunks.

BUFFALO ★

Population 310,548
Map p 6
Tourist Information ☎716-852-0511

Situated on the eastern tip of Lake Erie, New York's second-largest city anchors Western New York economically and culturally. Buffalo is also just 20mi south of one of the world's best-known attractions, Niagara Falls. While the "Queen

City" still may be best known for its formidable football team, its frigid winters and its namesake specialty food—Buffalo wings, the spicy, fried chicken wings first created in a Buffalo restaurant—the city's world-class art museum, historic architecture, downtown theater district and urban parks are well worth exploring.

Historical Notes

Iroquois Indians lived near the site of present-day Buffalo for thousands of years before French, and then Dutch, colonists staked their claim to the area. The Holland Land Co. established the first major settlement here in 1803. Soon afterward, surveyor Joseph Ellicott laid out Buffalo's radial street grid, based on Pierre Charles L'Enfant's plan for Washington, DC. During the War of 1812, Buffalo served as the US military's headquarters, and in 1813 the British torched the town. However, because of its strategic location as a shipping and transportation hub, Buffalo was quickly rebuilt. In 1825 the opening of the Erie Canal, which provided an east-west, all-water route across the state, instigated a huge growth spurt in Buffalo.

In 1840 the first steam-operated grain elevator was built here, helping make Buffalo the leading grain-handling port in the US, a distinction the city still enjoys. The second half of the 19C saw the city develop from a frontier outpost into a major industrial force, with its population quadrupling between 1860 and 1900. After the Erie Canal's decline, Buffalo became an essential conduit of rail travel across the US and into Canada. Factories sprang up along the eastern shores of Lake Erie, manned by European immigrants who poured into the city in the wake of famine and revolution abroad. Low-cost energy harnessed from Niagara Falls beginning in 1896 sparked a new wave of industrial growth, especially in the chemical and steel industries.

Buffalo continued to be an industrial powerhouse during the two world wars, manufacturing supplies and shipping them by boat and rail. The city's population peaked (at 580,132) in 1950. Since then, the opening of the St. Lawrence Seaway in 1959, the collapse of the steel industry in the 1970s and the great nationwide migration from city to suburbs have contributed to Buffalo's decline. In recent decades Buffalo officials have carried out a slew of urban renewal projects—including the construction of waterfront town houses, a downtown mall, a sport and entertainment arena, a conference center and a light-rail system—to stanch the flow of dollars out of the city, but full-scale revitalization of the city center has yet to occur.

★ DOWNTOWN   ½ day. Map p 147.

Grouped mainly around Pearl Street, Main Street and Niagara Square, the noteworthy buildings of Buffalo represent many of the leading styles in late-19C and early-20C civic and commercial architecture. Farther north on Delaware Avenue stands the mansion in which Theodore Roosevelt was inaugurated. And located just southwest of downtown, the Naval & Military Park draws tourists to its well-maintained battleships and submarine.

★ **Buffalo City Hall** – *65 Niagara Sq.* A tremendous example of the Art Deco style, this 30-story pile (1931, Dietel & Wade) is one of the city's most awe-inspiring structures. The mighty sandstone edifice is decorated inside and out with geometric designs typical of the Art Deco style, as well as friezes and murals depicting the history of the city from its pre-settlements days to the present. An eight-columned portico and intricate bronze doors grace the front entrance, breaking the powerful vertical lines in the main tower, the four surrounding towers and the two wings. A 28th-floor observatory *(open year-round Mon–Fri 8:30am–4pm, outside observation area open weather permitting; closed major holidays;* ✗ 🅿 *[$3.50/hr]* ☎*716-851-5991)* offers expansive **views** of the city and Lake Erie.

Directly in front of City Hall stands the **McKinley Monument [1]** (1907, Carrère & Hastings), a 62ft white-marble obelisk erected in honor of President William McKinley, who was assassinated in Buffalo in 1901.

Franklin Street – The Gothic Revival **Old County and City Hall** (1876, A.J. Warner) at 92 Franklin Street features a double-roofed clock tower, surrounded by four sculptures representing Justice, the Mechanical Arts, Agriculture and Commerce. Grover Cleveland presided here as mayor of Buffalo in 1881.
Constructed in 1833 as a Unitarian church, the Greek Revival **Title Guarantee Building** *(110 Franklin St.)* is the oldest surviving structure in downtown Buffalo.

President-elect Abraham Lincoln attended services here with President Millard Fillmore in 1861.

★ **Pearl Street** – This busy street offers tantalizing glimpses of fin-de-siècle Buffalo. At **nos. 76-92**, a series of cast-iron and brick storefronts built between 1870 and 1890 illustrates how the downtown sector appeared in its heyday. At 110 Pearl Street, the 10-story **Dun Building** (1893, E.B. Green and W.S. Wicks), built in the Renaissance Revival style, was Buffalo's first high rise. Constructed on a triangular plot, it served as the model for Daniel Burnham's Flatiron Building in New York City. The spectacular **Guaranty-Prudential Building**★★ (1896, Louis Sullivan and Dankmar Adler) on the corner of Church Street was one of the first buildings ever erected on an all-steel frame, making it one of the world's first skyscrapers. Thirteen stories tall, it boasts a richly embellished terra-cotta facade, punctured by a row of porthole windows around its capital. Be sure to peek in the lavish lobby, with its elaborate tile mosaics, art-glass skylight and iron balustrade.

Across Pearl Street, **St. Paul's Episcopal Cathedral** was built in 1849

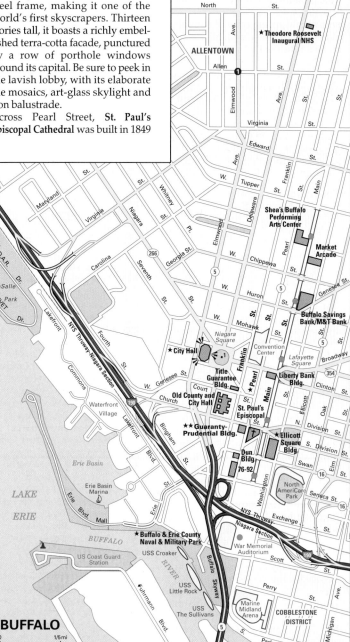

by noted architect Richard Upjohn, who preferred this relatively small creation to his masterwork, Trinity Church in New York City. Representative of the English Gothic Revival style, St. Paul's was almost completely destroyed in an 1888 fire; only the 274ft bell tower remained intact. Upon its reconstruction, clerestory windows were added and the chancel was lengthened.

Main Street – Forming the artery of the city's downtown shopping sector, this thoroughfare is open only to pedestrian traffic and Buffalo's light-rail line. Note at no. 201 the **Liberty Bank Building** (1925): the two 30ft replicas of the Statue of Liberty on the roof symbolize Buffalo's strategic position between the colonies to the east and the frontier to the west. At no. 295, the **Ellicott Square Building**★ (1895, Charles B. Atwood), built in the French Renaissance style, was the largest office building in the world at the time of its construction. Enter through the two-story arched doorway to admire the dazzling interior with its curving staircases, soaring atrium and colorful mosaic floor.

A few blocks down Main Street lies Buffalo's 20-block theater district, anchored by **Shea's Buffalo Performing Arts Center** (1926, Cornelius and George Rapp) at no. 646. The narrow facade of this richly appointed venue is deceiving; behind the opulent Baroque lobby stands a 3,000-seat auditorium where touring Broadway shows are often staged. Across the street, the **Market Arcade** (1892, E.B. Green and W.S. Wicks) at nos. 617-619 has been called the best surviving 19C retail structure in the city. Its brick and terra-cotta facades on Washington and Main Streets boast buffalo heads over the entrances. A visitor center, specialty shops and an art gallery are housed within. At no. 545, the **Buffalo Savings Bank/M&T Bank** (1901), also designed by Buffalo architects E.B. Green and W.S. Wicks, is a lovely example of the Beaux-Arts style. Its copper and terra-cotta dome, covered with gold leaf, gave rise to its nickname, "the Goldome Bank."

★ **Theodore Roosevelt Inaugural National Historic Site** – *641 Delaware Ave. Visit by guided tour (45min) only, Apr–Dec Mon–Fri 9am–5pm, weekends noon–5pm. Rest of the year Mon–Fri 9am–5pm, Sun noon–5pm. Closed major holidays. $3.* 🅿 ☎*716-884-0095. Recorded architectural walking tours of Buffalo are available here.* On September 14, 1901, after President William McKinley died from bullet wounds inflicted eight days earlier by the anarchist Leon F. Czolgosz at the Pan-American Exposition, Vice President Theodore Roosevelt took the oath of office in the ornate library of this stately Greek Revival mansion, one of only five inaugural sites outside of Washington, DC. Built around 1838 to house US troops when tensions with Canada were running high, the mansion is one of the oldest residential structures in the city. It passed into private ownership in the late 1840s; Ansley Wilcox, a prominent Buffalo lawyer and socialite—and a friend of the crusading reformer and trust-buster Teddy Roosevelt—acquired it in the 1880s. After serving as a restaurant for many years, it was named a National Historic Site in 1970 and was restored. Today the National Park Service (which manages the site) strikes a fine balance between relating the history of the assassination and inauguration—made colorful with artifacts such as the tattered handkerchief in which Czolgosz concealed his pistol—and presenting the mansion in all its Victorian finery.

1 **Elmwood Avenue**

Map p 147. Although SUNY-Buffalo moved from this neighborhood to the suburbs nearly a decade ago, this thoroughfare remains lively, trendy and fun. Outdoor cafes and restaurants cluster around the intersection of Allen and Elmwood, giving way to antique stores as Elmwood proceeds north. At no. 153, **Elmwood Outback**, a brew pub, is a popular local hangout. Farther north lies a succession of clothing boutiques and coffee shops, including the elegant **Le Metro** *(284 W. Utica)*, famed for its crusty, fresh-baked bread. One block west of Elmwood on Lexington Avenue stand a well-stocked health-food co-op, the playful **Savage Cat** cafe, and a superb used bookstore, **Rust Belt Books**. Two excellent eateries are located still farther north on Elmwood: **Kuni's Sushi Bar** *(no. 752)*, offering creative seaweed salads and noodle dishes in addition to raw fish, and **Sequoia** *(no. 718)*, specializing in California cuisine.

★ **Buffalo & Erie County Naval & Military Park** – *1 Naval Park Cove. Open Apr–Oct daily 10am–5pm. Nov weekends 10am–4pm. $6.* 🅿 ☎*716-847-1773.* Tucked beside the elevated Skyway just southwest of the downtown core, this six-acre waterfront park, flanked by a guided-missile cruiser, a destroyer and a submarine, is the only park of its kind on an inland freshwater port. It is accessible via a modern, two-story museum. Here, historic exhibits compete for the viewer's attention with a panoply of uniforms, medals, battle plans and firearms. A patriotic 10min video introduces the park and its attractions. Of special interest are the self-guided walking tours of the two docked ships and the submarine, which was awarded three battle stars and claimed eleven Japanese vessels during its six World War II patrols. Commissioned in 1943, the USS *The Sullivans* sports a shamrock on its stack in honor of its namesake—five Irish-American brothers who died with 700 others on the USS *Juneau* in 1942. On the USS *Little Rock*, note the shockingly cramped sleeping and eating quarters, the elaborate control rooms and the improvised niceties, such as a barbershop and post office, that made these mammoth vessels home for thousands of wartime sailors.

DELAWARE PARK AREA *½ day*

Frederick Law Olmsted, architect of New York City's Central Park, designed verdant **Delaware Park** *(Parkside and Elmwood Aves.)* in 1868 as a true getaway: in many areas, streets run below the surface of the 350-acre parcel, allowing visitors to escape from noise and cars. While its main draws are open space and woods, Delaware Park also hosts a 46-acre lake and, on its outskirts, the nation's third-oldest zoo, the **Buffalo Zoological Gardens**★ 🎟 *(300 Parkside Ave.; open May–Sept Mon–Fri 10am–6pm, weekends 10am–6:30pm; rest of the year daily 10am–5pm; closed Thanksgiving Day, Dec 25; $6;* ✗ ♿ 🅿 *[$3] www.buffalozoo.org* ☎*716-837-3900).* Established in 1876, this pretty, 23.5-acre zoo contains more than 1,000 animals, including a herd of shaggy buffalo, as well as dozens of well-marked trees and shrubs from around the world.

★★ **Albright-Knox Art Gallery** – *1285 Elmwood Ave. Open year-round Tue–Sat 11am–5pm, Sun noon–5pm. Closed Jan 1, Thanksgiving Day, Dec 25. $4.* ✗ ♿ 🅿 *($3) www. albrightknox.org* ☎*716-882-8700.* This is a truly world-class art museum. Best known for its extensive holdings of modern and contemporary painting and sculpture, the gallery also boasts smaller collections of Asian art, ancient sculpture and European painting of the 18C and 19C. Most of the museum's older work is appropriately housed in the Greek Revival main building (1905). Here, a grand atrium supported by Ionic columns contains sculpture from ancient times to the present. Side galleries feature permanent holdings in American and English painting, as well as Chinese sculpture, while a large room is devoted to Abstract Expressionists including Jackson Pollock, Mark Rothko and Robert Motherwell. **Clyfford Still** (1904-80) is represented by 33 paintings—the largest public collection of his work.

1957-D No. 1 by Clyfford Still

Albright-Knox Art Gallery, Buffalo N.Y., Gift of Seymour H. Knox, 1959

The heart of the museum lies in the modern addition (1962), where four narrow corridors encircling a sculpture garden are hung with works by the best-known artists of the century, from Monet, Degas and Renoir to van Gogh, Matisse and Picasso. Sculpture by Rodin and Giacometti, among others, is also found here. Large-scale prints and paintings by Pop artists Robert Rauschenberg, Andy Warhol and Jasper Johns enjoy more spacious viewing quarters. An underground tunnel links the addition to Clifton Hall, where exhibits on contemporary painting and sculpture are mounted.

Buffalo and Erie County Historical Society – *25 Nottingham Ct. Open year-round Tue–Sat 10am–5pm, Sun noon–5pm. Closed Jan 1, Thanksgiving Day, Dec 25. $3.50.* ♿ 🅿 *☎716-873-9644.* Dedicated to Western New York's cultural, economic and ethnic heritage, this museum is housed in a majestic Greek Revival edifice that served as the New York State Building in the Pan-American Exposition of 1901. A National Historic Landmark, it is the only structure left from that fair. The colonnaded portico in back of the building affords a beautiful **view** of a placid lake and Japanese garden. The large exhibit "Bflo. Made!" features more than 700 products, inventions and artifacts made in the region, from the motorized bicycle to the Buffalo wing to the kazoo. Another exhibit, "Neighbors: The People of Erie County," uses photographs and artifacts to tell the story of immigration, acculturation and the urban renewal projects of the 1950s. Other attractions include a Native American gallery and a turn-of-the-century model railroad.

EXCURSION *Map p 6*

★★ **Roycroft Campus and Elbert Hubbard-Roycroft Museum** – *2hrs. 20mi southeast of Buffalo in East Aurora.* A must-see for visitors to East Aurora, this turn-of-the-century crafts complex once buzzed with more than 500 furniture makers, metalworkers, bookbinders and other craftspeople plying their trades according to the Arts and Crafts principle, "Not how cheap, but how good." Today it contains craft and antique shops, a recently renovated hotel and a richly appointed house museum.

A charismatic leader and former marketing executive, **Elbert Hubbard** (1856-1915) founded the Roycroft movement in 1895, shortly after visiting William Morris' crafts community in England. Hubbard began with only a printing press, but his success in publishing both classic works and his own writings allowed him to quickly expand into making Mission-style furniture and other labor-intensive crafts. Because entrepreneurialism and artistry were so successfully wedded here, the Roycroft campus became a magnet for some of the greatest minds of the day, including Thomas Edison, Henry Ford, Clarence Darrow, Clara Barton, Booker T. Washington and Teddy Roosevelt. Hubbard and his wife died in 1915 aboard the *Lusitania,* a luxury ocean liner that was sunk by a German U-boat. Hubbard's eldest son, Elbert II, continued to manage the Roycroft corporation until it went bankrupt in 1938.

Visit – The **Elbert Hubbard-Roycroft Museum** *(363 Oakwood Ave.; visit by 1hr guided tour only, Jun–mid-Oct Wed, weekends 2pm–4pm; $2; ☎716-652-4735)* provides the best introduction to the work and philosophy of the Roycroft movement. Built in 1910 by Roycroft carpenters, the simple bungalow was the home and workplace of Roycroft leather craftsman George Scheide-Mantel until his death in 1979. Inside and out, it illustrates the finest in Roycroft artistry. Structurally, its deep

Roycroft Inn

40 S. Grove St., East Aurora. ☎716-652-5552. Modeled after a Gothic-style English country church, this superbly preserved inn (1895) captures the jubilant spirit and meticulous artistry of the Roycroft movement. Guests may choose from three-, four-, and five-room guest suites, available year-round. Timbered ceilings soar over the stunning lounge, which is decked with sturdy Roycroft chairs and tables, elegant lamps, and a sign that reads, simply, "Moderation." Stained-glass windows allow light to filter into the vaulted dining room, where lunch and dinner are served both to overnight guests and to visitors; and a vast peristyle offers a place to reflect on such aphorisms as "The love you liberate in your work is the love you keep," appropriately carved in the front door.

eaves, open front porch, prominent dormer and natural building materials (stone, clapboard and shingles) link it to the Arts and Crafts movement. Within, unpainted chestnut woodwork, hand-hammered copper fittings, and stained-glass lighting fixtures complement the rich variety of sturdy Roycroft furniture and specialty items, including andirons, hand-bound books, dishes and lamps. Named a National Historic Landmark in 1986, the shady **Roycroft Campus** *(along South Grove St. at Main St.; open daily year-round, building hours vary;* ☎716-652-3333) is an ideal place to stroll and browse. Nine of its fourteen former workshops and meeting halls are open to the public. Today the **Roycroft Copper Shop** (1902) contains stores that sell original and replica Roycroft items, hand-printed Elbert Hubbard epigrams and other locally made crafts. Antique stores, pottery shops and an art gallery are located in the large, utilitarian **Roycroft Furniture Shop** (1904). Other notable buildings, including the ivy-covered Roycroft Chapel (1899) and the Roycroft Print Shop (1901), have been converted for municipal and educational uses.

CHAUTAUQUA COUNTY★

Map p 6
Tourist Information ☎716-753-4304 or 800-242-4569

With slightly less than 40 percent of its area covered by fruit and vegetable farms, Chautauqua County is one of the most rural—and most beautiful—regions in the state. From the family-owned vineyards of the Erie Lowlands to the scores of roadside farmers' markets on the Allegheny plateau to the Amish shops and antique dealers clustered in its many small towns, the county offers plenty of opportunities to sample its bounty. The renowned Chautauqua Institution flanks the southern bank of 18mi-long **Chautauqua Lake**, which, interestingly, does not drain into Lake Erie, only 10mi away, but into the Gulf of Mexico, thousands of miles to the south. The lake's other shores have given rise to sleepy beach towns and popular resorts.

★★ CHAUTAUQUA INSTITUTION 2½hrs

Founded more than a century ago, this venerable institution won acclaim in the late 19C for spearheading a national movement based on self-improvement and continuing education. Since then nine US presidents and scores of diplomats, scholars and artists have come here to teach and learn, and today nearly 140,000 people attend concerts and lectures each summer. Surprisingly, Chautauqua's popularity has not diminished its unique appeal. Located in the sleepy town of **Chautauqua**, this 750-acre lakeside Victorian community retains a magical, almost

Chatauqua Institution

utopian atmosphere, where close-packed gingerbread houses rub shoulders with huge, dazzling performing spaces and hotels, and age-old religious ideas thrive alongside secular and artistic ones.

Historical Notes – The brainchild of Lewis Miller, an Ohio businessman, and John Heyl Vincent, a Methodist minister, the Chautauqua Institution got its start in August 1874 as a two-week training program for Sunday-school teachers and organizers, but its mission was never solely religious. Chautauqua's first general assembly promoted both spiritual enrichment and the idea of lifelong education in the arts and sciences. The combination clicked and Chautauqua flourished. Over the next few years the summer session was lengthened to two months, the curriculum grew to encompass dozens of subjects, and surrounding acreage was purchased to make room for new homes, churches, inns, libraries, lecture halls and performance spaces. In 1878 the Chautauqua Institution founded its Literary and Scientific Circle, the oldest continuously running book club in America. To date it has enrolled more than a million people in its self-study course. At its peak it sponsored 10,000 reading circles worldwide. By the 1880s Chautauqua was known nationwide as a spawning ground for the latest ideas in politics, economics, literature, science and religion. President Theodore Roosevelt described it as "typical of America at its best"—a place where democracy and diversity could both thrive. Traveling chautauquas—inspired by, but not connected to, the institution—criss-crossed the country between 1900 and the mid-1930s, offering spirited lectures, concerts and recitals under movable circus tents. At home, Chautauqua founded its own opera company and symphony in 1929, thus laying the cornerstone for its renowned summer concert program.

■ Western New York Wineries

When most people think of New York wine country, they imagine the rolling vineyards and posh wineries of the Finger Lakes area. But wine lovers looking for a touch of adventure—and some beautiful scenery—need not venture farther than Chautauqua County to sample some delicious reds and whites and learn how they are made. Wedged between Lake Erie and the Allegheny Plateau, this narrow fertile strip is ideal for grape growing, winemakers say, because of its well-drained gravel and shale soil (a remnant of the last Ice Age) and its unusually mild and sunny microclimate. Grape companies like Welch's, the largest local harvester of Concord grapes, have taken advantage of these conditions for 150 years. Winemakers, by contrast, have begun to establish roots here only in the last few decades, but already they have won prestigious awards for their homegrown varietals. Clustered around scenic Route 20 between Westfield and Dunkirk, the six wineries listed below are decidedly modest, mostly family-owned operations. A big wooden shack may house a store, tasting room and all winemaking equipment, and vineyards may be as small as 50 acres. But less, in this case, may be more: small, casual tours (often led by the site's proprietor or winemaker) and long, relaxing tastings are the order of the day, especially during the autumn harvest season *(Sept–Oct)*. Best of all, everything is free—except the bottles you'll want to take home.

Schloss Doepken Winery, *9177 Old Rte. 20, Ripley*; ☎716-326-3636 *(tastings and sales only)*.

Johnson Estate Winery, *W. Main Rd., Westfield*; ☎716-326-2191.

Vetter Vineyards, *E. Main Rd., Rte. 20, Westfield*; ☎716-326-3100.

Woodbury Winery, *3230 S. Roberts Rd., Dunkirk*; ☎716-679-9463.

Roberian Vineyards, *2614 King Rd., Sheridan*; ☎716-679-1620 *(tastings and sales only)*.

Merritt Estate Winery, *2264 King Rd., Forestville*; ☎716-965-4800.

VISIT

Cars aren't allowed on campus in the summertime. Shuttle buses run every 20min or so from the main gate to the lake. For details on 39 campus landmarks, see the Chautauqua Institution Walking Tour Guide, available at the bookstore (open late Jun–late Aug daily 7am–9pm; rest of the year daily 9am–5pm; & ▯ www.chautauquainst.org ☎716-357-6247). For information on the nine-week summer concert season, call ☎716-357-6250 or 800-836-ARTS.

While Chautauqua's architecture is always gorgeous, the atmosphere changes radically between the third week of June and the third week of

August. During the day nearly 7,500 student-residents—from grade-school kids to octogenarians—buzz about campus, attending courses ranging from pottery to investment banking. At night, thousands more visitors flock to campus to hear public forums on weekly historical, political and cultural themes, and performances of chamber music, pop, rock and jazz, as well as theater and dance. During the spring, winter and fall, however, the village is quiet. Only 400 Chautauquans reside here permanently, and many of the lakeside homes are closed. Still, the bookstore, cafe and library are open year-round, and the brick paths that wend through the grounds lend themselves to enchanting strolls.

A National Historic Landmark, the institution is made up primarily of performing facilities, gardens, lecture halls and whimsical Victorian cottages embellished with carpenter's lace and gingerbread. While some of these cottages are private homes, many serve as guest houses for summer residents and visitors. The palatial **Athenaeum Hotel**★★ mimics these in style if not in scale. The largest wood-frame building in the country at the time of its completion in 1873, this lakefront hotel boasts a distinctive mansard roof, a gigantic colonnaded verandah dotted with wicker furniture and a sumptuous interior bedecked in Victorian finery. It was wired for electricity by Lewis Miller's son-in-law Thomas Alva Edison *(p 184)*. Just behind the hotel, the 5,000-seat open-air **amphitheater** forms the hub of the summer's cultural activities. Another facility, the **Hall of Philosophy**★ is a true architectural wonder, with striking white Doric columns holding up a pediment roof made with a full acre of stainless-steel sheets. The colorful mosaic floor is bordered with names of literary greats like Dante and Tennyson. Down by the lake, the **Miller Bell Tower** (1911) has become the institution's signature structure. Standing 69ft tall, the red-brick campanile houses 14 bells and boasts a four-faced clock, added in 1969.

EXCURSION

★ **Fenton History Center** – *1hr. 17mi from Chautauqua in Jamestown. 67 Washington St. Open year-round Mon–Sat 10am–4pm, Sun 1pm–4pm (Dec only). $2.50.* 🅿 ☎*716-664-6256. Architectural walking-tour maps of Jamestown are available here.* Built for Reuben Eaton Fenton, a lumber tycoon who later served as the governor of New York (1865-69), as well as a US senator and representative, this imposing 1863 mansion recalls an Italian villa. Its exquisite period rooms and exhibits focus on quirky aspects of Jamestown and Chautauqua history. The stunning Renaissance Revival **drawing room** oozes Victorian excess with its multicolored, hand-painted ceiling and trim, sumptuous red-velvet curtains, Empire-style furniture and glowing gasolier. Less showy but considerably more cluttered, the family parlor is jam-packed with furniture, books, photo albums and Victorian gadgets. Among the center's dozen exhibits are "The Golden Age of Chautauqua Lake," which details lake activities from 1875 to 1910 with architectural photographs and mementos, and a military exhibit featuring war artifacts ranging from a Civil War bugle to World War I gas masks to machine guns. One room is devoted to locally born **Lucille Ball**; photographs and newspaper clippings chart the actress and comedienne's determined rise to fame. Jamestown's other famous personalities include world-renowned ornithologist Roger Tory Peterson, Supreme Court Justice Robert H. Jackson and singer Natalie Merchant (of the rock band 10,000 Maniacs).

Consult the practical information section at the end of the guide for travel tips, useful addresses and phone numbers, and a wealth of details on shopping, recreation, entertainment and annual events.

NIAGARA FALLS ★★★

Population 58,357
Map p 6
Tourist Information ☎716-439-7300 or 800-338-7890

Roughly halfway along its northward course from Lake Erie to Lake Ontario, the Niagara River suddenly plunges over a 170ft cliff, creating one of the world's greatest natural spectacles, Niagara Falls. Straddling the US-Canada border, three sets of falls—American and Bridal Veil Falls on the American side, and the awe-inspiring Horseshoe Falls on the Canadian border—make up what's known as Niagara. The falls have long been a magnet for daredevils, hucksters, honeymooners and sightseers, and today they attract upward of 14 million visitors a year. Boat and walking tours bring you into the damp mist of the raging waters, while a surprisingly tranquil state park allows you to take in this breathtaking sight from scenic overlooks.

Historical Notes

"The Universe Does Not Afford Its Parallel" – That statement, written by Father Louis Hennepin *(below)* in 1678, still rings true today. Indeed, Niagara Falls stun onlookers not for their height (the falls rank only 51st in the world in that category), but for their panoramic breadth, powerful roar and scenic beauty. Four of the five Great Lakes contribute to the mighty falls, whose waters eventually make their way to the Atlantic Ocean.

With a crest length of 2,500ft (1,000ft flank-to-flank), Horseshoe Falls channels more than 90 percent of the water at Niagara—some 315,000 to 675,000 gallons per second in the summertime, depending on how much water is being diverted for hydroelectric power. American Falls has a crest length of about 1,100ft; Bridal Veil Falls, 40ft. Together these two guide between 60,000 and 75,000 gallons of water over their edges every second. At the base of the falls the river is nearly as deep as the ridge is high: about 170ft.

In geologic terms the falls are not old. They were created at the end of the last Ice Age, about 10,000 years ago, when the waters of Lake Erie created an exit channel into what used to be Lake Iroquois. The edge of this ancient lake was the Niagara Escarpment, 7.5mi north of the present-day falls. As the newly formed Niagara River plunged into the lake, it eroded a thick, underlying layer of soft shale, which in turn undermined the top layer of harder dolostone. Over the millennia, as the dolostone continually broke off and washed away, the falls receded and a gorge was formed. Both American and Bridal Veil Falls were born between 600 and 700 years ago. In recent decades, upstream power projects (which divert one-half to three-quarters of the falls' water) and steel supports in the rock at Niagara's edge (added in 1969) have significantly reduced the falls' yearly erosion. For a good introduction to the huge hydroelectric operations, stop by the **Niagara Power Project Visitor Center** *(4.5mi north of the falls on Rte. 104; open Apr–Labor Day daily 9am–5pm;* 🅿 ☎*716-285-3211).*

Preserving a Natural Wonder – Native Americans discovered Niagara Falls thousands of years ago—the name Niagara is thought to be an Indian word meaning "bottleneck." The first European to see the falls was Father Hennepin, a Roman Catholic priest, who accompanied Robert LaSalle to the Niagara region in 1678. Throughout the 18C, the French and the British fought over the area, which was part of the holdings under dispute in the French and Indian War. The British finally won the land, only to cede it to the Americans after the Revolution. The 1814 Treaty of Ghent put the border between Canada and the US in the center of the Niagara River.

With peacetime came tourism and commerce. Entrepreneurs harnessed the river's energy to power the unsightly factories, mills and lumberyards that sprang up all around the natural wonder. Others concentrated on separating tourists from their money at the garish hotels and curiosity shops that crowded the region. At Niagara's nadir, tourists couldn't even see the falls without paying a fee.

In the 1870s a group including Hudson River school painter Frederic Church (who made the falls the subject of one of his most famous works) and landscape architect Frederick Law Olmsted pioneered the "Free Niagara!" movement, which would soon become a model for conservation programs nationwide. After lobbying the New York legislature and collecting signatures from nearly 700 notable Americans, movement proponents persuaded New York to buy back the land around the falls and return it to its natural state. In 1885 the Niagara Reservation State Park—the oldest state park in the US—was established on the American side of the falls.

Today a plethora of nearby hotels, thick crowds and full parking lots still give Niagara Falls away as one of the most popular tourist destinations in the world, but the park, landscaped by Olmsted in the 1880s, provides something of an oasis amid the hustle and bustle of the neighboring city. Secluded pedestrian paths twist amid a wide variety of trees and shrubs, which reach their fullest growth in the constant spray and mist, and the guided tours that bring visitors close to the falls can actually be a lot of fun.

Practical Information .... Area Code: 716

Getting There – Access from **Buffalo** (*20mi*) via I-190 west to Robert Moses Parkway (Route 18F). International and domestic flights service **Buffalo-Niagara Falls International Airport**. Closest Amtrak **train** station (☎*800-872-7245*) is in Niagara Falls. Greyhound **bus** service (☎*402-330-2055 or 800-231-2222*) runs to Buffalo.

Getting Around – Tours of Niagara Reservation State Park aboard the Viewmobile are offered May–mid-Oct (*weather permitting*). Visitors can board at any of the six stops located at major attractions. The same ticket allows free reboarding for the entire day (*$4.50; tickets available at state park visitor center, below*).

Visitor Information – Contact the following agencies for information and brochures on points of interest, seasonal events, recreation and accommodations: **Niagara Reservation State Park** (*PO Box 1132, Niagara Falls NY 14303-0132* ☎*278-1770*), **visitor center** located in Prospect Park (☎*278-1730*); **Niagara Falls Convention & Visitors Bureau** (*310 4th. St., Niagara Falls NY 14303* ☎*285-2400 or 800-421-5223*); **Niagara County Tourism** (*139 Niagara St., Lockport NY 14094 www.niagara-usa.com* ☎*285-9141 or 800-338-7890*). The **Niagara Master Pass** coupon book (*$20; available at state park visitor center, above*) provides discounted admission to area attractions, including Cave of the Winds (*p 156*), Maid of the Mist Boat Tours (*p 156*) and the Aquarium of Niagara (*p 157*).

Accommodations – (*p 358*) Area visitors' guides including lodging directories and campgrounds are available (*free*) from local tourism agencies (*above*). Hotels, motels and bed-and-breakfast inns can be found in the cities of Niagara Falls, Lockport and Towanda. **B&B reservation service**: International Bed & Breakfast Club (*7009 Plaza Dr., Niagara Falls NY 14304* ☎*696-6720*). State parks that allow **camping** in the Niagara Falls area include Four Mile Campsite (*Youngstown* ☎*745-3802*) and Golden Hill State Park (*Barker* ☎*795-3885*). Other public campgrounds can be found in and around neighboring cities.

Recreation – A variety of companies offer tours of the falls from the water, land and air. Many offer hotel pickup, including: **Maid of the Mist Boat Tour**; **Whirlpool Jet Boat Tours** (*depart from Lewiston Landing May–Oct; 1hr;* ☎*905-468-4800 or 888-438-4444*); **Rainbow Air Helicopter Tours** (*depart from 454 Main St. May–early Nov; 8-10min;* ☎*284-2800*); **Niagara Historic Walking Tours** (*depart from the base of Niagara State Park's Observation Tower Apr–Oct; 1hr 15min;* ☎*285-2132*). The **Niagara Historic Trail** loops around Niagara County highlighting historic sites (*for map and descriptive material, contact Niagara County Tourism, above*).
The city of Niagara Falls is home to two large outlet **malls**: Niagara International Factory Outlets (*1900 Military Rd.* ☎*297-2022*) and Rainbow Centre Factory Outlet (*302 Rainbow Blvd.* ☎*285-9758*). **Artpark** (*foot of S. 4th St., Lewiston* ☎*754-9000 or 800-659-7275*) is a 200-acre state park dedicated to visual and performing arts.

SIGHTS   *1 day. Map p 156.*

★★ **Niagara Reservation State Park** – *Open year-round daily, hours vary seasonally.* ✗ ♿ ▢ ☎*716-278-1796*. This strip of green, landscaped by Frederick Law Olmsted, stretches 3.5mi along the Niagara River and over the five islands located at the top of the gorge; within it lie all the attractions on the US side of Niagara Falls. **Prospect Point** affords a bird's-eye view of American Falls. The 282ft **New York State Observation Tower** (1961), located slightly northeast of Prospect Point, features a glass-walled elevator that descends 200ft to the craggy base of

American Falls. It also ascends 80ft above street level to an enclosed observation deck. Weather permitting, visitors can walk up one flight of stairs to an outdoor deck for a panoramic view of all of Niagara Falls.

A tree-lined pedestrian path follows the American bank of the Niagara River to bridges that lead to Green Island and **Goat Island**. Lush and tranquil, Goat Island, at a quarter-mile wide, is the largest of the islands at the top of the falls; it separates Horseshoe Falls from American Falls and got its name in the winter of 1770, when a farmer placed his farm animals on the island to protect them from predators. Only one goat survived. **Terrapin Point**, on the west end of Goat Island, affords the best view of Horseshoe Falls from the US. *(For information about sights on the Canadian side, see the Michelin Green Guide to Canada.)*

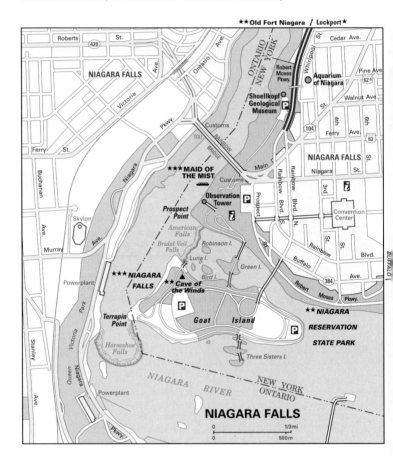

★★★ **Maid of the Mist Boat Tour** – [Kids] *Departs from Niagara Reservation State Park Apr–mid-May & Sept–late Oct Mon–Fri 10am–5pm, weekends 10am–6pm. Mid-May–late Jun daily 10am–6pm. Late Jun–Aug daily 9:15am–7:30pm. Hours may be extended during summer holidays. Round-trip 30min. Commentary. $8 cruise, 50¢ elevator.* ⅏ ⅏ ▯ *($4)* ☎716-284-4233. Launched in 1846, the first *Maid of the Mist* was a wooden-hulled, coal-fired steamboat. Today four all-steel, diesel-powered boats chug from the base of Prospect Point *(accessible via Observation Tower elevator)* past American and Bridal Veil Falls to bob at the tumultuous base of Horseshoe Falls. Visitors are given plastic hooded rain ponchos to protect them from the fantastic spray. With water pouring down on three sides, and rainbows often arcing above, a *Maid of the Mist* trip constitutes one of the most visceral experiences at Niagara Falls. It is also the most popular, so be prepared for long lines and crowded boats during peak season.

★★ **Cave of the Winds Trip** – *Goat Island. Visit by guided tour (30min) only, mid-May–mid-Jun daily 10am–5pm. Mid-Jun–Aug daily 10am–7:30pm. Sept–Oct daily 10am–5pm. $5.50.* ▯ ☎716-278-1796. This tour brings visitors within 25ft of roaring Bridal Veil Falls, which gushes over the terraced wooden walk-ways and covers them with a constant spray. Visitors are suited with heavy-duty slickers and booties in a stone building on Goat Island between Luna Island and Terrapin Point. An elevator descends 175ft into the Niagara Gorge, and a path flanked by rocks and shrubs brings visitors to the base of the falls. Rebuilt each year after being frozen over during the winter, the boardwalk culminates in the Hurricane Deck, which is bru-tally pounded with water when the wind comes from the east and lifts the mist off the falls. The trip actu-ally led behind the falls, into a shallow cave, until 1920, when a major rockfall closed off the route.

Aquarium of Niagara – **Kids** *701 Whirlpool St. Open Memorial Day–Labor daily 9am–7pm. Rest of the year daily 9am–5pm. Closed Thanksgiving Day, Dec 25. $6.25.* ⚬ 🅿 ☎ *716-285-3575.* Located half a mile down-stream from the falls, this small but well-organized aquarium boasts more than 40 exhibits showcasing 1,500 aquatic animals, including the largest collection of Great Lakes fish in the world, as well as a diverse collection of tropical fish, bottom-feeders, sharks, penguins, shellfish and anemone. All are displayed in simulated natural habitats and described with informative signs. A large round tankful of sea lions forms the centerpiece of the aquar-ium. These playful critters stop gliding around the tank only during demonstrations, when they enter-tain the crowds in exchange for whole fish.

A pedestrian bridge leads from the aquarium over the Robert Moses Parkway to the **Shoellkopf Geological Museum** **Kids**, housed in a funky 1971 building made from dolostone, sandstone and limestone from the Niagara Gorge. On the grounds, stop to view the Niagara River Gorge from the overlook. This was the site of a major rockfall that destroyed two-thirds of Schoellkopf Power Generating Station 3 on June 7, 1956. Inside, a 13min, three-screen slide presentation tells the story of the gorge and the falls, from their prehistoric formation to the work done in recent decades to preserve their beauty. Encircling the movie theater, exhibits include

■ Daredevils

One might think it hard to rival the thundering natural drama of Niagara Falls, but that hasn't stopped dozens of daredevils, hucksters and desperate souls from trying. The first known adventurers to tumble over Horse-shoe Falls—the preferred "stunt" falls, because there are no rocks at the bottom—were two bears, two foxes, a buffalo, a raccoon, an eagle, a dog and 15 geese, who were pushed to the edge in a wooden schooner in 1827, as some 30,000 rubberneckers looked on. Before long, stuntmen took their turn entertaining the masses. The most famous of these, **Jean François Gravelet**, also known as "the Great Blondin," traversed Niagara Gorge on a tightrope for the first time on June 30, 1859, in 17 minutes. In later feats, he rode across the rope on a bicycle, walked it blindfolded and made the trek with his manager on his back. During a tightrope competition, another enter-prising daredevil brought a small stove with him. Midway across the falls, he stopped, lit a fire and cooked two omelets, which he lowered down to passengers on a Maid of the Mist *(p 156)* boat.

Plunging over the waterfall in a barrel has become the most popular Niagara feat in the 20C, even though it is tech-nically illegal. In 1901 Annie Edson Taylor, a schoolteacher, was the first one to do it and survive. She encased herself in a regular oak barrel, but all others who have braved the drop in that most humble of containers have died. Daredevils in barrels made of steel, rubber, plastic, or a combination thereof have enjoyed a slightly higher success rate. The only exception was eight-year-old Roger Woodward, who on July 9, 1960, survived the plunge virtually unscathed in only a life jacket, after his boat capsized in the Upper Niagara River.

rock and mineral samples from the gorge and displays on hydropower, engi-neering and natural history. While the museum feels a bit dated, it is the most educational attraction in the Niagara area *(open Apr–late May daily 10am–5pm; Memorial Day–Labor Day daily 9am–7pm; early Sept–Oct daily 10am–5pm; $1;* ⚬ 🅿 ☎ *716-278-1770).*

EXCURSIONS *Map p 6*

★★ **Old Fort Niagara** – *2hrs. 15mi from Niagara Falls along Robert Moses Pkwy. to Youngstown.* Situated on a scenic promontory where the Niagara River feeds into Lake Ontario, this complex of 18C stone structures—including the oldest in the Great Lakes region—has alternately served as a French, English and American military stronghold over the centuries. Today, with its pristinely preserved buildings and its 22 acres of well-manicured emerald lawns resembling a golf course, the fort is as picturesque as it is historically significant.

Old Fort Niagara

Because it controlled water access from Lake Ontario to the four other Great Lakes, Old Fort Niagara enjoyed one of the most strategic positions in Western New York. It was also one of the most contested. The French established the first post here in 1679 and built the first permanent fortification, the "French castle," in 1726. The British captured the fort in 1759, during the French and Indian War, but were forced to surrender it to the Americans in 1796. Except for a brief stint of British rule during the War of 1812, Ft. Niagara has been maintained by the US ever since. Its power to control the movement of waterborne supplies to the west was greatly diminished by the completion of the Erie Canal in 1825. Although the fort's outer defenses were shored up during the Civil War, it has mainly served as a border post during peacetime and as barracks and a training station for American soldiers during World War I and II. Long recognized as a historic site, it was restored between 1926 and 1934 and later opened to the public.

Visit – *Open Jan–Mar & Oct–Dec daily 9am–4:30pm. Apr daily 9am–5:30pm. May Mon–Fri 9am–5:30pm, weekends 9am–6:30pm. Jun Mon–Fri 9am–6:30pm, weekends 9am–7:30pm. Jul–Aug daily 9am–7:30pm. Sept Mon–Fri 9am–5:30pm, weekends 9am–6:30pm. Closed Jan 1, Thanksgiving Day, Dec 25. $6.75.* よ 🅿 ☎716-745-7611. During the fort's early-20C restoration, each building was returned to its original appearance, and each was given a colorful plaque, representing the coats of arms of France, Britain or the US, to indicate the nation responsible for its construction. Cobblestone paths link the various structures, which range from the simple powder magazine (1757) and provisions storehouse (1762) to the striking south and north redoubts (1770-71), with their raised pagoda roofs. The crown jewel of the complex, the **French castle★** (1726) stretches luxuriously along the banks of Lake Ontario. On clear days it affords a stupendous **view★★** of Toronto on the other side of the lake. Although the castle was used only as officers' quarters from 1757 until World War I, it has been restored to its 1727 appearance, when soldiers' barracks, an officers' apartment, a chapel, a powder magazine, a storehouse and a trade room all crowded under its roof. Reproduction mid-18C furniture and stained-glass windows re-create the castle's Colonial heyday. Outside, daily musket-firing demonstrations, performed by staff in period garb, enhance the effect.

★ **Lockport** – *2hrs. 22mi from Niagara Falls via Rte. 31.* Completed in 1825, the 363mi Erie Canal *(p 94)* is famous for providing the first all-water route from the Atlantic Ocean to the Great Lakes and for spurring the young Republic's westward expansion. Perhaps less known is the fact that the canal also sparked significant development along its banks, giving rise to 19C boomtowns like SYRACUSE and Lockport. Here, the canal plunged some 50ft over the Niagara Escarpment, necessitating the construction of two flights of five locks (one for eastbound craft, one for westbound) to lift and lower boats.

Today the town celebrates its heritage at the **Canal Museum** *(80 Richmond Ave.; open May–Oct daily 9am–5pm;* ☎716-434-3140), located in the two-story former powerhouse at the foot of one of the two "flight of five" locks (the other flight was replaced in 1918 by two larger locks to accommodate bigger boats). Here visitors can watch a 10min video on early canal life and browse hundreds of historic photographs, which depict canal-boat families, lock operators and the construction workers who widened and deepened the canal in the early 20C. Also on display are canal-boat log books, repair tools, early-19C maps and massive traffic lights once used to control the boats coming in and out of the locks. **Riley's Way**, a guided walking tour *(.5mi)* of the area around the museum, connects 14 signs that relate historical and engineering facts about the locks, which are the last two on the Erie Canal. Daily **canal cruises** *(depart from 210-228 Market St. May–Oct daily 10am–7pm; round-trip 2hrs; commentary; reservations required; $9;* ✕ ♿ 🅿 *Lockport Locks & Erie Canal Cruises* ☎716-693-3260 or 800-378-0352) bring visitors through the locks, under the world's widest bridge and past Lockport's historic district.

ROCHESTER ★

Population 221,594
Map p 6
Tourist Information ☎716-546-3070 or 800-677-7282

The third-largest city in New York State, Rochester sits halfway between Buffalo and Syracuse near the famous FINGER LAKES region. For a town its size, Rochester is a cultural powerhouse: eight institutions of higher learning—including the private University of Rochester, with its famed Eastman School of Music—make their home here. Rochester also boasts a world-class orchestra, one of the finest regional art museums in the country and the unique Strong Museum. Although downtown Rochester has suffered somewhat from urban renewal schemes of the 1960s and 70s, the city's charming residential neighborhoods, where huge mansions crouch behind rows of century-old trees, preserve the city's fin-de-siècle elegance.

Historical Notes

The Seneca Nation occupied much of western New York until 1788, when Yankee speculators purchased 2.5 million acres from the Indians at bargain-basement prices. In 1789 the first European settler arrived at the Genesee River Falls, now called High Falls *(60 Brown's Race)*, and constructed the city's first flour mill there. Col. Nathaniel Rochester and two business partners acquired the mill in 1803 and began building others, using the falls to power the mills' waterwheels. Colonel Rochester officially founded the city in 1812.

Immigrant laborers hand-dug the Erie Canal through Rochester in the 1820s. In just two decades the city's population increased thirteenfold and its mills' production shot up twentyfold. By the 1830s Rochester was known as Flour City, and by the 1850s it earned the nickname Flower City as well, because of its expansive nurseries, parks and private gardens. Two of the nation's most promi-

---

■ **Lilac Festival**

Giving credence to Rochester's moniker, Flower City, this lively festival takes place the second week of May and runs for 10 days (☎716-256-4960). A veritable feast for the senses, Highland Park is resplendent with some 1,200 lilac bushes representing more than 500 varieties. Visually complementing the fragrant blossoms are more than 10,000 hand-planted pansies, 15,000 hand-planted tulips and myriad rhododendrons and azaleas. Musical performances, entertainment for kids, a parade and a 10K road race round out the event.

nent activists lived in the city during those prosperous years: early women's rights advocate Susan B. Anthony and black abolitionist Frederick Douglass. Anthony spent 40 years in Rochester, writing about and organizing for the women's suffrage movement. Douglass, an escaped slave and renowned orator, published his newspaper *The North Star* here.

Rochester continued to flourish throughout the 19C with the creation of three of the world's best-known companies: the optical-equipment giant Bausch and Lomb, the Xerox Corporation, and perhaps most famous, Eastman Kodak. The latter emerged as the city's largest employer by the turn of the century and its world headquarters continues to anchor Rochester's "imaging technology" scene, where dozens of high-tech firms produce everything from lenses to lasers. In the daytime, the blocks bounded by East and Park Avenues, Alexander Street and Culver Road—where most of the city's attractions can be found—are particularly beautiful. At night, a collegiate air pervades the cafes, bars and restaurants on Park Street.

SIGHTS *1 day*

★★ **Strong Museum** – **Kids** *One Manhattan Square. Open year-round Mon–Sat 10am–5pm, Sun 1pm–5pm. Closed Jan 1, Jul 4, Thanksgiving Day, Dec 25. $6.* ✗ ♿ 🅿 *www.strongmuseum.org* ☎716-263-2700. A one-of-a-kind institution, the Strong Museum (1982) dazzles visitors with selections from its enormous, eclectic collection of 19C and 20C miscellany, including the world's most comprehensive assemblage of **dolls**, numbering about 27,000. The Strong is also aggressively expanding as a state-of-the-art children's museum.

Courtesy Strong Museum
Dolls made by Izannah Wallace (c.1873)

Born into a wealthy New York family, **Margaret Woodbury Strong** (1897-1969) has been called "the collector's collector." By the age of eight she had already traveled the world with her parents. On extended trips to Europe and Asia she got her first taste of picking and choosing her favorite objects, which she could keep only if they fit in the small satchel she was allowed to fill—hence her taste for dolls and miniatures. Strong continued to collect throughout her life, and at the time of her death she had amassed more than 300,000 objects.

Some 7,000 pieces of the collection are now on permanent display in the museum. In addition to dolls and dollhouses, visitors will find, in row upon row of glass cases, American pressed glass, inkwells, beer steins, folk art, Tiffany glass, toy trains, animal figurines, miniature rooms and more. In recent decades museum curators have filled out the collection with larger objects, such as furniture and domestic appliances.

On the first floor of the museum, the 4,000sq ft "Kid to Kid" exhibit teaches children about communications by letting them experiment with walkie-talkies, Morse code, quill pens, computers, whisper dishes, Braille and sign language. "Can You Tell Me How to Get to Sesame Street?" reproduces some of the characters and scenery from the famous children's television show. The museum is also building a glass-atrium addition with a 1950s diner, a park and a restored carousel *(scheduled for completion in November 1998).*

★★ **George Eastman House/ Museum of Photography** – *900 East Ave. Open year-round Tue–Sat 10am–4:30pm, Sun 1pm–4:30pm. Closed Jan 1, Thanksgiving Day, Dec 25. $6.50.* ✗ ♿ 🅿 *www.it.rit.edu/~gehouse* ☎716-271-3361. *Live music recitals take place in the house during the first Sunday of the month at 3pm (free with museum admission).* George Eastman, the founder of Eastman Kodak Company, spared no expense in building his opulent Colonial Revival mansion in 1905. The house and gardens reflect Eastman's lavish tastes, while enormous collections of photographs, cameras and films pay homage to his pioneering role in photography.

Eastman was born in 1854 in Waterville, New York. He moved to Rochester with his family in 1860, but the death of his father two years later necessitated that he leave school at age 13 to become a messenger boy for an insurance company. After a brief stint as a bank clerk, Eastman began experimenting with photography in 1877. In 1880 he opened a factory to manufacture dry plates, or old-fashioned negatives for large-format cameras. Throughout the 1880s he worked on perfecting a hand-held camera that anyone could use; in 1888 he succeeded and by 1898 he was a millionaire. A lifelong bachelor, Eastman contributed more than $100 million to Rochester schools, arts programs, parks and hospitals. He died in 1932.

Visit – *2hrs.* A National Historic Landmark, Eastman's 50-room, 35,000sq ft former residence was the ultimate bachelor pad. Designed by local architect J. Foster Warner, with interior decorations supervised by the eminent New York firm McKim, Mead & White, it forms the centerpiece of a 12.5-acre estate that once boasted eight gardens, five greenhouses, stables, barns, pastures and a working farm. A grand mahogany staircase dominates the entrance hall. Marble and oak parquet floors throughout the house are set off by silk damask wall coverings, carved-oak paneling and elaborate plaster ceiling decorations. Some 85 percent of the furniture on display belonged to Eastman.

Four gardens encircle the mansion. Landscape architect Alling S. DeForest designed the **Terrace Garden** as an open-air living room where Eastman could entertain guests. The garden's 23 boxwood-edged flower beds contain more than 90 varieties of plants that blossom between early spring and late fall. A grove of Japanese maples, a sunken oval lily pool and two 17C Venetian wellheads complement the blooms.

Major additions to the back of the house contain the museum's impressive collections of photographs and camera equipment. Located in the Mees Gallery, the mesmerizing **technology exhibit★** charts the course of photography through the centuries with some 4,000 still cameras and more than 15,000 pieces of camera equipment. A photography gallery is crammed with selections from the museum's 500,000-piece collection of prints and negatives. Ansel Adams, Weegee, Paul Strand, Man Ray, Alfred Stieglitz, Edward Weston and Mary Ellen Mark are only some of the big names you'll find here. A cinephile's dream, the **Dryden Theatre★** presents a phenomenal lineup of movies—new and old, familiar and obscure, domestic and foreign, short and feature-length—including many from the museum's 15,000-film collection.

★ **Memorial Art Gallery** – *500 University Ave. Open year-round Tue noon–9pm, Wed–Fri 10am–4pm, Sat 10am–5pm, Sun noon–5pm. Closed Jan 1 & Dec 25. $5.* ✗ ♿ 🅿 *www.rochester.edu/mag* ☎716-473-7720. The Memorial Art Gallery's collection comprises 9,500 objects and spans 5,000 years, making it one of the most well-balanced museums in the state outside New York City. It's also one of the best organized and curated museums, full of bold and original viewing spaces tailored to show off the finest aspects of each piece of art. Founded in 1913, the gallery was given in trust to the University of Rochester and was expanded in 1926, 1968 and 1987. Its Classical Revival core appropriately houses the older artworks. The huge central space rimmed with clerestory windows is studded with ancient art ranging from a Roman sarcophagus (3C AD) to a 15C walnut credence with a French coat of arms carved on the front. Richly painted side rooms contain European art from the Renaissance period through the 20C; highlights include a gorgeous 1696 Italian harpsichord, painted gold with cherubs and landscape scenes, and Rembrandt's famous *Portrait of a Young Man*. The modern sections of the gallery contain temporary exhibitions, 19C and 20C American art and a small but eye-catching collection of American **folk art★**. The latter includes a carousel goat, and 19C custom-made signs, such as a colossal top hat for a New York City hatmaker and a giant glasses-and-mustache combination for an optometrist. In the 20C sculpture court, visitors can look through the glass atrium ceiling to see the soaring spire of the Gothic cathedral next door, which now houses the University of Rochester art school.

★ **Rochester Historical Society (Woodside Mansion)** – *485 East Ave. Visit by guided tour (45min) only, year-round Mon–Fri 10am–4pm. Closed Thanksgiving Day, Dec 25. $2.50.* 🅿 ☎716-271-2705. Two aspects of the stately Woodside Mansion compete for the visitor's attention: its sturdy, stately design, a textbook example of the Greek Revival tradition, and its wide-ranging collection of documents, photographs, furniture and curios stretching back to Rochester's pioneer period.

Woodside was completed in 1840 for merchant Silas O. Smith; its most prominent features are the front porch, supported by two Doric columns, and the balustraded deck and cupola. Within, a gracefully wrought spiral staircase ascends three stories from the wide main hall to the cupola. Downstairs, Woodside's simple but spacious rooms are furnished with period furniture—much of which, like the Rosewood player piano in the drawing room, originated in Rochester. Paintings of Rochester notables, selected from the society's 700-work collection, cover the walls. Upstairs, the small **smoking room ★** is a fabulously rich space lined with leather and mahogany walls and stuffed with ornately carved Herter Brothers furniture. In other parts of the mansion, the society maintains a collection of 20,000 historic Rochester photographs; large holdings of local architectural drawings, costumes and toys; and a reference library (formerly the kitchen) with a copy of the Pioneer Record.

Rochester Museum & Science Center

– **Kids** *657 East Ave. Open year-round Mon–Sat 9am–5pm, Sun & holidays noon–5pm. Closed Dec 25. $6. ✗ ⅋ ▣ www.rmsc. org ☎716-271-1880.* In this regional museum, archaeology, anthropology and hands-on science and technology exhibits explore the natural and cultural history of upstate New York. On the first floor, "Cabinets of Curiosity" shows how the natural sciences got their start with the work of self-taught scholars of the 19C and their pioneering collections of fossils, animals and birds. On the second floor, "At the Western Door" examines the relationship between Seneca Indians and 19C European explorers, and "Face to Face" features masks, clothes, headdresses, jewelry, baskets and rugs from various cultures around the world. Also on view is the Farview Mastodon, an unusually well-preserved, 11,600-year-old mastodon skeleton that was excavated in 1991 near Avon, New York. Next door, the **Strasenburgh Planetarium** (1968) projects films (both astronomy-related and not) on a four-story screen and conducts laser and star shows. Exhibits on display in the lobby include a 173-pound iron meteorite that landed in Arizona, several 18C telescopes and a walk-through electronic display about the solar system.

Park Avenue

Extending east from Alexander Street to Culver Road, this artsy 12-block corridor sprinkled with cafes, restaurants, pubs and boutiques is a great place to stroll, browse, eat or just hang out. The strip between Vassar and Somerton Streets is the liveliest section of Park Avenue. Try **Tivoli** *(no. 690)* for light and tasty Italian fare. The European-style coffee drinks served up at the **Tivoli Cafe** next door are a great way to round out a meal. At no. 682, the clamorous **Big Apple Cafe** draws college students and other locals with its hearty pasta, crepes and salads. Frittatas, fish specials, pasta and creative diner grub can be had at **Charlie's Frog Pond**, a local favorite that got its name from the frog-covered wallpaper that adorns its interior. Another classic, **Stever's Candies** *(no. 623)*, has been satisfying local sweet tooths for more than 50 years.

Susan B. Anthony House – *17 Madison St. Visit by guided tour (45min) only, year-round Thu–Sat 1pm–4pm. Closed Jan 1, Jul 4, Thanksgiving Day, Dec 25. $5. www.frontiernet.net/~1hurst/sbahouse/sbahome.htm ☎716-235-6124.* Leading advocate for women's rights and suffrage, **Susan B. Anthony** (1820-1906) lived in this red-brick Italianate house (c.1850) from 1866 until her death. Here, in the parlor, Anthony met with such reformers as Elizabeth Cady Stanton *(p 135)* and Frederick Douglass. It was also here that police arrested her for voting in the presidential election in 1872. In the attic, added c.1895, she helped write the groundbreaking *History of Woman Suffrage*. Today some of Anthony's personal possessions—including her signature black silk dress, her Morris chair and her autographed photograph of Buffalo Bill—are on display in the house, and a museum room tells the story of women's suffrage, which was won in the US with the passage of the 19th Amendment in 1920. As part of a major expansion and renovation, an education and visitor center is scheduled to open next door *(19 Madison St.)*, in the former home of Anthony's sister Hannah Anthony Mosher, in July 1998.

EXCURSIONS *Map p 6*

★ **Genesee Country Village Museum** – [Kids] *½ day. 20mi southwest of Rochester via Rte. 383 (Scottsville Rd.) to Rte. 36. Follow Rte. 36 south into Mumford, turn left onto George St., which becomes Flint Hill Rd. 1410 Flint Hill Rd., Mumford. Open mid-May–mid-Oct Tue–Sun & holidays 10am–4pm. $10.* ✗ ♿ ⃣P ☎716-538-6822. A re-created 19C village, an unusual wildlife art gallery and a 175-acre nature preserve (with 5mi of interpreted hiking trails) make up what's known as the Genesee Country Village Museum. Of these, the sprawling village, comprising 57 restored and furnished buildings staffed with costumed guides and craftspeople, offers the most comprehensive view of regional history. Before the advent of the modern city in the mid-19C, more than 40 hamlets and villages thrived in Genesee County, a six-million-acre tract that stretched from the Finger Lakes to the lower Great Lakes. The village preserves the full spectrum of domestic architecture common to Western New York in the 19C, from pioneers' log cabins to ornate Victorian mansions. In many of the dwellings and workshops, costumed guides ply 19C trades such as pottery, blacksmithing, tinsmithing and woodworking. Interestingly, the two most historically significant structures moved to this site—Col. Nathaniel Rochester's log cabin (c.1795) and George Eastman's small Greek Revival childhood home (c.1840)—are among the most humble. Tucked within the village is the **Carriage Museum★**, a real gem. Here, some 50 horse-drawn vehicles illustrate the range of 19C transportation options, from a rugged brewery hitch wagon to a lightweight sporting rig to an elegant park phaeton, with wheel guards to protect women's skirts from mud. Among the curvy sleighs is one that is thought to have belonged to the great showman P.T. Barnum. Also on the grounds is the **Gallery of Sporting Art**, one of the country's largest collections of wildlife and sporting art. Dating from the 17C to the present, several hundred paintings and bronze sculptures depict various animals and "gentlemen's sports" such as horseback riding, hunting and fishing.

★★ **Letchworth State Park** – *2hrs. 35mi south of Rochester in Castile. From Rte. 390, take Exit 7 and continue to Rte. 36 north to park entrance. Open year-round daily 6am–11pm. $4/car.* ⚠ ✗ ♿ ⃣P ☎716-493-3600. Forging its dramatic path toward Lake Ontario, the Genesee River flows over two sets of falls. One is flanked by flour mills and factories in Rochester; the other is preserved in gorgeous Letchworth State Park. Here, surrounded by 14,350 acres of lush forest, the Genesee cuts the deepest canyon east of the Mississippi River, the Genesee Gorge. A gently curving road traces the edge of the gorge, and a number of turnouts, including spectacular **Inspiration Point★**, afford splendid vistas of breathtaking 600ft cliffs and three separate waterfalls. At 107ft, Middle Falls stands the tallest and is best seen from a lookout deck beside the Greek Revival **Glen Iris Inn**, formerly the home of William P. Letchworth. A businessman, amateur historian and conservationist, Letchworth restored the area around the falls in the 1860s after it was ravaged by lumbering. Today the Glen Iris, with its welcoming, colonnaded porch outfitted with Adirondack chairs, houses a celebrated inn and restaurant. A steep but beautiful footpath—one of dozens of hiking trails in the park—leads from Middle Falls to the 70ft Upper Falls. The 1852 predecessor to the bridge that now stretches above the falls, the Portage High Bridge, bore the distinction of being the tallest wooden railroad bridge in the world at the time of its construction. Across the road from the Glen Iris stands the eclectic **William Pryor Letchworth Museum** *(open mid-May–Oct daily 10am–5pm; $1;* ♿ ⃣P ☎716-493-2760*)*. Opened in 1913, the stone museum contains a broad assortment of artifacts Letchworth amassed throughout his life. Highlights include a large Mastodon skull, discovered nearby in the 1860s, and a large collection of Native American artifacts. On a bluff behind the museum stands a log cabin built around 1800 by Mary Jemison, "the White Woman of Genesee," for her daughter, Nancy. After her family was massacred by Delaware Indians, Mary was taken in by the tribe and became an honorary member. Beside the cabin and a restored Seneca Indian Council House, last used in 1872, stands an 8ft statue of Mary, a fitting monument to this local legend.

Introduction to New Jersey

Resembling an elongated "S," New Jersey owes its official moniker, the Garden State, to its plentiful orchards, flower gardens and vegetable farms, located primarily in its northwestern valleys and southwestern plains. The state's key location between NEW YORK CITY and PHILADELPHIA brought it several unofficial titles as well: the Cockpit of the Revolution, for the more than 100 battles staged on its soil during the War of Independence; the Birthplace of Industrial America, for its many factories and historic skirmishes between labor and capital; and, most recently, the Commuter State, for the spider's web of highways that suck many of its suburban residents to work in neighboring New York and Pennsylvania.

Embracing 7,532sq mi, New Jersey is the fifth-smallest state in the nation, behind Hawaii, Connecticut, Delaware and Rhode Island, but with some 8 million residents, it is the most densely populated state in the US, and ninth in population overall. Fully 89 percent of New

New Jersey State Facts
Capital: Trenton
Land Area: 7,532 square miles
Population: 8,001,850
Nickname: Garden State
Motto: Liberty and Prosperity
State Flower: Purple Violet
State Bird: Eastern Goldfinch

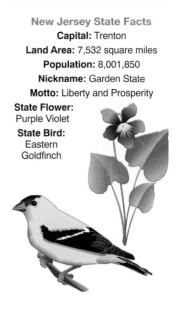

Jersey residents live in the nine metropolitan areas located partly or entirely in the state, yet 65 percent of its acreage remains farmland or forest. Except for the 50mi diagonal line that separates it from New York State, New Jersey is completely surrounded by water. The Delaware River and Bay largely define the state's western edge; the Hudson River and Atlantic Ocean limn its eastern border. Scores of navigable rivers penetrate New Jersey's interior, bringing settlers and powering industry as early as the 17C, while dozens of bays and inlets complicate its coastline, the famous "Joisey" Shore.

Geographical Notes

Regional Landscapes – New Jersey is made up of four main land regions *(map p 15)*, situated in diagonal bands running northeast to southwest. The northernmost strip belongs to the **Appalachian Ridge and Valley**, a large land mass stretching from New York to Alabama. The Kittatinny Mountains rise along the region's—and the state's—northeastern edge and contain New Jersey's highest point, the aptly named High Point (1,803ft). During the last Ice Age, the Delaware River cut through those mountains, creating the DELAWARE WATER GAP, a scenic gorge that measures 900ft at the widest point of its base, with sides up to 1,600ft tall. A crazy quilt of pastureland and farms, the Appalachian Valley, part of the Great Valley, sprawls eastward from the mountains.

The land region to the south, the **New England Upland**, also called the Highlands, extends into New York and Pennsylvania. Veined with scenic rivers and pocked with glacial lakes and ponds, the upland is named after its high, flat-topped ridges made up of tilted layers of Pre-Cambrian and Paleozoic rock.

Low plains broken up by traprock ridges rising 400ft to 500ft characterize the 20mi-wide **Piedmont Plateau**, which spreads east to the Hudson River, embracing New Jersey's major industrial centers (Paterson, Newark, Jersey City, Elizabeth) and suburban enclaves of New York City. The **Atlantic Coastal Plain**, made fertile from detritus left by retreating glaciers some 10,000 years ago, covers the southern three-fifths of the state. The land rises gradually from sea level along the Atlantic Ocean in the east to gentle slopes along the Delaware River in the west. Lower elevations feature salt marshes, cranberry bogs, swamps and the famous PINE BARRENS, while the rolling hills to the southwest are covered with produce farms.

Climate – For a state so small, New Jersey has a rather varied climate. Along the coast, the ocean depresses temperatures in the summer and increases them in the winter, while higher elevations in the north mean slightly colder temperatures year-round. Average July temperatures range from 70°F (21°C) in the north to 76°F (24°C) in the southwest. January averages range from 26°F (–3°C) in the north to 34°F (1°C) in the southeast. The greatest disparity between northern and southern climates is in snowfall, which measures about 13 inches per year in the south, compared with up to 60 inches in the north.

Historical Notes

Early Squabbles – Until the early 16C, approximately 8,000 Native Americans belonging to the Lenni Lenape ("the Real People") tribe of the Algonquian family lived in what is now New Jersey. Then came a slow but steady trickle of European explorers, beginning with Italian navigator Giovanni da Verrazano, who briefly explored the coast in 1524. In 1609 Henry Hudson, an Englishman working for the Dutch East India Company, probed the Sandy Hook Bay area and sailed up the river that now bears his name. Five years later, Dutch explorer **Cornelius Mey**, after whom CAPE MAY was named, became the first European to sail the Delaware River. Despite frequent Indian attacks, further Dutch exploration led to the establishment of New Jersey's first permanent white settlement, Bergen (now part of Jersey City), in 1660.

By that time European powers were frantically vying for control of the New World and its lucrative fur trade, and New Jersey was smack in the middle of the fray. Swedish settlers and traders filtered into the southern part of New Jersey from 1638 to 1655, when the Dutch drove them out. In 1664 the English seized all of the Dutch West India Company's substantial claims to North America, including what is now New Jersey, which King Charles II gave to his brother James, Duke of York. Naming the territory after the English Isle of Jersey, James gave the land to his friends Lord John Berkeley and Sir George Carteret.

Cheap land prices and political and religious freedom drew many settlers to New Jersey, but disputes over land and government led to its being officially split in half in 1676. West of the line drawn from north of Atlantic City to the Delaware Water Gap was Berkeley's territory, West Jersey. Here William Penn *(p 222)*, among others, founded an agrarian Quaker colony—the first in North America. In the shadow of New York City, Carteret's portion, East Jersey, became a manufacturing center. But a series of tenant revolts in the 1690s forced England to take over and reunite East and West Jersey in 1702. Ruled by New York for more than three decades, New Jersey gained political independence in 1738, though riots over land titles continued into the 1750s.

By the 1760s New Jersey boasted about 100,000 residents (mostly concentrated in the north) and two of the oldest universities in the nation, Princeton (1746) and Rutgers (1766, the only state university with a Colonial charter). But whatever

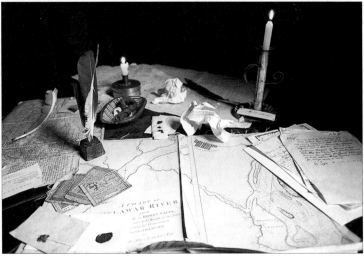

Wick House, Morristown National Historical Park

© Scott Barrow

fragile peace New Jersey had cobbled together was shattered with the coming of the Revolution. There were many New Jersey patriots: In 1774 a group of New Jerseyites staged a tax rebellion similar to the 1773 Boston Tea Party, burning a supply of British tea stored in a ship docked at Greenwich. Three years later New Jersey declared its independence from England. Even so, fully half of New Jersey soldiers fought for the Redcoats, not against them. Nonetheless, important battles at TRENTON (1776), PRINCETON (1777), Monmouth (1778) and Springfield (1780) eventually paved the way for self-rule. New Jersey became the third state of the new Republic on December 18, 1787.

Industry and Ingenuity – If the war tried New Jersey politically, it greatly strengthened the state economically. From the hills of the north came iron ore for munitions; produce from the south fed troops that were stationed here for hundreds of engagements and three bitter winters. Believing that the future of the Republic lay in industry, Alexander Hamilton helped to establish the first planned manufacturing district in Paterson in 1791. Although that effort was not entirely successful, industrial cities grew up all over northern New Jersey in the 19C. Textiles were woven in PATERSON; ships were built in Jersey City and Newark. Workers in Trenton mass-produced pottery. Sussex had its zinc mines, MORRISTOWN its iron forges. Glassmaking took root in southern towns on the Delaware River. In Camden, Elizabeth and Passaic, industry exploded as waves of European immigrants crashed on American shores. Improved roads, then two canals and finally a fast-growing network of railroads rushed raw materials to factories, finished goods to market—and tourists to the beach.

Strange as it may seem, New Jersey's tourist industry grew up at the same time its smokestacks and factories did. People had been flocking to Cape May to enjoy the healthful effects of "seabathing" since 1801, but it was the train that began arriving in ATLANTIC CITY in 1854 that made the latter city America's original beach resort: the birthplace of the wooden boardwalk (to keep sand out of hotel lobbies), the amusement park, saltwater taffy and the picture postcard. New Jersey was home to many more historic "firsts" in the 19C. In 1804 the first and most famous duel between American politicians took place at Weehawken, when Aaron Burr, the vice president of the US, fatally shot Alexander Hamilton, his political rival. In 1840 Joseph Henry transmitted the first radio impulse at Princeton. Eight years later the first federally funded lifeguard station was established on the Jersey Shore. The first dinosaur skeleton in North America was found buried in Haddonfield in 1858. Rutgers and Princeton competed in the nation's first intercollegiate football game in 1869. A decade later, Thomas Edison invented the electric light and the phonograph in his Menlo Park lab. Edison's 1887 invention, the kinetoscope (motion picture), brought the burgeoning silent-film industry—and stars like Mary Pickford and Fatty Arbuckle—to studios at Fort Lee.

Livestock Show

Social Strife and Reform – Despite these gains, New Jersey continued to be riven by political and economic forces. A testing ground for labor-management relations, the state was home to one of the first strikes in America, at the Paterson textile mills in 1828. Rising living costs and stagnant wages prompted more strikes throughout the 1830s, with shoemakers, hatters, textile workers, harness makers, construction workers and others battling for a living wage and, in some cases, the 10-hour day—which was finally won in 1851 along with a ban on child labor. The Civil War evinced conflicting allegiances in New Jersey, where slavery had existed since the Colonial era. Although the state eventually chipped in more than 80,000 troops for the Union cause, it was one of only three states to vote against the reelection of Abraham Lincoln in 1864.

In the late 19C, lax incorporation laws—coupled with corrupt urban political machines—drew many of the nation's biggest industrial monopolies to set up shop in the north. Not until 1910, when New Jersey voters elected the reform-minded Princeton alumnus Woodrow Wilson to the governorship, did any real trust-busting take place. Labor disputes continued, however. A six-month strike by 20,000 Paterson silk workers in 1913 drew widespread support of labor activists, including Upton Sinclair, but was eventually broken. In 1915 company-hired "deputy sheriffs" fired on peaceful pickets at a fertilizer factory in Carteret. Hiring strikebreakers, infiltrating unions, using police force and operating illegal sweatshops became industrial New Jersey's modus operandi. The Paterson silk and dye workers' strike in 1933-34 was one of the few strikes in New Jersey history that has been a clear-cut success.

The 20C has brought about startling transformations in New Jersey's social and physical landscape. Between 1900 and 1930, the state's population more than doubled, as immigrants streamed from Ellis Island into factory jobs and as railroad lines spurred the growth of suburbs. During World War II, northern shipbuilding cities like Newark attracted a huge influx of black workers from the South, adding yet another layer to New Jersey's diversity. In 1952 the New Jersey Turnpike opened, providing a fast and direct route between New York City and Philadelphia; the Garden State Parkway, running down the coast to Cape May, followed in 1955. To keep traffic flowing, both featured the cloverleaf, invented in New Jersey. Meanwhile, many industrial cities fell prey to urban blight, which was both a cause and an effect of the black riots that killed 26 and injured 1,500 in Newark in the summer of 1967. With the supposed aim of raising money for the disabled and the elderly, the first casino opened in Atlantic City in 1978, sparking a national trend. In recent years, charismatic politicians like Republican governor Christine Todd Whitman have been working to attract new business to the Garden State and to rebuild its schools and social infrastructure.

Economy

Natural Resources – Historically, New Jersey's rivers and ocean ports have been among its most important natural resources: the rivers for providing hydropower and transportation, and the ports for promoting trade. Still today miles of wharves along the Hudson and Delaware Rivers serve as important docks for oceangoing vessels, while Newark, Elizabeth, Hoboken and Camden host the state's chief ports. Other natural resources include minerals—crushed stone, sand and gravel are mined throughout the state—and the fruits of the sea. Indeed the sea has continually provided livelihoods for New Jerseyites, and today the commercial fishing industry is valued at $97 million a year.

Industry – More than a half-million New Jersey residents work in **manufacturing**, which generates 17 percent of the state's gross product. New Jersey leads the nation in the production of chemicals, particularly pharmaceuticals and detergents. Food products rank second among the state's manufactured goods; printed matter third. Oil refineries cluster around the area of Linden, Carteret and Bayway.

All those activities that keep the social fabric together—government, transportation, trade, communication, health care, utilities and the like—fall under the rubric of **services**. Together these make up 78 percent of gross state product in New Jersey. Thanks in large part to Thomas Edison's work in the state, New Jersey is known as a center for research and development; the area around Princeton in particular has garnered a reputation for high technology. Northern New Jersey ranks as a national leader in commercial real estate transactions. Ranking as the state's second-largest industry, **tourism** is valued at $17 billion, with glittering Atlantic City's 12 mammoth casinos and annual Miss America beauty pageant topping the list of attractions. Yet many travelers find the 50 other beach towns along the Jersey Shore—especially historic Cape May—more appealing for their wide sandy beaches and local color.

Agriculture – Although only one percent of the gross state product is generated by agriculture, it is nonetheless a vital industry for thousands of New Jersey farmers and millions of urban consumers. Greenhouse and nursery products, raised mostly in the northern part of the state, earn more money than any other agricultural goods; milk ranks second. Peaches, grown mostly in the south, are New Jersey's best-selling fruit, while the state's more than 3,000 acres of cranberry bogs make it the third-largest cranberry-producing state in the nation, after Massachusetts and Wisconsin.

The State Today

Modern New Jersey is nothing if not diverse. Some of the wealthiest suburbs and resorts in the nation are located here, as are some of the most decrepit ghettos. The result of centuries of immigration, the state's population is also a mix, with 79.3 percent of its people of European (predominantly Italian, Irish and English) descent; 13 percent of African descent; 9.6 percent Hispanic; and 3.5 percent Asian. A wide range of artists, politicians and intellectuals have called New Jersey home. Count Basie, Aaron Burr, Grover Cleveland, Stephen Crane, Paul Robeson, Philip Roth, Frank Sinatra and Bruce Springsteen were all born here, while Thomas Edison, Albert Einstein, Walt Whitman and Woodrow Wilson resided here for many years.

While it's true that some parts of the state are scored with highways and marred with smokestacks and factories, 65 percent of New Jersey is forested or farmland, and much of that is breathtakingly scenic. And New Jersey has taken pains to preserve its long history in many quaint towns along the Delaware River and its many tributaries: MOUNT HOLLY, founded in 1700 by Quakers; BURLINGTON, the birthplace of author James Fenimore Cooper; SALEM, the first Quaker colony in North America; GREENWICH, the site of the famous Colonial tea burning; Millville, an important 18C-19C glassmaking center *(p 208)*; and BRIDGETON, home of the largest historic district in the state, are just some of the villages worth a visit. In Swainton, Leaming's Run Gardens, the largest annual garden in the US, proves the enduring accuracy of the Garden State's nickname. And for recreation, more than 800 lakes and ponds, 40 state parks, 11 state forests, 127 miles of beaches and the 1.4 million-acre PINE BARRENS offer possibilities galore. Benjamin Franklin once called New Jersey "a barrel tapped at both ends," with much of its bounty flowing to New York and Philadelphia. The discerning traveler will find that much remains within.

Northern New Jersey

Jersey City – © Scott Barrow

A bove New Jersey's wasp waist, a confusing network of roadways, the roar of traffic and an industrial skyline mar the landscape. Such distractions, however, lend a special value to the north's many beautiful regions and historical sites. A march of mountains—the Watchung and Ramapo ranges and the Kittatinny ridge—proceeds northwest from the Hudson River to the Delaware, embossing the land with a lovely topography. Along the western border, quaint towns live quietly by the Delaware River, buffered by dairy, poultry, vegetable and fruit farms from the bustling megalopolis to the east. By the Atlantic seaside, seasonal civilization and sandy wilderness blend against a backdrop of pounding surf.

During the Revolution, as troops moved back and forth between New York and Philadelphia, more than 200 engagements ensued in northern New Jersey, and General Washington chose three times to winter his troops between the Hudson and Delaware rivers. By then men were exploiting the rich deposits of iron ore that lay in the hills, where mining and smelting continued well into the 20C. Such early wilderness enterprise established North Jersey's peculiar balance between natural beauty and the beast of industry. Along the Delaware, towns grew up

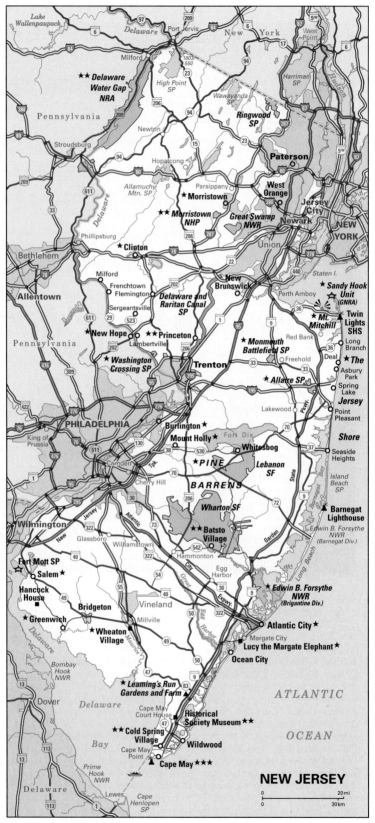

around commercial fishing, milling and, eventually, rubber making. Elsewhere, raging streams provided the hydropower for mills and factories, but nowhere more than in Paterson, which became the first planned manufacturing district in the US in 1791. The northeast corner of the state swelled with people as canals, trolleys and railroads began to outline a complicated urban geography. The Morris Canal, opened in 1836, transported coal and iron from the interior to the Jersey City docks, and other waterfront enterprises took root in the cities along the Hudson River. Newark (today the state's largest city) came of age in the 1830s as a manufacturing and transportation center. As rail—and later auto—travel became easier, suburbs sprouted around an ever-widening metropolis with its epicenter in Manhattan. In 1889 liberal corporation laws encouraged more industrial development (until contravening antitrust laws were enacted in 1913), and North Jersey's modern steel-and-smoke silhouette took shape. Today chemicals and oil top the product list, but the state still depends on a highly diversified manufacturing base that thrives largely in the north. At the same time, a considerable portion of the $17 billion generated annually by the state's tourism industry originates along the northern Atlantic coast, in the hill and lake country and at sites in between.

CLINTON ★

Population 2,380
Map p 172
Tourist Information ☎973-366-6889 or 800-475-9526

Situated comfortably at the center of lovely Hunterdon County, quaint Clinton straddles the confluence of the Raritan and Spruce Run Rivers. Rushing water and plenty of grist from the surrounding rich farmlands made it the perfect site for milling in the 18C, when it was known as Hunt's Mills. The two picturesque mills that flank the town's scenic waterfall now serve history and art.

SIGHTS *2hrs*

Hunterdon Historical Museum – *56 Main St. Open early Apr–late Oct Tue–Sat 10am–4pm, Sun noon–5pm. Nov–Dec 23 Sat 10am–4pm. Closed major holidays. $4.* ▣ *www.clintonnj.com/redmill.html* ☎*908-735-4101.* Hunterdon comprises a historic 10-acre compound that includes a mill and a limestone quarry site. The picture-perfect Red Mill was built in 1810 to manufacture woolens and grew over the years as its function changed. Today its four floors exhibit objects related to local

---

■ Down on the Delaware

The Delaware River sketches the western edge of bucolic Hunterdon County, indeed of the state itself, between Lambertville and Mount Joy. Across the river lies Bucks County, Pennsylvania, whose long-lived popularity is beginning to rub off on the Jersey side. Once a bustling commercial and industrial corridor augmented by the Delaware Canal and set about by paper mills, rubber factories and shad fisheries, the river today is the quiet haven of hawks, sycamores and cliff swallows. While some industry remains, the countryside retains its beauty. To sample it, plan a day to explore the old ferry towns of **Lambertville**, **Frenchtown** and **Milford** where an eclectic array of historic architecture, shops and restaurants makes lingering irresistible. The drive along the river is particularly lovely north of Milford on Old Mine Road/Route 521 *(access from Milford on Church St.)*. Down to one lane, the road makes its way under steep bluffs that loom above the river. Where the river splits to turn east/west, cacti grow on the hillside in the heat of the southern sun. Or, from Lambertville climb Route 523 to **Sergeantsville** through a rustic landscape that retains its 18C essence. The stone inn here was once a gathering place for Patriots, and a mile west down Route 604 (Rosemont Road) stands the only remaining covered bridge in the state, built in 1872. Farther along Route 523 you'll find **Flemington**, the county seat and site in 1935 of the trial of Bruno Hauptmann, who kidnapped and murdered Charles Lindbergh's infant son. Stop in the 1828 courthouse and enjoy a drink at the Union Hotel (1862) across the street, where reporters once congregated. The town is a center of Greek Revival architecture, as a stroll down Main Street will reveal.

agricultural and industrial history. Behind the mill, the 150ft cliffs that line the river's edge yielded limestone for whitewash as early as 1781, when the existing kilns were built. In 1848 the Mulligan family acquired the business, supplying fertilizer for local farms and stone for railway and road beds. Of the quarry works, only the stone crusher, quarry office and dynamite shed remain. The tenant house, where employees lived, also lodges a general store reminiscent of the period. Buildings not original to the property include the 1860 Bunker Hill Schoolhouse, carriage sheds, a replica log cabin and a springhouse.

Hunterdon Art Center – *7 Center St. Open year-round Wed–Sun 11am–5pm. Contribution requested.* ♿ ☎*908-735-8415.* An 1836 gristmill makes a wonderful gallery space, as this compact museum attests. Renovations in the 1980s saved the landmark from flood damage, and today its sturdy wooden floors and whitewashed stone walls enclose a cool and inviting space in which to enjoy painting, sculpture, photography and other contemporary art and crafts. Four floors display the works of well-known and emerging artists from New York, New Jersey and Pennsylvania in an ever-changing exhibit schedule.

EXCURSIONS

★ **New Hope, Pennsylvania** – *½ day. 24mi southwest of Clinton. Take Rte. 31 south 10mi to Flemington, then 12mi west on Rte. 202 to New Hope. Description p 259.*

★★ **Delaware Water Gap National Recreation Area** – *2 days. 33mi northwest of Clinton. Take Rte. 31 north 17mi to Rte. 46, then 10mi north to join I-80; continue 6mi west to park. Description p 267.*

JERSEY SHORE★

Maps p 11 and p 172
Tourist Information ☎908-929-2138 or 800-365-6933

From Perth Amboy, 90mi of coastline bends around the hip of New Jersey and plunges southward through dozens of beach communities, narrowing into a fragile wand of offshore barrier beaches that stretches from Point Pleasant to the tip of Long Beach Island. The north-facing bay shore between the Amboys and Sandy Hook affords spectacular vistas of New York City and the busy harbors of New York and Raritan Bays. Around the corner, empty ocean unfurls all the way to Portugal. Along the coast, fishing fleets and pleasure boats tuck into the mouths of the rivers that empty at regular intervals into the sea—the Navesink, Shrewsbury, Shark and Manasquan among them.

Early Dutch and English seafarers encountered the Lenni Lenape Indians here reaping the bounty of the ocean, and the treacherous coastline became the haunt of fishermen, whalers and privateers who put in at Barnegat and Egg Harbor bays. Lying broadside to the Atlantic's furious northeasterly storms, the Jersey Shore collected hundreds of shipwrecks as swelling maritime traffic headed to and from New York Harbor attempted to skirt its shoals. So large did this graveyard of the Atlantic grow that in 1848 the first federally funded manned lifesaving stations in the country were constructed along this coast—a nascent US Coast Guard—outfitted with the latest in rescue equipment. Today historic lighthouses from Sandy Hook to Barnegat still beam their warnings to ships at sea and wink a picturesque welcome to land-bound visitors. Known for its seaside resorts since the railroad came through in the 1870s, the Jersey Shore remains a primary destination for city-weary residents of Philadelphia, Trenton and New York City, as well as an active center of commercial fishing, clamming and crabbing.

SIGHTS   *1 day. Map p 172.*

★ **Mount Mitchill Scenic Overlook** – *Ocean Blvd., Atlantic Highlands. Open year-round daily 8am–dusk.* ♿ 🅿 *www.monmouthcountyparks.com* ☎*732-842-4000.* Getting here is half the fun, as the drive up Ocean Boulevard (Scenic Drive) climbs past houses with ever-expanding views. The small overlook park at the summit crowns the highest point on the Atlantic Seaboard north of the Yucatan Peninsula in Mexico. At 266ft, Mt. Mitchill hardly soars, but it nonetheless yields a sweeping panorama of the bays—Raritan, New York and Sandy Hook—as well as Staten Island to the northwest and Brooklyn to the northeast. On a clear day, the Manhattan skyline looms between. Just below lies the low, trim profile of the 6.5mi-long Sandy Hook peninsula.

★ **Sandy Hook Unit, Gateway National Recreation Area** – *Rte. 36, Highlands. Open year-round daily sunrise–sunset. $4/car Mon–Fri, $5/car weekends (Memorial Day–Labor Day only).* ╳ 🅿 *www.nps.gov/gate* ☎*732-872-5970. Lifeguards on duty Memorial Day–Labor Day.* Thrust between the wild Atlantic and the calmer bay waters, this salty, windswept landscape tenaciously survives storm and sea. Its barrier beaches—ocean on one side, bay on the other—are fragile, however, their sands shifting with the tides. Nonetheless, this narrow, 1,665-acre spit supports migratory birds, turtles, a variety of small mammals and an abundance of sea life. Lenni Lenape Indians once gathered wild plums here, and the Hook's holly forest *(visit by guided tour only)* is unsurpassed in age and size on the East Coast. Sandy Hook supports thousands of visitors as well, who come to enjoy swimming, fishing, hiking, windsurfing, beachcombing and picnicking. On summer weekends, rangers advise arriving before 10am, lest capacity crowds cause the gates to be closed.

Sandy Hook

Visit – *¹⁄₂ day.* To enhance a day of beaching, begin at the **Spermaceti Cove Visitor Center** *(open daily 10am–5pm)*, built in 1894 as the third lifesaving station to stand guard here. Exhibits provide an orientation to the Hook's environment. A particularly good display on the history of lifesaving along the Jersey Shore occupies one gallery with photographs and artifacts, including a breeches buoy, used to haul shipwreck survivors ashore. Spermaceti Cove was among the first of the lifeboat stations to be established in 1849; the original hut now resides at Twin Lights State Historic Site *(below).*

Pick up a brochure and walk the mile-long **Old Dune Trail**, which begins near the visitor center, for a glimpse of the barrier beach ecosystem. Farther north, the country's oldest operating **lighthouse**—funded by New York merchants distressed over profits lost at sea—towers over the tip of the peninsula, surrounded by the disintegrating fortifications of Ft. Hancock. When first lit with "48 oil blazes" in 1764, the lighthouse stood 500ft from the water's edge; shoaling has increased the distance by 1.5mi.

In 1874 this area became the first US weapons-testing ground, and in 1895 **Fort Hancock** was officially established as the last in a series of defenses to occupy this strategic point since the Revolution. At its peak in 1945, the fort comprised a community of 18,000 enlisted men and women whose duty it was to protect the coast. Among its oldest buildings, a tidy row of Colonial Revival officers' residences trims the parade ground and overlooks the bay. Most fascinating, however, are the hulking remains of the huge gun and mortar batteries that once safeguarded New York Harbor and now lurk like temple ruins in the underbrush. These various emplacements were built mainly between 1890 and 1910, and most were dismantled for scrap during World War II. The US Army deactivated the fort in 1974. On weekends, visit the Fort Hancock Museum, in the old post guardhouse, and the History House, located in a restored officer's residence, for exhibits about the fort.

Twin Lights State Historic Site – *Lighthouse Rd., Highlands. Open Memorial Day–Labor Day daily 10am–5pm. Rest of the year Wed–Sun 10am–5pm. Closed Jan 1, Thanksgiving Day, Dec 25. Contribution requested.* 🅿 ☎*732-872-1814.* The unusual

175

two-tower silhouette of the Navesink Lighthouse station looms precipitously over the village of Highlands. This high bluff made an ideal site for a lighthouse, and the first permanent structure was built in 1828. Thirteen years later it was equipped with the first Fresnel lens used in the US. The present towers were erected in 1862 (notice that they are not truly twins), and Navesink became the first primary seacoast light in the country to use electricity in 1898. Decommissioned in 1949, the lighthouse today occupies a small park and houses a museum devoted to the history of the lighthouse, lighthouse technology, navigation and the US lifesaving service. In a footnote to the light's history, Guglielmo Marconi first demonstrated wireless telegraphy here in 1899 by wiring the results of the America's Cup race from a vessel offshore to an antenna built on the north side of the lighthouse. Climb the 65 steps to the top of the north tower and enjoy the view.

Barnegat Lighthouse State Park – *At the northern tip of Long Beach Island on Broadway. Lighthouse open May Wed–Sun 9am–4:30pm. Memorial Day–Labor Day daily 9am–4:30pm (Sat in Jul–Aug until 9:30pm). Sept–Oct Wed–Sun 9am–4:30pm. Park open daily year-round. $1.* 🅿 ☎609-494-2016. Forming the centerpiece of this small 32-acre park, the archetypal **lighthouse** known as "Old Barney" is the second light to mark the top of Long Beach Island (the first fell into the sea in 1856). Rising to 168ft, the tower was designed by George G. Meade, later the commander of Union troops at GETTYSBURG. First lit in 1859, its kerosene lamp—refracted by 1,000 prisms—had a range of 30mi out to sea. A lightship replaced Old Barney in 1927. Climb 217 steps to the top to take in a stunning view★ all around, especially down the 18mi length of skinny Long Beach Island. The windswept park itself offers fishing; picnicking; bird-watching; a short, self-guided trail; and a view of Island Beach State Park across the inlet. *Barnegat* is Dutch for "inlet of breakers," and it is easy to see why it was thus named as the ocean rushes into the breech between the two land masses. For more on the light and local history, visit the **Barnegat Light Historical Museum** in a former one-room schoolhouse at Fifth and Central Streets just south of the lighthouse *(open Jun weekends 2pm–5pm; Jul–Aug daily 2pm–5pm; Sept weekends 2pm–5pm; contribution requested;* ☎609-494-8578). The museum features Old Barney's original lens.

■ **By the Sea**

From the faded elegance of Long Branch, through Victorian Ocean Grove and into the sandy wilds of Island Beach State Park, the destinations along the northern Jersey Shore have little in common but the ocean. Certainly, you can speed your way to stops along the shore via the Garden State Parkway, but to hear the surf and smell the salt, follow the shore drive, along Routes 36, 71, 35, 37 and 9. While **Long Branch** was once among America's most glamorous resorts and the refuge of presidents, only a shadow of its former splendor remains. Beginning in the 1870s, a race track, gambling casinos and a host of celebrity visitors gave the town a titillating reputation. South beyond the exclusive enclave of **Deal** lies **Asbury Park**, most recently famous as the haunt of rock star Bruce Springsteen. Begun as a temperance resort in 1870, Asbury Park ironically evolved into a honky-tonk beach town whose heyday in the 1930s and 1940s echoes only dimly from the boardwalk to the forlorn facade of the Palace Funhouse. By contrast, **Ocean Grove**, only recently delivered from the governance of the Methodist Camp Meeting Association that founded it in 1870, remains quiet and dry. Since 1894 the Great Auditorium *(54 Pitman Ave.)* has served as the center of local revival activities, and the town is renowned for its lovely Victorian architecture. Distinguished by its peaceful lake, the historically Irish town of **Spring Lake** retains a stately charm and offers particularly lovely hotels along its oceanfront. **Point Pleasant Beach** marks the head of the Barnegat Peninsula and, as home port to one of New Jersey's four commercial fishing fleets, serves wonderful seafood. Past several miles of magnificent homes and beyond the raucous boardwalk amusements at **Seaside Heights** lies Island Beach State Park. This 10mi stretch of shifting sands, windswept dunes and wildlife sanctuary is one of the last undeveloped barrier beaches along the North Atlantic coastline. Finally, 4mi offshore and a world away, rugged **Long Beach Island** takes the beach business seriously. No boardwalk or commercial development mars this pristine oceanfront, where sturdy houses armored in weathered shingles huddle behind the dunes.

EXCURSIONS

★ **Allaire State Park** – *2hrs. Rte. 524, Farmingdale. Open Jan–Apr daily 8am–4:30pm. May–Memorial Day & Labor Day–Oct daily 8am–6pm. Memorial Day–Labor Day daily 8am–8pm. Nov–Dec daily 8am–4:30pm. $3/car (Memorial Day–Labor Day & weekends & holidays).* △ ⅇ ᴘ ☎732-938-2371. It is hard to imagine the bustling industrial center that once inhabited this quiet forest. That these woods yielded up a harvest of iron is also difficult to picture, but such was the nature of the bog-iron industry that once flourished in the low, swampy plains of New Jersey. Here stand the remains of Allaire Village, purchased as Howell Iron Works by James P. Allaire in 1822. From the swamp, workers coaxed the yellowish iron ore that is a by-product of decaying vegetation. In a tall blast furnace, they burned the ore with charcoal to remove the oxygen and poured the molten metal into casts to form bars of "pig iron" *(p 307)*. Remelted, the iron could be molded into pots, stoves, screws and pipes by other village workers. Although Allaire was typical of New Jersey bog-iron works, the total self-sufficiency of the town was not, complete as it was with school, church, employee housing and even its own currency for use at the company store. At its peak, the works employed hundreds of workers, but the population dwindled to nothing by the 1850s when anthracite coal from Pennsylvania replaced charcoal in the smelting process. Today the hivelike blast furnace and several of the village buildings still stand; the latter are furnished in period style and occupied by costumed interpreters. Stop by the visitor center to view an exhibit on iron-ore mining. The 3,000-acre park that surrounds the village offers hiking, camping, canoeing, fishing, golfing and picnicking. Next door to the village, **Pine Creek Railroad**, the only narrow-gauge steam train in New Jersey, takes visitors on rides through the park *(depart from Purr Station Apr–Jun weekends noon–4:30pm; Jul–Aug daily noon–4:30pm; Sept–Oct weekends noon–4:30pm; 15min; $2;* ☎732-938-5524*).*

★ **Monmouth Battlefield State Park** – *Rte. 33, Freehold. Open year-round daily 8am–dusk.* ⅇ ᴘ ☎732-462-9616. From the bitter cold of VALLEY FORGE to the sweltering heat at Monmouth Courthouse, American Revolutionary troops endured the extremes of war. Although on paper the June 1778 Battle of Monmouth appears a draw, its great value lay in proving that the Continental Army could face down the British on the battlefield. The largest land artillery battle of the Revolution, the encounter at Monmouth would be the last between the two full-blown armies. The opportunity was perfect for an American attack as British general Henry Clinton marched his 20,000 men in an exposed phalanx across New Jersey bound for Sandy Hook. Plagued by heat and rainstorms, Clinton's troops made only about 6mi a day dragging 1,500 wagons over rough terrain, finally encamping, exhausted, at Monmouth Courthouse. It was then that Washington's second-in-command, Gen. Charles Lee, carried out his orders to attack the British rear guard with an advance force of 5,000 men. Lee had engaged the Redcoats when he

■ **The Heroine of Monmouth**

The heroics of Molly Pitcher are well known among the legends of the American Revolution. The tale of how a brave young wife, drawing water for the parched soldiers during the sweltering Battle of Monmouth, stepped in to load the cannon when her husband collapsed has swelled many a patriotic heart over the decades. But legend has also shrouded the details of Molly's story. She is most commonly believed to have been 24-year-old Mary Ludwig Hays, who, as was customary, traveled with her husband as his artillery regiment went about its wartime business. Although popularly portrayed as an avenging goddess, the real Mary Hays was described as hard-bitten, muscular and tough. One story reports her unconcerned when an enemy cannonball ripped through her petticoats. Both she and her husband survived the war and settled in Carlisle, Pennsylvania, where he died in the late 1780s. Mary later remarried and worked as a servant. She died in 1832. While the state of Pennsylvania awarded her an annual $40 pension for her service in 1822, it wasn't until the nation's centennial celebration in 1876 that Mary's bravery surfaced and the name "Molly Pitcher" gained its mythical status. In some ways, Molly probably represents a composite Revolutionary heroine, for patriotism undoubtedly drove many courageous women onto the fields of battle.

suddenly realized that half the British Army was returning to attack his troops. In the midst of a hasty retreat, Lee was intercepted by General Washington, who ordered the men to hold their position while he regrouped the forces.

Although Clinton and his men completed their march, the Americans had held their ground. Today the Park Service is restoring this historic landscape to its 18C appearance based on war journals, deeds and maps to give a sense of the topography that influenced the battle. At the visitor center, an exhibit describes the events of June 28, 1778, and the view takes in the entire battlefield. Walking trails crisscross the hilly terrain, which is still scattered with period farmhouses (occasional access available to the restored John Craig House), as well as wildlife habitats and the Owl Haven Nature Center (on Route 522, which bisects the park).

Just north of the park stands the **Old Tennant Presbyterian Church** atop a little hill. Built in 1751, the white shingle church served as a field hospital during the battle. Among the myriad souls in its peaceful churchyard rest British and American casualties of the Battle of Monmouth.

MORRISTOWN ★

Population 16,357
Maps p 11 and p 180
Tourist Information ☎973-366-6889 or 800-475-9526

Nestled in the heart of northern New Jersey's iron-rich hills, Morristown has lived an active life since the turn of the 18C. Expanding beyond its stately village green laid out in 1715, Morristown thrived on farming, forges and the commerce they inspired, and by 1740 the town served as county seat. Men who had grown comfortable on Morristown's good fortunes built generous houses and established a "pretty little village" surrounded by abundant farmland. General Washington made his winter encampments here twice during the Revolution. Its protected and strategic location, as well as its proximity to the manufactories of iron munitions, made the town ideal for his purposes. After the Revolution, the local iron industry faded, then revived with the canals and railroads through the 19C, until the discovery of ore in the Minnesota ranges in 1882 finally signaled the end. By then, however, Morristown was well-served by transportation routes and began to attract wealthy New Yorkers who flocked to the countryside to build grand summer estates. Among them came political cartoonist Thomas Nast and author Frank Stockton. As commuting became fashionable, Morristown swelled with year-round tycoons and businessmen who, by the turn of the century, made the town denser with millionaires than anyplace in the world. Today Morristown remains heir to a Gilded Age legacy of elegant Victorian homes and stately tree-lined streets. In addition, Morristown boasts a formidable concentration of historic sites, including the Morris Museum (6 Normandy Heights Rd.; ☎973-538-0454); Historic Speedwell Village, on the site of an early ironworks (333 Speedwell Ave.; ☎973-540-0211); Federal-style Macculloch Hall built by the "father of the Morris Canal" (45 Macculloch Ave.; ☎973-538-2404); and the Colonial Schuyler-Hamilton House (5 Olyphant Pl.; ☎973-267-4039).

★★ MORRISTOWN NATIONAL HISTORICAL PARK   ½ day. Map p 180.
$4 admission good for all park attractions. ☎973-539-2085.

By the time the winter of 1779-80 rolled around, Washington's army had survived three winter encampments. In 1777, in fact, they had billeted around Morristown, the general choosing to set up headquarters at the Arnold Tavern on the town green. That year, smallpox posed the biggest threat to the troops, and doctors battled it with a crude inoculation that induced a mild form of the disease to create immunity. When the army returned in 1779, it faced one of the cruelest winters of the 18C. A deep freeze settled over the land and 26 snowstorms smothered the countryside. Supply lines failed, food sources disappeared and clothing wore thin. Severely taxed, the army nonetheless survived with a miraculous loss of only 86 men out of more than 11,000. The multifaceted historic park at Morristown includes several sites related to the Continental Army's winters in the area. In the town of Morristown you can visit the Ford Mansion, site of General Washington's headquarters, the Historical Museum (at the rear of the mansion) and Fort Nonsense. Some 5mi to the southwest lies Jockey Hollow, site of the encampment.

© Scott Barrow

Colonial Soldier

★ **Ford Mansion and Historical Museum** – *10 Washington Pl.* ☎*973-539-2016.* In 1779 General Washington selected the commodious mansion of Mrs. Jacob Ford, Jr., as his headquarters. Considered the finest house in Morristown, the Georgian manse still graces its modest knoll with dignity, despite the encroachment of highways and traffic. Palladian fanlights and attached Ionic columns decorate the facade, where seamless wooden siding creates the appearance of marble.

Begin a visit in the **museum** located at the rear of Ford Mansion, near the parking lot *(open year-round daily 9am–5pm; ⅙ 🖪).* Here, two floors of exhibits explore the role and importance of Morristown during the Revolution. Clearly labeled and well-crafted displays speak to both adults and children about the tension between citizens and soldiers, the scourge of smallpox and the terrible winter of 1779-80. Other exhibits explore 18C life and present a stunning collection of 18C weapons. Leaving from the museum, guided tours of the **mansion** itself focus on life in the house during Washington's occupation *(visit by 45min guided tour only, year-round daily 10am–4pm; closed Jan 1, Thanksgiving Day, Dec 25).* The sparsely furnished rooms reflect Mrs. Ford's apprehensions regarding the quartering of the commander's retinue of aides-de-camp and servants, although through it all only one silver spoon was lost. She and her four children crowded into two rooms on the first floor, allowing the Washingtons (Martha joined her husband) the run of the others. The kitchen served at least 30 people a day, and a constant stream of messengers and dignitaries darkened the doorway. On the grounds outside, the 250-man Life Guard took up sentry duty. By all accounts, however, Washington was a mannerly and solicitous houseguest who spent much of his time attempting to ease the deprivations of his men encamped 4mi farther south.

Jockey Hollow – *Jockey Hollow Rd. Open year-round daily 8am–dusk. Closed Jan 1, Thanksgiving Day, Dec 25.* 🖪 ☎*973-543-4030.* Here, 10 infantry brigades logged the thick woods to build huts as meager protection from the elements. Arranged in orderly rows along the hillsides, nearly 1,000 log huts housed 13,000 men for six bitter months, making the encampment at Jockey Hollow tantamount to the sixth-largest city in the colonies. Though none of the huts survive today, the victims of farmers who scavenged their timber and nails, the site nonetheless quietly evokes that hard winter. At the visitor center *(open year-round daily 9am–5pm),* a dramatic film depicts the terrible hardships of life in camp. Just beyond, the restored **Wick House** *(p 167); open year-round daily 9:30am–4:30pm),* home of Henry Wick, served as the quarters of Maj. Gen. Arthur St. Clair and is furnished today with the simple household goods of the period and manned by costumed interpreters eager to answer questions and share information. You may choose to hike or drive through the hollow, now largely reforested to its pre-Revolutionary appearance. Signs identify the campsites of various brigades, as well as the grand parade ground where daily drills and reviews continued despite the awful weather. Reproductions of several huts stand on Sugar Loaf Hill, where dwelled the "backbone" of Washington's Army—the 1st and 2nd Pennsylvania brigades.

Fort Nonsense – *Off Ann St. on Mt. Kemble. Open year-round daily 8am–dusk. Closed Jan 1, Thanksgiving Day, Dec 25.* 🅿. On the way back to town, stop at Ft. Nonsense, so named for the persistent rumor that its construction was a make-work project during the encampment of 1777. However, because of its encompassing vista, the site made a logical location for a lookout post and beacon fires to signal a British attack from New York City, a scant two-day march away. The attack never came, however, and the redoubt served mostly as a guard post. Nothing remains today but a commemorative plaque and a timeless view.

EXCURSIONS

Lord Stirling Park and Environmental Education Center – *1hr. 7mi south of Morristown in Basking Ridge, via Rte. 287 (Exit 26). On Lord Stirling Rd. off S. Maple Ave. Open year-round daily 9am–5pm. Education Center closed major holidays.* ♿ 🅿 ☎908-766-2489. Edged by the Passaic River to the east, 897-acre Lord Stirling Park is a crazy quilt of meadows, marshes, thickets and woodlands traversed by 8.5mi of trails and boardwalks. The education center houses temporary exhibits, a bookshop and the highlight, a wonderful exhibit orienting both children and adults to the **"Secrets of the Great Swamp."** If you plan to visit the Great Swamp National Wildlife Refuge that lies just east of the Passaic River, this colorful and easy-to-follow exhibit provides a terrific introduction to its natural history and wonders.

Great Swamp National Wildlife Refuge – *2hrs. Just north of Education Center on Long Hill Rd., Basking Ridge. Open year-round daily dawn–dusk.* ♿ 🅿 ☎973-425-1222. A busy world of terrestrial and aquatic life inhabits the footprint of glacial Lake Passaic. Although it eventually drained down the Passaic River, the prehis-

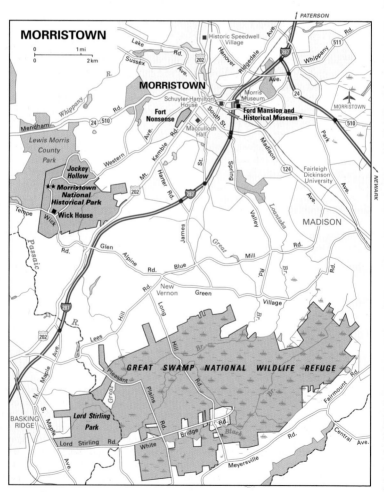

toric lake never quite dried up, leaving behind 7,000 acres of swamp woodland, hardwood ridges, cattail marsh and grasslands, and an incredibly rich collection of habitats. Fortunately, the swamp is now federally protected, split between wilderness and a wildlife management area. A walk from the trailhead at the Wildlife Observation Center covers about a mile of trail and boardwalk, complete with interpretive signage and observation blinds. For more extensive hiking, 8mi of trails penetrate the refuge wilderness area from several parking lots around the perimeter. With patience you may spot a member of the largest breeding population of bluebirds in the state, the endangered bog turtle or a river otter.

NEW BRUNSWICK

Population 41,534
Map p 172
Tourist Information ☎201-641-7632

The largest city on the banks of the Raritan River, New Brunswick began as a crossing place in the 1680s and developed into a center of shipping, an important link between New York City and Philadelphia. Pharmaceutical giant Johnson & Johnson has been headquartered here since 1885, but it is **Rutgers University** that is most associated with the city. Founded in Somerville in 1766, Rutgers is today the only state university with a Colonial charter. Moving to a vacant New Brunswick tavern in 1771, the college erected its first building, Old Queens, in 1809; the three-story brownstone still occupies a prominent campus location.

SIGHT   1hr

New Jersey Museum of Agriculture – *Off Rte. 1 and College Farm Rd., Cook College Campus. Open year-round Tue–Sat 10am–5pm, Sun noon–5pm. Closed major holidays. $3. ⓫ ◩ ☎732-249-2077.* Located on the grounds of Rutgers' Cook College of Agriculture and Environmental Science, this huge, barnlike museum houses an encyclopedic collection of historic agricultural equipment. Illustrating the blend of industry and agriculture that characterizes American farming, implements from crafting and mending utensils to planting and harvesting paraphernalia to animal-tending apparatuses (including a 19C oil-lamp incubator and chick-shipping box), fill the oversize rooms and dispel any sense of the simple agrarian life. To add the human dimension, several exhibits utilize the museum's wonderful collection of **photographs** documenting farming in the Garden State between 1880 and 1940. A particularly interesting exhibit explores the cultivation of Jersey produce, including apples, corn, blueberries and cranberries.

EXCURSIONS

Duke Gardens – *1hr. 14mi south of New Brunswick in Somerville via Rtes. 18, 287 and 22. From Rte. 22, turn south on Rte. 206. Gardens are located south of Somerville Circle. Visit by guided tour (1hr) only, Oct–May daily noon–3pm. Closed Jan 1, Thanksgiving Day, Dec 25. $5. Reservations suggested. ◩ ☎908-722-3700.* Only 15 gardeners tend this lush circuit of 11 greenhouse display gardens, each representing a different country, historic period or climate. Orchids in shades of purple, white and orange crowd the Edwardian conservatory; latticework encloses the showy formal French garden; and a variety of dainty English plantings includes a particularly beguiling 18C rock garden. Traditional Chinese and Japanese gardens encourage meditation, and the Persian terrace languishes in the fragrance of citrus trees. Greenhouses occupy a small corner of the estate of turn-of-the-century tobacco baron James Buchanan Duke, whose daughter Doris traveled the world to furnish them with plants. Entrance to the compound is closely guarded, but tours are available by advance reservation. Visitors are not permitted to wander unescorted on the grounds.

Wallace House/Old Dutch Parsonage Historic Site – *2hrs. 1.5mi north of Duke Gardens at nos. 38 and 65 Washington Pl. Visit by guided tour (1hr 30min) only, year-round Wed–Sat 10am–4pm, Sun 1pm–4pm. Closed major holidays. Contribution requested. ◩ ☎908-725-1015.* Sharing the same quiet residential block, these two historic houses tell different stories. Both are furnished to their period, but their importance lies in context rather than decoration. Begin at the **Wallace House**, of notable significance for one winter of its long life. Wealthy Philadelphia merchant John Wallace built the main portion of the home between 1775 and 1776, making it the largest to be constructed in New Jersey during the Revolution. Its size and strategic location made the Wallace House the choice of Gen. George Washington for his headquarters in the winter of 1778-79. Open to the public in 1897, the Wallace House is now being carefully restored to its 1770s appearance.

The **Old Dutch Parsonage** was moved 500yds to its present site when threatened by railroad construction in 1913. Built in 1751 by three Dutch Reform churches to house a common minister, it served as rectory until 1810, when the churches sold it. Its first occupant, the Reverend John Frelinghuysen, tutored students there, but he died several years later at age 27. One student, Jacob Hardenbergh, went on to marry Freylinghuysen's widow, Dinah, and eventually founded Queen's College—now Rutgers—in 1766 as a seminary for Dutch Reform clergy.

PATERSON

Population 150,270
Map p 183
Tourist Information ☎201-641-7632

Like many East Coast towns, Paterson began as a quiet Dutch farming settlement in the 17C, and, had it not been for the thundering falls over which the Passaic River plunges 77ft in a raging torrent, its history might have proceeded predictably. In 1791, however, Paterson became one of the country's first industrial cities, a designation it still reflects today in its gritty urban neighborhoods and working-class ethos.

Historical Notes – As part of his all-encompassing vision for the economic future of America, Secretary of the Treasury Alexander Hamilton recommended that the government establish a manufacturing city to provide the young country with industrial independence and self-sufficiency. Familiar with the Passaic's Great Falls, Hamilton had them in mind to power the mills of such a city. However, opponents (Thomas Jefferson among them) visualized an agrarian future for the US, and Congress rejected Hamilton's ideas. Turning to the private sector, Hamilton carried through his plan under the aegis of the Society for the Establishment of Useful Manufactures (SUM), which purchased 700 acres around the falls and sealed Paterson's—and New Jersey's—industrial destiny. Architect Pierre Charles L'Enfant (later to design Washington, DC) laid out a budget-busting scheme of which only the raceways (canals to channel the rushing river water) were built. Over the ensuing decades, Paterson's fortunes waxed and waned. Generation after generation of industry came and went, and the riverfront district thickened with mills. Out of Paterson rolled cotton and sailcloth, Colt pistols, locomotives, iron goods and silk. A series of floods and fire around the turn of the century sorely tested the town, and a strike against the silk mills in 1913 further undermined it. As rayon replaced silk in the 1920s, aeronautics manufacturers moved in, rejuvenating Paterson once again. When they departed after World War II, Paterson's economic base began to diversify, and today more than 700 industries operate there. The old mill district, however, fell into ruin. Happily, sheer civic determination is slowly reversing the decay, and numerous local and federal agencies and special-interest groups rallied to the cause after 119 acres around the Great Falls were added to the National Register of Historic Places in 1970. Today, with renewal far from complete, many surviving structures are being creatively adapted, while numerous others crumble from vandalism and fire. It is interesting to note that two of America's greatest poets, William Carlos Williams and Allen Ginsberg, drew, as residents of Paterson, considerable inspiration from its grit.

SIGHTS *2hrs. Map p 183.*

Despite its raw edge, tourists come to walk the old mill district, crossing the bridge over the spectacular **Great Falls**, viewing the remains of once-busy mills and imagining the bustle of America's original industrial city in its heyday. The **Great Falls Visitor Center** offers information and self-guided, walking-tour maps of this urban landmark *(65 McBride Ave. Ext.; open Apr–Oct Mon–Fri 9am–4pm, weekends noon–4pm; rest of the year Mon–Fri 9am–4pm; 🅿 ☎973-279-9587).*

Paterson Museum – *2 Market St. Open year-round Tue–Fri 10am–4pm, weekends 12:30pm–4:30pm. Closed major holidays. $2. ♿ 🅿 ☎973-881-3874.* Housed in the cavernous Thomas Rogers Locomotive Erecting Shop (1873), where 3,000 railroad engines took shape, the museum presents a hodgepodge of exhibits and displays of local interest, loosely addressing the various phases in Paterson's industrial history. A collection of silk looms, though not well labeled, bears mute testimony to the complexity of the process and the fineness of the work. Also on view are submarines invented and successfully tested in the Passaic River by Paterson resident John Holland around 1880 and a small exhibit of rare Colt firearms manufactured in Paterson in the 1830s.

Botto House National Landmark/American Labor Museum – *83 Norwood St. in Haledon, 2mi from downtown Paterson via Union Blvd. Open year-round Wed–Sat 1pm–4pm. Closed major holidays (open Labor Day). $1.50.* ♿ 🅿 *☎973-595-7953.* A modest house of great importance to the American labor movement, the home of Pietro and Maria Botto has come to symbolize both the plight and the power of the American worker. Built in 1908 by a skilled working-class family finally able to afford a comfortable home outside the city, the Botto House became the focal point for 20,000 Paterson silk workers out on strike in 1913. At the invitation of Haledon's mayor and the Bottos, the strikers met here for Sunday rallies, surrounding the house in huge, peaceful crowds to hear the exhortations of Upton Sinclair and others who spoke from the second-story balcony. With support from the International Workers of the World (IWW), the strikers endured for six months, distressed by low pay and harsh conditions and calling for an eight-hour day and regulation of child labor. Finally, strike funds expired, forcing them to return to work. Although immediate results were scant, improvements did come slowly. Today the Botto House is the home of the American Labor Museum. This 10-room Victorian home offers an extensive labor library, and is furnished with family photographs, heirloom furniture and keepsakes from the family's life in Biela, Italy.

EXCURSION *Map p 172*

Ringwood State Park – *3hrs. 20mi from Paterson, in Ringwood. Take Rte. 208N to I-287 at Exit 59. From I-287, take Exit 57 and continue to Skyline Dr. Turn right onto Rte. 511, then right again on Sloatsburg Rd. Visit by guided tour (45min) only, year-round Wed–Sun 10am–4pm. Closed major holidays.* 🅿 *($2 late May–Labor Day) ☎973-962-7031.* Just south of the New York State border lie the 5,000 acres of Ringwood State Park. Deep in the Ramapo Mountains, the park can be reached from the south by Skyline Drive. **Views** of the mountains and glimpses of Wanaque Reservoir from the drive's apex make this among the most scenic roads in the state. Ringwood Park itself offers plenty of the usual outdoor activities—hiking, swimming, fishing and picnicking—especially around Shepherd Lake. In addition, two man-made diversions are worth exploring.

New Jersey State Botanical Garden – Aptly named Skylands, the garden crowns the heights at the end of Morris Road. Passing through the eagle gates and up the long drive makes Skylands feel like a private estate; indeed, the property was developed and landscaped in the 19C and 20C by two private owners. Clarence McKenzie Lewis,

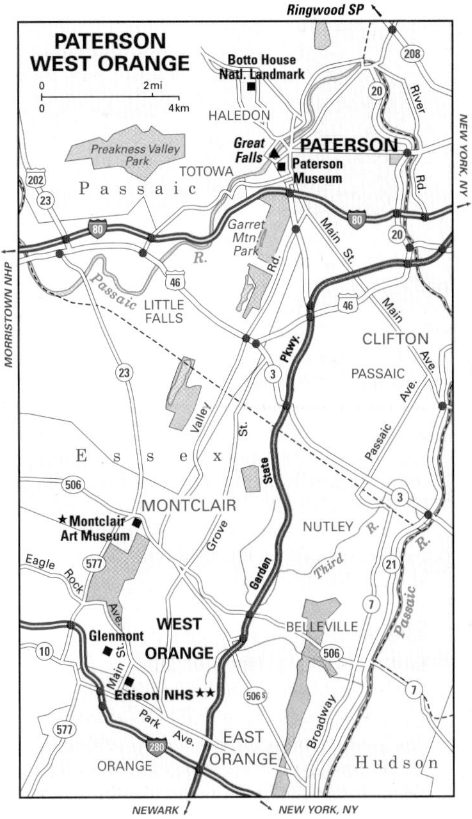

an investment banker, acquired it in 1922 and built the 40-room Tudor mansion that still stands at its center *(not open to the public)*. A trustee of the New York Botanical Garden, Lewis spared no expense in establishing formal gardens blooming with plants from New Jersey and around the world. Much of his horticulture remains today, including an arbor of magnolias rare in these northern climes and a selection of trees planted near the house for their winter color and beauty. Blossoming furiously in May, a half-mile of crab-apple trees promenades elegantly across the property.

★ **Ringwood Manor** – Ringwood Park boasts a second grand home located just off Sloatsburg Road. Ringwood Manor, an odd blend of gables, Gothic details and gingerbread in a sampler of Victorian styles, grew by accretion beginning in 1810 as the seat of an iron-mining empire known as the Ringwood Company. From 1740 until 1931, 12 mines on the 20,000 acres around Ringwood yielded 2.5 million tons of iron ore. For much of that time, furnaces and forges smelted away, providing matériel for every American war until World War I, including parts for the famous chain the Americans slung across the Hudson River to impede the British navy during the Revolution. Over the years a succession of able ironmasters ran the business; in 1807 Martin Ryerson bought the works and built the earliest portion of the existing house. The multitalented Peter Cooper (designer of the first American locomotive) purchased the ironworks in 1853 with partner Abram Hewitt, who soon married Cooper's daughter. So began the alliance that is today best recognized for the Cooper-Hewitt National Design Museum *(p 46)*, founded in New York City in 1897. The Hewitts added 41 rooms to the home over the years; in the sun parlor note the windows from Cooper Union, the technical school founded by Peter Cooper in New York. Today Ringwood Manor is furnished to the period of the Hewitt family's summer occupancy (1857-1936), and its pleasing array of furnishings, decorative arts and Hudson River school paintings comes as something of a surprise in this remote corner of New Jersey.

Planning a trip to New Jersey?
*Don't forget to take along the **Michelin Road Map (No. 474)***

WEST ORANGE

Map p 183
Tourist Information ☎908-527-4744

Located in Essex County in the foothills of the Orange Mountains, West Orange was incorporated in the 1860s, carved out of the larger Orange Township. The area had by then become famous for its numerous hat manufactories, the first of which had been founded around 1785. In the shadow of both Newark and New York City, West Orange early on became a commuter suburb as rail lines snaked west and north from the metropolitan area. To entice wealthy urbanites, developers created planned communities of large houses and spacious lots; West Orange's Llewellyn Park (1857) was among the first such developments in the country. Laid out by Llewellyn Haskell and renowned landscape architect Alexander Jackson Davis, the residential park helped to shape America's vision of suburban life.

SIGHT

★★ **Edison National Historic Site** – *Main St. and Lakeside Ave. Visit by guided tour (1hr) only, year-round daily 10:30am–3:30pm. Closed Jan 1, Thanksgiving Day, Dec 25. $2.* & 🅿 *www.nps.gov/edis* ☎973-736-0550.

The inventor of modern inventing, **Thomas Alva Edison** (1847-1931) established his "Invention Factory" at West Orange in 1887 after about a decade in Menlo Park. Of his total 1,093 patents, he developed more than half at this facility, working with 200 researchers sometimes 120 hours a week to perfect a "big idea every six months." When the West Orange laboratories opened, the hardworking 40-year-old Edison had already discovered how to record sound. He had fabricated the first lightbulb to last more than two hours. He had developed a system for delivering electricity to customers and built a dynamo to power it. For him, genius needed a practical application, and he established the West Orange compound as a place to both invent and manufacture. A visit here reveals Edison as a true trial-and-error experimenter who successfully married industry and science in the form of the corporate industrial research laboratory.

Thomas Alva Edison

Visit – *2hrs.* The park includes two sites: the West Orange laboratories and Glenmont, Edison's nearby home. The chemistry, physics and metallurgy laboratories constituted the heart of the operation, which was once surrounded by huge factories where 10,000 workers gave form to Edison's phonographs, recording cylinders, dictating machines, motion-picture equipment and storage batteries. Today four of the ten remaining buildings are accessible by guided tour. Exhibits in the **visitor center** *(open year-round daily 9am–5pm; &)* display the products of Edison's wide-ranging genius, including the 1868 stock ticker that was his first successful invention, the incandescent bulb, the storage battery and even talking dolls.

The world's first phonograph (1877), which recorded by imprinting tinfoil with the vibrations of sound, earned Edison the sobriquet "Wizard of Menlo Park." At West Orange he perfected the invention and launched a recording company. Peephole kinetoscopes and a screening room present early Edison movies (he invented a "moving-picture machine" and made films until 1918), including the popular *Great Train Robbery* produced in 1903.

The spirit of this site, however, lingers in the laboratories and workshops—playgrounds of genius that have been left much as they were when Edison died in 1931. In the musty **chemistry lab**, crowded with test tubes, beakers, elixirs and powders of ordinary and exotic origin, remnants of his final experiments to extract rubber from goldenrod remain. The **machine shop**, where prototypes and models were fashioned, smells of old wood, grease and metal; the complex network of drive shafts and pulleys has been recently renovated to working condition. A nearby storage area overflows with materials Edison collected—everything from elephant hide to bamboo—to use in his experiments. Edison's three-story **office-library**, filled with books and relics of his career, still feels lived-in, his desk as cluttered as the day he died.

Following the tour, drive to **Glenmont** *(visit by 30min guided tour only, year-round Wed–Sun 11am–4pm)* in Llewellyn Park, the salmon-colored Queen Anne mansion that Edison bought with his second wife, Mina, in 1886. The Edisons purchased the home and its high Victorian furnishings, changing little about the lush interior during their occupancy, although they were the first in the neighborhood to electrify with cables he ran from the plant in town. They also added the den, where figures painted on the ceiling represent their two loves: his for science and hers for music. Besides Edison's "thought library" upstairs, however, the home emanates little of his personality. Ironically, the great inventor had a kitchen so small and ill-equipped that the family catered its dinner parties. Visitors to the home must confine their exploring to the estate's 13 lovely acres (both Thomas and Mina are buried on the grounds), as the neighborhood enforces strict security against outsiders.

EXCURSION

★ **Montclair Art Museum** – *1hr. From Garden State Pkwy. take Exit 148 (Bloomfield Ave.). Continue west on Bloomfield Ave. for 2.7mi and turn right on S. Mountain Ave. 3 S. Mountain Ave. Open Jul–Sept Wed–Sun noon–5pm. Rest of the year Tue–Wed & Fri–Sat 11am–5pm, Thu & Sun 1pm–5pm. Closed major holidays. $5. ▣ www. montclair-art.com ☎973-746-5555.* Although this little jewel may seem out of place in the quiet suburb of Montclair, it is in fact legacy of the art colony that thrived here in the last century. With landscape painter George Inness in residence from 1885 to his death in 1894, artists gravitated to the town in droves. Thirty-six paintings from Inness' estate formed the basis of the museum, which opened in 1914 as the first public museum in New Jersey. Today the elegant Neoclassical museum houses 11,000 pieces of American and Native American art, including a strong selection of landscapes and portraits. Works by Colonial artists Gilbert Stuart and John Singleton Copley, Hudson River school painters Asher Durand and Thomas Cole, and Impressionist Mary Cassatt highlight the collection, which also includes examples of synchronism, American Scene painting and Abstract Expressionism. The museum also owns a fine variety of Native American arts and ethnographic artifacts from around the country, along with contemporary Indian paintings. Exhibits rotate through the museum's seven galleries, showcasing pieces from the permanent collection alongside traveling exhibitions of related interest.

Southern New Jersey

Victorian Homes, Cape May – © Alan Goldstein/FOLIO, Inc.

From the bright lights of coastal Atlantic City through the vegetable farms of the Delaware River Valley, South Jersey offers a range of natural and cultural attractions. Settled by Quakers, forged by the Revolution and fired by the growth of Philadelphia, South Jersey has always been the crossroads of America, a hybrid of north and south and a crucible of invention and industry. Benjamin Franklin called New Jersey "a keg tapped at both ends"—the north by New York City and the south by Philadelphia. Indeed, Southern New Jersey has been linked to Pennsylvania by the Delaware River Valley since the native Lenni Lenape tribes introduced pottery and farming a millennium ago. Henry Hudson first spied Delaware Bay in 1609, followed by Dutch explorer Cornelius Jacobsen Mey *(p 191)* in 1614. The Dutch built a series of forts and controlled trade in the valley through the mid-17C, but Swedish and English settlers infiltrated, and in 1638 the New Sweden colony was established by Swedish and Finnish settlers on both sides of the Delaware River.

In 1675 Quaker John Fenwick purchased the "Salem Tenth" of the colony and established the first permanent English-speaking settlement in the Delaware Valley. Sustained by agriculture, the young colony was characterized by the progressive Quaker theology that encouraged gender equality and eschewed violence. Settlers from New England set up whaling and fishing villages near Cape May in the 1680s, harvesting shad, sturgeon and cod from the Atlantic Ocean. By 1765 colonists occupied the entire area, pushing out the Lenni Lenape. America's first Industrial Revolution grew up in the backwaters of the Pine Barrens, as bog iron was forged into munitions for the Revolutionary War. Farmers produced food and fodder from fertile southwestern fields, trading heavily with their Quaker brethren in Philadelphia and earning New Jersey its sobriquet, "the Garden Colony." Coastal cities developed into bustling ship-building centers, and glassmaking blossomed in the interior.

Key Revolutionary War battles at TRENTON and PRINCETON and the state's cross-roads location made New Jersey a fulcrum of the new nation, as Yankees and Southerners alike patronized Princeton College and Cape May hotels. The Civil War saw the state firmly Union but torn by its Southern ties and slavery. As the nation grew rapidly in the 19C, Southern New Jersey's industries boomed, especially in Trenton, while the southwest remained a glassmaking center and the Pine Barrens were made fertile for cranberries and blueberries. In the 20C, industrial decline has affected its cities, but overall South Jersey suggests the rural charms of Colonial life and early-19C settlement, a quieter cousin to its northern half and a restful retreat for wealthy Philadelphians.

ATLANTIC CITY ★

Population 38,361
Maps p 11 and p 172
Tourist Information ☎609-348-7100

From the opening of the first amusement park to the christening of the first casino, Atlantic City's boardwalk has defined and redefined American recreation for more than a century and a half. The sometimes depressing city beyond Pacific Avenue grows dimmer against the glittering casino lights.

Historical Notes

The future site of Atlantic City was wilderness when Dr. Jonathan Pitney arrived here in 1820, determined to create a resort. His tireless promotion paid off in 1852 when he established the Camden & Atlantic Railroad and changed the name of Absegami Island to Atlantic City. In 1854 the first train arrived and an American resort phenomenon was born. Advertisements promoted the sea air as a cure for insanity, consumption and most other ills, and the tourists came in herds. On June 26, 1870, Jacob Keim of the Chester Hotel and railroad executive Alex Boardman opened the first **boardwalk** to help reduce the amount of sand in the hotel lobby. Others followed their lead, and the boardwalk soon became a regular feature of many Jersey Shore resorts. Atlantic City's widened timberway was declared an official street in 1894. By the turn of the century, Atlantic City was setting the standard for American recreation, having invented sand art, amusement parks, saltwater taffy and picture postcards. Steel Pier became the premier attraction with opera, theater, movies, animal circuses and stunts, including the famous horse-and-rider dive into a pool. John Philip Sousa, Glenn Miller, Stan Kenton and Tommy Dorsey played here. The Million Dollar Pier boasted a ballroom, skating rink and Venetian house when it opened in 1906, the same year the Ziegfeld Follies debuted. Hotels and speakeasies sprang up along the boardwalk in the 1910s and 20s, and locals coined the word "airport" in 1919 for nearby Bader Air Field. The first **Miss America** was crowned in 1921 as an offshoot

Roulette Chips, Caesar's Casino
© Scott Barrow

■ Atlantic City Casinos

Atlantic City's glitz and glamour lie primarily in its 13 large casino resorts (most located along the boardwalk), among the most popular and lucrative in the world. Over the last two decades, the allure of winning a fortune from slot machines, cards, dice and roulette wheels has drawn thousands daily to the brightly colored gaming rooms. Within the casinos, the majority of floor space is given over to slot machines surrounded by twinkling lights that dazzle the eyes. All casinos feature traditional and video electronic machines. Colored lights on top of each machine indicate which amounts the machine accepts *(5¢ to $5)*. Slot machines accept either coins or tokens, which are both available from change booths, roving change personnel or bill-changer machines.

For those wishing to stray beyond the coin-filled cups of the tour groups or emulate James Bond at Monte Carlo, the casinos provide instruction guides *(available throughout the casino)* for games such as blackjack (try to draw cards that total, but do not exceed 21); roulette (place your chips on any combination of numbers and watch the wheel); baccarat (wager on the Bank or the Player as to who will be dealt cards that equal nine); craps (roll for points in this complex dice game); and the popular card game poker. Wagers are made with chips that can be purchased at the casino cage or at the gaming tables (denominations range from $1 to $5,000). *Casinos are open 24hrs daily; admittance to the casino floor is restricted to adults age 21 and over*.

Competition among the dozen major casinos has spurred constant redecoration, ornamenting the gaming floors with architectural and artistic fantasies of theme-park proportions. Rows of white statues of Augustus Caesar herald the entry to **Caesar's Hotel Casino**, while the interior features an 18ft-high replica of Michelangelo's *David*. Life-size figures cavort on the gingerbread porches of **Showboat**, and exotic Indian architecture defines the luxuriant **Trump's Taj Mahal**. Casino buffet meals are very popular, as evidenced by long queues of tourists. Major variety shows with big-name entertainers carry on a century-old tradition that has witnessed generations of American crooners, comedians and dancers.

Atlantic City Casino Hotels

Atlantic City Hilton Casino Hotel *Boston & Pacific Aves.*	☎609-347-7111 or 800-257-8677
Bally's Park Place-A Hilton Casino Resort *Park Place & Boardwalk*	☎609-340-2000 or 800-225-5977
Caesar's Atlantic City Hotel Casino *Arkansas & Pacific Aves.*	☎609-348-4411 or 800-443-0104
Claridge Casino Hotel *Indiana Ave. at Brighton Park*	☎609-340-3400 or 800-257-8585
Harrah's Casino Hotel *1725 Brigantine Blvd.*	☎609-441-5000 or 800-242-7724
Resorts Casino Hotel *North Carolina Ave. & Boardwalk*	☎609-344-6000 or 800-336-6378
Sands Hotel & Casino *Indiana Ave. at Brighton Park*	☎609-441-4000 or 800-257-8580
Showboat Casino Hotel *Delaware Ave. & Boardwalk*	☎609-441-4000 or 800-257-8580
Tropicana Casino & Resort *Iowa Ave. & Boardwalk*	☎609-340-4000 or 800-257-6227
Trump Plaza Hotel & Casino *Mississippi Ave. & Boardwalk*	☎609-441-6000 or 800-677-7378
Trump's Castle Casino Resort *Huron Ave. & Brigantine Blvd.*	☎609-441-2000 or 800-365-8786
Trump Taj Mahal Casino Resort *1000 Boardwalk*	☎609-449-1000 or 800-677-7378
Trump World's Fair Casino Hotel *Florida Ave. & Boardwalk*	☎609-441-6000 or 800-677-7378

of the King Neptune pageant. The completion of the world's largest convention hall in 1929, with its 3,000-pipe organ, marked a high point as the Depression loomed. The hall hosted the 1964 Democratic convention during a spate of motel construction, but new resorts along the Jersey Shore soon eclipsed Atlantic City. Great hotels like the Traymore and Blenheim were demolished by the 1970s, when voters approved casino gambling in an effort to revitalize the city. The first casino opened in a restored hotel in 1978, sparking yet another trend in American entertainment. Today the city is on a roll, undergoing a $7 billion development plan.

Atlantic City Boardwalk (c.1890)

Corbis-Bettmann/Rau 1837INP

VISIT *2hrs*

Maps of the 4.5mi-long **Boardwalk**★ are available everywhere, and affordable jitneys travel the length of the town. The Boardwalk offers all of its trademark diversions, from souvenir shops flogging sand art, hermit crabs and saucy T-shirts to the whirring hubbub of casino lobbies and the thrills of carnival rides. Rolling chairs shuttle guests past seaside grills offering New York pizza and Philadelphia cheesesteaks, and shops featuring Atlantic City's own saltwater taffy, caramel corn, ice cream and fudge. One can still encounter Mr. Peanut, in top hat and tights, hawking legumes as he has since 1916, as well as fortune-tellers and caricaturists. The transitory nature of these amusements is broken by the solemn Art Deco facade of the **Boardwalk Convention Hall**, dedicated to "recreation, social progress and industrial achievement," facing a curving peristyle of columns that frame the seashore. **Ocean One** offers three levels of shopping and food on a pier across from Caesar's, while amusements and rides supplement shops at **Central Pier**. The famous **Steel Pier**, at Trump's Taj Mahal, features rollercoasters, a 100ft Ferris wheel, carousels and games. Housed in a modern building on Garden Pier *(north end of Boardwalk)*, the **Atlantic City Historical Museum** *(open year-round daily 10am–4pm; & ▯ www.nj.com/acmuseum ☎609-347-5839)* exhibits historic photographs and mementos from the city's glory years. Take time to watch the video, which includes footage of the Miss America Pageant and of the famed high-diving horses. Across from the museum, the Atlantic City Art Center features rotating exhibits of local art.

EXCURSIONS

★ **Lucy the Margate Elephant** – ▦ *30min. 4mi south of Atlantic City, at Atlantic and Decatur Aves. in Margate. Visit by guided tour (20min) only, Apr–mid-Jun weekends 10am–4:30pm. Mid-Jun–Labor Day daily 10am–8pm. Sept–Oct weekends 10am–4:30pm. $3. ✕ ▯ ☎609-823-6473.* Victorians loved frills and exoticism in their buildings, and it is nowhere more apparent than in Margate, where the six-story "elephant" was built by *Mayflower* descendant James Lafferty in 1881. One of the nation's oddest National Historic Landmarks, the 90-ton wood-framed folly with tin skin—topped by an Indian howdah for an observatory—was erected to promote South Atlantic City (now Margate). A guide leads the climb up 26 narrow stairs to the hollow belly of the elephant, full of exhibits and artifacts from her uses as a house, hotel, tavern and tourist attraction. A short video details how Lucy, based on P.T. Barnum's Jumbo the elephant, inspired imitators like the Colossus on Coney Island and the Light of Asia at Cape May. A 1929 storm forced Lucy to move back from the ocean, and in 1962, a northeaster accelerated her deterioration. These events led to the formation of the Save Lucy Committee, which helped move the landmark to city park land in the 1970s and restore it.

Ocean City – *1hr. 20mi south of Atlantic City. Take Garden State Pkwy. south and exit at Rte. 52E.* Founded in 1879 as a Christian retreat, the family alternative to Atlantic City still bans liquor sales but offers the other Jersey Shore attractions, including the 50ft-wide boardwalk running from Sixth to Sixteenth Streets. Kiosks sell beach access permits, while the inland side is lined with shops hawking food and souvenirs. The Mediterranean Revival **Music Pier** (1928) dominates the seaside and contains a visitor center, police station and 950-seat theater. To the north, miniature golf and water slides compete with the huge **Gillian's Wonderland** amusement center replete with Ferris wheel and carnival rides. Historic buildings in town include Queen Anne mansions on Fifth Street near the Tabernacle and three-story gabled cottages on Wesley Street between Eighth and Eleventh Streets.

CAPE MAY ★★★

Population 4,490
Maps p 11 and p 172
Tourist Information ☎609-884-5508

The tip of the Jersey peninsula, named for 17C Dutch explorer **Cornelius Jacobsen Mey**, attracted settlers from Plymouth and Yarmouth, Massachusetts, to early whaling and shipbuilding towns. In fact, there are still more *Mayflower* descendants in Cape May than in any other US county. During the early 19C, the warm climate helped the region become one of the young nation's first resort areas.

Historical Notes

Cape May's history as a tourist destination dates back to 1801, when the first ferry service to **Cape Island** brought vacationers seeking the healthful effects of "sea-bathing," which was little more than wading and splashing about in long woolen outfits. By mid-century the island ranked as the nation's premier resort, with huge wooden hotels packing in summer guests. Henry Clay's 1847 visit—to mourn his son's death in the Mexican War—extended the season, as thousands returned to see the popular statesman. The birth of ATLANTIC CITY, with its superior railroad connections dented Cape Island's appeal, and an 1856 fire devastated the town's largest hotel, the famed 2,100-room Mount Vernon Hotel. The railroad finally arrived in 1863 as speculative cottages joined the 20 established hotels in the rechristened city of Cape May. In 1869 another fire wiped out two blocks, and then on November 9, 1878, an arsonist's fire destroyed 35 acres, including 7 hotels and 35 cottages. Cape May was rebuilt at a smaller scale, forsaking giant hotels for affordable cottages and catering to Philadelphians and Southerners. From 1878 to 1903 the steamer *Republic* plied the waters from Philadelphia to Cape May, and the massive Hotel Cape May (demolished 1996) was erected in 1908, but the area never regained the popularity it had enjoyed in the late 19C. In 1954 the Garden State Parkway opened, offering quick and easy access to the once bustling town. Just as people were rediscovering Cape May's rich collection of 19C cottages, the 1962 northeaster destroyed the town's boardwalk. A large group of individuals inaugurated a preservation effort that led to Cape May's 1976 designation as a National Historic Landmark.

In recent years, the city has again become a tourist mecca, as thousands come to enjoy the reborn Victorian architecture, shop the Washington Street mall, and laze on the pleasant beaches devoid of boardwalk sideshows and kitsch. Featuring performances of work ranging from the Renaissance to the Jazz Age, the **Cape May Music Festival** in May and June heralds the onset of the busy summer season. April's **Spring Festival** and October's **Victorian Week** focus on Victorian architecture, fashions, antiques and music. Christmas events allow visitors to re-create century-old Yuletide traditions in a period setting.

Getting There

By Air – Closest airport is **Atlantic City International Airport**, 45mi north of Cape May; international and domestic flights. Rental car agencies *(p 358)* are located at the airport.

By Bus and Train – **Bus** service to Cape May is provided by New Jersey Transit *(609 Lafayette St.;* ☎*973-762-5100 or 800-772-2222).* Cape May Seashore Lines *(*☎*884-2675)* provide **train** service from Tuckahoe to Cold Spring Village.

Getting Around – Shuttles run to Cape May Lighthouse and Cape May State Park from downtown Cape May *(depart from bus depot at Elmira & Lafayette Sts. Apr–Oct; purchase tickets at Washington Street Mall Information & Ticket Booth, below).*

General Information

Visitor Information – Contact the **Chamber of Commerce of Greater Cape May** *(PO Box 556, Cape May NJ 08204* ☎*884-5508)* or visit the **Welcome Center** *(405 Lafayette St.; open year-round daily 9am–4pm;* ☎*884-9562)* for information and brochures on points of interest, seasonal events, recreation and accommodations. The **Mid-Atlantic Center for the Arts** (MAC), founded in 1970 to preserve the city's Victorian heritage, offers numerous walking and trolley tours of the historic areas, and features an extensive calendar of events *(PO Box 340, Cape May NJ 08204; www.beachcomber.com/capemay/mac.html* ☎*884-5404 or 800-275-4278).* MAC also operates the **Washington Street Mall Information & Ticket Booth** *(Ocean St. at Washington Street Mall; open Apr–May & Oct–mid-Nov daily 10am–4:30pm; Memorial Day–Sept & Thanksgiving–early Jan daily 10am–7:30pm; Jan–Mar weekends 11am–2pm).* Their publication, *This Week in Cape May (free),* is available at information centers and lodging facilities.

Accommodations – *(p 358)* Area visitors' guide including lodging directory is available *(free)* from local tourism agencies *(above).* Accommodations consist mainly of **guest houses** and **bed-and-breakfast inns** (although several hotels and motels are available); note that many inns do not permit children and may require a 3-night minimum stay. Discounted rates before Memorial Day and after Labor Day may be available. Rooms may be difficult to obtain on weekends between May and August; advance reservations are strongly encouraged. **Reservation services**: Chamber of Commerce of Greater Cape May *(above);* Cape May Reservation Service *(*☎*884-3191 or 800-729-7778).* **Campgrounds** are located throughoutthe area.

Sports and Leisure

Sightseeing – The popular neighborhood and house **walking** and **trolley** tours sponsored by the MAC *(above)* are available year-round *(depart from Washington Street Mall Information Booth).* Other MAC tours include the Fisherman's Wharf Tour *(meet at dock at Lobster House; Apr–mid-Oct; 45min; purchase tickets at dock);* and a nature tour of beach and marshlands *(depart from Nature Center of Cape May, 1600 Delaware Ave. Jun–Oct; 1hr 30min).* Self-guided **audio tours** are also available at the Washington Street Mall Information Booth. **Carriage** tours of the historic district depart from Washington Street Mall *(Mar–Dec, weather permitting; 30min; reservations required;* ☎*884-4466).*

Cruises – Companies offering sightseeing and whale-watching cruises include Cape May Whale Watch & Research Center *(depart from 1286 Wilson Dr.; 2 & 3hrs;* ☎*898-0055);* Cape May Whale Watcher *(depart from 2nd Ave. & Wilson Dr.; 2-3hrs;* ☎*884-5455);* Schooner Yankee *(depart from Ocean Highway Dock; 2-3hrs;* ☎*884-1919);* and Salt Marsh Cruise *(depart from Miss Chris Marina, 2nd Ave. & Wilson Dr. Mar–Dec; 2hrs 30min* ☎*884-3100).*

Recreation – Cape May Point is an excellent spot for **bird-watching** (especially during spring and fall migration); bird-sighting hotline: ☎884-2626. Recommended viewing areas include Cape May Migratory Bird Refuge *(off Sunset Blvd.);* Cape May Bird Observatory *(707 E. Lake Dr.;* ☎*884-2736);* and Cape May Point State Park *(off Lighthouse Ave.;* ☎*884-2159).* With its peninsular setting, Cape May offers a wide range of water sports. **Boat rentals** and **charter fishing** are available at Cape May Harbor. **Swimming** beaches are located on both the Atlantic Ocean *(lifeguards on duty Memorial Day–Labor Day)* and the Delaware Bay sides. Beach fee *($4/day)* may be charged.

SIGHTS *2 days*

Cape May's Victorian charm is concentrated in the downtown area, between Congress and Franklin Streets and Beach and Lafayette Avenues, and is best explored on foot. Begin your visit at the **Welcome Center** *(p 192)*, housed in a restored church just one block from the Washington Street Mall. The city center offers numerous spots for grabbing a quick bite or enjoying a more substantial feast.

In the early morning hours or at dusk, head west to **Sunset Beach** at Cape May Point, which is littered with Cape May Diamonds, the clear quartz pebbles that are subject to constant tourist scavenging. For a break from sightseeing, drive up to the **Wildwoods**, a popular shore resort occupying an isle just north of the city. Three separate communities share a 4mi stretch of boardwalk and accompanying amusements, including the early Bobs roller-coasters, Ferris wheels and other carnival rides. Attracting a younger, more eclectic crowd than Cape May, the Wildwoods is best known for its safe, sandy beaches and numerous cruises, ranging from narrated sightseeing tours to dolphin- and whale-watching excursions.

★★ Downtown Walking Tour *2hrs. 1.25mi. Map below.*

Begin at intersection of Hughes and Ocean Sts. and walk north on Hughes St.

★ **Hughes Street** – The **White Dove Cottage** at no. 619 features a detailed mansard roof, while no. 629 flaunts its decorative Cape May detailing, including fish-scale shingles. At no. 645 stands the 1868 **Joseph Hall House**, a Victorian Gothic confection of curving foliate verge boards, protruding dormers and a gingerbread porch. Around the corner on Stockton Place, the **Bell Bungalows [A, B]** reflect the seaside style of the 1920s. The 1865 **J. Stratton Ware House** at no. 655 exhibits skillful carpentry in its cornices and incised window hoods.

Turn right on Franklin St. and right again on Columbia Ave.

★ **Columbia Avenue** – Developer Peter McCullom commissioned Stephen Decatur (S.D.) Button to design a series of Victorian cottages along this charming street, including nos. 725 and 715; today both operate as bed-and-breakfast inns. Just east at Howard Street and Sewell Avenue, the **Chalfonte Hotel** (1875), an American Bracketed Villa built in 1875, stands as the oldest operating hotel in Cape May. Reminiscent of the Old South, the elegant, Italianate-style **Mainstay Inn [C]** (1872) at no. 635 was once a gambling house for Southern gentlemen. East on Stockton Place, the **Stockton Cottages** (1869) present a row of eight largely identical Carpenter Gothic designs with two-story porches and a wealth of wedding-cake ornamentation. Located at Columbia and Gurney Streets, **The Abbey** was designed for Philadelphia coal baron J.B. McCreary by S.D. Button in 1869.

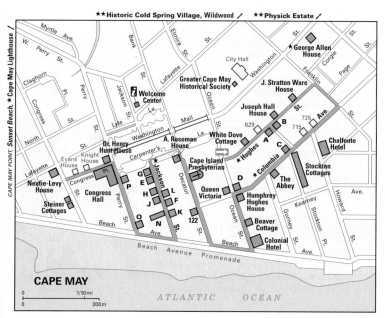

CAPE MAY

■ Victorian Architecture in Cape May

Devastated by the fires of 1869 and 1878, Cape May was rebuilt in the age of High Victorian architecture, when the picturesque qualities of a building were greatly exaggerated. Although the first hotels were undecorated barns, by the mid-19C, cottages in the popular **Gothic Revival** style began to sprout, as still seen today on Hughes Street. Steep center gables, pointed windows and dormers sported fanciful ornamentation, including elaborate cut-out balustrades along the porches and verge boards along the eaves. Each cottage competed with the next for visual interest and sought to attract summer tourists with

sweeping verandahs and gables adorned with finials and pendants. These gingerbread details began to define Cape May through the work of local architect **Stephen Decatur Button** (1813-97), who freely borrowed Gothic, Italianate and Renaissance elements with a penchant for the decorative. The familiar 1860s **Italianate** style, with overhanging eaves and brackets, is outnumbered in Cape May by its more ornate cousin, the **American Bracketed Villa**, which defines the Chalfonte Hotel *(p 193)*. Hallmarks of the style include elaborate brackets

and delicate filigree along overhanging porch roofs.

The 1870s brought the **Second Empire** style with the steep mansard roof, such as those found at The Abbey *(p 193)*, and subsequently the **Queen Anne** style, characterized by picturesque roof lines and heavily ornamented porches. This latter style represents a culmination of Victorian taste, with asymmetrical massing of buildings and fancy ornamentation creating a lush, romantic architecture with endless visual improvisations. Diverse and colorful paint schemes added to the allure of the buildings, while extra dormers and turrets provided further opportunities for decorative cresting in wood and iron. Cape May also boasts examples of the 1870s **Stick** style, which features attached wooden boards and decorative trusswork, as well as the later **Shingle** style with fish-scale (rounded) or shark's tooth (diamond-shaped) wooden shingles enlivening roofs and walls.

By the early 20C, revival styles like the Dutch Colonial, Renaissance Revival and Spanish Colonial appeared as a reaction to Victorian excess. Cape May examples, such as the Dutch Colonial Humphrey Hughes House *(p 195)*, nonetheless featured large porches and stained glass. Growing out of the turn-of-the-century Arts and Crafts movement, squat **bungalows** were built in the early decades of the 20C. The low-pitched roofs of these single-story homes feature exposed rafters and stone or shingle piers supporting the porch, as seen on Stockton Place *(p 193)*. In the mid-20C, Cape May was eclipsed by Atlantic City and other resort towns; as a result, the existing Victorian housing stock was not razed for new construction. While many structures fell into disrepair and commercial buildings on Washington Street were heavily altered, by the 1960s Cape May was ripe for historic preservation. In 1976 the entire downtown was listed on the National Register of Historic Places. The gradual reclamation of the town's "Painted Ladies" opened a new flow of tourism and has led to the recent construction of Victorian Revival structures throughout Cape May.

A Victorian Gothic delight, it sports a 60ft corner tower, arched windows and elaborate trim work. At the corner of Ocean Street, note **Dr. Ware's Drugstore [D]** at nos. 101-103, one of the few original commercial buildings left in the city. Facing it is the Second Empire **Queen Victoria**, at no. 102, built by Douglas Gregory in 1881 with elaborate brackets and a Victorian garden wrapped in wrought iron.

Turn left on Ocean St. and continue east to Beach Ave.

The Dutch Colonial **Humphrey Hughes House** (1913) at no. 29 features an expansive verandah, while the **Beaver Cottage** at no. 23 boasts a whimsical, tiny balcony in the turret. At the corner with Beach Avenue stands the expansive **Colonial Hotel** (1894-95), distinguished by shingle patterns in purple and gray.

Continue south on Beach Ave. and turn right on Decatur St.

The quaint Victorian cottage at **no. 122** proves that gingerbread ornament works on any scale, while the stone Gothic **Cape Island Presbyterian Church** (1898) relates to the city's dominant style. Turned balusters and stained glass distinguish the charming **Aaron Roseman House** (1895) at no. 132.

Turn left on Carpenter's Ln. and left again on Jackson St.

★ **Jackson Street** – Take time to absorb the details along this colorful street. From Colonial Revival elements adorning the Queen Anne-style **I. Leaming Shepart House [E]** *(no. 38)* to a bold, polychromatic slate roof topping the Second Empire-style **Poor Richard's Inn [F]** *(no. 17)*, these homes offer plenty to satisfy the senses. The **Merry Widow [G]** at no. 42 shows that restorationists today can be as exuberant with color as their Victorian predecessors. At no. 24, the 1905 **Windward House [H]** is a rare Shingle-style structure, while the **Inn at 22 Jackson [J]** exhibits typical Victorian turned spindles and an octagonal tower. At no. 15, note the half-timbering and cast-iron fence of 1883 **McConnell House [K]**, a stately Queen Anne manse. A smaller version of the Chalfonte, the **Carroll Villa Hotel [L]** is topped by a fancy Italianate cupola. Architect S.D. Button faced the simple **Seven Sisters [N]** cottages at nos. 10-20 (1891) toward a side courtyard, creating a pleasant retreat.

Turn right on Beach Ave. and right again on Perry St.

King Cottage [0] at 9 Perry Street was designed by Frank Furness in 1871 and rebuilt in 1878 with notable ceramic balusters and glazed tiles. At no. 33 stands the much photographed **Pink House [P]** (c.1882), distinguished by a bright profusion of carpenter's lace enlivening its two-story porch and gable.

Turn left on Congress Pl.

The L-shaped **Congress Hall** has existed on its beachfront site since the early 19C. The current edifice, rebuilt in brick after the 1878 fire, features a grand, marble-floored lobby arcade, now given over to specialty shops and boutiques. Note the **Dr. Henry Hunt House** at no. 209, an eclectic fantasy erected in 1881: the dormers and porches combine Victorian styles in a single breathless composition. The sturdy square masses of the Joseph Evans House (1882) at no. 207 and E.C. Knight House (1883) at no. 203 are enlivened with decorative porches. Among Cape May's oldest homes are the 1865 **Neafie-Levy House** *(at the intersection with Congress St.)*, with its elaborate two-story wraparound verandah, and the Carpenter Gothic **Joseph and John Steiner Cottages** (1848-51), located just east at nos. 22-24.

Additional Sights

★ **George Allen House (The Southern Mansion)** – *720 Washington St. Open year-round daily 11am–6:30pm. $10.* ✗ ▯ *www.capenet.com/capemay/allen* ☎609-884-7171. This massive 1863 Italianate villa was restored as a luxury country inn in the mid-1990s. Philadelphia merchant George Allen hired architect Samuel Sloan, whose famous Long Court Octagon in Natchez had been interrupted by the Civil War, to design the huge vacation home at a cost of $10,000. The mansion reveals its Southern influence with pocket windows that slide up to create doors onto the verandah. Inside, tours point out the mahogany staircase, brass chandeliers and a cupola with gorgeous views of sea and town. In the rear of the manse are servants' quarters (c.1890s) and a separate two-seater privy.

★ **Physick Estate** – *1048 Washington St. Visit by guided tour (45min) only, daily year-round. Closed Thanksgiving Day, Dec 25. $7.* ▯ *www.beachcomber.com* ☎609-884-5404 *or* 800-275-4278. Designed by noted Philadelphia architect **Frank Furness** for bachelor doctor Emlen Physick and his mother in 1878, the mansion—an Academy of Fine Arts design—took $20,000 and three years to build. The

Mid-Atlantic Center for the Arts (MAC) was formed to save the house and has operated it under a lease from the city since 1971. Guided tours begin in the impressive Victorian foyer with its square staircase and woven willow screen. Walls throughout the house are trimmed in reeded oak and covered with lincrusta, a combination of paper and linseed oil, while the ceilings are painted burlap. The gentlemen's parlor in front is furnished with games and books, while the ladies' parlor to the rear showcases an 1876 pianoforte. Long windows slide up into wall pockets, becoming doors in summer. William Morris wallpaper and a geometric mantelpiece—one of many interior elements designed by Furness—distinguish the dining room. Upstairs, a guest bedroom with a marble corner sink is furnished as a game room replete with billiard table and bookcase. Additional bedrooms include Furness-designed furnishings, some boasting the architect's signature bull's-eye design. The tour concludes in the museum shop on the sun porch.

Greater Cape May Historical Society – *Rear of Alexander Guest House next to City Hall at 653 1/2 Washington St. Open mid-Jun–mid-Oct daily 10am–2pm. $1.* ▯ ☎*609-884-9100.* The Society presents revolving exhibits in three reconstructed rooms in the town's oldest building, known as the Colonial House. Built by Memucan Hughes before the Revolutionary War, it was moved to this site in 1882 when the Italianate Alexander Guest House in front was built. Exhibits focus primarily on life on old Cape Island before 1840.

Cape May Point State Park

★ **Cape May Lighthouse** – *In Cape May Point State Park; 3mi south of Cape May, off Sunset Dr. Open May–late Oct Mon–Fri 10am–6pm, weekends 9am–6pm. Late Oct–mid-Nov Mon–Fri noon–3pm, Sat 10am–4pm. $3.50.* ▯ *www.beachcomber.com* ☎*609-884-5404 or 800-275-4278.* Located in the town of Cape May Point, just steps from a pleasant beach, state park and nature preserve, the lighthouse dates from 1857 and still guards the access to Philadelphia via the Delaware River. Climb the 199 steps to the top to view exhibits about the lighthouse and admire the vistas on each landing. The first lighthouse was built in 1823 and was located 800ft from the present shoreline, whose erosion has eliminated six blocks of the town. Today a 1,000-watt bulb has replaced the oil and kerosene lamps of old; the original Fresnel lens is displayed at the Cape May County Historical Society Museum *(p 197)*. Located in the adjacent oil house, a visitor center for the state park provides information on the 153-acre coastal dune and freshwater marsh nature preserve, which is laced with hiking and biking trails.

★★ **Historic Cold Spring Village** – *720 Rte. 9, 3mi north of Cape May. Open Memorial Day–late Jun weekends 10am–4:30pm. Late Jun–Labor Day daily 10am–4:30pm. Sept weekends 10am–4:30pm. $5.* ✗ ▯ *www.hcsv.org* ☎*609-898-2300. Carriage tours ($4; 20min) depart from front entrance.* A popular summer attraction opened in 1981, this reconstructed village offers first-person historical interpretation of the

Federal period (c.1790-1830). Educational demonstrations of life and trades share space with more commercial crafts. The 1894 **Welcome Center** focuses on maritime history with a 10min video history of Cape May and interactive exhibits on whaling, fishing and shipbuilding. Artifacts include a Jersey Shore "sneakbox" boat and a model of the *Republic*, the famous Cape May steamer.

Follow the long circular road from the visitor center to the various village sites. The one-room **Marshallville School** enlists child volunteers for lessons and the dunce cap, while the 1820 Willis Barn hosts weaving demonstrations. Built in 1825, the Spicer Leaming House is a classic Jersey farmhouse with gabled roof and lean-to addition; here, a farmwife in period dress spins wool. The **Dennisville Tavern★** (1775) features lively interpretation of the bartender's grilled-in cage and descriptions of how circuit judges would ask new attorneys to take their "bar" exams. Rope-, leather- and pewter-making demonstrations take place at the 1850 Cape May Jail, the Walter P. Taylor octagon—a curiously ornate henhouse—and at the Tin Shop. To the north across the road is the working Blacksmith Shop (1865). Another typical Jersey home, the 1878 Howard Norton House, serves as a bakery. Other village sites include a bookbindery, a pottery shop and a barn.

At the far end, the **Grange★**, a hall built by the fraternal and political farmers' group in 1867, is now a restaurant independent of the village and the only building in its original location. A hundred yards to the south stands the brick Neoclassical Cold Spring Presbyterian Church (1714) and adjacent graveyard.

EXCURSIONS *Map p 172*

★ **Leaming's Run Gardens and Farm** – *1hr. 16mi north of Cape May via Rte. 9 north. 1845 Rte. 9 in Swainton. Open mid-May–mid-Oct daily 9:30am–5pm. $4.50.* ♿ 🅿 ☎*609-465-5871.* Opened in 1978 by Jack and Emily Aprill, the largest annual garden in the US covers 30 acres surrounding the white frame Thomas Leaming House (1706). Two dozen discrete gardens linked by a mile-long path through a pine forest create a sense of discovery not found in didactic botanical sites. A large underground lake helps drain the sandy loam soil, and the plots are maintained without weeding or fertilizing. Several are organized by color, like the Yellow Garden with gladiolas and banana peppers. Endangered plants like the spindle tree and swamp hyacinth are preserved along stretches of thick forest carpeted with ferns. The English Cottage Garden is the result of "careful planning to create an unplanned look," while a Historical Village replicates frontier log-cabin life with a smokehouse, herb garden, barnyard animals and rows of tobacco, beans and cotton. Devoted to a single species are plots such as the Everlasting Garden with Pearly Everlasting, and the Hibiscus Garden.

★★ **Cape May County Historical Society Museum (John Holmes House)** – *2hrs. 14mi from Cape May via Rte. 9 north. 504 Rte. 9 in the town of Cape May Court House. Open Apr–Nov Tue–Sat 9am–4pm. Rest of the year Sat 9am–4pm. Closed major holidays. $2.50.* 🅿 ☎*609-465-3535.* This fascinating museum is housed in a structure built by Irish farmer John Holmes between 1778 and 1835 as an addition to a small 1755 home. The Historical Society purchased the building in 1976 to house its growing collection of historical artifacts, and maintains an adjacent library and genealogical research center here. Docent-led *(at 10:30am and 2pm)* and self-guided tours take in eclectic collections in the main house as well as in the barn. Start your tour in the main hall; the English mahogany tall-case clock (c.1820) here is the only piece original to the house. Upstairs several rooms display period clothing and fabrics as well as musical instruments. The peculiar Victorian hobby of hairworks is represented by hair arrangements covered by glass domes. Hair was gathered in a special collecting dish and crafted into intricate sculptures, including "mourning rings" made from the hair of deceased loved ones.

Downstairs, you'll find an 18C-appointed kitchen and an early-19C **dining room** replete with Hepplewhite sideboard and chairs, a Duncan Phyfe-style table and a painting of Henry Clay, who visited Cape May in 1847. Various rooms throughout the house are devoted to a specific theme, including history, medicine and toys (don't miss the elaborate doll house modeled on a Philadelphia mansion). In the rear of the house, a board-and-batten Jersey **barn** displays household and trade tools as well as a stagecoach, peddler's carriage and doctor's surrey. Highlighting the exhibits is the **1847 Fresnel lens★** from the Cape May lighthouse: hundreds of ground-glass louvers and bull's-eyes in an octagonal turret turned a simple whale-oil lamp into a 250,000-candlepower beam visible for 19mi. One room describes the 1690 whaling village settled by *Mayflower* descendants, while another is dedicated to the Lenni Lenape Indians.

PINE BARRENS ★

Named by early settlers who found the semi-forested area useless for agriculture, this unique ecological resource covers 1.4 million acres in seven counties. Pine, oak and cedar forests grow on sandy soil over a 17-trillion-gallon aquifer, surfacing in branching streams of potable "cedar water" that flow toward the ocean. Carnivorous plants, "pygmy pines," cedar swamps and some 400 varieties of wildflowers can be found in the 1.1 million-acre **Pinelands National Preserve**, created by Congress in 1978.

The pine barrens were ideal for early industries. Rivers provided waterpower, pitch pine was burnt for charcoal, and riverbeds yielded the bog iron ore that stoked the furnaces of Colonial industry and fed the flames of the American Revolution. These wilds also hid rebel privateers harassing the British navy and, later, renegade Tories and other outcasts who became known as the "Pine Robbers." The area's remoteness gave rise to the ongoing legend of the **Jersey Devil**, a marauding beast with a forked tail, horns and bat wings, supposedly born to a Mrs. Leeds in 1735. In the 1840s the bog-iron industry died, replaced by glassmaking and lumber, and then cranberry and blueberry farming in the late 19C. Still untamed, vast stretches of wilderness host only 15 persons per square mile in the nation's most densely populated state.

Practical Information .... Area Code: 609

Getting There – The Pine Barrens are located between Atlantic City and Philadelphia. The Atlantic City Expressway runs parallel to the southern end of Wharton State Forest. Route 70 cuts through the northwest corner of Lebanon State Forest. Many small roads branch off these routes to towns that border the recreation area. The closest airports, **Atlantic City International Airport** and **Philadelphia International Airport**, handle both international and domestic flights. Closest Amtrak **train** station (☎800-872-7245) is located in Philadelphia. **Bus** service to area towns is provided by New Jersey Transit (☎973-762-5100 or 800-772-2222).

Visitor Information – Contact the following agencies for maps, information and brochures on points of interest, seasonal events, recreation and accommodations: **Wharton State Forest** (744 Rte. 206, Vincentown NJ 08088 ☎268-0444); **Bass River State Forest** (PO Box 118, New Gretna NJ 08224 ☎296-1114); **Lebanon State Forest** (Box 215, New Lisbon NJ 08064 ☎726-1191); **Pinelands Commission** (PO Box 7, New Lisbon NJ 08064 ☎894-9342).

Accommodations – **Campgrounds** and **cabins** are located in the three state forests listed above. Reservations are recommended in the summer and over holiday weekends. Hotels, motels and bed-and-breakfast inns can be found in Mays Landing, Burlington, Mount Holly and Pemberton.

Recreation – The majority of recreational activities in the Pine Barrens, such as **canoeing**, **hiking** (p 364), **hunting** and **fishing**, are available in Wharton, Bass River and Lebanon state forests. Companies offering canoe rentals (advance reservations required) can be found in Green Bank, New Gretna, Chatsworth, Batsto and Mays Landing. Spring and fall, when the Batsto, Mullica, Oswego and Wading rivers are less crowded, are the best seasons for canoe trips. All outfitters provide maps and route information and may offer guide service. Naturalist-led tours of the Pine Barrens are offered periodically by the Pinelands Preservation Alliance (Pemberton ☎894-8000) and year-round by Pine Barren Tours (Southampton ☎859-3566).

DRIVING THROUGH THE PINELANDS   *1½ days. 75mi. Map p 199.*

Today the Pinelands National Preserve stretches for miles along the New Jersey shore, encompassing fascinating early-19C settlements as well as recreation areas that offer hiking, biking, swimming and canoeing opportunities. To the east, Oceanville hosts a wonderful wildlife refuge, while Mount Holly, to the west, is home to some of the state's most historic homes.

Begin at Oceanville. To reach Oceanville from the Garden State Pkwy., take Exit 48 and continue south on Rte. 9 for 6mi. Turn left (east) on Great Creek Rd.

★ **Edwin B. Forsythe National Wildlife Refuge (Brigantine Division)** – *(pp 164-165) Great Creek Rd. off Rte. 9 in Oceanville. Open year-round daily sunrise–sunset. $4/car.* ⚐ **₽** ☎*609-652-1665.* Odds are against a visitor to Atlantic City viewing the natural wonders only 11mi from the casino resort, but the Forsythe Refuge pays out with a host of migratory waterfowl winging their way above 20,000 acres of tidal marshland. There is a modern visitor center, a .25mi self-guided nature trail through upland pitch pine and oak forest, and a .5mi foot trail through salt marsh and forest. An information booth provides current waterbird surveys and tide charts. The self-guided **Wildlife Drive★** follows an 8mi rectangular route through three different wetlands as well as uplands of forest and field. Signs along the way describe the many varieties of geese, ducks, herons and egrets that migrate here. Stop by the observation tower to take in sprawling views of Atlantic City and a rare stretch of natural barrier beach.

Just outside the refuge, the **Noyes Museum of Art** *(Lily Lake Rd.)* exhibits fine art as well as folk art focusing on New Jersey and the Atlantic Coast. Four modern galleries overlook quiet woods and a pond *(open year-round Wed–Sun 11am–4pm; $3;* ⚐ **₽** ☎*609-652-8848).*

> *Continue north on Rte. 9 to New Gretna, then take Rte. 542 west for 11mi.*

★★ **Batsto Village** – *On Rte. 542, in Wharton State Forest. Open Apr–Oct Mon–Thu & Sun 9am–4:30pm, Fri & Sat 9am–9pm. Rest of the year daily 9am–4:30pm. Closed Jan 1, Thanksgiving Day, Dec 25.* △ **₽** *($3 Memorial Day–Labor Day weekends & holidays)* ☎*609-561-0024.* Batsto presents a rare view of an intact 19C rural industrial settlement, while adjacent fishing sites and nature trails in the 109,000 acre **Wharton**

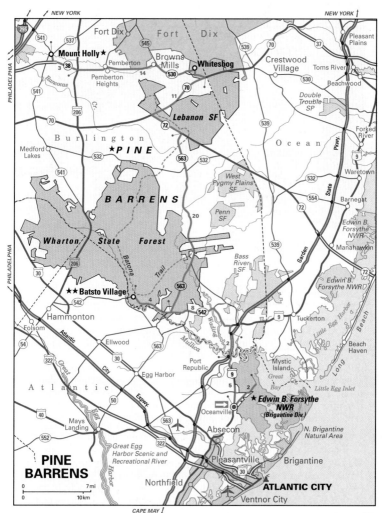

State Forest—the largest park in the state—allow an experience of the Pine Barrens. One of the first bog-iron furnaces in the Pine Barrens was founded at Batsto by Charles Read in 1766, and the town became an important source of cannonballs, kettles and other material during the Revolutionary War. William Richards rebuilt the furnace and town in 1784, and it grew to 1,000 people under the management of his son Jesse. After 1848 the iron industry shifted to Pennsylvania, and Batsto focused on window-glass production until 1867. The village was all but abandoned following an 1874 fire; but two years later, Philadelphia industrialist Joseph Wharton bought it and cultivated cranberries, sugar beets and other crops here until 1909. The state acquired Batsto and the forest in 1954.

Visit – ½ *day*. The **visitor center** offers a detailed history of the Pine Barrens and the glass and iron industries it spawned in the 18C. Displays are illustrated with artifacts, including cast-iron firebacks, stoves and pig-iron ingots. Old photos depict the glassmaking process and the successive agricultural industries of the Pine Barrens.

Begin your visit with the **mansion★**, as guided tours fill up quickly *(visit by 45min guided tour only Mar–Dec daily 10:30am–3:30pm; rest of the year weekends 10:30am–3:30pm; closed Jan 1, Thanksgiving Day, Dec 25; $2, tickets available at visitor center only;* ☎*609-561-3262)*. Built in the 1780s as a modest Federal-style ironmaster's home, the rambling structure was transformed by Wharton into a 36-room Italianate mansion in 1876. Tours begin in the foyer and continue to adjoining parlors and bedrooms appointed with period furniture. An informative 15min slide presentation on the Batsto industries is shown twice daily.

Batsto Village

Not far from the mansion lies the small **post office**, set up by Jesse Richards in 1852 and still functioning without a zip code. The current postmaster can hand-cancel mail on the original postmaster's desk and mail cabinet. Ruins of a 150-year-old iron-ore boat and a reproduction kiln illustrate how iron was made. Across the Batsto River, the large L-shaped clapboard **sawmill**, dating from 1882, still operates each Saturday and Sunday *(1:30pm, 2pm and 2:30pm)*. Beyond the mill are rows of neat clapboard **workers' houses**, built in the early-19C Federal style with bog ore and stone foundations, unpainted cedar siding and shingle roofs. These five-room houses rented to workers and their families for $2 a month plus morning chores. Sparsely furnished interiors serve as nature and craft centers, with demonstrations of pottery and weaving.

> *From Batsto Village, take Rte. 542 east to Rte. 563 and continue north toward Rte. 72.*

This section of the Pine Barrens is fairly scenic and typically rural, with roadside stands offering firewood and canoe rentals to park visitors. The surrounding forest is interrupted by great rectangular **cranberry bogs** watered by huge sprinklers. Visible along Route 563, the Ocean Spray cooperative processes the cranberries

Cranberry Harvest – © Michael Melford

■ Cranberries in New Jersey

The cranberry, a compact red perennial, grows in century-old bogs where vines take up to five years to bear fruit. In the flooded fall fields, farmers beat the bushes until ripe cranberries float to the surface for harvesting. More than 3,000 acres of bogs make New Jersey the third-leading cranberry state after Massachusetts and Wisconsin.

following the fall harvest. To encounter the famous **pygmy pine forest**, follow Route 539, accessible from Route 9 north, to Route 72: the thick forest stretches for miles on both sides of the highway with scrubby pines only 5ft tall. Follow Route 72 west and the pygmy pines give way to the taller pines of the **Lebanon State Forest**, a 31,879-acre preserve named for the Lebanon Glass Works (1862-67). There are several nature trails here, including the 49.5mi **Batona Trail** to Wharton State Forest. An informative visitor center near the intersection of Routes 72 and 70 stocks maps and brochures.

At the junction of Rtes. 72 and 70, follow Rte. 70 north to Rte. 530 and turn left (west).

Whitesbog – *North end of Lebanon State Forest along Rte. 530.* A large water tower looms silently over the tiny, turn-of-the-century agricultural settlement surrounded by abandoned cranberry bogs and blueberry fields. First developed as an experimental cranberry farm by Col. James Fenwick in 1857, the settlement was founded in 1882 by his daughter Mary and husband Joseph Josiah White. Their daughter, **Elizabeth White**, started blueberry cultivation in 1893 and turned it into a profitable venture by 1916, in partnership with Dr. Frederick Colville of the US Department of Agriculture. The state acquired the village in the 1960s, and it is now preserved by the Whitesbog Preservation Trust. A short nature trail leads past the abandoned bogs.

Continue west on Rte. 530/38, passing through Pemberton, to Mount Holly.

★ **Mount Holly** – Founded in 1700 by English Quakers, this charming town draws tourists to its quiet, shady streets and boasts a wealth of historic homes and businesses, including the oldest fire station and the oldest continuously operating courthouse in the US. Rows of narrow, Federal-style business blocks line the rising curve of **High Street★** downtown. One block north of Washington Street, Brainerd Street features the 1759 pattern-brick **John Brainerd Friends School** at no. 35, illustrating the early Quaker emphasis on education. Back on High Street, the oldest US county **Courthouse** (1796) still in use exemplifies Georgian Colonial architecture with its symmetrical white-brick facade, pediment and octagonal cupola. Set like a medieval bulwark back from the street at no. 128 is the **Burlington County Prison**, a National Historic Landmark built in 1808 by architect Robert Mills. Small Federal houses give way to large 19C brick Italianate mansions as the neighborhood grows more residential to the north.

East of High Street, the **Mill Street Hotel and Tavern** has been operating since 1723, hosting Hessians and Patriots during the Revolutionary War. South on Pine Street, an 1892 brownstone facade with cupola and widow's walk marks the oldest **Fire Relief Station** in the nation, founded in 1752.

PRINCETON ★★

"Princeton," F. Scott Fitzgerald wrote in 1927, "is in the flat midlands of New Jersey, rising, a green phoenix over the ugliest country in the world.... Around Princeton, shielding her, is a ring of silence certified with great estates of peacocks and deer parks, pleasant farms and woodlands." Indeed, the lush, rolling countryside surrounding Princeton gives the town a rarefied, patrician air appropriate to the residences of scholars and the retreats of politicians. Today the small town revolves around the Ivy League campus at its center, the nation's fourth-oldest institution of higher learning.

★★ PRINCETON UNIVERSITY *½ day. Map below.*

In 1746 a small group of Presbyterian ministers founded a college for the middle American colonies and named it the College of New Jersey. First established at Elizabeth, and then at Newark, it moved to the present site in 1756, after the completion of Nassau Hall. During the Revolution, the college buildings served successively as barracks and hospitals for British and American troops. Its capture by General Washington on January 3, 1777, marked the end of the Battle of Princeton, a victory for the colonists. In 1783 the college housed the Continental Congress for six months, and the final treaty of peace was signed here. On its 150th anniversary, the College of New Jersey (already called Princeton College) became a university; six years later alumnus **Woodrow Wilson** became its president. He established the preceptor system of small study groups, but he failed in his attempts to integrate the graduate and undergraduate schools and to abolish the exclusive eating societies where many upperclassmen still reside.

Since the 18C, Princeton has been noted for its teaching in political science and its programs of scientific research (the first chair of chemistry in the US was created here in 1795). In 1930 Louis Bamberger founded the Institute for Advanced Study, home to **Albert Einstein** from 1932 to 1955. Princeton graduates include presidents James Monroe, Grover Cleveland and Woodrow Wilson, writers Eugene O'Neill and F. Scott Fitzgerald, and businessman Malcolm Forbes. Women were admitted in 1969, and the school today claims 4,500 undergraduates and 1,600 graduate students.

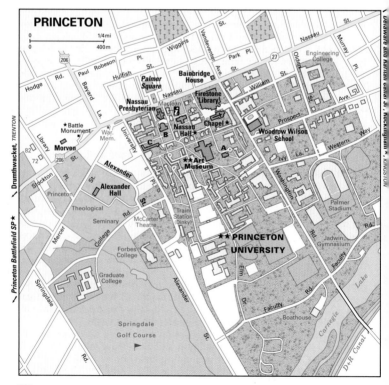

Campus – *Free guide service offered by students year-round; request a tour three days in advance. Information available at the Orange Key Guide Service, Maclean House.* ☎609-258-3603. Princeton's shady, 600-acre campus comprises over 130 buildings in a variety of styles, from Neoclassical to Modern, reflecting its growth from small Presbyterian college to world-renowned institution. Ivy planted by each graduating class covers the orange stone walls of **Nassau Hall★**, the largest collegiate building in the colonies when it was completed in 1756. This Neoclassical structure was twice rebuilt, once by Benjamin Latrobe after an 1802 fire and again in 1855. The marble foyer memorializes Princeton alumni killed in US wars, while the paneled **Faculty Room★**, modeled on the House of Commons, features Charles Willson Peale's portrait of George Washington at the Battle of Princeton.

The Georgian quadrangle of the campus behind Nassau Hall included East College (now demolished) and West College, both built in 1836. Nearby stand Whig Hall and Clio Hall, Greek Revival temples rebuilt in marble in 1893 by A. Page Brown. **Prospect [A]**, a picturesque Italianate mansion designed by John Notman, was added in 1849. Exemplifying the Romanesque style is **Alexander Hall [B]** (1892), a stately granite and sandstone landmark ornamented with sculpture and stained glass.

By the late 19C, England's Oxford and Cambridge inspired the American Collegiate Gothic style. **Blair Hall and Tower [C]** (1899) feature Gothic turrets, finials and grotesques in gray limestone. In 1907 noted Gothicist Ralph Adams Cram crafted a new campus plan. His triumphant **University Chapel★** (1928), modeled on King's College, Cambridge, with English oak paneling and stained glass, is the third-largest university chapel in the nation, seating 1,800. Containing some five million volumes, the **Harvey S. Firestone Library** (1948) is the largest of the 23 libraries on campus and includes a rare book display and the papers of F. Scott Fitzgerald, Woodrow Wilson and other graduates. Modern architecture defines the famous **Woodrow Wilson School of Public and International Affairs**, a sparkling concrete temple arcade designed by Minoru Yamasaki in 1966.

★★ **Princeton Art Museum** – *Open year-round Tue–Sat 10am–4:45pm, Sun 1pm–4:45pm. Closed major holidays.* ♿ ☎609-258-3788. Housed in a modern building behind Picasso's *Head of a Woman*, the museum was founded in 1882 to collect original objects for teaching. The collection's range and diversity are immediately apparent in the **American Painting and Sculpture gallery**, featuring Augustus Saint-Gaudens' *Diana* and *Coming through the Rye* by Frederic Remington. Formal portraits by Rembrandt Peale and John Singleton Copley are nicely balanced by landscapes by William Merritt Chase and George Inness.

The substantial ancient Greek ceramic collection in the lower gallery features the black-figure hydria *Apotheosis of Herakles* (c.530-520 BC) and the large red-figure volute-krater *Medea at Eleusis* (c.330 BC). Reconstructed wall and floor mosaics, many from Princeton's excavations at Antioch in the 1930s, and 2,300-year-old columns provide an authentic backdrop for the **Roman gallery**, featuring a 2C AD Roman sepulchral pediment, sepulchral friezes and fragments, and busts.

The **Asian galleries** trace four millennia of culture through a large collection of bronzes, prints and calligraphy, beginning with a 3,000-year-old bronze *kuang* (wine pitcher) in the form of a dragon. Ornate jade pendants and Tang dynasty Buddhist stelae give way to clay figurines from the Six Dynasties (AD 220-589) and hanging scrolls from the Northern and Southern Sung dynasties (12C AD). Ming and Ch'ing dynasty highlights include Wang E's *Winter in the Mountains* and Wang Hui's *Herd Boy*. Indian and Khmer art, as well as Japanese hanging scrolls from the Kamakura period, round out the assemblage.

European Art galleries on the upper level feature Northern Renaissance works by Peter Paul Rubens and Anthony Van Dyck. A Venetian Renaissance doorway heralds the **Medieval room** containing a stained-glass window from France's Chartres Cathedral and a 16C staircase and balustrade from Majorca, Spain. The **Impressionist gallery** features works by Ingres, Delacroix, Pissarro, Daumier, van Gogh, Degas and Toulouse-Lautrec. Among the 20C artists represented are Kandinsky, Moore, Lehmbruck, Modigliani, O'Keeffe, Rauschenberg, Warhol and Dine. Sculptures sited around the campus include works by Louise Nevelson, Alexander Calder and Jacques Lipchitz.

Additional Sights   ½ *day*

Princeton's modest downtown complements its quiet suburban atmosphere. Colonial and Federal buildings predominate, along with numerous Tudor Revival structures. **Nassau Presbyterian Church** (1836) near the university is an excellent example of Greek Revival architecture. Colonial Revival buildings from the 1930s line **Palmer Square** to the west, while modern structures define the north and east sides. Sculptor Frederick MacMonnies' **Princeton Battle Monument★** located at the end of Nassau Street depicts a cascade of contorted human figures surmounted by a statue of George Washington clutching his mantle.

Bainbridge House (Princeton Historical Society) – *158 Nassau St. Open Mar–Dec Tue–Sun noon–4pm. Rest of the year weekends noon–4pm. Contribution requested.* ♿ *www. princetonol.com* ☎*609-921-6748. The Society offers guided walking tours of Princeton every Sunday at 2pm; tours leave from Bainbridge House.* Built by Job Stockton in 1766, one of the few remaining Georgian homes in town retains its original central hall

Nassau Street, Downtown Princeton

© Scott Barrow

staircase and paneled walls. The home was leased by Dr. Absalom Bainbridge, whose son William was born here in 1774 and became a hero of the War of 1812. The Historical Society took over in 1967 and now offers revolving and permanent exhibits on the history of Princeton, along with a library and gift shop.

Morven – *55 Stockton St. May be closed for renovations in 1998. Call ahead for opening hours* ☎*609-683-1514.* Originally built c.1750 for Richard Stockton III, a signer of the Declaration of Independence, and his wife, poet Annis Boudinot Stockton, the house was a center of social life in the 18C. The current Federal structure dates from the 1790s, with major alterations made by Stockton's grandson Robert in the 1850s. In 1954 Governor Edge and his wife donated the house to the state. It was used as a governor's residence until 1982, when Drumthwacket *(below)* took over that role. Today Morven serves as a house museum.

Princeton Theological Seminary occupies the Federal **Alexander Hall** (1817) on Mercer Street. Nearby, Charles Steadman erected the narrow, two-story white clapboard houses (1834) that line tiny **Alexander Street**. These modest structures with Greek Revival details form a picturesque streetscape. Steadman also designed the 1836 Greek Revival house at 72 Library Place that was home to Woodrow Wilson before he built the Tudor Revival mansion (1882) at no. 82.

Drumthwacket – *354 Stockton St. Visit by guided tour (40min) only, year-round Wed noon–2pm. Closed Aug, Wed before Thanksgiving, Dec 25–Jan. Contribution requested.* ♿ 🅿 ☎*609-924-3044.* A stately example of the Greek Revival style, this white clapboard mansion distinguished by a grand portico was built by Gov. Charles Olden in 1835 and extended in 1893 and 1900 by Moses Taylor Pyne. Weekly guided tours of the manse take in the dining room with its 24-seat table and USS *New Jersey* silver service still used for state dinners; a parlor appointed with 18C antiques, many crafted in New Jersey; and the exuberant Gothic library with stone fireplace and ornate Medieval-style paneling. The tour continues to the governor's oval office and ends in the restored terraced garden.

★ **Princeton Battlefield State Park** – *500 Mercer St. Open year-round daily dawn–dusk.* 🅿 ☎*609-921-0074.* A broad sweep of grassy meadow against thick forest evokes the battlefield where generals George Washington and Hugh Mercer surprised Lord Cornwallis' troops on the morning of January 3, 1777. The Mercer Oak, near where the general lay mortally wounded, stands alone, while across the road, a portico of Ionic columns marks the graves of soldiers who fell that day. Located in the park, the **Thomas Clarke House** sits on land the family settled in 1696 and occupied until purchase by the state in 1946 *(open year-round Wed–Sat 10am–4pm, Sun 1pm–4pm; closed Jan 1, Thanksgiving Day, Dec 25)*. Revolutionary War arms and artifacts, and paintings of the battle are displayed in the 1840s wing of the Clarke House. In the 18C section, the bedroom where Mercer died has been restored. A short walk through the woods reveals the Friends Meeting House and cemetery where patriot Richard Stockton and Gov. Charles Olden are buried.

Delaware and Raritan Canal State Park – *Open year-round daily dawn–dusk.* ⚠ ♿ 🅿 ☎ *732-873-3050. The park's canal paths can be accessed from small parking areas located at regular intervals between the towns of Milford and Trenton.* The 75ft-wide canal opened in 1834 between the Delaware and Raritan Rivers, primarily to transport Pennsylvania coal to New York City. Mule-drawn boats negotiated 14 locks along the 66mi route. Canal traffic peaked in 1871 and the waterway closed in 1933. Listed on the National Register of Historic Places, the canal became a state park in 1973. Park access on Route 27 near Kingston features a lock, lock-tender's house and canoe launch. Rocky Hill *(at Rtes. 518 and 630)* is dotted with the foundations of 18C mills and early quarrying structures. The igneous rock diabase is still quarried along Route 603.

★ **Rockingham** – *Rte. 518 in Rocky Hill. Visit by guided tour (45min) only, year-round Wed–Sat 10am–noon & 1pm–4pm, Sun 1pm–4pm. Call for holiday hours.* 🅿 ☎ *609-921-8835.* Dating back to 1702, the clapboard house served as General Washington's headquarters and home during the final months of the Revolutionary War in 1783. After housing quarry workers in the 19C, the home was acquired by the Rockingham Association and moved twice due to encroaching quarrying. An upcoming third move (in 1999) will place it closer to its original site. The interior depicts the time when George and Martha Washington lived here.

Tours begin in the dining room, which is set for a meal with typical 18C tearing forks, marrow spoons and curving flat knives. Walls are hung with *papyrotamia*, or cut-paper silhouettes (a popular folk craft at the time), representing an exquisitely detailed 1780s village landscape. The parlor reveals the home's post-and-beam construction. Upstairs, the **study**★ is furnished with a writing table, quills, a whale-oil lamp, a chandelier and a clock, as it was when Washington wrote his farewell orders to his troops.

SOUTHWESTERN NEW JERSEY★

Map p 172
Tourist Information ☎ 609-825-6800

Mild winters and a long growing season on the southern Delaware River Valley fostered an agricultural hinterland that fed early settlers and is still known as the "Garden Spot of the Garden State." This area yields $500 million of produce a year, notably tomatoes, asparagus, blueberries, peaches and cranberries. Pioneered by Swedish and Finnish farmers, settlement began in earnest with the 1675 establishment of John Fenwick's Quaker colony, centered around the towns of Salem and Greenwich. The first successful glassworks in America was created in Salem County in 1739, soon joined by iron foundries and a penchant for freedom that pushed the colony into the heart of the Revolutionary War. Coastal regions today provide rare habitat and natural beauty in a series of parks and preserves, while the interior is punctuated by historic towns.

★ **SALEM** *2hrs*

The first Quaker colony in North America and the first permanent English-speaking settlement on the Delaware was founded by John Fenwick, who had purchased the "Salem Tenth" of New Jersey and named it for the Hebrew word for peace. He signed a treaty with Lenni Lenape tribesmen under an oak tree at Salem town in 1675 and planned the sister town of Greenwich along the coast. The early success of the West Jersey settlements served as an incentive to fellow Quaker William Penn *(p 222)*, who founded Philadelphia in 1682. Fenwick died in 1683, unsure of the success of his colony, but it sprung to life with settlement, industry and agriculture, growing in tandem with Philadelphia during the 18C. Along Broadway and Market Streets, Salem reveals layers of history that reach from the trunk of the Salem Oak through decorous 19C homes to modern government buildings.

★★ **Salem County Historical Society (Alexander Grant House)** – *79-83 Market St. Visit by guided tour (1hr 30min) only, year-round Tue–Fri noon–4pm & 2nd Sat of each month noon–4pm. Closed major holidays. $3. www.salemcount.com//historicalsociety* ☎*609-935-5004.* Alexander Grant built the Flemish pattern-brick house in 1721, incorporating a c.1690 structure in the rear. Acquired by the Historical Society in 1929, the house today is furnished with local collections to reflect a Salem home from the 1690s to the mid-19C. The museum also includes the attached Rumsey Wing (c.1790); the tiny octagonal **John Jones Law Office** (c.1735)—the oldest law office in the country; and a modern **barn**, which holds collections of farm implements, guns, carriages, maritime items and the H.J. Heinz cane collection.

The dining room in the 1721 residence displays 18C imported Canton and Staffordshire china. The main parlor's walls exhibit original paneling, and furnishings include a finely wrought Quaker chest-on-chest and a tall-case clock with music-box movement. In the rear 1690s house, a restored **keeping room** with the original hearth features a 17C chair that belonged to William Penn.

The large parlor of the 1790s edifice features changing exhibits. Second-floor rooms display specialized collections including toys, dolls and samplers. One room showcases items made by pioneering Salem County glassmaker Caspar Wistar *(p 208)*, while the costume collection features the dress Sarah Hancock Sinnickson wore to George Washington's first inaugural ball.

Other notable structures on Market Street include the Goodwin Sisters House *(private)* at no. 14, an Underground Railroad station with original 1821 clapboards, and the William Sharp House *(private)* at no. 31, an 1862 Italianate mansion. The **New Johnson Hall** (1806) at 94 Market Street was built by Col. Robert Gibbon Johnson, founder of the county agricultural society. Located next to 15 Market Street stands a reconstructed Swedish "survivor's" cabin and garden, typical of the type of housing built by settlers in the Delaware Valley in the mid-17C.

Guarded by the 500-year-old **Salem Oak** where Fenwick met with Indians in 1675, the Friends Burial Ground lies two blocks west of Market on Broadway. The Friends Meeting House (1772) is the oldest religious assembly in the state; note the twin entrances, locally made glass windows and pattern-brick gables.

Fort Mott State Park – *6mi northwest of Salem on Ft. Mott Rd. Open Memorial Day–Labor Day daily 8am–7:30pm. Rest of the year daily 8am–4pm. Closed Jan 1, Thanksgiving Day, Dec 25.* ☎*609-339-9702.* A pleasant drive west of Salem leads past the Finns Point Rear Range Light—an unusual, cylindrical, steel lighthouse—to the state park's entrance. Here, an ordnance building serves as a visitor center offering brochures, nature exhibits and a video on the New Jersey Coastal Heritage Trail *(below)*. Designed in 1872 as part of an elaborate system of coastal forts on the Delaware River, the original Ft. Mott was never completed. Revamped in 1896 in anticipation of the Spanish-American War, the fort never saw action and became a military reservation until 1947, when it was acquired by the state. Today a self-guided walking tour runs along the grounds and up to a 20ft-high, 750ft-long concrete-and-earth parapet, affording views from bunkers and gun emplacements. Interpretive panels describe disappearing gun carriages, ruined communications rooms and other features of the coastal defense system.

A small road leads to **Finns Point National Cemetery**, where 2,436 Confederate prisoners of war are buried under an obelisk of rusticated stone. More than 130 Union soldiers are interred along with veterans of numerous other wars, including 13 German POWs of World War II. The bucolic setting has been a National Cemetery since 1875.

> ■ **New Jersey Coastal Heritage Trail**
>
> Established by federal legislation in 1988, the trail promotes the interpretation and protection of significant natural and cultural resources on New Jersey's coast. Coastal Heritage Trail is a public/private partnership among the National Park Service, the State of New Jersey, and local communities and organizations that seek to manage and promote maritime history, waterfowl habitats and historic sites dating back to the first European contact in the New World. Attractions are marked with freestanding interpretive panels describing their historical and cultural significance. Regional welcome centers such as the one at Ft. Mott *(above)* provide more detailed information about sites along the trail.

Hancock House – *5mi south of Salem off Rte. 49. House is undergoing renovation, call for schedule.* ▯ ☎609-339-9702. This 1734 pattern-brick house exemplifies the style favored by Quaker colonists in the first half of the 18C: narrow gabled structures ornamented with zigzag patterning using vitrified bricks. The design included the date of construction and the owners' initials, in this case William and Sarah Thompson Hancock. The house made history on March 21, 1778, when American patriots were massacred here by the British in retaliation for their loss at nearby Quinton's Bridge.

BRIDGETON 2hrs

Quaker Richard Hancock built a sawmill and housing for workers on the bank of the Cohansey River in 1686, and in 1716 a bridge was erected over the river. Bridge Town prospered, owing to early industry, and became the county seat in 1749. It was a hotbed of patriotism in the 1770s, firing off broadsides and ringing the "South Jersey Liberty Bell" in celebration of the 1776 signing of the Declaration of Independence. An 1816 misspelling led to the present name, and by 1838 the town claimed some 475 buildings and 2,400 inhabitants. Industry grew throughout the 19C, and today the city boasts the state's largest historic district numbering 2,200 homes *(self-guided walking tours available from the Tourist Center at 50 E. Broad St.; open Apr–Sept Mon–Fri 9am–4pm, weekends & holidays 10am–4pm; rest of the year Mon–Fri 9am–4pm; & ▯ ☎609-451-4551 or 800-319-3379).*

Visit – Key historic buildings line Broad Street *(Rte. 49)*, from the 1792 gabled **Old Broad Street Church**★—a tribute to Georgian architecture—to the towering 1909 County Courthouse, which displays the **South Jersey Liberty Bell** in its lobby. The *Plain Dealer*, a patriotic broadside, was published in 1775-76 in the diminutive stone-and-frame **Potter's Tavern** (1767-68) at no. 49. Commerce Street includes the 1834 Greek Revival Dr. William Elmer House at no. 65, the David Sheppard House at no. 31 (1791), and the Seven Sisters, a row of commercial structures near the bridge. The George Woodruff Museum of Indian Artifacts *(150 E. Commerce St.)*, located in the town library, contains more than 20,000 Lenni Lenape artifacts. Larger historic homes lie west of Atlantic Avenue on the hill.

Bridgeton City Park encompasses 1,100-acres including two lakes; a relocated 19C school; the state's oldest zoo; and the **New Sweden Farmstead Museum** *(open May–Sept Sat 11am–4pm, Sun noon–4pm; $3; ▯ ☎609-455-9785)*, a reconstructed 1638 Swedish log cabin settlement. The Cumberland Iron and Nail Company office (1815) now houses the small **Nail Mill Museum** *(open Apr–Dec Tue–Fri 10:30am–3:30pm, weekends 11am–4pm; ▯ ☎609-455-4100)*, featuring local memorabilia and displays on glass and nail manufacturing.

★ GREENWICH 1hr

From Rte. 49 in Bridgeton drive south on Rte. 618 for 6mi, then bear left on Rte. 607. Continue on Rte. 650 (Cohansey Rd.) to Rte. 623, which is Ye Greate St. in Greenwich.

John Fenwick planned this sleepy village as a twin to Salem and laid out the 100ft-wide street that remains a compelling tribute to Colonial ambition. A principal port, whaling center and shipbuilding town, Greenwich (pronouced "GREEN-witch") was the site of a 1774 "tea party," when county patriots disguised as Indians burned a cargo of British tea. A sympathetic jury acquitted the Tea Burners in 1775, and one of the group's members became governor in 1792. The 1909 **Tea Burners Monument** commemorates the event.

East on Ye Greate Street stands the Georgian Friends Meeting House (1771), a fine example of the plain Quaker style with typical dual entrances. Also of note are the Richard Wood House, a 1686 gambrel-roof structure, the 1720 Bond House and the 1893 Kubler Bakery.

★ **Cumberland County Historical Society (Gibbon House)** – *Ye Greate St. Open Apr– mid-Dec Tue–Sat noon–4pm, Sun 2pm–5pm.* ▯ ☎609-455-4055. Built in 1730 by shipowner and merchant Nicholas Gibbon, the pattern-brick house remained in the Wood family 200 years before it was purchased by the Historical Society in 1968. Tours led by docents begin in the sitting room, with its original mantel, paneling and Gibbon's cyphering book. The dining room features restored portraits of Gibbon and his wife and cabinets laden with Canton china. Upstairs bedrooms exhibit locally made ladder-back rush-bottom chairs, along with samplers and toys dating back to the 18C. A glass case displays the well-preserved **figurehead** of the *St. John*, sunk here in 1797. In the rear of the house, a restored Swedish log **granary** (c.1650) is the oldest structure in the county.

Across the street, the John Dubois Maritime Museum *(open Sundays only)* presents artifacts from Greenwich's shipbuilding past.

★ **WHEATON VILLAGE** *2hrs*
1501 Glasstown Rd., Millville. Open Apr–Dec daily 10am–5pm. Rest of the year Wed–Sun 10am–5pm. Closed Jan 1, Easter Sunday, Thanksgiving Day, Dec 25. $6.50. ✗ ♿ ▣ www.wheatonvillage.org ☎609-825-6800 or 800-998-4552.

Druggist T.C. Wheaton came to Millville in 1883 and soon began manufacturing pharmaceutical and medical glassware, founding the T.C. Wheaton Glass Co. in 1892. By 1918 he employed 450 persons in a 20-acre plant. His son, Frank Wheaton, Sr., succeeded him in 1931 and remained on the board until his death in 1983 at the age of 102. Grandson Frank Jr. oversaw the expansion of Wheaton Industries to a multinational firm with 40 divisions. In 1970 he donated 88 acres for the creation of the Wheaton Village as well as the museum's initial glassware collection.

Visit – A wide, tree-lined boulevard connects the fourteen buildings that make up this re-created glassmaking community. To the right of the entrance, the **T.C. Wheaton Glass Factory**, a replica of the 1888 glass factory, offers glassmaking demonstrations in an amphitheater surrounding the kilns. The furnace runs 24hrs a day at temperatures above 2,000°F. *(Visitors can make a glass paperweight by appointment; call ☎609-825-6800, ext. 2754; $45 fee.)* The **Craft and Trades Buildings** feature artisans creating pottery, glass marbles and decoys. Other highlights include a tinsmith shop, the half-scale C.P. Huntington train and the 1876 Centre Grove schoolhouse. The left side of the village is composed of shops open to the public, including the Gallery of American Crafts, the evocative Victorian general store and a working stained-glass studio and gallery.

★★ **Museum of American Glass** – Showcase of the village is this comprehensive compendium of glass, housed in a replica Cape May hotel. The lavish Victorian lobby leads to 10 successive galleries displaying some 7,500 objects. Exhibits in the first gallery describe 18C glassmaking and illustrate the production of window glass by the English (bull's-eye) and German (broad) methods *(below)*. Adjacent space focuses on 19C bottles for cologne, smelling salts, proprietary medicines, whiskey and pharmaceuticals. Farther on, note the early art glasses created by heat activation, layering, and the addition of gold, silver, uranium and mercury oxides, and the display of household items such as Mason jars, oil lamps and light bulbs. The history of Wheaton's glass company is narrated through examples of the firm's glassware and "end-of-day" pieces like canes, chain links and bells. In the **Gallery of American Paperweights**, displays celebrate a 150-year-old design tradition with modern and historic paperweights, including the renowned Millville Rose, a red "rose" encased in glass. Don't miss the "World's Largest Bottle," capable of holding 188 gallons.

■ **Glassmaking in South Jersey**

"Down in Southern New Jersey they make glass. By day and by night, the fires burn on in Millville and bid the sand let in the light"—Carl Sandburg

In defiance of the British prohibition on Colonial manufacturing, **Caspar Wistar** started making glass in Alloway, New Jersey in 1739. The region proved ideal for the manufacture of glass because of its fine silica sand, crushed shells for lime, ash, abundant water power and timber fuel. A staple manufacture, glass windowpanes were produced by the German broad method of blowing a large cylinder to be cut in half and flattened, or the English bull's-eye method where glass is blown as a large flattened bowl. Experienced glassblowers also created a variety of drinking glasses and bottles for everything from perfume and liquor to mineral water and medicine, as well as whimsical pieces like canes, horns and linked chains. In 1852 Millville saw the creation of the American glass paperweight. It was here that glassmaking eventually came into the Industrial Age as glassblowers were replaced by mechanical glass-pressing machines and molds. Today the industry survives in modern facilities, a growing art-glass movement and the collections of local historical museums. Visitors can learn the ancient art of glassblowing and make a paperweight at Wheaton Village *(above)*, thereby reviving one of South Jersey's definitive craft industries.

TRENTON

Population 85,437
Maps p 172 and p 210
Tourist Information ☎609-777-1771

Situated at a fall in the Delaware River that required early travelers to portage their boats and cargo, Trenton grew into an industrial power and became the state capital in 1790. Approaches to the city betray the seamy effects of urban decay; nevertheless, Trenton remains home to important historic sites and cultural attractions. A short drive west of town lies the site of General Washington's historic crossing of the Delaware River in 1776. And some 17mi to the southwest, Burlington draws tourists to its quaint streets and fascinating historical museum.

Historical Notes

The falls of the Delaware were first harnessed with a grain mill built by Mahlon Stacy and a group of Yorkshire Quakers in 1679. In 1714 Philadelphia trader **William Trent** bought 800 acres from Stacy's son for a mill and summer home. He soon doubled his holdings and in 1721 laid out the streets and lots of "Trent's town." Trent died in 1724, but the city blossomed as an early industrial center and port on the Delaware. Its pivotal role in the Revolutionary War led the Continental Congress to briefly consider Trenton for the national capital in 1784. Topped by a statue of George Washington, the Battle Monument—a 155ft fluted granite column (*N. Broad and Warren Sts.*) erected in 1893—marks the spot where the general trained his guns on the Hessians during the Battle of Trenton.

During the 19C, Trenton was home to major manufactories. Colonial pottery evolved into "trent tile," and the city was known as the "Staffordshire of America." Thomas Maddock, a Trenton potter, produced the first porcelain toilet in America, and Woodrow Wilson—a former governor of New Jersey—brought Lenox china to the White House. In 1847 Peter Cooper built an ironworks here that produced the world's first I-beams capable of bearing loads for buildings higher than three stories. He was joined the following year by the John A. Roebling Co., which designed and built the 1883 Brooklyn Bridge and engineered bridges nationwide, including the George Washington in New York and the Golden Gate in San Francisco, before being absorbed by a conglomerate in the 1950s. Local rubber industries grew along with pioneering, open-hearth steelmakers Cooper-Hewitt, and by the early 20C, the motto "What Trenton Makes, the World Takes" was coined.

The city also developed as a cultural crossroads, with immigrants from Western Europe followed in the post-Civil War years by Eastern Europeans and in the 1920s by African Americans from the South. Recent Hispanic and Asian immigrations have created vibrant cultural enclaves throughout the city, though late-20C decline has left portions of the community impoverished and desolate.

SIGHTS ½ day (not including guided visit of State House). Map p 210.

A good starting point for a visit to the state capital is the Trenton Convention & Visitors Bureau, housed in the Old Masonic Lodge (1793) at the corner of Barrack and Lafayette Streets (*open year-round daily 10am–4pm; closed Jan 1, Jul 4, Thanksgiving Day, Dec 25; trentonnj.com ☎609-777-1771; 2hr guided walking tours offered Apr–Oct Sun 1pm; $7*). From here, a short walk north on Barrack leads to West State Street, a wide, pleasant avenue lined with an eclectic assortment of town houses, home to Trenton's wealthy elite during the late 19C.

★ **New Jersey State Museum** – *205 W. State St. Open year-round Tue–Sat 9am–4:45pm, Sun noon–5pm. Closed major holidays.* ♿ ▯ *www.state.nj.us/state/museum/musidx.html* ☎609-984-0676. This stark, modern building encompasses four floors of exhibits ranging from ancient archaeology to modern art, culled from the museum's collection of more than two million artifacts. Extending from the first-floor lobby, a spacious gallery is devoted to changing exhibits, with an emphasis on New Jersey, American and minority artists. Walk down to the basement to view the small planetarium (*$1 admission*), the Sisler collection of North American mammals and an intriguing assemblage of cultural and ceremonial artifacts from New Jersey's Delaware Indians. Displays dating from the Woodland period (c.1000) include pottery vessels in all shapes and sizes and describe the changing climate and shoreline of New Jersey through the pre-Columbian period.

On the second floor, fascinating exhibits on dinosaurs and other fossil treasures highlight the Hall of Natural Sciences; dioramas of New Jersey ecosystems from suburbs and seashore to pine barrens and mountains round out the natural history collection. The **Fine Arts Galleries** display American art since the 1930s, including works by George Segal, Louise Nevelson, Georgia O'Keeffe, Richard Hunt and Sam Gilliam.

Thomas Eakins bronze bas-reliefs depicting Revolutionary War scenes ornament the second-floor landing. Located on the second and third floors, the excellent **Decorative Arts Galleries**★ feature Jersey furniture, from the familiar country ladder-back rush-bottom chairs to high-style Chippendale pieces. One 1870s Jelliff armchair is refinished to show the restoration process, while another is cut away to illustrate horsehair upholstery. Additional galleries on the third floor feature local ceramics, silver and glassware, as well as prints, sculpture and paintings.

New Jersey State House – *125 W. State St. Open Jul–Aug Mon–Fri 10am–3pm, Sat noon–3pm. Rest of the year Tue–Wed & Fri 10am–3pm, Sat noon–3pm. Rooms may be closed periodically for legislative purposes. Closed major holidays.* ♿ 🅿 ☎*609-633-2709. Pick up a self-guided walking-tour brochure at the front desk or take a guided tour (call ahead to make reservations).* The second-oldest state capitol in continuous use in the US, this grandiose structure has borne witness to state politics for more than two centuries. The original Neoclassical building (1792) was enlarged in the 1840s by John Notman, who added a rotunda, dome and cupola. Further renovations in the late 19C and early 20C included the addition of wings for the state legislature and private offices for the governor. Today the gray limestone facade centers on a portico of six marble Corinthian columns, flanked by pedimented windows, pilasters and detailed fretwork. The interior features a dramatic stained-glass ceiling and an impressive art collection, period rooms and historical exhibits. Located next door, the State House Annex (1930) is a five-story, U-shaped building designed to match its Neoclassical parent with rusticated stone and Ionic columns.

★★ **Trent House** – *15 Market St. Visit by guided tour (1hr) only, year-round daily 12:30pm–4pm. Closed major holidays. $2.50.* 🅿 ☎*609-989-3027.* Built by wealthy Philadelphian William Trent as a summer home, this early (1719) and excellent example of Georgian architecture features a central hall plan, patterned Flemish

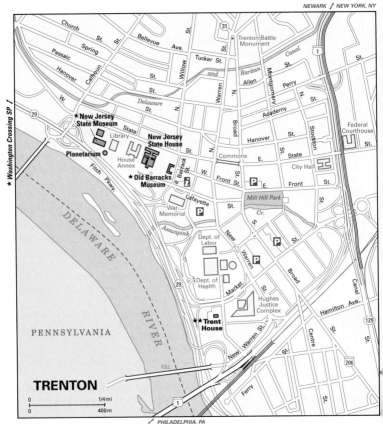

NEWARK / NEW YORK, NY

TRENTON

0   1/4 mi
0   400 m

PHILADELPHIA, PA

bond brick, 12-over-12 windows and an octagonal cupola. Donated to the city in 1929, the structure has been restored and furnished according to an original 1726 household inventory. Knowledgeable guides enhance the visit by offering fascinating insight into early Colonial life.

Tours begin in the drawing room, used for entertaining guests, and continue to the library; note the Bible box located near a window, a precaution in Colonial times in case fire broke out. The dining room features everyday pewter dinnerware and a lovely sharkskin and red velvet knife box. Upstairs rooms include a sitting room (note the Dutch Delft tiles on the fireplace); the master bedroom, which accommodated the entire family with a cradle and trundle bed in addition to the main rope bed; and a guest room furnished with a "necessary chair" and a lovely Dutch *kas* with wooden hinges.

★ **Old Barracks Museum** – *Barrack St. Visit by guided tour (45min) only, year-round daily 10am–5pm. Closed Jan 1, Easter Sunday, Thanksgiving Day, Dec 25. $2.* 🄿 *www.voicenet.com/barracks* ☎609-396-1776. Built in 1758 by the Colony of New Jersey for George II during the French and Indian War, these unfortified urban barracks were designed to replace the practice of quartering soldiers in colonists' homes. George III quartered Hessian mercenaries here in late 1776 when Washington attacked and defeated them at the **Battle of Trenton** *(p 212).* Converted into a rooming house after the war, the building was bisected by a road in the 18C, thereby razing a 40ft section of the U-shaped barracks. This section was rebuilt after 1917 when the state acquired and restored the structure. The original courtyard and cedar-shingle roofing have been restored to better approximate the barracks' original form.

Old Barracks Museum

Docent-led tours include the brick **officers' quarters**, built in 1759. A table set with silver, pewter and bone, and a bedroom outfitted with horsehair trunks and a canopy bed illustrate the comfortable life led by the aristocratic officers. Lowly enlisted men were housed in the adjacent **large barracks** inside 2ft-thick stone walls; here soldiers slept on straw or worse. During the Revolutionary War the barracks served as a hospital. Re-created period rooms on the first floor contain primitive hospital items used at a time when the majority of war casualties were caused by diseases such as smallpox. Additional displays in the barracks interpret the Revolutionary War with special emphasis on the critical battles of Trenton and Princeton.

EXCURSIONS *Map p 172.*

★ **Washington Crossing State Park** – *1hr. 8mi northwest of Trenton on Rte. 29, then northeast on Rte. 546. Open Memorial Day–Labor Day daily 8am–8pm. Rest of the year daily 8am–4:30pm. $3/car (Memorial Day–Labor Day weekends & holidays).* ♿ 🄿 ☎609-737-0623. This 841-acre park's importance stems from the dramatic river crossing that Gen. George Washington engineered here on Christmas night, 1776. An informative **visitor center** details the events surrounding the crossing and the pivotal battles of Trenton and Princeton with a collection of nearly 900 Revolutionary War artifacts *(open year-round Wed–Sun 9am–4:30pm, holiday hours may vary;* ♿ ☎609-737-9303).

From the visitor center you can walk historic Continental Lane to the **Johnson Ferry House**, a stone structure that served as Washington's New Jersey command post after the stormy trip of the Continental troops *(open year-round Wed–Sat 10am–4pm, Sun 1pm–4pm, holiday hours may vary;* ☎*609-737-2515)*. Today the structure reflects the style and furnishings of an 18C Dutch farmhouse. Located nearby, the Arboretum Overlook affords pleasant views of the Delaware River and Washington Crossing Historic Park *(p 260)* on the Pennsylvania shore.

West of Route 29 on the banks of the river, the actual crossing site—originally called Johnson's Ferry—features the small Nelson House.

■ **Ten Days That Changed the Revolution:**
December 25, 1776 to January 3, 1777

After a successful beginning, the American Revolution started losing steam in 1776. The British had taken New York and driven Washington's army out of New Jersey. Demoralized, Washington's ragtag troops retreated across the Delaware to Bucks County, Pennsylvania, on December 8. Five days later, Lords Howe and Cornwallis, confident that victory was at hand, established winter quarters for their forces, including 1,500 Hessians barracked at Trenton.

Most of Washington's 5,500 men were under contract only to the end of the year, and they were ready to go home. Poorly clad and ill fed, the troops suffered in the harsh Pennsylvania cold, and desertions were common. Realizing that the Continentals must score a victory to bolster morale, Washington devised a bold scheme to attack the Hessian troops in nearby Trenton when they would least expect it—on Christmas Day. Braving the ice-choked river and a sudden fierce snowstorm, Washington led his division of 2,400 men across the river at McConkey's Ferry *(p 260)* on Christmas night, but the storm prevented the two supporting divisions from making the crossing. Despite the lack of reinforcements, Washington and his troops surprised the Hessians the following morning, setting up 18 cannons on the hill and quickly routing the enemy. The Hessians suffered 106 casualties while only four Americans, including Lt. James Monroe (the future American president) were wounded.

Washington recrossed the river the same day with 900 prisoners of war, returning to occupy Trenton on December 28. This much-needed victory allowed him to borrow money and offer bonuses to keep his troops enlisted for 10 more days. With 5,000 soldiers, Washington occupied the south bank of Assunpink Creek at Trenton. Cornwallis advanced with 8,000 troops on January 2, 1777, but failed in three attempts to cross the creek and resolved to "bag the fox in the morning." Meanwhile, Washington slipped out of Trenton under cover of darkness and advanced to Princeton, joining Gen. Hugh Mercer and engaging the British rear guard on January 3. Bayoneted seven times, Mercer refused to leave the field until the battle was won. Washington took Princeton, achieving his first victory over British regulars and concluding a 10-day campaign that salvaged a flagging revolution.

★ **Burlington** – *2hrs. 17mi southwest of Trenton via Rte. 295 to Rte. 130 South.* Belgian Walloons came to Burlington Island in 1624, followed by Dutch, Finns and Swedes, before the town was permanently settled by English Quakers in 1677 as the capital of West Jersey. The city was a center of the textile industry and retains a high degree of historic integrity.

Broad and High Streets – A premier example of the Gothic Revival style, **New St. Mary's Episcopal Church★** (1854) was designed by architect Richard Upjohn. The square Norman central tower, pierced by arched windows and supported with stone buttresses, rises up from the surrounding cemetery, in romantic contrast to the original 1703 Colonial church next door. The **Boudinot-Bradford House** (1804) at 207 Broad Street was the home of Elias Boudinot—president of the Continental Congress—and his son-in-law William Bradford. Farther north, on High Street, the 1785 **Friends Meeting House** replaced a century-old octagonal structure and continues to serve city Quakers. In 1916 Temple B'nai Israel reworked the 1801 Federal mansion at no. 212 into an attractive house of worship. The 1839 Neoclassical **City Hall** at no. 432 features 1812 War hero Captain James Lawrence's *(p 213)* dictum, "Don't Give Up the Ship," inscribed in the pediment.

★ **Burlington County Historical Society** – *457 High St. Visit by guided tour (1hr 30min) only, year-round Mon–Thu 1pm–4pm, Sun 2pm–4pm. Closed major holidays. $5.* 🅿 *www.bc.emanon.net/org/bchs* ☎609-386-4773. This complex consists of three historic homes on High Street, a library and a fascinating museum, all providing an excellent introduction to South Jersey history and culture. Informative guided tours begin in the **James Fenimore Cooper House** (c.1780), where the author of *The Last of the Mohicans* and other frontier classics was born in 1789. Plastic panels outline the original wall and fireplace of the front rooms, which are decorated with a Cooper family chair and a portrait of the author. A second-floor bedroom commemorates Joseph Bonaparte, who lived in nearby Bordentown from 1817 to 1836. The tour continues into the attached **Captain James Lawrence House** (1742) with a narration of the early life of this American naval officer and his heroism during the War of 1812. Family artifacts include a desk and settee, a portrait and surveying tools. The handsome Georgian, pattern-brick **Bard-How House** (c.1743) has been restored with period furnishings to illustrate Colonial life; pieces include a rare writing desk with an enlarged arm, and a Burlington tall-case clock.

Behind the houses, the Corson Poley Center contains the Society's library and a spacious, modern **museum★**, which displays a substantial collection of artifacts ranging from the Colonial era through the early 20C. Galleries first include a bicycle and doctor's surrey, then a large assemblage of locally manufactured tall-case clocks, followed by an attractive display of Burlington County quilts and samplers dating from the 1790s.

Introduction to Pennsylvania

Roughly describing a rectangle with a jagged eastern edge, Pennsylvania became known as the Keystone State for its central position among the 13 original colonies and its key role as a political, economic and cultural leader. Pennsylvania's neighbors include six states and one of the Great Lakes. The state's northern border is formed by New York and a 40mi pod of land along Lake Erie; on the west Pennsylvania is bounded by Ohio and West Virginia; and to the south are West Virginia, Maryland and Delaware. New Jersey and New York lie to the east. Two major focal points, PHILADELPHIA and PITTSBURGH, define the state's eastern and western reaches. The former city forms part of the seaboard megalopolis stretching from Boston to Washington, DC, and the latter constitutes the shoulder of a westward-thrusting arm of industrial centers. Though at an area of 45,026sq mi the state ranks only 33rd in size, a population of just over 12 million makes Pennsylvania the nation's fifth most populous state.

Pennsylvania State Facts

Capital: Harrisburg
Land Area: 45,026 square miles
Population: 12,040,084
Nickname: Keystone State
Motto: Virtue, Liberty and Independence
State Flower: Mountain Laurel
State Bird: Ruffed Grouse

Geographical Notes

Geologic Past – During the Carboniferous period, starting some 365 million years ago, the land mass that would form the continent of North America lay just south of the equator, a position to which it had drifted over the aeons. The hot, steamy environment of that early location created swamps rife with vegetation throughout the area that is now Pennsylvania. Preserved in water, dead vegetation formed layers of peat, which compacted as flooding rivers and a rising sea level laid sediments over it. Then a new layer of peat would form, get squeezed down by more overlying sediments, and so on. Over time this pressurized peat turned into a carbon compound called coal—more than 100 veins stacked between layers of sandstone, shale and clay. From these rich deposits, Pennsylvania has supplied 20 percent of the country's bituminous (soft) coal and nearly all the anthracite (hard) coal over the past 200 years. The state now holds about seven percent of the nation's coal reserves, enough to last another three centuries at the current rate of use.

More recent geological history has been marked by periods of erosion and glaciation that have sculpted the state's present topography. In the most recent Ice Age, ending 10,000 years ago, glaciers crept down into the northern part of the state, scouring hilltops and deepening valleys.

Regional Landscapes – Pennsylvania's variegated land *(map p 15)* holds seven distinct physiographic provinces. The slender **Atlantic Coastal Plain** in the state's extreme southeast corner is part of the same low-lying, flat system that stretches from New York to Florida. Taking in a wider swath of the southeast, the adjacent **Piedmont Plateau** includes the limestone-enriched farmlands of Lancaster, Montgomery, Chester and Bucks counties. Rolling hills and gentle valleys characterize this region. The northern tip of the **Blue Ridge** extends just over the Maryland state line into south-central Pennsylvania near GETTYSBURG; its hills and mountains helped determine the course of the decisive Civil War battle. Another small region, the **Reading Prong**, is part of the New England Upland, here forming a narrow ridge that runs athwart Berks, Bucks, Lehigh and Northampton counties.

One of the state's most distinctive landscapes, the **Appalachian Ridge and Valley** curves in a broad band from the northeast down to the south-central section; viewed from overhead, its long, thin ridges and valleys look as if a great claw had raked parallel scars across the land. Though impressive to geologists, the region proved a labyrinth for early wayfarers, many of whom followed the Great Valley along the region's southern border, down to Maryland and Virginia. Covering more than half the state, the **Appalachian Plateau** spreads across northern and western Pennsylvania and wears a more rugged aspect than the Ridge and Valley region. Its broad tablelands and deep, narrow valleys are punctuated by glacial boulders in the north and forested highlands in the south—the state's highest point, Mt. Davis, rises 3,213ft near the Maryland border. The flat **Erie-Ontario Lowland** borders Lake Erie in the northwest corner of the state; its sandy soil provides fertile ground for grape growing.

Climate – Pennsylvania's climate varies only slightly from region to region, with average January temperatures ranging from 26°F (-3°C) in the northwest to 34°F (1°C) in the southeast and July temperatures rising from 70°F (21°C) in the northwest to 77°F (25°C) in the southeast. A relatively moist state, Pennsylvania averages 41 inches of precipitation a year, the highest amount falling in the southeastern part of the state.

Historical Notes

First Settlers – At the time of European arrival, the area that became Pennsylvania was inhabited by a number of Indian nations, among them the Lenni Lenape (or Delaware Indians), the Susquehannocks, the Shawnee and various Iroquois tribes. One of these groups, the peaceful Lenni Lenape ("the Real People") lived in small bands spread throughout what is now eastern Pennsylvania, New Jersey and southeastern New York, reaching as far afield as parts of Delaware and Connecticut.

Though the colony was eventually settled by peace-loving Quakers, relations with the natives inevitably soured, so that by 1790 only 1,000 Indians remained in a state that once claimed 20,000. Whites in 1790 numbered more than 400,000. The first known European to step on Pennsylvania soil was a Dutch sea captain named Cornelius Mey *(p 191)*, who landed along the lower Delaware River in 1614. Scores of explorers followed, and the first permanent Pennsylvania settlement occurred in 1643 when 400-pound governor Johann Prinz (called "Big Tub of Guts" by the Lenni Lenape) moved his band of Swedish settlers upriver from the site of present-day Wilmington, Delaware. Meanwhile, the governor of New Netherland, Peter Stuyvesant, grew worried about his new neighbors and led an expedition to the fledgling settlement in 1655. The Swedish flag came down, the Dutch went up. But in less than ten years, another flag would be raised and remain dominant for more than a century: The English had arrived.

Penn's Woods – At the age of 37, Englishman **William Penn** (1644-1718) persuaded King Charles II to grant him a tract of North America to pay off a debt the king owed Penn's deceased father. A Quaker, Penn had dreamed of a "holy experiment" where people could govern themselves, own property and worship as they pleased. The king offered Penn 50,000sq mi and insisted, to honor Penn's father, that the new colony incorporate his family name. Pennsylvania ("Penn's woods") was thus born in England in 1681. Full of bold plans and ideas, Penn arrived in the New World the following year, established Philadelphia, and held a general assembly. He also signed a friendship treaty with the Lenni Lenape and paid them for their land—moves that smoothed the way for his colony. French philosopher and writer Voltaire called the pact "the only treaty never sworn to" (Quakers were forbidden to swear)—"and never broken."

Thousands of settlers poured into the new colony in the next few decades, lured by the hope of a better way of life. Pennsylvania became a promised land for religious dissenters of every stripe—Quakers, French Huguenots, Scotch-Irish Protestants and more. In and around Philadelphia, fine examples of red-brick Friends meetinghouses and 18C homes in the popular Georgian Colonial style remain as testimony that the early settlers were serious about putting down roots. Along with the English and French came the German-speaking sects—Mennonites, Amish, Dunkards, Pietists, Lutherans, Moravians, Harmonists— enough German-speakers to compose nearly half of the state's population by the mid-18C. The Medieval-style, stone-and-timber buildings they erected in Bethlehem, Ephrata, York and other places endure.

Peace Shattered – While settlement was proceeding apace in eastern Pennsylvania, trouble was brewing in the west. A chain of French forts along Lake Erie's south shore raised British hackles in the colonies. Given that the pacifist Quakers refused to intervene, the governor of Virginia took matters into his own hands and sent 21-year-old provincial major George Washington to the frontier in 1753. In May of the following year, a 15-minute skirmish near present-day Pittsburgh ignited the protracted **French and Indian War**. Shortly thereafter, the British suffered a humiliating defeat at FORT NECESSITY. Not until 1758 did British forces gain the upper hand and succeed in routing the French from the Pennsylvania territory. Even so, France's Indian allies under Ottawa chief Pontiac continued to trouble settlers until the British squelched the Indians in 1763 at Bushy Run. French and British claims to the area were resolved that same year when, under the terms of the **Treaty of Paris**, France ceded to Great Britain Canada and all its territories east of the Mississippi River.

Reeling financially after the war, Britain decided to raise money by increasing taxes in America. Though governor John Penn (a grandson of William) was staunchly Loyalist, others in Pennsylvania sided with the movement for independence, and the first and second Continental Congresses convened in Philadelphia in 1774 and 1775. With the Revolutionary War well under way, Congress adopted the **Declaration of Independence** on July 4, 1776, in the Pennsylvania State House in Philadelphia.

By September the British had captured the new capital, forcing Congress to retreat to YORK. Pennsylvania became the ground of early British victories, including gruesome massacres near Philadelphia and Wilkes-Barre. During the so-called Paoli Massacre in 1777, British soldiers showed no mercy with their bayonets, slaughtering about 300 men; the following year, British and Indians swarmed upon settlers in the Wyoming Valley near Wilkes-Barre, killing more than 200 men, women and children, and spreading fear throughout the region. The Patriots were further crippled by the grim winter of 1777-78 that claimed 3,000 soldiers at VALLEY FORGE. Its mettle tested and its resolve strengthened, America went on to triumph over the British five years later, and in 1787 Philadelphia hosted the historic convention that produced the US Constitution. The city served as the nation's capital until 1800.

Pittsburgh (1845), Woodcut

Courtesy Historical Society of Western Pennsylvania

The Industrial Era – With the loss of its political clout in the early 19C, Pennsylvania saw its future in its vast natural resources. Already a pre-Industrial Age iron producer, the state became a powerhouse of iron and steel after the discovery of bituminous (or soft) coal in the west: Converted into a by-product called coke, soft coal fired the great furnaces of Pittsburgh. In the east, anthracite, first discovered in 1769, continued to stoke the nation's furnaces—the state's 500sq mi of anthracite fields yielded an average of 75 million tons a year into the early 20C. By the end of the 1800s, most of the nation's iron and steel was coming out of Pennsylvania.

To service this giant industrial machine, an equally impressive transportation system had to be developed. In the early 1800s, some 3,000mi of roads were built, and steamboats ferried passengers and freight on rivers in the east and west. But the most remarkable feat was the construction of a link between Philadelphia and Pittsburgh, 300 mountainous miles apart. Completed in 1834, the **Main Line Canal** system was either a delight or a misery depending on one's tolerance for modes of transportation. Consisting of a series of canals, bridges, tunnels, inclined planes and rails that carried portable canal boats, the Main Line reduced a 30-day trip across the state to a zippy five days. Steam railroads soon rendered the canals obsolete and heralded a modern age of heavy industry. In 1852 the Pennsylvania Railroad Company established a steam rail link from Philadelphia to Pittsburgh, and it was not long before the state was connected by train to the rest of the Eastern Seaboard.

Civil War Years – The state that gave birth to the nation was called on to play a key role again in the most critical conflict in US history. True to its Quaker origins, Pennsylvania opposed human bondage and passed a law in 1790 declaring blacks born in the state to be free. The border between Pennsylvania and Maryland—called the Mason-Dixon Line after its surveyors—became the dividing line between the North and the South, and thus the goal of many a runaway Southern slave. During the Civil War, Pennsylvania supplied 340,000 troops to the Union Army. At the height of the war in 1863, Confederate general **Robert E. Lee** invaded Pennsylvania with an army of 70,000, hoping for a crucial victory that would ulti-mately curtail the war. Lee's gamble at Gettysburg resulted in a humiliating defeat for the Confederates—which did, in fact, hasten the war's end. President Abraham Lincoln dedicated the battlefield and a national cemetery four months after the battle. Although he considered his Gettysburg Address "a flat failure," later critics have declared it a model of classical perfection.
As for subsequent conflicts on Pennsylvania soil, Confederate cavalry raided and burned Chambersburg in July 1864, but no further serious invasion occurred.

Into the 20C – In the late 19C and early 20C, Pennsylvania further solidified its position as an industrial leader, pumping out a prodigious quantity of coal, coke, oil, iron and steel to build the nation's infrastructure and later to support its efforts in World War I. The period was also marked by violent strikes at coal mines and steel mills as labor unions struggled to gain recognition here and around the country. Industrial barons like Andrew Carnegie and Henry Frick stood at one end of the food chain, throngs of immigrants fresh from Southern and Eastern Europe huddled at the other. The Great Depression of the 1930s put 4,000 coal mines out of business and left hundreds of thousands of workers—up to 80 percent of the labor force around Pittsburgh—without jobs.
World War II temporarily revived Pennsylvania's sagging economy, but from the 1950s to the 80s the state struggled to compete with steel and textile makers abroad and in other parts of the country. Layoffs and urban decay around the state led to a shift toward high-tech and service industries. An accidental partial meltdown at the Three Mile Island nuclear plant in 1979 focused national atten-tion on the Harrisburg area; technicians prevented disaster, but a costly cleanup and serious safety questions remained.

Economy

Natural Resources – Sizable deposits of anthracite and bituminous **coal** continue to top the state's list of important minerals, the former found mostly in eastern Pennsylvania, the latter in the west. Iron ore is extracted in quantity from near Reading, while natural gas fields dot the western region. Other mineral deposits scattered around the state include limestone, sand, slate and clay. About 60 per-cent of Pennsylvania is cloaked in **forest**, accounting for a $5 billion annual logging industry. Oaks, hickories, beeches and pines are prevalent. Pennsyl-vania's **soil** has also long been a key natural resource—well-drained land in the Piedmont and Coastal Plain harbors some of the country's most productive farms. Main **rivers** include the Allegheny, Ohio and Monongahela in the west; the Juniata and Susquehanna in the central region; and the Lehigh, Schuylkill and Delaware in the east. Although Pennsylvania does not border the Atlantic Ocean, the state nevertheless has access to the sea via the Susquehanna River, which flows to the Chesapeake Bay, and the Delaware River, which empties into Delaware Bay.

Industry – About three-quarters of Pennsylvania's economy centers around the **service** industries—business and community services, finance, insurance, tourism and the like. Though Pennsylvania is still the country's leading **steel** producer, the metal industry has taken a backseat since 1970 to food and chemical production; in fact, manufacturing as a whole accounts for only about 20 percent of the state's gross product. A pioneer in the field of **medicine**, the state claims the nation's first public medical facility and first medical school; some 500,000 Pennsylvanians work in medical-related industries. Another 500,000 are employed in the crossover field of **high technology**, which is growing in Pennsylvania at twice the national average. Among the latest technological endeavors, the customizing of recycled steel is helping the state compete in the global marketplace with a product that has been synonymous with Pennsylvania for more than two centuries. Nearly 1.3 million US and foreign visitors travel to Pennsylvania every year, fueling a $15 billion **tourism** industry. The expanding travel and tourism field provides jobs for more than 200,000 state citizens, or about four percent of the total workforce, and generates more than five percent of the gross state product. The Pennsylvania Dutch region is the top-ranking tourist destination, while the Pocono Mountains and the Philadelphia area also attract a considerable number of travelers. In addition to outdoor recreation, visitors come for the numerous Revolutionary and Civil War sites, historic industrial sites, cultural events and festivals, shopping outlets, and such regional culinary specialties as soft pretzels, shoofly pie and Pennsylvania Dutch smorgasbords.

Agriculture – Today generating only about one percent of the gross state product, agriculture nevertheless remains an important piece of the economic profile, with more than 50,000 farms blanketing one-third of the entire state. The historically rich farmlands of Lancaster, York and Berks counties continue to hold sway as the leaders in agricultural acreage. About 70 percent of Pennsylvania's farm income derives from **dairy** and livestock products—**milk** is the leading product, followed by eggs. The state's top crops are **mushrooms** (raised in indoor facilities in Kennett Square in the BRANDYWINE VALLEY), corn, hay, oats and potatoes. Pennsylvania ranks among the top ten national producers of mushrooms, milk, ice cream, cherries, apples and potato chips.

The State Today

Modern Pennsylvania looks increasingly like its East Coast neighbors as it rushes to compete in the complex game of technology and information; it faces similar problems and challenges in its environment, cities and workplaces. Around 1970, Pennsylvania's **population** growth began leveling off for the first time in the state's history. At the turn of the 20C, Pennsylvania claimed the second-highest percentage of foreign-born residents; by 1980 the trend had reversed, giving the state the highest percentage of native-born citizens. The massive waves of immigration—from the Quakers and Germans in the 18C and early 19C to the Italians, Poles and Southern blacks in the late 19C and early 20C—were finally over. Positions of power are to a large extent maintained by descendants of the earliest arrivals. With nearly one-third of its population still living in rural areas, Pennsylvania has one of the largest groups of non-urban dwellers in the country. **Recreational opportunities** from rafting and fishing to hiking and skiing abound in the 114 state parks and scores of other natural areas. Popular resort vacation areas include the Poconos in the northeast and the Laurel Highlands in the southwest. The **arts** flourish in Philadelphia and Pittsburgh with world-class symphony orchestras and distinguished art museums, and a host of fine historical museums are sprinkled throughout the state. Artists from Pennsylvania include Mary Cassatt, Alexander Calder and Andy Warhol; the list of writers counts Pearl S. Buck, Rachel Carson, John O'Hara, Mary Roberts Rinehart, James Michener and John Updike.

Having peaked early as the nation's political and industrial powerhouse, Pennsylvania now plays a less prominent role in the day-to-day life of the country. Yet from its beginnings as Penn's self-proclaimed experiment, the Keystone State has grown into a Commonwealth that draws strength from its diverse land and people and takes pride in its pivotal position in American geography and history.

Pennsylvania's moniker the "Keystone State" derives from the fact that it forms the center, or keystone, of the 13 original US colonies.

Liberty Bell – Joseph Nettis/Tony Stone Images

One of America's most historic pockets, Philadelphia, along with neighboring BUCKS COUNTY to the northeast and the BRANDYWINE VALLEY to the west, preserves a rich store of monuments to the past. Quakers, Patriots, industrialists and waves of immigrants have helped shape the area's history—from Independence Hall in PHILADELPHIA to Pennsbury (William Penn's country manor) in Bucks County, to Hagley (the first du Pont factory) alongside the Brandywine River. Also in the Brandywine Valley, members of the artistic Wyeth family—whose works are showcased in a renovated mill overlooking the river—have long been inspired by the valley's pastoral landscapes.

Long before any white man admired these landscapes, the Lenni Lenape Indians inhabited the area, and it was from this peaceful tribe that **William Penn** purchased tracts in the late 17C. Penn's city of Philadelphia became a natural meeting place for Colonial leaders discontented with the Crown. In 1776 they declared their independence from Britain and set up a new capital here. During the revolution that followed, the region became contested ground, now famous as the site of the Valley Forge encampment and Washington's crossing of the Delaware River. With independence came new growth, and 19C industrialism turned Philadelphia into a roaring engine of progress—and a land of promise for the millions of European immigrants who flocked here. Among those immigrants, the French du Pont family has bequeathed a valuable legacy to the Brandywine Valley, in sites such as Longwood Gardens and Winterthur (just across the border in Delaware). In more recent decades, the area has continued to evolve. In Philadelphia itself, universities, theaters, myriad restaurants, sporting events and museums set a lively, livable tone. And when they tire of too much activity, urbanites seek respite in the pastoral beauty of the rolling Brandywine Valley and the quaint towns lining the Delaware canal in nearby Bucks County. These charming monied enclaves remain among the most appealing rural areas in the mid-Atlantic region.

PHILADELPHIA ★★★

Population 1,478,002
Map p 11
Tourist Information www.libertynet.org/phila-visitor ☎215-636-1666 or 800-537-7676

Embodiment of the American spirit, William Penn's "City of Brotherly Love" splays out between the banks of the Schuylkill and Delaware Rivers. Seventeenth-century beacon of religious freedom and 18C cradle of national independence, the well-situated seaport went on to become an industrial powerhouse and a melting pot of cultures. Now skyscrapers pierce its skyline, looming above streets and squares pebbled with history but still rambunctiously alive with the present. The spirit of industry and culture that has been the city's legacy since Ben Franklin walked these streets still prevails, making Philadelphia one of the country's great destinations.

Historical Notes

City of Brotherly Love – The first recorded residents of this stretch of the Delaware River were the Lenni Lenape Indians, a branch of the Algonquian family. As early as the 1640s, they were joined by Swedes, who began filtering up the Delaware and establishing small outposts in the vicinity of present-day Philadelphia. More muscular in their claims to the inviting Delaware River Valley were the British and Dutch, who vied to control it. By the 1670s the British had won, and within a decade William Penn had begun his "holy experiment" in the New World.

Son of British naval hero Adm. Sir William Penn, the young Penn found himself powerfully attracted to the beliefs of the new Society of Friends. The Quakers—as their detractors called them because of the quaking gestures they made when moved by the Spirit—suffered harsh persecution in England. Penn's grant of land in the New World promised a new beginning for them and for other persecuted groups. "Ye shall be governed by laws of your own making," Penn proclaimed to his colonists, "and live a free, and if you will, a sober and industrious people." Penn sent his agents ahead of him, to lay out a "greene Countrie Towne, which will never be burnt and will allways be wholsome"—a herald of his new utopia. Philadelphia, he called it, borrowing a name with both classical and biblical connotations—"city of brotherly love." His commissioners chose a tract of land on the west bank of the Delaware, just above the confluence with the Schuylkill, and in 1681 they began laying out the town Penn himself had designed. The early gridiron of streets that was platted between the two rivers still characterizes the city today, as does the central park (City Hall Plaza) and four original town squares (Washington, Franklin, Rittenhouse and Logan).

Within only a few years, Penn's town was burgeoning, as not only Quakers but European immigrants of all persuasions flocked in, drawn by the promise of freedom and prosperity. Penn himself initially stayed only a scant two years. When he returned at the turn of the 18C, the City of Brotherly Love had grown to the second most populous in all the New World, topped only by Boston. Penn enjoyed almost two more years in the colony before rumors reached him that the British Parliament had plans to place his colony under control of the Crown. Hurrying back to England, he prevented this, but the rest of his life was fraught with problems: Defraudment of part of his fortune by a friend forced him to spend months in debtor's prison, and dissension from his colonists led him to seek to put his beloved colony under Crown control after all. Before that could happen, however, he died. The year was 1718; Penn was 73.

Seeds of Revolution – Though many of the commissioners Penn appointed to manage affairs in his colony proved incompetent, his able and talented secretary, **James Logan**, kept things on an even keel. Virtually all immigrants to Pennsylvania landed in Philadelphia and many settled there. To accommodate them, spacious town lots were divided and subdivided, and the brick row houses that still signify the old city began to line streets and alleyways. More a port city than the "wholsome" utopia Penn had envisioned, Philadelphia shipped out grain, hemp, tobacco and other farm produce that flowed down the Delaware from the fertile interior lands. Much of it went to the West Indies, in exchange for molasses, sugar or rum. Lumber, fur and copper also added to the city's export coffers, and by the mid-1700s iron furnaces dotted the Schuylkill, forging a new source of wealth. Culture and civic spirit were also being forged, in large part through the creativity of one man—**Benjamin Franklin** (p 230). The institutions he founded added an urbane appeal to the town's more sober Quaker aspect. As the 18C progressed, Philadelphia became the wealthiest and most populous city of British North

America. No wonder that in 1774 delegates to the First Continental Congress met here to discuss the colonies' troubled relations with Britain. By the summer of 1776, a Second Continental Congress had convened in town and set an irrevocable course for separation from Britain. The following year, the British marched on the city and seized it. The young commander in chief of the Continental Army, **George Washington**, tried to thwart the British, but after the unsuccessful October Battle of Germantown *(p 250)*, Washington admitted temporary defeat.

Though the British occupied Philadelphia for more than a year, they were never able to gain access to the city from the sea. What stopped them in part were the valiant Continentals manning **Fort Mifflin** *(along the Delaware River just east of the airport on Ft. Mifflin Rd.; open Apr–Nov Wed–Sun 10am–4pm; closed Thanksgiving Day; $4;* 🅿 ☎215-685-4192*)*. These Patriots endured a 40-day siege in the small mud fort (since rebuilt), now known as the "Alamo of the Revolution." In June 1778, the redcoats left Philadelphia for New York, and the Continental Congress returned from its exile in YORK, Pennsylvania. Three years later, after Washington's victory at Yorktown, Virginia, Philadelphia again witnessed history in the making, when the delegates of the Continental Congress passed the Articles of Confederation to govern their new nation.

In the postwar years Philadelphia leaped into the Industrial Revolution, with textile manufacturing, steam locomotives and cotton mills. The city's prestige only intensified when, in 1790, it was selected as interim capital of the new Republic. For the next decade, the area around Independence Hall served as the seat of federal and state government.

"Workshop of America" – At the turn of the century, Philadelphia lost its governmental clout, when the capital of the state was moved to more centrally located Harrisburg, and the US Congress moved, as planned, to the still incomplete national capital of Washington, DC. Still, the engines of industry, now powered by steam, raced on. The discovery of anthracite coal in Western Pennsylvania only fueled the industrial flames, and by mid-century Philadelphia had become an enormous caldron of expectation and refuge for thousands of Irish and German immigrants. Of its 400,000 residents, about a third were foreign-born. Cramped houses overlooked filthy alleyways, ethnic dissension erupted into occasional violence, and disease flourished. Yet the city, now known as the "workshop of America," toiled on.

The Civil War years made Philadelphia the arsenal of the North and a center of abolitionist activity. After the war, the wealthy began building showplace homes west of the city along the Main Line of the Pennsylvania Railroad, which had become the largest corporation in America. And a new, extravagant City Hall began going up on Penn's central park. In 1876 the city celebrated the 100th anniversary of the signing of the Declaration of Independence with a Centennial Exposition held in FAIRMOUNT PARK. Showcasing the industrial achievements of both Philadelphia and the nation, the exposition also gave rise to a museum of art that would grow into one of the finest in the US.

The late 19C saw another shift in the city's mix, as African Americans, Poles and Jews joined earlier immigrants who had sought refuge in the City of Brotherly Love. When World War I overtook the country, Philadelphia again profited from its industry. The city was not spared the deprivations of the Great Depression; nevertheless in 1932 the world's first modernist skyscraper and a harbinger of the International style, the **PSFS building**—housing the Philadelphia Saving Fund Society—rose in the heart of town at South 12th and Market Streets.

World War II brought the city's last great boom, followed by decades of decline as the middle class fled to the suburbs and industry at last slowed to a trickle. One ray of hope cast across the dismal inner-city scene was the arrival of the National Park Service in the early 1950s. Having acquired Independence Hall, the National Park Service began turning the core of buildings around Independence Square into one of the nation's most popular historical parks. Soon thereafter, urban pioneers, encouraged by government funding, began a slow renovation of the old Society Hill homes, just south of the park.

A Modern City Emerges – In the 1970s, career cop Frank Rizzo became the city's controversial mayor, engendering racial dissension with his strong-arm tactics. Wilson Goode, Philadelphia's first African-American mayor, took the reigns in 1984, promising progress and racial healing. Though he did precipitate new office building downtown, he could not bring an end to racial and ethnic tensions. By the late 1980s, Philadelphia was bankrupt, both financially and in some ways spiritually. But a metropolis of such deep roots would not stay down for long.

Getting There

By Air – **Philadelphia International Airport**: 8mi southwest of Center City; international and domestic flights; ☎937-6800. Information centers *(open daily 6am–11pm)* are located in all terminals. Southeastern Pennsylvania Transportation Authority (SEPTA) trains to Center City stations depart from pedestrian bridges at each terminal *(daily 5:30am–midnight every 30min; 20min; $5)*. Taxi service to Center City: 20min *($20/flat rate)*. Rental car agencies *(p 358)* located outside baggage claim area.

By Bus and Train – **Bus** service to Philadelphia is provided by Greyhound *(10th & Filbert Sts.;* ☎800-231-2222) and Peter Pan/Trailways *(55 N. 11th St.;* ☎413-3420). Amtrak **trains** come into the 30th Street Station *(30th & Market Sts.;* ☎800-872-7245). Regional rail service is available from New Jersey Transit *(30th Street Station;* ☎569-3752 or 800-582-5946), SEPTA Regional Rail *(below)* and Port Authority Transit Corporation (PATCO) *(8th & Market Street Station;* ☎922-4600).

By Public Transportation – The **Southeastern Pennsylvania Transportation Authority** runs an extensive network of transit and rail routes throughout the city and outlying areas. System fares: $1.60 base rate for subway and transit lines; commuter rail fare varies according to distance traveled and time of day. Exact change required. The SEPTA Day Pass entitles the user to one day of unlimited riding on all city transit vehicles *($5)*. SEPTA commuter rail between the city and suburbs services Suburban Station *(16th St. & John F. Kennedy Blvd.)*, Market East Station *(11th & Market Sts.)* and 30th Street Station. Tokens and passes are available at the SEPTA Information Center *(69th St. terminal)* and most stations. System maps may be difficult to obtain; contact **Transit Information** *(www.septa.org* ☎580-7800) for detailed route and schedule information.

Subway and Buses – Two main **subway** lines crisscross the city: Market-Frankford (east to west) and Broad St. (north to south). Both lines operate daily 5am–midnight. City Transit lines (**buses**, streetcars and trackless trolley) operate primarily within the city with routes extending into the suburbs. Most lines operate daily 5:30am–2am; 24-hour "owl" service is available on several routes.
The PHLASH people-mover system (easily recognized by its purple buses) makes a continuous loop from Logan Circle through Center City to the Waterfront and South St. *(mid-May–mid-Sept daily 10am–midnight, rest of the year daily 10am–6pm; every 10min; $1.50 one-way;* ☎636-1666).

By Car – Downtown Philadelphia is laid out in a grid between the Delaware and Schuylkill Rivers, with named streets running east-west and numbered streets running north-south. Major interstate access to the city is via I-95 and I-76. Limited metered parking *($1/hr)* is available downtown. Parking garages are located throughout the city *(average fee $13/day)*.

By Taxi – Olde City Taxi Coach Assn. *(☎247-7678)*; Quaker City Cab *(☎728-8000)*; United Cab Assn. *(☎238-9500)*; Yellow Cab *(☎922-8400)*.

General Information

Visitor Information – The **Philadelphia Convention & Visitors Bureau** *(1515 Market St., Philadelphia PA 19102; www.libertynet.org/phila-visitor* ☎636-1666 or 800-537-7676) operates two visitor centers that provide information on shopping, accommodations and seasonal events: 16th St. & John F. Kennedy Blvd., and 3rd & Chestnut Sts. *(both open Memorial Day–Labor Day daily 9am–6pm; rest of the year daily 9am–5pm; closed Thanksgiving Day, Dec 25)*.

Accommodations – *(p 358)* Area visitors' guide including lodging directory is available *(free)* from the Philadelphia Convention & Visitors Bureau. Accommodations range from elegant hotels in Center City to more modest hotels and motels in the airport and stadium areas. Bed-and-breakfast inns can be found in Center City and surrounding areas. **Reservation services**: Philadelphia Convention & Visitors Bureau *(above)*; Accommodations Express *(☎609-645-8688 or 800-941-7666)*; AmeriRoom *(☎609-383-0303 or 800-888-5825)*; Abby's Agency & Guesthouses *(☎610-692-4575)*; Bed & Breakfast Philadelphia *(☎687-3565 or 800-448-3619)*; Assn. of Bed and Breakfasts in Philadelphia *(☎610-783-7838)*. **American Youth Hostels**: Bank Street Hostel *(32 S. Bank St., Philadelphia PA 19106* ☎922-0222 or 800-392-4678) or Chamounix Mansion Youth Hostel *(Chamounix Dr., W. Fairmount Park, Philadelphia PA 19131* ☎878-3636 or 800-379-0017).

Local Press – Daily news: *Philadelphia Inquirer* (morning) and *Philadelphia Daily News* (afternoon); Friday entertainment section appears in both papers.

Foreign Exchange Offices – *(p 355)* Philadelphia International Airport, terminals A and B *(daily 6am–8pm)*; Thomas Cook *(1800 John F. Kennedy Blvd.* ☎*800-287-7362)*; CoreStates Bank *(Broad & Chestnut Sts.* ☎*786-8880)*; First Union National Bank *(Broad & Walnut Sts.* ☎*985-7068)*.

Sports and Leisure

Sightseeing – Tours of Philadelphia aboard **trolleys** are offered daily year-round *(10am–5:30pm, weather permitting; 1hr 30min)*; visitors can board (and reboard) at stops located at major attractions. For information, contact American Trolley Tours *(*☎*333-2119)* or Philadelphia Trolley Works *(*☎*923-8522)*. Gray Line narrated **city tours** *(depart from 30th Street Station, hotel pick-up service available, Apr–Oct daily; 2hrs 30min;* ☎*569-3666)* and the Foundation for Architecture tours *(Apr–Nov weekends; 2hrs; www.voicenet. com/~ffa/index.html* ☎*569-3187)* provide insight into Philadelphia and its neighborhoods. **Horse-drawn carriage** tours are available from '76 Carriage Co. *(depart year-round daily from Independence Hall and 2nd & South Sts., weather permitting; 15min-1hr;* ☎*923-8516)*; and Philadelphia Carriage Co. *(depart from Chestnut St. opposite Independence Hall year-round daily;* ☎*922-6840)*. Companies offering **boat tours** include Holiday Boat Tours *(depart from Delaware St. & Callow Hill year-round daily; 1hr 30min;* ☎*629-8687)*; Liberty Belle Paddlewheel Cruises *(depart from Lombard Circle, Penn's Landing;* ☎*629-1131)*; and Spirit of Philadelphia *(depart from Lombard Circle, Penn's Landing May–Sept daily; reservations recommended;* ☎*923-1419)*.

Entertainment – Consult the arts and entertainment section of local newspapers *(p 224)* for schedules of cultural events and addresses of theaters and concert halls. To purchase **tickets**, contact the box office; Upstages *(full and half-price tickets sold;* ☎*893-1145)*; or Ticketmaster *(*☎*336-2000)*.

Venue	Performances	☎
Academy of Music	Philadelphia Orchestra, Opera Company of Philadelphia, Philadelphia Ballet	893-1999
Mann Center for the Arts	Philadelphia Orchestra *(Jun–Jul)*	567-0707
Merriam Theater	Broadway shows, Philadelphia Ballet	732-5997
Painted Bride Art Center	Theater, dance	925-9914
Society Hill Playhouse	Off-Broadway shows	923-0210

Spectator Sports – Phillies baseball *(*☎*463-1000)*; **Eagles** football *(*☎*463-5500)*; **76ers** basketball *(*☎*336-3600)*; **Flyers** hockey *(*☎*336-3600)*.

Recreation – Philadelphia's primary recreation area is **Fairmount Park** *(p 245)*, offering over 100mi of paths for walking, biking and horseback riding *(Germantown & Northwestern Rds.;* ☎*685-9286)*. The park also includes tennis courts, golf courses and an in-line skating pathway along the Schuylkill River. Outdoor **ice-skating** is available at the Blue Cross RiverRink *(Columbus Blvd. between Market & Chestnut Sts.; late Nov–early Mar daily; rentals available;* ☎*925-7465)*.

Shopping – Major shopping areas in Philadelphia: Center City *(p 238;* ☎*545-7766)*; South Street *(p 237; between 10th & Front Sts.;* ☎*413-3713)*; Manayunk *(p 249; Main St. between Leverington & Ridge Sts.;* ☎*482-9565)* and Chestnut Hill *(p 250; 7900-8700 Germantown Ave.;* ☎*247-6696)*. **Jewelers' Row** *(Sansom St. between 7th & 8th Sts.;* ☎*627-1839)* is home to over 350 retailers. More than a dozen **art galleries** can be found in the Old City area *(p 232)*. Both **Antique Row** *(Pine St. between 9th & 12th Sts.)* and South Street *(between 3rd & 9th Sts.)* offer a large assortment of antique shops. **Malls** in Center City include The Shops at Bellevue *(Broad & Walnut Sts.;* ☎*875-8350)* and The Shops at Liberty Place *(16th & Chestnut Sts.* ☎*851-9055)*. Other area malls: Gallery at Market East *(9th & Market Sts.* ☎*625-4962)*; The Bourse *(111 S. Independence Mall East;* ☎*625-0300)*; Market Place East *(701 Market St.,* ☎*592-8905)*; Shops at Penn *(34th & Walnut Sts.;* ☎*222-8595)*; Franklin Mills *(1455 Franklin Mills Circle;* ☎*632-1500)*.

Useful Numbers   ☎

Police/Ambulance/Fire	**911**
Dental Referral *(Mon–Fri 9am–5pm)*	925-6050
Medical Referral *(Mon–Fri 9am–4:45pm)*	563-5343
24-hour Pharmacy *(CVS, locations throughout Philadelphia)*	
Main Post Office *(2970 Market St.)*	895-8000
Weather (recorded)	936-1212

Recent years have witnessed a lively rebirth of Center City, helped along by the opening of an enormous new convention center. To accommodate the million conventioneers that the center brings to the city annually, fine new hotels and refurbished old ones now add to the impressive skyline.

Far more than just a conventioneer's city, hospitable Philadelphia boasts a vibrant arts and theater scene and a wealth of fine museums. Its blue-collar, cheesesteak-style cuisine has now been joined by upscale restaurants to rival any in the country. Three major universities within the city—the University of Pennsylvania, Drexel and Temple—add a lively flavor of student life and easy sophistication. Ardent sports enthusiasts, Philadelphians support national teams in football (Eagles), baseball (Phillies), basketball (76ers) and hockey (Flyers).

Industry still persists in Philadelphia, though the smokestacks of old have given way to less sooty endeavors, and the city's major businesses revolve around health care and the service and professional industries. Sprawling far into the surrounding suburbs of Pennsylvania and New Jersey, greater Philadelphia now ranks as the nation's fourth-largest metropolitan area.

Sober but forbearing in his long coat, William Penn still looks down on all he wrought from his unassailable position atop City Hall, as though proclaiming as he once did: "And thou, Philadelphia ... what love, what care, what service, and what travail has there been to bring thee forth."

★★★ INDEPENDENCE NATIONAL HISTORICAL PARK   2 days. Map p 229.

Critical moments in America's struggle for independence and in her early nation-hood were played out here in the historic heart of the city. Now juxtaposed against the architecture and atmosphere of this century, Independence National Historical Park encompasses roughly 12 blocks—bordered by Second and Sixth Streets on the east and west, and Market and Walnut Streets on the north and south. The most important of the score of historic sights contained within this area is Independence Hall. Here, on July 4, 1776, delegates of the Second Continental Congress adopted the Declaration of Independence, and soon there-after, at the first public reading of the declaration, the bell in the building's cupola heralded liberty. Now one of the nation's most revered icons, the Liberty Bell serves as the symbolic centerpiece of the park.

Sights are organized roughly east to west beginning at the park's visitor center.

Visitor Center – *3rd & Chestnut Sts. Open year-round daily 9am–5pm. Closed Jan 1, Dec 25.* &. *Owing to ongoing renovation, some buildings in the park may be closed or not completely operational. Call for details. Guided tours are available at many park sights.www. nps. gov* ☎*215-597-8974.* The modern lines of this orientation and informa-tion facility were intended to harmonize with the sur-rounding historical area. An angular bell tower houses the **Bicentennial Bell [A]**, a gift from Great Britain. Inside the center, interactive computer sta-tions allow visitors to explore aspects of the US Constitution, and the 28min film *Independence*, directed by John Huston, features a host of familiar screen stars as America's Founding Fathers.

Independence Hall

Adjacent to the visitor center, the striking **Philadelphia Exchange** *(3rd and Walnut Sts.; not open to the public),* with its semicircular portico and Greek Revival facade, opened in 1834 as a merchants' exchange. **Welcome Park** *(behind the visitor center on 2nd St.),* the site where William Penn granted his "Charter of Privileges" (a revised constitution) in 1701, features a statue of Penn surrounded by wall panels explaining his hopes and dreams for the "Penn's Woods" colony.

First Bank of the United States [B] – *120 S. 3rd St. Not open to the public.* Establishing a national bank was one of the first orders of business for the newly confederated United States. Spearheaded by Secretary of the Treasury Alexander Hamilton, the country's first national bank (1794) was originally housed in Carpenters' Hall. In 1797 this dignified Greek Revival marble structure was built to house the bank; it is now considered the oldest extant bank building in the country.

New Hall Military Museum [C] – *Carpenters' Ct. on Chestnut St.* In 1791 the Carpenters' Company built the simple brick Federal-style New Hall as a meeting place, since their own hall was being used as the First National Bank. During this period, New Hall also housed the office of the first US Secretary of War, Henry Knox. A reconstruction of the two-story building now contains exhibits honoring the armed services of the US.

Carpenters' Hall [D] – *Carpenters' Ct. on Chestnut St.* Still owned by the Carpenters' Company of Philadelphia, the two-story Georgian brick structure was designed and built by members of that guild in the early 1770s as their meeting hall. In 1773 Benjamin Franklin's Library Company moved into the second floor. The following year, the hall was chosen as the meeting place for the **First Continental Congress**, whose 56 delegates convened here during September and October. During the subsequent war for independence, the hall was used as a hospital and arsenal. In 1956 the guild renovated Carpenters' Hall and opened it as the nation's first historic monument.

Todd House [E] – *4th & Walnut Sts. Visit by guided tour (1hr) only, year-round daily. Closed Jan 1, Dec 25. $2 (includes Bishop White House). Reservations required through park visitor center the day of your visit. www.nps.gov ☎215-597-8974.* This pleasant brick row house was home to Quaker couple John and Dolley Todd in the late 1700s and reflects the simple refinements of an educated couple of that period. After John, a lawyer, died in the 1793 yellow fever epidemic that besieged Philadelphia, Dolley married Virginia statesman James Madison, who would become the country's fourth president.

Around the corner off South Fourth Street, **St. Joseph's Church** *(entrance via Willing's Alley),* the city's first Roman Catholic church, traces its roots to 1734. Across the street, the stately brick headquarters of the **Philadelphia Contributionship [F]** *(212 S. 4th St.)* was designed by US Capitol architect Thomas U. Walter in 1835. The oldest property insurance company in the nation, the contributionship was founded by Benjamin Franklin in 1752.

Bishop White House [G] – *309 Walnut St. Visit by guided tour (1hr) only; same hours as Todd House (above). $2 (includes Todd House). Reservations required through park visitor center the day of your visit. ☎215-597-8974.* One of the most gracious homes still standing from the Federal period, the capacious multilevel brick row house (1787) was designed by its owner, respected Anglican bishop Dr. William White. Rector of both Christ Church *(p 232)* and St. Peter's *(p 235),* and chaplain of the Continental Congress, White was also a prominent member of the Philadelphia Society. The house tour showcases the urbanity and elegance of his life here at the turn of the 19C.

★★ **Second Bank of the United States/National Portrait Gallery** – *420 Chestnut St. Open year-round daily 10am–5pm. $2. ☎215-597-8974.* A superb example of Greek Revival architecture, this columned marble structure (1818) was designed by William Strickland and opened in 1824 as the Second Bank of the US. Functioning under a 20-year Act of Congress, it became one of the most powerful financial institutions in the world under the direction of Nicholas Biddle. When Andrew Jackson became president, however, he questioned the constitutionality of a national bank and vetoed its charter in 1832. From 1845 to 1935 the building served as the Philadelphia Custom House. Restored in 1974, it now devotes its space to the permanent exhibit "Philadelphia: Portraits of the Capital City." Prominent among the paintings here are more than 100 Charles Willson Peale portraits of delegates to the Continental Congress, signers of the Constitution and officers of the Revolution and War of 1812. These works form part of the collection that Peale once exhibited in his Museum of Philadelphia, which occupied the second floor of Independence Hall. A large gallery at the rear of the building displays street scenes and portraits that depict life in Philadelphia during the Federal period.

★★★ Independence Hall – *Chestnut St. between 5th & 6th Sts.*

Now world-renowned as Independence Hall, the steepled Georgian brick building, with its balustraded roof, was originally constructed as the Pennsylvania State House. Work began on the brick edifice in 1732, but construction was slowed by a lack of skilled labor. Though the legislative assembly began meeting here in 1735, the ambitious, 107ft-long building, with its two 50ft wings connected by piazzas, was not fully completed until 1756. In 1753 a steeple and belfry were completed, and the State House Bell, now famous as the Liberty Bell, was hung.

A Place to Plan Rebellion – On May 10, 1775, delegates of the Second Continental Congress convened in the Assembly Room of the State House to determine how the colonies should respond to increasing hostilities with Britain. As it met throughout that summer, the Congress assumed a more aggressive attitude toward the Mother Country, appointing Virginia delegate George Washington as commander in chief of the Continental Army.

In Britain, George III responded by proclaiming the colonists in "open and avowed rebellion." The following June, as the Continental Congress again met in the State House, Virginia delegate Richard Henry Lee presented a resolution for independence from Britain. Two days of debate ensued, and consideration of the resolution was tabled for several weeks while a committee worked to draft a declaration explaining why such a resolution was necessary. When the declaration was presented on July 2, more debate followed before Congress adopted the Declaration of Independence on July 4, 1776. Throughout the Revolutionary War the Second Continental Congress continued to convene in the State House, and in 1781, when victory and independence at last seemed imminent, the Articles of Confederation were also adopted here. In the summer of 1787, the 55 delegates of the Constitutional Convention met in the State House chambers to conceive a new government. On September 17 they adopted the US Constitution.

In the decades that followed, the building became the property of the city and was modified on several occasions, most notably when the original steeple and roof were replaced with a different design. In the early 1800s there was talk of demolishing the building, but the official visit of Revolutionary War hero the Marquis de Lafayette in 1824 focused attention on the historic significance of what he called the "Hall of Independence." At the turn of the century, the city of Philadelphia moved to restore Independence Square and Independence Hall to its Revolutionary War-era appearance.

The Assembly Room, Independence Hall

Visit – *30min.* Now a UNESCO World Heritage Site, the building retains its mid-18C appearance. Inside, a large central hall displays much of its original woodwork and separates the open chamber used by Pennsylvania's Supreme Court from the closed Assembly Room, where the Continental Congress and Constitutional Convention met. Ringed by a semicircle of desktops and Windsor chairs, the Speaker's original "rising sun" chair occupies the prominent central position in the Assembly Room. On a desk in front of the chair stands the silver **inkstand**, crafted by silversmith Philip Syng, Jr., and used during the signing of the Declaration of Independence. A staircase leads to the second floor's broad gallery, or "Long Room"; the Governor's Council Chamber, appointed in fine Colonial reproductions; and a smaller committee room.

Independence Square – *Located directly behind Independence Hall.* Once called State House Yard, the pleasant, shaded square stretching behind Congress Hall, Independence Hall and the Old City Hall is anchored by a statue of Revolutionary War naval hero Commodore John Barry. It was here, on July 8, 1776, that the Declaration of Independence was first read in public.

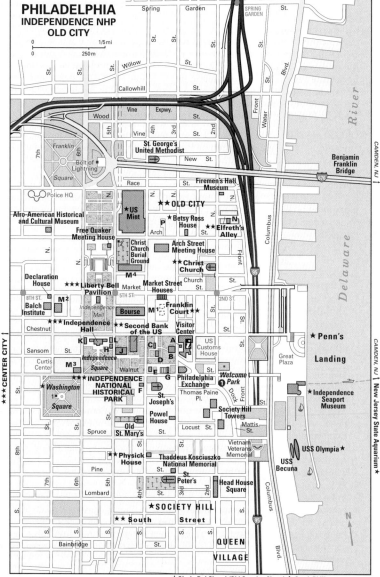

On the northeast side of the square, the unadorned red-brick **Philosophical Hall [H]** *(not open to the public)* has housed the American Philosophical Society since the 1780s. Founded by Benjamin Franklin as the nation's first learned society in the 1740s, the society counted Founding Fathers Washington, Adams, Jefferson and Madison as members. In 1959 the society erected its Neoclassical **Library Hall [J]** *(105 S. 5th St.)* across the street. Open to scholars, the hall houses a superb collection of books and manuscripts that trace the history of science and technology.

Catercorner across Walnut Street sits **Washington Square★** *(bordered by Walnut & 6th Sts.)*. The large, gracious city square was one of the four original town plazas planned by William Penn. During the Revolution, some 5,000 British and American soldiers were buried here and are commemorated by a **Tomb of the Unknown Soldiers of the Revolution [1]**. Later, casualties of the 1793 yellow fever epidemic were also buried in the square. In the late 19C, the square and its environs became the focal point of the city's prestigious publishing industry.

★ **Congress Hall [K]** – *6th & Chestnut Sts.* The Georgian brick building that was to serve as the Philadelphia County Courthouse was begun in 1787, but by the time of its completion two years later the building was needed for a much larger purpose. With the selection of Philadelphia as the interim federal capital, the building became Congress Hall, meeting place for the elected delegates of the fledgling United States. From 1790 to 1800 the House of Representatives met in the large first-floor chamber, while the Senate convened in the more elegantly furnished courtroom upstairs. A wide, three-tier semicircle of reproduction studded chairs and mahogany desktops now reflects the House chamber's appearance in the mid-1790s, when 105 congressmen met here. The podium from which the Speaker of the House presided serves as the centerpiece of the room, and a public viewing gallery overlooks the entire space. The smaller Senate chamber holds two tiers of desks and red leather armchairs, many of which are the original ones made by Philadelphia cabinetmaker Thomas Affleck.

★ **Old City Hall [L]** – *5th & Chestnut Sts.* Flanking the east side of Independence Hall, this building is a virtual mirror image of Congress Hall. Completed in 1791, it, too, was taken over by the federal government, to serve as home to the Supreme Court. The ground-floor chamber has been returned to its appearance during the early justices' nine-year tenure here. Presiding from a raised dais, the six justices then sitting on the court towered over a jury box and public gallery. Appointed by the president, most justices served only a two-year tenure, owing to the ardors of the job. In addition to convening in Philadelphia, judges rode a circuit that covered three Federal districts.

■ Benjamin Franklin

The 15th child of an English soapmaker who immigrated to Boston in the early 18C, Ben Franklin (1706-90) had only two years of formal schooling before he apprenticed to his brother James to learn the printing business in 1718. At age 17, Franklin left Boston and settled in Philadelphia. By his late 20s, Franklin had established himself as a successful Philadelphia printer and was financing other printing concerns throughout the colonies. But printing and business were not enough to fully engage his creative restlessness, and in 1732 he began writing his phenomenally popular *Poor Richard's Almanack*, homilies on the benefits of thrift, industry and other classically American virtues. Gradually he became a city leader, a man whose ideas shaped and refined the burgeoning town of Philadelphia and whose hand can be seen behind many city institutions: the extant Philadelphia Contributionship; the Library Company of Philadelphia; the Pennsylvania Hospital (the nation's oldest); the American Philosophical Society; and the Philadelphia Academy, which evolved into the University of Pennsylvania. For his part, Franklin was perhaps most proud of his scientific endeavors, and his experiments with electricity gained him fame in Europe.

In his fifties, Franklin was elected a delegate to the Pennsylvania Assembly, and politics, revolution, nationhood and long stays in Europe consumed much of his energy for the remainder of his life. While the nation now reveres him as a Founding Father, Philadelphians proudly claim him as their own "uncommon citizen" and his familiar image continues to inform much of the city's iconography and culture.

★ **Liberty Bell Pavilion** – *Open year-round daily 9am–5pm.* ♿. *When the building is closed, the bell is visible through the large glass panes.* Completed for the 1976 Bicentennial celebrations, the modern, glass-fronted building anchoring a broad greensward enshrines the revered **Liberty Bell**★★★ *(p 221)*. In 1751 a bell was ordered from Whitechapel Foundry in London, possibly to commemorate the 50th anniversary of William Penn's Charter of Privileges to his colony. Made from an alloy of copper and tin, it bears a biblical inscription from Leviticus 25:10: "Proclaim Liberty throughout all the Land unto all the inhabitants thereof." Soon after its arrival in Philadelphia, the bell developed a crack, and local metalsmiths John Pass and John Stow recast it. Their names now appear prominently on its face. In 1753 the 2,000-pound bell took its place in the State House belfry and was rung for official occasions for almost 100 years, until a crack again threatened its viability. Its finest moment occurred on July 8, 1776, when it was rung to announce the first public reading of the Declaration of Independence in the State House Yard. In 1846 it sounded its last public notes in commemoration of George Washington's birthday. In the mid-19C, abolitionists proclaimed it the "Liberty Bell" and adopted it as the symbol for their movement. Since that time it has gained increasing recognition as the national symbol of freedom.

Fronting the east side of Liberty Bell Pavilion on Fifth Street, the impressive red sandstone **Bourse** opened in 1895 as a country's first commodities exchange. Also one of its first steel-frame buildings, the Victorian structure was renovated in 1981; its old trading floor and spectator galleries now house eateries, shops and offices.

★ **Franklin Court** – *Entrance on Market St. between 3rd and 4th Sts.* Benjamin Franklin, Philadelphia's most prominent citizen, began building a substantial home here in the 1760s, when he and his wife, Deborah, were already middle-aged. Just as construction was under way, Franklin was called to serve as the colony's representative to London and did not return permanently to his new home for almost a decade. During his absence Deborah died, and Franklin lived out his last years in the home surrounded by his daughter and her family. Demolished long ago, the three-story brick house has been re-created as a steel-frame "ghost structure," as has the 1786 print shop Franklin built for his grandson. An underground **museum**★ **[M1]** houses an ingenious array of audio-visual presentations that celebrate Franklin's life and genius. An 18min film details Franklin's family life.

The north end of Franklin Court is edged by reproductions of the **Market Street Houses** that Franklin built as rental properties in the 1780s. At the west end, nos. 320-322 re-create the 18C printing office and bookbindery of Franklin's grandson and protégé in the printing business, Benjamin Franklin Bache. Next door, no. 318 showcases the architecture of these town houses. Colonial and Federal pottery and glassware recovered from excavations in Franklin Court are also exhibited. In keeping with Franklin's concern for the mail, the adjacent B. Free Franklin Post Office recalls Colonial decor and houses a small postal museum on the second floor. Mail sent from here bears the cancellation postmark "B. Free Franklin."

Declaration (Graff) House – *7th & Market Sts. Open year-round daily 10am–1pm. Closed Jan 1, Dec 25.* Entered from a quiet courtyard just off the commercial hubbub of Market Street, the small brick house is a reconstruction of the Colonial residence **Thomas Jefferson** occupied during the summer of 1776, while drafting the Declaration of Independence. Arriving in Philadelphia as a Virginia delegate to the Second Continental Congress, Jefferson rented upstairs rooms in the newly built home of bricklayer Jacob Graff, Jr. Along with four other delegates (Benjamin Franklin, John Adams, Roger Sherman and Robert Livingston) Jefferson was charged by the Congress to create a document that would explain the need for independence from Britain. The other committee members deferred to the learned, 33-year-old Jefferson, who produced the first draft of the Declaration of Independence. The Park Service reconstruction of Graff House (the original structure was demolished in the 1880s) re-creates Jefferson's parlor and bedchamber. Exhibits and an 8min film detail Jefferson's involvement with the Declaration of Independence.

Additional Sights

The Balch Institute for Ethnic Studies – *18 S. 7th St., next door to Graff House. Open year-round Mon–Sat 10am–4pm. Closed major holidays. $2. www.libertynet.org/~balch* ☎*215-925-8090.* Devoted to celebrating America's multiculturalism, the institute features well-researched changing exhibits *(ground floor)* that reflect ethnic traditions brought to the US from other countries, and document ethnic and racial discrimination. The second floor houses an extensive research library.

★ **Atwater Kent Museum [M²]** – *15 S. 7th St., across the street from the Balch Institute. Open year-round Wed–Mon 10am–4pm. $3.* & *www.philadelphiahistory.org* ☎*215-922-3031.* Official museum of the city's history, this modest exhibit space packs a great deal of information into its displays. Philadelphia's 300-year history—from Penn's dreams for a City of Brotherly Love to the city's meteoric rise to second-largest metropolis in the British Empire—are recounted in cases housing artifacts, dioramas and historic illustrations. The 1824 Greek Revival building, designed by John Haviland, originally housed the Franklin Institute *(p 242)*. The building's current namesake, Atwater Kent, was a radio pioneer.

Curtis Center of Norman Rockwell Art [M³] – *601 Walnut St., lower level. Open year-round Mon–Sat 10am–4pm, Sun 11am–4pm. Closed Jan 1, Easter Sunday, Thanksgiving Day, Dec 25. $2.* ✗ & ☎*215-922-4345.* This small gallery boasts a comprehensive collection of Rockwell lithographs, paintings and his complete series of *Saturday Evening Post* covers. In the course of his 25-year affiliation with the *Post*, Rockwell produced more than 300 of the magazine's covers, and his images came to symbolize the ideals of mid-20C American life. An 8min video captures Rockwell discussing his work. Curtis Publishing, creator of the *Saturday Evening Post* and *Ladies' Home Journal,* was once headquartered in this building.

National Museum of American Jewish History [M⁴] – *55 N. 5th St. Independence Mall East, between Market & Arch Sts. Open year-round Mon–Thu 10am–5pm, Fri 10am–3pm, Sun noon–5pm. Closed Jewish holidays. $2.50.* & ☎*215-923-3811.* Established in 1976, the museum collects, preserves and interprets artifacts related to the American Jewish experience. A new core exhibit, "Creating American Jews," scheduled to open in the fall of 1998, will explore the changing meanings of American Jewish identity, drawing on personal stories and extraordinary artifacts of the past 340 years. The Mikveh Israel synagogue, which shares a lobby with the museum, is home to the first Jewish congregation in the nation (c.1740). Outside the museum entrance, four marble pillars by sculptor Buky Schwartz commemorate the martyrdom of Jonathan Netanyahu, who led the 1976 commando raid to free Jewish hostages held in Entebbe, Uganda. Both Jonathan and his brother, Israeli Prime Minister Benjamin Netanyahu, spent part of their childhoods in Philadelphia.

★★ **OLD CITY** *½ day. Map p 229.*

The core of Penn's original city, this once bustling Colonial waterfront district just north of INDEPENDENCE NATIONAL PARK had fallen into serious neglect by the mid-20C. The development of the national park, however, precipitated a gradual turnaround, and hip restaurants and restored historic buildings are now scattered through the area, many housing performing arts groups, architectural firms, artists' studios, and galleries. On **First Fridays** *(the first Friday of every month Oct–Jun;* ☎*215-545-7766),* Old City galleries, showrooms and theaters extend their hours *(5pm–9pm)* to host an open house for the public *(galleries are clustered along N. 2nd & N. 3rd Sts. between Market & Race Sts.).*

★★ **Christ Church** – *N. 2nd & Church Sts. Open Mar–Dec Mon–Sat 9am–5pm, Sun 1pm–5pm. Rest of the year Wed–Sat 9am–5pm, Sun 1pm–5pm. Closed Jan 1, Holy Saturday, Easter Sunday, Thanksgiving Day, Dec 24–25, Dec 31. Contribution requested.* ☎*215-922-1695.* One of the nation's most historic churches, this parish traces its beginnings to 1695, when a small Anglican chapel was erected here. Construction on the elegant Georgian brick structure was begun in 1727. In 1754 the tower and "Philadelphia steeple" were added. The church's traditional Royalist congregation changed dramatically during the Revolution, when delegates to the Continental Congress, including George Washington and 15 signers of the Declaration of Independence, began to worship here, earning Christ Church its sobriquet "the nation's church."

Altered and Victorianized in the 19C, the church has since been returned to a more simplified decor. Elegant archways and fluted columns sweep toward the pulpit, backed by a Palladian window. Markers indicate the pews where Washington and Franklin worshipped. The 600-year-old walnut **baptismal font** originally served in an Anglican church in London, and the infant William Penn was baptized in it.

Christ Church

Four blocks west, **Christ Church Burial Ground** (*N. 5th and Arch Sts.; not open to the public*) dates back to 1719 and contains the graves of four signers of the Constitution, including Revolutionary War financier Robert Morris. **Benjamin Franklin's grave [2]** is visible through the fence along Arch Street and easily identifiable by the pennies that modern admirers toss onto it.

★ **Elfreth's Alley** – *Between N. 2nd and Front Sts.* Charming as well as historic, the narrow, block-long alleyway dates to the beginning of the 18C and lays claim to being the oldest continuously inhabited street in Philadelphia—and arguably the oldest in the nation. A few of its 33 narrow brick row houses have stood here since 1725 and today house urbanites. Now a National Historic Landmark, the alley was named for blacksmith Jeremiah Elfreth, its mid-18C owner. The **Mantua Maker's Museum House★ [N]** (*no. 126; open Mar–Dec Tue–Sat 10am–4pm, Sun noon–4pm; Jan–Feb Sat 10am–4pm, Sun noon–4pm; Closed Jan 1, Easter Sunday, Thanksgiving Day, Dec 25; $2; ☎215-574-0560*), built in 1755, depicts the working-class conditions of the two seamstress sisters-in-law who lived here. Its design is a classic "trinity," a residence with one room on each of three stories.

Firemen's Hall Museum – *147 N. 2nd St. Open year-round Tue–Sat 9am–4:30pm. Closed major holidays. Contribution requested. ☎215-923-1438.* An authentic 1876 firehouse, the museum now contains two floors of fire-fighting tools, historic fire marks (plaques once used to indicate which houses were insured) and fire wagons. The living quarters of an early-19C firehouse are re-created, as is the pilot house of a marine fire-fighting boat used to battle waterfront blazes.

1 Old City Eats

Map p 229. Old City's history carries over to a couple of restaurants in the area surrounding the national park. For Colonial victuals and atmosphere, try the **City Tavern** (*S. 2nd & Walnut Sts.; ☎215-413-1443*), a rebuilt version of the 18C tavern that served the city's founding fathers. Both lunches and dinners—served by wait staff in period dress—focus on well-prepared seafood, game and meat dishes. The tavern also offers a nice ale, brewed using Thomas Jefferson's own formula. Across the street, **Old Original Bookbinders** (*S. 2nd & Walnut Sts.; ☎215-925-7027*) has been a Philadelphia institution since 1865. Over the years, Bookbinders has hosted its share of political figures and Hollywood celebrities, whose photographs line the walls. Its hefty, always popular portions of salad, beef, seafood and desserts are served in a voluminous (the restaurant boasts seven dining rooms) and darkly ornate Victorian setting.

Jonathan Wallen

233

★ **Betsy Ross House** – *239 Arch St. Open year-round Tue–Sun & Mon holidays 10am–5pm. Closed Jan 1, Thanksgiving Day, Dec 25. Contribution requested. www. libertynet.org/iha/betsy* ☎*215-627-5343.* By long-cherished legend, the Quaker seamstress who lived here is credited with making the first version of the Stars and Stripes—though that fact is now disputed by scholars. Born Elizabeth Griscom in 1752, Betsy married a young upholsterer named John Ross, and the couple became ardent Patriots. John Ross died in 1776, after only a few years of marriage, and Betsy made "naval colors," or flags, as a means of support. The brick, gable-roofed home (c.1740) she lived in with the widow Lithgow now celebrates her talents and the making of the original Stars and Stripes. Her shop is preserved on the first floor, and living quarters are re-created on the upper two floors.

A block west on Arch Street, the facades of fashionable row houses now front **Loxley Court [P]**, the site where Benjamin Franklin flew his kite during a thunderstorm in his groundbreaking experiment on electricity. Also in this area of Arch Street stand two buildings that speak to the strong Quaker presence in Philadelphia: the simple brick **Arch Street Meeting House** *(no. 320)*, which dates from 1803; and the **Free Quaker Meeting House** *(5th & Arch Sts.)*, built in 1783, which houses a re-created meeting room on its first floor.

★ **United States Mint** – *5th & Arch Sts. Open Jul–Aug daily 9am–4:30pm. Sept–Apr Mon–Fri 9am–4:30pm. Closed Jan 1, Thanksgiving Day, Dec 25.* ♿ ☎*215-597-7350.* The modern pink granite building housing the world's largest mint is a direct descendant of the country's first mint, which began operations two blocks away in 1792. The current mint (1969), the fourth in Philadelphia and one of four now operating in the US, produces coins and national medals. A self-guided tour begins with a corridor featuring exhibits on US mints; commemorative medals and coins; and a re-created assayer's office. Windows in the adjacent corridor overlook the working floor of the mint. Audio- and videotapes explain the intricacies of the coining process, from blanking to annealing, riddling, upsetting, striking, inspecting, counting and finally bagging. Further historical exhibits are also offered in the David Rittenhouse Room on the second floor.

St. George's United Methodist Church – *235 N. 4th St. Open year-round Mon–Fri 10am–3pm, Sat by appointment only, Sun after services.* ☎*215-925-7788.* This unadorned brick building is the oldest extant Methodist church structure (c.1769) in the country. One of the most important Methodist congregations in America, the church hosted such luminaries as Francis Asbury, the father of American Methodism. The only **Asbury Bible** in the nation is now displayed in the exhibit rooms. Lined with white pews trimmed in brown, the church's simple sanctuary is overseen by clear, unadorned windows.

Afro-American Historical and Cultural Museum – *701 Arch St. Open year-round Tue–Sat 10am–5pm, Sun noon–5pm. Closed major holidays. $4.* ♿ 🅿 ☎*215-574-0380.* Since 1976, this museum has celebrated the accomplishments and history of the African-American community, which has had a strong presence in Philadelphia since the city's founding. Two floors of galleries are devoted to changing exhibits that have included the works of regional African-American artists such as Elizabeth Catlett and Clementine Hunter, and such national figures as photographer Gordon Parks.

★ **SOCIETY HILL**   *½ day. Map p 229.*

The streets stretching south of Independence Hall to Lombard Street, and bounded on the east and west by South Second and South Fifth Streets respectively, contain a plethora of 18C homes and churches that reflect the burgeoning spirit of the nation in the decades surrounding independence. Though Society Hill suffered serious urban decline from the late 19C to the mid-20C, revitalization—encouraged by federal grants to urban pioneers—has returned this area to its former glory. As part of the renewal effort, a design competition was held in the early 1960s to choose an architectural symbol of the area's rebirth. Internationally renowned architect **I.M. Pei** won the competition for his design of new Third Street town houses and the three landmark **Society Hill Towers** *(2nd and Locust Sts.)*, with their soaring rectilinear facades.

Powel House – *244 S. 3rd St. Visit by guided tour (45min) only, Jun–Oct Wed–Sat noon–5pm, Sun 1pm–5pm. Rest of the year Thu–Sat noon–5pm, Sun 1pm–5pm. $3.* ☎*215-627-0364.* Part of a line of distinguished houses called Mansion Row, the

Georgian brick structure (1765) retains its classic interior, with an arched and wainscoted center hall, delft and marble fireplace surrounds, and a broad mahogany staircase. The home's furnishings reflect the period of the second owners, prominent Philadelphians Elizabeth and Samuel Powel. Powel served as the city's last mayor under Crown rule, and its first after the Constitution was adopted. The couple entertained Washington, Jefferson, Franklin, Lafayette and other notables in their gracious home.

Old St. Mary's Church – *252 S. 4th St. Open year-round Mon–Sat 9am–4:45pm, Sun 8:15am–11:45am, holidays 9am–noon.* ☎215-923-7930. The stark red-brick church dates from 1763, when it became the principal Catholic church in the area. Members of the Continental Congress attended services here, and from 1810 to 1838 it served as the cathedral for the diocese. The interior houses a 1791 baptismal font and brass chandeliers that once hung in Independence Hall. Behind the church, the serene **cemetery** holds the remains of Commodore John Barry and other 18C and 19C notables.

★★ **Physick House** – *321 S. 4th St. Visit by guided tour (30min) only, Jun–Labor Day Thu–Sat noon–4pm, Sun 1pm–4pm. Rest of the year Thu–Sat 11am–2pm. $3. www. libertynet.org/iha/physick.html* ☎215-925-7866. Wine merchant Henry Hill built his elegant home in 1786. In 1815 esteemed "father of American surgery," Dr. Philip Syng Physick, took possession of the house and his descendants resided here until 1940, when it was willed to the Pennsylvania Hospital. For the 1976 Bicentennial celebration, philanthropists Walter and Lenore Annenberg purchased the property and funded an extensive renovation that has made the house one of the showpieces of the Federal period, with furnishings that reflect the Federal and Empire styles popular during Dr. Physick's tenure. The fanlight above the front door ranked as the largest in the colonies when Henry Hill imported it from England. In the front hall stands a Chippendale tall-case clock owned by Dr. Physick; and the parlor contains a silver cream pitcher crafted by Physick's maternal grandfather, Philip Syng, Jr. *(p 229).* Thomas Sully portraits of family members hang in the downstairs reception rooms, and more period rooms and an exhibit on Physick's accomplishments occupy the second floor. Behind the house, brick walkways edge 18C-style gardens.

St. Peter's Church – *S. 3rd and Pine Sts. Open year-round Mon–Fri 9am–4pm. Weekends by guided tour (20min) only, Sat 11am–3pm, Sun 1pm–3pm.* ☎215-925-5968. The stately Georgian church has serviced the Episcopal community since 1761 and retains its original design, with Palladian windows, a wine-glass pulpit and a 1764 Rococo organ case. The tower and spire, added in 1842, house bells cast at the same Whitechapel Foundry as the Liberty Bell. The **cemetery** contains the graves of artist Charles Willson Peale, banker Nicholas Biddle, 19C naval hero Stephen Decatur, Colonial chief justice Benjamin Chew and US vice president (1844-52) George Dallas.

Thaddeus Kosciuszko National Memorial – *301 Pine St. Open Jun–Oct daily 9am–5pm. Rest of the year Wed–Sun 9am–5pm. Closed Jan 1, Thanksgiving Day, Dec 25. www.nps.gov* ☎215-597-9618. Completed in 1776, this simple Federal-style brick residence briefly housed Polish Patriot and Revolutionary War hero **Thaddeus Kosciuszko** (1746-1817). A military engineer by training, Kosciuszko served with Continental forces throughout the Revolution and at its successful conclusion returned to Poland. In the 1790s he led an insurrection against Russian dominance of Poland. Defeated, he was forced into exile for the remainder of his life, though he continues to be revered as a great Polish figure. During his exile he lived for part of 1798 in this Society Hill house. An upstairs room re-creates his modest living quarters, and a 7min slide show details his contributions to the Revolution.

Head House Square – *S. 2nd & Lombard Sts.* Extending along South Second Street between Pine and Lombard is an open, brick-paved square backed by a two-story Georgian head house *(S. 2nd and Pine Sts.)* built in 1804 to house fire-fighting apparatus. Behind it stand restored 19C market sheds that once served as produce stalls and now house crafts markets on summer weekends. The collective structure is the oldest of its kind in the country.

★ **PENN'S LANDING AND SOUTH STREET** *½ day. Map p 229.*

William Penn's first settlers found shelter in caves they dug in the riverside cliffs above the Delaware on this tract of waterfront that now lies between Vine and South Streets. Later part of the port area, this slice of coastline devolved by the

1960s into a dilapidated bygone. At that time the city wisely instigated plans to turn Penn's Landing into a major recreational complex, featuring walking and jogging paths, sculpture, a skating rink and amphitheater. At its north end, the blue span of the **Benjamin Franklin Bridge** (1926, Paul Cret) soars 150ft above the Delaware. When the bridge was completed, its 1,750ft span ranked as the longest suspension bridge in the world. Be sure to see the bridge at night, when computer-operated lighting illuminates each cable. Four blocks south, the Landing's big draw is the seaport museum and the historic ships docked just beyond it. Anchoring the south end of Penn's Landing, trendy South Street fills at night with young hipsters, who frequent the area's numerous restaurants and nightclubs.

The Italian Market – © Robert Holmes

■ South Philly

Since the Swedes arrival in the early 17C, this area has been sought out by new immigrants arriving on the shores of the Delaware. During most of the 20C, Italians have dominated here and Mafia bosses have brought their share of notoriety to the area, particularly during the speakeasy days of Prohibition. Today its straight-line streets are edged by tidy awninged houses and most of the action centers around the boisterous **Italian Market★★** *(9th St. between Christian & Wharton Sts.; Tue–Sat 9am–5pm, Sun 9am–noon;* ☎*215-551-3054).* Stretching for five blocks is a gourmand's delight of vegetable stalls; meat, fish and poultry markets, with plucked geese and other game dangling by their feet; bins full of dried *bakala*, or salt cod; and delis filled with the rich aromas of cheeses, olives and salamis.

These days, Asian shopkeepers have elbowed in on the action, but the competition is good-natured. And so is the longtime rivalry between Philly's famously popular cheesesteak dons, **Pat's King of Steaks** and **Geno's Steaks** *(across from each other at the corner of Passyunk Ave. and 9th St.).* Pat's claims to have invented the culinary craze—a steak sandwich slathered in cheese and fried onions—but the jury is still out in the debate over which artist's offerings now reign supreme.

You can see the work of budding visual artists in a series of changing exhibitions at the **Samuel S. Fleisher Art Memorial** *(709-721 Catharine St.;* ☎*215-922-3456).* The memorial incorporates a hauntingly beautiful Romanesque Revival **church** from the 1880s, filled with religious art collected by the memorial's founder, Samuel Fleisher.

South Philly's signature museum, however, is unquestionably the **Mummers Museum** *(1100 S. 2nd St. at Washington Ave.;* ☎*215-336-3050),* filled with the glittering costumes worn in the city's annual Mummers parade. The Mummers trace their earliest roots to the area's original Swedish settlers, who celebrated the New Year with masquerades and noisy revelry. Subsequent ethnic groups, including the Germans and English, added their own elements to the festivities. Today neighborhood groups spend months preparing floats and costumes for the January 1 extravaganza, and the museum explains the effort—and fun—that goes into this Philadelphia frolic.

Sights described below are listed from north to south.

★ **Independence Seaport Museum** – *211 S. Columbus Blvd.; pedestrian access via Walnut St. walking bridge. Combination tickets for ship tours available with museum entrance fee. Open year-round daily 10am–5pm. Closed Jan 1, Thanksgiving Day, Dec 25. $7.50. & 🅿 ($5–$10) www.libertynet.org/~seaport ☎215-925-5439.* Formerly the Philadelphia Maritime Museum, located in Society Hill, this new addition to Penn's Landing opened on the waterfront in 1995. The contemporary 100,000sq ft facility offers three permanent exhibits and two historic ships, and hosts a variety of traveling exhibitions. On the first floor, "Home Port Philadelphia" traces the transatlantic crossing of early-20C immigrants and the industrial life of the Port of Philadelphia during that period; "Divers of the Deep" chronicles human attempts to explore the undersea world; and **"Workshop on the Water"** is a working boatbuilding facility where visitors can observe the construction of 19C and 20C wooden craft used in the Delaware River area.

Docked just south of the museum, the **USS Olympia**★ and the **USS Becuna** preserve different periods in American naval history. Last survivor of America's late-19C Great White Fleet, the steel-bodied *Olympia* served as the flagship of the Asiatic Squadron during the Spanish-American War. During the Battle of Manila Bay, Commodore George Dewey stood on her bridge and made his famous sangfroid proclamation, "You may fire when you are ready, Gridley." The ship's well-preserved, spacious interior retains much of its original woodwork, and exhibits recall life onboard. Docked alongside, the World War II Guppy-class submarine *Becuna* served in the 1940s as the flagship of the Southwest Pacific Fleet under Gen. Douglas MacArthur. A walk through her claustrophobic chambers offers a good idea of the cramped living conditions endured by the submarine's crew.

At Columbus Boulevard and Spruce Street, across from the museum, the **Vietnam Veterans Memorial** occupies a plaza dominated by a black granite wall etched with the names of Philadelphians who lost their lives in that war.

★★ **South Street** – Defining the southern perimeter of Penn's Landing, this trendy— and perpetually congested—street has retained its countercultural climate since it was a haven for hippies in the 1960s. Blocks of shops *(from the waterfront to 10th St.)*, specializing in everything from Latin-American jewelry to skateboards to hip-hop music, tempt locals and visitors alike. For gourmands, myriad restaurants offer a wide range of cuisines; cutting-edge clubs cater to the hip latenight crowd.

The area stretching below South Street between Second and Front Streets is the oldest occupied part of the city, where the early Swedes erected their log cabins. Now known as **Queen Village**, the small stone-paved pedestrian lanes are fronted by pristinely restored 18C and early-19C row houses.

★ **Gloria Dei Church/Old Swedes Church** – *Columbus Blvd. & Christian St. Open year-round daily 9am–5pm. & ☎215-389-1513.* Though isolated in a remote area and surrounded by the noise of freeway traffic, the small, simple church and its cramped churchyard are poignant reminders of the city's earliest days. Swedish Lutherans who had occupied the Delaware Valley since the early 17C built the brick structure between 1698 and 1700, making it the city's oldest church. Since 1845 Gloria Dei has been an Episcopal church, and its quaint interior contains such whimsical touches as a carved angel Gabriel and a ship's model hanging from the ceiling.

Excursion

★ **New Jersey State Aquarium** – 🄺🄸🄳🅂 *2hrs. On the east bank of the Delaware River at 1 Riverside Dr. in Camden. Open mid-Mar–mid-Sept daily 9:30am–5:30pm. Rest of the year Mon–Fri 9:30am–5:30pm, weekends 10am–5pm. Closed Jan 1, Thanksgiving Day, Dec 25. $10.95. ✗ & www.njaquarium.org ☎609-365-3300 or 800-616-JAWS. Access via Riverlink passenger ferry from Penn's Landing Apr–Dec daily 10am–5:30pm, every 30min; one-way 20min; $5; ✗ 🅿 ☎215-925-5465.* A short ferry ride across the Delaware River from Penn's Landing, the aquarium is housed in a large, two-story contemporary structure on the Camden waterfront. On the main level, touch baby sharks and visit an idyllic Caribbean beach and tropical shipwreck at **Ocean Base Atlantic**. And be sure to catch a dive show at **The Ocean Realm**★, where divers explain the diversity of marine life in this awesome 760,000-gallon tank that holds more than 1,400 aquatic animals *(check at information desk for show times)*.

Then proceed to the interactive second floor for a peek at cuddly-looking Water Babies and ominous Dangers of the Deep.

Complete your visit outside the main entrance, where you can watch seals frolic in an outdoor pool and trout swim in a rushing stream. *A variety of daily performances highlight different marine animals, including sharks and seals (check at information desk for show times).*

★★★ CENTER CITY   *1 day. Map p 240.*

The once worn-down area that radiates out from City Hall, bounded by Vine Street on the north and Pine Street on the south, has been remarkably revitalized in recent decades. Though part of Penn's layout, Center City did not become the chief commercial district until the 1870s, with the building of the current City Hall. By the mid-20C, decline had set in. In the late 1980s, the building of the gleaming, 960ft-high **One Liberty Place** *(1650 Market St.)* broke a long-held "gentlemen's agreement" to build nothing higher than Penn's statue atop City Hall's dome. The new high rise altered the city's appearance and spurred new growth; in 1993 the city opened the 1.3 million-square-foot, brick and limestone **Pennsylvania Convention Center** *(Arch & Race Sts. between N. 11th & N. 13th Sts.)*, which contributes millions of dollars to the city's coffers each year. Scattered among all this new development are pieces of outdoor sculpture by

Clothespin by Claes Oldenburg

such notable 20C artists as Jacques Lipchitz and Claes Oldenburg, whose landmark 45ft steel **Clothespin [1]** *(S. 15th & Market Sts.)* rises in Center Square Plaza across from City Hall.

One of William Penn's four public parks, **Rittenhouse Square** still sprawls across eight acres in the heart of the commercial district. A fashionable residential neighborhood in the 19C, the park is now fronted by upscale highrise condominiums and hotels. Nearby **South Broad Street** now bears the epithet "Avenue of the Arts," owing to the many performing-arts venues located on the blocks between Locust and South Streets. Chief among them is the **Academy of Music** *(232-46 S. Broad at Locust St.)*, a 1850s Baroque-style theater that is modeled after La Scala in Milan, Italy and serves as the winter home of the Phila-delphia Orchestra. Another

Broad Street landmark, **The Bellevue** *(Broad & Walnut Sts.)* has risen in French Renaissance splendor since it opened as the Bellevue Stratford hotel in the early 20C. Though it became notorious as the setting for the 1976 outbreak of Legionnaires' disease, its upper levels now house the gilded elegance of the Park Hyatt Philadelphia at the Bellevue, and shops fill its lower level. Several blocks southeast, more shops offer everything from gallery-caliber antiquities to old-fashioned curios along **Antique Row** *(Pine St. between S. 9th & S. 12th Sts.)*.

★★★ City Hall – *Broad & Market Sts. Interior rooms accessible by guided tour (1hr 30min) only, year-round Mon–Fri 12:30pm. Closed major holidays. Tours, which include the observation deck, depart from the information center in Room 121, East Portal. ☎215-686-2840.* Centerpiece of downtown Philadelphia, this massive 700-room French Renaissance extravaganza still ranks as the largest municipal building in the

country and the world's tallest masonry load-bearing structure. Constructed over a period of 30 years (1871-1901), City Hall was designed by John McArthur (with input from US Capitol architect Thomas U. Walter) and was intended to be the tallest and grandest building in the world. By the time of its completion, however, the enormous mansard-roofed structure with its solid masonry walls was almost obsolete, and early in this century there was talk of demolishing it. The very cost of demolition saved it, and City Hall continues to function as an administrative hub and ceremonial "palace" for the city. Its open central courtyard serves as an intersecting walkway for downtown's two main corridors, Broad and Market streets. The building's many porticos, archways and public rooms are adorned by the statuary

View down Market Street to City Hall

of Alexander Milne Calder, who depicted farmers, allegorical figures and leaders "to express American ideals and develop American genius." Calder also designed the 37ft **statue of William Penn** that surveys the city atop the building's 548ft tower. Just below the statue, an **observation deck** *(tickets available in information center or 9th-floor exhibit room; visit by 15min guided tour only, year-round Mon–Fri 9:30am–4:30pm; ☎215-686-9874)* offers panoramic views of the city and its environs. Other notable chambers include the **Mayor's Reception Room**, with rich mahogany wainscoting, coffered stenciled ceilings and a fireplace offset by Herculean caryatids; **Conversation Hall**, with its restored plaster and aluminum ceiling, and its statue of George Washington (1869, Joseph Bailly), which originally fronted Independence Hall; and the octagonal, stone **staircases** that occupy the four corners of the building.

■ Tea in the Grand Style

Celebrating the renaissance of a dignified old custom, several of Philadelphia's finest hotels have resurrected the British tradition of serving high tea in the afternoon. Each offers the classics: petite tea sandwiches, scones and cream, pastries, and a selection of first-class teas. *(Don't forget to call ahead for reservations.)*

Topping the tea-lovers' list is the **Hotel Atop the Bellevue** *(Broad & Walnut Sts.; ☎215-893-1776)*, whose 19th-floor Barrymore Room provides an idyllic tea setting; the circular room overlooking the city is swagged, muraled and domed in celestial fashion. At the elegant **Rittenhouse Hotel [A]** *(201 W. Rittenhouse Sq.; ☎215-546-9000)*, tea is served in the serene Cassatt Lounge, fronting a lovely courtyard. Styled after fine European hotels, the **Ritz-Carlton [B]** *(S. 17th & Chestnut Sts.; ☎215-563-1600)* devotes its intimate lobby lounge to tea, while at the **Four Seasons [C]** *(1 Logan Sq.; ☎215-963-1500)* you can sink into the generous sofas and armchairs of the Swann Lounge as you sip.

★★ **Masonic Temple** – *1 N. Broad St. Visit by guided tour (45min) only, Sept–Jun Mon–Fri 9am–4pm, Sat 9am–11am. Rest of the year Mon–Fri 9am–4pm.* & ☎215-988-1917. Spires, towers and the grand entrance portico of the handsome granite, Medieval Norman-style edifice give it a prominent presence on the north side of City Hall. Considered one of Freemasonry's most magnificent temples, it was conceived by 27-year-old Masonic brother James Windrim, who won a competition for the exterior design. Though it was dedicated in 1873, the building's elaborate interior rooms, designed by George Herzog, were not completed until 1908. Guided tours take visitors through halls whose motifs reflect the orders of Masonry: Moorish, Gothic, Ionic, Egyptian, Romanesque, Renaissance and Corinthian. The double Tennessee-marble Grand Staircase is overlooked by stained-glass windows and four large allegorical murals. Freemasonry has a long-established history in America; Founding Fathers Washington and Franklin were dedicated Masons. And Benjamin Franklin served twice as Grand Master of Pennsylvania.

★★ **Museum of American Art of the Pennsylvania Academy of the Fine Arts** – *Broad & Cherry Sts. Open year-round Mon–Sat 10am–5pm, Sun 11am–5pm. Closed major holidays. $5.95 (Sun free 3pm–5pm).* ✗ & *www.pafa.org/~pafa* ☎215-972-7600. The nation's first art school and museum was founded in 1805 by the respected portraitist Charles Willson Peale and others. Completed in 1876, the ornate limestone and brick Victorian building was designed by Philadelphians Frank Furness and George W. Hewitt to house both the academy and museum galleries. In the 1880s Philadelphia artist Thomas Eakins briefly served as the school's director before being dismissed for his controversial practice of having both male and female students paint from live nude models. This conservatism did not last, however, and in the early decades of the 20C, the academy spearheaded photography and avant-garde exhibitions that heralded new movements in the art world.

Visit – *2hrs.* A 1970s restoration returned the building to its original grandeur, and an imposing double staircase leads to the museum level, where the evolution of the academy's ideas concerning art are reflected. Front galleries *(nos. 1-5)* house works in the "Grand Manner," following the 18C tradition set by the academy's first honorary member, Benjamin West, and the Royal Academy of London. These works include large, heroic canvases by Peale, Gilbert Stuart and Thomas Sully. Also featured are paintings from the Colonial and Federal periods and works depicting the culture and commerce during Andrew Jackson's tenure as president. In the adjoining stair hall stand examples of 19C American sculpture. Progressing chronologically and moving toward the back of the building, works range from canvasses illustrating slavery and other "national" subjects *(gallery 6)* to the international styles and themes put into practice by American artists, such as William Morris Hunt and Mary Cassatt, who studied abroad in the late 19C *(gallery 7)*. Gallery 8 ushers in "A New Era at the Academy" with the realism of Winslow Homer, Thomas Eakins, George Bellows and members of the Ash Can school. Bringing visitors back to recent decades, the final galleries *(nos. 10 & 13)* introduce early-20C Modernism and post-World War II Abstract Expressionism.

Chinatown – *N. 8th to N. 11th Sts. between Arch and Vine Sts.* Packed with people, shops and eateries, the eight blocks of Chinatown offer an eclectic mix of Asian cultures and cuisines, from spicy Szechuan and Hunan to Thai and Vietnamese. Overarching the scene is the 40ft **Chinese Friendship Gate** *(10th St. between Arch & Cherry Sts.)*. The elaborately carved and painted landmark was created in 1984 by Chinese artisans, using materials from Tianjin, Philadelphia's Chinese sister city.

★ **Rosenbach Museum and Library** – *2010 Delancey St. Visit by guided tour (1hr 15min) only, year-round Tue–Sun 11am–4pm. Closed major holidays & Aug–mid-Sept. $5. www.libertynet.org/~rosenbl/* ☎*215-732-1600*. Renowned for its rare books and manuscripts, the museum occupies an 1866 brick town house that was once home to Philip and Abraham Rosenbach. Book dealers and antiquarians in the first half of the 20C, the Rosenbach brothers amassed an impressive collection of decorative arts, as well as some 30,000 books and 300,000 manuscripts and letters. One of the most prized pieces in the collection is James Joyce's handwritten **Ulysses manuscript**★. Found throughout the museum are paintings and sculptures by such masters as Thomas Sully and Henri Matisse; American and British silver; American and British antique furnishings; and Derby and Sèvres porcelain. Vitrines display such literary gems as illuminated medieval manuscripts, original illustrations by children's author Maurice Sendak, and manuscript pages from the poetry of Milton, Wordsworth, Keats and Shelley. The third-floor library *(open to researchers by appointment)* contains the museum's wealth of rare books. On the second floor, the Greenwich Village living room of mid-20C Modernist poet Marianne Moore is re-created with Moore's original furnishings.

❶ Reading Terminal Market

Map p 240. N. 12th St. between Filbert and Arch Sts. ☎*215-922-2317*. The only survivor of Center City's grand Victorian-era train stations, the Reading Railroad's red-brick and terra-cotta terminal has turned its face decisively away from the 1890s and toward the 1990s. No longer a grim coal-and-iron port, the arched train shed has been incorporated into the design of the Pennsylvania Convention Center, while the more elaborate Renaissance-style head house (designed by New York architect Francis Kimball) now contains a festive food bazaar. Here shop stalls sell fresh produce and gourmet delicacies, and restaurants keep the steak, seafood and cappuccino coming.

■ **Wanamaker's**

Philadelphia's first department store, **John Wanamaker's** *(1300 Market St.)*, a magnificent Italian Renaissance merchandising palace designed by Daniel Burnham, opened in 1911. Enclosing 1.9 million square feet, it dazzled Philadelphians with its 30,000-pipe organ, crystal chandeliers and a central court overlooked by the balconies of upper floors. A huge bronze eagle purchased from the 1904 Louisiana Purchase Exposition in St. Louis still stands in the central court. Named for its founder, Philadelphia merchant king John Wanamaker, the store dominated the retail scene for some 70 years, until it passed out of family hands in the 1980s. After downsizing to a few floors and changing ownership several times, the store is now owned by the May Company, which operates it as Lord & Taylor's.

Pennsylvania Hospital – *S. 8th & Spruce Sts. Open year-round Mon–Fri 8:30am–5pm. Closed major holidays.* ✕ ▣ *www.pahosp.com* ☎*215-829-3000. A walking-tour brochure is available at the information desk (accessible via the main entrance on 8th St.).* Occupying the square block between Spruce and Pine, and Eighth and Ninth Streets, the nation's first hospital was founded in 1751 by Benjamin Franklin and Dr. Thomas Bond. Its **Pine Street building**★, a fine example of Colonial and Federal architecture that evolved in stages between 1755 and 1804, embodies much of the institution's history. Twin staircases in the entrance hall lead to the country's first medical library *(2nd floor)* and the 1804 circular **surgical amphitheater** *(3rd floor)*, topped by a domed skylight. In the gallery pavilion hangs Benjamin West's *Christ Healing the Sick in the Temple*, the artist's gift to the hospital.

★★★ **BENJAMIN FRANKLIN PARKWAY**   *2 days. Map p 240.*

Modeled after the Champs Elysées in Paris, the Benjamin Franklin Parkway, which cuts a broad, pleasant swath from City Hall to the Pennsylvania Museum of Art, heralds the beginning of Fairmount Park. The parkway was designed by landscape architect Jacques Breber and constructed in 1917, serving as a diagonal route across Penn's original grid of smaller streets. On its southeast end, one of Penn's original town squares (since modified as Logan Circle) bears the name of the colony's early administrator, James Logan. In the 1920s, the elegant **Swann Memorial Fountain [2]** took its place in the square. Alexander Stirling Calder playfully designed it with bronze swans around the periphery, to honor Dr. Wilson Carey Swann, president of the Philadelphia Fountain Society. The fountain's three focal figures represent the city's three main waterways: the Schuylkill and Delaware rivers and Wissahickon Creek.

On the north side of the circle, the **Free Library of Philadelphia** *(1901 Vine St.;* ☎*215-686-5322)* was conceived as one of the civic buildings in the original parkway plan. In keeping with the parkway's French design, the massive library—designed by Horace Trumbauer in 1917—was modeled after the twin palaces on the Place de la Concorde in Paris. The parkway's northwest end is defined by **Eakins Oval**, named for Philadelphia painter Thomas Eakins. Occupying the oval's center, the **Washington Monument [3]** was originally created by German sculptor Rudolf Siemering for the 1896 Centennial in Fairmount Park and moved here in 1928.

Sights described below are organized from east to west beginning at Logan Circle.

★★ **Cathedral of Saints Peter and Paul** – *B.F. Pkwy. and N. 18th St. Open year-round daily 7am–3:30pm.* ☎*215-561-1313.* The flood of Irish Catholic immigrants that began settling in the city in the 1830s led to the construction of this cathedral beginning in 1844. Inspired by Rome's Church of San Carlo al Corso, the copper-domed Italian Renaissance edifice with its sober Corinthian portico was designed by local architects Napoleon Le Brun and John Notman. On the interior, enormous Corinthian pilasters surround the transept and nave, which is overarched by a coffered, barrel-vaulted ceiling. The dome occulus was done by Constantino Brumidi, who also painted the frescoes in the dome of the US Capitol in Washington, DC.

★ **The Academy of Natural Sciences of Philadelphia** – 🅺🅸🅳🆂 *1900 B.F. Pkwy. at Logan Circle. Open year-round Mon–Fri 10am–4:30pm, weekends & holidays 10am–5pm. Closed Jan 1, Thanksgiving Day, Dec 25. $7.75.* ✕ 🔥 *www.acnatsci.org* ☎*215-299-1000.* Founded in 1812, the Academy claims to be the oldest science research institution in the Western Hemisphere. The museum itself, which opened in its present building in 1876, is a great place to learn about dinosaurs. Its early founders began the assemblage of bones that has now grown into the museum's renowned collection. On the first floor, the acclaimed exhibit **Discovering Dinosaurs**★ displays skeletons (both fossilized and cast) of the enormous creatures and does a superb job of explaining their lives on earth, as well as the rigors paleontologists face in uncovering fossilized remnants. At the back of the first floor, you can walk through a humid, tropical garden where bright butterflies flit freely. Life-size dioramas throughout the museum showcase specimens of native animals and re-create habitats found in North America, Asia and Africa. On the third floor, visit **Outside-In**, a hands-on nature center for children. In addition to its permanent galleries, the museum also hosts changing exhibitions annually.

★★ **The Franklin Institute Science Museum** – *N. 20th St. & B.F. Pkwy. Open year-round daily 9:30am–5pm (Fri & Sat 9pm). Closed Jan 1, Thanksgiving Day, Dec 25. $9.50 (museum only), $7.50 (Omniverse Theater only), $12.50 (museum & theater* *combination ticket).* ✗ & ♿ ▯ *www.fi.edu* ☎*215-448-1200.* Founded in 1824 to teach artisans and mechanics basic science, the Franklin Institute and its museum have successfully turned the sciences into public entertainment. The current, cavernous 300,000sq ft museum is entered through the domed **Benjamin Franklin National Memorial**, dominated by a 122-ton marble likeness of a seated Franklin. The Science Center dazzles children and adults alike with its clever and informative exhibits.

On the first floor, a communications exhibit covers innovations ranging from the printing press to video technology, while the railroad hall reproduces a Victorian railway station and houses a Baldwin steam locomotive. Here also, the **Fels Planetarium** features a changing program of astronomy and laser shows. Major exhibits begin on the second floor, with a popular walk-through version of the human heart and other anatomical and bioscience exhibits, as well as displays on electricity and aviation. In the **Tuttleman Omniverse Theater**, 70mm Omnimax films are projected onto a 79ft-wide screen, producing a simulated experience full of thrills. The 20,000ft **Mandell Center**, devoted to traveling exhibitions, also houses a permanent new Cyberzone, where visitors can explore computer technology.

A staircase overlooking a sweeping pendulum leads to third-floor exhibits on shipbuilding, hands-on mechanics, weather and the changing earth. The fourth floor is devoted to math and astronomy and boasts its own small observatory and working ham radio station.

Surrounding the museum, the outdoor **Science Park** uses whimsical interactive elements to teach the fundamentals of science *(open May–Oct daily 9:30am–4pm).*

★ **Rodin Museum** – *N. 22nd St. & B.F. Pkwy. Open year-round Tue–Sun 10am–5pm. Closed major holidays. $3.* & ▯ *www.rodinmuseum.org* ☎*215-763-8100 or 800-537-7676.* Administered by the Philadelphia Museum of Art, the small 1920s Beaux-Arts building and surrounding gardens were designed by Paul Cret and Jacques Gréber and are devoted exclusively to the sculpture and drawings of French artist **Auguste Rodin** (1840-1917). Originally the collection of Philadelphia movie-theater magnate and philanthropist Jules Mastbaum, the 124 sculptures—the largest collection of Rodin's works outside France—include bronze casts of *The Burghers of Calais, Eternal Springtime* and *Gates of Hell. The Thinker* sits at the parkway entrance to the museum grounds.

★★ **Philadelphia Museum of Art** – *Allow 1 day to visit. N. 26th St. & B.F. Pkwy. Open year-round Tue–Sun 10am–5pm (Wed 8:45pm). Closed major holidays. $7.* ✗ & ▯ *www. philamuseum.org* ☎*215-763-8100 or 800-537-7676. The museum hosts a popular Wednesday-night program of movies, music, dance, lectures and art demonstrations.* Anchoring the northwest end of the parkway, this stately Greek Revival structure (1928, C. Clark Zantzinger, Horace Trumbauer and Charles L. Borie, Jr.) ranks

Philadelphia Museum of Art

© Robert Llewellyn

among the most significant art museums in the country. The collection housed within its three connected Minnesota dolomite "temples" is representative of the artistic achievements of humankind worldwide, fulfilling the goal set by its influential mid-20C curator, Fiske Kimball, whose intent was to "enable the visitor to retrace the great historic pageant of the evolution of art."

Historical Notes – The museum's establishment can be traced to the 1876 Centennial Exposition, when the state legislature called for the building of a permanent structure to be used as an art gallery during the exposition and, thereafter, to house the Pennsylvania Museum and the School of Industrial Art. Still standing in West Fairmount Park, Memorial Hall served this function until the early 1920s. Construction on the current Neoclassical building, with its ornately embellished columns and pediments, began in 1919 on a hill called Faire Mount, and the first galleries opened in 1924. Subsequent additions have followed as the museum has expanded its holdings, which now number more than 300,000 objects in four major departments: Asian, European, American and 20C collections. To supplement these, the museum also mounts a score of temporary exhibitions annually. In 1976 the grand flight of stairs leading to the museum's main entrance portico gained national fame as the high point in Sylvester Stallone's morning run in the original *Rocky* film. The museum's exterior and surrounding grounds are punctuated by a plethora of statuary, most with allegorical and classical themes.

First Floor – The museum's outstanding collection of Impressionist works forms the core of its first-floor wing devoted to **European Art 1850-1900**★★ *(galleries 150-165).* Setting the stage for the coming of Impressionism and the modern period, the initial galleries house works by Courbet, Fantin-Latour, Whistler and the traditional classicism of Delacroix. Within the Impressionist galleries, all the masters are represented: Degas *(Little Dancer* sculpture), Monet *(Water Lilies),* Renoir *(The Grand Boulevards),* Cézanne *(The Large Bathers),* van Gogh *(Sunflowers),* Rodin, Manet, Cassatt, Pissarro, Rousseau, Gauguin, Sisley and Bonnard.

Within the adjoining section devoted to **20C Art** *(galleries 166-188),* the modern period is represented by the Cubist works of Pablo Picasso, Georges Braque, Juan Gris and Marc Chagall; the sculpture of Constantine Brancusi; the whimsical Expressionism of Paul Klee and Wassily Kandinsky; and the Surrealism of Salvador Dalí and René Magritte. Moving into mid-century, the works of Americans Marsden Hartley and Georgia O'Keeffe are displayed, along with the Pop Art of Man Ray and Jasper Johns, the Dadaism of Marcel Duchamps, and the Abstract Expressionism of Robert Motherwell, as well as other contemporary works.

The wing containing **American Art** *(galleries 100-119)* is notable for its unsurpassed collection of paintings by 19C Philadelphia artist Thomas Eakins. An extensive assemblage of Colonial silver is also on display, including pieces by renowned silversmith Philip Syng, Jr. *(p 229)* Among the American furniture featured are fine examples of Shaker craftsmanship and a collection of rural 18C and 19C Pennsylvania-German decorative arts.

Second Floor – Take the **Great Stair Hall** to the second floor, where an ethereal statue of Diana, goddess of the hunt, by 19C sculptor Augustus Saint-Gaudens, presides at the top of the stairs. The work originally stood atop the first Madison Square Garden as a weathervane. Around the balcony hang 13 massive tapestries, by Dutch Baroque master Peter Paul Rubens and Italian artist Peitro da Cortona, depicting the life of the 3C emperor Constantine the Great. Hovering above the broad ceremonial staircase here is Alexander Calder's playful *Ghost* mobile.

Much of this floor is devoted to European art. The earliest period, **European Art 1100-1500**★ *(galleries 207-221)* is notable for its rare collection of architectural details from monasteries and chapels. A re-created Medieval cloister *(gallery 204),* with an arcaded walkway surrounding a marble fountain, fuses an amalgam of elements from several French monasteries. A massive French Romanesque stone portal from the 12C Abbey of St.-Laurent *(gallery 201)* leads into a re-creation of a small chapel. Throughout these galleries, paintings, altar panels, sculpture and stained glass recall the religious character of art during the Middle Ages, while the paintings and sculpture depict the gradual move toward secularism and include works by 15C Dutch masters Jan van Eyck and Rogier van der Weyden. Behind the staircase, the museum's extensive collection of **Arms and Armor** *(galleries 245-249)* focuses on European field armor, firearms, crossbows, swords and daggers from the 11C through the 16C.

The section devoted to **European Art 1500 to 1850** *(galleries 250-299)* begins with the decorative arts, paintings and sculpture of the Renaissance. An exceptional choir screen and altarpiece from the chapel of the 16C French Chateau of Pagny *(gallery 255)* depicts the passion of Christ. The strength of this section, however, lies in its re-created period rooms from English, French and Dutch homes and estates. Paneling, furnishings, portraiture and other appointments recall in vivid detail the changing decorative tastes of Europe, from the dark Tudor-style decor to the flourishes of the Rococo to the restraints of the Palladian and Adamesque styles.

Adjoining the early European art galleries, the **Asian Art**★★ wing *(galleries 220-244)* features a wide range of artistic traditions, from Persian mosaic tiles and carpets to small, exquisitely crafted Thai Buddhist pieces and watercolors to a pillared **temple hall** *(gallery 224)* from India—a rare example of Indian stone architecture. The bulk of the collection, however, is devoted to Japanese and Chinese works. A Chinese nobleman's **reception hall** *(gallery 226)* from 17C Beijing captures the splendor of the late Ming dynasty (1368-1644) in its elaborately carved and painted wooden beams and lacquered pillars. A more light-hearted motif is found in the decor of a Beijing scholar's study from the Ch'ing dynasty (1644-1911); other galleries display Ming, Sung and Yuan porcelain. Surrounded by interior gardens, the museum's **Japanese ceremonial teahouse** *(gallery 244)*—called *Sunkaraku*, or "Evanescent Joys"—was designed by early-20C architect Ogi Rodo; intricate Japanese scrolls from the 16C to the 20C are also represented.

Ground Floor – Several smaller galleries occupy this space, devoted to special and changing exhibits from the museum's own collection of **Prints, Drawings, and Photographs**. This group is rich in the works of old masters and 19C and 20C artists and photographers, notably Alfred Stieglitz. One corridor also displays contemporary American crafts, and the Great Stair Hall is backed by an enormous canvas painted by Marc Chagall as a backdrop for the ballet *Aleko*. Also on this level are a restaurant, cafeteria and gift shop.

■ **If Time Permits...**

If you have extra time in Philadelphia, the following sights cover a wide range of interests:

Civil War Library and Museum *(1805 Pine St.;* ☎*215-735-8196)* – This three-story repository of Civil War memorabilia includes life masks of Abraham Lincoln and the stuffed head of General Meade's horse.

Edgar Allan Poe National Historic Site *(532 N. 7th St.;* ☎*215-597-8780)* – The modest brick addition to a larger home in the Spring Garden area housed author Edgar Allan Poe for about a year in the early 1840s. Its basement is thought to have inspired Poe's story *The Tell-Tale Heart*.

The College of Physicians of Philadelphia *(19 S. 22nd St.;* ☎*215-563-3737)* – Dating back to 1787, this source of public health information features the **Mütter Museum**, which depicts medical history with artifacts and pathological displays. The adjoining College Gallery hosts changing exhibits relating to health today.

National Archives *(900 Market St., Room 1350;* ☎*215-597-3000)* – Changing exhibits showcase the archives' extensive collection of records dating from the First Continental Congress to the present.

Please Touch Museum Kids *(210 N. 21st St.;* ☎*215-963-0667)* – Fun is fundamental in this activity-packed museum geared to preschoolers.

★ **FAIRMOUNT PARK**   *1½ days*

With the establishment of the Faire Mount Water Works in 1815 to provide Philadelphia with drinkable water, the city became interested in acquiring surrounding lands to protect the purity of the water source and to provide recreation for residents. In 1844 city officials began the gradual purchase of nearby estates, and Fairmount Park became a reality. Sweeping across 8,900 acres from City Hall up the Benjamin Franklin Parkway, then northwest along the Schuylkill River and Wissahickon Valley into the suburbs, Fairmount Park ranks as one of the largest city parks in the world. Encompassed within its borders are the Museum of Art, a number of historic homes, a horticultural center and a wealth of recreational opportunities along the Schuylkill River and Wissahickon Creek.

In 1876 the park hosted the US Centennial Exposition, and some 250 buildings were constructed here for the event. The only major Centennial structure remaining is the colossal Beaux-Arts **Memorial Hall** *(42nd St. and N. Concourse Dr.)*. Its enormous square cast-iron and glass dome *(under renovation)*, originally lit by gaslights to glow at night, is topped by a statue of Columbia. The building now houses park administrative offices and a city recreation hall. At the far end of North Concourse Drive, the **Mann Music Center** serves as the summer home of the Philadelphia Orchestra and offers a dramatic outdoor venue for live performances.

Fairmount Water Works – *Off Kelly Dr. behind the Museum of Art. Visit by guided tour (45min) only, Jun–mid-Oct weekends 1pm–4pm.* ☎215-685-4908. Frederick Graff designed this steam-powered pumping station in 1812 to supply the city with potable water. Over time Graff and his son ornamented the exteriors of the buildings with porticos and columns meant to reflect Neoclassical and mill town motifs. The Schuylkill's polluted waters forced the water works to close in 1909. Today this National Historic Landmark is undergoing renovation.

Azalea Garden – *Off Kelly Dr. just north of the Water Works.* Designed in the English Romantic style with curving paths bordered by shrubs and accented by large trees, the four-acre garden was originally planted in 1952. A 1990 restoration added a variety of understory trees and hydrangea, franklinia, crape myrtles and other flowering species to extend the blooming season beyond the early spring blaze of azalea color.

★ **Boathouse Row** – *Off Kelly Dr., along the Schuylkill River north of the Azalea Garden.* Dating from the mid-19C to the turn of the century, this row of Victorian cottages is headquarters for the private boating clubs that make up the city's renowned "Schuylkill Navy." Since the founding of these amateur rowing clubs in 1835, their members have participated in rowing competitions on the river. Outlined in white lights by night, the old boathouses compose one of the city's most picturesque landmarks.

Horticulture Center – *N. Horticultural & Montgomery Dr. Open year-round daily 9am–3pm. $2.* & 🖪 ☎215-685-0096. The center's 22-acre **Centennial Arboretum**, originally planted for the 1876 Centennial Exposition, abounds with trees from Asia, Europe and North America, as well as demonstration and display gardens devoted to herbs, perennials and gardening techniques. A serene Japanese house-and-garden complex called **Pine Breeze Villa★** reflects the lifestyle of an upper-class Japanese family in the early 17C. The *shoin,* or main interior room, functions as both a study and reception room. A bridge connects the main house to a small teahouse; surrounding both are traditional Japanese gardens, punctuated by ponds and watercourses. Nearby a **greenhouse complex** displays flowering plants and cacti.

★ **Philadelphia Zoo** – 🄺🄳 *3400 W. Girard Ave. Open Apr–Oct Mon–Fri 9:30am–4:45pm, weekends 9:30am–5:45pm. Rest of the year daily 9:30am–4:45pm. Closed Thanksgiving Day, Dec 24–25, Dec 31–Jan 1. $8.50.* ✗ & 🖪 *($4) www.phillyzoo.org* ☎215-243-1100. Like so many other institutions in this city, the Zoological Society of Philadelphia was the first in the nation, established in 1859. Modeled on a Victorian pleasure garden, the zoo welcomes visitors through the original wrought-iron gates and turreted twin gatehouses (1874, Frank Furness & George Hewitt). Inside, the grounds have an intimate, inviting feel, with winding paths rambling over 42 acres and past more than 1,600 animals from across the globe, including some 50 endangered species. Africa is well represented with the usual complement of hoofed animals and big cats, including **white lions**, of which there are only a score surviving in the world. You'll also find such water-loving acrobats as penguins, giant river otters and polar bears. Behind the penguins stands the 18C Adamesque mansion built by William Penn's grandson, John, and now used as administrative offices. A Rare Animal House displays some of the world's most endangered species, and young visitors will enjoy discovering secrets of the natural kingdom inside the Treehouse *(10am–4pm; $1, children only).* The zoo's primate house burned in a much-publicized 1995 fire; a new primate house is scheduled to open in the spring of 1999.

Historic Houses – *Mount Pleasant, Cedar Grove, Strawberry Mansion, Sweetbriar and Woodford are open year-round. Other houses are open in summer only. For information about the houses or special tours, contact the Museum of Art Park Houses* ☎215-684-

7922. *Trolley tours (45min) featuring 2 mansions per day depart from the 16th St. visitor center year-round daily 10am–3pm every 30min. $8. Philadelphia Trolley Works* ☎215-925-8687. In the 18C and early 19C a number of well-heeled Philadelphians built rural retreats on the bluffs above the Schuylkill, an area described by one 18C observer as being "finely situated for prospect, health and pleasure." Now governed by the Fairmount Park Commission, these elegant homes represent fine examples of domestic period architecture. The houses are separately administered by a variety of organizations, including preservation societies, women's clubs and the Philadelphia Museum of Art.

★ **Cedar Grove** – *W. Fairmount Park off Landsdowne Dr. Open year-round daily 10am–5pm. Closed major holidays. $2.50.* ▣. This gray fieldstone farmhouse (1746) is the oldest of the park's historic homes. The modest interior holds three centuries of family furnishings.

Laurel Hill – *Off Edgely Dr. Open Apr–Dec Wed–Fri 10am–4pm. Closed major holidays. $2.50.* ▣. The original central Georgian portion of this house, completed in 1767, served as the summer home for pre-Revolutionary War mayor Samuel Shoemaker. Federal furnishings adorn the drawing and dining rooms.

★ **Lemon Hill** – *Off Kelly Dr. Open Apr–Dec Tue–Sun 10am–4pm. Closed major holidays. $2.50.* ▣. Merchant Henry Pratt built the Neoclassical gem *(privately owned)* in 1800 on land originally owned by Revolutionary financier Robert Morris. (The name derives from the lemon trees that Morris grew in his greenhouse.) The gracious interior showcases fine pieces by early-19C craftsmen.

★ **Mount Pleasant** – *Off Fountain Green Dr. Open year-round daily 10am–5pm. Closed major holidays. $2.50.* ▣. Quoined corners, double chimneys and the balustraded roof of this elegant stucco mansion reflect classic Georgian details. The interior retains its original elaborate woodwork as well as Rococo furniture from the collection of the Philadelphia Museum of Art.

Strawberry Mansion – *Off Dauphin St. Open year-round Tue–Sun 10am–4pm. Closed major holidays. $2.50.* ▣. This rambling manor began as a Federal-style country house completed in 1789 for Judge William Lewis. Fine woodwork in the entry hall and parlor still reflect the understated refinements of the Federal period.

Sweetbriar – *W. Fairmount Park off Landsdowne Dr. Open year-round Wed–Sun 10am–4pm. Closed major holidays. $2.50.* ▣. Built in 1797 by merchant Samuel Breck, the white Neoclassical stone mansion is furnished with pieces by respected period craftsmen from Philadelphia and New England.

★ **Woodford** – *Off Dauphin St. Visit by guided tour (30min) only, year-round Tue–Sun 10am–4pm. Closed major holidays. $2.50.* ▣ ☎215-229-6115. The first floor of the well-proportioned late Georgian home was built in 1756 by merchant William Coleman, a close friend of Benjamin Franklin; the second floor was probably added in the 1770s. The house is notable for its outstanding collection of **Colonial furnishings**.

RittenhouseTown – *206 Lincoln Dr.; entrance off Wissahickon Ave.* In 1690 Dutch immigrant Wilhelm Rittenhouse established the first paper mill in America on this site beside Monoshone Creek. Throughout the 18C, the village prospered as an industrial site, once boasting 40 structures. Today seven historic buildings remain. The three that are open to the public include the birthplace of pioneering 18C astronomer David Rittenhouse, after whom Rittenhouse Square is named; and the c.1720 Abraham Rittenhouse home, which features a 15min video detailing the history of the site, as well as exhibits that relate its development *(open Apr–Oct weekends noon–4pm; closed major holidays; $4;* ▣ ☎215-438-5711).

② **Valley Green Inn**

Map p 240. Springfield Ave. & Forbidden Dr. ☎215-247-1730. Picturesque in both setting and atmosphere, the Valley Green, with its broad, inviting porch and green shutters, has stood on the banks of Wissahickon Creek since the mid-19C. Now part of upper Fairmount Park, the inn overlooks a stone bridge leading down into the park and serves fare worthy of its lovely surroundings. Meals are served in three cozy, antique-filled dining rooms and feature fresh, artfully combined ingredients.

★ **UNIVERSITY CITY** *½ day*

Dominating the left bank of the Schuylkill in west Philadelphia, University City teems with the student life of both the University of Pennsylvania and Drexel University. The former, established by Benjamin Franklin in the mid-18C as The Academy and Charitable School of Philadelphia, has now grown to become one of the nation's most prestigious universities. Philanthropist and banker Anthony Drexel founded the latter institution in the 1890s, and its population now numbers 9,200 students. Drexel's original **Main Building** *(32nd and Chestnut Sts.)* still bristles with turrets and arches. Its interior, centered around a Rococo court overlooked by three levels, houses the **Drexel University Museum** (☎215-895-2424), a Victorian-style picture gallery housed beneath a coffered skylight.

★ **University of Pennsylvania** – *From S. 34th to S. 40th Sts., between Walnut & Spruce Sts. Campus maps and information available in admissions office in College Hall. Visitors to the Quadrangle must sign in with dormitory reception on Spruce St.* With some 21,000 students, the Ivy League institution sprawls across 260 acres. It moved to its present location in the 1870s, when west Philadelphia was still a rural enclave. The focal point then, as now, was **College Hall** *(central campus between 34th & 36th Sts.),* a green ashlar monument that set the tone for the Gothic style of the campus. An 1899 statue of Benjamin Franklin sits outside the hall, overlooking the bustle of students along **Locust Walk**, the major pedestrian thoroughfare cutting through campus. The nearby **Quadrangle** *(Spruce St. between 36th and 37th Sts.),* built at the turn of the century, was inspired by the design of Britain's Oxford and Cambridge universities, with ornate Jacobean Revival dormitories fronting a central courtyard. Three blocks away, the university's **Institute of Contemporary Art** *(118 S. 36th St.;* ☎215-898-7108) is dedicated to exhibiting and promoting the visions of working artists and has shown the works of such contemporary figures as Andy Warhol, Robert Mapplethorpe and Jose Bedia.

> **3** **White Dog Cafe**
> *Map p 240. 3420 Sansom St.*
> ☎215-386-9224. Gingham and lace create a homey setting in this 19C town house, which once belonged to Russian noblewoman and intellectual Madame Helena Blatavasky. Named for the white dog that mystically cured Blatavasky's ailing leg, the popular cafe recalls its namesake by complementing the decor with myriad canine memorabilia. Regional cuisine made with the freshest—and often organic—local ingredients tempts the palette. And the cafe stimulates minds as well as appetites by sponsoring an ongoing program of speakers addressing timely political topics.

★★ **University of Pennsylvania Museum of Archaeology and Anthropology** – *33rd and Spruce Sts. Open Sept–Memorial Day Tue–Sat 10am–4:30pm, Sun 1pm–5pm. Rest of the year Tue–Sat 10am–4:30pm. $5. ✗ & www.upenn.edu/museum/* ☎215-898-4000. The university's enormous, rambling museum was originally designed in the 1890s, with subsequent additions. Situated on 12 acres donated by the city, it combines in its eclectic largesse of architecture elements of Japanese, Byzantine, and Arts and Crafts design. Its 30-some galleries display artifacts that reflect the many cultures and civilizations that have been studied by university scholars.

On the first floor you'll find exhibits of Plains Indian feather and beadwork and a changing photographic gallery. A glass-walled mosaic gallery, featuring Turkish and Syrian tilework, overlooks inner courtyards. The second floor is devoted to the indigenous cultures of the American Southwest, Alaska, Polynesia and Africa. The Middle America gallery contains superb examples of carved limestone stelae, as well as sculpted greenstone and pottery. Large halls contain artifacts related to the archaeology and architecture of **Ancient Egypt★★** and include stelae, columns and figurines from sites excavated by the university. On the third floor you will find more displays of Egyptian artifacts, including a grouping of mummies and sculpted sarcophagi. Also represented are the sculpture, pottery and coins of ancient Greece, from the Bronze Age to the Hellenistic period; Roman statuary; Etruscan artifacts; and Hindu and Buddhist art from India, Tibet and other areas of Southeast Asia. Statuary, painted scrolls and porcelain deck the massive **China rotunda**. The renowned artifacts recovered from the Sumerian

Royal Tombs of Ur★ (in present-day Iraq) by university archaeologists in 1922 fill a large gallery with finely wrought gold, jewelry and vessels. A final exhibit is devoted to Ancient Near East pottery dating from 7000 BC.

Anne & Jerome Fisher Fine Arts Library – *Locust Walk at S. 34th St. Open Sept–May Mon–Fri 8:30am–8pm. Closed during university breaks.* ♿ 𝐏 ☎215-898-8325. Renowned Philadelphia architect Frank Furness designed this red-brick Victorian extravaganza, which was completed in 1890 as the university library. A portion of the structure is now devoted to the **Arthur Ross Gallery**, featuring changing exhibits from the university collection and elsewhere.

★ NORTHWEST *1½ days*

Alongside the 1,400 acres of undeveloped furrow known as the Wissahickon Valley, gracious neighborhoods of elegant stone mansions and Colonial homes mix with older pockets of urban decay. Cut by Wissahickon Creek and upper Fairmount Park, the northwest wedge of Philadelphia encompasses the historic sites of Germantown, the fashionable suburb of Chestnut Hill and the newly discovered charm of **Manayunk**. The latter, a 19C riverside textile town located 4mi up the Schuylkill River from Center City, now boasts an artsy, gentrified Main Street. Here the local cognoscenti go to browse in funky shops and galleries, and sample innovative cafe fare. Running through much of the Northwest is scenic, wooded **Lincoln Drive**, which follows the zigzag course of Wissahickon Creek up from the Schuylkill River and through the park before heading north toward Mount Airy and Chestnut Hill.

★ Germantown *Sights along Germantown Ave. are organized from south to north.*

Laid out in 1683, this township roughly 6mi north of Center City was settled by 13 German families, all of whom were Quakers or Mennonites. Through the decades the town developed into a manufacturing center famous for textiles and leather. In the mid-18C, wealthy Philadelphians began building elegant summer homes here, away from the crowds and heat of the city. During the Revolution, the town was thrown into tumult by the pivotal **Battle of Germantown**, fought between Washington's Continental Army and British forces led by General Howe. Turmoil has again marked recent decades, as Germantown has suffered urban decay and unrest. A number of the great houses and historic buildings of its illustrious past, however, still punctuate stone-paved **Germantown Avenue**, a former Indian trail that has long served as the main street through Germantown, Mount Airy and Chestnut Hill. Among the 500 historic structures remaining along the avenue are the low-roofed 1770 **Mennonite Meetinghouse** *(no. 6121)*; **Grumblethorpe** *(no. 5267)*, built in 1744 by German immigrant John Wister from Wissahickon schist quarried on the property; and **Wyck** *(no. 6026)*, a late-17C residence occupied by nine generations of the same Quaker family. The **Germantown Historical Society** *(5501 Germantown Ave.; open year-round Tue & Thu 10am–4pm, Sun 1pm–5pm; closed major holidays; $4;* ♿ 𝐏 ☎215-844-1683*)* provides information on historic sites throughout the area, and its changing exhibits feature displays on black history, as well as items from its collection of toys, furniture and clothing.

★ **Stenton** – *4601 N. 18th St. Visit by guided tour (1hr) only, Apr–Dec Tue–Sat 1pm–4pm. Rest of the year by appointment only. Closed major holidays. $5. Reservations suggested.* 𝐏 ☎215-329-7312. Now isolated in a remote southern corner of Germantown surrounded by abandoned factories, this three-acre plantation was the home of William Penn's secretary, **James Logan**. Logan designed and built the impressive late-Georgian structure—subsequently occupied by six generations of Logans—between 1723 and 1730. Its interior is handsomely furnished with pieces ranging from 1730 to 1830, including many family and Philadelphia-made items and an outstanding textile collection.

Deshler-Morris House – *5442 Germantown Ave. Visit by guided tour (30min) only, Apr–mid-Dec Tue–Sat 1pm–4pm. Rest of the year by appointment only. Closed major holidays. www.libertynet.org/~inhp* ☎215-596-1748. David Deshler purchased this residence from his uncle John Wister and began construction on a small summer house in 1751. By 1772 the house had become the nine-room structure that stands today. The home played a role in national history twice: in the 1777 Battle of Germantown, when British general William Howe headquartered here; and again in 1793-94, when President Washington resided here to escape the yellow fever epidemic raging in Philadelphia. The house is now interpreted to the period of Washington's stay.

★ **Ebenezer Maxwell Mansion** – *200 W. Tulpehocken St. at Greene St. Visit by guided tour only year-round Fri–Sun 1pm–4pm. $4.* ☎*215-438-0133.* The 1859 stone villa, built by textile merchant Ebenezer Maxwell, epitomizes eclectic Victorian tastes, combining Italianate, French, and English Gothic elements in its exterior. The interior offers a richly authentic look at the excesses of Victorian decor, including an array of faux finishes, ornate wallpaper and carpeting, and superb ceiling stenciling in the upstairs bedrooms.

★★ **Cliveden** – *6401 Germantown Ave., at Morton St. Visit by guided tour (1hr) only, Apr–Dec Thu–Sun noon–4pm. Rest of the year by appointment only. $6.* ☎*215-848-1777.* Situated on a six-acre sweep of forested grounds, the country manor of the Chew family was begun in the 1760s as a summer retreat by Colonial chief justice Benjamin Chew. Ten years after its completion, the elegant home found itself encircled by history, as the October 4, 1777, Battle of Germantown swirled in and around it. About 100 British soldiers commanded by Lt. Col. Thomas Musgrave barricaded themselves in the house, causing General Washington to order a full-scale attack on Cliveden. The Continentals' attack did little to dislodge the British, and Washington's troops withdrew in defeat. However, their tenacity here and at Saratoga, New York in the same year convinced the French to support their cause. Today the exterior of the house still bears the scars made by 18C cannon-balls. The elegant interior, featuring a broad central hall, contains furnishings spanning the Chew family's 200-year occupancy, including many pieces crafted by Philadelphia artisans.

Across the street from Cliveden, **Upsala** (*no. 6430*) is a 1798 Quaker farmhouse that stands on grounds that saw action during the Battle of Germantown, when Washington's forces fought here.

Additional Sights

Chestnut Hill – *Bounded by Lincoln Dr., Northwestern Ave., and Stenton and Ridge Aves.* Once an extension of Germantown, Chestnut Hill began as a modest farming community. With the arrival of the commuter railroad in the mid-20C, this lovely area, watered by Wissahickon Creek, quickly became a fashionable address, and it remains so today. Many of Philadelphia's prominent and monied citizens erected elaborate stone estates along Chestnut Hill's dipping, shaded streets. The eclectic architecture that resulted here is now preserved as a National Historic District. Centered around upper Germantown Avenue (*between Mermaid Ln. and Rex Ave.*), the commercial area is sprinkled with upscale shops and restaurants.

Woodmere Art Museum – *9201 Germantown Ave. Open year-round Tue–Sat 10am–5pm, Sun 1pm–5pm. Closed major holidays. $3.* 🅿 ☎*215-247-0476.* The Victorian home of self-made entrepreneur Charles Knox Smith now houses the art collection he amassed in the early decades of this century, as well as recent acquisitions. Within its limited gallery space the museum mounts changing and juried exhibitions, as well as rotating pieces from its permanent collection. The strength of the latter lies in its works by such American artists as Jasper Francis Cropsey (*The Spirit of Peace*), Benjamin West, Hiram Powers, Frederic Church, and Pennsylvania Impressionists, as well as 19C European paintings by Corot, Vuillard, Derain and Daumier. The distinctive frames of master craftsman **Frederick Harer** highlight many works, and two period rooms contain an impressive collection of 19C **Meissen** and **Sèvres** porcelain.

★ **Morris Arboretum** – *100 Northwestern Ave. Open Apr–Oct Mon–Fri 10am–4pm, weekends 10am–5pm. Rest of the year daily 10am–4pm. Closed Dec 25–Jan 1. $4.* ♿ 🅿 *www.upenn.edu/morris* ☎*215-247-5777.* Originally the late-19C estate of avid plant collectors John and Lydia Morris, the arboretum now operated by the University of Pennsylvania rolls across 175 acres at the edge of Wissahickon Creek. The 92 acres open to the public feature almost 10,000 labeled botanical species and include rose, herb, azalea and display gardens, as well as an English park and a picturesque **swan pond**★. A 19C-style **fernery**★ re-creates the romantic green-houses of the Victorian era. Fountains and large pieces of sculpture also stand throughout the grounds. In its research capacity, the arboretum maintains laboratories devoted to propagating rare plants.

EXCURSIONS

★★ **The Barnes Foundation** – *½ day. 5mi from Center City in Merion. From Philadelphia take the Schuylkill Expressway (I-76) west to City Ave. (Rte. 1) exit and continue south about 1.5mi to Old Lancaster Rd. Turn right, then left on N. Latch's Ln. to*

300 N. Latch's Ln. Street parking is limited. Open Sept–Jun Thu 12:30pm–5pm, Fri–Sun & holidays 9:30am–5pm. Closed Thanksgiving Day, Dec 25. $5. ☎610-667-0290. Physician and pharmaceutical manufacturer **Dr. Albert C. Barnes** (1872-1951) began his renowned art collection in 1912. Passionate both about his connoisseurship and his sociological ideals, Barnes hung some of his paintings in his factories and invited workers to participate in art discussions and seminars. In 1922 Barnes established the Barnes Foundation to "promote the advancement of education and the appreciation of the fine arts for people of all socioeconomic levels." Several years later he commissioned architect Paul Cret to design a gallery on a 13-acre arboretum he had purchased on the Main Line.

When Barnes died, he left his trusteeship of his foundation to Lincoln University, the country's oldest black college. Today the public may view works from the collection, which numbers more than 1,100 paintings. Housed in Cret's Italianate gallery, the collection encompasses a wealth of **Impressionist and Postimpressionist works★★**, with 180 pieces by Renoir, 69 by Cézanne and 60 by Matisse. Degas, Modigliani, Picasso, Monet, Manet and others are also represented. Barnes personally designed each of the 96 walls of paintings as an artistic tableau unto itself, hanging paintings in tiers interspersed with pieces of ornamental ironwork and occasionally offset by chairs, tables and other furnishings. As part of his method, he dispensed with labels listing the title, date and creator of the works and paid little heed to standard museum methods of organization, such as chronology or artistic style. He also collected African sculpture and Medieval works and positioned them to show their influence on modern painting.

The arboretum surrounding the gallery features compositions of flowering trees and shrubs—including lilacs, roses and magnolias—and a formal garden.

★★ **Valley Forge National Historical Park** – *Map p 10. 2½hrs. 20mi northwest of Center City via I-76 W. Take the Valley Forge exit (26B) and continue on N. Gulph Rd. 1.5mi to visitor center. Open year-round daily 9am–5pm. Closed Dec 25. $2. ♿ 🅿. Bus tours depart from the visitor center Memorial Day–Labor Day daily 9:30am–4pm; May–Jun & Sept–Oct Mon–Fri 9:45am & noon, weekends 9:30am–4pm. 45min. Commentary. $5.50. ☎610-783-1077.* Initiated into the national park system for the US Bicentennial, the 3,620-acre park preserves the fields and ridges where George Washington's struggling 12,000-man Continental Army camped from December 19, 1777, to June 19, 1778.

© Robert Llewellyn

Valley Forge National Historical Park

A Winter of Hardship – Exhausted by a grueling autumn campaign, Washington's army marched into Valley Forge in December 1777. Here, close enough to monitor the British troops in Philadelphia, the poorly provisioned troops hastened to erect log huts in which to weather the Pennsylvania winter. By late December, a combination of illness, hunger and improper clothing rendered the majority of the Continental soldiers unfit for duty. It was then that General Washington wrote an impassioned letter to Congress on behalf of his neglected forces, whom, he said, would be forced to either "starve, dissolve, or disperse" without an infusion of new provisions. The grim situation began slowly to brighten by the end of January, when congressional delegates visited the camp and took measures to improve the flow of supplies.

In late February, Prussian army veteran Baron von Steuben was appointed Acting Inspector General and set about rigorously drilling the poorly trained Continental troops in Prussian military technique. By spring the formerly dispirited army was better disciplined and reinvigorated with both new recruits and the news that France would support the Patriots' cause.

Visit – Begin at the **visitor center**, where tools and other artifacts of the Continental encampment, along with Washington's sleeping marquee, are displayed. An 18min film dramatizes the travails of the ragtag Continental troops. Once you're familiar with the site's history, take the 10mi self-guided **driving tour★** through woods and fields, past remains of earthworks and reconstructed log huts, including those of **Muhlenberg's Brigade**, where costumed guides interpret the life of a Continental soldier. Nearby, the marble **National Memorial Arch**, designed by Paul Cret and modeled after Rome's Arch of Titus, commemorates the struggles of the troops that wintered here. Along the river, a cluster of historic stone buildings stands in the former village of Valley Forge. **Washington's Headquarters** were set up in the 1760s fieldstone house owned by Isaac Potts, whose family operated the local saw- and gristmills. Period furnishings now re-create the atmosphere in the house during George and Martha Washington's occupancy. (Martha joined her husband on a rare visit to the field that winter.) In the open fields beyond the village, the modest fieldstone farmhouse used as **General Varnum's Quarters** now houses more military exhibits and an explanation of how the encampment affected the local population. The imposing stone **Washington Memorial Chapel** (1903) stands just to the east, a vision of Gothic arches and towers; beside it rises an equally impressive carillon. In the connecting structure, the **Valley Forge Historical Society Museum** offers a permanent exhibit on the encampment, including an impressive number of items belonging to both George and Martha Washington.

BRANDYWINE VALLEY ★★★

Map p 253
Tourist Information www.brandywinevalley.com ☎610-388-2900 or 800-228-9933

As the narrow but beautiful Brandywine Creek (locally known as the Bandywine River) weaves its way through Chester County, Pennsylvania, and into Delaware, it creates in its wake a valley so charming that it has spurred entrepreneurs to build elaborate mansions and artists to immortalize its verdant countryside on canvas. Situated between the metropolises of PHILADELPHIA and Wilmington, Delaware, the Brandywine Valley retains a rural, yet tony, atmosphere. A drive along its serene country lanes reveals lovely fieldstone houses set in a rolling pastoral landscape.

A French immigrant named Eleuthère Irénée (E.I.) du Pont realized the potential of the river as a source of hydroelectric power and established a black-powder mill on the Brandywine's banks early in the 19C. Du Pont's mill community, Hagley, would grow to be one of the world's largest manufacturers of black powder and would give rise to a family of philanthropists whose legacy has immeasurably enriched the region. Today you can follow the du Pont family trail from the outstanding Winterthur Museum; to **Nemours Mansion** *(1600 Rockland Rd.; ☎302-651-6912)*, the 102-room, Louis XVI-style home (1910) of Alfred I. du Pont; to renowned Longwood Gardens.

In the late 19C and early 20C, the quiet beauty of the Brandywine Valley attracted a growing number of artists, among them famed illustrator N.C. Wyeth. His works, along with those of his son Andrew and grandson Jamie, are now displayed at the Brandywine River Museum.

The area owes its ambience in part to the concerted efforts of the local citizenry, who in 1967 established the Brandywine Conservancy to prevent industrialization of the area and pollution of the river. The only large industry in the valley today is a clean one—the **Franklin Mint** *(on Rte. 1 in Franklin Center; ☎610-459-6168)*—whose museum displays the coins, dolls, porcelains and other commemorative collectibles produced at the mint.

★ **CHADDS FORD**   *½ day. Map below.*

The Lenni Lenape Indians greeted the first European settlers in this region in the late 17C. One of these pioneers was Francis Chadsey, who purchased 500 acres in the crossroads community now known as Chadds Ford. By 1707 Chadsey had established a corn mill along the river near the present site of the Brandywine River Museum. In the early 1720s, his son, farmer and ferryman John Chads, considered the founder of Chadds Ford, erected a substantial house built of local blue fieldstone. Some 50 years later, the **John Chads House** *(on Rte. 100, .25mi north of Rte. 1; visit by 1hr guided tour only, May–Sept weekends noon–5pm; $3;* 🅿 ☎*610-388-7376)* survived the fighting that raged nearby during the Battle of the Brandywine, a pivotal Revolutionary War battle lost by the Continentals.

Today the tiny village of Chadds Ford is noted for its craft shops and winery. **Chaddsford Winery** *(632 Baltimore Pike/Rte.1;* ☎*610-388-6221)* offers tastings and guided tours of its small facility, with in-depth explanations of fermentation and other aspects of the wine-making process.

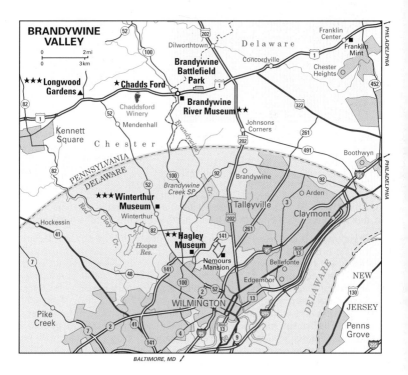

BALTIMORE, MD ╱

The Brandywine Valley Tourist Information Center (located outside the entrance to Longwood Gardens; p 254) provides maps and information on area attractions.

★★ **Brandywine River Museum** – *On Rte. 1, just south of intersection with Rte. 100. Open year-round daily 9:30am–4:30pm. Closed Dec 25. $5 (museum only), $7.50 (museum & N.C. Wyeth Studio).* ✗ & 🅿 *www.brandywinemuseum.org* ☎*610-388-2700.* Set on the banks of the meandering Brandywine River, this cavernous brick, Civil War-era gristmill has been converted into a striking museum, renowned for its collection of paintings by members of the local Wyeth family. The family's roots in the Brandywine begin with illustrator **Newell Convers (N.C.) Wyeth** (1882-1945), who came to the area in 1902 to study with renowned illustrator Howard Pyle at his art school in Wilmington, Delaware. Wyeth spent most of his life in the Brandywine Valley, settling in Chadds Ford and gaining fame for his powerful illustrations of Robert Louis Stevenson's novel *Treasure Island*.

In 1917 **Andrew** was born to Wyeth and his wife, Carolyn. As a young man, Andrew pursued a career as an artist himself, using watercolor and egg tempera to achieve the detail and texture for which his work is noted. After his father died unexpectedly in a car accident in 1945, Andrew's work changed dramatically; he began painting haunting portraits that evoke a sense of human isolation and

Courtesy Brandywine River Museum

Roasted Chestnuts (1956) by Andrew Wyeth

timelessness. Andrew's son **Jamie** (b.1946) represents a third generation of Wyeth painters in the Brandywine area. Jamie's paintings are characterized by a distinctive blend of realism and whimsy. Opened in 1971 as part of the Brandywine Conservancy, the three-story museum, surrounded by naturalized gardens, features the works of all three Wyeths, as well as other renowned artists. On the first floor, the **Brandywine Heritage Galleries**★ display landscapes by Delaware Valley artists and such noted illustrators as Howard Pyle, Maxfield Parrish, Charles Dana Gibson and Rockwell Kent. When not used for temporary exhibitions, the second floor features the bold illustrations of N.C. Wyeth, as well as such well-known paintings by Jamie Wyeth as his *Portrait of Pig*. The third floor houses the **Andrew Wyeth Gallery**★★,
where some 40 of the artist's paintings represent his career from 1938 to present. In 1996 the museum began offering tours of **N.C. Wyeth's studio** nearby *(accessible via shuttle bus from museum; visit by 40min guided tour only Apr–Oct Wed–Sun 10am–3:15pm; $2.50; &)*. Filled with his furniture, easels, props and books, the studio is lighted by large windows facing north across the Brandywine landscape.

Brandywine Battlefield Park – *On Rte. 1, 1.5mi west of Rte. 202. Open year-round Tue–Sat & holidays 9am–5pm, Sun noon–5pm. Guided tours (1hr) of Benjamin Ring House & Layfayette's Quarters offered year-round Tue–Sat & holidays 9:30am–3pm, Sun 12:30pm–3pm. $3.50/both houses. Closed Dec 25.* ✗ & **Ⓟ** *www.libertynet. org/iha/brandywine* ☎610-459-3342. A hilly, roadside park preserves two Quaker farmhouses associated with the September 11, 1777, Battle of the Brandywine, when George Washington's forces were outmaneuvered by those of General Howe. The British victory here enabled Howe's forces to march unopposed into Philadelphia two weeks later. **Lafayette's Quarters**★, a large restored stone farmhouse, served as headquarters for the Marquis de Lafayette, who saw his first military action in America in this battle. A reconstruction of the **Benjamin Ring House** re-creates the home General Washington used as his local headquarters. The battle itself actually occurred nearby along the Brandywine River. A 20min video in the visitor center recounts details of the conflict.

Additional Sight

★★★ **Longwood Gardens** – *Gardens are located off Rte. 1. just west of Rte. 52 in Kennett Square. Open Apr–Oct daily 9am–6pm. Rest of the year daily 9am–5pm. $12.* ✗ & **Ⓟ** *www.longwoodgardens.org* ☎610-388-1000. This world-renowned garden fills 1,050 rolling acres with extravagant European fountain gardens, quiet naturalized woodlands, superb conservatories and specialty gardens. The vision for this horticultural masterpiece came largely from one man: **Pierre S. du Pont** (1870-1954). A great-grandson of Hagley founder E.I. du Pont, Pierre grew up in nearby Wilmington, Delaware, and later worked for the family's DuPont Company, eventually becoming chairman of the board of both DuPont and General Motors. Despite his demanding career, he pursued his interest in horticulture. In 1906 he purchased the 200-acre core of the current garden, largely to save an arboretum established by Quaker brothers Joshua and Samuel Peirce in 1798. Du Pont used the Peirce family's 1730 brick farmhouse as a country home, eventually adding a conservatory and other rooms. He also began work on the grounds, planting an extensive flower garden below the house. For the next 30 years, he added more and more elaborations to the property, including vast, fountained water gardens, an amphitheater for outdoor productions and a four-acre Beaux-Arts conservatory—"designed," as he put it, "to exploit the sentiments and ideas associated with plants and flowers in a large way."

Visit – ½ *day. Map and schedule of events are available at the visitor center.* Embedded in a hill, the garden side of the visitor center melds into the scenery. As you enter the gardens, follow signs for the **Peirce-du Pont House★** on the north side of the grounds. An orientation film in the house explains du Pont's life and his development of Longwood; exhibits detail the building of various portions of the gardens. Behind the house, a path leads through a long allée of trees that formed part of **Peirce's Park**, the original arboretum. Continue downhill through a small woodland to the charming **Italian Water Garden★★**, based on that of a Florentine villa du Pont visited in 1913. Just south of the water garden, the Lake Area makes a serene understatement with its long lake and single weeping willow. Paths to the west of the visitor center pass through du Pont's original flower gardens and the 1913 Open-Air Theatre. From this point, head northwest toward the enormous **Conservatory★★★** that commands this side of the gardens. Inside these

East Conservatory, Longwood Gardens

Larry Albee/Longwood Gardens

graceful greenhouses, lush, showy floral plantings are changed seasonally. A 10,010-pipe Aeolian organ—one of the largest residential organs in the world—is located in the conservatory ballroom and played daily during the Christmas season. Below the conservatory is du Pont's **Main Fountain Garden**, where 380 fountainheads, colored lights and music—and occasionally fireworks—create a fantastical **Festival of Fountains★★** on summer evenings *(Memorial Day–Labor Day daily 9am–6pm; evening concerts Tue, Thu & Sat)*. To the west of the fountains, an Idea Garden offers visitors horticultural suggestions for their own gardens, and to the east lie the **Rose Garden** and **Topiary Garden**. Longwood's hilly southeast corner is devoted to a naturalized Hillside Garden and a stone Chimes Tower, which affords a sweeping view of the nearby 50ft-high waterfall.

DELAWARE EXCURSIONS   1 day. Map p 253.

★★ Winterthur Museum – ½ *day. On Rte. 52, 5mi south of Rte. 1, in Winterthur, Delaware. Open year-round Mon–Sat 9am–5pm, Sun noon-5pm. Closed Jan 1, Thanksgiving Day, Dec 25. $8; general admission fee includes the museum galleries & gardens.* ✗ ₾ ▣ *www.udel.edu/winterthur* ☎*302-888-4600 or 800-448-3883.* Premier showcase of American decorative arts in the nation, the former home of collector Henry

Francis du Pont occupies a green swale surrounded by a lush 965 acres on the out-skirts of Wilmington, Delaware. The estate dates back to the 1830s, when James Antoine Bidermann and his wife, Evelina Gabrielle du Pont, a daughter of E.I. du Pont, built the original three-story Greek Revival structure that forms the core of the current mansion. They named it after Winterthur, Switzerland, the ancestral home of the Bidermann family. About 30 years later, the Bidermanns' nephew, Henry du Pont, Sr., purchased the house for his son, Henry Algernon du Pont. Upon Henry Algernon's death in 1927, the estate passed on to his son, Henry Francis.

Initially interested in European antiques, **Henry Francis du Pont** (1880-1969) shifted his focus closer to home in the late 1920s to support his belief that "the early American arts and crafts had not been given the recognition they deserved." He spent the rest of his life amassing his unsurpassed **decorative-arts collection**★★★, adding on to the house periodically to accommodate it. In 1951 Winterthur opened to the public. Today the property includes the du Pont mansion, featur-ing 175 period rooms and a gallery addition, 60 acres of gardens, and a separate research library and gift shop. Winterthur's more than 89,000 objects represent pre-industrial decorative arts in America from 1640 to 1860 (the date du Pont con-sidered the beginning of industrialization).

Winterthur – *Visit by guided tour only. Reservations required. $5.* Options for visiting the mansion include a 1hr introductory tour, 1hr or 2hr decorative-arts tours, as well as special-interest tours *(limited to 5 people; reservations recommended; $5)* that require advance preparation. Special Yuletide tours are given during the holi-days. During 1998, the standard tours will cover a series of rooms not normally on view, while the high-style, fifth-floor rooms typically shown undergo renova-tion. The various house tours take in different combinations of the 175 re-created **period rooms**★★★. Du Pont frequently purchased entire rooms from homes and estates, including paneling, wallpaper and furnishings, and had them reassem-bled at Winterthur. The decorative arts displayed throughout the house represent the best in American porcelain, furniture, pewter and silver, and portraiture. Among the outstanding items in the collection are Chippendale furnishings by Newport cabinetmakers Townsend and Goddard; silver tankards crafted by Paul Revere; and paintings by Gilbert Stuart, John Singleton Copley and Charles Willson Peale.

The Galleries – This large, modern addition to the du Pont mansion features an interactive, first-floor exhibit that allows visitors to explore **"Perspectives on the Decorative Arts in Early America"**★. The second floor is devoted to Winterthur's **furniture study collection**★★ and to the reconstructed woodworking and clock-making shops of one Long Island family, including some 800 18C and 19C tools. Changing exhibits related to the decorative arts are also displayed on this level. In 1997 the new Dorrance Gallery premiered the Campbell Collection of Soup Tureens. Donated to Winterthur by the Campbell Museum, this 270-piece collec-tion features tureens from around the world dating from the 18C to present; 125 of the best examples have been selected for display.

A tram leaves every 20min from the mansion to take passengers on a narrated tour of the 60-acre **gardens**★, passing the homes of former du Pont staff and the naturalized azalea, rhododendron and evergreen plantings designed by Henry du Pont, a Harvard-trained horticulturist.

★★ **Hagley Museum** – *½ day. On Rte. 141 between Rtes. 100 & 202 in Wilmington, Delaware. Open mid-Mar–Dec daily 9:30am–4:30pm. Rest of the year Mon–Fri 1:30pm–4:30pm, weekends & holidays 9:30am–4:30pm. Closed Jan 1, Thanksgiving Day, Dec 25, Dec 31. $9.75.* ✗ ▣ *www.hagley.lib.de.us* ☎302-658-2400. Nestled into the forested, serene banks of the Brandywine River, the old granite buildings of this early-19C factory once roared with the noise and commotion of industry. In 1802 French immigrant and chemist **Eleuthère Irénée (E.I.) du Pont** (1771-1834) chose this spot for the establishment of a black-powder mill, and a year later he built a substantial Georgian home, Eleutherian Mills, adjacent to it. Quickly successful, the mill complex at Hagley eventually stretched for 2mi along the river and grew to be the largest producer of black powder in the world. Remaining in produc-tion until 1921, Hagley gave rise to the DuPont Company, an industrial behemoth that continues to thrive today. In 1957 the company opened Hagley's 230 acres to the public, thereby preserving a part of American's industrial era. *A shuttle bus leaves from the visitor center and stops at attractions along the 2mi museum drive; no cars are allowed past the visitor center.*

A former cotton mill, the 1814 **Henry Clay Mill** now serves as an orientation center, recounting the history of the site and the growth of industry in the US through videos and exhibits; a series of intricate small-scale wooden **models**★ depict, with moving parts and people, various milling activities. Standing along the river are the remains of stone mills, storehouses and waterwheels of the old **Powder Yard**. In the spit-and-polish **Machine Shop** volunteers explain and demonstrate 19C tools used at Hagley. From the shop, a short path leads up to **Blacksmith Hill**, where a couple of houses and a church re-create the modest but comfortable lives of the factory workers.

Crowning a hilltop upstream from the factory stands the stately Georgian **Eleutherian Mills**★. E.I. du Pont and his descendants occupied the house from its completion in 1803 to 1890, when a severe powder explosion forced the family to vacate the premises. In 1923 a final du Pont scion, Louise du Pont Crowninshield, took possession of the residence, which she gave to the Eleutherian Mills-Hagley Foundation in 1952. Today the first-floor rooms remain much as Mrs. Crowninshield left them; the second floor comprises a series of period rooms (Federal, Empire and Victorian) reflecting the entire du Pont tenure. On the grounds, a formal garden has been restored to E.I. du Pont's original design.

BUCKS COUNTY★★

Map pp 10-11
Tourist Information www.bctc.org ☎215-345-4552 or 800-836-2825

Much heralded for its quaint historic villages, covered bridges and artsy ambience, Bucks County has long been a haven for weekenders from neighboring Philadelphia and for the glitterati, who maintain fine country homes here. The county's 625 square acres—named for William Penn's birthplace of Buckinghamshire, England—were originally part of Penn's land grant from Charles II. Penn built his own Pennsbury Manor in what is now the county's southeastern corner. By the late 17C and early 18C, small villages dotted the banks of the Delaware.

The Delaware River, which defines the southern and eastern sides of the county, figured prominently in the Revolutionary War, when George Washington made his famous crossing in the winter of 1776. With the prosperity that infused the new country after its independence, canal building reached a fever pitch, and in 1832 the 60mi-long **Delaware Canal** was completed between Bristol and Easton. Though the canal saw its last paying boat in 1931 and is now only partially filled with water, the structure—with its 23 locks and 10 aqueducts—continues to provide a scenic corridor with a towpath seasonally frequented by bikers, hikers and cross-country skiers.

Lovely **River Road**★ *(Rte. 32)*, which parallels the canal and river for the length of the county, offers a scenic route to many county attractions. It was the area's waterways, particularly around New Hope, that attracted the late-19C artists who would become the acclaimed "Pennsylvania Impressionists." In the 1930s, such prominent New York writers and composers as Dorothy Parker and Oscar Hammerstein also discovered Bucks County and bought country homes here, giving the area its sobriquet "the genius belt." Today lovely estates still nestle into the county's dipping hills, and day-trippers flock here to browse in the antique stores that stretch along Route 202 from New Hope to Lahaska, to relax at the many upscale inns and restaurants or to canoe or "tube" down the river.

★★ DOYLESTOWN *1 day*

Seat of Bucks County since 1813, this pleasant town began as a stagecoach stop in the 18C. Today its streets are lined with Federal-style row houses and stately Victorians, some housing unique shops and fine restaurants. Doylestown has gained most fame as the home of architect, archaeologist and ceramist Henry Chapman Mercer. Visitors can view his legacy in the three imposing concrete structures he designed along the "Mercer Mile": Fonthill, the Mercer Museum and the Spruance Library. Another renowned Doylestown native is remembered nearby at the James A. Michener Art Museum.

Maps and information are available at the Central Bucks County Chamber of Commerce, 115 W. Court St. in the Fidelity Bank Building; ☎215-348-3913.

★ **Fonthill** – *E. Court St. off Swamp Rd. (Rte. 313). Visit by guided tour (1hr) only, year-round Mon–Sat 10am–5pm, Sun noon–5pm. Closed Jan 1, Thanksgiving Day, Dec 25. $5. Reservations required.* ▯ *www.libertynet.org:80/~bchs* ☎215-348-9461. A surprising castle-like vision standing at the east edge of town, Fonthill is the turreted, whimsical masterwork of Renaissance man **Henry Chapman Mercer** (1856-1930). Born into a prominent Doylestown family, Mercer studied law at the University of Pennsylvania but found archaeology more to his taste and eventually became a respected curator at the Museum of the University of Pennsylvania in Philadelphia. Although he traveled extensively throughout the world, in 1897 his interests turned to collecting American pre-industrial tools, implements and folk art—much of which is now displayed at the Mercer Museum. Inspired by folk designs, he began producing ornamental ceramic tiles re-creating these motifs. His Mercer tiles and extensive scholarly knowledge vaulted him into the vanguard of the American Arts and Crafts movement of the early 20C.

In 1908 he began designing Fonthill, a rambling, reinforced-concrete Gothic Revival extravaganza built entirely by manual labor—assisted by a horse named Lucy. Mercer's manipulation of concrete and use of features such as storm windows proved him to be a man ahead of his time. Tours through the house—which took four years to construct—take in less than half of Fonthill's labyrinthine 44 rooms. Cluttered with artifacts from its builder's travels and embedded with his tiles depicting scenes from history, myth and literature, Mercer's "concrete castle for the New World," as he dubbed it, stands as a living museum to the man himself.

★ **Moravian Pottery and Tile Works** – *130 Swamp Rd. on the Fonthill grounds. Visit by guided tour (45min) only, year-round daily 10am–4:45pm. Closed major holidays. $3.50.* ▯ ☎215-345-6722. In 1912 Mercer completed another concrete building behind Fonthill, this one modeled after California's Spanish mission cloisters. He called it the Moravian Pottery and Tile Works in deference to his appreciation of the Moravian designs on the Pennsylvania German stove plates that had first inspired him. The tiles from Mercer's small factory were a financial and critical success, and he was commissioned in 1904 to produce a series of ornamental tiles for the rotunda floor of the Pennsylvania State Capitol in Harrisburg. The factory continues to produce and sell handmade tiles based on Mercer's designs. A self-guided tour begins with a 17min video explaining Mercer's artistry and how the tiles are made; afterward, visitors may walk through parts of the tile-making operations and watch artisans at work.

> **Peddler's Village**
> *Rtes. 202 & 263 in Lahaska.* ☎*215-794-4000.* Shoppers won't want to miss these 70 specialty boutiques landscaped in a country-village setting. Here you'll find a plethora of merchandise ranging from jewelry and clothing to local crafts and fine English china. In addition, **Carousel World Museum** *(lower level of Carousel World gift shop, in north end of village;* ☎*215-794-8960)* features a whimsical collection of early-20C carousel animals and circus art, as well as a ride on an antique carousel. Eight restaurants and a bed-and-breakfast inn complete the complex.

★ **Mercer Museum** – *84 S. Pine St. Open year-round Mon–Sat 10am–5pm (Tue 9pm), Sun noon–5pm. Closed Jan 1, Thanksgiving Day, Dec 25. $5.* ▯ *www.libertynet.org: 80/~bchs* ☎215-345-0210. A mile away from Fonthill on the south side of Doylestown, the enormous concrete Mercer Museum is another Henry Chapman Mercer "castle." Built between 1913 and 1916, the cavernous museum houses Mercer's collection of American pre-industrial artifacts, which he called "The Tools of the Nation Maker." An introductory orientation exhibit on the ground floor explains the logic behind Mercer's frenzied collecting. Four of the five main exhibit floors wrap around a shared central court, while the sixth level and tower hold smaller exhibit rooms. The overwhelming accretion of artifacts stacked, hung from ceilings and crammed into display cases ranges from Moravian stove plates to mining, nautical and smithing equipment to farming, weaving, kitchen and food-preservation implements.

Connected to the museum, the **Spruance Library** completes the concrete extravaganza of the "Mercer Mile." A research library for scholars, it preserves historical and genealogical records of Bucks County.

★ **James A. Michener Art Museum** – *138 S. Pine St. Open year-round Tue–Fri 10am–4:30pm, weekends 10am–5pm. Closed major holidays. $5.* ✗ �& ▢ ☎*215-340-9800.* Named in honor of the late best-selling author (1907-97) and Doylestown native who endowed it, this modern museum occupies part of the 1884 Bucks County Jail. Its light, airy galleries hold both changing and permanent exhibits intended to reflect "Bucks County's artistic soul." Among the permanent exhibits on the main level, "James A. Michener: A Living Legacy" *(off the lobby)* displays Michener memorabilia and details the writer's commitment to racial equality. The **Nakashima Reading Room**★ re-creates the serenity of a Japanese study, with furniture designed by renowned Bucks County woodworker George Nakashima. Works in "Visual Heritage of Bucks County 1930-1990" range from one version of the *Peaceable Kingdom* (c.1837) by local Primitivist Edward Hicks to landscapes by Pennsylvania Impressionists Edward Redfield and Daniel Garber. The Mari Sabusawa Michener Wing, opened in 1996, was endowed by the novelist's wife. Its interactive **"Creative Bucks County"** gallery showcases the contributions of 12 famous county inhabitants: writers Pearl Buck, George S. Kaufman, Moss Hart, S.J. Perelman, Dorothy Parker and Jean Toomer; painters Edward Hicks, Daniel Garber, Edward Redfield and Charles Sheeler; architect and ceramist Henry Chapman Mercer; and composer Oscar Hammerstein II. The lower level hosts changing exhibits throughout the year.

Excursion

★ **Pearl S. Buck House** – *1½hrs. 8mi northwest of Doylestown. Take Rte. 313 west to Dublin; turn left at the Maple Ave. traffic light. Continue 1mi to the entrance to Green Hills Farm on the right. Visit by guided tour (1hr) only, Mar–late Dec Tue–Sat 11am, 1pm & 2pm; Sun 1pm & 2pm. Closed major holidays. $5.* ▢ *www.pearl-s-buck.org* ☎*215-249-0100.* This charming fieldstone farmhouse was the home of internationally acclaimed author **Pearl S. Buck** (1892-1973) and her second husband, publisher Richard Walsh. The daughter of American missionary parents, Buck was raised in China and lived there until her early forties, when she returned to the US and settled on this 50-acre estate in Bucks County. Distinguished by receiving both the Pulitzer Prize (in 1932 for her novel *The Good Earth*) and the Nobel Prize for Literature (1938), Buck wrote some 100 books during the 38 years she lived at her Green Hills Farm. An ardent supporter of orphaned and neglected children, Buck also adopted and raised a number of Amerasian children here.

Tours take visitors through the home, an expanded version of an 1835 farmhouse, filled with Buck's personal furnishings and memorabilia—much of the decor reflecting her years in China. The hand-carved **desk** in the library is the one on which she wrote *The Good Earth* while living in China. The tour ends in the adjoining building (c.1740s) that Buck and her husband used as an office. Buck, who lived here until her death at age 80, is buried on the estate grounds. Also on the grounds is the headquarters of the Pearl S. Buck Foundation that the author founded to aid displaced and disadvantaged children.

★ **NEW HOPE** *½ day*

Situated on the west bank of the Delaware River and cut by the Delaware Canal, New Hope must rank as one of the most picturesque villages in the mid-Atlantic region. The town's roots reach back to 1710, when Scotsman Robert Heath purchased 1,000 acres granted to his brother-in-law by William Penn and erected a gristmill here. About ten years later, John Wells started a ferry across the river and built the Ferry Tavern to house travelers. (New Hope's sister city of Lambertville [*p 173*], New Jersey, grew up as the ferry stop across the river.) Over the next few decades, the ferry—and the name of the town—changed according to its owner. After the American Revolution, Philadelphia entrepreneur Benjamin Parry began buying mills in the area. When one of his mill complexes burned to the ground in 1790, he replaced it with another he optimistically named New Hope Mills. Soon the town, too, became known as New Hope.

The one-square-mile village preserves its history in some 200 buildings that are listed on the National Register of Historic Places. Opposite the Revolutionary War memorial on Cannon Square *(intersection of Main & Ferry Sts.)*, the renovated **Logan Inn** incorporates the shell of the Colonial-era Ferry Tavern, which dates back to 1727. Down the street, the 1865 **Mansion Inn** *(9 S. Main St.)*—now a B&B—is the town's most notable Victorian landmark.

Early in this century, New Hope inspired its own school of Impressionists, which included such outstanding painters as Daniel Garber and Edward Redfield. That arts tradition continues today, with fine crafts galleries lining **Main Street** and the

1939 Bucks County Playhouse—housed in the old Parry gristmill—hosting a year-round schedule of Broadway musicals. These attractions, coupled with New Hope's tranquil setting and wide range of restaurants, bring a steady flow of travelers to town.

When visitors need a break from shopping, the **New Hope & Ivyland Railroad** offers steam-powered rides on vintage locomotives through the county's rolling hills to nearby Lahaska and back *(station at 32 W. Bridge St.; depart May–Nov Mon–Fri 11am–4pm, weekends 11am–5pm; rest of the year weekends noon–3pm; closed major holidays; round-trip 50min; commentary; $8.50;* ✗ ♿ 🅿 *[$5]* ☎215-862-2332).

> ### Gerenser's Exotic Ice Cream
> **Kids** *22 S. Main St.* ☎215-862-2050. One of New Hope's best places to beat the summer heat, this family-run ice-cream parlor has been a town institution for 35 years. Choose from 50 unique flavors, including such homemade exotica as Japanese Ginger, Caribbean Spice Tree Bark and Ukrainian Rose Petal.

The New Hope Information Center, at the corner of S. Main and Mechanic Streets, offers maps of the town and information about Bucks County attractions.

Parry Mansion – *S. Main and Ferry Sts. Visit by guided tour (1hr) only, late Apr–early Dec Fri–Sun & holidays 1pm–5pm. $4.* ☎215-862-5652. This two-story fieldstone house was built by wealthy Quaker mill owner Benjamin Parry in 1784, with a southern wing added in 1810. The decor spans the late Colonial period through the Victorian era (1775-1900), reflecting the tastes of the five generations of Parrys who lived here until 1966. Among the period and family furnishings are Duncan Phyfe and Hepplewhite pieces in the Federal-style parlor and two Edward Redfield paintings in the entry hall.

New Hope Mule Barge Excursion – **Kids** *New St. off S. Main St. Departs May–Oct daily 11:30am–6pm. Apr & Nov 1–Nov 15 Wed, Sat–Sun 11:30am–4:30pm. $7.50.* 🅿 ☎215-862-2842 *or* 800-592-2743. Take a leisurely ride back in time on a mule-drawn barge. These excursions transport passengers 2mi up the Delaware Canal, offering a peek at New Hope backyards, while onboard musicians sing the history of the canal.

Adjacent to the dock, the 19C **Locktender's House** details the life of lock tenders along the canal. During the canal's heyday in the 1860s, more than 3,000 boats a year locked through New Hope.

Additional Sights *1 day*

★★ **Washington Crossing Historic Park** – *On Rte. 32 south between New Hope and Yardley. Open year-round Tue–Sat & holidays 9am–5pm, Sun noon–5pm. Closed Presidents' Day, Thanksgiving Day. $4. Access to building interiors by guided tour (45min) only; tours leave hourly from the visitor center and take in the Hibbs House, Durham Boat House, McConkey Ferry Inn and the Mahlon Taylor House.* ♿ 🅿 ☎215-493-4076. Two parcels in this historic park preserve sites connected with George Washington's legendary crossing of the Delaware *(p 212)* in the winter of 1776 to launch a surprise attack on the Redcoats' Hessian forces across the river in TRENTON, New Jersey.

In the **Lower Park**, the **Memorial Building and Visitor Center** *(7mi south of New Hope on Rte. 32)* features a 25min documentary film recounting the Colonials' effort here. The center also contains a copy of Emanuel Leutze's well-known painting *Washington Crossing the Delaware (below)*, which captures the heroic conceit of an event that helped create a new nation. Adjacent to the visitor center, the former ferry-crossing village of Taylorsville now consists of a row of buildings dating from the 18C to the 20C. The original west side of the fieldstone **McConkey's Ferry Inn★** dates to the 18C and served as a guard-post during the Continental encampment in the area; it is now furnished as a Colonial-era inn. Washington and his officers are said to have had Christmas dinner here before crossing the Delaware. Open-hearth cooking techniques are occasionally demonstrated at the modest c.1830 **Hibbs House**, and the nearby **Durham Boat House** features replicas of the sturdy, flat-bottomed Durham craft used by the Continentals to cross the Delaware. Across Route 532, the c.1817 **Mahlon K. Taylor House** was constructed by one of the founders of Taylorsville. Next door, the family's **Taylorsville Store** was established by Mahlon Taylor in the late 1820s and has recently been restored to its original function as a general store.

The **Upper Park** *(3.5mi north of the visitor center on Rte. 32)* preserves the **Thompson-Neely House★**. John Pidcock built the central section of this rambling fieldstone structure in 1702. The west side and upper floor were added in 1757 by Robert Thompson. General Washington appropriated this house as headquarters for the Continental Army's Gen. Lord Stirling during December 1776. Now interpreted to that period, the house contains simple Colonial furnishings, some of them original. Nearby, the restored Thompson-Neely Gristmill was built by William Neely in the 1830s. Below the house at the edge of the Delaware lie the graves of America's first unknown soldiers.

Across Route 32, a gated road loops through the **Bowman's Hill Wildflower Preserve**, where trails amble through 80 acres of mixed hardwood forests, with their understory of wildflowers and other native vegetation *(open year-round daily: grounds sunrise–sunset; headquarters Mon–Sat 9am–5pm, Sun noon–5pm; closed Jan 1, Easter Sunday, Thanksgiving Day, Dec 25;* 🅿 ☎*215-862-2924). Trail maps with comprehensive listings of wildflowers are available at the headquarters building adjacent to the parking lot.*

Washington Crossing the Delaware (1851) by Emanuel Gottlieb Leutze – The Metropolitan Museum of Art, Gift of John S. Kennedy, 1897. (97.34)

On a hill behind the preserve, the stone **Bowman's Tower** *(accessible via Lurgan Rd. off Rte. 32 South;* ☎*215-493-4076)* rises 110ft, affording sweeping **views** of the river and surrounding countryside. Built in 1930, it commemorates the Revolutionary lookout post here.

★★ **Pennsbury Manor** – *400 Pennsbury Memorial Rd. Access via Rte. 1 or 13 to Tyburn Rd. Go east on Tyburn and turn right at light on New Ford Mill Rd. Turn right at dead end and take first left on Pennsbury Memorial Rd. Open year-round Tue–Sat 9am–5pm, Sun noon–5pm. Closed major holidays (except Memorial Day, Jul 4 & Labor Day). $5.* ⓵ 🅿 *www.libertynet.org/~pensbury* ☎*215-946-0400.* About 26mi north of Philadelphia, this 40-acre site on the banks of the Delaware re-creates the personal estate of Pennsylvania's founder, Quaker William Penn. Penn arrived in his new colony in 1682 and the following year began building Pennsbury on 8,400 acres purchased from the Lenni Lenape Indians. Penn's first visit was brief and politics forced him back to England in 1684, but construction on the stately Georgian house and surrounding dependencies continued. He returned in 1699 with his family and occupied the manor as a summer home for two seasons, before health concerns and politics sent him back to England. He never again set foot in America and his estate fell into neglect. In 1792 his heirs sold the land, and it passed through several hands in the ensuing years. The Crozier family purchased the property in 1835 and built a simple home on the original manor foundations. Between 1933 and 1942, the Pennsylvania Historical Commission reconstructed the estate, moving the **Crozier House** (now a gift shop) to another site on the grounds and re-creating the manor.

Today the Georgian **manor house**★★ *(visit by 1hr 30min guided tour only)* proudly stands as Penn built it, its brick facade overlooking formal English gardens and the Delaware beyond. Costumed tour guides take visitors through the two-story house, furnished in fine 17C and 18C English and Dutch decor with a number of original Penn family pieces. Though Penn was a Quaker, he felt no religious constraint to live in a plain style, and the rooms reflect his upper-class social status. Outbuildings, such as a **Bake and Brew House**, barn and smokehouse, faithfully depict conditions and activities on a Colonial plantation. A 20min introductory film in the visitor center explains the Penns' brief tenure at the estate. A reproduction of the ornate, six-oarsman barge that Penn used to travel the five hours downriver to Philadelphia is also displayed on the grounds.

Historic Fallsington – *4 Yardley Ave. at the intersection of S. Main St. and Meetinghouse Sq., Fallsington. 6mi northwest of Pennsbury Manor via S. Main St. off Tyburn Rd. Visit by guided tour (1hr) only, mid-May–Oct Mon–Sat 10am–4pm, Sun 1pm–4pm. $3.50.* 🅿 ☎*215-295-6567.* Begun as a Quaker village in the late 17C, the picturesque small town, now listed on the National Register of Historic Places, still boasts several Quaker meetinghouses as well as some 90 homes from the 18C and 19C. The local preservation society, headquartered in the early-20C Gillingham Store, offers tours of three historic sites that re-create various periods in the life of the town: the **Stagecoach Tavern**, which operated as an inn from 1799 to Prohibition days; the Federal-style **Burges-Lippincott House**, the home and office of a local doctor; and the 18C **Moon-Williamson Log House**. Self-guided walking-tour maps of the town are also available from the preservation society.

Pocono Mountains Region

The Delaware Water Gap – Jonathan Wallen

Traditionally noted for its anthracite coal mining and its honeymoon resorts, the northeastern corner of Pennsylvania has in recent years become a recreational mecca for urbanites from nearby NEW YORK CITY and PHILADELPHIA. The wooded Pocono plateau, a tableland cresting some 2,000ft above sea level, occupies a wedge of land within the Appalachian Ridge that is bounded by the Delaware River on the east, the Moosic Mountains on the west, and the Lehigh Gorge (near JIM THORPE) in the south; the northern edge of the Pocono plateau slopes down toward Honesdale. Take the time to explore beyond the plethora of golf and ski resorts here, and you will discover a wealth of small villages, coal-mining museums and natural areas tucked among the mountains.

In the early 19C, these rich woodlands were heavily exploited for their timber, as hemlock and oak were logged for the tannic acid needed by local tanneries. In the latter part of the century, logging gave way to mining, after the discovery of the nation's richest fields of anthracite coal in and around Scranton. In these early days, canals and gravity railroads were built to ship coal and other resources from the interior to the coast; picturesque remnants of such bygone modes of transportation now punctuate the landscape.

For practical information on the Delaware Water Gap area, see p 268.

Getting There

By Air – Closest airports are **Wilkes-Barre/Scranton International Airport** and **Lehigh Valley International Airport** *(Allentown)*; international and domestic flights.

By Bus – Martz Trailways *(☎821-3800 or 800-233-8604)* provides **bus** service to many cities in the Pocono Mountains region.

General Information

Visitor Information – Contact the **Pocono Mountains Vacation Bureau** *(1004 Main St., Stroudsburg PA 18360 www.poconos.org ☎424-6050 or 800-762-6667)* to obtain maps and information on recreation, accommodations and seasonal events. The vacation bureau operates ten manned information centers *(open year-round daily)*.

Accommodations – *(p 358)* Area visitors' guides including lodging directories are available *(free)* from the Pocono Mountains Vacation Bureau. Pocono **resorts** offer packages that can include room, meals, nightly entertainment, recreation (such as water sports, golf/tennis, skiing) and health club facilities. Hotels, motels, bed-and-breakfast inns and **cabins** can be found throughout the area, especially in Mount Pocono and Stroudsburg. The Pocono Mountains **hostel** provides inexpensive lodging *(LaAnna Rd., RR #2, Box 1026, Cresco PA 18326 ☎676-9076)*. **Reservation service**: Pocono Mountains Vacation Bureau *(above)*.

Camping – Campsites dot the region, in forests and along waterways. Consult the *Poconos Campgrounds Guide and Map (available free from Pocono Mountains Vacation Bureau)* for a comprehensive listing of campgrounds and facilities. State parks that allow camping in the area include Hickory Run *(White Haven; ☎443-0400)* and Promised Land *(Greentown; ☎676-3248)*; winter facilities are available.

Winter Activities – With an average winter snowfall of over 10 inches per month, the Poconos provide ample opportunities for winter recreation. **Snowmobiling** is offered at most ski resorts *(equipment rental available)*. Trail maps are available from the Pennsylvania Bureau of Forestry *(HC1, Box 95A, Swiftwater PA 18370; ☎424-3001)*. Stores offering snowmobile rentals and trail information can be found in Mount Pocono and White Haven. **Sledding** and **ice-skating** are offered at ski areas.

Skiing – Ski condition hotline: ☎421-5565. Poconos ski areas offer a wide variety of trails, from beginner to expert. Ski packages including equipment rental, lift tickets and instruction are available (child care and children's ski schools may also be included). **Downhill-skiing** areas: Alpine Mountain *(Analomink)*, Big Boulder *(Blakeslee)*, Blue Mountain *(Palmerton)*, Camelback *(Tannersville)*, Jack Frost *(Blakeslee)* and Mt. Airy *(Mount Pocono)*. Many of these resorts also offer **snowboarding**. **Cross-country** skiing on well-groomed trails can be found at most downhill ski areas, as well as at Lehigh Gorge State Park and Hickory Run State Park *(both in White Haven)*. *Ski the Poconos*, published by the Pocono Vacation Bureau, provides detailed information about ski areas and amenities.

Water Sports – **White-water rafting** excursions on the Lehigh River are offered by Jim Thorpe River Adventures *(1 Adventure Ln., Jim Thorpe PA 18229; ☎325-4960)*; Lehigh Rafting Rentals *(PO Box 296, White Haven PA 18661; ☎443-4441)*; Pocono Whitewater Adventures *(Rte. 903, Jim Thorpe PA 18229; ☎352-8430 or 800-944-8392)*; Whitewater Challengers *(PO Box 8, White Haven PA 18661; ☎443-9532)*; and Whitewater Rafting Adventures *(Rte. 534, Box 88, Albrightsville PA 18210; ☎722-0285)*. Some outfitters also feature guided **canoe** trips. **Boating** and **swimming** are available on Lake Wallenpaupack. Boats and recreational water equipment can be rented in Hawley and Greentown. Wallenpaupack **Scenic Boat Tours** depart from Paupack *(May–Sept; 30min; ☎226-6211)*.

Other Recreation – A wide variety of **hiking** trails are located throughout the area, especially in Lehigh Gorge State Park *(White Haven)* and Promised Land State Park *(Greentown)*. Many cross-country ski routes make excellent hiking trails after the snow melts; contact the Bureau of Forestry *(above)* for maps and information. Trail rides on **horseback** are available for the novice and experienced rider; stables are located in Cresco, Whitehaven, Mount Pocono and Honesdale. **Golf** enthusiasts can choose from more than 30 area courses *(contact the Pocono Mountains Vacation Bureau for locations)*.

Sightseeing – Companies offering **train** excursions include Rail Tours, Inc. *(depart from Jim Thorpe early Apr–Oct & Dec; 40min–2hrs 45min round-trip; ☎325-4606)* and Stourbridge Line Rail Excursions *(depart from Honesdale late Jun–Aug, Oct & Dec; 1hr 30min–3hrs 30min round-trip; ☎253-1960)*. Pocono Country Carriages conducts **sleigh** and **carriage rides** *(year-round; 20-30min; ☎424-6248)*.

Steam-powered railroads ushered in the Industrial Age in the late 19C. Money from coal and railroads made millionaires of many local entrepreneurs, and in former mining and railroad towns such as Jim Thorpe, the elegant, Gilded Age homes they built still line the streets.

As the industrial boom slowed, so did the need for anthracite, and by the mid-1920s the region's economy was faltering. Several decades later, however, revenues began to rebound as the high Pocono plateau became known for its resorts. Visitors were drawn to the more than 500 lakes that pock the area—evidence of glaciers that grated across the hills some 15,000 years ago—and to the series of 19 waterfalls formed by streams tumbling down the eastern edge of the mountains. Tourism continues to be a lucrative business here, where large resorts now mix with quaint inns, and a strong emphasis on conservation pervades. The **Pocono Mountains Vacation Bureau** (p 264) maintains ten information centers throughout the area.

COAL COUNTRY ★★

Maps p 10 and p 270
Tourist Information ☎717-457-1320 or 800-229-3526 or www.visitnepa.org

Underlying a 500sq mi swath through northeastern Pennsylvania just west of the Pocono plateau, seams of anthracite coal dictated the state's early industrial history. It wasn't long after this nearly pure carbon substance was discovered in the area in the late 18C that it came to be recognized as a clean-burning fuel, excellent for both domestic and industrial use. Stoked by the steam railroad boom, demand for anthracite blasted coal production from a paltry 22 tons in 1814 to 81 million tons 100 years later. During the late 19C, immigrants swarmed to eastern Pennsylvania to work the mines and occupy the hundreds of "patches," or mining villages, that dotted the landscape. Anthracite's heyday lasted until the end of World War I, when improvements in technology made oil and natural gas popular alternative fuels. By the mid-1920s anthracite

> "We do not ride the railroad; it rides upon us. Did you ever think what those sleepers are that underlie the railroad? Each one is a man, an Irishman, or a Yankee man. The rails are laid on them."
>
> Henry David Thoreau, *Walden*, 1854

coal use was in steep decline and the railroads, whose business centered on hauling hard coal to East Coast markets, went bankrupt. Today, even after 200 years of mining, some 65 billion tons of anthracite still line eastern Pennsylvania's hills. Although modern technology eventually outstripped the coal industry, Pennsylvania is proud to preserve the anthracite heritage that helped fuel its early prosperity. Much of this heritage centers around the city of **Scranton**, which lies just over the Moosic Mountains from the western edge of the Pocono plateau. Here visitors can learn about all facets of the anthracite industry, from the men who risked life and lung digging coal out of dark, dusty mines to the railroads that carried this precious commodity to distant cities.

SIGHTS   2 days. Map p 270.

★★ **Steamtown National Historic Site** – 🖾 *At the intersection of Lackawanna Ave. & Cliff St. in Scranton. Open year-round daily 9am–5pm. Closed Jan 1, Thanksgiving Day, Dec 25. $6. & 🅿 www.nps.gov/stea ☎717-340-5182 or 888-693-9391.* Occupying some 52 acres of the Scranton railroad yard of the Delaware, Lackawanna and Western (DL&W) Railroad, Steamtown celebrates the industry that has been heralded as "the biggest business of 19th-century America." In the decades following the advent of the steam locomotive in 1829, with merchants clamoring for more efficient ways of transporting goods, tens of thousands of miles of track were laid. Anthracite kept the early railroads chugging; hard coal made up 90 percent of the DL&W's freight by 1874. Pennsylvania's steam railroads prospered until the demand for anthracite coal plummeted in the 1920s. After World War II, the diesel engine revolutionized the flagging railroad industry; the era of steam was dead.

Visit – ½ *day.* The National Park Service has administered this site since it opened in 1986. Exhibits here surround the 90ft-diameter **turntable**, used to turn engines toward the roundhouse, in which locomotives were repaired. Begin at the **visitor**

center, where displays will orient you to the site and introduce the history of the DL&W railroad and the area's coal industry. The theater next door shows the 18min film *Steel and Steam* every half-hour. In the adjoining **history museum★★**, well-presented displays and interactive exhibits cover the history of steam railroading in the US, from how the rails were laid to how industrialists controlled them. Raised walkways in the 1902 **roundhouse★** provide a good view of a variety of standard-gauge steam locomotives. Proceed to the **technology museum** for a detailed look at the technological advancements made by railroads over the years. Outside, a number of historic train cars sit in the railyard.

A variety of tours and steam-train excursions are also available *(check at visitor center for seasonal schedules and fees)*.

★ **Lackawanna Coal Mine Tour** – *On Bald Mountain Rd. in McDade Park, Scranton. Visit by guided tour (1hr) only, Apr–Nov daily 10am–4:30pm. Closed Thanksgiving Day. $6.* ✗ 🅿 *www.visitnepa.org* ☎717-963-6463 or 800-238-7245. Ride old mine cars 300ft underground where you'll walk through the rock tunnels of what was once a working mine. Here, former miners explain how anthracite coal was dynamited from its subterranean seams. In these cold, dark passageways, you'll quickly come to understand the innumerable hazards to which 19C miners were constantly subjected.

Coal Miners, Scranton

Pennsylvania Anthracite Heritage Museum – *Adjacent to the coal mine in McDade Park, Scranton. Open year-round Mon–Sat 9am–5pm, Sun noon–5pm. Closed major holidays (except: Memorial Day, Jul 4, Labor Day). $3.50.* ♿ 🅿 ☎717-963-4804. Set in a 200-acre park, this museum relates the history of the area's mining industry. Panel displays and photographs illustrate the ethnic groups who came here to work the mines. A wealth of mining equipment illustrates the hazardous job of extracting coal from its underground seams, and a roomful of textile mill machinery depicts the jobs many women took to supplement their family's income.

Scranton Iron Furnaces – *159 Cedar Ave. between Lackawanna Ave. & Moosic St. Open year-round daily dawn–dusk.* ♿ 🅿 ☎717-963-4804. Four massive stone blast-furnace stacks stand in a park adjacent to downtown Scranton as vestiges of the Lackawanna Iron and Coal Company, once one of the busiest iron mills in the world. In its mid-19C heyday, the company used local anthracite to fuel these furnaces, which smelted iron for its most successful venture: making rails for the railroads. Panel displays on-site explain the smelting process and relate how the city of Scranton grew up around the iron industry.

★★ **Eckley Miner's Village** – *9mi east of Hazleton off Rte. 940E. Open year-round Mon–Sat 9am–5pm, Sun noon–5pm. Closed major holidays (except: Memorial Day, Jul 4, Labor Day). $3.50. Guided tours (1hr) available Memorial Day–Labor Day.* 🅿 ☎717-636-2070. This planned community, built in the rolling countryside some 40mi south of Scranton, preserves a typical 19C "patch," or company mining town. Settled in 1854, Eckley provided housing for the families of men—many of them immigrants—who worked in the nearby colliery, where coal was mined and processed. The town's stores, schools and churches satisfied most of the needs of its villagers; Eckley even had its own doctor—a relative rarity for a patch. After its boom in the 1880s, when the village's population numbered some 1,500 people, Eckley gradually declined as strip mining began to replace underground mining, starting in 1890. In 1969 a group of local businessmen purchased the defunct mining village and opened it as a museum; the site was deeded to the Commonwealth in 1971.

At the **visitor center**, a video presentation *(17min)* introduces Eckley and some of its early inhabitants. Exhibits here focus on the home life of the mining families. During the tour, guides recount the history of the 22 structures on-site: the original buildings; those relocated to Eckley; and those—like the "breaker" where coal was sorted—that were built as props for the film *The Molly Maguires*, which was shot here in 1968. The size of a family's dwelling at Eckley was determined by the man's job; those with higher rank merited larger homes. And religion also played a part in socioeconomic status: Protestants and Catholics lived in separate sections of the village.

★ **Museum of Anthracite Mining** – *17th & Pine Sts., Ashland; 20mi south of Hazleton via I-81. Take Exit 36 west (toward Frackville) and follow Rte. 61 west 7mi to Ashland. Open May–Oct Mon–Sat 10am–6pm, Sun noon–5pm. Rest of the year Tue–Sat 9am–5pm, Sun noon–5pm. $3.50.* ♿ 🅿 ☎717-875-4708. A series of informative displays, artifacts and historical photographs in this modest museum illustrate the coal-mining process from the formation of coal to the painstaking job of processing it. Highlights include a collection of 19C mining equipment that inspires respect for the backbreaking—and notoriously low-paying—job of extracting anthracite from the earth.

Pioneer Tunnel Coal Mine – *Just south of the Museum of Anthracite Mining on 18th St., Ashland. Visit by guided tour (30min) only, Apr Mon–Fri 11am, 12:30pm & 2pm. Memorial Day–Labor Day daily 10am–6pm. May & Sept–Oct Mon–Fri 11am, 12:30pm & 2pm; weekends 10am–6pm. $6.* ✗ 🅿 *www.easternpa.com/pioneertunnel* ☎717-875-3850. Open mine cars transport visitors into a horizontal drift mine dug 1,800ft straight into the side of Mahanoy Mountain. There guides explain the arduous task of coal mining and detail its many dangers. Visitors to the mine can also take a 30min ride on a restored 1920s steam train to the site of an abandoned strip mine a mile away *(departs Memorial Day–Labor Day daily 10am–6pm; May & Sept–Oct weekends 10am–6pm; commentary; $3.50).*

DELAWARE WATER GAP NATIONAL RECREATION AREA★★

Maps p 11 and p 271
Tourist Information ☎717-588-2451

Gateway to the Poconos, the national recreation area stretches along the Pennsylvania and New Jersey border, encompassing 10mi of the Kittatinny Mountain Ridge, more than 20 lakes and ponds, numerous waterfalls, 25mi of the Appalachian Trail, and 40mi of the Upper Delaware Scenic and Recreational River. Some four million visitors come here annually to hike, swim, fish, canoe, cross-country ski and sightsee.

Historical Notes – Initially formed about six million years ago as continental plates separated, this part of the Upper Delaware River Basin was further chiseled during the last Pleistocene glaciation. The water gap itself, a sweeping 300ft-wide southeast bend in the river, breaks through the quartzite rock of the Kittatinny Ridge. Since roughly 8500 BC, the area has been inhabited by humans. At the time of the first European contact here in the 17C, the Algonquian-speaking Lenni Lenape Indians were living in the valley. White settlers arrived in the area in the early 18C, but the population did not burgeon until the 19C, when artists, wealthy vacationers and recreationists discovered its scenic beauty.

In 1962 the US Congress authorized the building of the Tocks Island Dam that would have created a 37mi-long reservoir with a natural area surrounding it. However, local opposition, spiraling costs and environmental concerns caused the government to abandon the reservoir project. The idea for a park survived nonetheless, and the Delaware Water Gap National Recreation Area was established by Congress in 1965 as a unit of the National Park Service. It now encompasses roughly 70,000 acres, of which the federal government owns about 55,000 acres.

Practical Information

For additional practical information, see p 264.

Getting There – Interstate I-80 runs east to west across New Jersey and Pennsylvania, providing southern access to both Old Mine Road (NJ) and Route 209 (PA), the main north-south routes through the Delaware Water Gap. On the northern edge of the Water Gap, I-84 crosses New York into Pennsylvania, connecting with Route 209 via Route 6E near Milford, PA. International and domestic flights service **Wilkes-Barre/Scranton International Airport** and **Lehigh Valley International Airport** *(Allentown)*. Martz Trailways **bus** service *(☎821-3800 or 800-233-8604)* runs to area cities.

Getting Around – One-hour **trolley** tours of the national recreation area depart from the Trolley Depot in the town of Delaware Water Gap, PA *(Apr–Nov daily 10am–4pm, weather permitting; ☎717-476-9766)*.

Visitor Information – *Delaware Water Gap NRA is open year-round daily. $5.* △ ▣ *www.nps.gov/dewa* ☎717-588-2451. Contact **Visitor Services**, **Delaware Water Gap National Recreation Area** *(Bushkill PA 18324; ☎717-588-2451 or 908-496-4458)* for information on points of interest, seasonal events and recreation. Trail maps, recreational information and permits are available at park **visitor centers**: **Kittatinny** *(just off I-80 on NJ side of toll bridge; open May–Oct daily 9am–5pm, rest of the year weekends 8:30am–5pm; ☎908-496-4458)*; and **Dingmans Falls** *(1mi west of Rte. 209 in PA; closed until spring 1999)*. Park headquarters is located on River Road off Rte. 209 near Bushkill, PA *(open year-round Mon–Fri 8am–4:30pm; ☎717-588-2451)*.

Accommodations – *(p 358)* Facilities within the recreation area include Dingmans Campground on the PA side *(open Apr–Oct; reservations accepted; ☎717-828-2266)* and primitive campsites for through hikers on the Appalachian Trail and canoeists on extended river trips. The Old Mine **hostel** provides inexpensive lodging *(Old Mine Rd., south of Rte. 206; open year-round, reservations required; PO Box 172, Layton NJ 07851 ☎973-948-6750)*.

Recreation – Delaware Water Gap NRA offers year-round recreational opportunities. There are more than 60 **hiking** trails, including a 25mi section of the Appalachian Trail (marked with white blazes). Popular **biking** paths include Old Mine Road (NJ) and Big Egypt Road or Zion Church Road (PA); bicycles are not permitted on hiking trails. **Canoeing** and **rafting** trips depart from Marshalls Creek, Marskin Hills, Dingmans Ferry and Shawnee. Liveries rent equipment and provide transportation between access points, contact Visitor Services *(above)* for list of licensed companies and river maps. Boat rentals are available in Dingmans Ferry. **Swimming** is recommended at guarded beaches only: Milford Beach and Smithfield Beach *(guarded Memorial Day–Labor Day)*. Numerous small lakes and ponds provide excellent **fishing** year-round; from mid-April through early June, millions of shad pass through this portion of the Delaware River. **Hunting** is allowed *(permit required)*. **Cross-country ski** trails *(no equipment rentals available)* in the park include Slateford Farmhouse *(south of Kittatinny Point Visitor Center, PA)* and Blue Mountain Lakes *(north of Rivers Bend Group Campground, NJ)*. Downhill skiing is available at Shawnee Mountain Ski Area *(Shawnee, PA)*. **Bald eagles** winter in the area; best viewing times are between mid-morning and late-afternoon, January through February. Contact the Upper Delaware Scenic & Recreation River Assn. for more information *(☎717-685-4871)*.

PENNSYLVANIA SIDE *1½ days. Map p 271.*

Both **Dingmans Falls Visitor Center** *(off Rte. 209 in the northwestern portion of the park)* *and scenic* **Dingmans Falls** *are currently closed for construction and scheduled to reopen by the spring of 1999.*

The majority of points of interest lie on this side of the gorge, where Route 209 cuts through the national recreation area from the town of Delaware Water Gap— which anchors the south end of the park—north to Milford. Eight of the area's fourteen waterfalls are accessible via this road. Running parallel to the river, Route 209 passes through small towns, resorts and other attractions, and can become congested on summer and fall weekends. To avoid the densest traffic in the small towns on the southern end of the commercial route, take **River Road** *(accessible from the Pennsylvania Visitor Center on I-80)*. This shady, quiet road winds above the river before rejoining Route 209 just south of Bushkill. For a good view of the gap itself, take Route 611 east along the south end of the river to **Point of Gap Overlook**★, where the water gap slices through the Kittatinny Ridge.

Pocono Indian Museum – *Rte. 209 in Bushkill. Open year-round daily 9:30am– 6:30pm. $4.* ▣ *www.pocoindianmuseum.com* ☎717-588-9338. Housed in a former c.1840 homestead, the museum occupies one end of a commercial gift shop. Small dioramas and artifacts here trace the Native American culture in the Delaware River Valley from prehistory, through contact with the Europeans, to the resulting demise of the Delaware (also known as Lenni Lenape) Indians. An informative taped narrative *(30min)* accompanies the exhibits.

★★ **Bushkill Falls** – *On Bushkill Falls Rd., 2mi northwest of Rte. 209. Open Apr–Nov daily 9am–dusk. $7.* ✗ ▣ ☎717-588-6682. Waters of Bushkill and Pond Run Creeks race downhill through a rock-riven, hemlock-fringed canyon here, creating a series of scenic waterfalls that have been dubbed the "Niagara of Pennsylvania." First opened to the public in 1904 by Charles Peters, the falls remain in the hands of his descendants. The simple bridge and path Peters built to access the **Main Falls**★, a 100ft-high tumble of water, has been replaced by an extensive network of four trails. Ranging in length from .5mi to 2mi, these trails lead past different combinations of the eight falls on-site. The entrance to the falls is surrounded by a commercial complex that includes exhibits relating to Pennsylvania wildlife and the Lenni Lenape Indians.

■ Sojourns in the Poconos

Close to the metropolitan areas of New York and Philadelphia, the Poconos have long been known as a lovers' roost, featuring heart-shaped private pools and Jacuzzis made to resemble champagne glasses in many honeymoon suites. (At several resorts in the area, you can request a room tour of these classic Pocono extravaganzas.) In addition to its sprawling resort complexes, the area also boasts fine inns, picturesque small towns and a wealth of sporting opportunities, including skiing, snowmobiling, hiking, canoeing, kayaking, hunting, fishing and golf galore. The Delaware Water Gap National Recreation Area runs along the Pocono plateau's eastern edge, and seven state parks offer their own recreation: 15,483-acre **Hickory Run State Park** *(on Rte. 534 in White Haven;* ☎717-443-0400) is known for its 12ft-deep Ice Age **boulder field**; **Big Pocono State Park** *(off Rte. 715 at the end of Camelback Rd. in Tannersville;* ☎717-894-8336) occupies 1,306 acres at the top of Camelback Mountain, a ski area that commands spectacular **views**★ of the Pocono plateau; and **Promised Land State Park** *(on Rte. 390 in Greentown;* ☎717-676-3428) preserves two evergreen-edged lakes high in the Poconos. Nearby, the vast, 5,698-acre **Lake Wallenpaupack** abounds with fishing and boating opportunities.

Just beyond the lake's northern end on Route 6, tiny White Mills is home to the **Dorflinger Glass Museum** *(.5mi east of Rte. 6 on Long Ridge Rd.;* ☎717-253-1185) and the surrounding Dorflinger Suydam Wildlife Sanctuary. The museum, contained in Christian Dorflinger's 19C farmhouse, holds the collection of renowned cut glass produced by the Dorflinger glassworks that operated in White Mills from the mid-19C to the 1920s. Exhibits in the **Wayne County Historical Museum** *(810 Main St.;* ☎717-253-3240) in Honesdale recount the history of the Delaware and Hudson Canal. Set on the west bank of the Delaware River in Lackawaxen, the **Zane Grey Museum** *(access via Rte. 6 to Rte. 590;* ☎717-685-4871) occupies the house where the famous author of Western novels lived for four years.

★ **Raymondskill Falls** – *Between Dingmans Ferry and Milford; turn west on State Rd. 2009 off Rte. 209. Continue .5mi to dirt parking lot on left.* A .25mi trail from the parking lot threads through an evergreen forest to these lovely—and less trafficked—falls, formed as Raymondskill Creek cascades 165ft down over tiers of bedrock.

Excursions

★ **Grey Towers National Historic Landmark** – *1hr. 2mi south of the northern end of the national recreation area; take Rte. 209 north to Milford and pick up Rte. 6W. Follow signs to house (turn left off Rte. 6 at Old Owego Tpk.). Visit of mansion by guided tour (45min) only, Memorial Day–Labor Day daily 10am–4pm. Labor Day–early Nov Fri–Mon 10am–4pm; Tue–Thu by appointment only. Early Nov–Memorial Day by appointment only. $2.* 🅿 ☎717-296-9630. The stately French chateau-style stone

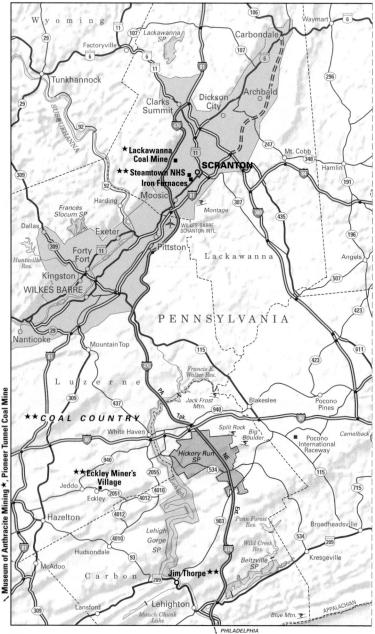

mansion served as the family home of prominent Pennsylvanian Gifford Pinchot. Pinchot's father, James, a Milford native, wealthy businessman and conservationist, commissioned respected architect and family friend Richard Morris Hunt to design the manse in 1885. The younger Pinchot—who later used Grey Towers as his summer home—served two terms (beginning in 1923 and 1931) as governor of Pennsylvania. Despite his political tenure, Gifford is probably best known as the founder and first chief of the National Forest Service, which now maintains the estate.

Tours cover several first-floor rooms of the three-story chateau (which is undergoing restoration, due to be completed by 2005). The house contains a collection of family antiques, some dating back to the 16C. In the library you'll find Gifford's early-20C French forestry texts, notable since no such books existed in English at the time. Shaded by trees planted by the Pinchots, the 102-acre grounds include a

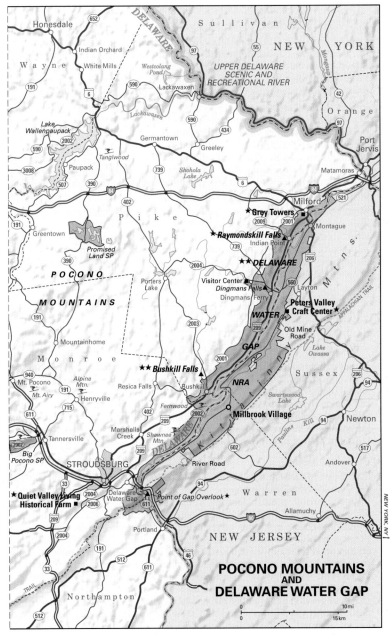

moat—in keeping with the chateau theme—and lovely formal **gardens**★. The gardens incorporate separate structures for Pinchot's office and his son's playhouse. Set inside an open-air gazebo near the house, a small raised pool called the **Finger Bowl** served as a dining table in which the family floated bowls of food.

★ **Quiet Valley Living Historical Farm** – 🎟 *2hrs. 1000 Turkey Hill Rd., in Strouds-burg. Take I-80 west to Exit 46A; take Rte. 209 west and turn right on Shafer School House Rd. Follow signs 1.5mi to Quiet Valley. Visit by guided tour (1hr 30min) only, Jun 20–Labor Day Tue–Sat & holidays 10am–5:30pm, Sun 1pm–5:30pm. $6.* 🅿 ☎717-992-6161. Tucked into the foothills of the Poconos, this peaceful farm was started in 1765 by German immigrant Johan Zepper. Visitors are spirited back to this period by costumed guides posing as farm family members—even the children had assigned tasks. During the informative 90min tour you'll go through a selection of the 14 buildings on-site (some are original; some are reconstructions), where daily chores such as tending animals, spinning and weaving, and smoking meat are explained and demonstrated.

NEW JERSEY SIDE   *½ day. Map p 271.*

On the New Jersey side of the Delaware River, picturesque **Old Mine Road** (which starts out as River Road on the south end of the Delaware) weaves through the largely undeveloped southeastern end of the national recreation area, skirting Worthington State Forest and affording views of the water gap. From there, the road continues north, following the course of the river.

★ **Peters Valley Craft Center** – *19 Kuhn Rd., off Rte. 560 in Layton. Open May–Jan Thu–Tue 11am–8pm.* 🅿 *www.pvcrafts.org* ☎973-948-5200. Occupying buildings of the turn-of-the-century village once known as Bevans, the craft center comprises seven studios, where classes and workshops in metalsmithing, ceramics, fibers, photography, woodworking and other arts and crafts are held during summer months. At the store and gallery on-site you can admire—and purchase—the work of more than 250 local artists. An annual crafts fair is held the last weekend of September.

Millbrook Village – *12mi north of I-80 on Old Mine Rd. Buildings open May–Oct daily 9am–5pm.* 🅿 *www.nps.gov/dewa* ☎908-841-9531. This group of re-created structures typifies a late-19C mill village as it would have appeared in these mountains, with its church, general store, and homes ranging from log cabins to farmhouses. Such traditional crafts as smithing and woodworking are demonstrated in some of the buildings.

JIM THORPE★★

Population 5,121
Maps p 10 and 270
Tourist Information ☎717-325-3673 or 888-546-8467

Snuggled against the side of Flagstaff Mountain, Jim Thorpe began as the mining town of Mauch Chunk. Steep, narrow streets that once bustled with commerce stoked by the coal industry now boast charming shops, inns and restaurants that cater to modern tourists. The town's 19C brick and stone structures, several of which now house museums, relate Jim Thorpe's colorful history. Whether your interests lie in history, architecture, shopping or a relaxing sojourn in the mountains, Jim Thorpe provides a pleasant day's diversion.

Historical Notes

Christened Mauch Chunk (Algonquian for "Mountain of the Sleeping Bear") in 1818, the 400-acre settlement on the Lehigh River revolved around the coal-mining industry during its early decades. In the 1820s engineer Josiah White, along with two partners, formed the Lehigh Coal and Navigation Company to ship local anthracite to East Coast cities via the Lehigh and Delaware canals. The organization was headquartered in the four-story brick building (1884, Addison Hutton) on the corner of Broadway and Route 209 that still bears the company's name.
In order to better haul coal from the mountain mines to the canals for shipping, Josiah White developed the **Switchback Gravity Railroad** in 1827. Cars full of coal descended from the mine atop Summit Hill on a system of wooden tracks by means of gravity; mules pulled the empty cars back up. By the 1870s, more efficient steam engines had replaced the Gravity Railroad. It continued to operate as a scenic railroad ride for tourists until 1933.

The advent of the steam railroad opened an opportunity for local entrepreneur and town benefactor **Asa Packer** to provide a more efficient way of transporting coal to market in Philadelphia. Packer funded construction of the Lehigh Valley Railroad and helped put Mauch Chunk on the map. Evidence of the town's late-19C heyday remains in the elegant homes that wealthy residents built along Broadway, now known as **Millionaires Row**.

When the coal industry began to crash in the 1920s, so did Mauch Chunk's economy. In an effort to revive the town, the boroughs of Mauch Chunk, Upper Mauch Chunk and East Mauch Chunk incorporated as Jim Thorpe in 1954. The widow of the famous Native American Olympian Jim Thorpe (1888-1953) lent the town her husband's name in exchange for a proper resting place for his remains (his native state of Oklahoma refused to build a suitable memorial). Today the black granite **Jim Thorpe Mausoleum** occupies a grassy plot just outside town *(1.5mi northeast of town on Rte. 903 north)*.

SIGHTS *1 day*

Begin your visit at Hazard Square *(at the foot of Broadway)* and work your way up Broadway (Race Street runs parallel to the first block of Broadway). The renovated New Jersey Central Railroad Station (1888) on the square now houses a tourist information center.

© David F. Wisse / DPA

Town of Jim Thorpe

★★ **Asa Packer Mansion** – *Off Rte. 209. Located a short walk up Packer Hill from Hazard Square. Visit by guided tour (45min) only, Apr–May weekends 11am–4:15pm. Memorial Day–Oct daily 11am–4:15pm. Nov weekends 11am–4:15pm. $5.* ☎717-325-3229. Distinguished by its first- and second-floor porches ornamented with graceful hand-carved fretwork, this Italianate mansion (1860, Samuel Sloan) overlooks the town of Jim Thorpe from its perch atop Packer Hill. Wealthy businessman **Asa Packer** (1805-79) commissioned the 20-room house. A Connecticut native, Packer arrived in Mauch Chunk in 1833—his pockets empty, but his heart full of ambition—and built his fortune in the coal industry. When Packer died, his daughter, Mary, inherited the mansion. In 1912 Mary Packer Cummings bequeathed the house and its furnishings to the borough of Mauch Chunk in memory of her father.

Tours take visitors through the first-, second- and third-floor rooms, which are furnished with Packer family pieces. Intricate, hand-carved oak and mahogany paneling lines the main hallway. It took 16 artisans 18 months to carve the 1,000 rosettes, each of which boasts a slightly different design. The **dining room** features a pair of pocket doors with glass insets etched in a dainty fleur-de-lis pattern. Upstairs in the hall separating the family bedrooms sits a rare example of a large Swiss-made Welte Cottage **orchestrion**.

Next door stands the handsome 18-room brick Victorian manse that Asa and his wife built as a wedding present for their son Harry in 1872. Now a B&B, the **Harry Packer Mansion** is open for occasional tours (☎717-825-8566).

★★ **St. Mark's Episcopal Church** – *21 Race St. Visit by guided tour (45min) only, Jun–Oct Mon–Sat 1pm–4pm. $2.* ☎717-325-2241. Hewn into the stone of Flagstaff Mountain, this unique 1869 Gothic Revival edifice—the second on this site—was designed by Richard Upjohn (noted ecclesiastical architect whose work includes the 1846 incarnation of Trinity Church in New York City). An adjoining parish hall, designed by Addison Hutton, was added to the church in 1881.

Tours begin in the **Mary Packer Cummings Memorial Chapel** *(1st floor, parish building)* with its windows by Louis Comfort Tiffany, hand-stenciled walls and white marble reredos. Visitors then board a wrought-iron birdcage Otis elevator (c.1912, now computerized) for the Great Hall on the third floor. Across from the hall is the **church**—built on the third floor to avoid flood damage—which is laid out in the shape of a Latin cross. Here black walnut pews provide seating for parishioners. The **reredos** incorporates sculpted French Caen stone panels copied from St. George's Chapel in Windsor, England; a stained-glass cross set in gold adorns the Italian marble altar. Music during services is provided by a grand, 1,600-pipe Austin organ. Two **Tiffany windows** pierce the wall to the right of the altar, and a rose window (notable for its use of cobalt glass, which is no longer made because it is slightly radioactive) lights the back of the church. Here, the **baptistery** features an octagonal baptismal font fashioned from white Italian marble and flanked by brass gas standards. The ceiling above the baptistery is painted with gold-leaf murals depicting four angels.

Adjacent to the church, **Stone Row** *(nos. 27–57 Race St.)* consists of 16 stone row houses that Asa Packer had built in 1848 for his engineers and foremen. Many of the residences have been restored as shops.

Mauch Chunk Museum and Cultural Center – *41 W. Broadway. Open mid–late Apr weekends 11am–5pm. May–Oct Thu–Sun 11am–5pm. Nov–mid-Dec weekends 11am–5pm. $3. www.jtasd.kl2.pa.us/switchbakc/sbmcm.htm* ☎717-325-9190. Jim Thorpe's oldest church building (1843) today houses a collection of artifacts relating to the town's early history and coal industry, and its namesake, Olympian Jim Thorpe. Be sure to catch a demonstration of the 30ft working **model Switchback Gravity Railroad** 🅺🅸🅳 and the working model of a canal lock.

★ **The Old Jail Museum** – *128 W. Broadway. Visit by guided tour (35min) only, Memorial Day–Oct Thu–Tue noon–4:30pm. $4.* 🅿 ☎717-325-5259. Built of hand-cut stone with 3ft-thick walls, this structure served as Carbon County's jail for 124 years (1871-1995). Prison architect Edward Haviland designed the building, which contains 29 regular cells, 16 dungeon cells and a warden's apartment. Criminals were discouraged from escaping by the 4in-thick, 1,000-pound oak door that still guards the entrance.

In 1877 the jail hosted its most famous prisoners: four men accused of leading the "Molly Maguires" *(below),* an organized group of Irishmen (precursors to modern labor unions) who protested the heinous conditions under which 19C coal miners were made to work. Despite their repeated denial of the crimes of which they were accused, all four men were hanged at the gallows here. Legend holds that before being hanged, one of these men left his handprint on his cell wall as a reminder of his innocence. The eerie print remains in cell no. 17 more than 100 years later—despite all efforts to remove it.

■ The Molly Maguires

Seventeenth-century Ireland saw the first use of the sobriquet "Molly Maguires," which identified a revolutionary peasant society formed to fight the oppression imposed by the country's British conquerors. Historians disagree about the term's origin: Some say the group is named for its founder; others maintain that it originates from the fact that its members disguised themselves in women's clothes during their attacks. In the mid-19C, coal-company owners adopted the name to label those miners who actively opposed the intolerable conditions under which they labored. The modern "Mollies" actually belonged to the Ancient Order of Hibernians, an Irish Catholic fraternal organization whose members were devoted to the welfare of their fellow Irishmen.

When pitiful working conditions and lack of regard for miners' safety on the part of the coal companies resulted in a workers' strike in 1875, mine operators were quick to crush the dissenters and exact harsh punishment on the miners. This led to a series of guerrilla attacks on mine operators for which the Mollies were blamed. Journalists echoed the sentiments of big business, and soon the term Molly Maguires became synonymous with murderers and assassins.

Determined to squelch such dissension once and for all, mine owners sent spies to infiltrate the ranks of their workers. The testimony of these agents in a two-year series of sensational trials beginning in 1875 resulted in the conviction and hanging of 10 members of the Molly Maguires for murder. Thus the Mollies were silenced, but thanks to their efforts, the voices of exploited workers would yet be heard.

Amish Boy – © Robert Llewellyn

F ertile, rolling farmlands and tidy front yards, roadside produce stands and horse-drawn buggies—all these are images of an area that, with the exception of tourism, has changed little in the past century. Looking for a place to practice their Protestant faiths undisturbed, groups of people began migrating from Switzerland and the Rhineland (in what is now southern Germany) to southeastern Pennsylvania in the early 1700s. By 1790, 40 percent of the region's population was German. Along with their religion, they brought their customs and language. Today in addition to English, many Amish still use Pennsylvania Dutch, a dialect that combines German and English. In fact, the term "Pennsylvania Dutch" evolved as a corruption of *Deutsch* ("German"), and the somewhat confusing name stuck.

Concentrated in LANCASTER COUNTY, the Pennsylvania Dutch influence is evident throughout the surrounding area up to the Schuylkill River and I-78. Colorful hex signs *(p 305)* still adorn barns, and family-style restaurants and homes advertising handmade quilts and crafts offer motorists further incentive to slow down and explore the scenic backroads. Largest inland city in the US from 1760 to 1810, LANCASTER never really grew to modern city status, and as the seat of a super-productive farming county it blends in harmoniously with its country cousins, its low skyline dominated as much by churches as by office buildings. The county itself contains the world's largest population of **Mennonites** and the

___etting There

By Car – Most tourist attractions are located on Route 30, which runs east to west through the heart of Lancaster County, offering access from **Philadelphia** and **York**. Major north-south roads that converge in the city of Lancaster are Routes 272, 222, 72 and 501.

By Air – Closest airports: **Lancaster Airport**, limited domestic flights; **Harrisburg International Airport** and **Philadelphia International Airport**, international and domestic flights.

By Bus and Train – **Bus** service to Lancaster is provided by Greyhound *(22 W. Clay St.;* ☎*800-231-2222)*. Amtrak **trains** come into the Lancaster station *(McGovern Ave. & Queen St.* ☎*800-872-7245)*.

Getting Around

Biking may be the best way to enjoy the leisurely pace of the Pennsylvania Dutch Country *(tours listed below)*. Bike rentals are available in Lititz, Lancaster and Ephrata. For a safe and relaxed ride, avoid major roads—especially Route 30— during rush hour. Red Rose Transit Authority provides local **bus** service throughout the county; for schedule and route information, call ☎397-4246.

General Information

Visitor Information – Contact the **Pennsylvania Dutch Convention and Visitors Bureau (CVB)** *(501 Greenfield Rd., Lancaster PA 17601; open year-round daily; www. 800padutch.com* ☎*299-8901 or 800-723-8824)* to obtain maps and information on sightseeing, accommodations and seasonal events. Other area information centers include **Downtown Lancaster Visitors Center** *(S. Queen and Vine Sts.; open Apr–Nov daily; rest of the year Mon–Fri;* ☎*397-3531)* and the **Mennonite Information Center** *(p 279). See also Visiting Amish Country, p 282.*

Accommodations – *(p 358)* Area visitors' guide including a lodging directory is available *(free)* from the Pennsylvania Dutch CVB *(above)*. Room rates tend to be higher from June through October. Hotels, motels, bed-and-breakfast inns and **farm homes** can be found in most area towns, especially in Lancaster, Bird-in-Hand, Strasburg, Intercourse and Ephrata. **Reservation service:** Pennsylvania Dutch CVB. **Campgrounds** are located near Lancaster, Denver and Strasburg.

Amenities – Most towns in Lancaster County offer a broad range of shops and restaurants. Several large **outlet malls** are located along Route 30 east of Lancaster and a large concentration of **antique shops** can be found on Route 272 near Adamstown. Handcrafted items such as **quilts**, pottery and woodcarvings are sold at roadside stands and shops throughout the area. Farmers' Markets *(p 288)* operate year-round.

Sightseeing

There are a wide variety of tours available in Lancaster County, many conducted by Amish or Mennonite guides. The staff at local information centers *(above)* can help you determine which tours will suit you best.

Guided Tours – Narrated bus and van tours of Lancaster County are offered by Amish Country Tours *(depart from Plain & Fancy Farm, p 283, Apr–Nov; 2hrs;* ☎*768-3600)*; and Gray Line *(depart from 30th Street Station, Philadelphia Apr–Oct; 10hrs;* ☎*215-569-3666 or 800-577-7745)*. Private auto tours, including a visit to an Amish farm, are conducted by Mennonite Information Center Tours *(depart from 2209 Millstream Rd. year-round; 2hrs;* ☎*299-0954)*; and Old Order Amish Tours *(depart from 63 East Brook Rd., Ronks year-round; no cameras allowed; 1-2hrs;* ☎*299-6365)*; advance reservations required for both. **Bicycle Tours** are given by Lancaster Bicycle Touring *(Mar–Nov; 1-day; advance reservations required; bike and helmet rentals available;* ☎*396-0456)*.

Buggy Rides – Travel scenic back roads and experience Amish country in a horse-drawn carriage. Tours generally operate year-round and range from 25-35min: Aaron & Jessica's Buggy Rides *(depart from Plain & Fancy Farm, p 283;* ☎*768-8828)*; Abe's Buggy Rides *(depart from 2596 Old Philadelphia Pike, Bird-in-Hand;* ☎*392-1794)*; Ed's Buggy Rides *(depart from 253 Hartman Bridge Rd., Strasburg;* ☎*687-0360)*.

Auto Tape Tours – Equipped with audio cassette tapes and detailed maps, visitors may tour the area at their own pace. The Pennsylvania Dutch CVB sells an assortment of taped auto tours, including Journey into Amish Life ($11.95) and Auto Tape Tour of Amish Country ($12.95). Tours last about 2hrs; cassette player rentals are available.

second-largest community (after Holmes County, Ohio) of **Amish** *(p 281)*. Sometimes called Plain People for their simplicity of dress and lifestyle, these two groups number more than 30,000 locally, making Lancaster County one of the few places in the nation where people are the main attraction. Ironically, the Plain People themselves stand far back in the tourism-dollar line—self-promotion would defeat their principles of modesty and separation from the world, the very reasons they are so intriguing to outsiders.

LANCASTER ★★

Population 53,597
Map p 10
Tourist Information www.800padutch.com ☎717-299-8901 or 800-723-8824

Seat of Lancaster County, this pre-Colonial burg anchors one of the richest farming areas in the country. Main roads lead like spokes on a wheel into the vibrant heart of Lancaster, magnet for farmers, businesspeople and tourists. The first known settler, George Gibson, owned an inn and brewery near present-day Penn Square as early as 1721. At first called Gibson's Pasture, the town grew quickly, and by 1730 a grid of streets was laid out around the square, which remains the city center. When the Continental Congress fled Philadelphia in 1777, they stopped here on the way to YORK and held a meeting in the courthouse, giving Lancaster the claim of being national-capital-for-a-day. Its tenure as state capital was longer—from 1777 to 1778 and again from 1799 to 1812. An 18C gun-making center, Lancaster produced the country's first "Kentucky rifles," and in the next century the city introduced the Conestoga wagon, which became an icon of overland travel.

Though automobile traffic has driven buggies back to the countryside, tourists are still likely to see Plain People—the women wearing bonnets, the men hats and beards—particularly on market days.

DOWNTOWN   *½ day. Map below.*

A walk around downtown affords a look at well-preserved examples of Colonial, Federal and Victorian architecture, both commercial and residential. In **Penn Square** *(King and Queen Sts.)*, alive with hot dog and T-shirt vendors, you can spot buildings from three centuries: the 1797 Old City Hall *(p 278)*; the 1889 Central Market *(below)*; and the 12-story Griest Building (1924), Lancaster's only skyscraper. In the center of the square, a **monument [1]** (1874) to Civil War soldiers and sailors rises where the courthouse once stood. Another city landmark, the restored 1852 **Fulton Opera House** *(King and Prince Sts.)* showcased the talents of W.C. Fields, Mark Twain, Sarah Bernhardt and many other 19C notables. At 28 Queen Street, the **Newseum** comprises a series of window displays that trace the evolution of newspapers, starting with early printing and including more than 25 pieces of equipment.

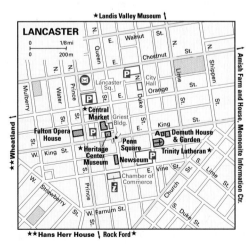

Guided 90min **walking tours★** of the city start at the Chamber of Commerce *(Queen and Vine Sts.; Apr–Oct Mon, Wed, Thu & Sun 1pm, Tue, Fri & Sat 10am & 1pm; 1hr 30min; $5;* ☎717-392-1776)*.

★ **Central Market** – *Northwest corner of Penn Sq. Open year-round Tue & Fri 6am–4:30pm, Sat 6am–2pm. Closed major holidays.* ☎717-397-3531. Erected in 1889 on the site of markets held there since the 1730s, this Romanesque-style brick building was noted for its architecture but loved for its ventilation and easily washed floor. Despite becoming a tourist attraction in recent years, Central Market remains an authentic farmers' market; a 1989 regulation requires that stands sell only "food products and farm-produced goods." Indeed, more than 80 vendors now ply a brisk trade in quilts, elderberry jam, shoofly pie (filled with a mixture composed mainly of molasses and brown sugar), smoked sausages, pepper cheeses and other local specialties; a few pre-regulation stands still hawk crafts and souvenirs.

★ **Heritage Center Museum of Lancaster County** – *Penn Sq. Open May–Dec Tue–Sat 10am–5pm.* ♿ ☎717-299-6440. Completed in 1797, the Georgian-style Old City Hall ranks as the oldest extant civic building in town. On the second floor of the museum, you'll find a good collection of locally crafted furniture, silver, clocks, quilts and other items from the 18C to the 20C. Plaques introduce visitors to the county's long-standing tradition of fine craftsmanship. The first floor houses changing exhibitions relating to the region's cultural heritage.

Charles Demuth House & Garden – *120 E. King St. Open Feb–Dec Tue–Sat 10am–4pm, Sun 1pm–4pm. Closed major holidays. Contribution requested.* ☎717-299-9940. This late-18C two-story home harbors changing art exhibits as well as artifacts and paintings of noted artist **Charles Demuth** (1883-1935), who was perhaps best known for his elegant watercolors depicting subjects such as fruit and flowers. Outside the house, a charming Victorian garden blooms from spring to fall. The adjacent **Demuth's Tobacco Shop [A]**, which has been in the family since 1770, claims a collection of antique firemen's parade hats.

★ **Trinity Lutheran Church** – *31 S. Duke St. Open year-round Mon–Fri 8:30am–5pm, weekends 10am–noon.* ☐ ☎717-397-2734. With a magnificent white Colonial tower and steeple rising 195ft, the oldest church (1761) in Lancaster announces its presence all over town. The tower features statues of the four evangelists—Matthew, Mark, Luke and John—replacements for the hand-carved, white-pine originals that withstood the weather for 154 years and now reside in the vestibule. The spacious sanctuary opens up to a stenciled, barrel-vaulted ceiling, while pews with wooden doors lend an aura of antiquity. Among brilliant stained-glass windows is one by Louis Comfort Tiffany *(front left)*, titled "Return from the Cross."

OUTSKIRTS OF LANCASTER *1 day. Map p 287.*

Amish Farm and House – 🧒 *4mi east of Lancaster on Rte. 30. Open Jan–Mar daily 8:30am–4pm. Apr–May & Sept–Oct daily 8:30am–5pm. Jun–Aug daily 8:30am–6pm. Nov–Dec daily 8:30am–4pm. Closed Dec 25. $5.75.* ✗ ☐ *www.dutchwonderland.com* ☎717-394-6185. Owned by the nearby Dutch Wonderland amusement park, this attraction is well positioned on the busy Route 30 corridor and draws a steady stream of visitors. Built by Quakers, the 1805 stone house *(visit by 30min guided tour only)* has been redesigned to illustrate the Old Order Amish lifestyle *(p 282)*, with a meeting room, simple country kitchen and upstairs bedrooms in which hang typical Amish clothes. Also on the 25-acre property are farm animals, a windmill and a waterwheel.

★★ **Hans Herr House** – *1849 Hans Herr Dr. (5mi south of downtown, off Rte. 222). Open Apr–Nov Mon–Sat & holidays 9am–4pm. Closed Thanksgiving Day. $3.50.* ☐ *www.netconexinc.com* ☎717-464-4438. Led by Hans Herr, the first white settlers in the county were a group of 27 Mennonites escaping religious persecution in Germany in the early 18C. In 1719 Herr's son Christian built the two-story Medieval German-style house, which ranks as the oldest in the county. Flanked by glorious farmland, the restored stone house with its apple orchard and herb garden creates an unforgettable picture of rural serenity. Artist Andrew Wyeth *(p 253)*, a Herr descendant, made several paintings of the house. Inside, rooms are laid out according to a standard German plan and include wide floorboards, a huge fireplace and simple pre-1750 furnishings. On one table sits a copy of *Martyrs Mirror (p 284)*, one of about 1,500 copies printed in the mid-1700s at EPHRATA. Roofing in the loft shows the carefully executed mortise-and-tenon joints used by Herr. An adjacent barn shelters an excellent exhibit on Mennonite farm life.

★ **Landis Valley Museum** – *2451 Kissel Hill Rd. (2.5mi north of downtown, off Oregon Pike/Rte. 272). Open Mar–Dec Mon–Sat 9am–5pm, Sun noon–5pm. Closed Thanksgiving Day & day after, Dec 25. $7.* ♿ ☐ ☎717-569-0401. This 16-acre, living-history village comprises some 20 restored or reconstructed buildings—some relocated from other farms—that interpret 18C and 19C Pennsylvania German rural life. Opened in the 1920s, the museum began with a collection of more than 75,000

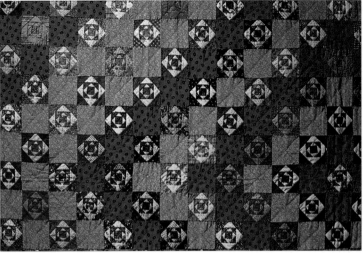

© Pete Souza

Amish Quilt

objects amassed by locals George and Henry Landis, whose German ancestors settled in Lancaster County in the early 18C. Some of the most interesting structures are original to the site: an 1815 Federal-style brick **farmhouse** and the 1856 Landis Valley House Hotel. In many of the buildings, craftspeople demonstrate trades and crafts such as shoemaking, quilting and weaving.

Mennonite Information Center – *2209 Millstream Rd. (4.5mi east of Lancaster, off Rte. 30). Open year-round Mon–Sat 8am–5pm. Closed Jan 1, Thanksgiving Day, Dec 25.* ♿ ▣ ☎*717-299-0954.* The informative center offers maps, brochures and a free film about the Amish and Mennonites. An interesting gallery of exhibits sheds light on Mennonite history and current lifestyles, with audio and video stations providing stories, hymns and information on modern missionary work. An unrelated guided tour on-site takes visitors through a life-size reproduction of the Jewish tabernacle chronicled in the Bible's Book of Exodus *(visit by 45min guided tour only, Apr–Oct Mon–Sat 8am–4pm; rest of the year Mon–Sat 11am, 1pm, 3pm; $4; ♿).*

★ **Historic Rock Ford Plantation** – *881 Rock Ford Rd., Lancaster County Park. Open Apr–Oct Tue–Fri 10am–4pm, Sun noon–4pm. $4.50.* ▣ *www.800padutch.com/rock ford.html* ☎*717-392-7223.* George Washington's adjutant general, **Edward Hand** (1744-1802), built this handsome four-story Georgian brick mansion (c.1794) along the winding Conestoga Creek. The house takes its name from a rocky spot in the creek that provided the only crossing in the days before bridges spanned the Conestoga's waters. In 1810 the estate passed out of family hands; the Rock Ford Foundation was formed in the late 1950s to restore the house and open it to the public. Today tours take in rooms furnished with period and family pieces and outfitted with original woodwork. A reconstructed stone barn on the sweeping landscaped grounds houses a collection of **Pennsylvania folk arts and crafts**, including Fraktur *(p 280)*, pewter, glassware and firearms.

★★ **Wheatland** – *1120 Marietta Ave. Visit by guided tour (1hr) only, Apr–Dec daily 10am–4pm. $5.50.* ▣ *www.wheatland.org* ☎*717-392-8721.* Built in 1828 for wealthy lawyer and banker William Jenkins, this elegant Federal-style mansion was home to **James Buchanan** (1791-1868), Pennsylvania's only US president, from 1848 until his death. Buchanan bought the estate—named by Jenkins after the neighboring wheat fields—when he was secretary of State under President James Polk, organized his 1856 presidential campaign here, and retired to Wheatland in 1861. After turning over the White House to Lincoln, Buchanan told his successor, "If you are as happy, my dear sir, on entering this house as I am in leaving it and returning home, you are the happiest man in this country!" When Confederate advance guards came to within 10mi of Lancaster in 1863, Buchanan refused to leave.

Furnishings throughout the house reflect Buchanan's tenure as head of state; a number of the decorative pieces were gifts from foreign dignitaries. Among high points on the tour are the library with the desk where Buchanan wrote his inaugural address; the formal dining room, set with the French porcelain he used in the White House; and the upstairs bedrooms of Buchanan and his niece Harriet Lane, who served as hostess for the bachelor president, both in the White House and at Wheatland.

EXCURSIONS   *Map p 286.*

★ **Watch and Clock Museum** – *1hr. 10mi west of Lancaster in Columbia. Take Rte. 30 west; turn left on Rte. 441 and left again on Poplar St. Continue two blocks to 514 Poplar St. Open May–Sept Tue–Sat 9am–4pm, Sun noon–4pm. Rest of the year Tue–Sat 9am–4pm. Closed major holidays. $3. & ₧ www.nawcc.org ☎717-684-8261.* The National Association of Watch and Clock Collectors maintains this cache of some 8,000 timepieces and other items tracing horology from the 1600s to the present. Constantly alive with ticking and chiming, the gallery begins with early sundials and hourglasses, as well as a capsule history of human awareness of the passage of time. Exhibits continue with an overwhelming variety of timekeeping devices, from American tall-case clocks and European pocket watches to clocks with exquisite inlays and modern clocks that use water and wood instead of metal mechanisms. Set off in a room by itself, the 1877 **Engle Monumental Clock** stands about 11ft high and features two barrel organs and 48 moving figures that become animated at various times during the day. Due to plans to remodel and add new exhibits by the end of 1998, the museum will be closed temporarily during part of 1998 *(call to confirm hours).*

■ The Fine Art of Fraktur

The Pennsylvania Dutch folk art known as Fraktur flourished from the Revolution to the Civil War, its practice a testimony to the close connection between religion and craft in the state's infancy. Fraktur (from the German *Frakturschrift* meaning "fractured writing") was a form of decorative calligraphy that originated in 16C German-speaking Europe and came with German immigrants to Pennsylvania, where it grew more elaborate, colorful and distinctively New World. The first known Fraktur produced in Colonial America came from Ephrata Cloister *(p 284)*, where it was used in hymnals and other religious books printed there. Illustrating birth and baptismal certificates, marriage certificates and bookplates, Fraktur as a graphic art consists of about two-thirds calligraphy—written in German—and one-third symbolic decoration. A Fraktur artist chose from a number of alphabets, each composed of fractured, or broken, letters. To illuminate the manuscript, the artist unleashed a fountainhead of birds, flowers, trees of life, hearts, six-pointed stars and abstract designs.

Fraktur (c.1833)

By the mid-19C, the art of Fraktur had spread well beyond Pennsylvania, extending as far as Indiana, North Carolina and Ontario, Canada. But the decline of parochial schools, the rise of the English language and a new national symbolism accompanying the age of industry spelled the end of this graphic link to the Old World. Today valuable collector's items, examples of Fraktur are found primarily in museums, private collections and antique stores.

York – *1 day. 25mi west of Lancaster via Rte. 30.* Situated on Codorus Creek, this agricultural and manufacturing community served as the US capital from September 1777 to June 1778, a pivotal period of the Revolution. Here Congress adopted the Articles of Confederation (a forerunner to the Constitution) and declared the first Thanksgiving Day. A reconstruction of the **York County Colonial Court House** *(205 W. Market St.; ☎717-846-1977)* features a multimedia show that helps dramatize the building's history.

Among downtown landmarks, the Romanesque Revival **Central Market** (*34 W. Philadelphia St.*) was built in 1888 and presents 80 vendors; and the 1766 **York Meeting House** (*135 W. Philadelphia St.*), the town's oldest house of worship, is still used by Quakers. The city's agricultural and industrial heritage is preserved at the **Agricultural and Industrial Museums of York County** (*Agricultural: 480 E. Market St.; Industrial: 217 W. Princess St.;* ☎717-852-7007), where adjacent 1874 factory buildings and warehouses maintain a hodgepodge of exhibits on York County's twin engines of growth.

★ **Historical Society of York County** – *250 E. Market St. Open year-round Mon–Sat 9am–5pm, Sun 1pm–4pm. Closed major holidays. $2.50* ⚬ ☎717-848-1587. Two floors of exhibits in this polished facility add luster to county history. Displays include a Conestoga wagon, a mock-up 19C street and a collection of early-19C watercolor drawings of York. The historical society also operates the **Bonham House** (*152 E. Market St.; visit by 40min guided tour only, year-round Tue–Sat 10:30am & 3:30pm; $2; 1-day advance reservation required;* ☎717-848-1587) just down the street. Built in 1840, the brick town house was occupied by artist Horace Bonham (1835-92) and contains Federal, Victorian and early-20C rooms.

★ **Golden Plough Tavern, General Gates House and Bobb Log House** – *157 W. Market St. Visit by guided tour (1hr 30min) only, year-round Mon–Sat 10am–4pm, Sun 1pm–4pm. Closed major holidays. $4.* ☎717-845-2951. Also maintained by the Historical Society of York County, this complex immediately catches the eye with the unusual half-timber and brick construction of the 1741 **Golden Plough Tavern**★, a rare example of German Medieval architecture. York's oldest building, the tavern contains an open-hearth kitchen, a public room and an upstairs communal sleeping room with wattle-and-daub walls. The adjacent stone **General Gates House**★ (1751) re-creates the buzz of activity and political intrigue at the birth of the nation. Here Revolutionary War officer Gen. Horatio Gates lived for a time and feted the Marquis de Lafayette in an unsuccessful attempt to gain his support for ousting George Washington as commander of the Continental Army. Moved to this site from a nearby location, the **Bobb Log House** (c.1812) illustrates with period furnishings a typical frontier dwelling.

Cornwall Iron Furnace – *1hr. 20mi north of Lancaster, off Rte. 72. Description p 303.*

LANCASTER COUNTY ★★★

Map pp 286-287
Tourist Information www.800padutch.com ☎717-299-8901 or 800-723-8824

An hour west of Philadelphia, this pastoral tableau of market towns and patchwork fields punctuated by silos and windmills lures visitors with the promise of immersion in a real-life Brigadoon, a people preserved unchanged for more than 200 years. Though the main roads are often clogged with traffic, particularly on sunny summer weekends, visitors who venture off in search of the perfect quilt, the freshest roadside vegetables or simply the best view can get a refreshing glimpse of that 19C world.

Historical Notes

A Sect Apart – Starting in the early 18C, a host of religious sects began trickling into the county—Quakers, Moravians, Pietists, Brethren, Mennonites and more. But it is the **Amish** who have captured the imagination of the outside world; their strong resistance to change has isolated them and given them the fascination value of a vanishing tribe, which they are not. The Amish and Mennonites grew out of the Anabaptist movement (whose members believe in adult baptism) during the Reformation in 16C Europe; those who followed Menno Simons were called Mennonites. By the late 17C, one Mennonite leader, **Jakob Amman**, felt that the Mennonite rule regarding excommunication was not strict enough—those who committed transgressions should be shunned not just at the communion table, but in all business and social interactions. His followers became the Amish, a more conservative sect than the Mennonites, and the Amish practice of shunning continues today.

Signs of an Amish farm are a windmill, a carriage and a farmhouse complex—created by adding one house to another to accommodate various family members and generations. What may seem to outsiders like a carefree existence, unfettered by modern distractions, actually amounts to a highly disciplined and prescribed life revolving around faith, farm and family. The women cook and sew, the men

Amish Family in Horse-drawn Carriage

© Sylvain Grandadam/Tony Stone Images

farm and the children help. Suspicious of the modern world and its temptations, the Old Order (most conservative) Amish do not use electricity, telephones or cars. Amish teenagers, interestingly, can drive or even own cars, since they do not become church members until they join of their own free will as adults.

Managing in the Modern World – For the most part, though, the Amish manage with horses and natural-gas generators and engines to power farm equipment and kitchen appliances. The women wear solid-colored dresses, black bonnets and no makeup; the men dress in dark broadfall trousers with suspenders and felt or straw hats. Married men grow beards but eschew mustaches as unsanitary and associated with the military. Children attend school in a one-room schoolhouse up to eighth grade; further formal education is considered unnecessary to farm life. One of the clashes between the Amish and the government was resolved in 1972, when their education system was finally approved by the US Supreme Court. In the decision, Chief Justice Warren Burger wrote, "A way of life that is erratic but does not interfere with others is not to be condemned because it is different." The Amish also carry only farm liability insurance; do not file lawsuits; do not contribute to Social Security (preferring instead to "take care of their own"); and have gained exemptions from military service because of their belief in pacifism. For visitors, some of the most rewarding experiences in Amish country come at mealtime. Fine, limestone-rich soil worked by expert farmers makes for an unsurpassed bounty at markets and family-run smorgasbords. Among indigenous specialties are shoofly pie *(p 278)*; deep-fried funnel cakes; sauerkraut served with pork and mashed potatoes; snitz and knepp (boiled cured ham with dried apples and dumplings); souse (pickled pork); chowchow (a pickled relish made with a variety of beans, peppers and corn); and homemade root beer.

> **Visiting Amish Country**
>
> The best way to gain an understanding of these gentle people and the way they live is to drive the back roads or visit towns on market day when the Plain People come to buy supplies. If you take it slow, maybe you'll be lucky enough to see an Amish farmer plowing his fields with his team of six, or to watch Amish children riding their homemade scooters.
>
> We offer the following words of advice for your tour of Amish Country:
>
> - Do not take photographs of the Amish (they respect the commandment against making any graven images).
>
> - On back roads, allow extra time for driving behind slow-moving buggies.
>
> - Pass only in passing lanes.
>
> - If you want to strike up a conversation with an Amish person, try talking about the weather or crops.

Back to the Future – Many people have questioned whether the Amish can remain here in the thick of 20C tourism and development without sacrificing more and more of their ideals. Rising taxes and property values have forced some Plain People off the farm into cottage industries and professions, while automobile traffic and other modern insults continue to put pressure on a self-sustaining 19C lifestyle. Despite it all, their numbers are growing: With 85 percent of young people choosing to stay on the farm, the Amish population has doubled in the past 20 years. Visitors lucky enough to steal a glimpse of this gorgeous land at its best—say, in the gentle light of sunset, or the unexpected hush of winter—can understand why a native would want to keep things the same.

★ **BIRD-IN-HAND**   *½ day. Map p 287.*

Like many towns in the area, this village took its name from an English-style tavern sign that once heralded travelers on the Lancaster-to-Philadelphia highway. Though the Plain People generally disapprove of alcohol, historically the area has enjoyed a long-standing relationship with it. More than 60 taverns lined the Philadelphia turnpike in the late 18C, and distilleries once outnumbered local gristmills. Several wineries and microbreweries keep the tradition alive. The farming community of Bird-in-Hand sits squarely in the midst of Amish country; turn north off Route 340 on Beechdale or North Ronks Road to explore picture-perfect farmlands and perhaps visit an off-the-beaten-path bakery, mill or natural foods store. Restaurants, motels and shops stand along the heavily trafficked Route 340 corridor.

Plain & Fancy Farm – **Kids** *3121 Old Philadelphia Pike (Rte. 340). Open Jun–Oct daily 8am–8pm. Rest of the year daily 10am–8pm. ✗ ⅃ ⊡ www.800padutch.com/millers.html* ☎*717-768-4400.* A shopping complex offers crafts, quilts, toys and other local prizes, while the family-style restaurant serves up hearty country fare. Buggy rides and Amish country tours are available.

Amish Country Homestead – **Kids** *On the site of Plain & Fancy Farm. Visit by guided tour (40min) only, Jul–Oct Mon–Sat & holidays 9:45am–6:45pm, Sun 10:45am–5:45pm. Rest of the year hours vary by season; call for schedule. $5. ✗ ⊡* ☎*717-768-3600.* Built specifically for tours and used as a set in the film *Jacob's Choice (below)*, this two-story house is furnished to illustrate the lifestyle of a typical Amish family; tours outline the history and modern culture of the Amish.

★ **Amish Experience Theater** – *On the site of Plain & Fancy Farm. Open Jul–Oct Mon–Sat & holidays 9am–8pm, Sun 11am–6pm. Rest of the year Mon–Sat & holidays 9am–5pm, Sun 11am–6pm. $6.50. ✗ ⅃ ⊡* ☎*717-768-3600.* An entertaining multimedia show, *Jacob's Choice (30min)* uses holographic images, film, bells, strobe lights and stage smoke to present the story of an Amish teenager's struggle to decide whether to remain true to his roots or leave the farm forever. Audiences sit on church benches, while images are projected on screens and barn-like walls. The show's refrain, "You can't live in both worlds," underscores the high stakes young Amish sometimes face.

★ **EPHRATA**   *3hrs. Map p 287.*

Commercial heart of a rich farm and livestock area in the northeast corner of the county, Ephrata came into existence in 1732, when German Pietist Conrad Beissel *(p 284)* started a monastic community here along the banks of Cocalico Creek. Christened with the old-style name for Bethlehem, the cloister grew to prominence by mid-century but declined after the death of its charismatic leader in 1768. The town, meanwhile, steadily increased in population, peopled by Mennonites and Brethren. Today its wide, shady streets lined by modest Colonial and Victorian homes exude an air of early Americana. Every Friday, the **Green Dragon Market** *(p 288)* enlivens the area with auctions and sales.

Artworks at Doneckers
100 N. State St., Ephrata. ☎*717-738-9503.* In the spirit of Ephrata's 250-year-old tradition of fine craftsmanship, the Artworks at Doneckers has converted an early-20C shoe factory into a four-floor warren of art studios and galleries, abuzz with the creation and sale of quilts and paintings, jewelry and art glass. Drop in for a chat with a kaleidoscope-maker and you could end up ordering a $3,000 custom-designed instrument. You might, on the other hand, be tempted by a piece of hand-thrown pottery for less than $50, or a Shaker-style chair that will last a lifetime. When you're through shopping, you can grab a bite to eat next door at the farmers' market.

★★★ **Ephrata Cloister** – *632 W. Main St.* One of the oldest and most unusual religious communes in the country prospered here from 1732 until 1813, when the last celibate sister died. More an experiment than a particular denomination, the community numbered 300 members in its heyday. Brothers and sisters, as they were called, followed the example of magnetic leader **Conrad Beissel** (1691-1768), who emphasized personal religious experience over intellectualism. Self-denial and hard work were the keys to spiritual purity. Celibate orders lived on the cloister property; "householders"—married farmers and craftsmen—resided a few miles distant. Ascetic cloister members slept from nine o'clock at night to midnight, rose for prayers, slept again from two to five, then spent the rest of the day

Larry Lefever / Grant Heilman Photography

Ephrata Cloister

in work and prayer. Sleep itself was hardly a luxury, since beds were bare wooden benches a mere 15in wide with wood blocks for pillows. Far from self-serving, the community ran one of the country's first printing presses, pouring out an acclaimed stream of books and tracts, including the 1,200-page masterwork *Martyrs Mirror*—a chronicle of sufferings endured by early Mennonites. They also made a fine art of Fraktur *(p 280)* and hymnody; Beissel's legendary skills as a composer and arranger resulted in the output of more than 1,000 hymns at the cloister, voiced for up to eight parts. When 250 sick and wounded soldiers were sent here from Valley Forge during the winter of 1777, the brothers and sisters cared for them in a makeshift hospital.

Visit – *1½hrs. Visit by guided tour (1hr) only, Mar–Dec daily 9am–5pm. Rest of the year Tue–Sun 9am–5pm. Closed major holidays. $5.* ♿ 🅿 ☎*717-733-6600.* Guided tours begin with a 15min slide show, then move on to visit several original buildings, constructed in 18C Germanic style with high-pitched roofs, and stone and half-timbered walls covered by clapboard. The austere **Saal**, or meetinghouse (1741), was used for worship services, which included preaching, a cappella singing, and the occasional foot-washing ceremony. Adjacent to it, the **Saron** (1743) served as the sisters' house and contains three identical floors, each with a kitchen, workrooms and tiny sleeping cells. Doorways are about 4ft high, forcing members to stoop in humility and reminding them of the narrow passage to heaven. After the tour, visitors are welcome to roam the grounds and see some of the other 12 buildings on-site, such as the bake house, academy and print shop; early cloister members, including Conrad Beissel, are buried in the graveyard here.

★ **INTERCOURSE** *2hrs. Map p 287.*

An absolute must for Amish country itineraries, Intercourse is a charming country village in the heart of Lancaster County's prime pasture- and farmland. Neatly tended Amish farms and houses sprawl just beyond the sidewalks where visitors and locals shop for quilts, antiques, tack and hardware. Among the 100 or so shops, restaurants and galleries, **Zimmerman's Store** *(on Main St./Rte. 340)* is the small grocery filmed in the 1985 movie *Witness*; stock up on dry goods, bulk items and chocolate here. Intercourse was founded in 1754 as Cross Keys (the name of a local tavern) and reportedly renamed in 1814 when the Old King's Highway from Philadelphia to Pittsburgh and the Wilmington-Erie Road intersected here—although some say the name derives from the entrance, or "entercourse," to a race course that was located nearby.

A visitor information center located at Cross Keys Village, a shopping complex *(on Old Philadelphia Pike/Rte. 340;* ☎*717-768-7171),* provides area maps and attraction brochures.

★ **The People's Place** – *3513 Old Philadelphia Pike (Rte. 340). Open Memorial Day–Labor Day Mon–Sat 9:30am–8pm. Rest of the year Mon–Sat 9:30am–5pm. Closed Jan 1, Thanksgiving Day, Dec 25. $7.* 🅿 ☎717-768-7171. The best place for a quick overview of the area, this well-conceived facility presents a 30min slide show, "Who Are the Amish?," a sensitive and balanced look at the history and current lifestyle of the Plain People. Upstairs, the exhibit "20 Q" focuses on the most-frequently-asked questions about the Amish and Mennonites, such as their education system, growth and conflicts. Displays also examine differences between sects and church districts, and offer a number of hands-on items. A bookstore contains a wide selection of literature on the Plain People.

★ **The People's Place Quilt Museum** – *3510 Old Philadelphia Pike (Rte. 340). Open Apr–Oct Mon–Sat & holidays 9:30am–5pm. $4.* 🅿 ☎717-768-7171. Cross the street to the **Old Country Store** quilt and crafts shop and head upstairs to the second floor. There you'll find changing exhibits of 19C and 20C (pre-1940) quilts. Hand-stitched by Amish and Mennonites, these quilted works of art display a dazzling array of patterns and colors.

★ **LITITZ** *½ day. Map p 287.*

Founded in 1757 by Moravians *(p 290)* from BETHLEHEM, Lititz was named for the barony in Bohemia where the Moravian church originated in the 15C. Until 1856 the religious, cultural and economic life of Lititz was directed by the church fathers, and only Moravians could live within the town. One of the country's oldest schools for girls, **Linden Hall** *(on Church Sq.)* was established here in 1746. And in 1861 Julius Sturgis opened his **Pretzel House**, the nation's first pretzel bakery *(219 E. Main St.)*; visitors can still tour the facility for a demonstration of how pretzels are made. A small industrial town, Lititz claims a quiet five-block **Main Street** lined with specialty shops, restaurants, and 18C and 19C architecture. Main Street ends at Broad Street *(Rte. 501)*, which stays busy with traffic to and from Lancaster.

★ **Moravian Church** – *8 Church Sq. (on Main St.). Open year-round Mon–Fri 8am–5pm. Go to church office (next door) for admission into church.* ♿ 🅿 ☎717-626-8515. The town's predominant landmark, this stalwart church and steeple have presided over the lovely green of **Church Square** since 1787, a reminder of Lititz's Moravian heritage. The church's **Archives and Museum** *(open Memorial Day–Labor Day Sat 10am–4pm; contribution requested)* contain early manuscripts, community artifacts and a noteworthy collection of antique musical instruments. Spreading peacefully behind the church, the **cemetery** holds the grave of **Gen. John A. Sutter** (1803-80). At one time the richest man in California, Sutter lost his holdings after gold was discovered on his property in 1848, precipitating the great gold rush and bringing hordes of squatters. He lived in Lititz while trying unsuccessfully to gain recompense from the US Congress.

Lititz Museum – *145 E. Main St. Open Memorial Day–Oct Mon–Sat 10am–4pm. Rest of the year by appointment only. $1.50.* ♿ 🅿 ☎717-627-4636. Exhibits in this small museum run by the Lititz Historical Foundation begin with a timeline illustrating the growth of Lititz from Indian settlement to modern town. A highlight, the Sutter Room contains furnishings that belonged to the town's famous local resident Gen. John A. Sutter. The remainder of the displays are devoted to antique furnishings and local artifacts.

Foundation docents give tours of the 1792 **Johannes Mueller House** ★ *(137-139 E. Main St.; visit by 45min guided tour only, same hours as museum; $3)*, a restored two-story stone dwelling with dormers and white shutters. Residence of local tanner and dyer Johannes Mueller, the house and its period furnishings give visitors a peek at the life of a tradesman in 19C Pennsylvania.

Wilbur Chocolate Company

🄺🄸🄳🄸 *48 N. Broad St.*
☎717-626-3249. Started in Philadelphia in 1884, Wilbur Chocolate Co. has been operating in Lititz since 1930. Inside the gift shop, a gallery displays a model of an early candy kitchen, old advertisements, cocoa tins, molds and the like. A video explains the process of chocolate-making that goes on in the adjoining factory—about 120 million pounds are produced here every year. The heady aroma of fresh chocolate makes it hard to resist buying edible souvenirs.

★ **Heritage Map Museum** – *55 N. Water St. Open year-round Mon–Sat 10am–5pm. Closed major holidays. $4.* ▣ *www.carto.com* ☎*717-626-5002.* Fans of geography and cartographic art will enjoy this compendium of maps dating from the 15C to the 20C. On display are scores of rare and original maps and charts, including one of the first printed maps of Europe (1493), a 1630 map of Virginia, and a 1720 map of North America showing California as an island. The polished 7,500sq ft space includes a retail corner, with prices ranging from $25 for local maps to $8,000 for gems from the 16C.

★ **STRASBURG** *1 day. Map p 287.*

A link between York and Philadelphia since 1793, Strasburg began as settlement of French Huguenots, then became a copper-mining village and later a predominantly German immigrant community named Peddlehausie ("Beggartown"). A tourist center with quaint shops and small houses surrounded by Amish and Mennonite farms, Strasburg is noted for its many railroad attractions. In a restored 18C building, the **Strasburg Country Store and Creamery** *(1 W. Main St.; ☎717-687-0766)* sells a large variety of items, including baskets, dolls, penny candy, deli sandwiches and homemade ice cream.

★ **Railroad Museum of Pennsylvania** – Kids *Rte. 741 (1mi east of Rte. 896). Open year-round Tue–Sat 9am–5pm, Sun noon–5pm. Closed Jan 1, Thanksgiving Day, Dec 25. $6.* & ▣ ☎*717-687-8629.* Railroad buffs will be in their element in this tremendous shed-like structure filled with trains, depot noises, whistles and videos. Scattered at random through the **Hall of Locomotives**★, special exhibits include a re-created 1915 depot; a machine shop with hands-on heavy tools and a pit for viewing the underside of a 62-ton freight locomotive; a walk-aboard World War II-era coach; and a freight engine you can board. A bridge offers an overhead view of the mighty locomotives (steam, electric and diesel), and a working model train on the second floor proves irresistible to children. Outside, an impressive display of more than 30 railroad cars and engines—including box cars, observation cars and switching locomotives—is arrayed around a working 1928 Reading Company turntable.

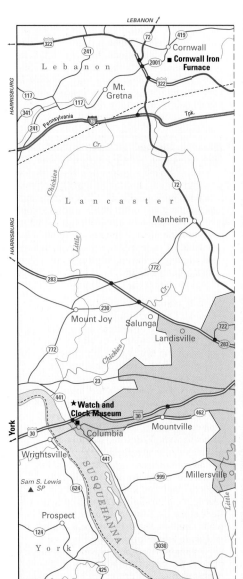

Those who get the urge to ride the rails should cross Route 741 to the **Strasburg Rail Road** *(trains generally depart daily Apr–Oct, weekends only Mar & Nov–Dec; call for schedule; $7.75;* ✗& ▣ ☎*717-687-7522),* featuring a coal-fired locomotive that powers 45min trips through the Amish countryside. Two model-train attractions in the vicinity are also worth a visit: At **Choo Choo Barn** Kids *(Rte. 741, just west of Strasburg Rail Road;* ☎717-687-7911) 17 trains run through a 1,700sq ft miniature countryside with more than 135 animated figures; the **Toy Train Museum** Kids *(Paradise Ln., just north of Rte. 741;* ☎717-687-8976) offers five push-button-operated layouts and glass cases filled with hundreds of antique and modern toy trains.

★ **Mill Bridge Village** – Kids *S. Ronks Rd., 2mi north of Rte. 741. Visit by guided tour (1-3hrs) only, Apr–May & Sept–Oct daily 10am–5pm. Jun–Aug daily 9:30am–5:30pm. $10.* △ ✗ P ☎717-687-8181. *Buggy rides are included in the admission fee.* The main attraction of this tourist complex, a restored four-story fieldstone **gristmill** *(visit by guided tour only)* was constructed here on Pequea Creek in 1803 to replace the burned-out mill built in 1738 by John Herr (grandson of pioneer Hans Herr, *p 278*); the 15ft overshot waterwheel was constructed in 1982. A National Register building, the mill holds 19C ledgers, typewriters and other original items; the working gears and crankshaft assembly operate with original or rebuilt parts. Also of interest, a 30min documentary *Understanding the Amish (shown in the upper level of the barn)* plays continuously throughout the day. Elsewhere on

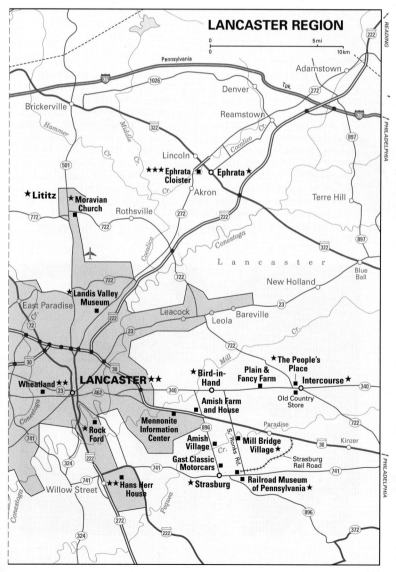

the property, craftsmen demonstrate broom making, quilting and blacksmithing *(Apr–May & Sept–Oct weekends noon–4pm; Jun–Aug daily noon–4pm)* and tours take in a replica Amish house and a collection of Victorian musical instruments.

Amish Village – 🧒 *Rte. 896 (2mi north of Rte. 741 in Strasburg). Visit by guided tour (25min) only, Jan–Feb weekends 10am–4pm. Mar–Memorial Day & Sept–Oct daily 9am–5pm. Memorial Day–Labor Day daily 9am–6pm. Nov daily 9am–4pm. Dec daily 10am–4pm. Closed Dec 24–25. $5.50.* 🅿 ☎717-687-8511. This site features an 1840 farmhouse furnished in the Old Order Amish style, with propane lamps and modest appointments. Guided house tours focus on Amish history, clothing and lifestyle. After the tour, take time to wander around the farm to see the animals and various outbuildings, such as a smokehouse, blacksmith shop and replica one-room schoolhouse.

Gast Classic Motorcars Exhibit – *421 Hartman Bridge Rd. (Rte. 896, .5mi north of Rte. 741 in Strasburg). Open year-round daily 9am–5pm. Closed Jan 1, Easter Sunday, Thanksgiving Day, Dec 24–25. $8.* 👍 🅿 ☎717-687-9500. An Amish country anomaly, this sleek display of 50 vintage and classic automobiles offers an interesting change of pace from farm- and shop-hopping. Although the exhibit changes regularly, such models as a 1911 Maxwell touring car and a 1930 Austin Roadster have been included in the past.

■ Farmers' Markets

Popping up in town and country, Lancaster County's farmers' markets show off the area's celebrated agricultural riches. **Central Market** *(p 277)* in Lancaster, the county's oldest, has been drawing customers since the 1730s. Frequented by Amish, Mennonites and other locals, the lively **Bird-in-Hand Farmers Market** *(just west of the intersection of Rte. 340 & N. Ronks Rd.;* ☎717-393-9674*)* is redolent of frying funnel cakes and fresh-baked soft pretzels. For an out-of-the-ordinary bazaar experience, drive out to Ephrata's **Green Dragon Market** *(995 N. State St.;* ☎717-738-1117*)*. Started in 1932 on the site of the Green Dragon nightclub, which folded during Prohibition, this sprawling outdoor country fair attracts some 400 vendors and thousands of customers from more than 100mi away. Other area markets include the **Farmers Market at Doneckers** *(100 N. State St., Ephrata;* ☎717-738-9503*)*; **Meadowbrook Farmers Market** *(345 W. Main St., Leola;* ☎717-656-2226*)*; and **Roots Market and Conestoga Auction** *(Graystone Rd., Manheim;* ☎717-898-7811*)*.

Central Market, Lancaster

Southeastern Pennsylvania

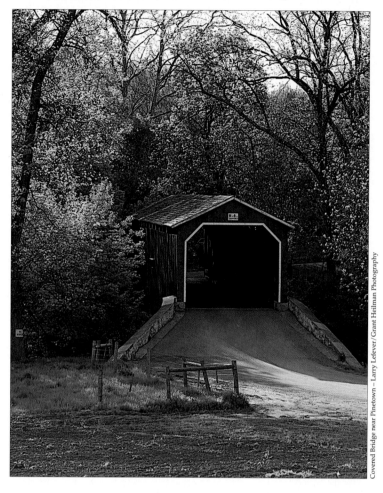

Covered Bridge near Pinetown – Larry Lefever/ Grant Heilman Photography

M arked by the blood and sweat of generations, this corridor of Pennsylvania, curving along the northeast-southwest alignment of the Piedmont ridges from BETHLEHEM west to GETTYSBURG, has played a key role in the nation's history. Easton and READING were both founded by sons of William Penn in the 1750s, and, positioned on broad rivers that flow to Philadelphia, they became important supply depots during the French and Indian War and the American Revolution. In their town squares, locals felt the first stirrings of patriotism listening to public readings of the Declaration of Independence in 1776. With their healthy populations of hardworking German immigrants and ready natural resources, Reading and Bethlehem flourished as centers for iron and steel production. By the mid-19C, this section of the state was a thriving blend of agricultural bounty and industrial muscle. Then in July 1863, Southeastern Pennsylvania became the proving ground for the nation's future—the biggest battle the continent has ever known took place at tiny Gettysburg. The climactic Union victory turned the war toward its ultimate outcome and gave hope, as President Abraham Lincoln eloquently expressed it not long after the battle, "that government of the people, by the people, for the people, shall not perish from the earth."

In the 20C, the region has grown beyond its blue-collar roots. While HARRISBURG honors the area's industrial heritage in the heroic statues and murals of the state capitol, the city has also learned to let its hair down here and there. Today Jet Skis ply the Susquehanna and late-night restaurants revive the spirits of weary lawmakers and conventioneers. Neighboring Hershey sprang to life in the early 20C as a factory town, much like the old self-supporting iron communities. But its sweet product quickly turned Hershey into a year-round tourist center, sporting half a dozen family-style attractions. West Reading's trendy shops and cafes and Bethlehem's music festivals have helped the region defy small-city homogeneity. And a liberal sprinkling of museums spotlight such pieces of local history as canals, tall-case clocks, Conestoga wagons, Germanic architecture and, of course, industry.

BETHLEHEM ★

Population 70,245
Map p 10
Tourist Information ☎610-868-1513 or 800-360-8687

Built along the shores of the Lehigh River, this industrious little city has flourished for more than 250 years and has managed, despite modern growth, to preserve its identity in a downtown that smoothly meshes three centuries of architecture, beginning in the 18C.

Historical Notes

Persecuted in Moravia and Bohemia (in the present-day Czech Republic), a group of Moravians moved in 1722 to Herrnhut, Germany, on the estate of Count Ludwig von Zinzendorf, who was to become their patron and leader. Founded in 1457 in Bohemia by followers of reformer John Hus—who was burned at the stake for his beliefs in 1417—the Moravians are a Protestant sect whose doctrine emphasizes the life of the historical Jesus. Missionaries from Herrnhut arrived in Southeastern Pennsylvania in 1741, making Bethlehem the oldest Moravian settlement in the country.

Named by von Zinzendorf during a Christmas Eve vigil, Bethlehem was a planned religious commune, its structures housing "choirs" of socially equivalent people—married couples lived in one building, while others housed single women, single men, widows and so forth. A walk along **Church Street ★** takes you past these sturdy, multistoried stone and wood buildings, one of the largest collections of early Germanic architecture in the US. Used as a hospital during the Revolutionary War, the 1748 **Brethren's House** (corner of Main & Church Sts.) now serves as the music department for Moravian College. Across the street stands the tremendous **Moravian Church** (1806), where services are still held—about five percent of Bethlehem's present population is Moravian. Just up the street is the 1741 **Gemeinhaus** (no. 66), now the Moravian Museum. Part of the same complex of buildings, the **Widows' House** (1768) and **Sisters' House** (1744) are still owned by the Moravians and occupied by widows, single women and retired clergy. **God's Acre**, a serene, shady square on Market Street (one block west of New St.), contains 2,700 graves, the flat stones a reminder that all are equal in death.

East on Market rise the Victorian mansions of the steel tycoons. Long associated with iron and steel making, Bethlehem operated under high security during World War II as an important armament producer. Though headquarters of Bethlehem Steel remain here, the factories have moved farther out and pollution controls have helped clean up the air. Visitors today will find a busy but manageable community, its Main Street gift shops and cafes especially popular during the Christmas season when the town is illuminated with thousands of lights, candles and the ubiquitous city motif, the Moravian star (p 291). Bethlehem's rich music tradition, originating with the Moravians, includes Christmas concerts, the renowned **Bach Festival** in May and a Musikfest in August.

SIGHTS 1 day

Walking-tour brochures are available at the Bethlehem Visitors Center, 509 Main St. ☎610-868-1513 or 800-360-8687.

★ **Eighteenth-Century Industrial Quarter** – 429 Old York Rd. Enter from Union Blvd., just west of Main St. Open year-round Mon–Fri 8:30am–5pm. Closed major holidays. ☐ ☎610-691-0603. Though still undergoing reconstruction, the few restored buildings in this ten-acre park along Monocacy Creek attest to the ingenuity of the Moravians. On a visit in 1777, John Adams said that the Moravians had "carried the mechanical arts to greater perfection here than in any place which I have seen." Particularly impressive is the 1762 **Waterworks** (open for group tours only), a National Historic Landmark. The limestone structure contained the first pumped municipal water system in the colonies. An undershot waterwheel powered pumps that delivered springwater through pipes all the way up the hill and into town. Also in the park are a 1761 tannery and the 1869 Luckenbach Mill. Built on the site of a 1743 mill, the latter houses scale models of the waterworks and old mill, as well as exhibits on archaeology and early Moravian industry. Further restoration of the site is planned, beginning in 1998.

Kemerer Museum of Decorative Arts – *427 N. New St. Visit by guided tour (45min) only, Jan–Nov Tue–Sun noon–5pm. Dec daily noon–5pm. Closed major holidays. $3.* ☎610-882-0450. Two floors of period rooms, galleries and changing exhibits hold a treasure trove of furnishings, folk art, paintings, maps, prints, textiles and decorative pieces that illustrate lifestyles from the past 250 years. Among the holdings are collections of cast-iron toys and antique dolls, an 1860 pianoforte, and landscapes and portraits by Reuben Luckenbach and other 19C regional artists. A flower garden and Victorian herb garden grace the grounds.

★ **Moravian Museum** – *66 W. Church St. Visit by guided tour (30min) only, Feb–Dec Tue–Sat 1pm–4pm. Closed major holidays. $5.* ☎610-867-0173. The Moravians began building their Gemeinhaus ("community house") upon arriving here in 1741, and used it for living quarters and worship services. Covered with clapboards during the Civil War, the five-story log structure is the oldest building in Bethlehem and now houses the museum. Guided tours of the 12 rooms outline the first 100 years of cultural, religious and community life in the village. Included are the worship room, conference room, school room and a pilgrim room for wayfaring missionaries. The Moravians' own brand of Protestantism, while it promoted fine craftsmanship, did not call for the plain, severe styles popular with the Shakers *(p 86)* and the Amish *(p 281).* Among the items on exhibit are elegant handmade silver and pottery, etched glass, needlework, a wonderful collection of old musical instruments and a 1652 Nuremberg Bible.

★ **Sun Inn** – *564 Main St. Visit by guided tour (1hr) only, year-round Mon–Fri 11am–4pm, Sat 11am–5pm. Closed Dec 25.* ✗& ☎610-866-1758. Writing to his wife, John Adams called this "the best inn I ever saw." The three-story fieldstone, tile-roof hostelry dates to 1758 and was owned by the Moravians until 1855. Serving as a way station for Philadelphia and New York travelers, the inn hosted George and Martha Washington, Benjamin Franklin, the Marquis de Lafayette and a delegation of 51 Indians. Costumed guides take you through the gentlemen's meeting room—a typical bedroom suite with period furniture—and the restored 18C kitchen with its walk-in fireplace. Gourmet fare is served at lunch and dinner in three upstairs dining rooms.

The Moravian Star

On the first Sunday in Advent, many Moravian families decorate a hall or porch with a multipointed star that symbolizes both the original star of Bethlehem and the Christ child, who is described in the Bible's Book of Revelation as "the bright and morning star." Moravians usually display the star until the Day of the Epiphany (January 6), when the Wise Men, who followed a star to Bethlehem, are thought to have arrived at the manger. No one knows who made the first Moravian stars, but they likely originated around 1850 in the Moravian settlement at Niesky, Germany. In the 1880s, Peter Verbeek of nearby Herrnhut learned to make the stars at a school in Niesky and began manufacturing them back in his hometown. He and his son later experimented with the design, settling on the tapered, pyramidal points joined with paper fasteners, similar to those made today. Soon the Verbeeks began shipping the stars far and wide. Although Moravian stars now come in a variety of sizes and materials, the most popular are the old-fashioned paper stars. If you're looking for a souvenir, the Moravian Bookshop *(428 Main St.;* ☎*610-866-5481)* boasts the best variety of stars in town.

Lehigh University – *Maps and information are available at the Alumni/Admissions Building, Brodhead Ave. and Memorial Dr. W; open year-round Mon–Fri 8:15am–4:45pm. ♿ ☎610-758-3100.* Founded by railroad magnate Asa Packer *(p 273)* in 1865, the venerable private university known for its school of engineering now sprawls more than 1,600 acres on the hilly south side of the Lehigh River. One of the university's three contiguous campuses, the original **Asa Packer campus★** stretches along Memorial Drive West, where ivy-clad, late-19C Gothic buildings crowned by spires and gargoyles vie for attention with flowering trees and gently rolling greenswards. Among noteworthy buildings are the Packer Memorial Church *(corner of Memorial and University Drs.)*; Packer Hall *(Library Dr.)*; Linderman Library *(on Library Dr. next to Packer Hall)*, sporting an impressive rotunda skylight of stained glass; and the 1928 Packard Laboratory *(across University Dr. from Packer Memorial Church)*, which was donated by the motorcar maker and displays an 1899 Model A Packard on the first floor.

EXCURSION

★ **Two Rivers Landing** – *3hrs. 10mi east of Bethlehem at 30 Centre Sq. in Easton. Take Rte. 22 east and exit at 4th St.; follow 4th St. south to Northampton St.; turn left on Northampton and continue two blocks east to Centre Sq. At the square, turn right on 3rd St. and take next right onto Pine St. ✗ ☎610-515-8000.* Opened in 1996, this three-floor attraction gathers under one roof the area visitor center, a canal museum and a hands-on children's museum. Begin on the first floor, where you can watch a 6min orientation film *(free)* and enjoy a gallery of Lehigh Valley history.

Sprawling over 20,000sq ft on the second floor, the **Crayola Factory★** Kids is a popular kids' play space that replaces tours of the actual factory, some 10mi north. In the glassed-in demonstration area, workers pour out vats of hot colored wax into molds and explain the process of crayon making. Then move on to the extensive hands-on stations, which include a curving glass wall that kids can draw on with special markers, an airy studio with craft tables, and a dark room for mixing colored light beams. Throughout wafts the unmistakable fragrance of crayons *(open Memorial Day–Labor Day daily 9am–6pm; rest of the year daily 9:30am–5pm; closed Jan 1, Easter Sunday, Thanksgiving Day, Dec 24–25; $7, tickets for the day are sold on a first-come, first-served basis; ♿ ☎610-515-8000).*

On the third floor, the **National Canal Museum★** *(open Memorial Day–Labor Day Mon–Sat 9am–6pm, Sun 11am–6pm; rest of the year Tue–Sat 9:30am–5pm, Sun noon–5pm ♿)* offers a variety of displays relating to the waterways that formed the prevalent means of transporting goods between Easton and Philadelphia in the mid-19C. Mules, often driven by children, hauled the canal boats; the trip took an arduous three days. Exhibits provide insight on boat life, locks, and the inclined-plane system used to haul goods and people over the steep Alleghenies.

During the summer, visitors may take a **canal boat ride** and explore the **Locktender's House Museum** down at Hugh Moore Park *(3mi southwest of Two Rivers Landing, between the Lehigh River and Lehigh Canal; depart from Hugh Moore Park May Tue–Sun; Memorial Day–Labor Day daily; Sept weekends; $5; commentary; ♿ P).*

Consult the practical information section at the end of the guide for travel tips, useful addresses and phone numbers, and a wealth of details on shopping, recreation, entertainment and annual events.

GETTYSBURG ★★★

Population 8,735
Maps p 10 and below
Tourist Information www.gettysburg.com ☎717-334-6274

Rolling farmlands and forests surrounding this crossroads town witnessed the worst carnage of the Civil War in July 1863—and five months later, one of the greatest oratories in the nation's history. Today visitors flock here to see the preserved battlefield and the many small private museums that recount the events of the battle and commemorate Lincoln's Gettysburg Address.

Historical Notes

The Tide Turns – In the late spring of 1863, Robert E. Lee, commander of the Army of Northern Virginia, made a strategic decision to invade the North, hoping to eventually capture the Pennsylvania state capital at HARRISBURG. Suffering from recent losses at Chancellorsville and Fredericksburg, the Union army was already demoralized. To counter Lee, Union commander Maj. Gen. Joe Hooker, dispirited and discredited by a string of defeats, slowly moved his own Army of the Potomac north. Neither general anticipated the collision that began on a drizzly July 1 morning, when two Confederate divisions entered Gettysburg. When a Union picket spotted them, a skirmish broke out. The fighting intensified as other troops in the region heard of the action and raced toward the town, where nine roads converged. Just as the battle caught fire, Hooker was replaced by Maj. Gen. George Meade, who would command the 93,000 Union troops against 75,000 Confederates during the three-day conflagration.

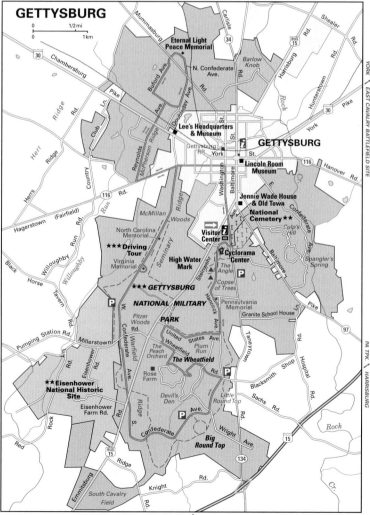

At the end of the first day of fighting, the Confederates had the upper hand. On July 2, however, the tide of the battle turned, after Lee's failed attempts to take out first the left, and then the right flanks of Meade's forces. By July 3 Lee realized that the Union held the strategic high ground and that desperate measures were necessary. That afternoon, 12,000 Confederates under Gen. George Pickett attacked the Union center, well positioned on Cemetery Ridge. As the Rebels surged across more than a half-mile of open, unprotected fields, they were mowed down by Union fire. **Pickett's Charge** cost the Confederacy 6,000 men. The following day, Lee ordered his soldiers to retreat. Never again would Lee's army launch an offensive on northern soil; it was the beginning of the end of the Southern cause.

A Final Resting Place – In all, the Battle of Gettysburg claimed some 27,000 Confederate and 24,000 Union casualties and left the town and surrounding countryside in shambles. Families of soldiers and agents from Northern states converged here, hoping to claim their dead from the shallow graves where they lay. Two local lawyers, David Wills and David McConaughty, quickly realized the need to preserve the battlefield and create a national cemetery to give the dead proper recognition. Funds were solicited from northern states, an interstate commission was formed, and architect William Saunders was hired to design the cemetery. The dedication ceremony was set for November 19, 1863, and popular orator Edward Everett was asked to deliver the speech. As an afterthought,

---

Practical Information .... Area Code: 717

Getting There – Access to Gettysburg National Military Park visitor center from the east (**Lancaster**, 56mi; **Philadelphia**, 124mi) or west: take Route 30 to Route 134/Taneytown Road south. From the north (**Harrisburg**, 38mi) or south: take Route 15 to Route 30 west to Route 134 south. Domestic and international flights service **Harrisburg International Airport**. Closest Amtrak **train** station (☎800-872-7245) is located in Harrisburg. Greyhound **bus** service (☎402-330-2055 or 800-231-2222) runs to Harrisburg.

Getting Around – The **Gettysburg Trolley** provides service to attractions on the perimeter of the national park and in the town of Gettysburg (Apr–Oct daily).

Visitor Information – Gettysburg is most crowded from Memorial Day through mid-October, especially during the anniversary of the battle, July 1-3. Contact the following agencies for information and brochures on points of interest, seasonal events, sightseeing and accommodations: **Gettysburg National Military Park** (97 Taneytown Rd., Gettysburg PA 17325 ☎334-1124); **Gettysburg Convention and Visitors Bureau** (35 Carlisle St., Gettysburg PA 17325; open daily year-round; www.gettysburg.com ☎334-6274).

Accommodations – (p 358) There are no public lodging facilities located within the park. Area visitors' guides including accommodation directories are available (free) from local tourism agencies (above). Hotels, motels and bed-and-breakfast inns can be found nearby in the town of Gettysburg. **Campgrounds** are located on the outskirts of the city.

Sightseeing – Visitors can chooses from a variety of tours of the battlefields and associated sights in town. Maps and additional information are available at the visitor centers listed above. **Gettysburg Licensed Battlefield Guides** offer walking and auto tours that examine the battles and their aftermath (depart from park visitor center year-round; 30min-2hrs). Self-guided Auto Tape Tours allow visitors to tour the battlefield at their own pace (available at the National Civil War Wax Museum, 297 Steinwehr Ave.; and Gettysburg Tour Centers, 778 Baltimore St. & 200 Steinwehr Ave.). Tours last about 90min; cassette player rentals available. Other guided battlefield tours include **bus** tours (depart from Gettysburg Tour Center, 778 Baltimore St.; 2hrs; year-round; ☎334-6296); **bicycle** tours (depart from 448 S. Baltimore St. Apr–Oct; 2hrs; bike & helmet provided; ☎691-0236 or 800-830-5775); and **horseback** tours (depart from Artillery Ridge Campground, 610 Taneytown Rd. Apr–Nov; 1hr; reservations required; ☎334-1288). **Trails** are located throughout the park (maps available at park visitor center). Scenic **Gettysburg Railroad** excursions travel a loop from Gettysburg to Biglerville (depart from station on N. Washington St. Apr–Oct; 1hr 30min; ☎334-6932).

President Lincoln was invited to attend and add a "few appropriate remarks." On the day of the ceremony Everett held forth for two hours. Then Lincoln rose and began his speech with the now-familiar words: "Four score and seven years ago our fathers brought forth on this continent a new nation conceived in liberty and dedicated to the proposition that all men are created equal." At the end of the three-minute speech the crowd responded with weak applause, but history has been more generous. The **Gettysburg Address** remains one of the nation's most revered and inspirational statements.

© Robert Llewellyn

Civil War Re-enactment at Gettysburg

SIGHTS   *1 day. Map p 293.*

★★ **Gettysburg National Military Park** – *Open year-round daily 6am–10pm. Closed Jan 1, Thanksgiving Day, Dec 25.* 🖪 *www.nps.gov/gett* ☎717-334-1124. Encompassing hills, fields, woods and orchards, the 5,900-acre park preserves the landscape where the pivotal battle raged in 1863. Much of this land was originally set aside by the Gettysburg Battlefield Memorial Association, founded in 1864. Thirty-one years later, the battlefield was given to the federal government, and in 1933 it became part of the National Park Service. Almost 100 historic structures, mostly farmhouses and barns *(not open to the public)*, are still scattered across the site and serve as the homes of National Park Service personnel.

Visitor Center – *Access via Taneytown Rd. or Steinwehr Ave./Business Rte. 15. Open year-round daily 8am–5pm.* This large brick structure grew from a small museum erected in the 1920s by the Rosensteel family, avid collectors of Civil War artifacts. In the 1970s, the much-expanded structure was sold to the park and the family's collection donated. Roughly ten percent of the Rosensteel's 40,000 artifacts are now displayed in the **Gettysburg Museum of the Civil War★★**, including a wealth of uniforms, firearms, local furniture bearing bullet holes from battle, musical instruments, signaling equipment and personal memorabilia. Audiotaped explanations accompany several of the exhibits. Also in the visitor center, a 750sq ft **Electric Map** presentation *(30min; year-round daily 8:15am–5pm every 45min; $2.50)* traces the movement of troops across the local terrain during the protracted battle. A variety of battlefield tours led by licensed park guides leave from the visitor center.

Cyclorama Center – *Across the south parking lot from visitor center. Same hours as visitor center.* Inside this circular concrete building opened in 1962, you can view the 1884 **mural★★** titled *Pickett's Charge*, by French artist Paul Philippoteaux. The immense 360ft-by-26ft circular canvas is the focus of the **Cyclorama Program★** *(20min; $2.50)*, in which sound and lights trace the battle action across the mural's field, accompanied by a guide's explanation of aspects of the painting and its history. The Cyclorama Center also shows two contemporary documentaries: *Gettysburg (20min)* and *The American Civil War (20min)*.

★★ **National Cemetery** – *Across Taneytown Rd. from the visitor center; self-guided walking-tour maps are available at the visitor center.* It was at the dedication of this cemetery on November 19, 1863—five months after the battle—that President Abraham Lincoln delivered his famous Gettysburg Address. More than 3,500 Union casualties of the battle are interred in the 17-acre plot, half of them unknown soldiers. Graves form concentric semicircles around the towering **Soldiers' National Monument**, an allegorical figure of Liberty surrounded along its base by statues representing War, History, Peace and Plenty. The statue stands near the site where Lincoln immortalized the Union dead with the words, "The world will little note, nor long remember what we say here, but it can never forget what they did here."

★★★ **Driving Tour** – *18mi; allow 2hrs. Maps available at visitor center, where tour begins.* Trace the steps of Civil War soldiers along this self-guided driving tour, which recounts events of the three-day battle in chronological order. First stop is McPherson Ridge, where the skirmish began. Nearby, the **Eternal Light Peace Memorial** *(on N. Confederate Ave.)* commemorates the Union dead with a 40ft limestone and granite shaft topped by an eternal flame. Allegorical figures on the monument depict Columbia pointing a young America to her destiny. The route continues past such well-known areas of action as **Big Round Top** (take the short loop trail here for a commanding view of the battlefield and the boulders of Devil's Den); the **Wheatfield**, where heavy fighting left more than 4,000 soldiers dead and wounded; and the **High Water Mark**, ground held by the Union center that repulsed the bulk of Pickett's men. For those who wish to venture a bit farther, the tour concludes at the East Cavalry Battlefield Site *(off Rte. 30, 4mi from visitor center)*, where Lee's cavalry commander, Gen. "Jeb" Stuart, was forced to withdraw in defeat. Throughout the battlefields stand some 400 cannon and more than 1,300 monuments, erected to memorialize men of various states, regiments and brigades, both North and South.

★★ **Eisenhower National Historic Site** – *Accessible via shuttle bus from Gettysburg National Military Park Visitor Center Apr–Oct daily 8:30am–5pm. Rest of the year Wed–Sun 8:30am–5pm. Closed Jan 1, Thanksgiving Day, Dec 25. $5.25. www.nps. gov/eise* ☎717-338-9114. The 690 acres of rolling pastureland here preserve the farm and only permanent home of President **Dwight D. Eisenhower** (1890-1969) and his wife, Mamie. Eisenhower grew up in Kansas and joined the military as a way to finance a college education. Instead the military became his life. During World War I, he and Mamie were stationed at Camp Colt, located on the Civil War battlefields of Gettysburg. During World War II, "Ike" was named Supreme Allied Commander of Operation Overlord and implemented the successful Normandy Invasion. In 1950 he and Mamie purchased a 189-acre dairy farm overlooking the South Mountains outside Gettysburg. When the farmhouse on the site proved unsound, the Eisenhowers commissioned a new brick and stone home to be constructed around a salvaged section of the old house. In the meantime, Eisenhower had become the 34th president of the US. The Gettysburg farm, a short helicopter ride from the official presidential retreat at Camp David, often functioned as a de facto White House, where such historic figures as Nikita Khrushchev and Charles de Gaulle were entertained.

After serving two terms as president, Eisenhower retired here, raising his black Angus show cattle, working on his memoirs and continuing his role as elder statesman. After Eisenhower's death in 1969 at the age of 78, Mamie remained on the farm until her own death ten years later.

Visit – *2hrs.* After a short orientation to the grounds given by park personnel, visitors can walk through the Eisenhower home on a self-guided tour. Decorated exactly as it was in the Eisenhowers' day, the comfortable but unpretentious two-story home is notable for its formal **parlor**, filled with gifts given to the Eisenhowers by heads of state and grateful dignitaries. The porch, where the couple spent most of their time, displays one of Ike's oil paintings (others hang upstairs). Grounds include a complex of buildings and a "show barn," used in the care of Eisenhower's black angus herd. A larger four-story barn near the house holds vintage automobiles and farm equipment; the small cottage beside it was used as a guest house. In the lower level of the rustic barn, you can view a short video relating the highlights of Eisenhower's presidency and his life on the farm. Alongside the barn, the **reception center** houses exhibits on Eisenhower's life, as well as a bookstore.

Jennie Wade House & Old Town – *547 Baltimore St. Open Mar–Nov daily 9am–5pm. Closed Thanksgiving Day. $5.25.* 🅿 ☎717-334-6100. Twenty-year-old Jennie Wade, the only civilian casualty of the Battle of Gettysburg, died in this modest 1820s brick duplex on July 3. A stray bullet ripped through two doors and struck her in the back as she was making bread for Union soldiers. The interior of the duplex, decorated in c.1863 furnishings, contains the original bread bowl Wade was using at the time of her death. Behind the museum, Old Town re-creates a Gettysburg square surrounded by five shops illustrating various trades.

Lee's Headquarters & Museum – *.7mi west of Lincoln Sq. on Rte. 30. Open Mar–Nov daily 9am–5pm. $2.* ✗ 🅿 *www.visitgettysburg.com* ☎717-334-3141. On July 1, 1863, Gen. Robert E. Lee commandeered this one-and-a-half-story stone house (c.1830s) as his quarters. He chose it for its strategic position at the crest of

Little Round Top, Gettysburg National Military Park – © Dick Dietrich

Seminary Ridge. Exactly how much time Lee spent here is unknown, though he did hold a counsel of war with his commanders in the house that night. Today the kitchen is decorated in period furnishings; Civil War artifacts fill cases in the two other rooms.

Lincoln Room Museum – *12 Lincoln Sq. in the Wills House. Visit by guided tour (30min) only, Apr–Sept daily 9am–6pm. Rest of the year Mon–Sat & holidays 9am–4pm. $3.25.* ☎*717-334-8188.* This prominently positioned brick structure (1806) on Lincoln Square was the home and office of Judge David Wills, a prime mover behind the establishment of the National Cemetery *(p 296).* At Wills' invitation, Lincoln—along with speechifier Edward Everett and Maryland's Governor Curtin—spent the night here prior to the cemetery dedication. The bedroom where Lincoln stayed and worked on his famous address has been replicated with period furnishings and a life-size mannequin of the president. Recorded narration explains events of that night and the following day, and a small museum displays Lincoln memorabilia.

HARRISBURG ★

Population 50,886
Map p 10
Tourist Information www.visithhc.com ☎717-975-8161 or 800-995-0969

Overlooking the broad Susquehanna River, the state capital flourishes as a center of government, transportation and light industry. In the early 18C, Englishman John Harris developed a trading post and ferry service into a thriving little settlement called Harris' Ferry. In 1785 his son, John Harris, Jr., and son-in-law, Sen. William Maclay, laid out the town and called it Louisburg after Louis XVI, the French king who had helped America defeat Britain in the Revolutionary War. The younger Harris later reputedly refused to sell the land to the Commonwealth of Pennsylvania unless the town's name was changed to Harrisburg. In 1812 the newly christened city became the capital of Pennsylvania

---

Practical Information .... Area Code: 717

Getting There – **Harrisburg International Airport**: 8mi south of city. Transportation to downtown via hotel shuttles and taxis *($20)*. Rental car agencies *(p 358)* are located at the airport. Amtrak **train** station is located at 4th & Chestnut Sts.; ☎800-872-7245. **Bus** service to Harrisburg is provided by Greyhound *(411 Market St.; ☎402-330-2055 or 800-231-2222).*

Getting Around – Local **bus service**: Capitol Area Transit Authority *(Mon–Sat 5am–10pm).* Transit Authority trolley buses operate in the downtown area *(Mon–Sat 11am–2pm; free).* Transit schedule and route information: ☎238-8304. Ample metered street and garage **parking** is available downtown.

Visitor Information – Contact the **Harrisburg/Hershey/Carlisle Tourism & Convention Bureau** *(114 Walnut St., Harrisburg PA 17108-0969; www.visithhc.com* ☎*975-8161 or 800-995-0969)* for information and brochures on points of interest, seasonal events, recreation and accommodations. The staff at **Historic Harrisburg Resource Center** *(p 299)* will help plan individualized itineraries and arrange sightseeing tours.

Accommodations – *(p 358)* Area visitors' guide including lodging directory is available *(free)* from the Harrisburg/Hershey/Carlisle Tourism & Convention Bureau. Accommodations range from hotels and motels to bed-and-breakfast inns spread out around the downtown and airport areas.

Entertainment – Consult the arts and entertainment section of the *Patriot News* or *CityBeat* for schedules of cultural events. The Harrisburg **Symphony Orchestra** performs at the Forum *(5th & Walnut Sts.; ☎232-2539).* The Market Square **Chamber Music Series** runs from October through May *(2nd & Chestnut Sts.; ☎697-6224).*

Sports and Leisure – Harrisburg's primary recreation area is **City Island** *(p 301).* **Shopping**: boutiques and specialty shops are located downtown at Strawberry Square *(Walnut & Market Sts.* ☎*236-5061).* Harrisburg East Mall features over 100 stores *(Rte. 83 & Paxton St.* ☎*564-0890).*

and began growing into a hub of river, canal and rail traffic. The Confederate Army under Gen. Richard S. Ewell briefly threatened Harrisburg in 1863, but the attack was called off by Gen. Robert E. Lee when he opted not to invade the Susquehanna Valley.

Following World War II, the city fell into a period of deterioration, with a lack of adequate housing and funds for urban redevelopment. The population began declining in 1970 as many people moved to the suburbs. But the last few years have put a new spin on downtown—the restoration of a splendid capitol, the recognition of seven historic districts, a spate of new buildings and other improvements have turned Harrisburg into a very visitable city. Though some buildings on the skyline hunker like modern misfits among the churches and older architecture, there is a sense of vitality at the core. Restaurants, bars and shops along Second and Third Streets stay open late, while **River Park**, extending 5mi along Front Street, delights walkers and joggers with its memorials, sunken garden and views of the Susquehanna. Among Front Street mansions are those built by city fathers John Harris, Jr. *(p 301)* and William Maclay *(no. 401)*, the latter now headquarters for the Pennsylvania Bar Association. Both Harris and Maclay are buried at the 1740 **Paxton Presbyterian Church** *(Paxtang Blvd. & Sharon St.)*, located in the upscale neighborhood of Paxtang.

SIGHTS *1 day. Map p 300.*

One of the country's oldest continuously running farmers' markets, the **Broad Street Market** *(3rd and Verbeke Sts., Bldg. 2; open year-round Thu–Fri 7am–5pm, Sat 7am–4pm; closed major holidays; ✗ ♿ P ☎717-236-7923)* began operations downtown in 1860. A far cry from its 1920s heyday of 725 vendors, the three-block-long stone and brick building now houses more than 30 vendors selling specialties ranging from fresh fish and produce to ice cream, baked goods and ethnic foods. Across Third Street, the **Historic Harrisburg Resource Center** *(1230 N. 3rd St.; open year-round Mon–Thu 9am–9pm, Fri 9am–5pm, Sat 9am–1pm; closed major holidays; ☎717-233-4646)* occupies a restored Romanesque bank building (1893) and offers information on the city's historic districts and structures.

★★ **State Capitol** – *Capitol Hill. Open year-round Mon–Fri 8:30am–4:30pm. Visit by guided tour (30min) only, weekends & holidays 9am–4pm. ✗ (Mon–Fri) ♿ www.pasen.gov ☎717-787-6810 or 800-868-7672.* At the dedication of this magnificent Italian Renaissance-style structure in 1906, Teddy Roosevelt declared it "the handsomest building I ever saw." Built to replace the original capitol, destroyed by fire in 1897, the new capitol was designed by Joseph M. Huston. Its five-story exterior is fashioned of Vermont granite and roofed with green glazed tile. Inside the rotunda, the capitol's **dome**, decorated with coffers and inlays, shoots up 272ft and weighs 52 million pounds; nearly 4,000 lights illuminate this focal point. A mosaic of some 400 brightly colored Mercer tiles *(p 258)* adorns the floor of the rotunda and its two adjoining corridors. And adding to the structure's palatial feel, the Italian marble **staircase** evokes the grandeur of the stairway in the Paris Opera House, which inspired it. Little wonder, then, that the **Senate** and **House of Representatives** chambers feel as Baroque as Old World theaters, their gold-leaf chandeliers and other opulent ornamentation a visual banquet for visitors up in the galleries. The Senate contains murals by Pennsylvania artist Violet Oakley, including prominent scenes of George Washington in Philadelphia and Abraham Lincoln at Gettysburg. More Keystone State iconography hangs on the House side; the murals in the House of

Brian D. Hunt

Grand Staircase, Capitol Rotunda

Representatives and in the rotunda were painted by prominent late-19C painter Edward Austin Abbey. You may also be able to view the **Supreme Court Room** and **Governor's Suite** reception room, if they are not in use.

Opened in 1987, the Neoclassical **East Wing** (1986) holds a skylit minidome, a plaza with a 68ft fountain, and a **welcome center** *(open year-round Mon–Fri 8:30am–4:30pm)*. Here visitors can learn about state history and lawmaking in 18 interactive exhibits that illustrate the legislative process.

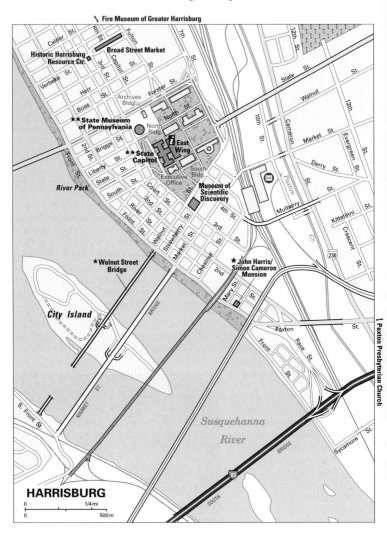

★★ **State Museum of Pennsylvania** – 🧒 *3rd and North Sts. Open Jun–Mar 28 Tue–Sat 9am–5pm, Sun noon–5pm. Rest of the year Mon–Sat 9am–5pm, Sun noon–5pm. Closed major holidays.* ♿ ☎*717-787-4978.* A wealth of Pennsylvania memorabilia occupies this circular four-story building just north of the capitol. Stop by the information desk on the ground floor for a museum plan; then view the orientation video and head up to the first floor, where you'll find an 18ft statue of William Penn, as well as a re-created 1790s dining room and Victorian parlor *(much of this floor is undergoing renovation).*

Focusing on state history, the second floor begins with the **Hall of Anthropology**★ and its evocative Lenni Lenape village; life-size scenes depict Indians smoking fish, tending fires, making clothes and burying their dead. A gallery of military history concentrates on the Civil War and showcases Peter F. Rothermel's monumental 1870 history painting, **The Battle of Gettysburg – Pickett's Charge**. The adjoining **Hall of Industry and Technology** covers 300 years of vehicles and machines, ranging from an 1840 Conestoga wagon to a 1940s Piper Cub airplane. In the third floor's **Hall of Geology★** you walk through a realistic reproduction of a dripping, croaking Carboniferous forest of 310 million years ago. And you could spend an hour in front of the **Dino Lab**, a relatively new glassed-off corner where staff members painstakingly labor over a Coelophysis skeleton excavated at Ghost Ranch, New Mexico. A 7min video and informative panels explain what's going on, and you can ask the technician questions. Adjacent sits the nearly complete skeleton of a 12,000-year-old **mastodon** found in a Monroe County bog in 1968. The updated **Hall of Mammals** shows dioramas of bear, deer, fox and beaver; and the natural science hall next door explores the state's various ecosystems. A planetarium offering weekend shows rounds out the museum.

★ **John Harris/Simon Cameron Mansion** – *219 S. Front St. Visit by guided tour (1hr 30min) only, year-round Tue–Sat 10am–4pm. Closed major holidays (except Presidents' Day). $7. Reservations suggested.* ▯ ☎717-233-3462. City founder John Harris, Jr., built his attractive four-story limestone house overlooking the river in 1766. In the 1860s, the house was purchased by US senator Simon Cameron, Lincoln's first secretary of war and minister to Russia. Cameron turned the Georgian structure into a Victorian mansion, adding the two-story back wing to hold a dining room, solarium and guest rooms, and replacing the Colonial stairs with an elegant curved staircase. Highlights of the tour include the 14ft ceilings, gilded Rococo chandeliers, Colonial and Victorian furnishings, decorative arts and textiles.

Museum of Scientific Discovery – ▦ *Strawberry Sq., entrance at 3rd & Walnut Sts. Open year-round Tue–Fri 9am–5pm, Sat 10am–5pm, Sun noon–5pm. Closed major holidays. $5.* ఉ *www.msd.org* ☎717-233-7969. Located downtown in the Strawberry Square shopping complex, the museum encompasses three floors and more than 100 hands-on exhibits, including a Bernoulli blower, a virtual basketball arena and an ultrasonic height measurer. In addition to the many high-tech activities, there are good displays on building construction, the Susquehanna River and city water. The third floor (*not accessible from first two floors; ask attendant for directions*) features a giant Van de Graaff generator, an artificial cave and an astronomy center.

City Island – *Access via Market St. Bridge or Walnut St. Bridge. Open year-round daily 6am–10pm.* ⛾ఉ ☎717-255-3020. Stretching for nearly a mile at Harrisburg's front door, the city's playground boasts hiking and biking trails, eateries, miniature golf, a carousel, train and carriage rides, swimming and minor-league baseball games. The *Pride of the Susquehanna* paddle wheeler offers cruises (*depart May–Oct daily, call for schedule; round-trip 45min; commentary; reservations suggested; $4.95;* ⛾ఉ ▯ ☎717-234-6500) along the river. Many people choose to walk to the island over the picturesque **Walnut Street Bridge★**, one of the country's few remaining multispan Phoenix trusses. "Old Shaky" was closed to car traffic after flood damage in 1972, then restored for pedestrians only.

■ **Covered Bridges**

Romantic symbols of a lost way of life, covered bridges remain tucked away in Pennsylvania's hidden corners, crossing rural streams and rivers ignored by modern highways. These bridges were built with roofs and sides for good reason—to protect the wooden framework from weather. Massachusetts millwright Timothy Palmer built the country's first long covered bridge over the Schuylkill River in Philadelphia around 1800. It no longer stands, but more than 200 old bridges remain scattered around the state, some 63 in the south-central region alone. They range in length from just under 25ft to nearly 300ft. Although covered bridges have a variety of structural designs, all are based on the use of triangles. The oldest and simplest design, the king post truss consists of one large triangle with supporting timbers on each side—these bridges rarely span more than 35ft.

Since 1972 at least 60 of Pennsylvania's covered bridges have been lost to arson, development, floods and neglect. But historic preservation groups have been working diligently to save those that are left. Many regional tourist offices offer maps and brochures to help visitors locate the area's covered bridges. As you walk through these quiet corridors over burbling country creeks, it's easy to imagine the clip-clop of horses' hooves and the roll of carriage wheels echoing from the planks.

Fire Museum of Greater Harrisburg – Kids *1820 N. 4th St. Open year-round Tue–Fri 10am–4pm, Sat 10am–5pm, Sun 1pm–5pm. Closed mid-Dec–early Jan. $2.50.* ☎717-232-8915. Recently restored, the Victorian Reily Hose Company fire station (1899) now houses a wonderful collection of fire-fighting memorabilia and exhibits. Here, life-size dioramas illustrate the evolution of equipment from hand-pulled pumpers to horse-drawn wagons to modern ladder/pumper trucks. A new wing on the back of the building boasts a video wall and an extensive collection of trucks. Upstairs you'll find a complete 1920s Gamewell alarm system with its multitude of switches and breaker panels.

HERSHEY ★

Map p 10
Tourist Information www.visithhc.com ☎717-232-1377 or 800-995-0969

A planned community built around the world-famous chocolate factory, Hershey is both a summer theme park and a clean, small town. Reminders of the factory's product are everywhere, from the aroma of chocolate that pervades the town to the streetlights shaped like Hershey "kisses."

Milton S. Hershey (1857-1945) grew up on a Mennonite farm in the area, apprenticed himself to a Lancaster candy maker, and by the age of 19 had opened his own candy shop in Philadelphia. After three big-city business failures in a row, Hershey returned to Lancaster in 1886 and started a caramel company; 14 years later he sold the company for $1 million and decided to devote his efforts to chocolate. Hershey built a factory out in the country, close to supplies of fresh milk, ready labor and rail transport. By mass-producing a few items—milk chocolate bars, "kisses," baking chocolate and cocoa—the entrepreneur was able to spread his name around the nation, making Hershey synonymous with chocolate. Of course, he also knew the value of taste: "Give them the quality," Hershey once said. "That's the best kind of advertising in the world." As recreation for his workforce, he built **Hersheypark** Kids *(Park Blvd.;* ☎717-534-3830), a 110-acre amusement park, in 1907 and subsequently added a hotel, theater, arena and other attractions to the town. Today the Hershey Foods Corporation leads the US in production of confectionery and pasta products.

© Roger Tully/Courtesy Hershey's Entertainment & Resorts

SIGHTS *1 day*

Hershey's Chocolate World – Kids *800 Park Blvd. Open year-round daily 9am–5pm, hours are often extended throughout the year. Closed Dec 25.* ✗ ✦ ▣ ☎717-534-4006. Serving as the source for information on the town of Hershey, the official visitor center of Hershey Foods Corp. offers a free 12min **ride ★** that has replaced tours of the factory, which were phased out in 1973 because of overpopularity. The simulated tour details the chocolate-making process from roasting and shelling the beans to turning out

Kids Love Hershey's Kisses

wrapped "kisses"—Hershey's signature candy—and ends with a free sample. Piqued appetites can be satisfied at tour's end in the mega gift shop and food court, or at the Chocolate Town Cafe.

★ **Hershey Museum** – *170 W. Hersheypark Dr., adjacent to Hershey Arena. Open Memorial Day–Labor Day daily 10am–5pm. Rest of the year daily 10am–6pm. Closed Jan 1, Thanksgiving Day, Dec 25. $5. ✦ ▣ ($5/summer) www.microserve.net/~hmuseum* ☎717-534-3439. An eclectic gathering of artifacts and displays sheds light on the Hershey empire, regional folklore and Indian culture. A highlight is the **"Built on Chocolate"** exhibit, depicting the rise of a penniless candy maker to a household name. A time line chronicles the factory town, with reference to a violent five-day strike in 1937. And glass cases show off sumptuous furnishings from Hershey's

High Point mansion (now offices for Hershey Foods). Though not a collector himself, Hershey wanted a museum, so in the 1930s he bought a collection of 3,000 Pennsylvania German objects and a similarly massive stash of North American Indian artifacts. Textiles, ceramics, tools, baskets and ceremonial objects from these collections fill the other part of the museum.

ZooAmerica – [Kids] *Park Blvd., adjacent to Hersheypark. Open daily mid-Jun–Aug 10am–8pm. Rest of the year daily 10am–5pm.* ◻ ☎717-534-3860. More than 200 animals representing 75 species are displayed in this compact 11-acre wildlife park. Originating with Hershey's private collection of animals, the zoo closed in the late 1960s, opening again in 1978 with a more up-to-date look. Highlights include Cactus Community, home to Gila monsters and tarantulas; and Big Sky Country, featuring elk, bison and a lively prairie dog town. A variety of other animals inhabit the Grassy Waters, Gentle Woodlands and North Woods areas.

Founders Hall – *On the grounds of Milton Hershey School; turn south on Homestead Ln. off Rte. 322. Open year-round daily 10am–4pm. Closed during school holidays.* ♿ ◻ *www.hershey.pvt.k12.pa.us* ☎717-520-2000. A tall white cylinder rising from immaculate, sweeping grounds serves as the visitor center for the school that Milton S. Hershey (who was childless) founded in 1909 with his wife, Catherine. Originally created for orphan boys, the Milton Hershey School now enrolls more than 1,100 needy students from around the US. Inside, the marble rotunda soars 74ft and is outfitted with snowflake chandeliers. On the floor below the dome, a marble mosaic medallion depicts the 12 significant aspects of Hershey's life. A 45min video presentation *The Vision*, shown in the Heritage Room *(on the hour beginning at 10:15am)*, details the school's history and profiles its founder, whose statue adorns the landing outside the auditorium.

★ **Hershey Gardens** – *170 Hotel Rd., off Hersheypark Dr. Open mid-Apr–Oct daily 9am–6pm (Fri & Sat 8pm Memorial Day–Labor Day). $5.* ♿ ◻ ☎717-534-3492. First opened in 1937, this vibrant botanical display across from the Hotel Hershey now encompasses 23 acres, which include an extensive rose garden, ornamental grasses, a traditional Japanese garden, a collection of dwarf and weeping conifers, and many other unusual plants. Among the 450 varieties of **roses**, numbering some 8,000 individuals, are grandiflora, hybrid tea and old garden. Azaleas, rhododendrons and perennials bloom in June, while summer annuals begin appearing in July.

Across the street, the upscale **Hotel Hershey** (1933) features a Mediterranean-style lobby with a tile floor and fountain. A formal dining room serves elegant fare with a view of the tailored grounds; the stylish Fountain Cafe offers a lighter menu.

EXCURSION

Cornwall Iron Furnace – *1hr. 15mi east of Hershey on Rte. 322 in Cornwall. Visit by guided tour (45min) only, May–Aug Tue–Sat 9am–5pm, Sun noon–5pm. Rest of the year Tue–Sat 10am–4pm, Sun noon–4pm. Closed major holidays (except Memorial Day, Jul 4, Labor Day). $3.50.* ◻ ☎717-272-9711. A trip to this peaceful village rewards visitors with a glimpse into the low-tech nature of 18C and 19C rural industrial life, the Gothic Revival buildings more reminiscent of quaint country parsonages than a molten-iron factory. The iron furnace established here in 1742 stayed in operation until 1883. Originally the Charcoal House, the visitor center contains exhibits outlining charcoal making, iron making and mining. Tours take visitors through the furnace building and explain how iron was made.

A short drive down Boyd Street brings you to **Minersvillage** and its charming lane of sturdy two-story stone houses *(not open to the public)*, continuously occupied by miners and their descendants since the 1860s.

READING

Population 75,723
Map p 10
Tourist Information ☎610-375-4085 or 800-443-6610

Spread along the banks of the Schuylkill River, this small industrial city was laid out in 1748 by Thomas and Richard Penn, sons of colony founder William Penn and named for the family's hometown in England. Despite Britain's attempts to limit the local manufacture of iron, Reading and environs quickly became a major producer of iron and steel goods, supplying the Continental Army with cannons, rifles and ammunition. At the start of the Civil War, Reading sent one of the first companies of soldiers, the Ringgold Light Artillery, to Washington, DC. The completion of the Philadelphia and Reading Railroad in 1884 kept the town in the mainstream of commerce, its factories cranking out tremendous quantities of military equipment and supplies. When the iron industry began to fade in the late 19C, textile mills began filling in the gaps. Reading today maintains the look and feel of a factory town, its apparel manufacturers and outlet malls generating a steady source of income, while a few cool parks and fashionable eateries provide pockets of 1990s sophistication.

■ Merchandise Mecca: Reading's Outlet Malls

In the late 19C, apparel factories began cutting costs by opening up small stores to sell flawed items and overruns to employees; it wasn't long before the general public caught on to this bonanza of bargains. Evolving from these early factory stores, four outlet centers—each one like a monster mall—now attract hordes of discount-hunters to Reading. Numbering more than 200, the outlets feature dozens of such high-end retailers as Laura Ashley, Ralph Lauren, London Fog and Coach. Discounts of up to 75 percent and the lack of a sales tax on clothing provide a strong incentive for serious shoppers. The four complexes are **VF Outlet Village** *(801 Hill Ave.; ☎610-378-0408)*; **Reading Outlet Center** *(801 N. 9th St.; ☎800-568-8538)*; **The Outlets on Hiesters Lane** *(755 Hiesters Ln.; ☎601-921-8130)*; and **Reading Station** *(951 N. 6th St.; ☎601-478-7000)*. Maps are available at the Reading and Berks County Visitors Bureau; ☎610-375-4085.

SIGHTS *½ day*

Penn Square *(5th and Penn Sts.)* remains the focal point of downtown. To the north, the **Centre Park Historic District** *(Centre Ave., 5th St., and 6th St. from Buttonwood to Spring Sts.)* showcases a large number of fine Victorian homes with turrets, wide stone porches and elaborate woodwork, while to the south of Penn Square stand well-kept 19C laborers' houses, commercial structures and factories. Dotting the town are the much-publicized factory outlets *(above)*, drawing bargain hunters from all over the East Coast. Atop Mount Penn on the east edge of town, the seven-story **Pagoda** houses galleries of the Berks Arts Council and affords good views of the city and surrounding countryside. Built in 1908, the Japanese-style building remains a prominent city landmark.

Historical Society of Berks County – *940 Centre Ave. Open year-round Tue–Sat 9am–4pm. Closed major holidays. $2.50. & www.berksweb.com/histsoc/ ☎610-375-4375.* A horn of plenty for local history boasts three floors of exhibits, including some wonderful historical photographs of Reading's early skyline with its manifold smokestacks and church spires. Also on display are an 1890 scissor-grinder's cart, a collection of Gaudy Dutch china (1780-1820) and a scale model of Reading c.1800. Be sure not to overlook the basement, with its 19C horse-drawn trolley, rugged Conestoga wagon, stylish black carriage and collection of antique toys and marionettes. Temporary exhibits and a children's hands-on room complement the museum's bill of fare.

★ **Reading Public Museum** – *500 Museum Rd. Open year-round Tue–Sat 11am–5pm (Wed 8pm), Sun noon–5pm. Closed Dec 25. Admission charged. & ▣ www.berks.net/ museum/ ☎610-371-5850.* This impressive limestone building of Italian Renaissance design is set in a 25-acre park with flowering trees, shrubs and a delightful waterway favored by ducks, geese and swans. Undergoing renovation, the museum's first floor will open in mid-1998 with new history and interactive science exhibits. The **second floor** features gorgeous Chinese ink-on-silk drawings dating from the 10C to the 18C; 14C to 15C Italian religious paintings; 19C French landscapes; as well as works by such noted European artists as Rodin, Degas, Courbet, Corot, van Ruysdael and Reynolds. Also presented are American landscapes by Frederic Church, Benjamin West and John Twachtman. A 20C gallery focuses on Abstract Expressionist works, and a Pennsylvania German gallery holds colorful paintings, boxes, butter molds, tall-case clocks and blanket chests.

EXCURSIONS

Berks County Heritage Center – *2hrs. 5mi northwest of Reading on Rte. 183, then left on Red Bridge Rd. Visit by guided tour (1hr) only, May–Oct Tue–Sat 10am–4pm, Sun noon–5pm. $3, $5 for Heritage & Canal Centers.* ✕ 🅿 ☎*610-374-8839.* A 50-acre spread along the Tulpehocken Creek makes a peaceful setting for an interpretive complex anchored by the 1882 **Gruber Wagon Works**, moved from nearby Mount Pleasant in 1976 and designated a National Historic Landmark. Visitors may walk through the various assembly rooms and view more than 19,000 artifacts from the heyday of wagon making. The **Hiester Canal Center** *(visit by 1hr guided tour only, same hours as Heritage Center; $3)* limns another early form of transportation with some 1,400 items, including a houseboat, toll booth and pilot

■ Hex Signs

One of the most visible of the Pennsylvania Dutch folk arts, hex signs brighten barns, houses, silos and restaurants throughout the southeast corner of the state. These colorful geometric designs come in a number of different forms, mostly variations of the six-pointed star and the whirling swastika, some embellished with tulips, birds and hearts. Though symbolic representations of the sun and the stars similar to hex signs showed up in pre-Christian Europe, scholars are uncertain how the signs came to Pennsylvania. Lutherans and other Reformed peoples decorated their furniture and tombstones with hex signs in the 18C and likely began putting the signs on their barns in the early to mid-19C. Contrary to popular misconception, the Amish do not use hex signs—in fact, their no-frills policy sometimes means whitewashing barns adorned with old hex signs. Consequently, there are very few hexes in Lancaster County; neighboring Berks County claims the highest concentration.

The meaning of hex signs remains a mystery. Photographer Wallace Nutting wrote the first account in 1924, declaring them a spiritual lightning rod to protect the barn and cattle from witches. A later theory held that "hex" was simply a misunderstanding of the German word *sechs* (meaning "six"), as in six-pointed star, and that the signs were intended only for decoration. Most likely, hex signs originally did have some pagan or Christian symbolism—for some people they were talismans both to ward off bad luck and to bring good luck.

The golden age of hex signage reigned from about 1900 to 1960. Since then a handful of painters have kept the art alive, often now painting on a wood or metal disk rather than bothering with the cumbersome scaffolding needed for painting directly on a barn.

house. Also on-site are a relocated gristmill (1888) and **Wertz's Red Bridge**, the longest single-span covered bridge in the state. Stretching 204ft across the creek, the bridge is open to pedestrians only; a 4.5mi walking and biking trail runs between the creek and the remains of the Union Canal.

★ **Daniel Boone Homestead** – *1hr. 10mi east of Reading off Rte. 422 in Birdsboro. Open year-round Tue–Sat 9am–5pm. Sun noon–5pm. Closed major holidays (open Memorial Day, Jul 4, Labor Day). $4.* ♿ 🅿 ☎*610-582-4900.* Legendary frontiersman **Daniel Boone** (1734-1820) was born here and spent the first 15 years of his life in this verdant backcountry before moving with his family to North Carolina. Though little is known of Boone's formative years, he likely helped with farming and blacksmithing and was fond enough of the place to return twice as a grown man, when travel was still a time-consuming ordeal. The 579-acre property contains seven 18C structures, including the **Boone House**. Originally a log dwelling built by Squire Boone in 1730, the house was enlarged by the Boones or subsequent owners around 1750. Another owner tore down the log section in 1779 and gave the house its present two-story stone appearance. Guided tours take in the 11 period-furnished rooms. Outbuildings include a smokehouse, blacksmith's shop and barn, as well as a log house, bake house and sawmill; a small lake on the grounds provides a good spot for picnicking.

Hopewell Furnace National Historic Site

★★ **Hopewell Furnace National Historic Site** – *Map p 10. 2hrs. 14mi southeast of Reading on Rte. 345, in French Creek State Park in Elverson. Open year-round daily 9am–5pm. Closed major holidays. $4.* 🅿 ☎*610-582-8773.* One of numerous iron plantations that littered the Pennsylvania countryside, this pastoral-looking village was once filled with colliers, farmers, craftsmen, storekeepers and housewives, all working toward the common goal of making iron. The 18C equivalent of a factory, the plantation geared up in 1771 and operated for more than 100 years, turning out pig iron *(p 307)*, cast stoves, plates and other products. More than a dozen well-preserved structures remain, with audio stations to explain the process and evoke the primitive dawn of American industry. Of particular interest is the high-ceilinged **casting shed** and **furnace**, the heart of the community. Walk into this cool, dirt-floored space and try to imagine the almost unbearable heat, noise and soot the laborers suffered. The waterwheel still turns outside, and piles of slag and stacks of wooden molds lend an eerie sense that the workers still linger about. A visitor center offers site maps, informative exhibits and an introductory film.

Conrad Weiser Homestead – *1hr. 12mi west of Reading on Rte. 422 in Womelsdorf. Open year-round Wed–Sat 9am–5pm. Sun noon–5pm. Closed major holidays (open Memorial Day, Jul 4, Labor Day). $2.50.* ⓚ 🄿 ☎610-589-2934. Though time has nearly erased the nation's memory of Conrad Weiser (1696-1760), his accomplishments as a diplomat made him a legend in his day. In his early years, in New York, Weiser became an encyclopedia of Iroquois language and customs, so that when he moved at age 33 to the Pennsylvania frontier and bought 200 acres of farmland he was constantly sought out as an Indian negotiator. His travels, treaty negotiations and land deals helped keep the region peaceful for both Indians and whites until the outbreak of the French and Indian War in 1754. After Weiser's death, one Indian leader lamented, "We are at a great loss and sit in darkness." Designed by the sons of Frederick Law Olmsted in 1928, the 26-acre park features rolling grounds, the Weiser gravesite and monument, a visitor center and several 18C and 19C stone buildings. Although only the masonry is original to the Weiser house (1729) on-site, the interior, with its creaky floorboards and 18C furnishings, retains an authentic feel.

■ **Pennsylvania Recipes: Iron and Steel**

Four ingredients found in abundance in Pennsylvania's hills and valleys helped the state become the country's leading iron maker in the 18C. Using a process that originated around 1200 BC, skilled laborers mixed iron ore, limestone and charcoal (made from burning wood), used waterpower to help heat the mixture, and ended up with metal.

Here's how a cold-blast furnace worked: First, workers constructed a pyramid-shaped furnace, about 25-35ft high, made of brick and stone. Then into the chimney (the narrow top of the furnace) they loaded the raw ingredients—the Hopewell Furnace *(p 306)* recipe called for 400-500 pounds of iron ore, 30-40 pounds of limestone, and 15 bushels of charcoal (greater in volume than the iron ore, but less in weight). Like feeding a ravenous beast, the same amount had to be dumped in every half-hour, around the clock. Once the furnace was fired up it had to keep roaring, except for occasional cleaning and repairing periods. Down in the crucible, the hottest part of the furnace, a pipe funneled in blasts of air from a huge bellows contraption powered by a waterwheel. These blasts pushed the furnace temperature up to 3000°F. The tremendous heat caused the carbon monoxide from the charcoal to react with the ore's oxygen, producing iron and carbon dioxide (the latter rose from the chimney). The limestone acted as a flux, drawing out the ore's impurities and fusing them into a rock by-product called slag.

Twice a day, a founder tapped the red-hot molten iron that dripped down the sides of the furnace. This liquid iron could be cast on-site into molds and turned into stoves, kettles and so forth, or it could be shipped out as rough bars of "pig iron" to refineries, where it would be made into wrought iron and steel. Supporting the work of the furnace at an iron-making community, a large cast of specialists—fillers, molders, colliers, miners, teamsters and woodcutters—toiled amid the constant noise, soot, dust and polluted air. At the top of the heap was the ironmaster, who managed the forge.

Some 55 iron furnaces dotted the Pennsylvania countryside in the late 1700s, but by the middle of the next century much of the iron and steel making was centralized in cities close to railroads that brought in carloads of coal and ore from the west. Old-fashioned cold-blast iron furnaces were replaced by big steam-powered, hot-blast furnaces fueled by anthracite coal and coke instead of charcoal. Such new technology spelled the end of the rural industrial era, and it ushered in the dawn of the Age of Steel.

*The basic product of the blast furnace
became known as "pig iron" owing to the fact
that the molds into which the molten iron was channeled
resembled a litter of pigs nursing at a sow's belly.*

Central Pennsylvania

Fallingwater – © Paul Rocheleau

R ich with early American history and natural beauty, this broad swath of forests and rolling farmland covers more than 1,500sq mi from the Susquehanna River west to Allegheny National Forest *(p 318)*, and south to the border of Maryland. Though the region is sparsely populated—its largest urban center, Altoona, contains just over 50,000 people—visitors who take the time to explore it will find a rich array of historic battlefields and towns that seem frozen in Colonial or Victorian times.

By the mid-18C, settlers were beginning to drift westward from Philadelphia into central Pennsylvania as tensions were heating up between the English and the French, prior to the French and Indian War. As people migrated farther west into the state, the great challenge was forging transportation routes over Pennsylvania's rugged Allegheny Mountains, both to usher pioneers out West and to plunder the area's copious lumber, oil and coal reserves. During the 19C, central Pennsylvania saw Conestoga wagon trails replaced by the nation's first National Road; later, the Main Line canal system between Philadelphia and Pittsburgh gave way to the Pennsylvania Railroad.

Agriculture and industry thrived here from the late 19C through the mid-20C, with land-grant colleges such as Penn State supporting the former and moguls such as Henry Clay Frick *(p 340)* and Andrew Carnegie *(p 338)* spearheading the latter. The area's rich natural resources helped fuel the state's leading oil, coal and lumber industries prior to 1900. In the early to mid-20C, steel mills put the city of JOHNSTOWN on the map. Though a few mines and steel mills still operate, the region's economy now relies on service industries (health care, banking, retail trade)—which make up nearly three-quarters of the gross state product—and tourism.

Skiers and other outdoor enthusiasts will find a wide range of recreational activities in the highlands here—where you'll find the state's highest point, 3,213ft Mt. Davis—and history buffs will enjoy exploring the region's wealth of historic sites. Crisscrossed by miles of scenic back roads, central Pennsylvania lends itself to meandering, especially during the warmer months and in the fall, when the foliage is stunning.

JOHNSTOWN ★

Population 26,149
Maps p 9 and p 311
Tourist Information ☎814-536-7993 or 800-237-8590

Nestled in a hole between Chestnut Ridge and Laurel Hill, where the Little Conemaugh and Stony Creek rivers meet, this once-thriving steel town is perhaps best known for the most macabre chapter in its history: the deadly flood of 1889, which wiped out 4sq mi of its downtown and killed more than 2,000 people in less than an hour.

Johnstown was founded in 1794, after the 1768 Treaty of Fort Stanwix opened up southwestern Pennsylvania for development. In 1834 the small mountain outpost served as the connecting point between the Main Line Canal and the Allegheny Portage Railroad, and in 1852 it became a stop on the Pennsylvania Railroad. Cambria Iron Company (forerunner of Bethlehem Steel) also came to town in 1852. Soon Johnstown was ablaze with steel mills, which produced two-thirds of the country's iron and steel. Changes in the economy eventually tempered the local steel industry. Today Bethlehem Steel's mills, located in the heart of downtown, are owned by six separate companies. Light manufacturing, tourism and other service-sector industries keep the city's economy afloat.

SIGHTS *1 day. Map p 311.*

★★ **Johnstown Flood Museum** – *304 Washington St. Open May–Oct Sun–Thu 10am–5pm, Fri–Sat 10am–7pm. Rest of the year daily 10am–5pm. Closed Jan 1, Thanksgiving Day, Dec 25. $4. & www.ctcnet.net/jaha ☎814-539-1889.* The tragic story of the 1889 flood is told inside this former Carnegie Library (1891) in three floors of outstanding exhibits and an Academy Award-winning film. The Johnstown Flood has been called the worst natural disaster of the 19C, but human error no doubt contributed to its horror. Some 14mi upstream from predominantly working-class Johnstown stood the tony South Fork Fishing and Hunting Club, where Pittsburgh steel and coal magnates had built elaborate summer "cottages." The club was situated on the banks of 3mi-long Lake Conemaugh, which had been created by an 1830s dam that had been constructed, and later abandoned, by the state. Once it fell into the hands of the club, the dam was not properly maintained. In fact, changes made to this dam—which held 20 million gallons of water poised 450ft above Johnstown—by club members actually weakened the structure.

In 1889, after 11 days of rain, the dam burst. With the force of Niagara Falls, a 36ft-high wall of water thundered down the valley, reaching speeds of 40mph and carrying with it everything in its path: uprooted trees, homes, boulders, barbed wire, freight cars. The deadly wave broke over Johnstown at 4:07pm. It "snapped off trees like pipestems," "crushed houses like eggshells," claimed 2,209

Aftermath of the 1889 Johnstown Flood

Corbis-Bettmann

lives and caused $17 million in damages. No one was ever held accountable. Begin your visit by viewing Charles Guggenheim's 26min documentary that elegantly recounts the disaster. Highlights in the museum include a three-dimensional wall of wreckage and an animated relief map showing the path of the floodwaters. Other exhibits cover the sensational worldwide publicity that followed the flood; the relief effort spearheaded by the Red Cross's Clara Barton; and the history of Johnstown.

★★ **Johnstown Flood National Memorial** – *Off Rte. 219 10mi northeast of Johnstown; take St. Michael/Sidman exit and go east on Rte. 869. Turn left onto Lake Rd. at flood memorial sign. Open Jun–Sept daily 9am–6pm. Rest of the year daily 9am–5pm. Closed Dec 25. $2. &* 🅿 *www.nps.gov/jofl* ☎*814-495-4643.* Overlooking what was once Lake Conemaugh, this small red barn-like structure houses displays that illustrate the damage done to Johnstown with dramatic before-and-after photographs. Exhibits here also raise the question of whether the South Fork Fishing and Hunting Club's members should have been held liable for the catastrophe. The museum features the 35min film *Black Friday*, which melodramatizes the death toll of the flood.

From the memorial, visitors can hike .5mi to a boardwalk that leads out to the ruins of the north abutment of the dam; an interpretive sign describes how the dam was engineered and neglected. Also nearby is the 1889 **Historic District of St. Michael** *(off Rte. 869 in the town of St. Michael),* where South Fork's clubhouse, annex and eight remaining Victorian cottages *(not open to the public)* recall the elite resort area that residents abandoned after the tragic flood.

Johnstown Inclined Plane – *Downtown station located on Rte. 56 between Union and Walnut Sts. Open year-round Mon–Thu 6:30am–10pm, Fri 6:30am–midnight, Sat 7:30am–midnight, Sun & holidays 9am– 10pm. Closed Jan 1, Dec 25. $1.75/one-way, $3/round-trip.* ✕ & 🅿 ☎*814-536-1816.* The steepest vehicular incline in the world, Johnstown's inclined plane was built in 1891, prompted by residents' newfound appreciation for high ground. Since then, two 38-ton cars, which counterbalance each other, have ascended the 71.9 percent grade of Yoder Hill, providing transportation to and from **Westmont**, the gracious suburb developed by Johnstown's onetime largest employer, Cambria Steel. The 2.5min ride up the 896.5ft hill commands a spectacular **view**★ of Johnstown and the surrounding valley. At the summit, a small visitor center features a glassed-in observation deck with a map identifying local landmarks. At the base of the hill, the 1.4mi James Wolfe Sculpture Trail is dotted with eight colorful contemporary steel sculptures, commissioned for the flood's centennial.

■**Additional Sights in Central Pennsylvania**

Within an hour's drive of State College are several sights that limn different aspects of local history:

Slifer House★ *(One River Rd., Lewisburg; visit by 1hr guided tour only;* ☎*717-524-2245)* – Inspired by a Tuscan villa, this refurbished mansion (1863, Samuel Sloan) houses a fine collection of Victoriana that reflects the life and work of local entrepreneur Eli Slifer.

Packwood House *(15 N. Water St., Lewisburg; visit by 1hr guided tour only;* ☎*717-524-0323)* – Rooms in this rambling, three-story frame house, which began as a log cabin in 1799, contain a wide-ranging collection of antiques and collector's items that belonged to its former owners, artist Edith Fetherston and her husband, John.

Peter J. McGovern Little League Museum★ 🅺🄸🄳🄳 *(on Rte. 15, just south of downtown Williamsport;* ☎*717-326-3607)* – Named after the first president of Little League Baseball, this two-story museum celebrates the popular American pastime that began as a three-team league in Williamsport in 1939.

Joseph Priestly House *(472 Priestley Ave., Northumberland; visit by 1hr guided tour only;* ☎*717-473-9474)* – The stately Federal manor and adjoining lab pays homage to the life and work of scientist **Joseph Priestley** (1733-1804), the English-born "father of modern chemistry."

Mifflinburg Buggy Museum *(523 Green St., Mifflinburg; visit by 1hr 30min guided tour only;* ☎*717-966-1355)* – This original 19C craft shop preserves the coachworks and repository run from 1883 to 1920 by William Heiss in Mifflinburg's heyday.

Grandview Cemetery – *From downtown Johnstown, take Rte. 271 (Menoher Blvd.) to top of hill, turn right on Geneva Ave. and right again on Millcreek Rd. Entrance is on the right.* Twisting roads wend among nearly 60,000 headstones, crypts and obelisks in Grandview's hilly, 235-acre burial ground, founded in 1885. Many of the 2,209 victims of the 1889 flood rest here, including 777 unidentified bodies that are buried side by side in the cemetery's centerpiece, the **Unknown Plot**. A striking memorial to the disaster, separate white stone headstones mark each anonymous grave, and a 30ft-tall angel looms over them.

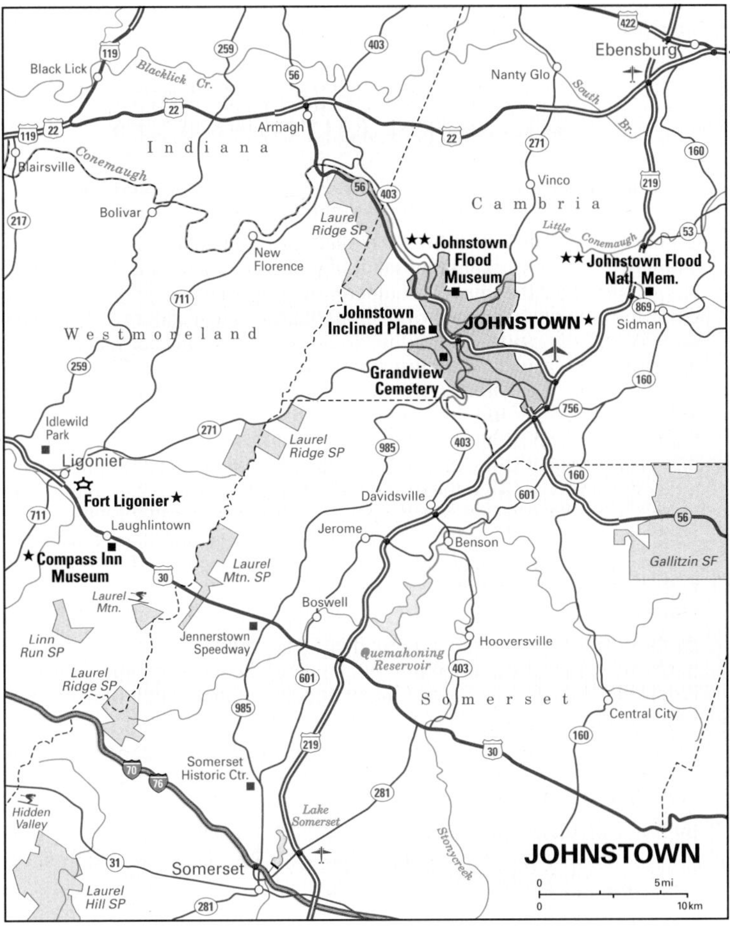

EXCURSIONS

★ **Fort Ligonier** – *2hrs. 21mi southwest of Johnstown at intersection of Rtes. 711 & 30 in Ligonier. Open Apr–Oct Mon–Sat 10am–4:30pm, Sun noon–4:30pm. $5.* ♿ P ☎*412-238-9701.* Situated just blocks away from Ligonier's charming downtown shopping district, this reconstructed fort evokes the site's history as a British outpost during the French and Indian War. Gen. John Forbes ordered the construction of Ft. Ligonier in 1758 for British troops traveling along Forbes Road, the route he cut across the Alleghenies on his successful mission to overthrow Ft. Duquesne in present-day Pittsburgh. Ft. Ligonier saw action during Pontiac's uprising *(p 323)* in 1763 and housed Pennsylvania troops during the Revolutionary War. It was gone by 1800. Today a full-scale reconstruction of the fort and a **museum** stand on the site. In the small museum, exhibits range from 18C weapons and Colonial pewter and silver to a re-creation of the sumptuous, Georgian-style drawing room of Field Marshall John Louis Ligonier, for whom the fort is named. The fort itself comprises a handful of log buildings, including replicas of the soldiers' barracks, officers' quarters and commissary.

★ **Compass Inn Museum** – *2hrs. 3mi east of Ligonier on Rte. 30 in Laughlintown. Visit by guided tour (1hr 30min) only, May–Oct Tue–Sat 11am–4pm, Sun noon–4pm. Nov–mid-Dec Fri–Sat 2pm–5pm. Closed Memorial Day & Labor Day. $4.* 🄿 ☎412-238-4983. This meticulously preserved and interpreted former stagecoach stop recalls Pennsylvania's early frontier days. Wagoners and drovers were the first patrons of the inn (1799), but after the Pittsburgh-Philadelphia Turnpike was completed in 1817, stagecoaches came to dominate business. In its heyday Laughlintown boasted 13 inns; the completion of the Pennsylvania Railroad in 1855 marked the end of the era. The last of its ilk, the two-story, Federal-style Compass Inn Museum is furnished with rustic period pieces; on the grounds, a blacksmith shop, barn and freestanding cook house illustrate the inn's many functions.

LAUREL HIGHLANDS AND
SOUTHERN ALLEGHENIES★★

Map p 9
Tourist Information ☎412-238-5661 or 800-925-7669 (Laurel Highlands)
814-943-4183 or 800-842-6866 (Southern Alleghenies)

Centering on 2,700ft Laurel Hill in the Allegheny Mountains, this region was populated by Native Americans thousands of years before settlers arrived in the 18C. From 1754 to 1763 the area was studded with forts used in the French and Indian War. After the British emerged victorious, the Laurel Highlands became a gateway to the West. Exchanging stagecoaches for canal boats for railroads for automobiles, Americans have marched their way across southern Pennsylvania with unflagging determination. Today the area preserves its history with re-created 18C forts, restored stagecoach stops and monuments to the almighty railroad. Its rugged beauty can be best appreciated from the Youghiogheny River, home to the best strip of white water in the east, or at Fallingwater, Frank Lloyd Wright's architectural masterpiece set amid the hardwoods of Bear Run Nature Reserve.

PRACTICAL INFORMATION
Getting There

By Car – The Pennsylvania Turnpike (I-70/76) runs east to west across the Laurel Highlands, offering access to many attractions in the southern part of the region. North-south access is provided via I-99 through Altoona and Route 219 through Johnstown.

By Air – Closest airports: **Altoona/Blair County Airport** and **Johnstown/Cambria Airport**, both with limited domestic flights; or **Pittsburgh International Airport**, international and domestic flights.

By Bus and Train – Greyhound (*☎402-330-2055 or 800-231-2222*) buses service many cities in the Laurel Highlands and Southern Alleghenies. Amtrak trains (*☎800-872-7245*) come into Altoona.

General Information

Visitor Information – Contact the following agencies to obtain maps and information on recreation, accommodations and seasonal events: **Laurel Highlands Visitors Bureau** (*120 E. Main St., Ligonier PA 15658* ☎412-238-5661 or 800-925-7669) operates **visitor centers** located at Ohiopyle State Park (*in old train station at trailhead*) and in Somerset (*601 N. Center Ave.*); and the **Allegheny Mountains Convention & Visitors Bureau** (*Logan Valley Mall, Rte. 220 & Goods Ln., Altoona PA 16602; www.amcvb.com* ☎814-943-4183 or 800-842-5866). The **Allegheny Traveler Passport** (*$12.50; available from Allegheny Mountains Convention & Visitors Bureau or at heritage attractions;* ☎814-696-9380 or 800-898-3636) entitles the holder to admission at nine designated "Pennsylvania Heritage" sites, including Allegheny Portage Railroad National Historic Site (*p 316*), Horseshoe Curve National Historic Landmark (*p 317*) and the Johnstown Flood Museum (*p 309*).

Accommodations – (*p 358*) Area visitors' guides including lodging directories are available (*free*) from local tourism agencies (*above*). Hotels, motels, bed-and-breakfast inns and mountainside **resorts** can be found throughout the region. Hosteling International **hostels** are located in Ohiopyle State Park (*Ferncliff Peninsula, PO Box 99, Ohiopyle PA 15470* ☎412-329-4476) and Shellsburg (*RD #1, Box 206, Schellsburg PA 15559* ☎814-733-4212).

SIGHTS *3 days*

★★★ **Fallingwater** – *(p 308). 9mi north of Rte. 40 on Rte. 381.* Widely considered one of the greatest works of 20C American architecture, Fallingwater distills the essence of master builder **Frank Lloyd Wright's** (1867-1959) vision of an organic building composition, of the marriage of nature and artifice, interior and exterior. This spectacular house seems at once to grow from the rocky terrain on which it sits and to float above it. Indeed, the centerpiece of Wright's design is the 20ft waterfall over which Fallingwater's stacked terraces are ingeniously balanced. What at first seemed like a sacrilege—building the house on top of the falls rather than facing them—turned out to be what the *New York Times* architecture critic called Wright's "most sublime integration of man and nature." Visitors to Fallingwater don't merely see the waterfall; they experience it, from the roar of the water that fills the spacious living room to the motifs throughout the house that echo its dramatic force.

The House at Bear Run – In 1935 Edgar J. Kaufmann, a wealthy Pittsburgh department store owner, hired Wright to design a year-round weekend retreat on Kaufmann's property in the rural, mountainous area of Bear Run, some 42mi southeast of Pittsburgh. As the story goes, Wright, who was 68 years old at the time, sketched out the design for the house in a single inspired morning. Kaufmann, whose son had been one of Wright's many architecture apprentices, was taken aback by the unusual design, which was based on the use of cantilevers that jutted out from the main structure well beyond the point of direct support. However, his tug of war with Wright focused not on design, but on finances, for in the end the house went five times over budget.

Fallingwater took nearly two years to build (the guest wing was not completed until 1939), and the construction was not without its mishaps. Pittsburgh engineers, who deemed Wright's concept impossible, tried to persuade Kaufmann to abandon it; local stonemasons, who quarried the rock on-site, were reluctant to carry out the unusual project; and the head builder occasionally altered

Camping – Campsites are scattered throughout the region along rolling hills and waterways. Contact local tourist agencies *(p 312)* for a comprehensive listing of area campgrounds. State parks that allow camping include Blue Knob *(Imler;* ☎*814-276-3576)*; Keystone *(Derry;* ☎*412-668-2939)*; Ohiopyle *(Ohiopyle;* ☎*412-329-8591)*; and Shawnee *(Schellsburg;* ☎*814-733-4218)*.

Recreation

White-water Rafting – *(p 316)* Several companies based in Ohiopyle State Park offer guided river trips: Mountain Streams *(PO Box 106, Ohiopyle PA 15470-0106 www.pennet.com/mst* ☎*412-329-8810 or 800-732-8669)*; Wilderness Voyageurs *(PO Box 97, Ohiopyle PA 15470* ☎*412-329-5517 or 800-272-4141)*; Laurel Highlands River Tours *(PO Box 107, Ohiopyle PA 15470* ☎*412-329-8531 or 800-472-3848)*; and Whitewater Adventures *(PO Box 31, Ohiopyle PA 15470* ☎*412-329-8850 or 800-992-7238)*. After-trip picnics are available for an additional fee. These and other organizations located in Ohiopyle also rent raft, canoe and kayak equipment for self-guided trips *(launch permit—available from Ohiopyle State Park—required for the Lower Youghiogheny)*.

Hiking and Biking – This mountainous region provides ample opportunities for hiking and biking. Area trails include Rails-to-Trails Lower Trail *(11mi)* from Williamsburg to Alfarata *(*☎*814-832-2400)*; Laurel Highlands Trail *(70mi)* from Ohiopyle to Johnstown through Laurel Ridge State Park *(*☎*814-455-3744)*; and Allegheny Highlands Trail *(19mi)* from Garrett to Fort Hill *(*☎*814-445-6431)*. Most white-water rafting companies offer bike rentals. Bicycles are permitted on many roads and trails, except for the Laurel Highlands Trail. Forbes State Forest *(Laughlintown)* is a popular destination for mountain bikers.

Skiing – Laurel Highlands ski areas offer a wide variety of trails, from beginner to expert. Ski packages including equipment rental, lift tickets and instruction are available. **Downhill skiing** areas: Blue Knob State Park *(Imler)*, Hidden Valley Ski Resort *(Hidden Valley)*, Nemacolin Woodlands Resort *(Farmington)*, Seven Springs Mountain Resort *(Champion)*. Many of these resorts also offer **snowboarding**. Well-groomed **cross-country-skiing** trails can be found at many downhill ski areas, as well as at Forbes State Forest *(Laughlintown)*, Keystone State Park *(Derry)*, Laurel Hill State Park *(Somerset)* and Ohiopyle State Park *(Ohiopyle)*.

Wright's plans to disastrous effect. While there were structural problems—the parapets initially cracked, due to excessive stress from the cantilevered terraces—the house ultimately proved itself sound. Upon completion, Fallingwater established Wright as the preeminent architect of the day and relaunched his career amid a flurry of gushing magazine articles—including a cover story in *Time* magazine—and a host of new commissions.

Visit – ½ *day. Visit of house by guided tour (45min) only, Apr–mid-Nov daily 8:30am–4pm. Mid-Nov–Mar weekends 8:30am–4pm. $8 (Mon–Fri); $12 (weekends). Reservations suggested. In-depth tour (1hr 30min) offered year-round daily 8:30am.* ✗ ▯ ☎412-329-8501. Nestled amid the 5,000-acre Bear Run Nature Reserve, Fallingwater peeks through the trees beside a rushing stream. A meandering path leads from an attractive, gazebo-like visitor center to the house. Once inside, visitors can see Frank Lloyd Wright's ideas in action, for the architect attended to nearly every detail of design and decoration. Anchored into a back wall made of sandstone, the 800sq ft **living room★** is Fallingwater's most spectacular space. Occupying most of the largest of three cantilevered surfaces, it is almost entirely enclosed by glass, allowing stupendous views of the woods outside. Note Wright's early use of recessed lighting, the clever glass "hatch" that covers a flight of stairs leading down to the stream, and the striking boulder, original to the site, that protrudes through the floor near the fireplace. On your way up to the second floor, feel Wright's vaunted "compression and release" philosophy at work: narrow, dark, almost cave-like passageways give way to brightly lit bedrooms that draw attention to the outdoors, which can be appreciated on broad, poured-concrete terraces that nearly double the rooms' size.

Wright's notion of "exploding the Victorian box" can also be appreciated in a study on the second floor. Here, one of 17 small casement windows incorporated into a three-story masonry tower can be opened so that the physical corner of the house literally disappears. Throughout the house, cantilevered bookshelves and desks reiterate Fallingwater's overall design, and spartan, Wright-designed furniture, including built-in seating and black walnut wardrobes, meticulously balance form and function. Out back, a final cantilever takes form as a curved canopy that shelters a walkway leading to the guest house and servants' quarters.

★★ **Kentuck Knob** – *On Chalk Hill-Ohiopyle Rd., 6mi north of Rte. 40; 2.5mi southwest of Ohiopyle. Visit by guided tour (1hr 30min) only, Apr–Nov Tue–Sun 10am–5pm. Rest of the year weekends only 10am–5pm (weather permitting). Closed major holidays. $10. Reservations suggested.* ▯ ☎412-329-1901. This graceful Frank Lloyd Wright design, opened to the public in 1996, demonstrates many famous Wright principles and exudes a cozy, lived-in charm cultivated by its present owners, Lord and Lady Palumbo of London. Crouched some 2,000ft above sea level, Kentuck Knob was designed in 1953—when Wright was 85 years old—for the I.N. Hagan family of Uniontown, Pennsylvania. Built on a hexagonal grid, the house is composed of red cypress and 800 tons of fieldstone, which was quarried on the property. Outside, 8ft eaves wrap around the house's exterior. Punctured with hexagonal skylights, they cast dazzling shadows and boast some of the house's most impressive woodworking. Inside, the hexagonal theme is continued with a panoply of six-sided rooms distinguished by flagstone floors, cypress window treatments and vaulted ceilings. Enthusiastic collectors, the Palumbos have

---

■ **Frank Lloyd Wright**

Born in Richland Center, Wisconsin in 1867, Frank Lloyd Wright credited the Froebel geometric blocks, given to him by his parents, as his earliest influences toward the design of form and space. After briefly attending the University of Wisconsin, Wright moved to Chicago in 1887 and was hired as a draftsman by the firm of Adler & Sullivan. He quickly became "a good pencil in the Master's hand" to Louis Sullivan, the only architect whose influence Wright ever acknowledged. The restless Wright, fired from Adler & Sullivan in 1893 for violating his contract, began designing on his own and developing his distinctive Prairie style of architecture over the next decade. His architecture became more expressionistic in the 1910s and 20s, and in 1931 he established Taliesin in Wisconsin to train other architects. Following the construction of Fallingwater, Wright opened his Taliesin West studio in Arizona and remained in the limelight, refining his iconoclastic image until his death in 1959 at age 92.

stocked the house with Frank Lloyd Wright tables, chairs and dishes; sculpture by Calder and Noguchi; and knickknacks such as dinosaur bones and eggs. The expansive grounds are studded with such oddities as a piece of the Berlin Wall and a British telephone booth, and just east of the house, the "knob" affords a fabulous panoramic **view**★★★ of the Youghiogheny River Gorge and the surrounding mountains.

★ **Fort Necessity National Battlefield** – *On Rte. 40 in Farmington, 11mi east of Uniontown.* When 22-year-old major George Washington saw the meadow that would become the site of Ft. Necessity, he called it "a charming field for an encounter." It didn't turn out to be so charming for him: here, in 1754, Washington experienced the only surrender of his military career, in the battle that saw the opening salvos of the French and Indian War.

A Fort of Necessity – The French and English had been fighting over the Ohio River Valley region since 1689, but the situation came to a head when the French stepped up their attacks (often carried out by their Native American allies) on English settlers in the 1750s. In the winter of 1753-54 Washington asked the French to leave the Ohio River Valley, but was rebuffed. In April he returned with a ragtag, 132-man military force, setting up camp in his "charming field." When he got word that the French were nearby, Washington and a group of 40 men ambushed 50 French soldiers at **Jumonville Glen** *(7mi west of Ft. Necessity off Rte. 40)* at dawn on May 28. During the 15-minute battle, Washington's men killed 10 Frenchmen—including the commander, Joseph Coulon de Villiers, Sieur de Jumonville—and took 21 prisoners, but one man escaped to alert the French at Ft. Duquesne (in present-day Pittsburgh).

Awaiting retribution, Washington and his men returned to their camp and constructed a circular, palisaded "fort of necessity." Reinforcements arrived several weeks later, but they were insufficient to withstand the July 3 attack by 600 Frenchmen and 100 Indians. After eight hours of fighting, Washington surrendered; he left the next day, and the French burned Ft. Necessity to the ground. In 1755 Washington joined British general Edward Braddock with 2,400 men in an attempt to capture Ft. Duquesne, but they were surprised by the French 6mi east of the fort and suffered devastating losses. Braddock himself was killed; he was buried under Braddock Road, the route he blazed through the wilderness. In 1804 his remains were moved to the present site of **Braddock's Grave** *(1mi west of the fort on Rte. 40)*. Ft. Duquesne was not taken until 1758; the war finally ended in 1763 with the expulsion of French rule in North America and India.

Visit – *2hrs. Open year-round daily 8:30am–5pm. Closed Dec 25. $2.* ♿ 🅿 *nps.gov/fone* ☎412-329-5512. At the **visitor center**, a 10min slide show and exhibits provide a good general overview of the French and Indian War, the Battle of Ft. Necessity, and the 1950s excavation and reconstruction of the fort. Out back in the quiet meadow stands a crude stockade fence (53ft in diameter) surrounding a replica of the log store house, which held powder, provisions and kegs of rum for Washington's troops. A steep, 200yd path leads from the parking lot to the two-story brick **Mount Washington Tavern** (1828), a former stagecoach stop now filled with period furnishings and exhibits about the National Road, the first highway built with federal funds.

Nemacolin Castle – *Entrance between Brashear & Front Sts. (Rte. 40) in downtown Brownsville. Visit by guided tour (1hr) only, Jun–Aug Tue–Sun 11am–5pm. Easter Sunday–mid-Oct weekends 11am–5pm. $5.* 🅿 *www.primepage.com* ☎412-785-6882. If Brownsville, situated where the National Road met the Monongahela River, was once known as "the gateway to the West," then Nemacolin Castle, distinguished by a crenelated octagonal tower, was its formidable gatehouse. Named for the Indian chief who charted the trail upon which the National Road was built, the 22-room, Tudor-style mansion began as a two-room trading post in 1789. Its owner, Jacob Bowman, built additions to the simple structure in the early 1800s as his family grew and his business expanded into manufacturing and banking. Around 1850 his heirs added the Victorian wing and the distinctive tower to the house. Today Nemacolin Castle reflects the three distinct historical periods during which construction took place. The dark, musty trading-post section, which contains Bowman's huge 18C desk, captures the pioneer period; two bedrooms, with their "witch's doors" and Ben Franklin stove, reflect the Colonial period; and the remaining rooms depict the high Victorian style. Many of the finest pieces, such as the magisterial "Bishop's bed," are original to the house. Some 20 fully furnished rooms are open to the public.

★★ **Allegheny Portage Railroad National Historic Site** – *Off Rte. 22, 10mi west of Altoona; take Gallitzin exit and follow signs. Open Memorial Day–Labor Day daily 9am–6pm. Rest of the year daily 9am–5pm. Closed Dec 25. $2. ☁ ☎814-886-6150.* This well-presented historic site, situated near Cresson Summit in the Alleghenies, pays homage to the railroad-canal system that opened up the west to development. Completed in 1834 as the final link of Pennsylvania's Main Line canal system, the 36mi-long Allegheny Portage Railroad used stepped planes, stationary steam engines and locomotives to physically carry (hence the name "portage") canal boats over the 2,400ft Allegheny Mountain range. Along with 276mi of canals, the mini-railroad operated for 23 years, helping to cut the travel time between Pittsburgh and Philadelphia from 20 days to 5 days. Ultimately the Pennsylvania Railroad, completed in 1854, made the portage system obsolete by making the same trip in 12 hours.

Opened in April 1991, the spacious **visitor center** features an excellent 20min introductory film and a host of informative interpretive exhibits about the railroad. Out back, a boardwalk zigzags its way to **Engine Room No. 6**, where a shed-like structure shelters the excavated foundations of the original engine house as well as a roomful of high-tech, hands-on exhibits that further illustrate how the innovative system worked (and, at times, did not work). Also nearby stands the restored 1832 **Lemon House**, which was used as a tavern during the railroad's peak years.

■ **White-water Rafting**

Leave the beaten path for a day and raft down the roiling waters of the famed Youghiogheny River. It was here, in 1964, that commercial white-water rafting—negotiating rapids in sturdy rubber boats—got its start in the eastern US. Cutting its way through the dramatic Youghiogheny Gorge, "the Yough" offers rafting opportunities for the novice and the expert alike. The most popular trip, on the Lower Yough *(5-6hrs; minimum age 12)*, leaves from scenic **Ohiopyle State Park** overlooking Ohiopyle Falls *(from the PA Turnpike, take Exit 9 and follow Rte. 381 south to Ohiopyle; open year-round daily dawn–dusk; △ ⚒ ☁ ☎412-329-8591)*. The voyage takes you 7.5mi down river and includes 22 frothy Class III and IV rapids. The Middle Yough offers a scenic 9mi float trip *(5hrs; minimum age 4)* that's perfect for families with its mild, Class I and II rapids. The Upper Yough *(minimum age 16)*, which courses through Maryland, provides the ultimate challenge: One section of the river drops 115ft in a mile, churning through Class V and VI rapids with names like Meatcleaver and National Falls. Four Ohiopyle-based outfitters offer guided trips of the river *(p 313)*. For information and reservations, call the Ohiopyle State Park office ☎412-329-8591.

White-water Rafting, Youghiogheny River

Holt Confer/Grant Heilman Photography

★ **Horseshoe Curve National Historic Landmark** – *On Rte. 4008 (Kittanning Point Run) in Altoona. Follow signs from Rte. 22 or Rte. 764. Open 1st Sun Apr–last Sat Oct daily 10am–6pm. Rest of the year Tue–Sun 10am–3:30pm. Closed Jan 1, Thanksgiving Day, Dec 25. $3.50.* ♿ 🅿 ☎*814-941-7960.* Widely regarded as the railroad engineering feat of the 19C, Horseshoe Curve forms the tightest of all curves on the Pittsburgh-Philadelphia Main Line. In the 1850s, when surveyors set out to plan Pennsylvania's Main Line railroad, they faced a formidable obstacle: 2,300ft Allegheny Mountain. Because the mountain was far too steep to ascend head on, engineer J. Edgar Thompson designed this 220-degree, 2,375ft curve, which climbs 122ft, or 1.8 degrees, from east to west. The design was perfect: although three additional tracks were added over the years, the original track alignment has remained unchanged since its completion in 1854.

Today an attractive, 4,600sq ft visitor center explains "the Amphitheater of the Alleghenies," with a 7min film, historical photographs, artifacts and a topographical map of the area. A funicular climbs the steep banks of the mountain to a grassy observation area level with the tracks. Here, visitors can take in the magnificent **view** of the valley and, with any luck, witness a train make its panoramic journey around this engineering marvel *(Amtrak trains traverse the curve every 20-30min en route from Johnstown to Altoona; call for schedule* ☎*800-872-7245).*

NORTH CENTRAL PENNSYLVANIA
Map pp 9-10
Tourist Information ☎814-726-1222 or 800-624-7802

This long, mountainous strip of land, stretching across the northern third of the state is largely covered by federally protected forests—including the 513,000-acre Allegheny National Forest. Part of the Appalachian Plateau, this area was carved by retreating glaciers 10,000 years ago. Deep, narrow furrows separated by plateau-like divides that can reach heights of more than 2,500ft characterize its geography. Rich in natural resources such as lumber, oil and coal, the area led the nation in these industries throughout the 19C and early 20C. Today second-growth forests give way to rolling farmland throughout the sparsely populated region, which is ideal for scenic drives and outdoor recreation.

SIGHTS   *1½ days*

Penn-Brad Historical Oil Well and Museum – *On Rte. 219 3mi south of Bradford at Custer City. Visit by guided tour (1hr) only, Memorial Day–Labor Day Mon–Sat 10am–4pm, Sun noon–5pm. $5.* ♿ 🅿 *www.bradford-online.com/penn-brad* ☎*814-362-1955.* Commemorating Pennsylvania's oil-rich past, the Penn-Brad Museum stands beside the only working 1890s-style wooden drilling rig in the country and contains a wide array of local oil-industry memorabilia. Oil was discovered in Bradford in 1871. By the 1880s, Pennsylvania was providing nearly three-quarters of the country's oil and gas, and as many as 1,000 drilling rigs were pumping "black gold" from the ground in Bradford alone. After nearly a century of drilling, the town could claim the world's first billion-dollar oil field. Today oil-industry veterans bring that history to life by describing how the 72ft oil rig operates and by pointing out highlights of the museum's collection, which includes an 1875 horse-drawn steam fire engine, "yellow dog" cast-iron lanterns, photographs and drilling tools.

Pennsylvania Lumber Museum – *On Rte. 6, 11mi east of Coudersport (opposite Denton Hill Ski Area). Open Apr–Nov daily 9am–5pm. Closed major holidays. $3.50.* ♿ 🅿 ☎*814-435-2652.* Set on 160 acres near the site where two of the world's largest sawmills once operated, this museum complex memorializes 19C lumbering with exhibits and a re-created logging camp, which includes a working steam-powered circular sawmill. Inside the museum, one large gallery contains interpretive displays about bark-peeling, tree-felling and the history of the industry's boom years; another room pays homage to the Civilian Conservation Corps, which replanted 200 million trees in the US during the Great Depression. Out back, a half-dozen wooden buildings filled with period artifacts simulate the type of crude logging camp that was common in this area around 1910.

★ **Kinzua Bridge State Park** – *4mi north of Mount Jewett on Rte. 3011. Open year-round daily dawn–dusk. Amenities limited Nov–Apr.* ♿ 🅿 ☎*814-965-2646.* The centerpiece of the 316-acre park, **Kinzua Bridge** once ranked as the highest railroad viaduct in the world. Today this National Historic Civil Engineering Landmark is only the fourth highest in the world, but it remains an awesome example of engineering know-how. Commissioned by Gen. Thomas L. Kane so a branch of the Erie Railroad could haul out the area's lumber, oil and coal reserves, the original bridge was built by a 100-man crew in 1882 in just 94 days. Although no accidents took place on the 301ft-high, 2,053ft-long trestle bridge, it swayed so much, especially on windy days, that trains had to slow to 5mph to cross it. In 1900 the bridge was rebuilt, its original ironwork replaced by 3,357 tons of steel to accommodate heavier trains. Today the Knox & Kane Railroad (☎814-927-6621) offers daily steam-powered train excursions across the span. Wood-plank footbridges running along either side of the tracks afford visitors a phenomenal **view**★ of the Kinzua Valley. An informative interpretive display about the history of the bridge is located in a steel-frame kiosk between the bridge and the parking lot.

★★ **Pine Creek Gorge** – *Accessible from Colton Point State Park or Leonard Harrison State Park (below).* Known as the Grand Canyon of Pennsylvania, lushly forested Pine Creek Gorge reigns as one of the state's most spectacular nature areas. The gorge, measuring 47mi long and up to 1,450ft deep, was formed 20,000 years ago, when retreating glaciers left a residue of gravel, sand and clay that blocked Pine Creek's northeasterly current and forced the creek to cut a new path south. Throughout the 19C and early 20C, the forest around the gorge was ravaged by logging and fires, but a second-growth forest has since covered the region. Two state parks, both established in 1922, now face each other across the precipice: rustic, 368-acre **Colton Point State Park** *(5mi south of Rte. 6 at Ansonia; open daily year-round;* ⚠ ▣ ☎*717-724-3061)* on the western rim, and 585-acre **Leonard Harrison State Park** *(9mi west of Wellsboro on Rte. 660; open daily year-round;* ⚠ ▣ ☎*717-724-3061)* on the eastern rim. In the latter, a small visitor center features exhibits about the region's geology, history and wildlife. Just yards from the visitor center, terraced wooden decks afford the area's best **view**★★ of the gorge and the creek 830ft below.

© Larry Ulrich/Tony Stone Images

Colton Point State Park, Pine Creek Gorge

★ **Allegheny National Forest** – *Open daily year-round.* ⚐ ▣ ☎*814-726-1291. Kinzua Point Information Center (13mi east of Warren on Rte. 59) open Memorial Day–Labor Day daily 10am–5pm. Bradford Ranger District Station (22mi east of Warren at the junction of Rtes. 59 & 321) open Memorial Day–Labor Day Mon–Fri 7am–4:30pm, weekends 10am–5pm. Rest of the year Mon–Fri 7am–4:30pm.* Pennsylvania's only national forest, the deep woods of the Allegheny span four counties and more than a half-million acres and offer recreational activities galore: 180mi of hiking trails and 500mi of streams wend their way through hardwood forests, and beaches and campgrounds grace the 90mi of shoreline along the Allegheny Reservoir. For thousands of years the area was home to Native American tribes. Settlers arrived in the area in the early 19C, and over the next century they harvested the immense virgin forest, decimating the local wildlife population and the watershed. In 1923 President Calvin Coolidge established Allegheny National Forest to protect the region. Kinzua Dam now forms the centerpiece of the forest. Completed in 1965, it has allegedly prevented flood damages in excess of $350 million. The 27mi-long Allegheny Reservoir now hosts a variety of water sports, including some of the best fishing in the state. Spectacular views and shoreline access are available along the 29mi loop of the Longhouse National Scenic Byway. Elsewhere in the forest, 300 species of wildlife, including black bears and bald eagles, make their home amid protected stands of black cherry, red maple, yellow poplar and white ash trees. *If the Kinzua Point Information Center is closed, you can get brochures and information at the Bradford Ranger District Station (p 318).*

STATE COLLEGE★

Population 39,400
Map p 10
Tourist Information www.visitpennstate.org ☎814-231-1400 or 800-358-5466

A quintessential college town, State College encompasses block after block of sandwich shops, clothing stores, bars, cafes and bookstores, all of which serve Pennsylvania State University's students during the school year. The borough of State College was founded in 1896 to meet the needs of the growing university. Today students account for over half of State College's population, and a panoply of research and development companies, attracted to Penn State's growing reputation as a high-tech hub, have recently taken up residence here, fueling the local economy by making everything from television picture tubes to defense equipment.

SIGHTS *1 day*

★ **Pennsylvania State University** – *University Park campus bounded by College Ave. and N. Atherton St. Maps are available at any of the information kiosks scattered around campus.* ☎814-865-4700. The crown jewel of Pennsylvania's land-grant university system, Penn State's historic main campus, studded with 1920s and 1930s Beaux-Arts and Georgian Revival buildings, sits on 390 picturesque acres and is attended by nearly 40,000 full-time students. Penn State got its start as one of the nation's first agricultural colleges in 1862. With the addition of graduate programs, Penn State finally attained university status in 1953. Today the university boasts nationally acclaimed schools of engineering, business and science, as well as strong liberal-arts programs. It is also a sports powerhouse: its Big Ten football team packs the 93,000-seat Beaver Stadium during home games, and a limestone sculpture of the school's prowling mascot, the **Nittany Lion** (1942, Heinze Warnecke), located at the corner of Burrowes and Curtin Roads, is the most photographed landmark on campus.

★ **Palmer Museum of Art** – *On Curtin Rd. between Allen & Shortlidge Rds. Open year-round Tue–Sat 10am–4:30pm, Sun noon–4pm. Closed major holidays.* ♿ *☎814-865-7672.* Thirty-five centuries of world art are displayed here in a gorgeous new facility (1993, Charles Moore with Arbonies King Vlock). The largest art museum between Philadelphia and Pittsburgh, the Palmer was named for local benefactors Barbara and James Palmer, who donated money toward its substantial facelift and expansion. The new structure wraps around the modernist slab that formerly housed the university's art collection. Its semicircular entrance loggia is flanked by two giant lion paws and ornamented with blue stained-glass windows that recall the Gothic cathedrals of Europe.

Eight of the museum's ten galleries, comprising some 50,000sq ft, generally display 1,500 pieces of the Palmer's 4,500-piece permanent collection, which is dominated by works on paper and 19C and 20C American art. Downstairs, the collection of Near Eastern coins contains relics from the 4C BC to AD 1; the Baroque gallery juxtaposes staid Northern European works such as *Portrait of a Lady* (1617, Michiel van Mierevelt) with dramatic Italian religious works inspired by the Catholic Counter-Reformation; and a gallery of Asian and African art houses an extensive collection of ceramics. Upstairs hang post-World War II works by Richard Diebenkorn, Willem de Kooning, Robert Motherwell and Roy Lichtenstein. The Palmer's largest permanent exhibition space contains portraits, landscapes and works on paper by such 19C and early 20C American greats as John Sloan, Robert Henri, John Singer Sargent and Edward Hopper. Also on the second floor is a grand gallery where the museum mounts four to six internationally renowned temporary and site-specific installations per year.

★ **Old Main** – *E. College Ave. Open year-round Mon–Fri 8am–5pm.* ♿ *☎814-865-7517.* Penn State's landmark building, the Federal Revival-style Old Main (1930, Charles Z. Klauder) occupies the site of the original college building, which was competed in the 1860s but showed structural flaws and was dismantled in 1928. Home of Penn State's administrative core, the present structure is fashioned from the original Old Main's local limestone and retains a similar cupola bell tower, which still peals every quarter hour. Eight smooth Tuscan columns grace the front portico, which overlooks a sloping green lawn. Inside, the second floor of the elegant two-story lobby is flanked by historic land-grant **frescoes** painted by Henry Varnum Poor in the 1940s. Depicting the development of Penn State from its origins as an agricultural college though its growth into the industrial age, the boldly drawn frescoes are anchored by a 12ft image of Abraham Lincoln. In 1862 Lincoln signed the Morrill Land Grant Act "to promote liberal and practical education," thus allowing Penn State to expand into engineering and other utilitarian subjects.

Other sights of note on campus include the **Matson Museum of Anthropology** (*2nd floor of Carpenter Building, near the corner of Burrowes & Curtin Rds.;* ☎*814-865-3853*), where exhibits range from plaster casts of prehistoric skulls to modern-day artifacts from cultures around the world; and the **Earth and Mineral Sciences Museum** (*Steidle Building, Pollock Rd.;* ☎*814-865-6427*). In addition to the 3,000 minerals, culled from Penn State's 22,000-specimen collection, which are arrayed in glass cases flanking the halls, the museum displays a collection of **paintings** (*1st floor*) depicting Pennsylvania's mining and mineral industry heyday in the 1930s and 40s. And sports fans won't want to miss the **Penn State Football Hall of Fame** (*Greenberg Indoor Sports Complex; corner of McKean & Pollock Rds.;* ☎*865-0411*), showcase for the esteemed Heisman Trophy awarded to fullback John Cappelletti in 1973; the 1994 Big Ten trophy; and the 1995 Rose Bowl trophy, among other accolades. *University museums are generally open 9am–4pm Mon–Fri and are closed during university breaks; call for individual schedules.*

The Creamery

Kids *Corner of Shortlidge & Curtin Rds.* One of Penn State's most popular sites, this one-story brick creamery and ice-cream shop recalls a savory addition to Penn State's utilitarian curriculum. In 1892 the university became the first institution in the US to offer collegiate instruction in ice-cream manufacturing. Since then, the program has brought Penn State to the fore of frozen-confections research, claiming ice-cream afficionados Ben Cohen and Jerry Greenfield (of Ben & Jerry's) as former students. Don't miss the ice-cream counter, where you can order up huge scoops of the rich home-made dessert in a variety of flavors.

Centre Furnace Mansion – *1001 East College Ave. at Porter Rd. Visit by guided tour (1hr) only, year-round Mon, Wed, Fri & Sun 1pm–4pm. Closed Dec 25–Jan 1.* ☎*814-234-4779.* Situated beneath a canopy of trees on two rolling acres, this stately brick Georgian home (1830) anchored the first charcoal iron-making settlement in the county. Built by two Philadelphia businessmen, Centre Furnace went into blast in 1792. By the 1830s more than a dozen iron furnaces dotted Centre County, creating a new, elite class of ironmasters. Centre Furnace Mansion served as the home of the furnace's various owners for nearly a century. Here in 1855, papers were signed to donate 200 of Centre Furnace's 10,000 acres for the Farmers' High School that would later become Penn State.

Today much of the house has been restored to appear as it did in the late 19C, replete with graceful period antiques. Gingerbread detailing, pocket doors and elaborate mantelpieces reflect its 1860s Victorianization. Upstairs, a model of an iron furnace illustrates how the pig iron once made here got its name (*p 307*). Outside, visitors can discover the Centre Furnace ruins.

EXCURSIONS

Boalsburg – *½ day. 3mi east of State College on Business Rte. 322.* Boalsburg was settled by the Scottish and Irish in 1808 and served as a stagecoach stop during the early 19C. Today, a stroll along the town's pristinely preserved Main Street reveals Federal and Colonial homes, B&Bs, shops and restaurants.

Pennsylvania Military Museum – *On Business Rte. 322 and Rte. 45. Open Apr–Oct Tue–Sat 9am–5pm, Sun noon–5pm. Rest of the year Thu–Sat 10am–4pm, Sun noon–4pm. Closed major holidays (open Memorial Day). $3.50.* ☎*814-466-6263.* The history of Pennsylvania's involvement in military conflicts from Colonial times to the Gulf War is told here. Highlights of the collection include *L'embuscade* ("The Ambusher"), a bronze cannon given to George Washington by General Lafayette in 1778; an 1848 Mexican flag, captured by US soldiers during the Mexican War; and an extensive collection of post-Civil War era machine guns. One room of the museum is devoted to a walk-through trench that cuts across a simulated World War I battlefield, brought to life by flashing lights and sounds of gunfire. Outside, 65 smoothly landscaped acres are studded with tanks, cannons and picnic tables.

★ **Columbus Chapel and Boal Mansion Museum** – *Old Boalsburg Rd. off Business Rte. 322 (across from the military museum). Visit by guided tour (1hr 30min) only, May–mid-Jun Tue–Sun 1:30pm–5pm. Mid-Jun–mid-Sept Tue–Sun 10am–5pm. Mid-Sept–Oct Tue–Sun 1:30pm–5pm. $5.* ◻ *www.vicon.net/~boalmus* ☎*814-466-6210.* Just off the highway, this privately owned site boasts a fascinating array of personal effects that belonged to **Christopher Columbus** (1451-1506), as well as artifacts collected by nine generations of the wealthy Boal family. The Boals became connected to Columbus through the propitious 1893 marriage between Theodore Davis Boal, an architecture student at the École des Beaux Arts in Paris, and Mathilde Denis de Lagarde, whose aunt Victoria married Don Diego Columbus, a direct descendent of the famous explorer. When Victoria died, she willed the chapel and its relics to her niece, Mathilde. In 1909 Theodore Davis Boal brought the entrance door, the interior of the chapel and its contents from the Columbus family castle in northern Spain to his estate in Boalsburg. In 1912 he built a limestone structure to hold the precious heirlooms.

The one-room **chapel★★**, which now stands on the estate grounds, houses a dizzying variety of artifacts, some more than 500 years old. Highlights include Christopher Columbus' admiral's desk, studded with gilt cockleshells; several "surveyor's crosses" with which the explorer would stake his claim to newly discovered lands; two tiny shards believed to be from the Cross on which Christ was crucified; and a number of 15C religious vestments and statues; as well as thousands of Columbus family documents, dating back several centuries.

First-floor rooms of the **Boal Mansion**, which was built over the course of a century around a 1789 stone cottage, are also open to visitors. Decorated in its original Victorian finery, the mansion contains numerous family curios, including a tiny lock of Napoleon's hair.

★ **Penn's Cave** – ▦ *2hrs. 18mi east of State College. Follow Rte. 26 northeast to Rte. 144 in Pleasant Gap; take Rte. 144 East to Centre Hall and turn east on Rte. 192; follow signs 5mi to cave. Visit by guided tour (1hr) only, Jun–Aug daily 9am–7pm. Rest of the year daily 9am–5pm. Closed month of Jan, Thanksgiving Day, Dec 25, Dec weekends. $9.* ✗ ◻ ☎*814-364-1664.* Gliding by boat through the chambers of this all-water cave hidden in the hills of rural central Pennsylvania makes for a unique visit. The cave was formed some 30 million years ago, when an underground spring dissolved the limestone rock. This spring still waters the cavern, requiring visitors to float through a half-mile of subterranean darkness in small, guided boats. During the tour, guides point out a variety of colorful limestone columns, cascades, pillars and other formations.

Western Pennsylvania

Downtown Incline Overlooking the Golden Triangle © Web Urbino

efined on the west by the Ohio border and on the east by a line running due south from the western edge of ALLEGHENY NATIONAL FOREST, Western Pennsylvania contains the state's only Great Lakes shoreline and Pennsylvania's largest natural lake, Conneaut Lake. More famous than its topography, though, is Western Pennsylvania's major city, PITTSBURGH. The former steel- and iron-making capital maintains its high-achiever image with a modern skyline and a bustling, fully diversified economy.

In 1753 George Washington, a 21-year-old major, not only scouted out the future location of Pittsburgh, but delivered a message from his British superiors to the French stationed at Ft. Le Boeuf (near present-day ERIE) asking them to stand down. The French refused, and the resulting hostilities led to the French and Indian War. Several years and many burned forts later, when the French, Indians, and even the British were gone, American settlers trickled into the Pennsylvania frontier. By the mid-19C, Western Pennsylvania was leading the nation into the Industrial Age, thanks to its ample coal mines and oil fields. Pittsburgh's legendary iron, steel and glass works, supported by immigrant labor, set the tone for the region's great productivity. The establishment of the world's first successful oil well to the north, in Titusville, in 1859 brought an overnight boom to the northwest corner of the state.

Today the region is still prospering, with a mix of manufacturing, high-tech industries and tourism. Up on the shore of Lake Erie, the beaches of Presque Isle can draw 30,000 to 40,000 people on a nice summer day. Erie's natural beauty, bountiful vineyards and growing number of tourist attractions are slowly turning it into a year-round destination. Pittsburgh has already attained that distinction within the last decade, polishing its once-tarnished image to a vibrant shine.

Population 350,363
Map p 9
Tourist Information www.pittsburgh.net ☎412-281-7711 or 800-366-0093

One of the largest inland ports in the US, Pittsburgh spreads over the hills and flats where the Monongahela and Allegheny rivers join to form the Ohio River. More than 700 bridges stitch together a hardworking city of modern skyscrapers, magnificent old churches, Industrial Revolution-era neighborhoods, and busy highways and railroads that quicken the city's pace. Offsetting Pittsburgh's historically insatiable drive to achieve and produce, the city boasts a high number of cultural attractions that range from serious history museums to playful contemporary art spaces.

Historical Notes

A Good Point – The narrow point of land from which the city rises was considered favorable living ground by the Indians long before the arrival of Europeans in 1753. In that year George Washington beheld a blufftop view of the Point and wrote, "I spent some time viewing the rivers, and the land in the fork, which I think extremely well situated for a fort." Within a year Ft. Prince George was built. Four months later, however, the French destroyed the small stockade and replaced it with **Fort Duquesne**. In 1758 they burned their own creation prior to the arrival of a British force of 6,500, thereby saving Gen. John Forbes the trouble of destroying it himself. **Fort Pitt**, the largest British fort in the New World, succeeded Ft. Duquesne and spelled the end of French control of the area for the remainder of the French and Indian War. Like the fort, the surrounding garrison town of Pittsburgh was named for England's secretary of state (and later prime minister), William Pitt.

In 1763 Native American tribes rebelled against the inhospitable treatment they had received at the hands of the British, their former allies. Led by Ottawa war chief Pontiac, the Indians captured eight British forts within two months and blocked supply lines at each end of Lake Erie. After a group of warriors attempted to lay siege to Ft. Pitt, the British crushed the Indians at nearby Bushy Run, outside present-day Pittsburgh. This battle spelled the turning point of Pontiac's war and opened up Western Pennsylvania for settlement. Interpretive trails and a small museum at **Bushy Run Battlefield** recount the story *(Rte. 993 West, near Jeannette;* ☎*412-527-5584).*

By the end of the century, Pittsburgh was a bustling frontier town of some 400 houses, a post office, a courthouse and six taverns. Its revenue depended on its production of boats, hats and rope, as well as flour milling and whiskey distilling. Keelboats and paddle wheelers plied the rivers as pioneers stopped for supplies in the gateway town and then headed west. The town grew steadily and undramatically in the first half of the 1800s, with one exception: the Great Fire of 1845, the result of crowding houses too close to factories, wiped out 1,000 buildings.

Hell with the Lid Blown Off – The next hundred years catapulted Pittsburgh into its position as the nation's forge, leaving a grimy workhorse image that the city had a hard time shaking long after its mills were torn down and its air and rivers cleaned up. Situated close to the ingredients for iron making—coal, iron ore and limestone—as well as the rivers necessary for transportation, Pittsburgh was a natural for production of iron and steel. During the Civil War, Iron City (as it became known) kept the Union Army supplied with ammunition and supplies, its largely Irish and Scottish labor force supplemented by a tremendous influx of German immigrants. Following the war, high numbers of freed blacks made cheap labor even more readily available. By 1868 the city claimed 46 foundries, 50 glass factories, 53 oil refineries, and hundreds of other production centers. Half the country's steel and one-third of its glass were being produced here after the Civil War.

With so much commerce and energy pumping in one place, Pittsburgh banker Thomas Mellon maintained that anybody who could not get rich in Pittsburgh in ten years was a fool. The age of the great industrialists was at hand. At the summit of the steel world, **Andrew Carnegie** and **Henry Clay Frick** joined their steel-making and coal-production enterprises into one industrial juggernaut that made the former the richest man in the world. When Carnegie sold his concerns to J.P. Morgan's U.S. Steel in 1901 for the equivalent of several billion dollars, 89 of his top executives suddenly became millionaires. Carnegie and Frick—like their associates Henry Phipps and Charles M. Schwab—made their fortunes here before moving on to New York City, but their names remain imprinted upon

Getting There

By Air – **Pittsburgh International Airport**: 16mi west of downtown; international and domestic flights; ☎472-3525. Greater Pittsburgh Convention & Visitors Bureau information centers are located Landside on the lower level *(open year-round daily 8am–8pm)*, and Airside on the main level *(open year-round daily 7:30am–6:30pm)*. Port Authority "Airport Flyer" bus (28X) departs from lower level, near baggage claim *(daily 5:30am–midnight, every 45min; $1.95)*. Airport shuttle service to downtown departs from lower level *(daily 6am–11:40pm; $12;* ☎471-2250)*. Taxi service to downtown: 1hr–1hr 30min *($28-$31)*. Rental car agencies *(p 358)* located on the lower level.

By Bus and Train – **Bus** service to Pittsburgh is provided by Greyhound *(11th & Liberty Ave.; ☎392-6514 or 800-231-2222)*. Amtrak **trains** come into The Pennsylvanian terminal downtown *(1100 Liberty Ave.; ☎800-872-7245)*.

Getting Around

The network of color-coded signs of Pittsburgh's Wayfinder System directs visitors to attractions and points of interest around the city *(contact visitor centers, below, for more information)*.

By Public Transportation – The **Port Authority of Allegheny County** operates an extensive public transit system of subway and buses throughout Pittsburgh and the county *(daily 4am–1am)*. System fares: free until 7pm when traveling between Grant St. and the Triangle; $1.25 rest of city. The **"T" Light Rail** line operates within the downtown area *(free)*, with three stations along 6th St. and Liberty Ave. The rail also crosses the river to Station Square *(75¢)*. Schedules and route information: ☎442-2000.

By Car – The triangular lay of the land and streets that shoot off in odd directions can cause some initial disorientation. Remember that the numbered avenues are aligned roughly east-west, and that the lower two-thirds of the triangle is organized in an orderly street grid. At Liberty Avenue, however, there is another grid oriented northeast to southwest that stretches to the Allegheny River. Metered street parking is available downtown *($2/hr)*. Parking garages are located throughout the city *(average fee $8/day)*. Parking information: Pittsburgh Parking Authority *(☎456-2770)*.

By Taxi – Yellow Cab *(☎665-8100)*; Peoples Cab *(☎681-3131)*.

General Information

Visitor Information – The **Greater Pittsburgh Convention & Visitors Bureau** *(Four Gateway Center, Pittsburgh PA 15222, www.pittsburgh-cvb.org ☎281-7711 or 800-366-0093)* operates four visitor centers that provide information on shopping, accommodations and seasonal events: Downtown *(Liberty Ave. next to Gateway Center; open Mar–Dec Mon–Fri 9am–5pm, weekends 9am–3pm; rest of the year closed Sun)*; Oakland *(Forbes Ave. on University of Pittsburgh campus; open year-round Mon 9am–4pm, Tue–Sun 10am–4pm)*; Carnegie Library *(Grandview Ave., lower level; open year-round Mon 9am–5pm; Tue–Wed & Fri–Sat 10am–5pm)*; Pittsburgh International Airport *(above)*.

Accommodations – *(p 358)* Area visitors' guide including lodging directory is available *(free)* from the Greater Pittsburgh Convention & Visitors Bureau. Accommodations range from elegant hotels downtown and along the South Side waterfront to more modest hotels and motels in the Oakland area and out near the airport. The Pittsburgh **hostel** provides inexpensive lodging *(830 E. Warrington Ave., Pittsburgh PA 15210 ☎431-1267)*.

Local Press – Daily news: *Pittsburgh Post-Gazette* (morning), Sunday entertainment section; *Pittsburgh Tribune-Review* (morning), Friday entertainment section.

Foreign Exchange Offices – *(p 355)* Pittsburgh International Airport, 2nd floor near ticket counters *(open daily 6am–10pm; ☎472-5151)*; Mellon Bank *(5th Ave. & Smithfield St.; ☎234-4215)*; PNC Bank *(5th Ave. & Wood St.; ☎762-2090)*.

Sports and Leisure

Sightseeing – Gray Line provides narrated historic or cultural **city bus tours** *(Apr–early Nov daily; 2hrs; reservations suggested; hotel pickup available; $16; ☎741-2720)*; combination tours (including Gateway Clipper Cruise) available. The Pittsburgh History and Landmarks Foundation features a history and architecture **walking tour** of downtown (*depart from USX Tower Plaza on Grant St. Jun–Sept Wed noon; 1hr; $3; ☎471-5808*). **Boat tours** on Pittsburgh's three rivers are offered by Gateway Clipper Fleet (*depart from Station Square Dock May–Oct Mon–Sat; 2hrs; ☎355-7980*).

Entertainment – **Cultural Events Hotline**: ☎800-366-0093. Consult the arts and entertainment section of local newspapers (*p 324*) for schedules of cultural events and addresses of theaters and concert halls. To purchase **tickets**, contact the box office or **Ticketmaster** ☎323-1919.

Venue	Performances	☎
Heinz Hall for the Performing Arts (*p 329*)	Pittsburgh Symphony Orchestra, Broadway shows	392-4800
Benedum Center for the Performing Arts (*p 329*)	Pittsburgh Opera, Pittsburgh Ballet	281-0912
Byham Theater	Touring shows, concerts	456-1350
Carnegie Music Hall	Concerts, opera	268-2372
Civic Arena	Concerts	642-1800
Three Rivers Stadium	Concerts	321-0650

Spectator Sports – **Pirates** baseball (*☎321-2827*); **Steelers** football (*☎323-1200*); **Penguins** hockey (*☎624-1800*). Gateway Clipper (*above*) provides ferry service to baseball and football games at Three Rivers Stadium (*departs 2-3hrs pre-game to 30min post-game; 15min; $2 one-way, $4 round-trip*).

Recreation – Pittsburgh's primary recreation area is **Schenley Park** (*p 340*), offering miles of paths for walking, biking, horseback riding and cross-country skiing. The park also includes tennis courts, baseball fields and a golf course. Outdoor **ice-skating** is available at the Schenley Oval on Overlook Road (*weather permitting; rentals available; ☎422-6523*). Most of the city's major annual festivals are held downtown at **Point State Park** (*p 327*).

Shopping – The major shopping area in Pittsburgh is the downtown Golden Triangle (*p 327*), which incorporates major **department stores** and retail centers such as the Shops of One Oxford Center (*Grant St. & Fourth Ave.; ☎391-5300*); Fifth Avenue Place (*Fifth & Liberty Aves.; ☎456-7800*); and PPG Place (*Third Ave. & Stanwix St.;*

■ **Pittsburgh Just for Kids**

From toddlers to teens, kids of all ages will find something to amuse them at the following sights:

Pittsburgh Children's Museum Kids (*10 Children's Way on the West Commons of Allegheny Center, North Side, Pittsburgh; ☎412-322-5058*) – Three action-packed floors of hands-on activities await kids inside this 1894 Italian Renaissance-style former post office building.

Kennywood Park Kids (*4800 Kennywood Blvd., in West Mifflin outside Pittsburgh; ☎412-461-0500*) – Created by Andrew Mellon in 1898, this 90-acre National Historic Landmark amusement park will thrill the whole family with classic roller coasters and rides galore.

☎434-1900). Over 60 shops and restaurants can be found on the South Side in the Shops at Station Square (*p 332*). Airmall, at Pittsburgh International Airport, offers a large collection of specialty shops (*☎472-5180*). Other shopping areas include the Strip District (*p 331*), with its open-air marketplace and **art galleries**; the historic South Side district **antique** and specialty stores (*East Carson St. between 10th & Brady Sts.*); and the major chains and specialty shops located in Shadyside (*Walnut St., east of Oakland*).

Useful Numbers	☎
Police/Ambulance/Fire	911
Dental Referral (*Mon–Fri 5am–6pm, Sat 5am–2pm*)	800-917-6453
Medical Referral (*Mon–Fri 9am–5pm*)	321-5030
24-hour Pharmacy (*Eckerd, locations throughout Pittsburgh*)	
Main Post Office (*1001 California Ave.*)	359-7500
Weather (recorded)	936-1212

the city's memory. Other 19C Pittsburgh barons include brothers Andrew and Richard Mellon (sons of Thomas), with their banking and oil interests; H.J. Heinz, whose bottling and food-processing works clustered on the North Side; and George Westinghouse, known for his work in electric systems.

While some people were cashing in on Pittsburgh, the city was fast becoming a churning cauldron of noxious fumes. Clanging blast furnaces spouted eye-sting-ing gases into the air, blackening the sky and surrounding buildings with soot and smoke to the point where winter middays were frequently indistinguishable from night. One writer in 1883 observed that "Pittsburgh is a smoky, dismal city, at her best. At her worst, nothing darker, dingier or more dispiriting can be imag-ined." And a 19C English journalist gave the city a moniker that stuck for many decades: "Hell with the lid taken off."

To stoke this seething inferno were thousands of immigrants fresh from Italy, Poland, Austria-Hungary, Russia and the Balkans. With all the level ground reserved for mills and factories, houses began perching on the steep surrounding slopes, and inclined railways carried workers to and from the city. Attempts to organize labor were fruitless. A railroad strike in 1877 left several people dead or wounded, and blacks were brought in by the railroad owners to break the strike. Then in 1892 the Amalgamated Association of Iron and Steel Workers tried to strike at the Homestead plant. Violence ensued, but Henry Frick and his 300 hired Pinkerton guards so successfully capitalized on the situation that the demoralized union remained powerless for 45 more years. With the labor move-ment crushed, wages plummeted.

The city nevertheless continued to build and expand, architectural styles switch-ing from stately Greek Revival to the more fanciful Gothic Revival and then to a muscular Romanesque Revival, as though to echo the solidifying fortunes of the ruling class. These same fortunes helped create some of the city's enduring cul-tural institutions. In 1895 Andrew Carnegie opened his Carnegie Institute complex (now called The Carnegie), which included museums of art and natural history, as well as a music hall and library.

By World War II, steel production was already on the decline, but the city rallied for the war effort and exhausted itself in its record-breaking output of munitions. After the war, instead of limping into some sad, unknown future, a worn-out city began to plan for smoke and flood control and a new phase of building, usher-ing in the much-touted Pittsburgh Renaissance.

Rebirth – When asked what should be done with Pittsburgh in the 1930s, archi-tect Frank Lloyd Wright tersely suggested, "Abandon it." Luckily, city fathers ignored his advice, and an unprecedented cooperation between public and pri-vate enterprise began to alter the look of the city. Led by Mayor David Lawrence and backed by wealthy banker Richard Mellon, Pittsburgh became a model for urban redevelopment. Dams were put in upstream to control flooding, and new regulations were enacted to reduce pollution. Buildings began coming down with increasing frequency, although preservationists managed to save many of the finest old structures.

A great deal of attention was focused on the Point, which by the 1950s had devolved into an unsightly web of bridges, railyards, warehouses and alleys. Among plans was one by Frank Lloyd Wright himself, calling for a tremendous 13-story shopping-office complex topped by a giant aviary. Instead, everything but the old Ft. Pitt blockhouse was cleared out, making way for green Point State Park that stands here today. At the park's tip, a fountain fed by an underground aquifer shoots 150ft into the air, a symbol of rebirth.

Tallying up a score of new skyscrapers, the $500 million renaissance culminated with the completion in 1971 of the 64-story **USX Tower** (former U.S. Steel Building). The next 20 years brought a mini-boom of new buildings including PNC Plaza (1976), PPG Place (1984), One Mellon Center (1983), the CNG Tower (1985), and Fifth Avenue Place (1987), as well as the lively shopping-restaurant complex at Station Square on the south shore of the Monongahela.

The New Pittsburgh – When Rand-McNally's 1985 *Places Rated Almanac* listed Pittsburgh as the nation's most livable city, it was as though the city had finally shaken off its dark mantle and stepped out into the limelight. The city has been on the upswing ever since. Pittsburgh ranks just behind New York City and Chicago in its number of *Fortune 500* corporate headquarters, and it holds offices for about 220 foreign companies—nearly half of them US or world headquarters.

The city's economy has shifted from manufacturing to service and retail, with less than five percent (down from 40 percent) of the workforce engaged in steel and other metal making. In addition to the service industries, a significant percentage of jobs are in medicine, biotechnology, software and finance. Visitors today are greeted by a bold and fully modern city, with clean air and rivers—the county's tally of 26,000 registered boats makes it second only to Florida's Dade County. The new $800 million Pittsburgh International Airport, opened in 1992, features its own shopping mall.

Pittsburgh's cultural offerings encompass a wide spectrum of tastes. The world-class Pittsburgh Symphony Orchestra plays a 24-program series in elegantly restored Heinz Hall, while nearby Benedum Center hosts local opera and dance productions as well as touring Broadway shows. Innovative small theater companies, scattered around town, present classical and contemporary drama. The city also maintains a strong jazz tradition in numerous nightclubs.

Home of the renowned Carnegie museums, Carnegie Music Hall, the University of Pittsburgh and Carnegie-Mellon University, the Oakland neighborhood is a cultural enclave unto itself. And since 1990, more than 35 major films have been shot in Pittsburgh, including *Silence of the Lambs*, *Lorenzo's Oil* and *Hoffa*.

Recreational opportunities begin with the city's 2,500 acres of parkland, providing lush respite from urban living. Allegheny County offers an additional 11,900 acres where visitors can hike, picnic and fish. The Pittsburgh Steelers play professional football at Three Rivers Stadium, while the Pirates take over during baseball season. Down at the Civic Arena, the Penguins present big-league hockey excitement.

With its low crime rate and close-knit neighborhoods, its thriving businesses and attractive riverfront setting, Pittsburgh looks poised to prosper as never before in the next decade. Visitors will discover a city on the move, but one that has not turned its back on the past. In the midst of a glittering 21C city, you can sometimes picture the old Pittsburgh. Clouds can gather in the hills for days, painting the sky an endless slate gray; and on such a day, when you come across a tarnished building and hear a coal-laden train grind along the river, you can almost imagine the old industrial town, long gone.

★★ DOWNTOWN & SOUTH SIDE   *1 day. Map pp 330-331.*

Sometimes referred to as the Golden Triangle, Pittsburgh's downtown fills in and rises high above the acute wedge of land between the two rivers. A wonderful mix of buildings designed by some of the country's foremost architects stands knee to knee here, from sturdy brick and stone edifices more than a century old to shimmering splinters of glass and steel built within the past 15 years. Less than one mile from Point State Park to the wall of skyscrapers along Grant Street, the Golden Triangle is easily covered on foot. Several bridges, used by motorists and pedestrians, link downtown with the North and South Sides, and a clean and easy-to-use subway stops at central locations.

One of the most striking landmarks on the west end of downtown, **Fifth Avenue Place** *(5th and Liberty Aves.)* is topped by a pyramid from which shoots a pencil-thin tower. Headquarters of Hillman construction company, the 1987 building features a public plaza and upscale shopping arcade.

Just south, **Market Square★** *(Forbes Ave. and Market St.)*, dating back to 1784, once held a courthouse, city hall and market buildings. Now a bustling, open grassy area surrounded by brick sidewalks and streets, the square is bordered by early commercial buildings such as a Civil War-era pub, and the 1902 Landmark Tavern. One block south, **PPG Place★★** (Pittsburgh Plate Glass) merits special attention as an eye-catching city icon. Designed by Philip Johnson and John Burgee and completed in 1984, the dark reflective glass tower and its flanking buildings, all surmounted by pointy turrets, were modeled after London's Houses of Parliament. Rising 635ft, the building also pays tribute to the Gothic architecture found in the Oakland neighborhood and the forts that stood on the Point in the 18C.

★ **Point State Park** – *At the southern end of Penn Ave., bordered by Commonwealth Pl. Open year-round daily 7am–11pm.* & 🅿 ☎412-471-0235. Set aside in 1946 for redevelopment as part of the city's effort to revitalize the sooty industrial riverfront, this tree-bordered park today offers an oasis for office workers as well as a venue for annual festivals. The Point's history, including the three successive stockades (forts Prince George, Duquesne and Pitt) that have occupied this site, is told here in the **Fort Pitt Museum** *(open year-round Wed–Sun 10am–5pm; $2;* & 🅿 ☎412-281-

9284). In this reconstructed bastion, dioramas, artifacts and detailed information panels depict the clash between the French, British and Indians for control of the Ohio Valley. In the middle of the park sits the outline of the most recent stronghold, five-sided Ft. Pitt, as it stood in 1765. The adjacent **Fort Pitt blockhouse** (which now houses the museum gift shop) dates from 1764, making it the city's oldest building *(open year-round Wed–Sun 10am–5pm;* 🅿 ☎*412-471-1764).* At the park's tip, the landmark **fountain** replaces the bygone smokestacks with plumes of sparkling water.

Downtown Skyline

© Walt Urbina

★ **Fourth Avenue** – Formerly the Wall Street of Pittsburgh, Fourth Avenue claims a dozen banks that once held vast iron, steel, oil and glass fortunes. Next to mighty PPG Place, the Greek Revival **Burke Building** *(no. 209)* stands as the oldest commercial structure downtown. The three-story building was erected in 1836 and survived the Great Fire of 1845. At the corner of Fourth and Wood, the 1902 **Arrott Building**, designed by local architect Frederick Osterling, rises 15 stories to a cap of arched windows and ornamental cornices; the lobby showcases marble, brasswork and mosaic tile. Catercorner across Fourth Avenue, the row of stolid bank buildings (now combined into Union National Bank), with their serious columns and pediments, dates from 1903 to 1907. Down at the corner of Smithfield Street, the 1870 **Dollar Bank**★ enlivens the block with its ostentatious Baroque details and a pair of regal stone lions guarding the bank's entrance.

★ **Sixth Avenue** – Among prominent structures along this must-stroll street, the 30-story **Alcoa Building** *(at Smithfield St.)* stands, like PPG Place, as a striking example of one of the city's signature buildings—those that advertise their product by their construction. Aluminum encases this still modern-looking 1953 building. Across the street, lively **Mellon Square** offers a landscaped retreat in the midst of a skyscraper forest.

Just west, **Trinity Episcopal Cathedral**★ (1872) claims a splendid Gothic Revival exterior, blackened by pollution over the years. By contrast, the interior is remarkably simple; the churchyard, located on an Indian burial ground, is the only cemetery within the city limits. Next door, the **First Presbyterian Church**★ (1905), also in the Gothic style, is graced by elegant stone tracery and an outdoor pulpit. Inside are 13 brilliantly colored Tiffany stained-glass **windows**.

Directly across the street in the classic brownstone **Duquesne Club** *(not open to the public)*, Pittsburgh's business and civic leaders have been mapping out the city's progress since 1889. And on the corner of Wood Street, the 300 Sixth Avenue Building displays on its facade an illuminated glass **mural [A]** depicting an iron-worker and titled *The Puddler* (1942).

★ **Heinz Hall** – *6th St. and Penn Ave. Open for performances only.* ☎412-392-4800. A 1926 vaudeville movie palace was restored in 1971 into an opulent showcase for opera, dance and theater. Now venue for the famous Pittsburgh Symphony Orchestra, the hall features terra-cotta embellishments outside and an interior rich with red and gold paint, marble accents and crystal chandeliers.

★ **Benedum Center** – *7th St. and Penn Ave. Visit by guided tour (45min) only. $2. Reservations required. www.pgharts.org* ☎412-456-6666. Also in the burgeoning cultural district, Benedum Center is another lavish 1920s theater, reclaimed from neglect in 1986. An English Renaissance exterior of terra-cotta, brick and limestone gives way to an Etruscan-style feast within, highlighted by aluminum-leaf details that were a luxury in the 20s. Be sure to note the **sculpture group** in the plaza between the two theaters: A realistic representation of business patronizing the arts, a man in a suit looks across to two violinists, all three posed as though they were part of the downtown crowd.

★★ **Grant Street** – Some of the city's most noteworthy historic and modern buildings line this corridor, beginning with Henry Hobson Richardson's Romanesque Revival masterpiece, **Allegheny County Courthouse and Jail**★★ *(at Forbes Ave.)*. Considered one of the country's preeminent 19C buildings, the muscular 1888 edifice, like its creator, is big and full of masculine bluster. A castle-like tower divides the symmetrical wings, while three grand arches provide entry. Arches and massive piers continue inside, where you'll find pointillist murals of industry, war, peace and justice. Also note the architect's initials, worked into the base of pillars and wherever else he could. The courthouse encloses a courtyard, outfitted with benches, plantings and a fountain.

Across the street stands the **Frick Building** (now occupied by Mellon Bank), a successful attempt by Henry Frick to overshadow the buildings of his partner and rival, Andrew Carnegie. Designed by Daniel Burnham, the skyscraper dates from 1902. When the street level was lowered in 1912, the upper lobby became a balcony and the basement the main lobby, where a hallway leads to a fine stained-glass panel by John La Farge titled *Fortune's Wheel*. North on Grant, across Fifth Avenue, **Two Mellon Bank Center**★ (formerly the Union Trust Building) is another Frick landmark, this one from 1916. Its Gothic filigree, stone dormer and mansard roofline cut neat figures against the sky, while inside, a vast lobby opens to a breathtaking center where balconies form ascending circles up to the ten-story, eye-shaped dome light. Frick also built the 1916 **William Penn Hotel**★ *(at Oliver Ave.)*, a triumph of elegance and pampering. The restored hotel boasts a 17th-floor Italianate ballroom with black Carrara glass walls, gilt moldings and a ceiling fresco. High tea in the formal Georgian-style lobby remains a popular daily event *(year-round Mon–Sat 3pm–6pm, Sun 2:30pm–6pm; $14.75; reservations requested;* ☎412-281-7100).

Across Grant looms the dark **USX Tower**, the city's tallest structure. Its exposed steel I-beams and skeletal framework make an austere statement; the coat of brownish purple rust actually protects the steel. At night from the Top of the Tower restaurant on the tower's 64th floor, you can see diamond chains of lights stretching along the city's north and west sides.

Up at Liberty Avenue, the restored railroad passenger terminal now known as **The Pennsylvanian**, with its terra-cotta details and Beaux-Arts rotunda, was designed by Daniel Burnham in 1898 and financed by painter Mary Cassatt's brother. An Amtrak and subway station, the building also serves as a residential and commercial complex.

★★ **Senator John Heinz Pittsburgh Regional History Center** – *1212 Smallman St. Open year-round daily 10am–5pm. Closed Jan 1, Thanksgiving Day, Dec 25. $6.* ✗ ⌕ 🅿 *($4)* ☎412-454-6000. Opened in 1996, this deluxe treatment of area history resides in the 1898 Chautauqua Lake Ice Company warehouse, renovated to the tune of $13 million. The massive building's three floors and stairways are exposed to views of vaulted brick ceilings and heavy wood beams and iron braces. The first floor, a showplace for the building's architecture, holds a Conestoga wagon, a walk-on 1949 streetcar and an impressionistic **mural**, titled *The Visible City* (1992-95), by local artist and professor of architecture Douglas Cooper. Located on the second floor, the permanent **Points In Time**★ exhibit covers Western Pennsylvania from 1750 to the present. Starting with a 10min video, you proceed chronologically from the Indian and Ft. Pitt periods to the age of steelworkers and entrepreneurs and on through the Pittsburgh Renaissance. More than 1,000 artifacts, photos and documents, as well as audio and video stations, make this a compelling walk through history. Included are exhibits on early travelers, industrial-era injuries, immigrant religions and the Hill District. **Discovery Place** Kids, a hands-on history center for children, occupies the third floor, while temporary exhibits are installed on the fourth. The sixth floor contains a library and archives.

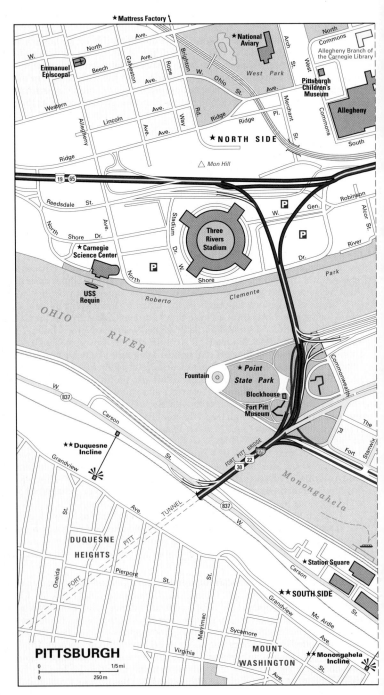

PITTSBURGH

★ **Strip District** – *Smallman St. & Penn Ave. from 16th St. to 22nd St.* A tradition since the 1920s, the wholesale produce and open-air markets along this narrow strand make for a festival atmosphere every day, and especially on Saturday mornings. The area, which was occupied at the turn of the century by the city's early iron forges, now bustles with a streetside smorgasbord of fruit and flower stalls, meat and fish markets, and smells of fresh-baked bread and sizzling meat. Within one block you can buy a cheap sweatshirt, Starbuck's coffee and a Korean shish kebab. The hip **Society for Contemporary Crafts**, located in the two-story brick Pennsylvania Railroad Fruit Auction and Sales Building *(corner of Smallman & 21st Sts.)*, displays temporary shows as well as a variety of items for sale. Diagonally

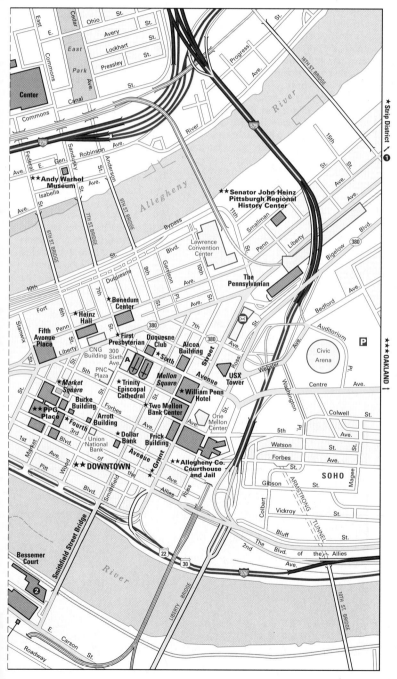

across the street squats the dignified St. Stanislaus Kostka Church, built by Poles in 1892.

★ **Station Square** – *On W. Carson St. just across the Smithfield Street Bridge from downtown. Shops open year-round Mon– Sat 10am–9pm, Sun noon–5pm; restaurant hours vary.* ✕ & ▣ *(parking fees $4-$12.50) www.stationsquare.com* ☎ *800-859-8959 or 412-261-2811.* Reached via the 1883 **Smithfield Street Bridge**—a rare lenticular truss that ranks as the oldest bridge in Pittsburgh—Station Square is a 1970s reworking of the Pittsburgh & Lake Erie Railroad Company's turn-of-the-century terminal and freight yard. The 52-acre complex on the south side of the Monongahela encompasses some 65 shops and restaurants, as well as offices and a hotel. On display in **Bessemer Court** *(adjoining the Sheraton's parking lot)* along the river are a 10-ton Bessemer converter (from a 1930 blast furnace), Victorian trolleys, railroad cars and other industrial artifacts. Station Square is also the headquarters for the Gateway Clipper Fleet, whose six riverboats offer a variety of sightseeing cruises on Pittsburgh's rivers (☎412-355-7980).

★★ **Monongahela Incline** – *W. Carson St. opposite Station Sq. Open year-round Mon– Sat 5:30am–12:45am, Sun & holidays 8:45am–midnight. $1/each way.* & ▣ *trfn. clpgh. org/patransit* ☎412-442-2000. The oldest of 17 funiculars that once ascended Pittsburgh's steep hills, the Monongahela opened in 1870 and still functions as a commuter route for residents of Mount Washington. Climbing at a precipitous 35-degree angle, the car takes about two minutes to cover the 635ft, its cable driven by two 75-horse

1 Primanti Brothers

Map p 331. Smallman & 18th Sts. ☎*412-263-2142.* This Pittsburgh institution got its start here in the 1930s catering to truck drivers and workers loading and unloading produce in the Strip. Although locals complain the shop has become commercialized (there are now several locations around the city), the Primantis still serve up sandwiches 24 hours a day. As in its early days, when it served truckers on the run, meals— coleslaw and all—are served on wax paper, not plates.

2 Grand Concourse Restaurant

Map p 331. One Station Square. ☎*412-261-1717.* With its stained-glass, barrel-vaulted ceiling and faux marble pillars, the Grand Concourse makes splendid use of the former waiting room of the Pittsburgh & Lake Erie Railroad Company's terminal. Designed by William George Burns in 1901, the palatial room now rates as one of the most elegant restaurants in the city. Fresh seafood— served grilled, broiled, blackened or fried—is the specialty here. And the adjacent Gandy Dancer Saloon and raw bar attracts the young professional set at happy hour.

South Side

power motors. German immigrants once mined coal from this hill, and vistas of the smoky city were almost nil. Now prime real estate, Mount Washington commands unparalleled **views**★★★ of the Golden Triangle; visitors can savor the scenery from a platform projecting from the cliff.

★★ **Duquesne Incline** – *W. Carson St. west of Ft. Pitt Bridge. Open year-round Mon–Sat 5:30am–12:45am, Sun & holidays 7am–12:45am. $1/each way.* ☎*412-381-1665.* Dating from 1877, this incline also offers a spectacular **view**★★★ *(p 322)*. Situated just west of the Point, the Duquesne gives somewhat less of an architectural panorama than the Monongahela, but more of a geographical one. From the observation deck on the summit, near where George Washington once surveyed the lay of the land, you get a bird's-eye perspective of the two rivers merging into the Ohio. (A number of neighboring restaurants also offer great views.) The 800ft incline features cars with original hand-carved cherry panels, maple trim and amber-glass transoms. The original waiting room displays historical photographs of Pittsburgh.

★ **NORTH SIDE** *1½ days. Map pp 330-331.*

Originally set aside as land grants for veterans of the Revolutionary War, the North Side area soon evolved into the industrial town of Allegheny, which was slated to become the county seat. But Pittsburgh usurped that honor for itself, and in 1907 the city annexed Allegheny (though the latter fought the decision all the way to the Supreme Court). During the late 19C and early 20C, the hilly town's riverside factories churned out iron, textiles, glass, pottery, brassware and other products in tremendous quantities. Noteworthy residents of Allegheny during its prime were industrialists Andrew Carnegie and H.J. Heinz, scientist Samuel Pierpont Langley, poet Robinson Jeffers, painter Mary Cassatt, and writers Gertrude Stein and Mary Roberts Rinehart.

Today the North Side's handful of attractions constitute some of the highlights of a visit to Pittsburgh. Two of its more popular sites, the Carnegie Science Center and the Andy Warhol Museum, now fall under the umbrella of The Carnegie's renowned museums *(p 336)*.

Occupying the core of North Side, **Allegheny Center** was a 1950s commercial and residential project that never took off. A large, underutilized shopping mall remains, and the whole area has a transitional feel. But the venerable 1889 Allegheny Branch of the Carnegie Library and other nearby Gothic-style buildings lend the neighborhood some solidity, as does the lovely surrounding park. Overlooking the Allegheny, one of the city's principal sports venues, **Three Rivers Stadium**, hosts professional football and baseball games.

★ **Carnegie Science Center** – 🏫 *1 Allegheny Ave. Open year-round daily 10am–5pm (Sat 9pm). Closed Jan 1, Thanksgiving Day, Dec 25. $6 (combination tickets available for Omnimax, Planetarium & USS Requin).* 🍴 🅿 *($3) csc.clpgh.org* ☎*412-237-3400.* Set on the north bank of the Allegheny River next to Three Rivers Stadium, this slick science museum began as the Buhl Science Center in the 1940s; it was modernized and added to The Carnegie's domain in 1991. The Science Center has been drawing crowds to its Omnimax theater, planetarium, World War II submarine and hands-on exhibits ever since. More than 45,000sq ft of exhibit space, spread over four floors, is housed within an oddly somber contemporary structure. Large south-facing picture windows throughout the museum provide expansive views of the Ohio River and the Pittsburgh skyline.

Visit – *½ day. Information desk located on first floor. Obtain tickets first for submarine tour and Omnimax and Planetarium shows, and plan your visit around these.* Much of the first floor is devoted to the **Omnimax Theater**★, an aluminum dome four stories high and 79ft across upon which large-format films are projected. Also on this floor, the **SciQuest Exhibit Gallery** demonstrates principles of waves, flight and force, with exhibits such as a walk-in wind tunnel where you can literally test your wings. In the **Science & Sport** area you can try ice climbing and measure the speed of your baseball pitch. The Health Science Theater presents frequent demonstrations on chemistry and other topics.

On the second floor, the **Planetarium**★ explores the solar system and galaxies. Special exhibits occupy half (about 6,000sq ft) of the remaining space on this level. A big hit here, the **Miniature Railroad and Village** portrays how people lived, worked and played in Western Pennsylvania at the turn of the century. The 30ft-by-85ft display includes some 100 animated pieces, including such wonderful details as a carnival, hot air balloons and an incline.

The third floor contains two areas especially for children, one for ages 7 to 13 and another for ages 6 and under. Across the hall, **Sea Life Aquarium** contains more than 100 ocean species in several tanks. On the fourth floor you can learn about weather as well as food packaging and consumption. **The Works** electronic exhibit theater presents multimedia lab shows dramatically demonstrating robotics, lasers, cryogenics, lightning and metal making.

Moored in the Ohio River behind the museum, the 312ft **USS Requin** submarine served in the last months of World War II but never saw action. Not for the claustrophobic, tours *(45min)* begin in the torpedo loading room and crawl through raised hatches to the officers' quarters and control room.

★★ **The Andy Warhol Museum** – *117 Sandusky St. Open year-round Wed & Sun 11am–6pm, Thu–Sat 11am–8pm. Closed major holidays. $6.* ✻ ⅖ *www.warhol.org/warhol* ☎*412-237-8300.* Opened in 1994, this comprehensive single-artist museum sprawls over seven floors and 35,000sq ft of gallery space; it is a big dynamic space for an artist of long-lasting fame. The latest star in The Carnegie's constellation of cultural venues, the Andy Warhol Museum displays more than 500 works of art and archival artifacts, a fraction of its total collection of more than 3,000 paintings, drawings, sculptures and photographs.

Born of Eastern European immigrant parents, **Andy Warhol** (1928-87) grew up in the Oakland neighborhood of Pittsburgh. While his father labored in heavy construction, Andy began collecting autographed photos of movie stars and attending free art classes at the Carnegie Institute, eventually graduating from the Carnegie Institute of Technology's College of Fine Arts. He then moved to New York City and achieved almost immediate success as a commercial artist. It was not long before the fame-conscious Warhol was welding avant-garde art to pop culture in his multiple Elvises and Campbell's soup cans, surrounding himself with celebrities and hangers-on, and creating a provocative persona that

Marilyn (Three Times), 1962, by Andy Warhol

earned him an enduring place in the world of 20C art. In the 1960s he turned to filmmaking, producing such titles as *Eat*, *Haircut* and *Sleep*—the latter containing five hours of footage of poet John Giorno lying in bed. Warhol founded *Interview* magazine in 1969, and in the 70s and 80s he returned to painting and made forays into television production.

Visit – *1hr. Begin on the 1st floor, then take the elevator to the 7th floor and work your way down.* The first floor, themed **Heritage**, introduces Warhol and his oeuvre with large-format self-portraits and commissioned portraits of such celebrities as Mick Jagger, Dennis Hopper, Judy Garland and Liza Minnelli, mostly combinations of silkscreen, polymer paint and urine on canvas. A theater screens films by Warhol and others. Take the elevator to the seventh floor—**Fame, Fortune, Fashion**—where you can view Warhol's experiments with shadows, torsos and diamond dust, as well as his early commercial drawings. **Success, 1950s** is the topic on the sixth floor, with still fresh-looking pop images of Elvis, Jackie, Liz, Marilyn, and Campbell's soup cans. The popular fifth floor, **Silver Factory, 1960s**, includes pink and yellow cow wallpaper and a room full of mylar pillow-shaped helium balloons that you can bat around while a sound track scratches quietly in the background. In **Enterprise, 1970s** on the fourth floor, varicolored paintings of skulls and Chairman Mao are displayed. The third floor contains an archives, and the second floor explores the **Legacy** Warhol left. Late works, collaborative efforts and temporary shows by current artists fill this space.

★ **National Aviary** – 🧒 *Allegheny Commons West. Open year-round daily 9am–4:30pm. Closed Dec 25. $4. ♿ 🅿 www.aviary.org ☎412-323-7235.* The nation's largest indoor bird facility not associated with a zoo gives out the warm breath of the tropics, a blessing on chilly Pittsburgh days. Home to about 150 species, the aviary runs a captive breeding program for rare and endangered birds. Self-guided tours proceed through various environments like desert, woodland and tropics, each featuring appropriate foliage and each alive with birds flying, walking, honking and twittering. The lush **fountain room** is especially appealing with its peacocks; and the **marsh room** houses a host of bright residents such as roseate spoonbills, parrots and flamingos. An outdoor enclosure holds Pennsylvania game birds and Andean condors.

★ **Mattress Factory** – *500 Sampsonia Way (entrance to parking lot at 505 Jacksonia St.). Open Sept–Jul Tue–Sat 10am–5pm, Sun 1pm–5pm. Closed major holidays. $4. ♿ 🅿 www. mattress.org ☎412-231-3169.* Helping transform a dreary stretch of the North Side, this perspective-altering art space exhibits works that are created specifically for

© The Andy Warhol Foundation for the Visual Arts, Inc.

installation on one of the six floors of a turn-of-the-century warehouse. Fifteen artists from around the world are chosen each year to display their creations, and they arrive not knowing exactly what form their work will take. They are encouraged to raise floors, tear down walls, add walls—in short, to do anything they want. The results range from the ridiculous to the brilliant. Materials have included tremendous polka-dot balloons, 6,600 cans of Budweiser, bales of hay, human hair and black light. In one permanent installation by James Turrell, viewers walk through pitch-black corridors to a dark gallery where, after fifteen minutes, a mysterious light begins to emanate from the far wall. An outdoor sculpture garden and separate gallery a few doors down round out this feast for the imagination.

Emmanuel Episcopal Church – *957 W. North Ave. Open year-round Mon–Wed & Fri 10am–4pm, Sun 8am–1pm. ♿ ☎412-231-0454.* Sometimes called the bake-oven for its shape, the church that Henry Hobson Richardson designed in the mid-1880s forms a brick-solid presence with its clean lines, Romanesque arches and unadorned gable roof. A bit more ornate inside, the church boasts dark wood, Tiffany stained glass and an Italian marble reredos. Jazz vespers are held here once a month.

★★★ **OAKLAND**   *3 days. Map p 336.*

Packed onto a 700-acre plateau 3mi east of the Golden Triangle, Pittsburgh's cultural and educational nerve center arose as a kind of high-minded counterpart to a decaying city. First settled as farmland, the area became a haven for wealthy families fleeing downtown cholera epidemics in the 1830s. Factories

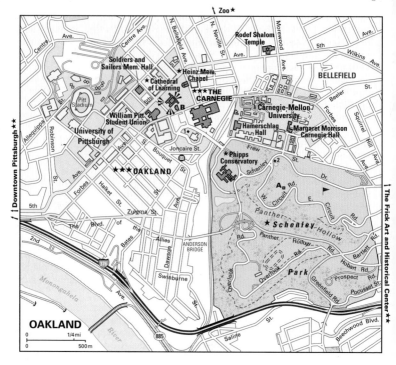

soon began appearing this far upriver, and Oakland, annexed to Pittsburgh in 1869, was well on its way to becoming another of the city's blue-collar districts. Twenty years later, expatriate Mary Schenley became the object of special attention as holder of a prime parcel of Oakland farmland. Schenley had eloped with a British sea captain in 1840 and left the country. As legend has it, city reps beat out developers in an 1889 transatlantic dash to reach her first, and convinced her to donate 400 acres of her land for the creation of a park. Thus Schenley Park was born on the eastern edge of the neighborhood.

In an effort to re-create Pittsburgh and leave a lasting legacy of his goodwill, Andrew Carnegie began the construction of his museum-library-music hall complex, the Carnegie Institute (now called The Carnegie), on the park's border in 1890. Other industrialists followed his lead, taking for their architectural inspiration the grand Neoclassical buildings of the 1893 World Columbian Exposition in Chicago.

Built in the early 1900s, the Carnegie Technical Schools that evolved into **Carnegie-Mellon University** were Carnegie's generous contribution to higher learning. Today the university is widely known now for its computer science, engineering and drama departments. On the north end of the grassy Mall, the old campus is anchored by **Hamerschlag Hall** (1912), an engineering building topped by a tall, temple-like tower. Another impressive sight, **Margaret Morrison Carnegie Hall** (1907) was the women's college named for Carnegie's mother. The building is recognizable by its three-story oval-shaped forecourt, with balcony and pilasters.

Among the 52 buildings of the **University of Pittsburgh** (1908), the handsome 10-story tan brick **William Pitt Student Union** *(Forbes Ave. & Bigelow Blvd.)* started out as the posh Schenley Hotel (1898, Rutan & Russell). For a taste of college-flavored coffeeshops and bookstores, stroll Forbes and Fifth Avenues between Atwood and Bouquet Streets.

★★★ The Carnegie

Located on Forbes Avenue, the city's premier cultural attraction opened in 1895 as the Carnegie Institute. Deemed too small, the five-acre Italian Renaissance-style sandstone **building**★ (designed by the local firm of Longfellow, Alden & Harlow) was expanded in the showier Beaux-Arts style and reopened in 1907 with 13.5 acres of floor space, including 6,000 tons of marble. Andrew Carnegie's grand vision of a center combining literature, art, science and music under one roof was thus realized. Though he funded thousands of foundations around the world, he declared that "the success of the Library, Art Gallery, Museum, and Music Hall … is one of the chief satisfactions of my life. This is my monument." Carnegie's legacy was extended to the North Side in the 1990s with the addition of the Carnegie Science Center *(p 333)* and Andy Warhol Museum *(p 334)*.

Befitting the cache of treasures within, the triumphal building—housing the museums of art and natural history, as well as the music hall and library—rambles for 800ft along Forbes Avenue and extends back to Schenley Drive. Outside the two wings fronting Forbes Avenue stand allegorical bronzes of *(right to left)* literature, music, art and science. Galleries in the museums of art and natural history ramble somewhat aimlessly side-by-side on the three floors of the building's east and west wings.

Unlike the museums, the adjoining **Carnegie Library of Pittsburgh** *(entrance on Schenley Dr.)* is supported by tax dollars, in accordance with Carnegie's philosophy that people should feel that they own the library. Having received little formal education, Carnegie often slipped off to a library in Allegheny to educate himself; he later acknowledged the importance of books by founding some 2,500 libraries. The Carnegie Library, one of the most important in the country, contains more than four million items. Its barrel-vaulted reading room, wall medallions and murals create an understated elegance. Adjacent to the library, **Carnegie Music Hall★** *(entrance on Forbes Ave.)* is home to the Pittsburgh Chamber Music Society, the Mendelssohn Choir and the River City Brass Band. It boasts a joyously ornamented foyer of brass and molded plaster, green marble columns, and a 45ft gilded ceiling—the grandest interior in the complex.

★★ **Carnegie Museum of Art** – In keeping with Carnegie's wishes, the museum concentrates on European and American art from the late 19C to the present. A sampling of Asian and African art, as well as architecture and decorative arts, is also offered. Though most galleries are on the east *(left)* side of the second floor, the Hall of Sculpture and Hall of Architecture are actually on the west side of the first floor, surrounded by rooms of the natural history museum *(follow museum maps, available at the reception desks)*.

Visit – *2hrs. Entrance on Forbes Ave. Open Jul–Aug Mon–Sat 10am–5pm, Sun 1pm–5pm. Rest of the year Tue–Sat 10am–5pm, Sun 1pm–5pm. Closed major holidays. $6 (ticket includes admission to both art and natural history museums).* ✗ ♿ 🅿 *($1/hr) www. clpgh.org* ☎412-622-3131. Based on the Mausoleum at Halicarnassus (one of the Seven Wonders of the Ancient World), the **Hall of Architecture★** holds more than 140 plaster casts of architectural masterpieces, plus numerous bronze replicas. Such copies were once held in great esteem, and the Carnegie retains one of the world's finest collections, including such works as a carved portal from a 13C Gothic cathedral in Bordeaux, France, and a holy water basin from a 16C church in Siena, Italy.

© Walt Urbina

Sculpture Hall, Carnegie Museum of Art

Likewise, the adjacent **Hall of Sculpture★**, resembling the interior of the Parthenon, displays copies of statues from ancient Greece arrayed around the loggia. Bathed in skylight, this roomy hall also harbors a sparkling collection of ceramic, metal, and glass objects (18C to 20C) from America, Europe and Asia on the second-floor balcony.

From here, cross the main corridor to the grand stairway. Walking up this elaborately carved staircase affords a look at John White Alexander's mural *The Apotheosis of Pittsburgh* (1905-08). On the second floor, the **Alisa Mellon Bruce Gallery** *(to the right)* showcases decorative arts, from 17C French tapestries and 18C English silver and French ceramics to early-19C American tall-case clocks. Go through the Hall of Sculpture balcony to the **Heinz Architectural Center**, which features changing exhibitions highlighting Pennsylvania and worldwide architecture. The south doorway leads to the Heinz Galleries, also reserved for temporary exhibits. Continue around to the **Sarah Scaife Galleries★**, which begin with an omnium-gatherum of world art from ancient Egypt to early 19C Europe. On display in these perimeter galleries are reliefs from the Temple of Isis (4C BC), a 3C BC Roman coffin, Medieval icons, a 1530 Austrian suit of armor, masks and figurines from Cameroon, and Tang dynasty carvings.

The middle of the Scaife Galleries consists of a free-flowing maze of more than 20 large rooms. Browse your way through works by Tintoretto and Rubens to Impressionists Monet, Pissarro, Renoir, van Gogh, Degas and Cézanne and on to Whistler, Homer and other American masters. Nearly every important European and American artist from 1800 to 1950 is represented here. Contemporary art is well represented with a series of bold canvases by the likes of Rothko, Pollock, de Kooning, Rauschenberg, Warhol and others. Final rooms are devoted to paintings and multimedia installations by emerging talents.

★★ Carnegie Museum of Natural History – 🧒 Known for its outstanding collection of dinosaur skeletons, this compendium of the sciences holds more than 17 million specimens. In addition to its displays and education programs, the museum is actively involved in research and fieldwork in the earth sciences, life sciences and anthropology.

Visit – *3hrs. Entrance on Forbes Ave. Open same hours as Carnegie Museum of Art. $6 (ticket includes admission to both art and natural history museums).* 🍴 ♿ 🅿 *($1/hr)*

Corbis-Bettmann

■ **Andrew Carnegie**

Born in Dunfermline, Scotland, **Andrew Carnegie** (1835-1919) moved with his family to Allegheny (Pittsburgh's North Side) when he was 13. Since his parents' wages as a weaver and a cobbler's assistant were not sufficient to support the family, Andrew found work first in a cotton factory, then as an engine tender and telegraph messenger and operator. As he began to learn his way around Pittsburgh, he developed a talent for recognizing who was important in the business world. He started working for the Pennsylvania Railroad in 1853, steadily climbing the ladder of success and amassing a small fortune in railroads and oil. In 1865 he quit the railroad and began the Keystone Bridge Company, and by the early 1870s he had settled on steel as the wave of the future. By 1888 Carnegie was the chief owner of Homestead Steel Works, which he consolidated—along with his other steel interests—into Carnegie Steel Company in 1899. When he sold his holdings to U.S. Steel in 1901, Carnegie was far wealthier than any of the other industrialists in the country. He spent the rest of his life as a philanthropist, putting into practice the ideas he espoused in his 1889 essay, "The Gospel of Wealth." He believed that the rich should plow their surplus capital back into the pockets of the general public; in his lifetime Carnegie gave away a total of $350 million.

www.clpgh.org ☎*412-622-3131.* A downstairs **Discovery Room** allows children and adults the chance to handle the kinds of objects they see behind glass on the floors above. First floor exhibits begin with a changing gallery of artwork related to natural history and proceed into the **Hall of Geology**, a lively center decked out with interactive computers, videos and a rock wall with pull-out drawers full of samples from various geologic layers.

Next comes a room full of Paleozoic fossils displayed in life-like dioramas. Through the right-hand door, the **Hall of Minerals and Gems**★ presents more than 1,000 specimens from around the world. This overwhelming gallery begins with informative panels and ends in rooms darkened to intensify dazzling display cases. Among geologic wonders shown here are meteorites, flower-like geodes and a 21in chunk of bright yellow hemimorphite.

Then on to **Dinosaurs**★★ *(docents here offer regular talks).* What makes these 11 skeletons one of the country's best collections is that they consists of 95 percent original fossil material. Arrayed in order of age, the tremendous specimens include a spiny-backed stegosaurus, an 84ft-long diplodocus (the longest animal to have walked the earth), a 20ft-tall tyrannosaurus and a three-horned triceratops. The rooms just beyond contain North American **Fossil Mammals** from the Cenozoic, and **Birds**, a gallery that impresses you with the tremendous abundance and variety of avian life.

On the second floor, the **Hall of African Wildlife**★ opens with a dramatic diorama created in 1867—now-extinct Barbary lions attack a North African nomad on camelback. The adjoining **Hall of North American Wildlife** features sparring Rocky Mountain elk, bear, pronghorns and Dall sheep. In the adjacent **Botany** wing you'll see 17 kinds of fungi, including the fatal destroying angel.

Third-floor exhibits begin with the **Insect** display, which sports rows and rows of bugs and butterflies, including 45 bright-green, jewel-like scarabs. Walk through a long corridor called "Hobby Hall," and you arrive at the **Hall of Ancient Egypt**★, a slick new corner containing video stations, hieroglyphic reliefs from 3000 BC, pottery, and adult and child mummies (300 BC) with x-rays of their skeletons. Neighboring **Polar World** explores arctic life with Inuit artifacts, including soapstone and whalebone carvings, and a walk-in igloo. Due to open in June 1998, the **Hall of American Indians** will display some 1,000 artifacts.

Additional Sights in Oakland

★ **Phipps Conservatory** – *On Schenley Dr. just across the Schenley Park Bridge from The Carnegie. Open year-round Tue–Sun & holidays 9am–5pm. Closed Thanksgiving Day, Dec 25 & prior to flower shows. $5.* ♿ *www.phipps.conservatory.org* ☎*412-622-6914.* A delightful refuge of exotic flora, the 43,500sq ft Victorian glass house opened in 1893 as a gift from Henry Phipps, a childhood neighbor and eventual business partner of Andrew Carnegie. Filling the 13 rooms are tropical palms, miniature orchids, desert plants and ferns. The **Sunken Garden** deserves special mention for its pierced brickwork, hanging baskets and flower-bordered pools splashed from a tall central planter. Tasteful background music complements the plantings. Don't forget to visit the outdoor bonsai collection, as well as the perennials, annuals, herbs and aquatic plants.

★ **Cathedral of Learning** – *On the Quadrangle at Forbes Ave. & Bigelow Blvd. Open year-round Mon–Fri 9am–3pm, Sat 9:30am–3pm, Sun & holidays 11am–3pm. Closed Thanksgiving Day, Dec 24–Jan 1. $2.* ✗ ♿ *www.pitt.edu/~bdobler/rooms/natrooms.html* ☎*412-624-6000.* Oakland's most visible landmark rises 42 stories in Gothic and Art Deco splendor. A monument to education, the stone tower (1937) was designed by Charles Klauder, with ironwork by Samuel Yellin (the same duo that did the Stephen Foster Memorial and Heinz Memorial Chapel), to hold offices and classrooms of the University of Pittsburgh. Though not a cathedral, this building stands up to its name, particularly in the 200ft-long Commons Room, where massive piers soar 60ft up to vaulted ceilings and stone tracery. A chapel-like hush hangs about niches where instead of marble saints, you find students hunched over books.

In the 1930s the university's chancellor invited Pittsburgh's immigrant groups to design rooms reflecting their countries' history, art, traditions and folklore. Audiotape tours *(90min)* of the resulting 24 **Nationality Classrooms**★ *(19 are located on the ground floor; 5 are upstairs on the 3rd floor)* explain architectural styles and ethnic customs. Especially appealing are the Irish Room, which represents a 12C oratory; the red and gold Chinese Room, styled after an 18C reception hall in the Forbidden City; and the Syria-Lebanon Room, boasting the intact library from an

18C villa in Damascus. *Taped tours available at the Information & Nationality Room Gift Center, located on the ground floor near the 5th Ave. entrance.* Take the elevator to the top floor for a great **view**★ of Oakland and environs.

★ **Schenley Park** – *Access via Schenley Dr. or Panther Hollow Rd. Open year-round daily 6am–11pm.* ▣ ☎412-622-6904. Now expanded to 456 acres, one of the city's most beloved greens started in 1889 as a 400-acre gift from expatriate Mary Schenley *(p 336).* Designed by British landscape architect William Falconer, Schenley Park provides a popular venue for local joggers, golfers, tennis players, picnickers and ice-skaters. At the park's northern end, the 1918 **Mary Schenley Fountain [1]** *(across Schenley Park Dr. from Carnegie Library)* is crowned by bronzes of Pan and Harmony. Farther on sits the **Westinghouse Memorial [2]** *(W. Circuit Rd. and Schenley Dr.),* sculpted by Daniel Chester French and Paul Fjelde in 1930. Nestled in a wooded hillside, the memorial includes a tableau inscribed with the many accomplishments of prolific inventor **George Westinghouse** (1846-1914). Also in the park, the one-room **Neil Log House [A]** *(W. Circuit Rd.)* dates back to the late 18C.

Stephen Foster Memorial [B] – *4301 Forbes Ave., in front of the Cathedral of Learning. Open year-round Mon–Fri 9am–4pm.* ☎412-624-4100. Completed in 1937, the Gothic-style structure honors songwriter and Pittsburgh native Stephen Foster (1826-64), known for such folk songs as "O Susanna," "Camptown Races" and "My Old Kentucky Home." A museum displays several of Foster's instruments, copies of his 200 compositions, programs, broadsides and other memorabilia of pop culture from 1850 to the 1930s. Holdings in the research library include more than 30,000 items. A concert hall hosts performances of the University of Pittsburgh's Center for American Music, as well as other programs.

Soldiers and Sailors Memorial Hall – *4141 5th Ave. (at Bigelow Blvd.). Open year-round Mon–Fri 9am–4pm, weekends 1pm–4pm. Closed major holidays.* ♿ ☎412-621-4253. This stately Beaux-Arts **building** (1907), built to heroic scale by Henry Hornbostel, was erected to honor Civil War veterans; it now also pays tribute to veterans of all succeeding American wars. Arranged along the building's four corridors, exhibits contain weapons, uniforms and other military memorabilia, beginning with the Civil War and covering all armed conflicts that the US participated in up to the Gulf War. A 2,500-seat auditorium hosts band concerts and lectures.

★ **Heinz Memorial Chapel** – *5th and S. Bellefield Aves. Open year-round Mon–Fri 9am–4pm, Sun 1pm–5pm. Closed on university holidays.* ♿ ☎412-624-4157. A memorial from H.J. Heinz and his children, this 1938 model of French Gothic elegance rises like a castle 253ft above the ground. The mannerist elongation continues inside with a 93ft ceiling that seems even higher because of the long, narrow nave (146ft) and truncated transept. A carved wood reredos and Numidian marble altar add graceful notes to the front of the church, but the tours de force are the 73ft-high stained-glass windows, whose deep blues create an otherworldly beauty. The 23 windows total 4,000sq ft and contain nearly 250,000 pieces of glass—a fitting tribute from the king of bottlers.

Rodef Shalom Temple – *4905 5th Ave.* Pittsburgh architect Henry Hornbostel, whose works include the Soldiers and Sailors Memorial and Carnegie Mellon University, won a commission to design the 1907 house of worship, a massive presence with its ornamented arched doorway and hulking four-sided dome. Beside the temple, a small biblical garden *(open Jun–Sept Sun–Thu 10am–2pm, Sat noon–1pm;* ♿ ▣ ☎412-621-6566) presents more than 150 kinds of plants.

★★ **The Frick Art and Historical Center** – *7227 Reynolds St. (at S. Homewood Ave. opposite Frick Park). Open year-round Tue–Sat 10am–5:30pm, Sun noon–6pm. Closed major holidays. Combination tickets available.* ✗ ♿ ▣ ☎412-371-0600. This six-acre estate, with its elegantly appointed 23-room Victorian mansion and greenhouse, was the home of industrialist Henry Frick from 1882 to 1905. Today the site also includes an art museum and a car and carriage museum, as well as a museum shop and a cafe serving gourmet meals and high tea.

Henry Clay Frick (1849-1919) grew up near Pittsburgh, and by the age of 21 he was borrowing money to start a coke-making company to supply processed coal to the growing steel industry. He began buying up coal fields during the financial panic of 1873, and by age 30 he had reached his goal of becoming a millionaire. He began traveling to Europe and indulged his passion for art collecting—many of his purchases now hang in The Frick Collection *(p 45)* in New York City. In the 1880s Frick teamed up with Andrew Carnegie, eventually becoming the chairman of Carnegie Steel Co. Whereas Carnegie was known for his exuberance and philanthropy, Frick was considered icy and reserved. A series of reversals left permanent scars on the family, starting with the death of Frick's six-year-old daughter Martha in 1891. The next year, shortly after the Homestead strike, an outraged anarchist burst into Frick's office, shot him twice and stabbed him three times. With utter sangfroid, the bloodied chairman finished his day's work and dictated a letter to the press saying the company would continue its labor policy no matter what. He then went home to recuperate; 11 days later, his new baby boy died. Frick never lost his fabulous wealth, but he did fall out of favor with Carnegie. Shortly before his death, Carnegie reputedly sent a message to Frick asking for a reconciliation. "Tell Mr. Carnegie," Frick replied, "that I'll meet him in Hell." Fourteen years Carnegie's junior, Frick died the same year as his former partner.

Pach/Corbis-Bettmann

Henry Clay Frick

★★ **Clayton** – *Visit by guided tour (1hr) only; tour departs from gift shop. $6. Reservations required 24hrs in advance.* Built just after the Civil War, this Italianate residence was redesigned in the 1890s by Pennsylvania architect Frederick Osterling, who added two stories and 13 rooms to the existing structure. Owned and lived in by Frick's daughter Helen until her death in 1984, the restored house is filled with family furnishings and memorabilia. Tours begin with the entrance foyer, decorated with carved oak paneling and coffers, and matching furniture. The rooms in which guests were entertained were all designed *en suite* and boasted the latest accoutrements of the period, such as faux-leather friezes made of paper, and aluminum-leaf ceilings. In the small but opulent **dining room**, with its tooled leather friezes and built-in buffet, Frick once hosted an eight-course luncheon for President Theodore Roosevelt. After a look through the parlor, kitchen and breakfast room, the tour continues upstairs with the bedrooms of Frick, his wife Adelaide, and daughter Helen, whose long-lasting affection for the house led to its preservation as a museum. In the richly furnished **library and sitting room** hang paintings by Hassam and Monet. The tour ends on the porch with a demonstration of the family's 1890s Swiss orchestrion.

★ **Frick Art Museum** – *412-371-0600.* European works collected by Helen Frick fill the intimate Italian Renaissance-style museum that she had built in 1970 as a gift to the city. The Alabama limestone building, floored with Italian marble, opens to a rotunda surrounded by eight pairs of teakwood columns and decorated with four early-16C Flemish tapestries. Among paintings in this small museum are works from the Italian Renaissance as well as canvases by Rubens, Fragonard and Boucher. A replica French salon holds early-18C decorative arts, including a gilt-bronze mantel clock, an Aubusson tapestry and a tulip-wood candelabra table. Three rooms are reserved for temporary exhibits.

Car and Carriage Museum – *$4; 412-371-0600.* Just behind the art museum, the carriage museum offers further insight into the Fricks' lifestyle by displaying their 15 horse-drawn carriages and such luxuries as a gleaming black 1914 Rolls Royce Silver Ghost and a 1931 Lincoln. A new adjoining classic car collection displays some 35 vintage autos, all owned or manufactured in Pittsburgh between 1890 and 1940.

★ **Pittsburgh Zoo** – 🖼 *Off Butler St. near Highland Park Bridge. Open Memorial Day–Labor Day daily 10am–6pm. Rest of the year daily 9am–5pm. Closed Dec 25. $6.* ✗ ♿ 🄿 *zoo.pgh.pa.us* ☎*412-665-3640.* This 77-acre facility exhibits more than 4,000 animals, representing 400 species. First opened in 1898, the zoo underwent major renovations in the 1980s to create naturalistic environments for its animal population. Today the zoo is engaged in breeding programs and currently displays 39 endangered species. A paved trail leads by every exhibit, beginning with the Asian Forest, with its snow leopards and Siberian tigers, and continuing past the African Savanna, home to lions, zebras, elephants and giraffes. The popular Tropical Forest displays monkeys and gorillas, while an AquaZoo harbors a window for watching the underwater antics of flightless penguins. The most enchanting exhibit area, **Kids Kingdom**, adds adventure to the zoo with raised boardwalks and swinging bridges over various animal habitats. A new play-and-learn **Discovery Pavilion** features permanent interactive exhibits such as the Bat Flyway and Walk-Through Aquarium, and hosts traveling exhibits from national institutions. In addition, educational programs are presented daily in the pavilion's outdoor amphitheater.

EXCURSIONS   *Map p 9*

★ **Old Economy Village** – *2hrs. 15mi northwest of Pittsburgh. Take Rte. 65 north and turn right on 13th St. in Ambridge. Turn left on Church St. to entrance at the corner of Church & 14th Sts. Visit by guided tour (1hr 30min) only, year-round Tue–Sat 9am–5pm, Sun noon–5pm. Closed major holidays (except Memorial Day, Jul 4 & Labor Day). $5.* ☎412-266-4500. Here on a bluff of the Ohio, a Christian communal society called the Harmonists built a village during the 1820s and became widely known for their fine wool, cotton and silk textiles. Originally from Germany, the 800 devout farmers and craftspeople left their homeland to seek religious freedom, settling first in nearby Harmony in 1804; ten years later they moved to Indiana to found New Harmony, then returned in 1824 to this site. After the death of their leader, Father George Rapp, in 1847, the society dwindled. Its celibate members finally disbanded in 1905. Informative tours led by costumed guides begin with a 20min video, then take in the 17 buildings remaining from a spread that once covered 3,000 acres. High points include the Feast Hall, a long two-story building where the Harmonists held holiday "love feasts"; a well-stocked general store (goods were free to society members); a typical household; a wine cellar; the European-style formal garden; and Father Rapp's house, in which the society's gold was once stashed.

★ **Hartwood** – *1½hrs. 15mi northeast of Pittsburgh. Take Rte. 28 North to Exit 5B. Travel north on Rte. 8 1mi to Saxonburg Blvd., turn right and continue to Hartwood Acres County Park, 5.5mi on left. Visit of house by guided tour (1hr) only, year-round Wed–Sat 10am–3pm, Sun noon–4pm. Closed major holidays. $3. Reservations required one week in advance.* 🅿 ☎412-767-9200. A rolling 629-acre park in the foothills of the Alleghenies provides the magnificent **setting**★ for this re-creation of a 16C Tudor-style manor house constructed of Indiana limestone and roofed with Vermont slate. Son-in-law and daughter of industrialist and US Senator William Flinn, John and Mary Lawrence built their dream house in 1929 and lived a fantasy life of no-holds-barred decorating, gardening, entertaining and riding to the hounds. Even the stables, with their wood paneling and brass hardware, show spit-shine polish and sophistication. Among European and American antiques original to the mansion are a 1620 carved oak chimneypiece, a large 1890 Bijar Persian rug, and a 1901 mahogany Steinway grand piano.

Washington – *½ day. 25mi south of Pittsburgh via I-79.* Laid out in 1780, this compact town of hills and Greek Revival houses is the home of Washington and Jefferson College (1793). Designed by Frederick Osterling in 1900, the ebullient Neoclassical **Washington County Courthouse** (*Courthouse Sq. on Main St.*) boasts a curved, columned portico, a triple-arched entrance, and a dome topped by a bronze of George Washington. Inside, the ceiling rises 60ft to a stained-glass skylight. The **Duncan Miller Glass Museum** (*525 Jefferson Ave.;* ☎412-225-9950) displays 1,500 pieces of fine-pressed and hand-blown glass near the site of a 19C glassmaking company.

Bradford House – *175 S. Main St. Visit by guided tour (1hr) only, May–mid-Dec Wed–Sat 11am–4pm, Sun 1pm–4pm. Closed major holidays. $4.* 🅿 ☎412-222-3604. Prominent lawyer and landowner David Bradford built this two-story Federal-style house in 1788. A few years later, as leader of the Whiskey Rebellion, he was robbing mail carriers and calling for secession to protest the new tax on whiskey. High on the most-wanted list, Bradford fled to New Orleans in 1794, returning seven years later to sell his house and gather up his family. The first stone house in town, this National Historic Landmark showcases fine woodwork, 18C furnishings and a small garden.

LeMoyne House – *49 E. Maiden St. Visit by guided tour (1hr) only, Feb–mid-Dec Tue–Fri 11am–4pm, weekends & holidays noon–4pm. $4. www.camconet.com/lemoyne* ☎412-225-6740. Home of the Washington County Historical Society, this early Greek Revival structure (1812) was built by Dr. John LeMoyne and became the residence of his son Francis, a physician as well as an ardent abolitionist. Tours cover the in-house apothecary shop/doctor's office, which displays 19C surgical equipment, medicinal herbs, and ashes from the country's first crematory, established near here by Francis. One upstairs room contains artifacts commemorating military history. And fugitive slaves were once hidden in the bedroom across the hall in this National Historic Landmark for the Underground Railroad.

West Overton Museums – *40mi southeast of Pittsburgh between Mount Pleasant and Scottdale. Take I-376 west to Rte. 30 east to the Pennsylvania turnpike (I-76). Take the turnpike east to Exit 8 at New Stanton and follow Rte. 119 south 10mi to Rte. 819. Go south on Rte. 819, approximately .5mi to museum. Open mid-May–Oct Tue–Sat 10am–4pm, Sun 1pm–5pm. Closed major holidays. $3.* ⚒ & 🅿 ☎412-887-7910. Featuring a restored, early-19C homestead and a former whiskey distillery (1859) now filled with regional antiques, this site is best known as the humble birthplace of millionaire industrialist **Henry Clay Frick** *(p 340)*. Frick's great-grandfather, Henry Overholt, a German Mennonite, established a farming community here in 1800; in the 1830s Frick's grandfather, Abraham Overholt, built the three-story brick home and distillery/gristmill that stand today. A 20min film, shown in the distillery, explains the coke-making process and tells the story of Frick's rise to prominence. A vast assortment of domestic implements and industrial/agricultural tools occupies two floors of the red-brick structure. Also open to the public are the tiny 1803 stone springhouse in which Frick was born and several rooms of the neighboring Overholt homestead, each restored to a different historical period.

■ **Western Pennsylvania Industry**

If any region can claim to be the birthplace of the American industrial revolution, Western Pennsylvania can. In the mid-1800s, Pittsburgh was pumping out iron and steel in mass quantities, the Civil War proving big business for the area's 50 iron foundries and factories.

With the mills clanging in Steel City, an even more important story was quietly unfolding 100mi north in the small lumber town of Titusville. Locals had long known of the "rock oil" (petroleum) in their creek. The strong-smelling oil had been bottled for medicine, and early experiments had proved it could be used for fuel. But no one had imagined a world run by oil, because getting it out of the ground in massive quantities seemed impossible. Then, in 1857, the Seneca Oil Company of Connecticut sent a 38-year-old former railroad conductor named Edwin Drake out to Titusville to try to boost the output. After failed attempts to hire well drillers, Drake finally struck on William Smith, a blacksmith and salt-well driller from near Pittsburgh. Improvising machinery as they went, the two tapped a deposit of oil at 67ft in 1859, and the world's first oil well began to flow.

The **Drake Well Museum**★★ *(off Rte. 8S in Titusville; open May–Oct Mon–Sat 9am–5pm, Sun noon–5pm; rest of the year closed Mon; $4;* & 🅿 ☎814-827-2797*)*, located alongside Oil Creek at the site of that first well, honors Drake's achievement. A 1954 film *(27min)*, with Vincent Price playing Edwin Drake, brings to life the story of perseverance against the odds. More than 70 exhibits detail the formation of oil, drilling, refining and the uses of oil. Among the many displays on the grounds, a working replica of Drake's derrick uses a steam engine to pump recirculating oil. The original well went dry in 1861, two years after Drake struck it.

Not far south, **Pithole City** *(off Rte. 227, 4mi northeast of Plumer; open Jun–Aug Wed noon–5pm, Thu–Sun 10am–5pm; $2.50;* 🅿 ☎814-589-7912*)* was an oil boomtown of 15,000 people in 1865. Within two years, the frenzy had moved elsewhere, leaving a bare shell. The remaining cellar holes and abandoned wells evoke the ghosts of that era. By the 1890s, Pennsylvania's oil production had peaked and began giving way to richer wells in the West.

ERIE★

Population 105,270
Maps p 9 and pp344-345
Tourist Information www.erie.net/~chamber ☎814-454-7191

As early as 1753, Europeans recognized the value of Presque Isle, the peninsula that hooks into Lake Erie and forms the best natural harbor on the Great Lakes. In that year the French built forts on the peninsula and at Le Boeuf (present-day Waterford, to the south). Within six years, during the French and Indian War, the British had driven the French out. In 1795 the Commonwealth of Pennsylvania bought the land making up Erie County from the US government, thereby gaining a foothold in the growing Great Lakes commerce. The town of Erie began spreading out along the shore of the protected harbor and soon became a major shipbuilding center. Shifting from the waterfront to the railroads in the late 19C, Erie branched out into metalworking and other industries. As you drive along 12th Street from I-79, you pass endless brick warehouses from that era. Manufacturing continues to support the local economy with General Electric's locomotive plant and many plastics companies, and the rising tourism trade is slowly turning the bayfront into a year-round attraction. A new 187ft **observation tower** at **Dobbins Landing** *(foot of State St.)* offers fine views of Presque Isle Bay, and the new **Erie Maritime Museum** *(150 E. Front St.; open year-round Mon–Fri 9am–5pm; closed major holidays; admission fee; ✕ & ▣ ☎814-452-2744)*, preserves Pennsylvania's Great Lakes maritime history. A bayfront hotel and shopping area are slated to be added in the near future. Just up the main drag of **State Street** you'll find restaurants, museums, historic buildings and houses, and the charming green of **Perry Square**.

SIGHTS *1 day. Map p 345.*

Erie Art Museum – *411 State St. Open year-round Tue–Sat 11am–5pm, Sun 1pm–5pm. $1.50. www.erie. net/~erieartm* ☎814-459-5477. Fluted columns and marble steps grace this 1839 Greek Revival building that served as a branch of the US Bank of Pennsylvania. Now housing temporary exhibitions of regional photographers, painters, sculptors and other artists, the museum also exhibits a permanent soft sculpture installation, *The Avalon Restaurant*, an endearing piece of local color by Lisa Lichtenfels.

★ **Erie Historical Museum** – *356 W. 6th St. Open Jun–Aug Tue–Fri 10am–5pm, weekends 1pm–5pm. Rest of the year Tue–Sun 1pm–5pm. Closed major holidays & last 2 weeks in Jan. $2.* ▣

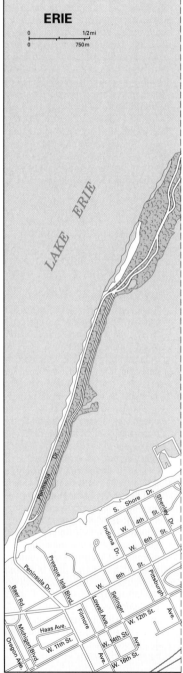

☎814-871-5790. Industrialist Harrison F. Watson had this dark stone pile built in the Richardsonian Romanesque style in 1889-91. The 24-room mansion now showcases upper-class life in late-19C Erie. Self-guided tours begin in the main hall, an elegant preface of oak paneling, gold mosaics and a coffered ceiling. Other rooms show off stained glass, marble fireplaces, fine woodwork and original antiques. A downstairs display on maritime Erie includes paintings, models and ships' artifacts, and the third-floor ballroom boasts a musicians' gallery and rotating exhibits of paintings by local artist Eugene Iverd, whose work adorned many *Saturday Evening Post* covers in the 1920s and 30s.

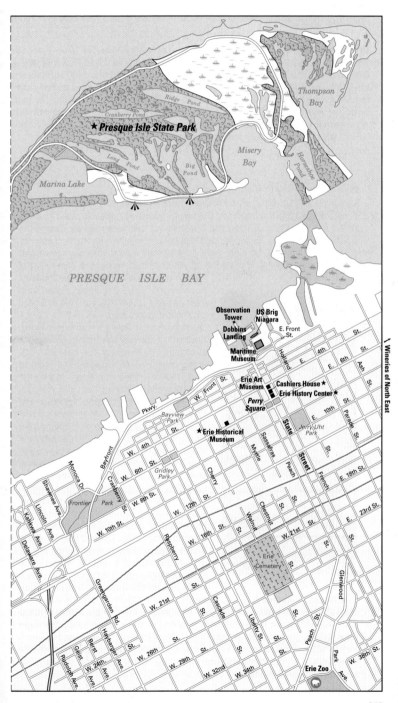

In the mansion's carriage house, the planetarium presents a variety of programs on astronomical themes *(year-round Sun 2pm & 3pm; $2)*.

★ **Erie History Center** – *419 State St. Open year-round Tue–Sat 9am–5pm. Contribution requested.* & ☎*814-454-1813*. An 1840 commercial building, renovated in 1992 for the headquarters of the Erie County Historical Society, offers informative exhibits on shipping, industry and architecture. The center includes the adjacent **Cashiers House**★, an 1839 Greek Revival town house once occupied by the chief officer of the bank next door (now the Erie Art Museum). Short tours take in the formal front rooms, with 14.5ft ceilings, then the more modest dining room and upstairs Victorian bedrooms. A museum since the 1970s, the home has also served as a boarding house and a girls' school *(visit by 30min guided tour only year-round Tue–Sat 1pm–4pm;* & ☎*814-454-1813)*.

Erie Zoo – 🄺🄸🄳🄼 *423 W. 38th St. Open May–Labor Day Mon–Sat 10am–5pm, Sun 10am–6pm. Rest of the year daily 10am–5pm. Closed Jan 1, Dec 25. $4.75.* ✗ & 🅿 ☎*814-864-6272*. A small but pleasant 15-acre park displays more than 400 animals representing some 110 species. Among the dozen endangered species are red-ruffed lemurs, white tigers and western lowland gorillas. Recently renovated, the main building features tropical plants and glassed-off views of African animals. A perennial favorite, the **Children's Zoo** area holds pygmy goats, wallabies, pot-bellied pigs, Mouflon sheep and arctic foxes.

■ Wineries of North East

A tradition for 150 years, area viticulture owes its existence to the unique micro-climate of Lake Erie's south shore. Cold winds from the frozen lake make for a late spring and virtually guarantee that buds will not open prematurely. During the growing season, the summer-warmed lake helps delay the early frosts of autumn, giving the shore up to 30 days more growing time than farms only a few miles south. Though Prohibition put a halt to wine-making, the Limited Winery Act of

© Robert Holmes

1968 brought new ferment to the industry. Accordingly, wines must be made from Pennsylvania-grown fruit and sold in limited quantities and locations.

Driving up scenic Route 5 from Erie to **North East**, you'll see row after row of grapevines stretching into the distance—nearly 14,000 acres of vineyards. Growers sell most of their produce—Concord grapes—to the local Welch's processing plant. But some of these, as well as other American varietals and French hybrids, end up in North East's wineries. Of the 30 to 40 kinds of grapes grown locally, natives include Cayuga, Catawba and Niagara; among European vinifera that do well here are Chardonnay, Pinot Noir and Riesling. More than a dozen wineries line the shore of Lake Erie, four of them in North East. All have gift shops and offer free tours and tastings. Tours cover the wine-making process from harvesting to crushing and stemming, fermenting and bottling. Opened in 1968, **Penn Shore Winery** *(12mi east of Erie on Rte. 5;* ☎*814-725-8688)* is one of the largest in the state, bottling up to 15,000 gallons of wine a year. Just up the road, the Mediterranean-style **Mazza Vineyards** *(11815 E. Lake Rd.;* ☎*814-725-8695)* offers a slide show and 15 to 20 kinds of wine, including champagne and ice wine (a sweet wine made from grapes that are harvested once they freeze late in the season). **Heritage Wine Cellars** *(I-90 and Rte. 20;* ☎*814-725-8015)* dates its family-owned fruit farm back to 1833; among its products are several fruit and dessert wines. **Presque Isle Wine Cellars** *(5mi west of North East on Rte. 20;* ☎*814-725-1314)* specializes in supplies for home winemakers.

US Brig Niagara – *Berthed along the north facade of the Erie Maritime Museum (p 344). Often not in port; call for schedule.* 🅿 ☎814-452-2744. The seaworthy brig is a reconstruction of the square-rigged, two-masted warship that formed part of Commodore Oliver Hazard Perry's fleet when he defeated the British in the Battle of Lake Erie in 1813. His famous report followed the battle: "We have met the enemy and they are ours." Scuttled in Misery Bay, the ship was raised in 1913 and rebuilt in celebration of the victory's centennial. Some original timbers were used in the 1990 reconstruction. Guided 45min tours cover the decks, quarters and nautical equipment.

Presque Isle State Park

★ **Presque Isle State Park** – *Access via Peninsula Dr. Open Memorial Day–Labor Day daily 5am–11pm. Rest of the year daily 5am–9pm.* ✗ ♿ 🅿 *www.presqueisle.com* ☎814-833-7424. Comprising 3,200 acres on the thumb of land jutting into Lake Erie, this gorgeous park is named for its geography—Presque Isle means "almost an island" in French. Red fox, white-tailed deer, great blue heron and many other animals roam its woods and shoreline. While beaches front the lake, several miles of hiking and jogging trails rim the bay side and lace the interior. Numerous turnouts give motorists the chance to get out and enjoy splendid **views**★ of water and the Erie skyline. Summer swimming and windsurfing give way in winter to cross-country skiing, ice fishing and skating on a frozen lake. A **nature center** houses exhibits on flora and fauna.

Practical Information

Calendar of Events

Listed below is a selection of the most popular events in New York, New Jersey and Pennsylvania. Some dates may vary from year to year. For detailed information, contact local tourism offices (☎ numbers listed under individual entry headings) or the state tourism offices (*p 352*).

Date	Event	Location
Spring		
early Mar	**Flower Show Week**	*Philadelphia, PA*
mid-Mar	**St. Patrick's Day Parade**	*New York City, NY*
late Mar	**Pennsylvania National Arts & Crafts Show**	*Harrisburg, PA*
mid-Apr	**Spring Festival** (*p 191*)	*Cape May, NJ*
late Apr	**Shad Festival**	*Lambertville, NJ*
late Apr–mid-May	**Philadelphia Open House**	*Philadelphia, PA*
early May	**Bach Festival** (*p 290*)	*Bethlehem, PA*
	Hudson River White Water Derby	*North Creek, NY*
May–Jun	**Music Festival** (*p 191*)	*Cape May, NJ*
mid-May	**Lilac Festival** (*p 159*)	*Rochester, NY*
	Spring Festival	*Naples, NY*
late May	**Mayfair Festival of the Arts**	*Allentown, PA*

Rhinebeck Dutchess County Fairgrounds – © Scott Barrow

Date	Event	Location
Summer		
Memorial Day–Labor Day	**Festival of Fountains** (*p 255*)	*Kennett Square, PA*
Memorial Day weekend	**Irish Festival**	*East Durham, NY*
	Jam on the River	*Philadelphia, PA*
early Jun	**Belmont Stakes**	*Belmont, NY*
	Syracuse Jazzfest (*p 141*)	*Syracuse, NY*
	Riverfest	*Red Bank, NJ*
mid-Jun	**Allentown Art Festival**	*Buffalo, NY*
	Antique Festival	*Kinderhook, NY*
	Fresh Seafood Festival	*Atlantic City, NJ*
late Jun	**Cherry Fair**	*Schaefferstown, PA*
	Heritage Days Festival	*Towanda, PA*
	National Quilting Show	*Syracuse, NY*
	The Season at Chautauqua (*p 152*)	*Chatauqua, NY*
	US Equestrian Team Festival of Champions	*Gladstone, NJ*
late Jun–early Jul	**Lake Placid Horse Show**	*Lake Placid, NY*
	Oswego County Fair	*Sandy Creek, NY*
	Pennsylvania Dutch Kutztown Folk Festival	*Summit Station, PA*
July 4	**Fourth of July Celebration**	*Pittsburgh, PA*
Jul-Aug	**Glimmerhouse Opera Festival** (*p 96*)	*Cooperstown, NY*
	Racing Season (*p 119*)	*Saratoga Springs, NY*

mid-Jul	Corn Hill Arts Festival	*Rochester, NY*
	Duck, Decoy & Wildlife Art Show	*Clayton, NY*
	French Festival	*Cape Vincent, NY*
	Taste of Buffalo	*Buffalo, NY*
	The Return to Beaver Creek Pow-Wow	*Belvidere, NJ*
late Jul	Empire State Games	*Albany, NY*
	Festival of Ballooning	*Readington, NJ*
	St. Ann's Italian Festival	*Hoboken, NJ*
early Aug	Antique Boat Show	*Clayton, NY*
	Antique Festival	*Old Chatham, NY*
	Bluegrass Ramble	*Sandy Creek, NY*
	Hambletonian Day	*East Rutherford, NJ*
	Riverside Festival	*Coxsackie, NY*
	Rodeo	*Gerry, NY*
	Sussex County Farm & Horse Show	*Augusta, NJ*
mid-Aug	Dutchess County Fair	*Rhinebeck, NY*
	Musikfest *(p 290)*	*Bethlehem, PA*
	Washington County Agricultural Fair	*Washington, PA*
late Aug	Columbia County Fair	*Chatham, NY*
	Hampton Classic Horse Show	*Bridgehampton, NY*
	Scottish Festival	*Amherst, NY*
	Travers Stakes	*Saratoga Springs, NY*
late Aug– early Sept	Polish American Festival	*Doylestown, PA*
	Arts & Crafts Fair	*Danville, PA*
Labor Day weekend	Celebration of the Arts	*Delaware Water Gap, PA*
	Fiddle and Folk Music Festival	*Stony Brook, NY*
	Great Allentown Fair	*Allentown, PA*
	Hoss's Keystone Country Festival	*Altoona, PA*
	Long's Park Art & Craft Festival	*Lancaster, PA*
	Pennsylvania Arts & Crafts Colonial Festival	*Greensburg, PA*
	Wild Wind Folk Art & Craft Festival	*Pittsfield, PA*

Fall

Sept	Miss America Pageant *(p 188)*	*Atlantic City, NJ*
mid-Sept	Adirondack Antiques Show	*Blue Mountain Lake, NY*
	Irish Festival	*Pittsburgh, PA*
	Niagara County "Fall Classic" Fishing Derby	*Lake Ontario, NY*
late Sept	Adirondack Balloon Festival	*Glen Falls, NY*
	Old Time Barnegat Bay Decoy & Gunning Show	*Tuckerton, NJ*
	Penn's Colony Festival	*Pittsburgh, PA*
	Revolutionary Times at Brandywine	*Chadds Ford, PA*
	Wings'N Water Festival	*Stone Harbor, NJ*
Oct–Nov	Water Color Club Exhibit	*Wallingford, PA*
early Oct	Applefest	*Warwick, NY*
	Flaming Foliage Festival	*Renovo, PA*
	Folk Festival	*Springs, PA*
	Pennsylvania National Horse Show	*Harrisburg, PA*
mid-Oct	Letchworth Arts & Crafts Show	*Letchworth State Park, Castile, NY*
	Pumpkin Days	*Media, PA*
	Shawnee Festival	*Shawnee on Delaware, PA*
	Victorian Week *(p 191)*	*Cape May, NJ*
early Nov	Apple Festival	*Lahaska, PA*
	New York City Marathon	*New York City, NY*

Winter

mid-Nov–Jan	Magic of the Season	*Pittsburgh, PA*
Thanksgiving Day	Macy's Thanksgiving Day Parade	*New York City, NY*
	Run for the Diamonds	*Berwick, PA*
late Nov	Christmas Parade	*Greenville, PA*
	Festival of the Trees	*Erie, PA*
early Dec	Lighting of the Giant Christmas Tree	*New York City, NY*
mid-Dec	Candlelight House Tour	*Harrisburg, PA*
Dec 25	George Washington Crossing the Delaware	*Titusville, PA*
Dec 31	New Years Eve Celebration	*New York City, NY*
Jan 1	Mummers Parade *(p 236)*	*Philadelphia, PA*
early Jan	Pennsylvania State Farm Show	*Harrisburg, PA*
mid-Jan	Ice Classic Carving Competition	*White Haven, PA*
	Winterfest	*Forksville, PA*
early Feb	Winter Carnival	*Pawling, NY*
	Winter Carnival	*Saranac Lake, NY*
Feb 2	Groundhog Day	*Punxsutawney, PA*
last week in Feb	Flower & Garden Show	*Somerset, NJ*

The following symbols are used throughout this section:

⑨ **New York**   ⑩ **New Jersey**   ⑫ **Pennsylvania**

Consult the pages shown for detailed practical information about the following areas:

Adirondacks *(pp 108-109)*; **Allegany State Park** *(p 144)*; **Cape May** *(p 192)*; **Catskills** *(p 70)*; **Delaware Water Gap National Recreation Area** *(p 268)*; **Gettysburg** *(p 294)*; **Harrisburg** *(p 298)*; **Hudson River Valley** *(p 77)*; **Laurel Highlands & Southern Alleghenies** *(pp 312-313)*; **New York City** *(pp 22-23)*; **Niagara Falls** *(p 154)*; **Pennsylvania Dutch Country** *(p 276)*; **Philadelphia** *(pp 224-225)*; **Pine Barrens** *(p 198)*; **Pittsburgh** *(pp 324-325)*; **Pocono Mountains** *(p 264)*; and **Thousand Islands** *(p 123)*.

Planning Your Trip

Tourist Information

State tourism offices provide information and brochures on points of interest, seasonal events and accommodations, as well as road and city maps. Local tourist offices (telephone numbers and Websites listed under each blue entry heading in the text) provide additional information, free-of-charge, regarding accommodations, shopping, entertainment, festivals and recreation.

State	Tourism Office	☎
⑨	**Empire State Development** Travel Information Center One Commerce Plaza Albany NY 12245	518-474-4116 *or* 800-225-5697 iloveny.state.ny.us
⑩	**New Jersey Division of Travel & Tourism** CN 826 20 W. State St. Trenton NJ 08625	609-292-2470 *or* 800-537-7397 www.state.nj.us/travel
⑫	**Pennsylvania Department of Community & Economic Development** Office of Travel, Tourism & Film Promotion Room 404, Forum Building Harrisburg PA 17120	717-787-5453 *or* 800-847-4872 www.state.pa.us

Tips for Special Visitors

Children – *In this guide, sights of particular interest to children are indicated with a* 🧒 *symbol.* Many of these attractions offer special children's programs. Most attractions offer discounted (if not free) admission to visitors under 12 years of age. In addition, many hotels and resorts boast special family discount packages, and some restaurants provide a special children's menu.

Travelers with Disabilities – *Full wheelchair access to sights described in this guide is indicated in admission information by* &. Federal law requires that existing businesses (including hotels and restaurants) increase accessibility and provide specially designed accommodations for the disabled. It also requires that wheelchair access, devices for the hearing impaired, and designated parking spaces be available at newly constructed hotels and restaurants. Many public buses are equipped with wheelchair lifts; many hotels have rooms designed for visitors with special needs. All national and most state **parks** have restrooms and other facilities for the disabled (such as wheelchair-accessible nature trails). Many attractions can make special arrangements for disabled visitors.

Passengers who will need assistance should give 24-48hrs advance notice; also contact the following transportation providers to request their informative literature for riders with disabilities:

Amtrak / *Access Amtrak*	☎800-872-7245 (TDD) 800-523-6590
Greyhound / *Greyhound Travel Policies*	☎800-231-2222 (TDD) 800-345-3109
New Jersey Transit / *Guide to Accessible Service*	☎201-762-5100 (TT) 800-772-2287

Reservations for hand-controlled cars at rental companies should be made well in advance. For information about travel for individuals or groups, contact the Society for Advancement of Travel for the Handicapped, 347 Fifth Ave., Suite 610, New York NY 10016 ☎212-447-7284; or Access-Able Travel Source's Website: www.access-able.com.

Senior Citizens – Many hotels, attractions and restaurants offer discounts to visitors age 62 or older (proof of age may be required). For further information, contact the American Association of Retired Persons, 601 E St. N.W., Washington DC 20049; www.aarp.org ☎202-434-2277.

When to go

The states of New York, New Jersey and Pennsylvania offer a diverse climate that is determined by elevation and proximity to the ocean and to the Great Lakes. Most attractions in major cities are open year-round.

The Seasons – A brief and generally unpredictable season, **spring** brings a mixture of warm days and cold nights. Snow remains a possibility (especially in the higher elevations) well into April. Many sights remain closed until mid-April or early May. **Summer** in the Adirondacks, Catskills and Pocono mountains tends to be comfortable and warm with temperatures averaging in the low to mid-70s; bring a light jacket or sweater for the cool evenings. In the lower elevations and along the

Temperature Chart

	January avg. high	avg. low	precip.	June avg. high	avg. low	precip.
🗽 **New York**						
Buffalo	30°F (-1°C)	17°F (-8°C)	3.0in (7.6cm)	75°F (24°C)	56°F (13°C)	2.7in (6.8cm)
New York City	37°F (3°C)	26°F (-3°C)	3.1in (7.9cm)	79°F (26°C)	63°F (17°C)	3.5in (8.9cm)
Poughkeepsie	34°F (1°C)	15°F (-9°C)	2.7in (6.9cm)	79°F (26°C)	56°F (13°C)	3.4in (8.6cm)
Rochester	31°F (-1°C)	16°F (-9°C)	2.3in (5.8cm)	82°F (28°C)	60°F (16°C)	2.5in (6.4cm)
Syracuse	31°F (-1°C)	15°F (-9°C)	2.6in (6.6cm)	82°F (28°C)	60°F (16°C)	3.8in (9.7cm)
Tupper Lake	25°F (-4°C)	3°F (-16°C)	2.5in (6.4cm)	73°F (23°C)	49°F (9°C)	3.5in (8.9cm)
🗽 **New Jersey**						
Atlantic City	40°F (5°C)	28°F (-2°C)	3.2in (8.1cm)	74°F (23°C)	62°F (17°C)	2.9in (7.4cm)
Cape May	41°F (5°C)	27°F (-3°C)	3.3in (8.4cm)	78°F (26°C)	61°F (16°C)	3.1in (7.9cm)
Newark	38°F (3°C)	24°F (-4°C)	3.1in (7.9cm)	80°F (27°C)	62°F (17°C)	2.9in (7.4cm)
🗽 **Pennsylvania**						
Bethlehem	35°F (2°C)	19°F (-7°C)	3.3in (8.4cm)	80°F (27°C)	58°F (14°C)	3.4in (8.6cm)
Erie	31°F (-1°C)	18°F (-8°C)	2.5in (6.4cm)	74°F (23°C)	55°F (13°C)	3.7in (9.4cm)
Harrisburg	37°F (3°C)	22°F (-8°C)	3.0in (7.6cm)	82°F (28°C)	65°F (18°C)	3.3in (8.4cm)
Philadelphia	39°F (4°C)	24°F (-4°C)	3.2in (8.1cm)	82°F (28°C)	62°F (17°C)	3.9in (9.9cm)
Pittsburgh	34°F (1°C)	19°F (-7°C)	3.0in (7.6cm)	79°F (26°C)	57°F (14°C)	3.8in (9.7cm)
State College	33°F (0°C)	18°F (-8°C)	2.6in (6.6cm)	78°F (26°C)	57°F (14°C)	3.7in (9.4cm)

Atlantic Coast, summer days are considerably warmer and humid. The summer season, from Memorial Day through Labor Day, brings an increased number of tourists to attractions and accommodations. Advance reservations are recommended. Most sights offer expanded summer hours.

Blazing **autumn** colors start in the higher elevations in late September and work their way down along the coastal areas through early November. Foliage reports track the procession of color. Autumn days are pleasantly mild and give way to cool nights. Hints of the impending winter may appear with the occasional early frost. Many attractions located in smaller towns operate with an abbreviated schedule, closing for the season at the end of October.

Winter typically lasts from mid-November into April. Southeastern Pennsylvania and southern New Jersey receive the least amount of snow—less than 36 inches a year. Central Pennsylvania and northern New Jersey can count on some 36-60 inches of snow a year. And in western Pennsylvania and upstate New York, an average of 60-100 inches of snow falls each winter. Lake-effect storms hit areas along Lake Erie and Lake Ontario, bringing some of the heaviest snowfalls in the three-state region (over 100 inches annually). All this snow attracts a host of skiers and other winter-sports enthusiasts to the nearly 100 ski resorts (p 368) in the three-state area. Opportunities also abound for ice-skating and snowmobiling. Many attractions normally closed during the winter offer special events during the Christmas holidays.

International Visitors

Planning the Trip

Visitors from outside the US can obtain information from tourism agencies (p 352), or from the nearest US embassy or consulate in their country of residence. Many countries have consular offices in New York City and Philadelphia.

Entry Requirements – Citizens of countries participating in the Visa Waiver Pilot Program (VWPP) are not required to obtain a visa to enter the US for visits of less than 90 days. For a list of countries participating in the VWPP, contact the US embassy or consulate in your country of residence. Citizens of non-participating countries must obtain a visa. Upon entry, non-resident foreign visitors must present a valid passport and round-trip transportation ticket. Canadian citizens are not required to present a passport, although identification and proof of citizenship may be requested (the best proof of citizenship is a passport, but a Canadian birth certificate and photo ID are usually acceptable). Naturalized Canadian citizens should carry their citizenship papers. Inoculations are generally not required, but check with the US embassy or consulate before departing.

Customs – All articles brought into the US must be declared at the time of entry. The following items are **exempt** from customs regulations: personal effects; one liter of alcoholic beverage (providing visitor is at least 21 years old); either 200 cigarettes, 50 cigars or 2 kilograms of smoking tobacco; and gifts (to persons in the US) that do not exceed $100 in value. **Prohibited items**: plant materials, firearms and ammunition (if not intended for sporting purposes) and meat and poultry products. For further information regarding US Customs, contact the US embassy or consulate before departing. Visitors should also contact the customs service in their country to determine reentry regulations.

Health Insurance – The United States does not have a national health program. Before departing, check with your insurance company to determine if your medical insurance covers doctors' visits, medication and hospitalization in the US. Prescription drugs should be properly identified and accompanied by a copy of the prescription.

Getting Around by Car – Visitors bearing a valid driver's license issued by their country of residence are not required to obtain an International Driver's License to drive in the US. Drivers must carry vehicle registration and/or rental contract and proof of automobile insurance at all times. Rental cars in the US are usually equipped with automatic transmission, and rental rates tend to be less expensive than overseas. **Gasoline** is sold by the gallon (1 US gallon = 3.8 liters) and is cheaper than in most other countries. Gas stations are usually found in clusters on the edge of a city, or where two or more highways intersect. Self-service gas stations do not offer car repair, although many sell standard maintenance items. **Road regulations**

(p 358) in the US require that vehicles be driven on the right side of the road. Distances are posted in miles *(1 mile = 1.6 kilometers)*. Travelers are advised to heed posted speed-limit signs.

Selected US Embassies ☎

Australia	Moonah Place, Yaraluma ACT 2600 APO AP 965 49	(61) 2-6270-5000
Canada	100 Wellington St., Ottawa ON K1P 5T1	613-238-4470
France	2, ave. Gabriel 75008 Paris, France PSC 116 B210 APO AE 09777	(33) 1-43-12-22-22
Germany	Deichmanns Aue 29 D-53170 Bonn, Germany	(49) 0228-339-1
Japan	1-10-5, Akasaka, Minato-ku 107 Unit 45004, Box 258, APO AP 96337-0001	(81) 3-3224-5000
Mexico	Paseo de la Reforma 305 Colonia Cuauhtemoc, 06500 Mexico	(52) 5-211-0042
United Kingdom	24 Grosvenor Square, United Kingdom W1A 1AE PSC 801 Box 40, FPO AE 09498-4040	(44) 71-499-9000

Basic Information

Currency Exchange, Credit Cards & Travelers Checks – Most main offices of national banks will exchange **foreign currency** and charge a small fee for this service; contact main or branch offices for exchange information and locations. Philadelphia International Airport, Pittsburgh International Airport, John F. Kennedy International Airport and LaGuardia Airport all have currency exchange offices. Almost all US banks are members of the network of **Automated Teller Machines** (ATM), allowing visitors from around the world to withdraw cash using bank cards and major credit cards. ATMs are located at banks, airports, train stations and some tourist attractions. Check with your bank before departing to obtain a Personal Identification Number (PIN); transaction fees may be charged to your account. Most banks will cash **travelers checks** and process cash advances on major credit cards; you must provide proper identification. Travelers checks are accepted at most stores, restaurants and hotels. To report a lost or stolen **credit card**: American Express ☎800-528-4800; Diners Club ☎800-234-6377; MasterCard ☎800-627-8372 (or the issuing bank); Visa ☎800-339-8472.

1 penny = 1 cent   10 dollar bill   1 dollar bill = 100 cents   dime = 10 cents   5 dollar bill   nickel = 5 cents   quarter = 25 cents   20 dollar bill

Electricity – Voltage in the US is 120 volts AC, 60Hz. Foreign-made appliances may need AC adapters (available at specialty travel and electronics stores) and North American flat-blade plugs.

Mail – First-class postage rates within the US: letter 32¢ (1oz); postcard 20¢. Overseas postage: letter 60¢ (1/2oz); postcard 50¢. Letters and small packages can be mailed from most hotels. Stamps and packing material can be purchased at post offices, grocery stores and businesses offering postal and express-shipping services. Most post offices are open Monday–Friday 9am–5pm. *See yellow pages of the phone directory under "Mailing Services" or "Post Offices."*

Telephones/Telegrams – In case of an **emergency** (police, fire, ambulance), dial **911**. For **long-distance** calls in the US and Canada, dial 1+area code+number. To place an **international call**, dial 011+country code+area code+number. Most hotels add a surcharge for local and long-distance calls. Telephone numbers that start with **800** or **888** are toll-free *(no charge)* and may not be accessible outside North America. The charge for numbers preceded by **900** can range anywhere from 50¢-$15/minute. Instructions for using **public telephones** are listed on or near the phone. Some public telephones accept credit cards, and all will accept long-distance calling cards. The cost for a local call from a pay phone is typically 25¢-35¢ *(fees vary regionally; use any combination of nickels, dimes or quarters).* You can send a **telegram** or wire money, or have money wired to you, via the Western Union system ☎800-325-6000.

Temperature and Measurement – In the US, temperatures are measured in degrees Fahrenheit and measurements are expressed according to the US Customary System of weights and measures.

Equivalents

Degrees Fahrenheit:	95°	86°	77°	68°	59°	50°	41°	32°	23°	14°
Degrees Celsius:	35°	30°	25°	20°	15°	10°	5°	0°	-5°	-10°

1 inch = 2.54 centimeters
1 foot = 30.48 centimeters
1 mile = 1.609 kilometers

1 pound = 0.454 kilogram
1 gallon = 3.785 liters
1 quart = 0.946 liter

Time Zone – *p 360.*

Getting There & Getting Around

By Air – Airports, receiving domestic flights from US airlines, are located throughout the three-state area, offering easy access to points of interest. Most international flights come into LaGuardia and John F. Kennedy International Airport outside New York City; Newark International Airport in New Jersey; and Philadelphia International Airport and Pittsburgh International Airport in Pennsylvania.

By Train – The **Amtrak** rail network offers a relaxing alternative for the traveler with time to spare. Advance reservations are recommended to ensure reduced fares and availability of desired accommodations. Passengers can choose from first class, coach, sleeping cars and glass-domed cars allowing a panoramic view. Daily service is provided on the **Northeast Direct** (from Virginia through New Jersey to New York City); **Empire Service** (from New York City to Niagara Falls); the **Adirondack** (from New York City to Plattsburgh NY); the **Keystone** (from Washington DC through New York City to Pittsburgh); and the **Three Rivers** (from Pittsburgh to New York City). **All-Aboard Pass** allows up to 45 days travel nationwide (limited to three stops). **North America Rail Pass** links Amtrak routes with Canada's VIA Rail system for 30 days of unlimited travel. **USA RailPass** (not available to US or Canadian citizens) offers unlimited travel within Amtrak-designated regions at discounted rates; 15- and 30-day passes are available. Schedule and route information: www.amtrak.com or ☎800-872-7245 (accessible in North America only; outside North America, contact your travel agent).

Local rail service is provided by **New Jersey Transit**, in all three states *(☎201-762-5100);* and **Metro-North**, from Connecticut through New York City to Poughkeepsie NY *(☎973-762-5100 or 800-772-2222).*

Scenic Rail Excursions – Traveling by train across historic rail lines provides the visitor an opportunity to see farmlands and wilderness areas that might be otherwise inaccessible.

Adirondack Scenic Railroad, Adirondacks *(p 109)*	☎315-369-6290
Delaware & Ulster Rail Ride, Catskills *(p 73)*	☎607-652-2821
Pine Creek Railroad, Allaire State Park *(p 177)*	☎732-938-5524

Bellefonte Historical Railroad, Bellefonte .... ☎814-355-0311
East Broad Top Railroad, Rockhill Furnace .... ☎814-447-3011
Gettysburg Railroad, Gettysburg *(p 294)* .... ☎717-334-6932
Knox & Kane Railroad, Kinzua Bridge State Park .... ☎814-927-6621
Middletown & Hummelstown Railroad, Middletown .... ☎717-944-4435
New Hope & Ivyland Railroad, New Hope *(p 260)* .... ☎215-862-2332
Oil Creek & Titusville Railroad, Oil City .... ☎814-676-1733
Rail Tours, Inc., Jim Thorpe *(p 264)* .... ☎717-325-4606
Steamtown National Historic Site, Scranton *(p 266)* .... ☎717-340-5182
Stourbridge Rail Excursion, Honesdale *(p 264)* .... ☎717-253-1960
Strasburg Rail Road, Strasburg *(p 286)* .... ☎717-687-7522
Tracks Through Time–
     Johnstown Flood National Memorial, St. Michael .... ☎814-495-4643
West Shore Rail Excursions, Lewisburg .... ☎717-524-4337

By Bus – **New Jersey Transit** *(p 356)* and **Greyhound** offer access to most cities in New York, New Jersey and Pennsylvania at a leisurely pace. Overall, fares are lower than other forms of transportation. Some travelers may find long-distance bus travel uncomfortable due to the lack of sleeping accommodations. Advance reservations suggested. Greyhound's **Ameripass** allows unlimited travel for 7, 14 or 21 days. Schedule and route information: ☎800-231-2222. *See p 352 for information for disabled riders.*

By Car – New York, New Jersey and Pennsylvania have an extensive system of well-maintained interstates and freeways that provide easy access from cities in the US and Canada. In remote areas, minor roads may be unpaved but are well marked in New York and Pennsylvania. Major **north-south routes** include I-87 *(toll road between Albany and New York City)* from the Canadian border near Lake Champlain to New York City; I-81 from the Thousand Islands Region in New York down through eastern Pennsylvania; the New Jersey Turnpike *(toll road; information & road conditions ☎732-247-0900)* from Fort Lee, near New York City, to Delaware; and the Garden State Parkway *(toll road; information & road conditions ☎732-727-5929)* from New York to Cape May, NJ.

Route 6, New Paltz, NY

© Scott Barrow

Major **east-west routes** include I-90, the New York State Thruway *(toll road; information & road conditions ☎800-847-8929)*, which runs from New England through Albany and across northern New York State, eventually skirting the northwestern corner of Pennsylvania near Erie; I-76, the Pennsylvania Turnpike *(toll road; information & road conditions ☎717-939-9551)* from Philadelphia across southern Pennsylvania to Pittsburgh; I-78 from Newark, NJ into southeastern Pennsylvania near Harrisburg; I-80 from northeastern New Jersey through the mid-section of Pennsylvania; and the Atlantic City Parkway from Atlantic City to Philadelphia.

Rental Cars – Most large rental companies have offices at major airports and downtown locations. Packages offer unlimited mileage and discounted prices. If a vehicle is returned at a different location from where it was rented, drop-off charges may be incurred. A major credit card and valid driver's license are required for rental. Minimum age for rental is 21. Be sure to check for proper insurance coverage, offered at an extra charge. Liability is not automatically included in the terms of the lease.

In addition to the national rental agencies listed below, there are local companies that offer reasonably priced rentals. *See the yellow pages of local telephone directories for phone numbers.*

Alamo	☎800-327-9633	**Avis**	☎800-831-2847
Budget	☎800-527-0700	**Hertz**	☎800-654-3131
National	☎800-227-7368	**Thrifty**	☎800-367-2277

Toll-free numbers are valid worldwide.

Road Regulations and Insurance – The maximum speed limit on interstate highways is 65mph; on state highways the speed limit is 55mph unless otherwise posted. Speed limits are generally 25-35mph within city limits, and average 25mph in residential areas. Motorists may turn right at a red light after coming to a complete stop, unless otherwise indicated. State law requires that headlights must be turned on when driving in fog and rain. Unless traveling on a divided road, state law requires that motorists in both directions bring their vehicle to a full stop when the warning signals on a **school bus** are activated. Parking spaces identified with ♿ are reserved for persons with disabilities only. Anyone parking in these spaces without proper identification will be ticketed and/or their vehicle will be towed.

In Pennsylvania, left turns may be completed at a red light when traveling from a one-way route to another one-way route. In New Jersey motorists are not permitted to pump their own gas. The use of **seat belts** is mandatory for: 🚗 all passengers in the front seat, and passengers under 10 in the back seat; 🚗 all passengers in the front seat; 🚗 all passengers in the front seat and passengers between 4 years and 18 years old in the back seat. Child safety seats are required for: 🚗 🚗 children under 4; 🚗 children under 3. *Safety seats are available at most rental car agencies; indicate need when making reservations.*

In Case of Accident – If you are involved in an accident resulting in personal or property damage, you must notify the local police and remain at the scene until dismissed. If blocking traffic, vehicles should be moved as soon as possible.

Accommodations

New York, New Jersey and Pennsylvania offer accommodations suited to every taste and pocketbook. Choose from large **hotels** in major cities (including Atlantic City's **casino hotels**), luxury **resorts** in the Poconos or Catskill Mountains or the **great camps** of the Adirondacks. For the budget-minded, try a roadside **motel**, **hostel** or **campground**. **Bed-and-breakfast inns** and **country inns** are usually located in historic houses in residential or rural areas. **Cabin** and home rental can be arranged by contacting local property management agencies. **Campgrounds** offering sites in wilderness locations, or swimming pools and tennis courts near tourist attractions, are plentiful.

© Cosmo Condina /Tony Stone Images

Mirror Lake Inn, Lake Placid, NY

In general, rates peak during the summer season (*Memorial Day–Labor Day*), Christmas and winter holiday weekends (especially near ski resorts). Advance **reservations** are also recommended during these times. Many of the more elegant hotels and resorts also offer entertainment, gourmet dining, health clubs, private golf courses and skiing. Contact local tourist offices to request free brochures that give details about area accommodations (*telephone numbers and Websites, where available, are listed under each blue entry heading in the main section of this guide*).

Hotels/Motels – Accommodations range from luxury hotels to moderate motels. Rates vary greatly according to season and location and tend to be higher during holiday and peak seasons. In most hotels, children under 18 stay free when sharing a room with their parents. In-room efficiency kitchens are available at many small hotels and motels. Packages, which can include meals, passes to local attractions, and weekend specials are often available. Typical amenities at hotels and motels include television, smoking/non-smoking rooms, restaurants and swimming pools. Always advise the reservations clerk of late arrival; unless confirmed with a credit card, rooms may not be held after 6pm.

Reservation services: 🏨 🏨 🏨 StayUSA (☎*813-895-4410 or 800-782-9872*) and Accommodations Express (☎*609-391-2100 or 800-444-7666*).

Major chains with locations throughout New York, New Jersey and Pennsylvania include:

Best Western	☎800-528-1234	**Crowne Plaza**	☎800-227-6963
Days Inn	☎800-329-7466	**Hilton**	☎800-445-8667
Holiday Inn	☎888-223-2323	**Marriott**	☎800-228-9290
Radisson	☎800-333-3333	**Ramada Inn**	☎800-272-6232
Sheraton	☎800-325-3535	**Westin**	☎800-228-3000

See the yellow pages of local telephone directories for phone numbers of additional establishments.

Bed-and-Breakfast Inns and Country Inns – Most B&Bs and country inns are privately owned historic residences. Bed-and-breakfast inns are usually cozy homes with less than 10 guest rooms; breakfast is generally the only meal provided. Country inns are larger establishments, offering over 25 guest rooms; full-service dining is typically available. In both types of establishments, private baths are not always available. Smoking indoors may not be allowed. Reservations should be made well in advance, especially during holiday seasons; be sure to ask about minimum stay, cancellation and refund policies. Most establishments accept major credit cards. The **Pennsylvania Travel Council** publishes a directory of bed-and-breakfast inns, country inns and host farms (*free; include self-addressed stamped envelope; 902 N. 2nd St., Harrisburg PA 17102; www.patravel.org* ☎*717-232-8880*). The *New Jersey Bed & Breakfast Directory* is available from the B&B Innkeepers Assn. of New Jersey (*free; PO Box 108T; Spring Lake NJ 07762; www.bbianj.com* ☎*908-449-3535*). **Reservation services:** 🏨 B&B Assn. of New York State (☎*315-474-4889*); 🏨 🏨 Abby's Agency & Guesthouses (☎*610-692-4575*).

Farm Vacations – Host farms allow paying visitors the chance to participate in the daily activities of a working farm. Opportunities for horseback riding, swimming, hiking, hunting and fishing are available at most locations. For a list of participating farms, send a self-addressed, stamped envelope to the Pennsylvania Department of Agriculture, Commodity Promotions Division, 2301 N. Cameron St., Harrisburg PA 17110-9408, www.pafarmstay.com; or the Pennsylvania Travel Council (*above*).

Hostels – Simple, budget accommodations are offered at close to 20 hostels in the three-state area. Dormitory-style rooms range from $10 to $15 per night for members; an additional $3 is charged to non-members. Private rooms are available at an additional charge. Amenities include common living room, laundry facilities, fully equipped self-service kitchen and dining room. Blankets and pillows are provided; linens may be available for rent. Many hostels offer special programs and activities. Reservations are suggested. For more information, contact **Hostelling International - American Youth Hostel**, 733 15th St. N.W., Suite 840, Washington DC 20005; www.hiayh.org ☎202-783-6161.

Camping – *See state park list, p 363.* Campsites, located in national and state parks, state forests, and in private campgrounds, offer a range of features from full recreational-vehicle hookups to cabins and rustic backcountry sites. Most camping areas provide recreational amenities, such as fishing, hiking and children's playgrounds.

Canoe sites are available on many area waterways. Year-round camping is available; reserve campsites from Memorial Day through Labor Day weekend. Reservations for cabins are recommended year-round. Contact the organizations below for directories listing sites and amenities:

Campground Owners of New York   ☎716-335-2710
PO Box 497, Dansville NY 14437-0497

New York State Department of Environmental Conservation   ☎518-457-2500
50 Wolf Rd., Room 679, Albany NY 12233-5253

New Jersey Campground Association   ☎609-465-8444
29 Cooks Beach Rd., Cape May Court House NJ 08210   or 800-222-6765

Pennsylvania Campground Owners Association   ☎610-767-5026
PO Box 5, New Tripoli PA 18066 or
www.rvcamping.com/pa/pcoa

Basic Information

Business Hours – In general, most businesses operate Monday–Friday 9am–5pm. Banking institutions are normally open Monday–Thursday 9am–5pm, Friday 9am–6pm. Some banks in larger cities may open on Saturday morning. Malls and shopping centers are usually open Monday–Saturday 10am–9pm, Sunday 10am–6pm.

Fax Services – Many hotels and businesses that offer copying or mailing services will send or receive faxes for a per-page fee *(see the yellow pages of the phone directory under Mailing Services)*.

Liquor Laws – The minimum legal age for purchase and consumption of alcoholic beverages is 21; proof of age may be required. Local municipalities may limit and restrict sales. Liquor stores and many drug stores sell liquor. Almost all grocery stores sell beer and wine; hours of sale vary by county. Liquor stores sell beer, wine and liquor. Beer and wine may also be purchased in package-goods stores and grocery stores. Hours of sale are generally daily 9am–10pm. Wine and liquor are sold at state-operated Wine & Spirits Shoppes; beer is sold by licensed distributors. Hours of sale are generally Monday–Saturday 9am–9pm.

Lottery – New York, New Jersey and Pennsylvania all have statewide lottery games that are available to individuals 18 years or older. State lotteries consist of several number-matching games (prize amounts are determined by total sales for each drawing and number of prize winners), and a multitude of instant "scratch-and-win" games. Depending on the game, drawings are held throughout the week; check local newspapers for prize amounts and winning numbers. Lottery tickets *($1-$5)* are sold at convenience stores, gas stations, drug stores and supermarkets.

Major Holidays – Banks and government offices are closed on the following legal holidays:

New Year's Day	January 1
Martin Luther King, Jr. Day*	3rd Monday in January
Presidents' Day*	3rd Monday in February
Memorial Day*	Last Monday in May
Independence Day*	July 4
Labor Day*	1st Monday in September
Columbus Day*	2nd Monday in October
Veterans Day*	November 11
Thanksgiving Day	4th Thursday in November
Christmas Day	December 25

*Many retail stores and restaurants remain open on these days

Taxes and Tips – General sales tax: 4%; 6%; 6%. Some municipalities add an additional sales tax of 2¾% to 4½%. Clothing and food items are exempt from taxation in all three states *(clothing tax will become effective in NY in 1999)*. It is customary in restaurants to tip the server 15-20% of the bill. At hotels, porters should be given $1 per suitcase; maids $1 per day. Taxi drivers are usually tipped 15% of the fare.

Time Zone – New York, New Jersey and Pennsylvania are on Eastern Standard Time (EST), which is five hours behind Greenwich Mean Time. Daylight Saving Time is observed from the first Sunday in April (clocks are advanced one hour) to the last Sunday in October.

Shopping

From large complexes that incorporate national chains, entertainment and restaurants to roadside booths displaying handcrafted kitsch, New York, New Jersey and Pennsylvania will satisfy the most ardent shopper. New York City's Fifth Avenue, Philadelphia's Center City and Pittsburgh's downtown Triangle shopping areas tempt travelers and residents alike with department stores, boutiques, galleries and restaurants. Small-town main streets offer charming antique and specialty shops. Handmade quilts are sold throughout Lancaster County. Moravian stars *(p 291)* are available in Bethlehem, PA. Fine glassware can be found in Corning, NY. King of Prussia *(20mi northwest of Philadelphia near Valley Forge;* ☎*215-265-5727)* boasts one of the largest shopping complexes on the East Coast with over 450 stores under one roof.

Flea Markets and Antiques – Whether displayed in elegant shops or simple roadside stands along rural roadways, this region's antiques will delight both the seasoned and novice collector in variety and quality. Auctions and flea markets are a bargain-hunter's dream. Meadowlands Marketplace in East Rutherford, NJ sponsors over 1,000 vendors. Pennsylvania's Renninger's Antique & Farmers Market in Kutztown and Stoudtburg Antique Mall in Adamstown attract hundreds of dealers.

Outlet Stores – Bargains galore (reductions up to 75%) can be found in outlet stores throughout the three-state area, including Niagara Factory Outlet Mall and Rainbow Centre Factory Outlet in Niagara Falls, NY and Secaucus Shopping Outlets in Secaucus, NJ. Franklin Mills *(p 225)*, outside Philadelphia, claims over 200 outlet stores. In Pennsylvania, both Reading *(p 304)* and Lancaster *(p 276)* offer a large assortment of manufacturer's outlets.

© Robert Llewellyn

Farmers' Markets – *p 77; p 236; p 288*. During harvest time, many farmers sell fresh-grown produce at modest prices at roadside stands and farmers' markets (some are even open year-round). Visitors can also pick their own fruits and vegetables (for a small fee) at farms open to the public. Contact the following agencies for a list of roadside stands and "pick-your-own" farms: ⓝ New York State Department of Agriculture & Markets publishes the *Guide to Farm-Fresh Goods (1 Winners Circle, Albany NY 12235-0001 www.agmkt.state.ny.us/farmsearch.htm)*; ⓝ New Jersey Department of Agriculture offers the *New Jersey Roadside & Urban Markets Directory* and the *Guide to Pick-Your-Own Farms in New Jersey (PO Box 330, Trenton NJ 08625; www.state.nj.us/agriculture/publ.htm)*.

Wineries – *pp 136-137; p 152; p 346*. Many wineries offer self-guided tours. To fully experience the wine regions, it is best to select no more than four wineries per day for tasting. Some wineries feature restaurants, or shops selling take-out fare for a picnic lunch.

Sports & Recreation

Nature and Safety

In most natural areas, tampering with plants or wildlife is prohibited by law. When visiting any natural areas, remember that while the disturbance of a single person may be small, the cumulative impact of a large number of visitors may be disastrous. Avoid direct contact with any wildlife; an animal that does not shy from humans may be sick. Northern New York State is undergoing a rabies epidemic within the wild raccoon population. **Mosquitoes**, flies, ticks and other biting insects are prevalent throughout the area. Cases of **Lyme disease**, resulting from tick bites, are at an all-time high in New York, New Jersey and Pennsylvania. Caught early enough, the Lyme infection can be completely cured by taking oral antibiotics. Typically, the initial infection is accompanied by an expanding red rash at the site where the tick was attached. The rash often resembles a bull's-eye.

Tips for Visiting Public Lands

- Spray clothes with insect repellent (particularly around cuffs and waistline) and check for ticks every 3-4 hours when participating in outdoor activities.
- Use extreme caution and wear bright colors when hiking during hunting season. Deer hunting is widespread between mid-November and December.
- Do not feed wild animals; they may become ill and die.
- Do not litter; pack out everything you pack in.
- Boil (5min) or chemically treat water from streams and lakes.

Fauna, Great and Small – The varied landscape of the three-state area is home to a rich diversity of animals and birds. In north central Pennsylvania, a wild **elk** herd roams state game lands in Elk County. **Whale-watching** cruises depart from coastal towns in New Jersey and Long Island, NY.

Bird-watching – The coastal marshes of New Jersey are on the main Atlantic flyway for migrating birds. Hawks and other raptors can be seen during their semiannual migration *(Jan–Feb)* in the Delaware Water Gap NRA *(p 268)*. Other viewing areas include Montezuma National Wildlife Refuge *(Seneca Falls NY)*; Edwin B. Forsythe National Wildlife Refuge *(p 199)*; Wetlands Institute *(Stone Harbor NJ)*; Cape May Bird Observatory *(Cape May NJ)*; Hawk Mountain Sanctuary *(Kempton PA)* and Presque Isle State Park *(p 347)*. For additional and other viewing locations, contact the **National Audubon Society**, mid-Atlantic Office, 1104 Fernwood, Suite 300, Camp Hill PA ☎717-763-4985.

National and State Lands

A wide variety of recreational opportunities are available year-round in the regions' parks and forests. Most amenities such as lifeguards and boat rentals are provided between Memorial Day and Labor Day. Contact the following agencies for maps and additional information:

- Ⓝ **Office of Parks, Recreation & Historic Preservation**, Empire State Plaza, Albany NY 12238 ☎518-474-0456; **Department of Environmental Conservation**, Public Information & Publications Unit, 50 Wolf Rd., Room 679, Albany NY 12233-5253 ☎518-457-3521.
- Ⓝ **Department of Environmental Protection**, Division of Parks & Forestry, CN 404, 501 E. State St., Trenton NJ 08625-0404 ☎609-292-2733.
- Ⓟ **Department of Conservation & Natural Resources**, www.dcnr.state.pa.us; **Bureau of State Parks**, PO Box 8551, Harrisburg PA 17105-8551 ☎717-772-0239 or 888-727-2757; or **Bureau of Forestry**, PO Box 8552, Harrisburg PA 17105-8552 ☎717-787-2703.

Fall Foliage and Scenic Drives – The display of brilliant autumn colors generally begins in mid-September in the higher elevations of the Catskills and the Adirondacks and moves to the Allegheny and Pocono mountains by early October. By mid-October, trees in central Pennsylvania, northwestern New York and northern New Jersey are bathed in color. The Hudson River Valley, southern Pennsylvania and southern New Jersey are at their peak by late October, followed by coastal New Jersey and Long Island into early November.

The **Seaway Trail** scenic byway *(454mi)* runs along the shoreline of Lake Erie, the Niagara River and Lake Ontario to the St. Lawrence River. Trail blazes are located along the route. The *Seaway Trail Bicycling* guidebook *($8.95)* includes detailed maps.

Selected National and State Parks

	☎	△	禾	!	⤚	⬤
🗽 New York						
Fire Island Natl. Seashore	516-289-4810	•	•	•	•	•
Allegany SP (p 144)	716-354-9121	•	•	•	•	•
Bear Mountain SP (p 87)	914-786-2701		•	•	•	•
Connetquot River SP (p 60)	516-581-1005			•		•
Clarence Fahnestock SP	914-225-7207	•	•	•	•	•
Four Mile Campsite SP	716-745-3802	•				•
Golden Hill SP	716-795-3885	•	•	•		•
Harriman SP	914-786-2701	•	•	•	•	•
Jones Beach SP (p 63)	516-785-1600		•		•	•
Letchworth SP (p 163)	716-493-2611	•	•	•	•	•
Mills-Norrie SP	914-889-4646	•	•	•		•
Mine Kill SP (p 74)	518-827-6111		•	•	•	•
Niagara Reservation SP (p 155)	716-278-1770		•	•		•
Orient Beach SP (p 63)	516-323-2440		•	•	•	•
Robert Moses SP -						
Long Island (p 64)	516-669-0449		•	•		•
Robert Moses SP - 1,000 Islands	315-769-8663	•	•	•	•	•
Saratoga Spa SP (p 120)	518-584-2950		•	•	•	•
Sunken Meadow SP (p 61)	516-269-4333		•	•	•	•
Taughannock Falls SP (p 131)	607-387-6739	•	•	•	•	•
Watkins Glen SP (p 132)	607-535-4511	•	•	•	•	•
🏛 New Jersey						
Delaware Water Gap NRA (p 267)	908-496-4458	•	•	•	•	•
Gateway NRA (p 175)	908-872-0115		•	•	•	•
Allaire SP (p 177)	908-938-2371	•	•	•		•
Barnegat Lighthouse SP (p 176)	609-494-2016		•			•
Cape May Point SP	609-884-2159		•	•		
Delaware & Raritan						
Canal SP (p 205)	908-873-3050		•			•
Fort Mott State Park (p 206)	609-935-3218		•			•
Liberty SP (p 55)	201-915-3400		•	•		
Ringwood SP (p 183)	201-962-7031		•	•	•	•
Washington Crossing SP (p 211)	609-737-0623		•	•		
🏔 Pennsylvania						
Delaware Water Gap NRA (p 267)	717-588-2435	•	•	•	•	•
Big Pocono SP (p 269)	717-894-8336		•	•		
Blue Knob SP	814-276-3576	•	•	•	•	•
Colton Point SP (p 318)	717-724-3061	•	•	•		
Hickory Run SP (p 269)	717-443-0400	•	•	•		•
Keystone SP	412-668-2939	•	•	•	•	•
Kinzua Bridge SP (p 317)	814-965-2646		•			
Laurel Hill SP	814-445-7725	•	•	•	•	•
Laurel Ridge SP	412-455-3744			•		
Leonard Harrison SP (p 318)	717-724-3061	•	•	•		
Ohiopyle SP	412-329-8591	•		•		•
Presque Isle SP (p 347)	814-871-4251		•	•	•	•
Promised Land SP (p 269)	717-676-3428	•	•	•	•	•
Shawnee SP	814-733-4218	•	•	•	•	•
Black Moshannon SP	814-342-5960	•	•	•	•	•
Caledonia SP	717-352-2161	•	•	•	•	
French Creek SP	610-582-9680	•	•	•	•	•

Symbols on the above chart indicate: ☎ *telephone number;* △ *camping;*
禾 *picnic grounds;* ! *hiking;* ⤚ *swimming;* ⬤ *fishing.*

For this and other publications, contact **Seaway Trail, Inc.,** 109 Barracks Dr., Sackets Harbor NY 13685 ☎315-646-1000 or 800-732-9298. Itineraries for other scenic routes are available from state tourism offices *(p 352)*.

Golf – With over 600 public courses throughout the three-state area, golfers can practice their driving and putting expertise at numerous public courses. Many hotels and resorts include access to golf facilities, and some private courses allow non-members to play. Most courses offer golf clinics and private instruction. Contact state and local tourism offices for a list of public courses.

© Robert Llewellyn

Hunting & Fishing – With an abundance of game and fish (including white-tailed deer, pheasant, trout and walleye), New York, New Jersey and Pennsylvania are a sportsman's paradise in all seasons. Many state and national lands are open for hunting and fishing; maps are available from park offices. Specialized **guides** and charter services provide gear and tackle, and take clients to productive fishing waters year-round. Contact the agencies listed below for a list of licensed guides. Licenses are required for hunting and freshwater fishing in all three states. One-day non-resident fishing licenses are available in fishing supply stores (some offer rental equipment). Non-resident hunting licenses tend to be considerably more expensive than resident licenses. Many fish are in season year-round, whereas most game can only be hunted seasonally. When transporting a rifle or shotgun it must be unloaded and in a secure case *(no permit required)*. Contact the following agencies for additional information (including regulations on transporting game out of the state):

- 🏞 **New York State Outdoor Guide Association**, PO Box 4704 NYS, Queensbury NY 12804 ☎518-798-1253; **Department of Environmental Conservation**, 50 Wolf Rd., Albany NY 12233-4790; www.dec.state.ny.us ☎518-457-5400.
- 🏞 **New Jersey Division of Fish, Game & Wildlife**, PO Box 400, Trenton NJ 08625-0400; www.state.nj.us/dep/fgw ☎609-292-2965.
- 🏞 **Pennsylvania Game Commission**, 2001 Elmerton Ave., Harrisburg PA 17110-9797; www.state.pa.us/PA.Exec/PGC/index.htm ☎717-783-7507; **Pennsylvania Fish Commission**, PO Box 1673, Harrisburg PA 17105-1673 ☎717-657-4519.

Hiking and Biking – The region's varied terrain of winding river valleys and steep mountain peaks offers abundant opportunities for hiking and biking on the many trail systems and public lands that lace the area. Guided wilderness vacations are offered by the New York State Guides Assn., PO Box 4704 NYS, Queensbury NY 12804 ☎518-798-1253. Bicycles may be prohibited on unpaved trails. Bicyclists are required by state law to wear approved safety helmets: 🏞 🏞 under the age of 14; 🏞 under the age of 12. A section of the **Appalachian Trail** cuts through southeastern Pennsylvania to northwestern New Jersey and southern New York. Major trail systems include:

- 🏞 **Erie Canal** from Lockport to Erie Canal State Park; **Long Path** from New York City to Albany; **Mohawk-Hudson Bikeway** from Albany to Schenectady along the Hudson and Mohawk Rivers; Long Island's **Greenbelt Trail** and throughout the **Adirondacks** *(p 106)*.

🌐 **Coastal Heritage Trail** *(p 206)* from Perth Amboy along the coast past Cape May; along the **Delaware & Raritan Canal** *(p 205)*; **Heritage Highlands** from Newburgh NY to northern Morris County NJ; and the **Batona Trail** through Wharton and Lebanon state forests *(p 201)*.

🌐 **Susquehannock Forest Hiking Trail**; **Laurel Highlands Trail** from Ohiopyle to Johnstown; and throughout the **Allegheny National Forest** *(p 318)*.

Trail Information – In addition to the agencies listed under "National and State Lands" *(p 362)*, the following agencies can also provide maps and trail information: Appalachian Trail Conference *(PO Box 807, Harpers Ferry WV 25425* ☎*304-535-6331)*; New York-New Jersey Trail Conference *(PO Box 2250, New York NY 10016* ☎*212-685-9699)*; Long Island Greenbelt Trail Conference *(23 Deer Path Rd., Central Islip NY 11722* ☎*516-360-0753)*; Adirondack Mountain Club *(814 Goggins Rd., Lake George NY 12845* ☎*518-668-4447)*; New Jersey Coastal Heritage Trail c/o National Park Service *(PO Box 118, Mauricetown NJ 08329* ☎*609-447-0103)*; Susquehannock Trail c/o Potter County Recreation, Inc. *(PO Box 245, Coudersport PA 16915)*; Rails-to-Trails Conservancy *(1400 16th St. N.W., Suite 300, Washington DC 20036* ☎*202-797-5400)*. **Biking guides** are available from the New Jersey Department of Transportation, CN 600, Trenton NJ 08625 ☎609-530-8062; and Pennsylvania Department of Transportation, Distribution Services Unit, PO Box 2028, Harrisburg PA 17105 ☎717-787-6746.

Horseback Riding – Many of the hiking trails and public lands mentioned above also allow riders on horseback. State parks often have well-maintained horse facilities. Public riding stables, specializing in trail rides for beginning through advanced riders, are located throughout the three-state area. Pennsylvania's **Horse-Shoe Trail** travels from Valley Forge and joins the Appalachian Trail north of Hershey, PA. For maps and information, contact the Horse-Shoe Trail Club, Warwick County Park, RD 2, Pottstown PA 19464 ☎215-469-9461.

Water Sports

With the hundreds of miles of prime coastline bordering the Atlantic Ocean, Lake Erie and Lake Ontario and the multitude of inland lakes and waterways, New York, New Jersey and Pennsylvania offer a variety of water sports year-round. Lifeguards generally patrol **swimming** areas between Memorial Day and Labor Day. Keep in mind that northern waters stay cool during the summer months. Visitors can **scuba dive** and **snorkel** along the New York and New Jersey coasts. Consult these publications for listings of operators and dive sites: 📖 *Scuba Dive Site Directory ($13)* available from Seaway Trail, Inc. *(p 364)*; 📖 *Scuba & Skin Diving in New Jersey ($2)* from New Jersey Department of Community Affairs, Division of Community Resources, CN 814, Trenton NJ 08625 ☎609-984-6654.

The New York State **Canal System** incorporates 500mi of waterways on the Erie, Oswego and Seneca-Cayuga canals that are open to water traffic from May through November *(special permission is required for night passage)*. **Canal cruises** travel from Rhode Island to the Hudson River and up the Erie Canal to the St. Lawrence Seaway *(Jun–mid-Oct; American Canadian Caribbean Line* ☎*401-274-0955 or 800-556-7450)*, and along the route of the Erie Canal *(mid-May–mid-Oct; Mid-Lakes Navigation* ☎*315-685-8500 or 800-545-4318)*. For maps and additional information, contact the **New York State Canal Corporation**, PO Box 189, Albany NY 12201-0189.

Selected Ocean Beaches	☎	$	✚	🎣	⚓	📷
🌐 **Long Island**						
Cedar	516-451-6100	•		•	•	
Cupsuge	516-854-4949	•		•	•	•
Gilgo	516-893-2100	•		•	•	
Heckscher Park	516-581-2100	•		•	•	
Jones Beach SP *(p 63)*	516-785-1600	•		•	•	
Meschutt	516-852-8205	•		•		
New Suffolk	516-765-5182	•		•		
Robert Moses SP *(p 64)*	516-669-0449	•		•	•	•
Sears Bellows	516-852-8290	•		•	•	
Smith Point	516-852-1313	•		•	•	•
South Jamesport	516-727-5744	•		•		
Sunken Meadow SP *(p 61)*	516-269-4333	•		•	•	

Selected Ocean Beaches	☎	$	✚	🐟	🏄	🤿
⑩ Jersey Shore						
Asbury Park	908-775-7676	•	•	•		
Atlantic City *(p 188)*	609-449-7130		•	•	•	•
Avalon	609-967-3936	•	•	•	•	
Avon	908-502-4510	•	•	•	•	
Barnegat	609-698-6658		•			
Barnegat Light	609-494-7211	•	•	•	•	
Bay Head	908-899-2424	•	•	•	•	
Beach Haven Beaches	609-494-7211	•	•	•	•	
Belmar	908-681-2900	•	•	•	•	•
Berkeley Township	908-244-7400	•	•	•	•	
Bradley Beach	908-776-2994	•	•	•	•	•
Brant Beach	609-494-7211	•	•		•	
Brick Township	908-477-3000	•	•		•	
Brigantine	609-266-7600	•	•		•	•
Brighton Beach	609-474-7211	•	•		•	
Cape May *(p 191)*	609-884-5508	•	•	•		
Cape May Point	609-884-5603	•	•	•		
Deal	908-531-1454	•	•	•		
Harvey Cedars	609-494-7211	•	•	•	•	
Holgate	609-494-7211	•	•			
Island Heights	908-270-6415	•	•	•		
Keansburg	908-787-0215		•			
Lavellette	908-793-7477	•	•	•	•	
Long Beach	609-494-7211	•	•	•	•	
Long Branch	908-222-0400	•	•	•	•	•
Longport	609-823-2731	•	•	•	•	
Loveladies	609-494-7211	•	•	•		
Lower Township	609-886-2005		•			
Manahawkin	609-494-7211	•	•			
Manasquan	908-223-0544	•	•	•	•	
Margate	609-823-2731	•	•	•	•	
North Beach	609-494-7211	•	•			
North Wildwood	609-522-1407	•	•	•	•	
Ocean City *(p 191)*	609-399-6111	•	•	•	•	•
Ocean Grove	908-775-0035	•	•	•	•	
Ortley Beach	908-341-1000	•	•	•		
Peahala Park	609-494-7211	•	•			
Point Pleasant Beach *(p 176)*	908-899-2424	•	•	•	•	
Sandy Hook *(p 175)*	908-872-0115	•	•	•	•	•
Sea Bright	908-842-0099	•	•	•		
Sea Girt	908-449-7079	•	•	•		
Sea Isle City	609-263-8687	•	•	•		•
Seaside Heights	908-349-0220	•	•	•		
Seaside Park	908-793-0234	•	•	•	•	•
Ship Bottom	609-494-2171	•	•	•	•	•
Somers Point	609-927-5253	•	•			
Spray Beach	609-494-7211	•	•	•		
Spring Lake	908-449-8005	•	•	•		
Stone Harbor	609-368-6805	•	•	•		
Strathmere	609-628-2011	•	•	•		
Surf City	609-494-7211	•	•	•		
Toms River	908-641-1000		•			
Union Beach	908-264-2277		•			
Ventnor	609-823-7948	•	•	•		
West Wildwood	609-522-4845		•			
Wildwood *(p 193)*	609-522-1407	•	•	•		
Wildwood Crest	609-552-3825	•	•	•		

Symbols on the above chart indicate: ☎ *telephone number;* $ *admission/parking fee;*
✚ *lifeguard (seasonally);* 🐟 *fishing;* 🏄 *surfing;* 🤿 *scuba/snorkeling.*

Arthur C. Smith III/Grant Heilman Photography

Rafting, Canoeing and Kayaking – Whether gently coasting down a serene river or riding the rapids, the scenic waterways of the region provide ample opportunities for rafting, tubing, canoeing and kayaking. Most establishments offer instruction, route maps and guides to lead boaters along the course. Wear layered clothing, a windbreaker and soft-soled shoes, and bring an extra set of clothes to change into after the trip.

Heavy spring rains and melting snow create excellent conditions for **white-water rafting**. Wet suits are generally required when the air and water temperature added together equal less than 100 *(many outfitters offer rentals)*. Picnic lunches are often available for an additional charge. Minimum age allowed depends on the difficulty of the specific course. Rafting and kayaking excursions are available at Delaware Water Gap NRA, on the Esposus River in New York and on Pennsylvania's Youghiogheny *(p 316)* and Lehigh rivers. Other scenic waterways include: ⑲ the Adirondack Canoe Route and the St. Regis Canoe Area *(p 109)*; ⑱ the Pine Barrens *(p 198)* and the Delaware & Raritan SP; ⑳ the Delaware and Susquehanna rivers.

Winter Activities

Skiing – Although resorts are located throughout the three states, the primary ski areas are the Catskills and North Country of New York, northwestern New Jersey, as well as the Pocono Mountains, Laurel Highlands and Southern Alleghenies of Pennsylvania.

Most ski areas offer a variety of accommodations including bed-and-breakfast inns, alpine lodges and major hotel chains. In addition, many places feature discount packages, which can include lift tickets and equipment rental. The ski season generally extends from mid- November through early April. Most ski areas offer instruction for children and adults. Some resorts even have nurseries and inside play areas for children. New York State's "Learn to Ski" downhill and cross-country program *($60 downhill/ $40 cross-country)* includes lessons, lift tickets/ trail fees and rental equipment; reservations required. Many ski areas also feature cross-country trails and snowparks for snowboarders.

© Richard Quataert/FOLIO, Inc.

Selected Ski Areas	City	☎	Vertical Drop (ft)	Total Runs	Downhill Trails Beginner	Downhill Trails Intermediate	Downhill Trails Advanced	Cross-Country Trails	Snowboarding

🗽 New York

Name	City	Phone	Vertical Drop (ft)	Total Runs	Beginner	Intermediate	Advanced	Cross-Country Trails	Snowboarding
Adirondack Loj	Lake Placid	518-523-3441						20km	
Alder Creek	Alder Creek	315-831-5222						24 km	
Allegany SP	Salamanca	716-354-9121						43km	
Ausable Chasm	Ausable Chasm	518-834-9990						36km	
Bark Eater	Keene	518-576-2221						20km	
Belleayre Mountain	Highmount	914-254-5600	1,404	33	11	9	13	Y	Y
Big Tupper	Tupper Lake	518-359-7902	1,152	28	6	13	9	Y	Y
Bobcat	Andes	914-676-3143	1,050	19	2	7	10	Y	Y
Bristol Mountain	Canandaigua	716-374-4600	1,200	22	3	14	5	N	Y
Byrncliff	Varysburg	716-535-7300						25km	
Cascade	Lake Placid	518-523-9605						20km	
Catamount	Hillsdale	518-325-3200	1,000	25	11	7	7	Y	Y
Cockaigne	Cherry Creek	716-287-3223	430	15	4	7	4	N	Y
Cold River Ranch	Tupper Lake	518-359-7559						100km	
Cortina Valley	Haines Falls	518-589-6500	725	18	5	11	2	N	Y
Cunningham's Ski Barn	North Creek	518-251-3215						25km	
Dewey Mountain	Saranac Lake	518-891-2697						25km	
Fern Park	Inlet	315-357-5501						22km	
Friends Lake Inn	Chestertown	518-494-4751						32km	
Frost Valley	Claryville	914-985-2291						35km	
Garnet Hill	North River	518-251-2821						56km	
Gore Mountain	North Creek	518-251-2411	2,100	46	4	33	9	Y	Y
Greek Peak	Cortland	607-835-6111						27km	Y
Hickory	Warrensburg	518-623-2825	1,200	15	3	7	5	N	Y
Holiday Mountain	Monticello	914-796-3161	400	15	5	6	4	N	Y
Holiday Valley	Ellicottville	716-699-2345	750	52	16	19	17	N	N
Holimont	Ellicottville	716-699-2320	620	45	13	16	16	N	N
Hunter	Hunter	518-263-4223	1,600	53	16	16	21	N	Y
Kissing Bridge	Glenwood	716-592-4963	550	36	13	13	11	N	Y
Labrador	Truxton	607-842-6204	700	22	6	10	6	N	Y
Lake Placid Nordic Center	Lake Placid	518-523-2556						20km	
Lapland Lake	Northville	518-863-4974						48km	
Letchworth SP	Castile	716-493-3600						40km	
McCauley Mountain	Old Forge	315-369-3225	633	14	2	8	4	20km	Y
Minnewaska SP	New Paltz	914-255-0752						65km	
Mohonk Mountain House	New Paltz	914-255-1000						40km	
Mountain Trails	Tannersville	518-589-5361						35km	
Mt. Peter	Warwick	914-986-4992	400	12	4	5	3	N	Y
Mt. Van Hoevenberg	Lake Placid	518-523-2811						50km	
Oak Hill Farms	Esperance	518-875-6700						30km	
Oak Mountain	Speculator	518-548-7311	650	13	5	5	3	N	Y
Osceola/Tug Hill	Camden	315-599-7377						30km	
Pechler's Trails	Palmyra	315-597-4210						20km	
Peek'n Peak	Clymer	716-355-4141	400	27	2	20	5	35km	Y
Pineridge	Petersburgh	518-283-5509						35km	
Royal Mountain	Caroga Lake	518-835-6445	550	14	2	8	4	N	Y
Salmon Hills	Redfield	315-599-4003						38km	
Scotch Valley	Stamford	607-652-2470	800	26	5	10	6	Y	Y
Shu-Maker Mountain	Little Falls	315-823-4470	750	22	6	13	3	N	Y
Ski Plattekill	Roxbury	607-326-3500	1,000	27	5	11	11	Y	Y

Selected Ski Areas City ☎		Vertical Drop (ft)	Total Runs	Downhill Trails			Cross-Country Trails	Snowboarding
				Beginner	Intermediate	Advanced		

⑩ New York *continued*

Ski Tamarack	Colden	716-941-6821	500	15	2	6	6	N	Y
Ski Valley	Naples	716-374-5157	700	12	4	5	3	N	Y
Ski Windham	Windham	518-734-4300	1,600	33	10	15	8	Y	Y
Snow Ridge	Turin	315-348-8456	500	22	3	6	14	Y	Y
Song Mountain	Tully	315-696-5711	700	24	14	7	3	N	Y
Swain	Swain	607-545-6511	650	18	7	5	6	N	Y
Thunder Ridge	Patterson	914-878-4100	600	30	10	8	12	Y	Y
Titus Mountain	Malone	518-483-3740	1,200	26	10	6	10	N	Y
Toggenburg	Fabius	315-683-5842	650	18	7	5	6	N	Y
Tree Haven Hills	Hagaman	518-882-9455						45km	
West Mountain	Glens Falls	518-793-6606	1,010	22	8	12	2	N	Y
White Birches	Windham	518-734-3266						35km	
Whiteface Mountain	Wilmington	518-946-2223	3,216	65	22	23	20	N	Y
Whiteface Nordic Center	Lake Placid	518-523-2551						35km	
Willard Mountain	Greenwich	518-692-7337	505	14	2	9	3	N	Y
Williams Lake	Rosendale	914-658-3101						20km	
Woods Valley	Westernville	315-827-4721	500	12	3	6	3	N	Y

⑩ New Jersey

Campgaw Mountain	Mahwah	201-327-7800	250	8	4	2	2	Y	Y
Craigmeur	Newfoundland	973-697-4500	250	4	4				Y
Hidden Valley	Vernon	973-764-6161	620	12	1	5	6	N	Y
Vernon Valley/ Great Gorge	Vernon	973-827-2000	1,040	32	16	11	5	N	Y

⑳ Pennsylvania

Alpine Mountain	Analomink	717-595-2150	550	17	4	9	4	Y	Y
Big Boulder	Blakeslee	717-722-0100	475	14	6	5	4	Y	Y
Blue Knob	Claysburg	814-238-5111	1,072	21	8	8	4	Y	Y
Blue Marsh	Bernville	610-488-6399	315	11	3	6	3	N	Y
Blue Mountain	Palmerton	610-826-7700	1,082	20	7	6	7	N	N
Camelback	Tannersville	717-629-1661	800	32	12	13	7	N	Y
Delaware Canal SP	Upper Black Eddy	610-982-5560						97	
Doe Mountain	Macungie	610-682-7100	500	15	5	6	5	N	Y
Elk Mountain	Union Dale	717-679-2611	1,000	26	7	8	12	N	Y
Elk State Forest	Emporium	814-486-3353						40	
Forbes State Forest	Laughlintown	412-238-9533						80	
Hidden Valley	Hidden Valley	814-443-2600	610	17	6	6	5	Y	Y
Jack Frost Mountain	Blakeslee	717-443-8425	600	21	4	8	8	Y	Y
Lackawanna State Forest	Scranton	717-963-4561						39	
Laurel Ridge SP	Rockwood	412-455-3744						32	
Lehigh Gorge SP	White Haven	717-443-0400						32	
Montage	Scranton	717-969-7669	1,000	21	5	9	7	N	Y
Moshannon State Forest	Clearfield	814-765-0821						87	
Mount Tone	Lake Como	717-798-2707	450	11	4	4	2	Y	Y
Ohiopyle SP	Ohiopyle	412-329-8591						48	
Oil Creek SP	Oil City	814-676-5915						80	
Ricketts Glen SP	Benton	717-447-5675						35	
Seven Springs	Champion	814-352-7777	750	30	15	10	5	N	Y

Selected Ski Areas City ☎	Vertical Drop (ft)	Total Runs	Downhill Trails			Cross-Country Trails	Snowboarding
			Beginner	Intermediate	Advanced		

☎ Pennsylvania *continued*

	City	☎	Vertical Drop (ft)	Total Runs	Beginner	Intermediate	Advanced	Cross-Country Trails	Snowboarding
Shawnee Mountain	Shawnee-on-Delaware	717-421-7321	700	23	6	12	6	N	Y
Ski Big Bear	Lackawaxen	717-685-1400	650	10	3	4	3	N	Y
Ski Denton	Coudersport	814-435-2115	650	20	7	7	7	Y	Y
Ski Liberty	Carroll Valley	717-642-8282	600	16	5	6	5	N	Y
Ski Roundtop	Lewisberry	717-432-9631	600	15	5	5	5	N	Y
Ski Sawmill Mountain	Morris	717-353-7521	515	10	4	4	3	N	Y
Susquehannock State Forest	Coudersport	814-274-8474						48	
Tanglewood	Tafton	717-226-9500	415	10	3	5	3	Y	Y
Tiadaghton State Forest	S. Williamsport	717-327-3450						88	
Whitetail Resort	Mercersburg	717-328-9400	935	17	4	9	4		
Wyoming State Forest	Bloomsburg	717-387-4255						32	

Snowmobiling – Miles of well-maintained trails on both public and private lands can be found throughout the region. Rental equipment is available in many areas. Snowmobiles are allowed on designated roads and trails from mid-November through March. The Adirondack Snowmobile Assn. *(Hamilton County Dept. NYG, PO Box 771, Indian Lake NY 12842 ☎518-648-5239)* provides trail maps with membership *($10)*. Snowmobile permits and trail information can be obtained from: ☎ Bureau of Marine and Recreational Vehicles *(Office of Parks, Recreation & Historic Preservation, p 362)*; ☎ Snowmobile/ATV Unit *(Dept. of Conservation & Natural Resources, p 362)*.

Professional Team Sports

Sport/Team	Season	Venue	☎ Information
⚾ **Baseball**	**Apr–Oct**		
New York Mets		Shea Stadium	718-507-8499
New York Yankees		Yankee Stadium	718-293-6000
Philadelphia Phillies		Veterans Stadium	215-463-1000
Pittsburgh Pirates		Three Rivers Stadium	412-321-2827
🏈 **Football**	**Sept–Dec**		
Buffalo Bills		Rich Stadium	716-648-1800
New York Giants		Meadowlands	201-935-8222
New York Jets		Meadowlands	516-560-8200
Philadelphia Eagles		Veterans Stadium	215-463-5500
Pittsburgh Steelers		Three Rivers Stadium	412-323-1200
🏀 **Basketball**	**Oct–Apr**		
New Jersey Nets		Meadowlands	201-935-3900
New York Knicks		Madison Square Garden	212-465-5867
Philadelphia 76ers		CoreStates Spectrum	215-339-7676
🏒 **Hockey**	**Oct–Apr**		
Buffalo Sabres		Memorial Auditorium	716-856-8100
New Jersey Devils		Meadowlands	201-935-3900
New York Islanders		Nassau Coliseum	516-794-9300
New York Rangers		Madison Square Garden	212-465-6741
Philadelphia Flyers		CoreStates Center	215-465-4500
Pittsburgh Penguins		Pittsburgh Civic Arena	412-642-7367

Index

MANUFACTURE FRANÇAISE DES PNEUMATIQUES MICHELIN

Société en commandite par actions au capital de 2 000 000 000 de Francs

Place des Carmes-Déchaux - 63 Clermont-Ferrand (France)

R.C.S. Clermont-Fd B 855 200 507

© Michelin et Cie, Propriétaires-Éditeurs 1998

Dépôt légal mai 1998 - ISBN 2-06-154901-2 - ISSN 0763-1383

Printed in the EU 05/98/1

Impression : I.M.E., Baume-les-Dames - Brochage : I.F.C. ASKREA, St-Germain du Puy

Cover illustration by Richard BATSON